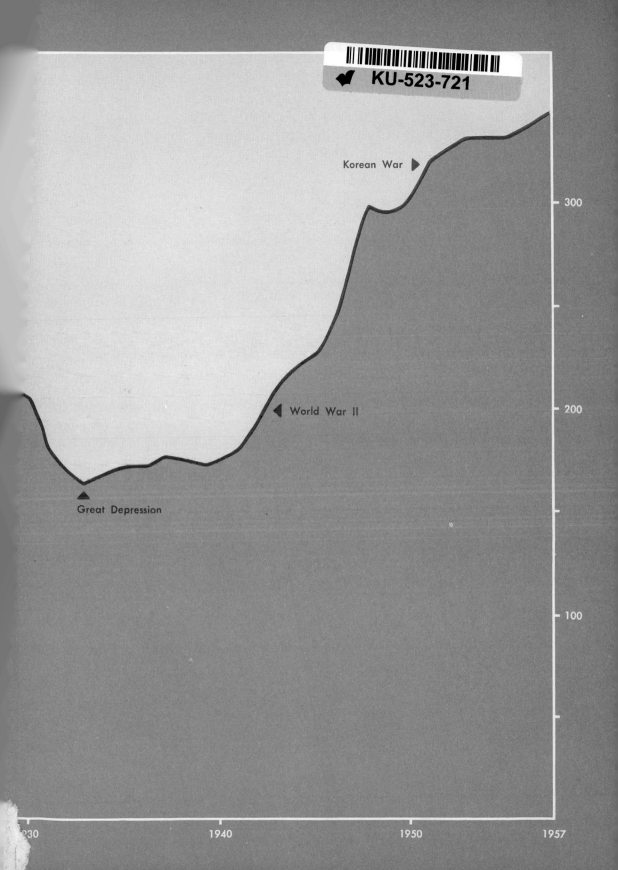

Korean War ▶

300

World War II ◀

200

Great Depression ▲

100

230   1940   1950   1957

ECONOMICS

An Introductory Analysis

E C O N O

Introductory

FOURTH EDITION

McGRAW-HILL BOOK COMPANY, INC.

MICS An
Analysis BY PAUL A. SAMUELSON

PROFESSOR OF ECONOMICS, MASSACHUSETTS INSTITUTE OF TECHNOLOGY

NEW YORK   TORONTO   LONDON   1958

This book is set in linotype

Baskerville, a typeface

originally designed by the

English printer and type

founder John Baskerville in

the middle of the eighteenth century.

The headings and chapter titles

are set in Spartan heavy. The

charts and graphs are drawn by

Evelyn Urbanowich.

PREFACE

This is an introduction to economics. It is designed for a half-year or a full-year beginning course, and for students who may or may not go on to do further economic study.

Economics is an important subject. It is also an exciting subject. Being a professional economist, I naturally think this. But repeated surveys of opinion show that a well-designed economics course almost always scores near the top in any popularity rating, and very often in life you meet up with people who bemoan their regret that they never had the chance to learn economics.

When I wrote the first edition of this book, I said to myself: "What should an intelligent person know about economics in this last half of the twentieth century? A reader will probably find those subjects interesting that are likely to be most important to him twenty years from now when he will himself begin to be in a position of power and responsibility."

The result has been successful beyond my fondest hopes. Economic teachers —here and abroad, in junior colleges and great universities, in night schools and training courses for government and business—were apparently ripe for a textbook which concentrated on the big, vital economic problems. On inflation and depression. On family income and national income. On prices, wages, profits, and the stock market. And, most important of all, on *the tools which help to analyze* the conditions leading to rapid economic progress and security, to efficient pricing and economical use of all our resources.

In the fourth edition, I've tried even harder to present the principles of economics so that a serious reader will find them both understandable and

v

worth understanding. No previous knowledge of the subject is assumed. Each topic is developed leisurely and at length in recognition of the principle: Short writing makes long reading. For me this has meant the job of writing, and rewriting. And rewriting once again—whenever experience with hundreds of thousands of readers has shown where improvements could be made. I have tried to shirk no difficulty intrinsic to an elementary introduction, knowing that beginners resent being written down to as much as more advanced students do. But I have never understood why an economics textbook should be *unnecessarily* difficult or dull!

McGraw-Hill has cooperated magnificently in producing a book whose print, color diagrams, and layout have been designed with the *sole purpose of aiding in mastery of the economics subject matter.* If the result is also a handsome book, worth keeping in a student's lifetime library, that is simply a bonus. It was the book's teaching function we concentrated on. We planned the careful chapter summaries; the clear introductions; the searching discussion questions; the final check list of key concepts at the end of each chapter; the occasional chapter appendixes marked off by double-column format, designed to handle material that can easily be skipped in a short course or in one concentrating on the basic fundamentals.

This book provides no recipes or panaceas. It has no single Great Message. Of course, the author has opinions, and these predilections may sometimes show through. Nonetheless, the book's genuine aim is *that understanding of economic principles and facts from which policy opinions and convictions can be intelligently formed.* I like to think that the book's wide use abroad and translation into foreign languages—French, Spanish, German, Italian, Portuguese, Arabic, and others—is a reflection of the fact that there do exist certain objective principles of economics which are relevant to societies of quite different institutional development.

What I said in the last edition still stands. An author never knows his own book. Literally hundreds of teachers and other readers have written me detailed letters of comment and criticism. All of these have been of incalculable benefit to me in this revision. They have enabled me to post a Stop, Look, and Listen sign at any point where the discussion becomes (1) difficult to understand or (2) controversial as far as policy is concerned. If the result is a more teachable and objective book—and I hope it is—the credit must go to this legion of helpful critics.

The present edition is a complete revision of the three earlier editions. Every chapter has been extensively rewritten; some—such as the chapter on national income, the chapters on central banking and fiscal policy, the chapters on production, capital theory, and international comparative advantage—have been completely rewritten. (These are now easier chapters—as the author gradually learns more about the craft of textbook writing.) A new chapter on a timely subject, the economics of nuclear energy and automation, has been added, and also an appendix giving a thumbnail sketch of the history of economic doctrines.

Those familiar with the earlier editions will notice the following changes:

The chapters dealing with "microeconomics," principally, Parts Three and Four, show the greatest reshaping. For the first time, the subjects of goods pricing and factor pricing have been given an organic unity by demonstrating throughout just how the market mechanism is contributing to the solution of society's triad of basic economic problems: What shall be produced, How, and For Whom. This makes for a much more understandable and significant treatment of both perfect and imperfect competition.

Monetary policy and problems of inflation have been given new emphasis—in accord with the times.

Repeatedly throughout the book I have set forth what I call a "grand neoclassical synthesis." This is a synthesis of the valid core of modern income determination with the classical economic principles. Its basic tenet is this: Solving the vital problems of monetary and fiscal policy by the tools of income analysis will *validate* and bring back into relevance the classical verities. This neoclassical synthesis does something equally important for the teacher of economics. It heals the breach between aggregative macroeconomics and traditional microeconomics and brings them into complementing unity. In my judgment it greatly enhances the utility of the "national income approach" to introductory economics and I only wish that my first editions could have had the benefit of its repeated use.

Once again, because of my personal phobia against books whose statistical facts and issues are already a few years old at date of publication, I have strained (again perhaps to a ridiculous degree) to bring the material up to as late a date as possible. This is not a book of 1929. Or of 1939. Or of 1955. I only wish I had the crystal ball to gear it more closely to 1965.

New, harmless verses or quotations now head some chapters.

The present book should provide material enough for a full-year course. It can be supplemented, if desired, and the material has been arranged in such a way that chapters and appendixes can be omitted without breaking the continuity. Many institutions will want to use the book for a one-semester course; a suggested outline for such a course (such as that used at my own institution, the Massachusetts Institute of Technology) is included.

Each chapter has been planned to constitute a unit of understanding. Where a chapter tends to be long, it has been broken into Sections A, B, and so forth; these can be assigned like chapters. In several places, material has been put in chapter appendixes. A straw vote showed that most instructors have approved of the extra flexibility provided by this method; such material is not necessarily more difficult, but it is usually something that can be eliminated if time is short or at a first reading.

The discussion has been carefully arranged so that the instructor can, if he wishes, alter the order of assignments. Thus, although at M. I. T. we prefer not to do so, there is no reason why Part Three on Pricing Theory could not precede Part Two on Income Determination. In fact, we often assign Part Three's introductory chapter on Supply and Demand as soon as the first three introductory chapters of Part One have been covered. (The book has been so arranged that knowledge of ten basic chapters—namely, 2, 3, 10, 11, 12, 15, 16, 18, 19, and 24—permits a reader to understand any other chapters.)

My coworkers and I have spared no pains to make this new edition understandable and teachable. Every diagram has been carefully drawn, labeled, captioned, and integrated with the text and with the numerical tables. In addition, the McGraw-Hill Book Company has available a set of a dozen silent filmstrips to provide a valuable classroom supplement.

Writing a beginning textbook is hard work. But its rewards have been tremendous—and I do not mean simply pecuniary rewards. Contact with hundreds of thousands of minds of a whole generation is an experience like no other that a scholar will ever meet. And writing down what we economists know about economics has been truly an exciting experience. I can only hope that some of this excitement will rub off on the reader.

When it comes to final acknowledgments for help received, I am again a hopeless bankrupt. I cannot even begin to enumerate the names of the hundreds of teachers and readers who have sent me suggestions for revision. To name all of my M. I. T. colleagues would be tedious, but Professors Robert L. Bishop, E. Cary Brown, and Francis M. Bator have to be named. And from other colleges, Professors Romney Robinson (Brandeis), Arthur M. Okun (Yale), George A. Kleiner (University of Illinois), John F. Due (University of Illinois), Richard S. Eckaus (Brandeis), and George B. Baldwin (Vanderbilt) have all been especially helpful. Mrs. Inez J. Crandall rendered efficient and patient secretarial aid. And David S. Staiger joined that growing list of able assistants who have enabled me to keep the successive editions abreast of the changing times.

A textbook should be dedicated to one's children—of whom I have my share—but I feel I must above all speak of my debt to Professor Ralph Evans Freeman, past Chairman of the Department of Economics and Social Science at M. I. T., who first suggested that this book be written. Neither he nor any of the above should be blamed for the result; any credit is due my wife.

PAUL A. SAMUELSON

CONTENTS

ix

Part 2 DETERMINATION OF NATIONAL INCOME AND ITS FLUCTUATIONS

Part 3 THE COMPOSITION AND PRICING
OF NATIONAL OUTPUT

Part 4 DISTRIBUTION OF INCOME: THE PRICING OF THE PRODUCTIVE FACTORS

SUGGESTED OUTLINE FOR
A ONE-SEMESTER COURSE

ECONOMICS

An Introductory Analysis

part

1

BASIC ECONOMIC

CONCEPTS AND

NATIONAL INCOME

INTRODUCTION

The age of chivalry is gone; that of sophisters, economists, and calculators has succeeded.

EDMUND BURKE

▶ **FOR WHOM THE BELL TOLLS**

A well-known college dean used to address the entering class: "Take a good look at the man on your right and the man on your left, because next year one of you won't be here."

If the future should be like the past, then of any three readers of this book, a similar statement can be made: There is a strong probability that one, at some period of his life, will be hard hit by a depression or may have his lifetime savings wiped out by price inflation. And all three will find that economic events play a dominant role in their everyday lives.

From a purely selfish point of view, then, it is desirable to gain understanding of the following overwhelmingly important problems of modern economics: the causes of depression, unemployment, and inflationary booms; and the causes of prosperity, full employment, and rising standards of living. But no less important is the fact—clearly to be read from the history of the twentieth century—that the political health of a democracy is tied up in a crucial way with the successful maintenance of stable high employment and living opportunities.

It is not too much to say that the widespread creation of dictatorships and the resulting World War II stemmed in no small measure from the world's failure to meet this basic economic problem adequately. And our world still stands on trial.

3

▶ **POVERTY MIDST PLENTY**

Modern economics tries to explain, among other things, how it is that nations are alternately afflicted with the dizzy ups and downs of business activity. Back in the old days, before the Industrial Revolution had developed our tremendous technology, there were often periodic famines. Statistics showed that the number of marriages moved inversely with the price of bread: when bread became dear, marriages had to be postponed. Millions died as a result of floods, droughts, or other easily recognized natural catastrophes. Everyone knew the causes of disasters, but nobody could do much about them.

Today it is just the opposite. Now we know how to produce a fair abundance of goods, but we are subject to periodic depressions of obscure causation. Bread is cheap in depression; but present-day marriages follow job opportunities rather than the cost of food. Famine due to crop failure in one part of the world can now be relieved by shipments from elsewhere. People go hungry in modern slumps, not because we can produce too little, but seemingly because we can produce too much.

A man from Mars or a Rip Van Winkle from an earlier century would have been at a loss had he returned to the world of the 1930's. He would have thought that everybody had lost his senses. Little pigs were plowed under while families did without meat. Because we had new efficient factories, we did without production. Because we had too many skilled and willing hands, unemployment prevailed. Everybody tried to save and hoard money, with the result that everyone got poorer and poorer. So it might have seemed.

The man from Mars would have been even more surprised to observe that the onset of history's most destructive and bloody war, instead of depressing American business conditions further, had just the opposite effect. Despite shortages, the American civilian standard of living surpassed all previous levels. And since the war, he would have observed all over the world mad inflationary spirals, in which wages chased after prices and prices chased after wages.

▶ **AMONG THE SOUVENIRS**

A man now sixty has a record of his life. Among his souvenirs he has his birth certificate, the picture of his first girl, a 1917 diploma from Siwash, and a Prussian helmet from Flanders field. He carries on his body a scar from a boyhood ski jump; in his mind, a scar from a frustrated desire to build ships rather than fan belts.

Figure 1 shows something else that economic life has engraved on his memory and on his very soul: It shows the ups and downs of the prices he has had to pay in the 60 years of his life. The pre-1914 rise of prices that saved

Grandpa from bankruptcy. World War I's inflationary burst that melted Aunt Jane's widow's pittance and made everyone talk about the H.C.O.L. (the "high cost of living"). The 1920 collapse of prices, when even Sears Roebuck almost went to the wall. The roaring 1920's—jazz, hooch, Lindbergh, and the stock-market boom. Whose silk shirt was lost in the 1929 stock-market crash? And what happened to Junior when he left Siwash with his still-wet 1932 diploma, to face a world that seemed overflowing with unemployed civil engineers?

All this—and World War II, with its aftermath—can be seen in the nation's price barometer. Ups and downs? Yes. But perhaps equally important: Can you make out an upward drift in prices? When granddaughter reaches sixty, how much will she be able to buy with the $10,000 endowment insurance policy she is now taking out in her premarriage working years? Did man come down from the trees, learn to stand, to walk, to conquer even the nucleus of the atom—only to find that he cannot control the stability of the price level?

In short, modern nations must worry lest total money spending and national income be too little, thus creating mass unemployment. But they must also worry lest total national income and money spending be too much, thus creating general price inflation.

The price level winds its way through our lives:

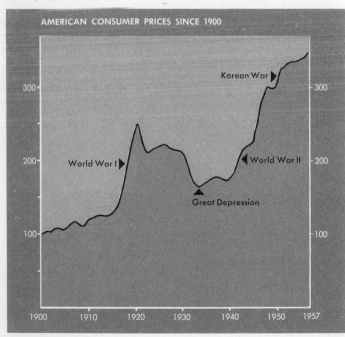

AMERICAN CONSUMER PRICES SINCE 1900

Korean War

World War I

World War II

Great Depression

Fig. 1. Wars and depressions make prices rise and fall. But the general drift has in this century been upward. (By using 1900 as our base, setting the price index equal to 100 in that year, we interpret the latest year's figure of 352 to mean that prices have gone up three and a half times, nearly quadrupling, during the life of a sixty-year-old.)

► ECONOMIC DESCRIPTION AND ANALYSIS

It is the first task of modern economic science to describe, to analyze, to explain, to correlate these fluctuations of national income. Both price inflation and depression unemployment are our concern. This is a difficult and complicated task, but still an obvious one.

A second task is equally difficult, but perhaps not so obvious. We must study the economic principles that tell us how productivity can be kept high and that tell us how people's standards of living can be improved. It is not enough to make jobs plentiful so that economic resources do not go unemployed. We must also make sure that our economic resources are fruitfully employed in such a way as to be efficiently producing the goods and services that people really want and need. So fully half this book is concerned with the composition of national production and not simply with its total.

Because of the complexity of human and social behavior, we cannot hope to attain the precision of a few of the physical sciences. We cannot perform the controlled experiments of the chemist or biologist. Like the astronomer we must be content largely to "observe." But economic events and statistical data observed are, alas, not so well behaved and orderly as the paths of heavenly satellites. Fortunately, however, our answers need not be accurate to several decimal places; on the contrary, if only the right general *direction* of cause and effect can be determined, we shall have made a tremendous step forward.

Knowledge and understanding of nature and society are worth while for their own sake. Just as it is interesting to know the paths of planets and the antics of atoms, it is worth while to know how banks create money, how inflations behave, how supply and demand help to determine prices. But in addition to knowledge for its own sake—and, to most people, of far greater importance—there is the hope that the findings of physics may help engineers make useful improvements, that the study of physiology may promote medical advancement, and that dispassionate analysis of the economic facts will enable society to devise ways to keep some of the more unpleasant ones from happening.

► ECONOMIC POLICY

This brings us to the important problem of economic policy. Ultimately, understanding should aid in control and improvement. How can the business cycle be diminished? How can economic progress be furthered? How can standards of living be made more equitable?

At every point of our analysis we shall be seeking to shed light on these policy problems. But to succeed in this, we must all try to cultivate an objective and detached ability to see things as they *are,* regardless of our likes or dislikes. The fact must be faced that economic issues are close to everybody emotionally. Blood pressures rise and voices become shrill whenever deep-seated beliefs and prejudices are involved, and some of these prejudices are thinly veiled rationalizations of special economic interest.

We know that a doctor passionately interested in stamping out disease must first train himself to observe things as they are. His bacteriology cannot be a different one from that of a mad scientist out to destroy the human race by plague. Wishful thinking is bad thinking and leads to little wish fulfillment. "Where it is a duty to worship the sun, the laws of heat will be poorly understood."

In the same way, there is only one valid reality in a given economic situation, however hard it may be to recognize and isolate it. There is not one theory of economics for Republicans and one for Democrats, not one for workers and one for employers. On the basic economic principles concerning prices and employment, most economists are in pretty close agreement.

This does not mean that economists always agree in the *policy* field. Economist *A* may be for full employment at any cost. Economist *B* may not rank it of primary importance. Basic questions concerning right and wrong goals to be pursued cannot be settled by economists as such. Each citizen must decide them for himself, and an expert is entitled to only one vote along with everyone else. All the expert can do is point out the true costs that may be involved in the different decisions.

▶ **COMMON SENSE AND NONSENSE**

Economics is not an easy subject. True, it does not require the mental application of, say, mathematics. But there is a definiteness in mathematics despite its complexity. So most people feel that, by gritting their teeth and applying themselves sufficiently, they can learn to solve such things as quadratic equations just as other ordinary mortals have done.

Economics at first seems less definite. The world of prices, wages, interest rates, stocks and bonds, banks and credit, taxes and expenditure is a complicated one. Every question seems to have two (or more!) sides, and often the right answer seems to be only that of the last man to buttonhole you.

Now no one can understand a complicated subject like chemistry prior to long and careful study. This is an advantage and a disadvantage. The man on the street or behind a newspaper desk cannot possibly consider himself a final authority on these subjects—which is all to the good. On the other hand, the new student of chemistry must be made familiar with all the basic concepts for the first time, all of which takes a good deal of time.

From childhood days on, everyone knows something about economics. This is both helpful and deceptive: helpful, because much knowledge can be taken for granted; deceptive, because it is natural and human to accept uncritically the truth of superficially plausible views. Everyone of college age knows a good deal about money, perhaps even more than he realizes. Thus he rightly laughs at the child who prefers the large nickel to the small dime or the shiny quarter to the paper dollar bill; and at the Basque peasants who murdered the visiting artist for his book of blank checks.

But a little knowledge may be a dangerous thing. On closer examination common sense may prove to be really nonsense. Because a union leader has successfully negotiated several labor contracts, he may feel that he is an expert on the economics of wages. A businessman who has "met a payroll" may feel that his views on price control are final. A banker who can balance his books may conclude that he knows all there is to know about the creation of money. And an economist who has studied the business cycle may be under the illusion that he can outguess the stock market.

Each individual naturally tends to look only at the immediate effects upon himself of an economic event. A worker thrown out of employment in the buggy industry cannot be expected to reflect that new jobs may have been created in the automobile industry. But we must be prepared to do so.

In an introductory survey, the economist is interested in the workings of the economy *as a whole* rather than in the viewpoint of any one group. Social and national policies rather than individual policy are his goals. Too often, everybody's business is nobody's business. It is just as well, therefore, to understand at the beginning that an elementary course in economics does not pretend to teach one how to run a business or bank, how to spend money wisely, or how to get rich quick from the stock market. But it is to be hoped that general economics will provide a useful background for many such activities.

Certainly the economist must know a good deal about how businessmen, consumers, and investors behave and think. This does not mean that those individuals must use the same language and methods in coming at their decisions as economists find useful in describing their behavior—any more than the planets need know that they are following the elliptical paths traced by the astronomer. Just as many of us have been speaking prose all our lives without knowing it, so many businessmen would be surprised to learn that their behavior is capable of systematic economic analysis. This unawareness is not necessarily to be deprecated. It does not help a baseball pitcher to know the laws of aerodynamics; in fact, if we become self-conscious about how to button our shirts, we may find it harder to do.

▶ THE TYRANNY OF WORDS

Peculiarly in a field where such an everyday concept as "capital" may have ten or more different meanings, we must watch out for the "tyranny of words." The world is complicated enough without introducing further confusions and ambiguities because (1) two different names are unknowingly being used for the same thing, or because (2) the same one word is being applied to two quite different phenomena.

Jones may call Robinson a liar for holding that the cause of depression is oversaving, saying, "Underconsumption is really the cause." Schwartz may enter the argument, asserting, "You are both wrong. The real trouble is underinvestment." They may go on arguing all night; but really if they stopped to analyze their language, they might find there were absolutely no differences in their opinions about the facts and only a verbal confusion was involved.

Similarly, words may be treacherous because we do not react in a neutral manner to them. Thus a man who approves of a government program to ration housing will call it a program of "sensible planning" while an unsympathetic opponent will describe the same activity as "totalitarian bureaucratic regimentation." Who can object to the former, and who could condone the latter? Yet they refer to the same thing. One does not have to be an expert in *semantics*—the study of language and its meaning—to realize that scientific discussion requires us to avoid such emotional terminology, wherever possible.

▶ **THEORY VERSUS PRACTICE**

The economic world is extremely complicated. As we noted, it is usually not possible to make economic observations under controlled experimental conditions characteristic of scientific laboratories. A physiologist who wishes to determine the effects of penicillin on pneumonia may be able to "hold other things equal" by using two test groups who differ only in the fact that they do and do not get penicillin injections. The economist is less fortunately placed. If he wishes to determine the effect of a gasoline tax on fuel consumption, he may be vexed by the fact that, in the same year when the tax was imposed, pipe lines were first introduced. Nevertheless, he must try—if only mentally—to isolate the effects of the tax, with "other things being equal." Otherwise, he will understand the economic effects neither of taxation, nor of transportation improvements, nor of both together.

The difficulty of analyzing causes when controlled experimentation is impossible is well illustrated by the confusion of the savage medicine man who thinks that both witchcraft and a little arsenic are necessary to kill his enemy, or that only after he has put on a green robe in spring will the trees afterward do the same.[1] As a result of this limitation and many others, our quantitative economic knowledge is far from complete. This does not mean that we do not have great amounts of accurate statistical knowledge available. We do. Bales of census data, market information, and financial statistics have been collected by governments, trade associations, and business concerns.

---

[1] In logic this is sometimes called the *post hoc, ergo propter hoc* fallacy (after this, therefore because of this).

Even if we had more and better data, it would still be necessary—as in every science—to *simplify,* to *abstract* from the infinite mass of detail. No mind can apprehend a bundle of unrelated facts. All analysis involves abstraction. It is always necessary to *idealize,* to omit detail, to set up simple hypotheses and patterns by which the mass of facts are to be related, to set up the right questions before we go out looking at the world as it is. Every theory, whether in the physical or biological or social sciences, distorts reality in that it over-simplifies. But if it is a good theory, what is omitted is greatly outweighed by the beam of illumination and understanding that is thrown over the diverse empirical data.

Properly understood, therefore, theory and observation, deduction and induction cannot be in conflict. And the test of a theory's goodness is its usefulness in illuminating observational reality. Its logical elegance and finespun beauty are irrelevant. Consequently, when a student says, "That's all right in theory but not in practice," he really means "That's not all right in theory," or else he is talking nonsense.

▶ BRIEF SUMMARY

Let's sum up what we can all agree on. (1) Economics concerns us all; depressions and inflations hit us where it hurts. (2) Beyond the problem of maintaining a high-level total output, we are all equally concerned that the detailed composition of output shall be in line with what people really want. Efficient work and not leaf raking is what we are after. (3) By its nature, economics is an inexact science in which emotions play a big role and controlled experiments play almost no role. (4) Nonetheless, we must undertake to formulate useful theories; these need not fit all the facts down to the last decimal place; their final worth must be reckoned in terms of the *factual insight* they give us, not their finespun beauty. Without sound principles or theories we can neither describe the economic system nor prescribe remedies for it.

But now let's go on to describe two special and strange features concerning economic principles: (1) the so-called "fallacy of composition," and (2) the fact that, in a world of great unemployment, the truth may be the reverse of what appears to be the simple truth.

▶ THE WHOLE AND THE PART: THE "FALLACY OF COMPOSITION"

The first lesson in economics is: things are often not what they seem. The following true statements may illustrate this:

1. If all farmers work hard and nature cooperates in producing a bumper crop, total farm income *may fall.*

2. *One* man by great ingenuity in hunting a job or by a willingness to work

for less may thereby solve his own unemployment problem; but *all* cannot necessarily solve their problems in this way.

3. Higher prices *for one industry* may benefit its members but, if the prices of *everything* bought and sold increased in the same proportion, no one would be any better off.

4. It may pay the United States to reduce tariffs charged on goods imported even if *other* countries refuse to do likewise.

5. It may pay a firm to take on some business at much *less than full costs*.

6. *Attempts* of individuals to save more in depression *may lessen the total of* the community's savings.

7. What is prudent behavior for an individual or a single business firm may at times be *folly* for a nation or a state.

Let us emphasize: Each of the above statements is true. But they are paradoxical. In the course of this book, each of the seeming paradoxes will be resolved. Once explained, each is so obvious that you will wonder how anyone could ever have failed to notice it. This again is typical of economics. There are no magic formulas or hidden tricks. Anything that is really correct will seem perfectly reasonable once the argument is carefully developed.

At this point it is just as well to note that many of the above paradoxes hinge upon one single confusion or fallacy, called by logicians the "fallacy of composition." In books on logic, this is defined as follows:

► A fallacy in which what is true of a part is, on that account alone, alleged to be also true of the whole.

Very definitely, in the field of economics, it turns out that what seems to be true for each individual is not always true for society as a whole; and conversely, what seems to be true for all may be quite false for any one individual. For everybody to stand on tiptoes to watch a parade does no good, albeit a single person may gain a better view in so doing. Countless similar examples can be given in the field of economics. You might amuse yourself by checking over the previous seven examples to see which are probably related to the fallacy of composition. Or better still, try your luck at finding new examples.

► **THROUGH THE LOOKING GLASS**

There is one very important situation in which any sensible person's beliefs are likely to turn out to be the reverse of the actual economic truth. When is that? It is not during times of high or substantially full employment; it turns out that at such times one's common-sense notions usually are confirmed by the facts. *It is when there is substantial unemployment that things often go exactly into reverse.* We then move into a topsy-turvy wonderland where right seems left and left seems right; up seems down; and black, white.

Mathematicians tell us that in addition to ordinary Euclidean geometry there exist non-Euclidean geometries. In these non-Euclidean worlds, two parallel lines may meet—an example is the spherical surface of the earth, where two "parallel" lines perpendicular to the equator meet at the pole. What is true of one kind of world may be false of another. Similarly, for a world of unemployment, the conclusions of the old classical or Euclidean economics may have to be carefully reformulated before they can become applicable.

This difference between what is true when there is full employment and when there is unemployment may be illustrated by three examples, all of which will be fully explained later and need not be understood at this point:

1. Men mine gold from the bowels of the earth only to have it go back to the earth in the vaults at Fort Knox, Kentucky. How good or bad is this strange procedure? The answer depends in an important way upon whether or not there is full employment.

2. Nations try in the worst way to raise their standards of living by exporting goods and by *not* importing them from other countries. This anxiety to give away goods would be merely stupid under conditions of full employment, but it does make some sense in a world of unemployment.

3. Thriftiness and parsimony may be individual and social virtues during a war or boom period. During a depression these same individual virtues may be self-defeating social vices that intensify our ills and represent the height of folly. Individual virtues can be restored to being social virtues, provided we are able to restore a healthy environment of adequate aggregate demand for the product of business.

After one has thoroughly mastered the analysis of national income determination, it is not hard to steer one's way with confidence in these seemingly difficult fields. The important hard kernel of truth in the older economics of full employment can then be separated from the chaff of misleading applications. Moreover, we shall again and again meet in later chapters what is called the "neoclassical synthesis." According to this: if modern economics does its task well so that unemployment and inflation are substantially banished from democratic societies, then its importance will wither away and the traditional economics (whose concern is *wise* allocation of fully employed resources) will really come into its own—almost for the first time.

▶ THE WORLDLY PHILOSOPHERS

A final question: Who are the economists from whom modern economics comes? Robert L. Heilbroner wrote a fascinating book calling them *The Worldly Philosophers* (Simon and Schuster, New York, 1953). Let's follow him down the picture gallery.

First comes Adam Smith, a Scotch bachelor with powdered wig like George Washington, who gathered together the earlier wisdom of business pamphleteers and philosophic system builders in his *Wealth of Nations* (1776). He recognized the virtues of free markets, and the times were ripe for his doctrines to become the bible of the rising middle classes.

David Ricardo, a practical broker who became a millionaire within 12 years after his father cut him off with £800 for marrying outside his faith, spun the most abstract of theories; but his friend Parson Malthus, who didn't know enough about practical affairs to follow Ricardo's advice to make a killing by speculating on Napoleon's Waterloo defeat—this impractical fellow put his finger on the real-world problems of population and depression.

John Stuart Mill, the last of the great classical economists, was taught Greek by his father at age three. (By age twenty he of course had a nervous breakdown.) But though he developed the eighteenth-century classical system to its logical conclusion, he was led by the end of his life—some say through respectable love for a married woman, whom he later married—to a kind of Christian socialism. (Just to confuse matters, Mill had always been—even at age three! —an atheist.)

Then our picture gallery comes to a black sheep, who was beyond the pale of the true classical tradition. Karl Marx, an exile from Germany, worked away in the British Museum vowing that the *bourgeoisie* would pay for the suffering his boils caused him as he sat working out his theories of the inevitable downfall of capitalism. (His own biography reads like a Balzac novel, not like sociological science.)

You must turn to Heilbroner's book for the full story of the economists. Suffice it only to mention here John Maynard Keynes (Lord Keynes), an all-round genius, who produced the most controversial book of recent years. In his *General Theory of Employment, Interest, and Money* (1936), there is a passage that happens to answer the question: Why study economics?

The ideas of economists and political philosophers, both when they are right and when they are wrong, are more powerful than is commonly understood. Indeed the world is ruled by little else. Practical men, who believe themselves to be quite exempt from any intellectual influences, are usually the slaves of some defunct economist. Madmen in authority, who hear voices in the air, are distilling their frenzy from some academic scribbler of a few years back. I am sure that the power of vested interests is vastly exaggerated compared with the gradual encroachment of ideas.

▶ A PREVIEW

Here in Part One we deal with the facts, institutions, and analysis necessary to an understanding of national income or output.

In Part Two we analyze the causes of prosperity and depression: how the processes of saving and investment interact to determine the level of monetary purchasing power, income, and employment—and how monetary and fiscal policies can stabilize business activity at a healthy level of progressive growth.

Part Three is concerned with the forces of competition and monopoly which act through supply and demand to help determine the composition of the national income, in terms both of goods and services to be produced and of their prices.

Part Four treats distribution of income: wages, rent, interest, and profits.

Part Five discusses international trade, in both its monetary and real aspects.

Its last chapter and the three chapters of Part Six deal with some of our most vital current economic problems. Nasty problems like war. Exciting problems like the development of backward countries. Challenging problems like automation and nuclear energy.

QUESTIONS FOR DISCUSSION

1. If another major depression like that of the 1930's should occur, do you think you would be affected (*a*) seriously, (*b*) moderately, or (*c*) not at all?

2. Why does the physicist often talk about a frictionless system, when there is no such thing? Is there any justification for this?

3. Discuss the emotional content of the following words: regimentation, planning, usury, monopolist, gambling, speculation, American way of life, free enterprise, cartels, thrift, hoarding.

4. Give examples of the fallacy of composition and of the *post hoc, ergo propter hoc* fallacy.

5. Give an example of an economic principle that may be valid when there is full employment but misleading when there is unemployment.

6. Review your understanding of the following concepts:

inflationary price rises	*tyranny of words*
poverty midst plenty	*controlled experiment*
analysis and policy	*fallacy of composition*
practice and theory	post hoc *fallacy*
wishful thinking	

2 CENTRAL PROBLEMS OF EVERY ECONOMIC SOCIETY

> To get land's fruit in quantity
> Takes jolts of labor ever more,
> Hence food will grow like one, two, three . . .
> While numbers grow like one, two, four . . .
>> Song of Malthus: A Ballad
>> on Diminishing Returns
>> ANONYMOUS

At the foundations of any community there will always be found a few universal economic conditions. Certain background problems hold as much for our present-day economy as they did in the days of Homer and Caesar. And they will continue to be relevant in the "brave new world" of the years ahead.

In this chapter we shall see what some of these universal conditions are: (A) how every society must meet a triplet of *basic problems of economic organization;* (B) how technological knowledge together with limited amounts of economic resources defines the available choices between goods and services open to a community, and how these *production possibilities* are subject to changing costs and to the law of diminishing returns; (C) finally, the *underlying population or human basis of any economy.*

The above topics form the three parts of this chapter. We leave to Chapter 3 those important special economic features characteristic of our own mixed system of private and public enterprise.

A PROBLEMS OF ECONOMIC ORGANIZATION

Any society, whether it consists of a totally collectivized communistic state, a tribe of South Sea Islanders, a capitalistic industrial nation, a Swiss Family Robinson or Robinson Crusoe—or, one might almost add, a colony of bees—must somehow meet three fundamental economic problems.

15

1. *What* commodities shall be produced and in what quantities? That is, how much and which of alternative goods and services shall be produced?

2. *How* shall goods be produced? That is, by whom and with what resources and in what technological manner are they to be produced?

3. *For Whom* are goods to be produced? That is, who is to enjoy and get the benefit of the goods and services provided? Or, to put the same thing in another way: How is the total of national product to be *distributed* among different individuals and families?

These three questions are fundamental and common to all economies. But different economic systems try to solve them differently. In a primitive civilization, custom may rule every facet of behavior. *What, How,* and *For Whom* may be decided by reference to traditional ways of doing things. To members of another culture, the practices followed may seem bizarre and unreasonable; the members of the tribe or clan may themselves be so familiar with existing practices as to be surprised, and perhaps offended, if asked the reason for their behavior. Thus, the Kwakiutl Indians consider it desirable not to accumulate wealth but to give it away in the *potlatch*—a roisterous celebration. This deviation from acquisitive behavior will not surprise anthropologists; from their studies they know that what is correct behavior in one culture is often the greatest crime in another.

In the bee colony, all such problems, even those involving an extraordinarily elaborate cooperative division of labor, are solved automatically by means of so-called "biological instincts."

At the other extreme we can imagine an omnipotent, benevolent or malevolent dictator who by arbitrary decree and fiat decides What, How, and For Whom. Or we might imagine economic organization by decree, but with decrees drawn up by democratic vote, or, what is more likely in view of the multiplicity and complexity of economic decisions, with decrees drawn up by selected legislative or planning authorities.

Finally, as Chapter 3 develops at length, in a so-called "capitalist free enterprise economy," a system of prices (of markets, of profits and losses) primarily[1] determines What, How, and For Whom goods and services shall be produced.

▶ **THE LAW OF SCARCITY**

What to produce, How, and For Whom would not be problems if resources were unlimited: if an infinite amount of every good could be produced, or if human wants were fully satisfied, it would not then matter if too much of any particular good were produced. Nor would it then matter if labor and materials were combined unwisely. Since everyone could have as much as he

---

[1] There never has been a 100 per cent purely automatic enterprise system. Even in our capitalistic system, the government has an important role in modifying the workings of the price system.

pleased, it would not matter how goods and incomes were distributed among different individuals and families.

There would then be no *economic goods, i.e.,* no goods that are relatively scarce; and there would hardly be any need for a study of economics or "economizing." All goods would be *free goods,* like water or air.

In the world as it is, even little children are supposed to learn in growing up that "both" is not an admissible answer to a choice of "which one." Compared with backward nations or compared with previous centuries, modern industrial societies seem very wealthy indeed. But even the richest of such nations, the United States, would have to be scores of times more productive than it now is to give everybody as comfortable a standard of living as is enjoyed by our most fortunate few.

Higher production levels always seem to bring in their train higher consumption standards. People feel that they want and "need" steam heat, indoor plumbing, refrigerators, education, movies, radios and television, books, automobiles, travel, music, fashionable clothes, etc. The biological scientist may tell them that they can be well nourished on a thin porridge for a few cents a day,[1] but that leaves them as cold as the information that the chemicals in their bodies are worth only a couple of dollars. Anyone who has kept a family budget knows that the necessities of life—the absolute musts—have little to do with the minimum physiological needs of food, clothing, and shelter necessary to keep life flickering.

During the Great Depression that followed the stock-market crash of 1929, it was fashionable for popular writers to announce the repeal of the "law of scarcity." They claimed we had moved into a new scientific era in which the economic system knew how to produce more than could be consumed.

This was dead wrong. Such observers were perfectly right in pointing out that the system could produce more than we were *then* consuming. They were right that the problem of technological unemployment could not be shrugged off lightly. They were also right in pointing out that "freedom from (physical) want" could be achieved for the more productive parts of the globe if only unemployment could be banished.

But they should also have realized what the postwar period has since helped to confirm: Even with all resources working at top efficiency, the average standard of living would be a quite moderate one compared with what we please to call the "American way of life," as revealed, for example, in rosy magazine advertisements. It is shown later that dividing up equally our highest full-employment income among every man, woman, and child would still yield less than an average of $45 per person per week.

---

[1] Statisticians have shown that the best modern standards of adult nutrition (vitamins A, B, . . . , calories, proteins, etc.) could be bought in 1958 for less than $100 per year! But what a diet this implies: kidneys, lima beans, peanut butter, and not much else.

Releasing atomic energy will still not bring us near to the state of "bliss." You need never fear that no useful work remains to be done. An infinite number of tunes are still to be written. If ever consumption needs should be sated—which is unlikely—there would always remain the alternative of leisure, recreation, and the other elements that go to make up the good life.

B THE TECHNOLOGICAL CHOICES OPEN TO ANY SOCIETY

▶ THE PRODUCTION-POSSIBILITY OR TRANSFORMATION CURVE

We have discussed the basic economic fact that *limitation* of the total resources capable of producing different commodities necessitates a choice between relatively scarce commodities. This can be illustrated quantitatively by simple arithmetic examples and by means of geometrical diagrams. Students have found that diagrams and graphs are important visual aids in many parts of economics. A little care at the beginning in understanding them will be rewarded manyfold later on.

Let's examine an economy with only so many people, only so much technical knowledge, only so many factories and tools, only so much land, water power, and natural resources. In deciding What shall be produced and How, the economy must really decide just how these resources are to be allocated among the thousands of different possible commodities. How much land should go into wheat cultivation? Or into pasturage? How many factories are to produce hairpins? How much skilled labor should go into machine shops?

These problems are very complicated even to discuss, much less to solve. Therefore, we must simplify. So let's assume there are to be produced only two economic goods (or classes of economic goods). For dramatic purposes, we can concentrate on the famous pair, guns and butter. These two commodities

Full employment of scarce resources means society must choose between more guns or more butter:

Table 1. Alternative possibilities in the production of butter and guns. Economic resources can be shifted from butter production to gun production, in effect enabling us to convert butter into guns.

Possibilities	Guns, thousands	Butter, millions of pounds
A	15	0
B	14	1
C	12	2
D	9	3
E	5	4
F	0	5

are commonly used to illustrate the problem of choosing between civilian and war goods. But the same analysis applies to any choice of goods: thus the more resources the government uses to build public roads, the less will be left to produce private houses; and the more the public chooses to consume of food, the less it can consume of clothing.

But let us stick to the example of guns and butter. Now, suppose that all resources are thrown into the production of civilian goods, or butter. There will still be at most some maximum amount of butter that can be produced per year. (The exact amount depends upon the quantitative and qualitative resources of the economy in question and the technological efficiency with which they are used.) Let's suppose that 5 million pounds of butter is this maximum amount which can be produced in the existing state of the technological arts.

At the other extreme, imagine that 100 per cent of society's resources had instead been devoted to the production of guns.[1] Only some maximum number of guns could then be produced: 15,000 guns of a certain description can perhaps be produced if we are willing to produce no butter.

These are extreme possibilities. In between there are still others. If we are willing to give up some butter, we can have some guns; if we are willing to give up still more butter, we can have still more guns. A schedule of a number of possibilities is given in Table 1, with F being the extreme where all butter and no guns are produced, and A being the opposite extreme where all resources go into guns. In between, at E, D, C, and B, butter is increasingly being given up in return for more guns. Butter is "transformed" into guns, not physically but by diverting resources from one use to the other.

Table 1 can also be represented diagrammatically by Fig. 1, which should be self-explanatory.

[1] Of course, this could not really happen. Without some civilian production society could not live. But we are considering possibilities—the subjunctive mood, not the indicative.

This can be shown pictorially . . .

ALTERNATIVE PRODUCTION POSSIBILITIES

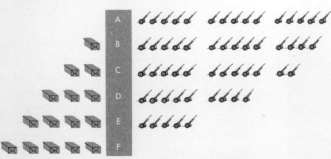

Fig. 1. The cost of getting extra guns can be reckoned as the extra butter we are forced to sacrifice.

BUTTER
(millions of lb)

GUNS
(thousands)

It may be even more illuminating to represent this same production-possibility or production-transformation schedule by measuring butter along the horizontal axis and guns along the vertical, as in Fig. 2.

The student should now be able to go directly from the numerical table to the final diagram; by counting over 5 butter units to the right in *F* and going up 0 gun units; in *E,* by counting over 4 butter units to the right and going up 5 gun units; and finally in *A* by going to the right 0 butter units and up 15 gun units.

We may fill in all intermediate positions, even those involving fractions of a million pounds, or of a thousand guns, as in the so-called production-possibility curve shown in Fig. 3.

The curve that we now have represents this fundamental fact:

▶ *A full-employment economy must always in producing one good be giving up something of another.* This assumes, of course, that at least some resources can be transferred from one good to another; *e.g.,* steel is used for guns and also for butter via farm machinery.

   Substitution is the law of life in a full-employment economy.

But what if there had been widespread unemployment of resources: idle men, idle land, idle factories? We have already warned that our economic laws may then be quite different. And this is one such instance.

With unemployment we are not on the transformation or production-possibility curve at all, but somewhere *inside* it; say at *U,* producing only 2 million pounds of butter and 4 thousand guns. If resources are idle, by putting

Or, it can be shown graphically by plotting the points on a grid . . .

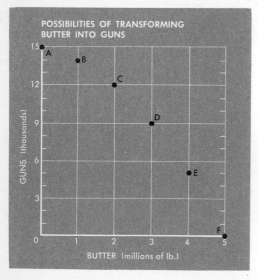

Fig. 2. Each marked point is a careful plot of each gun-and-butter numerical combination from Table 1. (Can you guess where the point midway between *B* and *C* might approximately fall? Can you read off its guns-butter numbers and pencil them into Table 1 at about the right place?)

them to work we can have more butter *and* more guns. We can move from *U* to *D* or *E*, thereby getting more butter and more guns.

This throws important light on the different historical wartime experience of three countries: the United States, Germany, and Russia. After 1940, how was the United States able to become the "arsenal of democracy" and to enjoy civilian living standards higher than ever before? Largely by taking up the slack of unemployment. On the other hand, Hitler Germany's war effort began in 1933, long before any formal declaration. It stemmed from a period of unemployment acute enough to win him the votes to get into power peacefully. Almost all the extra output made possible by taking up unemployed workers and plants was siphoned into German war goods rather than into higher civilian consumption. Still a third case is that of the Soviet Union in World War II. The Russians had little unemployment before the war and were already on their rather low production-possibility curve. They had no choice but to substitute civilian for war goods—with consequent privation.

Two questions will help to emphasize that the production-possibility curve is drawn up as of (1) fixed totals of resources and (2) given technological knowledge. First, what will happen to the production-possibility curve if a country's population and labor force grows over the years? And second, what will happen to it if scientists and engineers discover better ways of producing guns and butter? It is clear that, in both of these cases, the production-possibility curve will shift outward. More guns and more butter will then be

Or we can picture production possibilities by drawing a smooth curve:

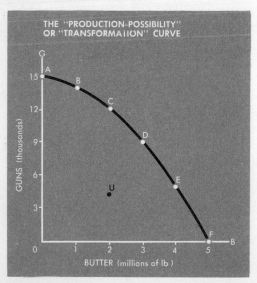

THE "PRODUCTION-POSSIBILITY" OR "TRANSFORMATION" CURVE

GUNS (thousands)

BUTTER (millions of lb)

Fig. 3. This shows how society can choose to substitute "guns" for "butter," assuming a given state of technology and a given total of resources. Any point *inside* the curve, such as *U*, indicates that resources are not being fully employed in the best known way. (Source: Table 1. A smooth curve has been passed through the points of the previous figure.)

possible, as the last few centuries of economic history confirm. (Try penciling in a new curve on Fig. 3 to show the effect of growth in productivity.)

▶ INCREASING COSTS

Our production-possibility curve, sloping as it does rightward and downward (*i.e.,* from northwest to southeast), summarizes the fact of substitution and choice between commodities at full employment.

But curving out as it does, it depicts a further important economic principle:

> ▶ As we want more of any good, we must usually pay a higher cost for it; we must give up more and more of other goods.

Table 1 and Figs. 1, 2, and 3 all illustrate this law of increasing cost. A very first unit of butter requires a sacrifice of only one unit of guns. But how much of guns must we sacrifice to get one more unit of butter? A full *two* units of guns! Our numerical table shows that each extra unit of butter becomes more and more expensive in terms of necessary extra sacrifices of guns.

This law of increasing *extra* cost applies in the case of butter production. Does it also apply in the case of gun production? Yes, using the same argument on the bloated, or convex, shape of the curve in Fig. 3 shows that the law of extra cost does apply to guns too. It applies perfectly symmetrically to either good. Here's the argument to show this. A first extra gun requires the sacrifice of very little butter when we are near the point *F*. But as we move toward *E* and *D* (sacrificing butter for guns), each additional gun requires giving up a greater amount of butter than did the preceding one. By the time we reach the vicinity of *A* and *B*, each additional gun requires the sacrifice of a great amount of butter, as shown by the flattening out of the curve.

What is the common sense of this law of increasing cost? Note that the first few guns can be produced in part with the kind of resources that are no good for butter anyway. But if more guns are wanted, we must use resources that are quite valuable for butter production. And if we insist upon having all guns, we must be prepared to take farmers and farm land, which are very efficient in the production of butter, and transform them to the production of guns even though they can produce only very little in this sphere. Thus increasing costs are to be expected.[1]

▶ THE FAMOUS LAW OF DIMINISHING RETURNS

The law that one good's cost tends to rise in terms of another good is itself closely related to an even more famous technological economic relationship

---

[1] Even if resources could be divided into two uniform classes, such as homogeneous land and homogeneous labor, increasing costs would still result from the fact that guns and butter

—the so-called "law of diminishing returns." This law states a relation, not between two goods (such as guns and butter), but rather between an input of production (such as labor) and the resulting output of a good produced (such as butter or, in the traditional examples, corn).

More specifically, the law of diminishing returns refers to the amount of *extra output* that we get when we successively add equal *extra* units of a *varying input* to a *fixed* amount of some *other input*. (Note the emphasized words.)

Here is an example to illustrate the law. We make the following controlled experiment. Given a fixed amount of land, say 100 acres of land, we will first add no labor at all. We note that there is then no corn output. So we record zero output.

Now we make a second related experiment. We add 1 extra unit of labor to the same fixed amount of land. How much output do we now get? Pure reason cannot tell us: we must look to the facts of the experiment. So this we do, observing, let us say, that we now have produced positive output of corn exactly equal to 2,000 units (bushels or whatever units you choose to measure corn in). We now write down the result of this second experiment, giving this summary: Adding 1 extra unit of labor to fixed land gives us extra output of +2,000 units.

Now to observe the law of diminishing returns, we must make a third controlled experiment. Still we hold land fixed. Again we vary the labor input, making sure to again add exactly the same extra unit of labor as before: *i.e.*, we now go from 1 unit of labor to 2 units of labor. We breathlessly await the outcome of the experiment in terms of extra corn produced. Will we now have a total of 4,000 units of corn, which would again represent exactly 2,000 extra output produced by the extra unit of the varying labor? Or will we find *diminishing* returns, with the new extra unit of input adding less than the 2,000 extra units of output that it previously did?

If the law of diminishing returns does in fact hold, our experiment can have but one result: the second extra labor unit will add less extra output than did the first. And adding a third extra unit of labor will, if diminishing returns does hold, result in still less extra output. And so forth.

Table 2 on the following page gives numbers to illustrate exactly what diminishing returns means.

The law of diminishing returns is an important, often-observed, economic and technical regularity. But it is not universally valid. Often it will hold only *after* you have added a considerable number of equal doses of the varying factor. Beyond that point, we say, the law of diminishing returns has set in.

---

do not require the same proportion of these resources, butter taking more land and guns requiring relatively more labor. But such an explanation belongs in a more advanced text.

Diminishing returns is a fundamental law of economics and technology:

Man-years of labor	Total product, bu	Extra output added by additional unit of labor
0	0	
		2,000
1	2,000	
		1,000
2	3,000	
		500
3	3,500	
		————
4	3,800	
		100
5	3,900	

Table 2. Returns of corn when units of labor are added to fixed land. Law of diminishing returns refers to successively lower extra outputs gained from adding equal doses of a variable input to a constant amount of a fixed input. (Pencil in the extra output of the fourth laborer.)

Before such a point it is invalid, since up until then we find that adding extra varying inputs to a fixed input leads to increasing rather than diminishing returns.[1]

Why does the fact of diminishing returns often seem plausible? We feel that if you had added land and labor together, with no input being fixed and all being varied in the same proportion, then in many cases you would have got extra outputs that did not diminish. For, why should the extra outputs diminish if each of the inputs always has as much of the other inputs to work with? On the other hand, *when we do hold one input or group of inputs constant and vary the remaining inputs, we see that the varying inputs have less and less of the fixed inputs to work with.* So we are not too surprised that such extra varying inputs begin to add less and less extra product. In effect the fixed factor of production, land, has decreased in proportion to the variable input, labor. If we crowd the land even further, we may by intensive cultivation of the soil still get some extra corn; but the amount of extra corn will become less and less.

In conclusion, we may summarize the law of diminishing returns as follows:

▶ An increase in some inputs relative to other comparatively fixed inputs will cause total output to increase. *But after a point the extra output resulting from the same additions of extra inputs will become less and less.* This falling off of extra returns is a consequence of the fact that the new "doses" of the varying resources have less and less of the fixed resources to work with.

[1] If you changed Table 2, replacing 2,000 by 900, you'd find that the law of diminishing returns becomes valid only after the second row; at first there would actually be increasing returns.

▶ ECONOMIES OF SCALE AND MASS PRODUCTION: A DIGRESSION

In Section C of this chapter we shall show how the law of diminishing returns can throw much light on world population problems. But before leaving this section, we ought to take note of a partial countertendency to the law of diminishing returns. In many industrial processes, there is an increase in efficiency as their scale increases. When you double labor, land, and *all* other inputs, you may find that your output is more than doubling: this is called "increasing returns to *scale*."

Actually, our law of diminishing returns always referred to cases where some factors were being varied with some being fixed. So this case of increasing returns to scale is not a direct refutation of the law of diminishing returns.

Increasing returns to scale, or so-called "economies of mass production" are often related to the following circumstances: (1) use of nonhuman and non-animal power sources (water and wind power, steam, electricity, turbines and internal-combustion engines, internal atomic energy); (2) automatic self-adjusting mechanisms (lathes, jigs, servomechanisms); (3) use of standard-ized, interchangeable parts; (4) breakdown of complex processes into simple repetitive operations; (5) specialization of function and division of labor; and many other technological factors. The automobile-production assembly line or the historical development of modern textile spinning and weaving typify these diverse factors.

Upon thought it will be evident that *each of these economies or savings comes into full play only if a large enough number of units is being produced to make it worth while to set up a fairly elaborate productive organization.* If only a few guns are to be produced, they might just as well be produced by hand; but if resources are available to produce many thousands, it will pay to make certain elaborate initial preparations which need not be repeated when still more units are to be produced.

Thus, it might come about that, unlike our simplified picture above, we would have to pay two butter units for our first gun unit; but to get still another gun unit we would have to pay only one butter unit because of the efficiency of mass production. This would be a case of decreasing rather than increasing costs.[1]

Economies of scale are very important in explaining why so many of the goods we buy are produced by large companies. We'll see they are important in helping explain "the division of labor" and pattern of "specialization." They raise questions to which we shall return again and again in later chapters.

---

[1] When strong increasing returns to scale overweigh diminishing returns and the law of increasing costs, advanced texts show you have to redraw Fig. 3 to be concave rather than convex.

C THE UNDERLYING POPULATION BASIS OF ANY ECONOMY: PAST AND FUTURE POPULATION TRENDS

▶ THE MALTHUS THEORY OF POPULATION

The law of diminishing returns has an important and interesting application in the field of population. Around 1800, Thomas Robert Malthus, a young English clergyman, used to argue at breakfast against his father's view that "every day in every way, the human race is getting better and better." Finally the younger Malthus became so agitated that he wrote a book about it. His famous *Essay on the Principle of Population* (1st ed., 1798) was an instantaneous best seller. It went through several editions and for a century influenced the thinking of people all over the world (including Charles Darwin, the expositor of the famous doctrine of biological evolution). It is still a living influence today. Malthus' views depend directly on the law of diminishing returns, and they continue to have relevance.

Malthus first took the observation of Benjamin Franklin that, in the American colonies where resources were abundant, population tended to double every 25 years or so. Malthus postulated, therefore, *a universal tendency for population—unless checked by food supply—to grow at a geometric progression.* Now anyone who lets his imagination roam knows how rapidly geometric progressions grow—how soon 1, 2, 4, 8, 16, 32, 64, 128, 256, 512, 1,024, . . . , becomes so large that there is not space in the world for all the resulting off-spring to stand.[1]

To all this Malthus, Sr., said only, "So what?" Consequently, at this point Malthus in effect unleashed the devil of the law of diminishing returns.

As population doubles and redoubles, it is exactly as if the globe were halving in size until finally it has shrunk so much that food and subsistence fall below that necessary for life. Because of the law of diminishing returns, food tends *not* to keep up with the geometric-progression rate of growth of population.

Mind you, Malthus did not say that population *would* increase at these rates. This was only its *tendency* if unchecked. He considered it an important part of his argument to demonstrate: In all countries in all times, checks are operating to hold population in. In the first edition of his work he put emphasis on *positive* checks that operate to increase the death rate: pestilence, famine, war,

---

[1] At 6 per cent compound interest, money doubles in value every 12 years. It has been estimated that the $24 received by the Indians for Manhattan island would, if deposited at compound interest, be today worth at least as much as all real property on the island. At 6 per cent, Sir Francis Drake's plunder of Spanish gold would today equal Britain's wealth.

etc. Later he relented from this gloomy doctrine to hold out hope for the human race through *preventive* checks operating on the birth rate. Although the birth-control movement is often called Neo-Malthusianism, Malthus, himself an early nineteenth-century clergyman, advocated only *moral restraint* with prudential postponement of early marriages until a family could be supported. In fact, to him the struggle for existence was an illustration of the wisdom of the Creator, and we can picture him discussing over a hearty breakfast with his own daughter how diminishing returns keep poor people from getting soft and lazy and how great are the advantages of "virtuous celibacy."

This important application of diminishing returns illustrates what profound effects a simple theory can have. Malthus' ideas had widespread repercussions. His book was used to support a stern revision of the English poor laws, whereby destitution was considered a result of laziness and unemployment a state to be made as uncomfortable as possible. Also he bolstered the argument that trade-unions could not improve the welfare of workers, since any increase in their wages would only cause them to reproduce until there was again barely enough to go around.

Despite the tons of statistics covering many countries in his later editions, it is today recognized that his views were oversimplifications. In his discussion of diminishing returns, he never fully anticipated the miracles of the Industrial Revolution. In the next century technological innovation *shifted* production-possibility curves *outward* and made possible better standards of living for more people. At the same time medical advances were prolonging human life and further lessening the positive checks to population. Nor did he realize that after 1870 in most Western nations, including the United States, family *fertility* as measured by actual number of children would begin to fall far short of family *fecundity,* or biological reproductive capacity.

Nevertheless, the germs of truth in his doctrines are important still for understanding the population behavior of India, China, and other parts of the globe where the balance of numbers and food supply is a vital factor.

Table 3 shows how much world population has increased. This increase was made possible mainly through the declining death rate, resulting from scientific advances in medicine and from the improved living standards made

World population has tripled since 1800:

	1800	1940	1955
Europe (including all of U.S.S.R.)	188	572	609
North, South, and Central America	29	277	366
Asia, Africa, and Oceania	702	1,396	1,717
World	919	2,245	2,692

Table 3. Population of the world (in millions). (Sources: W. S. Thompson, *Plenty of People,* Ronald, New York, 1944; United Nations *Statistical Year Book.*)

possible by the Industrial Revolution. Life expectancy of a new baby has increased from 18 years in 1800 to over 70 years at present, and standards of living far exceed those of any previous century. Moreover, the parts of the world where population is held in by food supply are shown in the table to have been of declining percentage importance. But will the Malthus devil of overpopulation stay chained? In India alone, one of the fruits of modern science has been a great increase in average life expectancy. In the 20 years from 1931 to 1951, India's population grew by about 93 million, an amount equal to the combined populations of France and England!

What if modern medicine were to keep people free of disease only to let them face starvation? The next-to-the-last chapter brings all the tools of economic analysis developed throughout this book to bear on the vital challenge of growth of underprivileged countries.

▶ DO AMERICA AND EUROPE FACE DEPOPULATION?

At the end of World War I men still feared the Malthusian curve of overpopulation. They wrote books with such alarming titles as *The World Faces Over-population* and *Standing Room Only!* But just as these books were coming off the presses, Western Europe and the United States were undergoing a profound revolution in population.

Only a generation later was this beginning to be understood. The pendulum then swung to the other extreme; the best sellers carried such flashy titles as *The Twilight of Parenthood* and *England without People.*

How can we account for this sudden change of tune? Have births fallen below deaths in modern England, France, Sweden, Germany, or the United States? The records show they have not. Why then were the experts afraid, before World War II, that a decline in population was just around the corner?

The answer is not hard to find. Since 1870—even earlier in France—birth rates began to drop in most countries of Western European civilization. After World War I, and especially after the Great Depression of the 1930's, the drop became precipitous. But curiously enough, the alarming nature of the crisis in births was hidden for a time.

Why did a comparison of births and deaths give a misleading feeling of security? Crude births and deaths were misleading because they ignored the fact that the United States and Western Europe *temporarily* have had an unusually large number of women in the childbearing groups. Why this bulge in these ages? Because our grandparents had larger families than our parents were having. With so many women of the age to be a mother, births may temporarily hold up; and yet the number of births per mother may be low—so low that, if the same rate continues, the future growth of the population will eventually end and turn into a decline.

▶ THE NET REPRODUCTION RATE

The true state of affairs as to prewar population trends was revealed to us by a little arithmetical trick. Instead of concentrating on crude births and deaths, someone got the bright idea of asking, "What is the total number of daughters that will have been born to 1,000 newborn girl babies by the time the latter have all completed their life spans?" If this total of daughters is exactly 1,000, then we say that the *net reproduction rate* (NRR) is 1.0, and the population will just hold its own in the long run.

If only 900 girl babies are born to each 1,000 girl babies throughout their lives, then the NRR is only 0.9—and ultimately the population will begin to decrease at the rate of 10 per cent per generation. On the other hand, if each 1,000 women leave 2,000 daughters behind them (who will leave 4,000 daughters behind them, etc.), then the NRR is equal to 2.0 and the population will ultimately grow at a rate of 100 per cent increase per generation. (A "generation" is about 27 years, the average age of a mother.)

The computation of the net reproduction rate for a given group is not too difficult if the necessary statistical data are available. From past mortality data collected by insurance companies, we know what fraction of the original 1,000 women are likely still to be alive at the ages of 15, 20, 25, . . . , and 50 years. From data on the number of likely births to women of each of these ages—data that this country has often neglected to collect—we are able to calculate just how many babies our group of women will have throughout their entire lives. A little less than half of these will be girls, and this number of girls divided by 1,000 is the NRR.[1]

The population crisis of our age was summarized in the statement that before World War II the net reproduction rate dropped far below unity in England, France, Germany, Sweden, and many other countries. The United States was balanced just under unity. South America, Eastern Europe, and Russia continue to have very high net reproduction rates. India and the Orient tend to have high fertility rates, but so few girls survive to adulthood and through the years of childbearing that until recently their net reproduction rate did not greatly exceed unity.

▶ OUR AMAZING POPULATION UPSURGE

Before World War II there was every good reason for the population expert to despair for the future of the population of Western nations. Moreover, the

---

[1] The NRR can increase only if the birth rate per woman of each age rises or if fewer women die in infancy and prior to the completion of the childbearing ages. Keeping older people alive or having the *same* number of babies at an earlier age will increase the population in the short run, but it cannot alone raise the NRR above 1.0 and check an ultimate declining trend in population.

problem did not appear to be directly economic. Everyone knows that the rich used to have fewer children than the poor. Before the war, Harvard and Vassar students were not reproducing themselves. Neither were Michigan State and Oberlin students or high-school graduates or urban groups generally.[1]

But then something remarkable happened to jar the expert. Nobody yet knows quite how to explain it. During and after World War II the pattern of fertility began steadily to climb, reaching new heights. Every year now brings us a crop of more than 4 million babies!

Some of the reasons are, of course, obvious. With the war came prosperity, and with prosperity the backlog of depression-deferred marriages began to melt. Also the Selective Service Act had something to do with the increase in marriages. With many more recent marriages, it was only natural to expect the birth rate to leap upward. But more than that, prosperity and the war seem to have stepped up the rate at which newly married couples have children.

For a long time, the population expert tended to pooh-pooh the new trend. He kept insisting that the increases in births represented only a flash in the pan, that most of these births represented either the backlog of the depression or a borrowing against the future. He argued: "Instead of having their children in the 1930's or 1950's, people are having them in 1948. The increased births are primarily increases in first and second children; clearly, the reproduction rate can be lifted above unity only if married couples average more than two or three children during their years of childbearing."

But finally the expert had to admit that at least temporarily there was an important break in the falling trend of the net reproductive rate. All over the Western world, in the neutral as well as the warring countries, there was this same increase in fertility. Part can be explained by full employment and marriages. Still, other factors are important—such as accumulated wartime savings, unavailability of automobiles during the war, lessened fear of childbirth now that its pains and dangers have diminished, government encouragement, veterans' benefits, and family allowances.

But to explain the increased fertility of marriages, one had to explore deeper psychological factors such as fear of death in battle and a desire to achieve a kind of personal immortality by leaving behind offspring. In the face of a world grown more dangerous, people's attitudes and values seemed to turn inward toward the home.

---

[1] Most authorities believe the decline is to be explained by social rather than biological factors. Thus, the French Canadians, who have high birth rates, came from just those rural regions of France with lowest rates. Second-generation Italian and Jewish city dwellers show greatly reduced rates, as do Negroes who move from the South to the North. Some of the highest net reproduction rates are among the white people in the Southern hillbilly regions. Ironically, the highest rates of all are to be found among—of all peoples—the American Indians, suggesting that we may yet give the country back to the Indians.

Net reproduction rates make correction for changing age distribution:

Table 4. Net reproduction rates for various countries. A NRR (net reproduction rate) always greater than one means ultimate population growth. A NRR less than one means ultimate population decline. The NRR for the United States has since the war risen to substantially above one. (Source: *Population Index*, Office of Population Research, Princeton, N.J.)

United States	*Total*	0.98	(1930–40)	Belgium	0.86	(1939)
		1.65	(1954)		1.05	(1954)
	White	0.96	(1935–40)	Netherlands	1.15	(1935–40)
		1.60	(1954)		1.41	(1954)
	Nonwhite	1.14	(1935–40)	Australia	0.96	(1932–4)
		2.06	(1954)		1.47	(1953)
United Kingdom		0.77	(1931–5)	Palestine *Moslems*	2.17	(1940)
		1.03	(1954)	*Jews*	1.61	(1945)
France		0.90	(1931–5)	Israel	1.64	(1954)
		1.25	(1954)	Japan	1.57	(1930)
Sweden		0.73	(1933–5)		1.18	(1953)
		1.03	(1954)	India	1.25	(1931)
Germany		0.70	(1933)		1.31	(1941)
		0.95	(1954)	Soviet Union	1.72	(1926)
					1.54	(1938)

Moreover, a man is a very imitative animal. Once it began to be fashionable for a middle-class family to have numerous children, many began to do the same. A glance at any college faculty—young, old, and middle-aged—will show the changing trends in this regard: the assistant professors already have more children than the full professors, and the race isn't over yet.

As a result of the new trend, many countries of Western Europe whose net reproductive rates were far below unity are now hovering around the critical level of unity. The United States, has come to have a net reproductive rate that is considerably in excess of unity.[1] Table 4 shows some interesting contrasts in net reproductive rates.

Will the present American trend continue? This nobody knows. It depends upon whether the number of *un*married adults continues to remain at the present low levels, never before reached in the modern history of any country. It depends upon whether the typical married couple thinks that a boy and a girl are enough or whether they aspire toward having a large family.[2] So far the odds favor larger families.

---

[1] The present fashion among experts is to recognize the volatility of net reproductive rates. They prefer to analyze the trends in the ages at which people get married and the trends in the patterns of fertility of marriages of different ages. The 1949 report of the British Royal Commission on Population reflects this change of approach.

[2] Some experts admit that middle-class families now often want third and fourth children, but they think this will be outweighed by lower income groups no longer having as large families as they used to.

▶ ECONOMIC EFFECTS OF POPULATION GROWTH

The economic impact of population changes is already very noticeable. Our suburbs teem with children, and our schools are overcrowded. The bulge of war births has already begun to hit our colleges: by 1973 we expect college enrollment to be double that of 1958! Bubble gum and piano sales mirror the rise in youths; gypsum board to finish attic bedrooms is in high demand.

Fig. 4 shows the rising proportion of dependent children. Those of working age will decline in relative importance: caught between the growth of the dependent old and the dependent young, they must each support more nonworkers. As we shall see in Part Two, economists stress the importance of population trends for business activity, and events have confirmed their theories.

From the military manpower viewpoint, time seems to be working against the countries of Western Europe. Table 5 shows estimates of future populations for certain countries. Note the high estimate for the Soviet Union, where net reproduction rates have a long way to fall until they reach unity; and note the pessimistic figures for Sweden and England.

Is our population upsurge a good thing? By economics alone you can't hope to answer such a general question. The joys and aches of family life are not to be measured in mere dollars and cents. Yet we can study certain economic as-

The old and young are gaining on the productive age group:

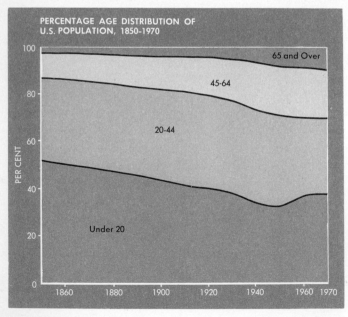

PERCENTAGE AGE DISTRIBUTION OF
U.S. POPULATION, 1850-1970

65 and Over

45-64

20-44

Under 20

PER CENT

Fig. 4. As couples have larger families and length of life increases, each person of working age will have more dependents to support. (Will labor scarcity be tomorrow's watchword?) (Source: National Resources Committee, 1938, and Bureau of the Census.)

United States and Soviet populations gain relative to rest of Europe:

	1958	1970
United States	174	204
United Kingdom	52	53
France	44	46
Soviet Union	206	260
Sweden	7.4	7.5
Italy	49	54
European Satellites of U.S.S.R.	93	99
Free Europe	339	363

Table 5. Estimated future population of different countries in 1970 (all data in millions). (Source: OEEC and Library of Congress Legislative Reference Service.)

pects of population growth. And when we come to do so in later chapters, we shall find that the answers are rarely simple.

Population growth makes for much money spending, as people buy cribs and homes. So it acts against unemployment—which is certainly a point in its favor. But population growth also threatens us with the law of diminishing returns; it fills our cars with people and fills our roads with cars; it spoils the countryside and ruins privacy. The economist has to weigh carefully the pros and cons of so complex a matter as population change. Only when he has analyzed the various aspects of the problem can he provide the citizen and statesman with the knowledge needed for understanding.

SUMMARY

▶ A. PROBLEMS OF ECONOMIC ORGANIZATION

1. Every economy must somehow solve the three fundamental economic problems: What kinds and quantities shall be produced of all possible goods and services; How economic resources shall be used in producing these goods; For Whom the goods shall be produced—*i.e.,* what the distribution of income among different individuals and classes is to be.

2. Different societies meet these problems in different ways—by custom, instinct, fiat and decree, and in our own system partially through a price and market system.

3. The basic problems are important because of the fundamental fact of all economic life: with limited resources and technology, standards of living are limited. Economic goods are *scarce* rather than free; society must choose among them because not all needs and desires can be fulfilled.

► **B. TECHNOLOGICAL CHOICES OPEN TO SOCIETY**

4. With given resources and technology, the production choices open to a nation between two such goods as butter and guns can be summarized in the production-possibility curve or schedule. This indicates the way in which butter can be transformed into guns by transferring resources from butter to gun production.

5. Production-possibility curves are usually drawn bloated out or convex to reflect the common tendency for a *law of increasing relative cost* to hold: measuring the cost of extra guns in terms of the extra butter we have to sacrifice for it, we note a tendency toward increasing costs.

6. The *law of diminishing returns* asserts that, after a point, as we add more and more of a variable input (like labor) to a fixed input (like land), the amount of extra product will fall off. This law is really just a matter of proportions—the varying input has less and less of the fixed input with which to work.

7. Just as the law of diminishing returns is related to, but not the same thing as, the law of increasing relative costs, so there is a related but distinct third law or tendency. *Economies of mass production or of scale* are often described as "increasing returns *to scale.*" The word "scale" is a warning that all inputs are being varied, with none held fixed as in the law of diminishing returns. Many modern processes do pass through an initial stage of increasing returns to scale, making it possible for the laws of diminishing returns and increasing costs to be at first overpowered.

► **C. UNDERLYING POPULATION BASIS OF ANY ECONOMY**

8. The Malthus theory of population rests on the law of diminishing returns. He thought that a population—if unchecked!—would tend to grow in geometric rate, doubling every generation or so. However, each member of the growing population would have less resources to work with. Therefore, because of diminishing returns, income would have a tendency to fall so low as to lead to starvation and pestilence.

9. For a century and a half after Malthus, populations grew by leaps and bounds everywhere. But so successful were the improvements of technology and in medicine that improved death rates caused most of the increase.

10. After 1870 birth rates began to fall. Prior to World War II, advanced nations had net reproduction rates below one and faced depopulation. Since that time the American middle classes have swung back toward a larger-family pattern, a trend that was predicted by few and that has momentous future consequences.

QUESTIONS FOR DISCUSSION

1. Without looking at the next chapter, can you anticipate how our price system through supply and demand solves the three problems of economic organization?

2. Explain what economists mean by "scarcity." By "free goods."

3. Instead of choosing between war goods and peace goods, society may choose between *consumption* goods and *capital* goods. Draw a hypothetical production-possibility or transformation curve indicating this choice.

4. What would happen to society's production-possibility curve if all services (population, land, etc.) increased in amount? What would happen to it if scientific inventions increased the productivity of given resources? What if these improvements were only in butter production and not in guns?

5. If land were increased in a number of steps and labor were held constant, would the law of diminishing returns hold? Illustrate and tell why.

6. Describe and contrast the laws of (*a*) diminishing returns; (*b*) increasing costs; (*c*) increasing returns to scale.

7. How many were there in your grandparents' family? In your parents' family? How many do you think there will be in your own family?

8. "Population pressure doesn't cause war as is commonly believed. Careful study suggests cause and effect are just the reverse. Nations that want to expand try to persuade their citizens to grow in numbers so the nation will be militarily strong and will have a pretext for expansion. Examples are Italy, Germany, and Japan." Discuss.

9. Review your understanding of the following concepts:

economic and free goods	*NRR*
substitution and law of scarcity	*Malthusian population theory*
production-possibility or transformative curve (and schedule)	*total product or output vs. extra product*
law of increasing cost, diminishing returns, and increasing returns to scale	*productive factors or inputs*
	age distribution

3 FUNCTIONING OF A "MIXED" CAPITALISTIC ENTERPRISE SYSTEM

> *Every individual endeavors to employ his capital so that its produce may be of greatest value. He generally neither intends to promote the public interest, nor knows how much he is promoting it. He intends only his own security, only his own gain. And he is in this led by an invisible hand to promote an end which was no part of his intention. By pursuing his own interest he frequently promotes that of society more effectually than when he really intends to promote it.*
>
> ADAM SMITH, *Wealth of Nations* (1776)

▶ A MIXED ENTERPRISE SYSTEM

Most of our attention will be devoted to the special features of economic life found in twentieth-century industrial nations (with the exception of Soviet Russia). In most of these countries, there was a trend in the past few centuries toward less and less direct governmental control of economic activity: gradually feudal and preindustrial conditions were replaced by greater emphasis on what is loosely called "free private enterprise" or "competitive capitalism."

Long before this trend had approached a condition of *laissez faire* (*i.e.*, of complete governmental noninterference with business), the tide began to turn the other way. Since some time in the nineteenth century, in almost all the countries under consideration there has been a steady increase in the economic functions of government. We must leave to historians the task of delineating the important factors underlying this significant and all-pervasive development. Suffice it to say here that ours is a "mixed" free enterprise economic system in which both public and private institutions exercise economic control.

The first part of this chapter shows how our mixed system tackles the three problems of economic organization that must be answered by all societies. The last section of this chapter deals with some fundamental characteristics of the present economic order.

A HOW A FREE ENTERPRISE SYSTEM SOLVES THE BASIC ECONOMIC PROBLEMS

In a system of free private enterprise, no individual or organization is consciously concerned with Chapter 2's triad of economic problems: What, How, and For Whom. This is really remarkable. To paraphrase a famous economic example, consider the city of New York. Without a constant flow of goods in and out of the city, it would be on the verge of starvation within a week. A variety of the right kinds and amounts of food is involved; from the surrounding counties, from 48 states, and from the far corners of the world, goods have been traveling for days and months with New York as their destination.

How is it that 10 million people are able to sleep easily at night without living in mortal terror of a breakdown in the elaborate economic processes upon which the city's existence depends? For all this is undertaken without coercion or centralized direction by any conscious body!

Everyone notices how much the government does to control economic activity—tariff legislation, pure-food laws, utility and railroad regulations, minimum-wage regulations, fair-labor-practice acts, social security, price ceilings and floors, public works, national defense, national and local taxation, police protection and judicial redress, zoning ordinances, municipal water or gas works, etc. What goes unnoted is how much of economic life goes on *without* direct government intervention. Hundreds of thousands of commodities are produced by millions of people more or less at their own volition without central direction or master plan.

▶ NOT CHAOS BUT ECONOMIC ORDER

This alone is convincing proof that a competitive system of markets and prices —whatever else it may be, however imperfectly it may function—is not a system of chaos and anarchy. There is in it a certain order and orderliness. It works. It functions. Without intelligence it solves one of the most complex problems imaginable, involving thousands of unknown variables and relations. Nobody designed it. Like Topsy, it just growed; and like human nature, it is changing; but at least it meets the first test of any social organization—it is able to survive.

A dramatic example of the importance of a pricing system is postwar Western Germany. In 1946–1947 production and consumption had dropped away to almost nothing. Neither wartime bombing damage nor postwar reparation payments could account for this breakdown. The paralysis of the price mechanism was clearly to blame: Money was worthless; factories closed down for lack of materials; trains could not run for lack of coal; coal could not be mined because miners were hungry; miners were hungry because peasants would not sell food for money and no industrial goods were available to give them. Prices were legally fixed, but little could be bought at such prices; a black market characterized by barter or fantastically high prices existed. Then in 1948 a "miracle" happened. A thoroughgoing currency reform set the price mechanism back into effective operation. Almost immediately production and consumption soared; again the What, How, and For Whom were being resolved by markets and prices.

The fact to emphasize is that such so-called miracles are going on all around us all the time—if only we look around and open our eyes to the everyday functioning of the market. A revolutionist out to destroy the capitalistic system could ask nothing better than a great inflation or deflation that would paralyze the price mechanism.[1]

▶ THE INVISIBLE HAND

Students of economics must avoid the error of thinking that a price mechanism has to work chaotically if it is not controlled by somebody. Having learned this lesson, they must not go to the other extreme and become enamored of the beauty of a pricing mechanism, regarding it as perfection itself, the essence of providential harmony and beyond the touch of human hands.

Adam Smith, whose *Wealth of Nations* we noted previously as representing the beginning book of modern economics or political economy, was thrilled by the recognition of an order in the economic system. Smith proclaimed the principle of the "invisible hand"; each individual in pursuing only his own selfish good was led, as if by an invisible hand, to achieve the best good of all, so that any interference with free competition by government was almost certain to be injurious. (Smith did recognize its realistic limitations.)

Actually some of the praise of perfect competition is beside the point. As has been discussed earlier, ours is a mixed system of government and private enterprise; as will be discussed later, it is also a mixed system of monopoly and competition. It is neither black nor white, but gray and polka-dotted.

A cynic might say of perfect competition what Bernard Shaw once said of Christianity: The only trouble with it is that it has never been tried. Historians quarrel over whether there ever was a golden age of free competition, and certainly competition is not now perfect in the economist's sense; we don't even know whether, because of the fundamental nature of large-scale production and technology, consumers' tastes, and business organization, competition is becoming less or more intense. The statistics suggest at least a slight weakening of monopoly power. But in any case, we need not accept as inevitable any trend toward big business, mergers, trusts, and cartels such as began to swell in

[1] In the late 1950's writers in the Soviet and Satellite countries are rediscovering some virtues of a pricing system. Imitation is the most sincere form of flattery.

the 1890's. The challenge is to work out laws and customs that help to improve the working of our less-than-perfect competitive system.

▶ THE PRICE SYSTEM

Just how does the unconscious automatic price mechanism operate? The bare outlines of a competitive profit-and-loss system are simple to describe. *Everything has a price*—each commodity and each service. Even the different kinds of human labor have prices, usually called "wage rates."

Everybody receives money for what he sells and uses this money to buy what he wishes. If more is wanted of any one good, say shoes, a flood of new orders will be given for it. This will cause its price to rise and more to be produced. Similarly, if more is available of a good like tea than people want, its price will be marked down as a result of competition. At the lower price people will drink more tea, and producers will no longer produce so much. Thus equilibrium of supply and demand will be restored.

What is true of the markets for consumers' goods is also true of markets for *factors of production* such as labor, land, and capital inputs. If welders rather than glass blowers are needed, job opportunities will be more favorable in the welding field. The price of welders, their hourly wage, will tend to rise while that of glass blowers will tend to fall. Other things being equal, this will cause a shift into the desired occupation. Likewise an acre of bottom land will go into sugar cultivation if sugar producers bid the most for its use. In the same way, machine-tool production will be determined by supply and demand.

In other words, we have a vast system of trial and error, of successive approximation to an *equilibrium system of prices and production*. We shall see later that the matching of supply and demand and price and costs helps to solve our three problems simultaneously. The bare outlines of the process can be briefly sketched.

1. What things will be produced is determined by the votes of consumers— not every 2 years at the polls but every day in their decisions to purchase this item and not that. Of course, the money that they pay into business cash registers ultimately provides the payrolls, rents, and dividends that consumers receive in weekly income. Thus the circle is a complete one.

2. How things are produced is determined by the competition of different producers. The method that is cheapest at any one time, because of both physical efficiency and cost efficiency, will displace a more costly method. The only way for producers to meet price competition and maximize profits is to keep costs at a minimum by adopting the most efficient methods. For example, synthetic rubber will be made from petroleum rather than from grain alcohol if the price of the one is in a certain relation to the price of the other, or electric power will be generated by steam rather than atomic power if the price of coal

is below some critical level. The large, tractor-operated farm will displace the family-size farm if this leads to lower costs of production.

International example: Bob Jones farms with much American land relative to each hour of labor; Pierre Reny uses much labor to each hectare of French land. Who orders these sensible How decisions, which properly adjust to the fact that France is more densely populated than America? Congress? The Chamber of Deputies? The UN? Of course not. The price system is society's signaling device. Like a master who gives his donkey carrots and kicks to coax him forward, the pricing system deals out profits and losses to get the What, How, and For Whom questions answered.

3. For Whom things are produced is determined by supply and demand in the markets for productive services: by wage rates, land rents, interest, and profits, all of which go to make up everybody's income—relative to everyone else and relative to the whole. (Of course, the character of the resulting distribution of income is highly dependent upon the initial distribution of property ownership and acquired or inherited abilities.)

Note this. Consumer votes don't by themselves determine What goods are produced. When a man courts a girl, it takes both to make the marriage. Similarly, it takes the business cost and supply decisions along with consumer demand votes to determine What. Just as a marriage broker may help arrange a match between groom and bride, the auctioneer who figuratively runs the goods market acts as the go-between, who reconciles the consumer votes and business supplies that impinge on the market. In the same way, you can think of the auctioneer who presides over the skilled-labor market as being the go-between who helps reconcile the business demand for labor with the public's supply of it. And the profit seeker is society's agent to determine How, seeking least factor costs for producing each good and being punished by ruthless competition if he fails to use best methods.

All this is highly simplified. Figure 1 gives a bird's-eye view of the way market pricing reconciles public demand and supply with business supply and demand. Real life is of course a good deal more complicated.

A competitive system is impersonal but not completely so. The consuming families face business enterprises on two fronts, with only prices in between. One front is the widely dispersed one, the retail market on which consumers buy thousands of small items from a score of different retail establishments: grocery, drug, and department stores; movie theaters; gasoline stations; and electric-power companies, government post offices, landlords, railroad lines, and insurance companies.

On the other front—the market for labor and other productive services— relations are not always so peaceful. To the family breadwinner his wage is not simply another price. It is the difference between luxury and comfort, between comfort and privation. The laborer feels inferior to the large corporation in bargaining power, and he may turn to collective bargaining by means of trade-unions. By doing this he may at times be helping to restore competition, while at other times he may be causing conditions to deviate still further from competition.

The price system uses supply-demand markets to solve the basic economic problems: What, How, and For Whom:

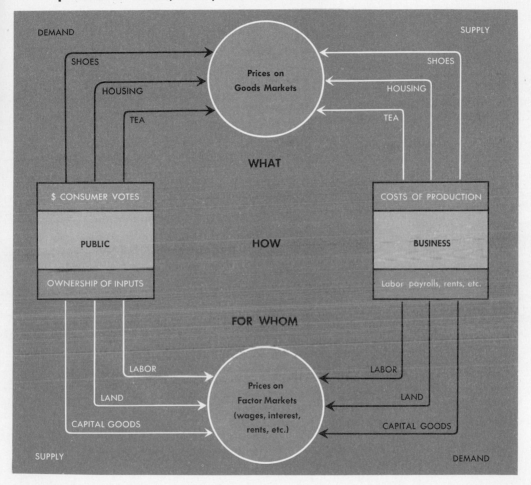

Fig. 1. All demand relations are shown in black; all the supply relations in white. See how consumer dollar votes of demand interact in the upper goods markets with business-cost supply decisions, thus helping determine What is produced. And business demand for inputs or productive factors meets the public's supply of labor and other inputs in factor markets to help determine wage, rent, and interest income—or For Whom goods are produced. Business competition to buy factor inputs and sell goods most profitably helps determine How goods are to be produced. (Warning: All parts of the diagram interact together. What depends on the lower part, just as For Whom depends on the upper part—carpenter wages depend on housing demand, and demand for yachts depends on oil-land royalties.)

The above picture of competition tending toward lowest costs is a highly oversimplified one. Even if the system worked perfectly as described above—which everybody knows to be not the case—many would not consider it ideal. In the first place, goods go where there are the most votes or dollars. A rich man's dog may receive the milk that a poor child needs to avoid rickets. Why? Because supply and demand are working badly? No. Because they are doing what they are designed to do—putting goods in the hands of those who can pay the most, who have the most money votes.

Or, to take another example, suppose the invention of automatic machines should cause the competitive price of labor to fall and thereby reduce incomes of the poor. Is there anything necessarily right in that? And should the fact that a man inherited 500 square miles of range land, for which oil companies offer a million dollars per year, necessarily justify so large an income? These questions you hear discussed in Congress every day. Whether incomes should be completely determined by a competitive struggle—the survival of the survivors—is an ethical question that goes beyond the mechanics of economics.

▶ IMPERFECTIONS OF COMPETITION

As we said earlier, one drawback to the picture of the price system as described above is the fact that, in the real world, competition is nowhere near perfect. Firms do not know when consumer tastes will change; therefore, they may overproduce in one field and underproduce in another. By the time they are ready to learn from experience, the situation may have again changed. Also, in a competitive system many producers simply do not know the methods of other producers and costs do not fall to a minimum. One can sometimes succeed in the competitive struggle as much by keeping knowledge scarce as by keeping production high.

An even more serious deviation from perfect competition results from *monopoly elements*. These—as we shall see more fully later on—may result in wrong pricing, incorrect and wasteful resource allocation, and monopoly profits. We shall also see later how strict is the economist's definition of a "perfect competitor"; the mere presence of a few rivals is not enough for perfect competition. Actually, the economic definition of an "imperfect competitor" is this: *anyone who buys or sells a good in large enough quantities to be able to affect the price of that good.* To some degree that means almost every businessman, except possibly the millions of farmers who individually produce a negligible fraction of the total crop. All economic life is a blend of competitive and monopoly elements. Imperfect, or monopolistic, competition is the prevailing mode, not perfect competition. This is a realistic fact, not a moral condemnation.

Of course, as we shall later see, a businessman cannot set his prices completely as he pleases and still make profits. He must take into account the prices of goods that are substitutes for his own. Even if he produces a trade-marked coal with unique properties, he must reckon with the prices charged for other coals, for oil and gas, and for house insulation.

Businessmen, farmers, and workers both like and dislike competition. We all like it when it enables us to expand our market, but we may be the first to label it as "chiseling," "unfair," or "ruinous" when the knife cuts the other way. The worker whose livelihood depends on how the market prices his labor may be the first to howl when competition threatens to depress wages. Farm groups, aware of what competition can do to agricultural prices, are constantly bringing pressure to bear on the government to restrict production and thereby raise prices.

Some of the basic factors responsible for monopoly-creating bigness in business may be inherent in the economies of large-scale production. This is especially true in a dynamic world of technological change. Atomistic competition by numerous producers would simply not be efficient in many fields and could not last. Trade-marks, patents, and advertising are often responsible for still other market imperfections. It would be humanly impossible, therefore, to attempt to create *perfect* competition by law. The problem is one of achieving reasonably effective "workable competition."

We shall return in Part Three to a more microscopic examination of supply and demand. After that discussion we shall be in a position to appraise the workings of the price system more judiciously. We have seen enough already to avoid the errors of both extremes. A competitive price system is one way of organizing an economy, but it is not the only way. Still it is of interest that some socialists plan to continue to use a price mechanism as one part of their new society. A price system is not perfect, but neither are its alternatives.

▶ ECONOMIC ROLE OF GOVERNMENT

It was said earlier that ours is not a pure price economy but a mixed system in which elements of government control are intermingled with market elements in organizing production and consumption. The economic role of government is now so important that Chapters 6 and 7 are devoted to it.

The broad outlines of its influence can be briefly indicated here. Democratic countries are not satisfied with the answers to the three questions, What, How, and For Whom given by a perfectly unrestrained market system. Such a system might dictate that certain people starve from lack of income and that others receive inadequate or excessive incomes. Therefore the government steps in with its own expenditure to supplement the real or money incomes of some individuals; *e.g.,* it may provide hospital beds for its citizens or may present the more needy of them with monthly allowances in times of unemployment or old age. Minimum standards of life are widespread as goals of government in this century.

More than this, government provides certain indispensable *collective* services without which community life would not be thinkable, and which by their nature cannot appropriately be left to private enterprises. Government came into existence once people realized, "Everybody's business is nobody's business." Obvious examples are the maintenance of national defense, of internal law and order, and the administration of justice.[1]

By and large in its expenditure of money, government is behaving exactly like any other large spender. By casting sufficient votes in the form of dollar bids in certain directions, it causes resources to flow there. The price system works much as if these were individual rather than collective needs.

If governments financed all their expenditure by printing paper money or by endless borrowing, that would be almost the whole story. Actually most government expenditure is paid for out of taxes collected. It is here that an important element of *coerci*on enters in. It is true that the citizenry as a whole imposes the tax burden upon itself; also each citizen is sharing in the collective benefits of government. But there is not the same close connection between benefits and tax payments as holds when the individual citizen puts a nickel into a gum machine or makes an ordinary purchase. I need not smoke Luckies or buy nylon stockings if I do not wish to, but I must pay my annual taxes whether or not I choose to.

Moreover, a second important form of coercion is involved in the universal custom of passing governmental laws: thou shalt not smoke opium, thou shalt not sell false weight, thou shalt not employ child labor, thou shalt not burn houses, thou shalt not charge more than the ceiling price for food, and so forth. This set of rules gives the framework within which private enterprise functions; it also modifies the direction of that functioning. Together with government expenditure and taxation, the decrees of government are hardly less important than the price system itself in determining the economic fate of the nation.

It would be fruitless to debate whether public enterprise or private enterprise is the more important—as fruitless as to debate heredity versus environment. Without either our economic world would be an entirely different one.

Finally, as we shall see in Part Two, it is part of the government's function

---

[1] Here is a famous example of government service: lighthouses. These save lives and cargoes. But lighthouse keepers can't reach out to collect fees from skippers. "So," says the more advanced economic texts, "we have here a divergence between *private* advantage and money cost (as seen by a man crazy enough to try to make his fortune running a lighthouse business) and true *social* advantage and cost (as measured by lives and cargoes saved in comparison with 1. total costs of the lighthouse, and 2. extra costs that result from letting one more ship look at the warning light). Philosophers and statesmen have always recognized the needed role of government in such cases of 'external-economy divergence between private and social advantage.'" Naturally, a beginning text will only mention such issues.

to alleviate one of the most important causes of acute and chronic cycles in unemployment or inflation. Especially in wealthy communities like our own, individuals as a whole may try to save much more or much less than the private enterprise can profitably or usefully invest in new real capital goods. Defense and war may require more output than civilians will voluntarily give up. We shall see that this will result in inflation or deflation and a distortion of the economy's long-run rate of progress. Necessarily the government must try to use its constitutional fiscal and monetary powers to enable private enterprise to maintain a steady level of high employment and rising productivity. And then our "classical" principles of economics—dealing with markets and pricing—will have their validity assured.

B CAPITAL, DIVISION OF LABOR, AND MONEY

There are three further important features of modern economic society:

1. Modern advanced industrial technology rests upon the use of vast amounts of capital: elaborate machine equipment, large-scale factories and plants, stores and stocks of finished and unfinished materials. Our economy receives the name "capitalism" because this capital, or "wealth," is primarily the private property of somebody—the capitalist.

2. The present-day economic system is characterized by an almost incredibly elaborate degree of *specialization* and intricate *division of labor*.

3. Finally, ours is a system that makes extensive use of *money*. The flow of money is the lifeblood of our system. It also provides the measuring rod of values.

All these features are interrelated—with each other and with the price mechanism described in Section A of this chapter. Thus we shall see that, without the great facility for trade and exchange which money provides, an elaborate division of labor would be impossible. Money and capital become related through the credit activities of the banking system and through the organized capital markets upon which securities can be transformed into money by sale or vice versa. And of course the relationship between the price mechanism and money is immediate and obvious.

▶ CAPITAL AND TIME

First, let us survey the important economic role of capital. If men had to work with their hands on barren soil, productivity and consumption would be very low indeed. But gradually over time our economic system has been able to amass a tremendous stock of instruments of production, of factories and housing, of goods in process, of drained and fertilized land.

Men learned very early that the simple, direct methods of production can be improved upon by using *time-consuming indirect* methods. We who are inside the economic system are not conscious of how roundabout productive processes now are. An outside observer would be struck with the fact that almost no one in our system is producing *finished* goods. Almost everyone is doing work of a preparatory nature, with final consumption a distant future goal. The farmer spends his time in fattening hogs, the truck driver in carrying them toward market, the packer in advancing them further toward the last stage of consumption. A steel worker prepares pig iron, part of which will become a hammer to build a house; another bit will become part of a pig-iron furnace, which in turn will prepare pig iron to be used in making further hammers and more pig-iron furnaces, and so forth.

And so the economic process goes—around and around like air inside the pipes of a French horn, or like the egg-chicken-egg-chicken-egg sequence of biological evolution.

Each person is unconscious of the roundabout character of production: all he has to do is to perform his own job and not worry himself as to where his output will ultimately go or whence come the raw materials to which his activity has added value. Once all the circular paths had become established and activity became synchronized, even an outside observer of the system might not notice its complexity. In such a steady state each day would look like the previous one, and it would appear that the work of each day was producing the output of that same day.

But this is an optical illusion. Time was required to get the process going in the first place. Human and nonhuman resources had to be put to work for a long time before any output came out from each new process. It is as if one had to blow into a huge French horn for some time to get the air pressure up before the note could be sounded. Gradually a steady state is reached when one is pumping air constantly in and receiving out a constant tone. Finally, if one stopped pumping air in, one would not incur the penalty of losing the note for some time. So in the economic world, we can stop replacing capital and begin to loaf for a while and still can hope to leave output undiminished for a spell while "milking capital."

The fact that it takes time to get things started and synchronized is important. It explains why society does not automatically replace all direct processes by more productive indirect ones; and all indirect processes by still more indirect processes. The advantage in doing so is balanced by the initial disadvantage of having *to forego present consumption goods* by directing resources from current production to uses that will bear fruit only after some time.

To the extent that people are willing to save—to abstain from present consumption and wait for future consumption—to that extent society can devote resources to new capital formation.[1] And to the extent that people are irresponsible as to the future, they may at any time try to "dissave"—to snatch present pleasures at the expense of the future. How? By diverting resources away from the endless task of replacing and maintaining capital and to the job of producing extra present-day consumption goods. There is an old Chinese proverb: "He who cannot see beyond the dawn will have much good wine to drink at noon, much green wine to cure his headache at dusk, and only rain water to drink for the rest of his days."

We may summarize as follows: The bulk of all economic activity is directed toward the future. By the same token, the bulk of current economic consumption is the consequence of past efforts. *It is the primary role of current productive efforts to produce for the future, so as to repay the past for present consumption.* Also, in progressive societies some fraction of current productive efforts is devoted to the new or net capital formation, whereby current consumption is sacrificed to increase future production.

▶ CAPITAL AND PRIVATE PROPERTY

Physical capital goods are important in any economy because they help to increase productivity. This is as true of Soviet communism as it is of our own system. But there is one important difference. By and large, private individuals own the tools of production in our capitalistic system.

What is the exception in our system—government ownership of the means of production—is the rule in a socialized state where productive property is collectively owned. The returns from such real capital goods accrue to the government and not to individuals directly. The government then decides how such income is to be distributed among individuals. The communist government also decides how rapidly resources are to be invested in new capital formation: the government decides by how much *present* consumption should be curtailed in order to add to the total of factories, equipment, and productive stocks of goods that are necessary if *future* output is to rise.

In our system individual capitalists earn interest, dividends, and profits, or rents and royalties on the capital goods that they supply. Every patch of land and every bit of equipment has a deed or "title of ownership" that belongs to somebody directly—or if it belongs to a corporation, then indirectly it belongs to the individual stockholders who own the corporation. Moreover, each kind of capital good has a money market value. Hence each claim or title to ownership of a capital good also has a market value. A share of common stock of

---

[1] We shall later see that, *sometimes* in our modern monetary economy, the more people try to save, the less capital goods are produced and, paradoxically, the more people spend on consumption, the greater the incentive for businessmen to build new factories and equipment.

General Electric is quoted at some certain price, a New York Central bond at another price, a mortgage on a house is valued at some amount, the deed to a house and lot is appraised by the real-estate market at some given level, etc.

Clearly, in taking a census of the nation's total capital, we must avoid fallacious double counting. Nobody could be so foolish as to declare that his total capital was $20,000 if he owned a $10,000 house on Main Street and also had under his mattress a $10,000 deed to that house. Nor would three brothers who owned a small corporation manufacturing electric toasters ever be under the illusion that the million dollars of common stock of the company could be *added* to the million dollars' worth of capital goods (factory machines, wire, etc.) held by the corporation.

These cases are too simple to give rise to confusion and need not be discussed further at this point. It is enough to point out that the everyday term "capital" has many different meanings. It may refer to a capital good; it may refer to a bond, stock, security or deed, or any document that represents a claim to an income-producing capital good. Often in everyday parlance, it is thought of as a sum of money. We say, "Jones is in need of $100,000 of capital which he hopes to raise from the bank." Actually, of course, when Jones borrows that sum from the bank, he will not continue to hold it in the form of a liquid cash asset. He will convert his assets into tangible capital assets, such as tools, or into intangible capital assets, such as an important patent.

It should be pointed out that the government does own a good deal of the national real capital; *e.g.,* Hoover Dam. In addition, its agencies, such as the Federal Housing Administration (FHA), are important sources of capital loans for private individuals and business.

Also, we note that the legal property rights of an individual are relative and limited. Society determines how much of his property a man may bequeath to his heirs and how much must go in inheritance and estate taxes to the government. Society determines how much the owners of public-utility companies —such as electric and gas firms—can earn and how they must run their business.

Even a man's home is not his castle. He must obey zoning laws and, if necessary, make way for a railroad or slum-clearance project. Interestingly enough, most of society's economic income cannot be capitalized into private property. Since slavery was abolished, human earning power is forbidden by law to be capitalized.[1] A man is not free to sell even himself.

> ### ▶ SPECIALIZATION, EXCHANGE, AND DIVISION OF LABOR

We turn now to the second of the three characteristic features of the present-day economy. The economies of mass production upon which modern standards of living are based would not be possible if production still took place in self-

---

[1] Maybe organized baseball should be listed as a partial exception.

sufficient farm households or self-sufficient provinces. *Specialization* of function permits each person and each region to use to best advantage any peculiar differences in skill and resources. Even in a primitive economy men learn that, rather than have everyone do everything in a mediocre way, it is better to institute a *division of labor*—it is better for fat men to do the fishing, lean men to do the hunting, and smart men to make the medicine.

Besides resting upon any interpersonal differences in ability, specialization accentuates and creates differences. Hunting makes a man thin and good at stalking prey; a region with no resources especially adapted to hat making may nevertheless develop skills which give it advantages in this trade.

Finally, even with no natural or acquired differences in skills, specialization will sometimes pay: often in this way alone can a large enough volume of activity be reached to realize all the economies of large-scale production mentioned in the preceding chapter.[1] Two identical Indian twins might find it better for one to make all bows and the other all arrows—even if they had to draw lots to see which would make which—because only in this way could each be making enough of each item to warrant introducing improved techniques.

To illustrate the increased productivity of specialization, Smith provided the classical example of pinmaking. One man could at best make a few dozen imperfect pins per day. But when a small group of men are subdivided with respect to function so that each performs simple repetitive operations, they can turn out hundreds of thousands of perfect pins in the same period of time.[2]

---

[1] In his famous book, Adam Smith recognized that specialization and division of labor were limited by the extent of the market, *i.e.*, by the volume that can be sold. Smith would have approved of the six-nation Common European Market scheme, which aims to lower the tariff barriers to international trade so as to create a market big enough to support fruitful mass production and specialization.

[2] The following passage describing the extent of specialization in meat slaughtering has often been quoted: "It would be difficult to find another industry where division of labor has been so ingeniously and microscopically worked out. The animal has been surveyed and laid off like a map; and the men have been classified in over thirty specialties and twenty rates of pay, from 16 cents to 50 cents an hour. The 50-cent man is restricted to using the knife on the most delicate parts of the hide (floorman) or to using the ax in splitting the backbone (splitter); and, wherever a less skilled man can be slipped in at 18 cents, $18\frac{1}{2}$ cents, 20 cents, 21 cents, $22\frac{1}{2}$ cents, 24 cents, and so on, a place is made for him, and an occupation mapped out. In working on the hide alone there are nine positions, at eight different rates of pay. A 20-cent man pulls off the tail, a $22\frac{1}{2}$-cent man pounds off another part where good leather is not found, and the knife of the 40-cent man cuts a different texture and has a different 'feel' from that of the 50-cent man. Skill has become specialized to fit the anatomy. . . .

"The division of labor grew with the industry, following the introduction of the refrigerator car and the marketing of dressed beef, in the decade of the seventies. Before the market was widened by these revolutionizing inventions, the killing gangs were small, since only the local demands were supplied. But when the number of cattle to be killed each day increased to a thousand or more, an increasing gang or crew of men was put together; and the best men were kept at the most exacting work." From J. R. COMMONS, *Quarterly Journal of Economics,* vol. XIX, 1904, pp. 3, 6.

Moreover, the simplification of function made possible by specialization lends itself to mechanization and the use of labor-saving capital. At the same time it avoids the wasteful duplication of tools that would be necessary if every man had to be a Jack-of-all-trades; and it also saves time lost in going from one job to another. The modern conveyer system of automobile assembly illustrates the efficiency of specialization. Today automation is the watchword.

▶ SPECIALIZATION AND INTERDEPENDENCE

Clearly, however, specialization and division of labor involve one serious problem—that of *interdependence*. A single-celled low form of life such as the amoeba or paramecium is not particularly efficient, but it can live alone and like it. In higher animals such as man, every cell will die if once the heart cells fail. When all goes well, the extreme specialization of cells is very efficient— but at the cost of extreme interdependence.

In modern economic society this process is carried to the nth degree. No one man makes the smallest fraction of the commodities that he consumes. In medieval times the artisan made one article and exchanged it for many others. Today a worker produces not even a single good; he may make only shoe tongues or simply turn bolt 999 on the Ford assembly line. Such may be his whole life work. For performing this he will receive an income adequate to buy goods from all over the world. But hidden costs could be involved. Specialization may breed half men—anemic clerks and brutish truck drivers.

Thus, specialization involves complete mutual dependence. A bank in Austria fails, and the natives in Fiji, who carry water in empty Standard Oil cans and clothe their infants in Pillsbury flour bags, lose their livelihood—yes, and may even starve. In the backwash of a war a breakdown in transportation and the economic fabric of exchange reveals how perilously modern economic life depends upon exchange. Would we, if we could, turn the clock back to a simpler and poorer life? Or can we keep the advantages of division of labor and find policies that will prevent breakdown?

▶ BARTER VERSUS THE USE OF MONEY

Along with capital and specialization, money is a third aspect of modern economic life. Without the use of money our present division of labor would be impossible. But we could imagine a state of *barter,* where one kind of merchandise is traded directly for another. In primitive cultures it is not uncommon for food to be traded for weapons, or aid in the building of a house exchanged for aid in clearing a field. Even in the most advanced industrial economies, if we strip down exchange to its barest essentials, peeling off the obscuring layer of money, we find that trade between individuals or nations pretty much boils down to barter—transforming one good into another by exchange rather than by physical production.

Barter represents a great improvement over a state of affairs in which every man had to be a Jack-of-all-trades and master of none. And a great debt of gratitude is owed to the first two ape men who suddenly perceived that each could be made better off by giving up some of one good in exchange for some of another. Nevertheless, simple barter operates under such great disadvantages that a highly elaborate division of labor would be unthinkable without the introduction of a new great improvement—the use of money.

In all but the most primitive cultures men do not trade one good against another. Instead they sell one good for money, and then use money to buy the goods they wish. At first glance this seems to complicate rather than simplify matters, to replace a single transaction by two transactions. Thus, if I have apples and want nuts, would it not be simpler to trade one for the other rather than to sell the apples for money and then use the money to buy nuts?

Actually the reverse is the case: the two transactions are simpler than one. Ordinarily there are always people ready to buy apples and always some willing to sell—at a price—nuts. But it would be an unusual *coincidence* to find a person with tastes just opposite to my own, with an eager desire to sell nuts and buy apples. Such a coincidence would be as unlikely as the chance of picking two winning horses in a row. Even if the unusual should happen—as occasionally it must—there is no guarantee that the desires of the two parties with respect to the exact quantities and terms of the exchange would coincide.

To use a classical economic phrase: Instead of there being a double coincidence of wants, there is likely to be a want of coincidence; so that, unless a hungry tailor happens to find a farmer who has both food and a desire for a pair of pants, neither can make a trade.

▶ COMMODITY MONEY, PAPER MONEY, AND BANK MONEY

If we were to reconstruct history along hypothetical, logical lines, we would naturally follow the age of barter by the age of commodity money. Historically a great variety of commodities have served at one time or another as a medium of exchange: cattle (from which comes the Latin stem of "pecuniary" and also the words "capital" and "chattel") , tobacco, leather and hides, furs, olive oil, beer or spirits, slaves or wives, copper, iron, gold, silver, rings, diamonds, wampum beads or shells, huge rocks and landmarks, and cigarette butts.

Each of the above has some advantages and disadvantages. Cattle are not divisible into small change; but while it is being hoarded such money is likely to increase by reproduction, giving the lie to the doctrine of Aristotle that "money is barren." Beer doesn't improve with keeping, although wives and wine may. Olive oil provides a nice liquid currency which is as minutely divisible as one wishes. Iron will rust and is of so little value that one would need a cart instead of a pocketbook. The value of a diamond is not proportional to weight but varies with its square; therefore, if cut up into pieces it loses value.

The yearly additions to (by mining) or subtractions from (by use in teeth or jewelry) the accumulated stock of precious metals are small in percentage terms; so the total amounts and value of these substances do not fluctuate wildly. Silver has luster but will tarnish in air. Gold keeps its attractive sheen, but unless mixed with an alloy is very soft. Gold's high specific gravity makes detection of counterfeiting and admixture easy; but through most of historical time, gold's scarcity value has been so great per ounce as to require inordinately minute coins for small purchases.

Most kinds of money tended once to be of some value or use for their own sake. Thus, even wampum had decorative uses, and paper money began as warehouse or mint receipts for so much metal. But the intrinsic usefulness of the money medium is the least important thing about it.

The age of commodity money gives way to the age of paper money. The essence of money, its intrinsic nature, is typified by paper currency. *Money, as money rather than a commodity, is wanted not for its own sake but for the things it will buy!* We do not wish to use money up directly; but rather to use it by getting rid of it; even when we choose to use it by holding it, its value comes from the fact that we can spend it later on.

Money is an artificial, social convention. If for any reason a substance begins to be used as money, all people will begin to value it even if they happen to be teetotalers or vegetarians or disbelievers in its intrinsic usefulness. As long as things can be bought and sold for a given substance, people will be content to sell and buy with it. Paradox: money is accepted because it is accepted!

The use of paper currency (dollar bills, fives, tens, etc.) has become widespread because it has many conveniences as a medium of exchange. Currency is easily carried and stored away. By the printing of more or fewer zeros on the face value of the bill, a great or small amount of value can be embodied in a light, transportable medium of little bulk. By the use of decimal points it can be made as divisible as we wish. By careful engraving, the value of the money can be made easily recognizable and can be protected from counterfeiting and adulteration. The fact that private individuals cannot create it at will in unlimited amounts keeps it scarce, *i.e.,* an economic rather than a free good.

Given this limitation in supply, modern currencies have value—*i.e.,* can buy things—independently of any gold, silver, or government backing. The public neither knows nor cares—and needs not know or care—whether its currency is in the form of so-called "silver certificates," federal reserve notes, or in copper or silver coin. So long as each form of money can be converted into any other at fixed terms, the best is as good as the worst.[1]

Along with the age of paper money there is finally also the age of bank

---

[1] A century ago it was the exception rather than the rule for bank notes and coins to exchange for each other at par. Each had different prices which varied from day to day so

money, or bank checking deposits. Today at least nine-tenths of all transactions, by value if not number, take place by checks. A professor will have his salary paid directly into his bank account, after income and social security taxes have already been withheld at the source by his employer. His rent or dentist bills will be paid by check, which his wife may not even give him the privilege of signing. Except then for a little petty cash for lunches and carfare, he may hardly handle any hard cash at all in the course of a year's time.

▶ PRICE RATIOS AND MONEY PRICES

In every transaction, whether for barter or money, each person gives something up and receives something in exchange. If 5 apples are traded for 25 nuts, the price of apples in terms of nuts is 25 to 5 or, briefly, 5 to 1; the price of nuts in terms of apples is 5 to 25 or 1 to 5, or $\frac{1}{5}$, or in terms of decimals 0.2. Similarly, if 5 apples sell for 25 cents, then the price of apples in terms of money is 5 cents. It would be equally true, but not very customary or familiar, to say that a penny costs $\frac{1}{5}$ or 0.2 of an apple.

Every price is really a price ratio involving a numerator and a denominator. Each depends upon the way in which the two quantities are measured: thus, eggs are quoted at 5 cents apiece, 60 cents a dozen, or $7.20 a gross; likewise we may say that eggs sell for $\frac{1}{20}$ dollar, "get-away automobiles" for $1\frac{1}{2}$ "G's," and haircuts for "10 bits."

If we relied completely on barter, we should have to keep in mind a great number of price ratios—as many as the number of pairs that could be formed mathematically from the number of commodities. Thus, for only 5 different goods there would be 10 different price ratios to remember, just as there are 10 different tennis matches to be played in a round robin of 5 different men. For 1,000 commodities, you'd have to remember almost 500,000 price ratios.[1]

A little reflection will convince us that many of these price ratios are unnecessary, being deducible from a much smaller number. For example, if the price of apples in terms of nuts is 5 and the price of oranges in terms of nuts is 10, then is it necessary for us to be told what the price of oranges is in terms of apples? Because 10 nuts is twice 5 nuts, we know already that 2 apples must be paid for 1 orange.

By use of the elementary axiom, "things equal to the same thing are equal to each other," the reader can convince himself that, once he knows the price ratios of all goods in terms of any *one* good, he can easily get the price ratio

---

that it was necessary for storekeepers to keep daily lists of values; and it became a profession in itself to change money, buying and selling it at a profit.

[1] By elementary algebra, the number of pairs that can be selected from n different objects is no less than $n(n-1)/2$, or about $\frac{1}{2}n^2$ all together.

between *any two goods* by division. For 5 commodities we need only remember 4 price ratios, not 10; the other 6 ratios are redundant, being deducible from these 4. For 1,000 goods, only 999 price ratios are needed, not 500,000.[1]

▶ MONEY AS A MEDIUM OF EXCHANGE OR AS A UNIT OF ACCOUNT

There are two distinct functions of money: as a medium of exchange, and as a standard unit of value. This distinction is illustrated by a perfect clearing system, where careful record of all transactions is kept and where finally what each person has coming to him is canceled against what he owes, with the balance credited to his account. In such a system no medium of exchange whatever is needed! But a common denominator of value, telling us how to compare and weigh such diverse items as a stick of gum and an automobile, would certainly still be necessary.

Actually an African tribe once existed which used as its unit of money the so-called "macute." This was not a shell or commodity; it had no corporeal existence as a medium of exchange but represented simply a standard unit of value or money of *account*. Until recently the Paraguayan unit of money was based upon a long-obsolete, extinct Argentine coin. Similarly, fashionable London shops quote prices in terms of "guineas" even though that coin no longer exists. I buy a 1-guinea hat by actually paying 21 shillings; it is fashionable to pretend guineas still exist. Americans can thank Franklin and Jefferson that the decimal system was adopted for our money. Imagine doing arithmetic problems with heterogeneous English small coins such as the farthing, penny, shilling, half crown, etc. This is almost but not quite so bad as having to do long division with Roman numerals.[2]

---

[1] This is only one illustration of a general principle applying to all price ratios. When we come to examine the exchange rate at which the moneys of different countries can be converted into each other, we find the same principle applies. If 4 dollars used to make 1 British pound sterling and $\frac{1}{50}$ of a dollar equaled 1 Italian lira, then the number of lire in a pound is perfectly determinate (equal to $4 \div \frac{1}{50}$ or 200). When the Allied military authorities first took over Italy in World War II, they overlooked this fundamental economic truth and set three independent rates. The result was what one might expect: by using currency *A* one could buy currency *B* which could then be exchanged for an amount of currency *C*—an amount that would buy more than the initial amount of *A*. This is just what happened. *Arbitragers* (*i.e.*, people who speculate on a sure thing) went round and round the circuit making a profit at each whirl. Of course, the military authorities suffered a corresponding loss. Finally they noticed what was happening and did what they should have done in the first place—set the third price ratio in proper relation to the other two. See Part Five.

[2] Of course, any system of reckoning which a child has been taught seems easiest to him, and it is natural for people to think their own methods best. But the real test is whether it would be easier for us to learn their system than for them to learn ours. The decimal system is an obvious winner in such a contest, as strangers to both England and the United States all testify.

In earliest schooling, we are taught never to add apples to oranges or to combine dimensionally heterogeneous quantities. In economics it is the function of money prices to make all values commensurable. We cannot add apples to oranges. But if we multiply the number of apples by their price per apple, we get a dollar quantity. If we do the corresponding thing with respect to oranges and their price, we again get a dollar magnitude. And of course two dollar magnitudes can be added together. Aesthetically bread and flowers may be incommensurable, but in economics money reduces them to comparability. It does the same for diverse capital goods—hammers and looms.

▶ MONEY AND TIME

The two essential functions of money—(1) as a *medium of exchange* and (2) as a standard *unit of account* or common denominator of values—are both tied up with the passage of time.

First, there is always a time interval between receiving and spending money. Normally this is not more than a week or month. To hold any substantial amount of money idle for longer than a few months means you are earning no interest return. If there were any securities or bonds that were sure to pay a positive interest rate, no sensible man would long continue to use money as a store of value. (We return often to this important question in later chapters.)

But whether the period be a day or a decade, it is clear that money must be held for some period of time. And what if prices should generally rise or fall during that time?

Also the use of money will always play an important role in serving as a *standard unit of reckoning* between financial transactions over time. When a man borrows $10,000 for 5 years, he is, of course, getting present money and agreeing to pay back future money. But suppose all prices have doubled in the meantime; or, what is another way of saying the same thing, suppose the value of money has halved? Is it not unfair that the lender should receive much less in real purchasing power than he has given to the borrower?

Obviously, when prices are very unstable over time, when there is extreme inflation or deflation, money serves very badly as a "standard of deferred payment" (over time). Inflation favors debtors at the expense of creditors; in deflation, when prices fall, debtors are hurt and creditors are benefited—if they can collect!

This completes the discussion of the way in which money performs its two essential functions between points in time. In Part Two, we shall examine in detail the monetary and credit operations of banks and the government to see how they bear on fluctuations in prices and production.

SUMMARY

Even though it deals with facts subconsciously familiar to every person, this is one of the most difficult chapters in the whole field of economics. We are too near our own system to appreciate how it works.

▶ **A. PRICING AND MIXED ENTERPRISE**

1. In our mixed private enterprise system, the price mechanism, working through supply and demand in competitive markets, operates to answer the three fundamental problems of economic organization. The system is not perfect, but it works to solve the What, How, and For Whom.

2. The dollar votes of people affect prices of goods; these prices serve as guides on the amounts of the different goods to be produced. Whenever the price of a good exceeds its cost of production, a businessman can make a profit by expanding production of that good. Under competition, the business-man must find the cheapest method of production, using labor, land, and other factors that are relatively cheap and economizing on the use of relatively expensive factors. Otherwise he will make losses and be eliminated.

At the same time that the What and How problems are being resolved by prices, so is the problem of For Whom. The distribution of income is deter-mined by competitive bidding up or down of prices of the factors of produc-tion—wages of each kind of labor, of each kind of land, royalties of books, etc. Anyone lucky enough to own much fertile well-located land or possess widely admired crooning ability will be supplied with many dollar votes for his use in the markets for consumer goods. Anyone without property and with skills that the market cares little about will receive a very low annual income.

3. Our system is mixed in at least two senses: Governments modify private initiative; monopolistic elements condition the working of perfect competition.

▶ **B. CAPITAL, DIVISION OF LABOR, AND MONEY**

4. Capital goods—such as machinery, housing, and inventories of goods in process—add tremendously to a nation's output. Roundabout, time-consuming methods take time to get started; hence, adding to the stock of capital goods requires a temporary sacrifice of present consumption goods.

5. Under a system of capitalism, capital goods are owned as private property and the incomes they produce belong to their owners. Under communism, ownership of capital goods is by the state. In no system are private-property rights unlimited.

6. Specialization and extreme division of labor characterize modern economies. This raises productivity, but at the cost of mutual interdependence.

7. Without exchange, division of labor could not be highly developed. Simple barter is inefficient and tends to be superseded by the use of money. Commodity money in its turn is superseded by paper money and bank money. Unlike other economic goods, money is valued because of social convention; we value it indirectly for what it buys rather than for its direct utility.

8. The two main functions of money are (a) as a medium of exchange and (b) as a unit of account or common-denominator standard of value. Related to these two functions of money by the passage of time are two subsidiary functions: (c) while money is held, it is a "store of value" whose ultimate worth depends on the trend of prices; (d) contracts concerning the future are usually expressed in terms of money, which is why it is often called "a standard of deferred payment."

QUESTIONS FOR DISCUSSION

1. During World War II did we let consumers' dollar demand determine their sugar consumption? Why not? What did?

2. Could supply and demand for labor work so as to distribute to salesmen with a "gift of gab" ten times as much income as to competent surgeons? At other times could it operate so as to give surgeons ten times the income of accountants?

3. Do you think that an "instinct of craftsmanship" and a "sense of social responsibility" could ever replace the "profit motive"? Read the chapter head's "invisible hand" quotation aloud. What do you think Smith is trying to say?

4. List a number of cases where the government modifies the working of an automatic price system. Also list a number of cases where monopoly elements modify the workings of the price system.

5. Assuming she cannot borrow abroad, what must China do if she wishes to become an efficient industrialized nation in the next few generations?

6. "Lincoln freed the slaves. With one pen stroke he destroyed much of the capital the South had been able to accumulate over the years." Comment.

7. Would ice cubes make a good unit of money? Why not? What about radium? How would people's spending habits be changed if every dollar bill decreased 10 per cent in value with each month that has elapsed since its date of printing?

8. What are some of the advantages of using bank checks rather than paper or metal money? List some of the disadvantages.

9. Late in 1947, Russia called in old rubles and issued one new one for ten

old ones. And early in 1957 Russia suspended payment on its domestic bonds. How do such actions affect people's desire to hold wealth in the form of money? To hold wealth in the form of bonds? To abstain from today's consumption?

    10. Review your understanding of the following concepts:

mixed enterprise system	*division of labor*
demand-and-supply markets for goods and for factors of production	*interdependence*
	extent of the market
minimizing cost and maximizing profit	*exchange*
	barter
perfect and imperfect competition	*money prices*
collective services of government	*price ratios*
roundaboutness of production	*commodity, paper, and bank money*
abstinence and waiting	
dissaving by failure to maintain and replace capital goods	*medium of exchange*
	unit of account
various capital concepts	*store of value*
specialization	*standard of deferred payment*

4 INDIVIDUAL AND FAMILY INCOME

F. SCOTT FITZGERALD: *You know, Ernest, the rich are different from us.*
ERNEST HEMINGWAY: *Yes, I know. They have more money than we do.*

One does not have to know anything about the laws of economics to have a lively appreciation of the importance of income. The expression "Clothes make the man" would be more nearly right if it were "Income makes the man." That is to say, if you can know but one fact about a man, knowledge of his income will prove to be the most revealing. Then you can make a rough guess as to his political opinions, his tastes and education, his age, and even his life expectancy. Furthermore, unless a steady stream of money comes into the family's hands every week, every month, and every year—even though it be made up of saints—that family is sick. Not only its materialistic activities, but its nonmaterialistic activities—the things that convert existence into living—must suffer: education, travel, health, recreation, and charity, to say nothing of food, warmth, and shelter.

It is a commonplace to state that the American standard of living and level of family income are the highest in all the world. But few people have more than a hazy conception of just how small the average American income really is, or how great is the range between the highest and the lowest incomes, or even how great are the fluctuations over time in the levels of income.

This chapter presents some basic facts about the distribution of incomes.

▶ **DISTRIBUTION OF INCOME IN THE UNITED STATES**

As a matter of fact any poll of students will show that they are not very certain as to what their own family incomes really are. Usually it turns out that students have a slightly exaggerated notion as to how much their fathers earn.

And despite the recent (quite justified) claim of a prominent clubwoman that "women spend 70 per cent of the national income, and we soon hope to get hold of the rest," an astonishing number of wives have no conception of their husbands' pay checks. In addition there are some people so inept at keeping records and with such variable earnings that they do not themselves know how much they make. Even where income is known within the family, there is a quite natural reticence to reveal it to outsiders, so much so that investigators who made a 1939 survey of the birth-control habits of native white Protestants of Indianapolis often found it harder to get financial data than intimate personal information.

In the absence of statistical knowledge, it is understandable that one should form an impression of the American standard of living from the full-page magazine advertisements portraying a jolly American family in an air-conditioned home with a Buick and a station wagon and all the other good things that go to make up comfortable living. Actually, of course, this sort of life is still beyond the grasp of 95 per cent of the American public and even beyond most families from which the selected group of college students comes.

In 1957, at the pinnacle of American prosperity, the amount of per capita income in the United States was around $2,000 per year per person, or about $39 per week. Such an average figure has not very much meaning, inasmuch as it is derived by pretending that all the income in the United States is divided equally among every man, woman, and child. Of course, in real life income is distributed far from equally, as we shall see; and there is no guarantee that the attempt to divide income in this way would leave the total unchanged.

If the members of a classroom, or of the whole country, write down their family income on a card, these cards may be sorted into different income classes; *i.e.,* some cards will go into the $0-to-$1,000 class, some into the $1,000-to-$2,000 class, and so forth. In this way we get the *statistical frequency* distribution of income. At one extreme will be the very poor, who have drawn a blank in life; at the other extreme, the very rich, who have hit the jack pot. In between will fall the vast majority of the population.

Table 1 summarizes recent statistics on this subject. Column (1) gives the *income class interval.* Column (2) shows the percentage of families and individuals in each income class. Column (3) shows the percentage of the total of all income that goes to the people in the given income class. Columns (4) and (5) are computed from (2) and (3), respectively. Column (4) shows what percentage of the total number of families and individuals belong to each income class *or below.* Column (5) shows what percentage of total income goes to the people who belong in the given income class or have still lower incomes.

Table 1 shows it would be a great mistake to think that the poor and the rich are equally distributed around the middle. The Biblical statement, "For ye have the poor always with you," gives no inkling of their vast numbers. Abraham Lincoln pointed up this fact picturesquely in his statement, "The Lord prefers common people. . . . He made so many of them." A glance at the income distribution in the United States shows how pointed is the income pyramid and how broad its base. "There's always room at the top," is certainly true; this is so because it is hard to get there, not because it is easy. If we made an income pyramid out of a child's play blocks with each layer portraying $1,000 of income, the peak would be far higher than the Eiffel Tower, but almost all of us would be within a yard of the ground.

Moreover, the middle, or "median," income class (which divides the upper from the lower half) corresponds to a modest income. In 1955 the median income class, for an average American family of two adults and a number of children, was only about $4,600. Table 1 shows that such an income falls short of the average (or "arithmetic mean") income per family of $5,520. This is primarily because the unequal distribution of incomes gives so much more to the families lying above the median.

Let's see how adequate the income level enjoyed by the typical American

Few families in America reach income level of $10,000:

Table 1. Distribution of Incomes of American families and individuals, 1955. Half of these families and individuals are below the median income of $4,600. The average (or arithmetic mean) income which each would get if total income were distributed exactly equally is about $5,500. More families and individuals have incomes around the mode of $4,000 than around any other income. (Source: U.S. Department of Commerce.)

Income class (1)	Per cent of all families and individuals in this class (2)	Per cent of total income received by families and individuals in this class (3)	Per cent of families and individuals in this class and lower ones (4)	Per cent of income received by this class and lower ones (5)
Under $1,000	6	1	6	1
$ 1,000–$ 2,000	10	3	16	4
2,000– 3,000	12	5	28	9
3,000– 4,000	13	9	41	18
4,000– 5,000	14	12	55	30
5,000– 7,500	26	28	81	58
7,500– 10,000	11	16	92	74
10,000– 15,000	5	10	97	84
Over $15,000	3	16	100	100
	100	100		

family is today. Social-service workers a few years ago made careful estimates of certain minimum budgets as follows:

1. Bare subsistence—no movies, practically no meat, no dental care, no newspapers, little clothing, etc.

2. Minimum health and decency—occasional movie or recreational expenditure, cheap cuts of meat at intervals, some medical and dental care, etc.

3. Minimum comfort—adequate diet, occasional vacation and amusement, some tobacco and books, etc.

We may roughly estimate the cost of the first of these in 1955 at $2,300. Now, if we examine the actual 1955 statistics in Table 1, it appears that 20 per cent of the population did not even reach this level of income and 30 per cent earned less than the $3,200 needed for the second budget. Even allowing for the fact that it costs less to live in the country than in town, we see why there is public concern for the "lower third" of the population.

From the same table, we can compute that only 59 per cent have incomes reaching above the $4,000 needed for the comfort budget. If we revert to our typical American family of the slick-paper magazine ads, even after stripping them of their station wagons and mink coats, we still find that only 5 per cent of the population have the $13,000 pretax income which we can conservatively estimate was the minimum necessary in 1955 to rough it out at such an existence. The number of American families who have the $35,000 per year which magazines assure us is absolutely necessary in order to make ends meet just east of Fifth Avenue in New York City is minuscule.

Moreover, the upper crust is losing ground relative to the rest of the population. Careful studies by the Census and by the private nonprofit National Bureau of Economic Research suggest that the American income pyramid is becoming less unequal. Since 1929 the share of total income of the upper-5-per-cent group has gone down: today that group probably gets only about one-fifth of the total income instead of getting about one-third as it did back in 1929. Figure 1 shows how the different income classes fared in the last 20 years. The modern "welfare state" is no doubt part of the reason for this trend toward equality; but the trend is evident here and abroad and seems to be only partly explained by government actions.

▶ THE DECLINE OF POVERTY

It is now more than a century since Karl Marx and Friedrich Engels in 1848 issued the Communist Manifesto containing the lines: "Workers of the world, unite! You have nothing to lose but your chains." Some of the Marx predictions as to the future of industrial capitalism were proved correct in the intervening years, but one of his most famous has proved to be quite wrong. His assertion that the rich will become richer and the poor will become poorer cannot be

Postwar prosperity has raised income of every class:

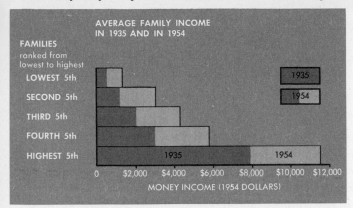

AVERAGE FAMILY INCOME
IN 1935 AND IN 1954

FAMILIES
ranked from
lowest to highest

LOWEST 5th

SECOND 5th

THIRD 5th

FOURTH 5th

HIGHEST 5th

1935

1954

0   $2,000 $4,000 $6,000 $8,000 $10,000 $12,000

MONEY INCOME (1954 DOLLARS)

Fig. 1. The average family income of all groups has increased greatly from the prewar period. The fifth of all families having highest incomes received the largest increase in dollars but smallest relative increase. (Source: National Resources Planning Board and U.S. Department of Commerce.)

sustained by careful historical and statistical research. In Europe and in America there has definitely been a steady secular improvement in minimum standards of living whether measured by food, clothing, housing, or length of life. This fact about capitalism is clear from statistics to be presented shortly.

Not very long ago it was fashionable for economic historians to dwell on the evils of the Industrial Revolution and the poverty-ridden condition of the masses in the disease-producing cities. In point of fact no Dickens novel does justice to the conditions of child labor, length of the working day, and conditions of safety and sanitation in early nineteenth-century factories. A work week of 84 hours was the prevailing rule, with time out for breakfast and sometimes supper, as well as lunch. A good deal of work could be got out of a six-year-old boy or girl, so long as one didn't care about his health or existence beyond the age of twelve. If a man lost two fingers in a machine, he still had eight left.

However true their lurid picture of industrial factory towns, the earlier historians erred in thinking that conditions were worse than in the preindustrial era. The earlier "putting-out" or domestic system, in which wool or yarn was provided to workers for them to spin or weave in their homes, brought the worst conditions of the sweatshop into the home. Sleep and need battled for the week's 168 hours. The whole family, not just the breadwinner, was figuratively forced to run on the treadmill to keep alive. For these reasons labor unions have always opposed this system of production, even more than the factory with all its evils.

Furthermore, poverty is never so obvious in the country as in the industrial cities where it forces itself on the observer. The idyllic picture of the healthful happy countryside peopled by stout yeomen and happy peasantry is a mirage in most parts of the world. Even today, nothing in New York's Hell's Kitchen or Harlem, nothing in Boston's south or north end, nothing "behind the

Yards" in Chicago or in its black belt can overshadow the poverty and squalor of our rural problem areas: the Tobacco Road of the deep South, hillbilly regions of the Appalachian Plateau, dust bowls and ghost mining towns.

Modern historians therefore emphasize that the conditions of the industrial present, inadequate as they may seem, are nevertheless great improvements over the previous periods of commercial enterprise and agrarian feudalism. How far we have come is illustrated by the following quotation describing a period some men can still remember:

In the middle of the nineteenth century there lived in the parish of Marsham, Norfolk, a couple of poor people by the name of Thomas and Mary Edwards. It was on October 5th, 1850, that Mary Edwards bore her last baby boy. At the time of my birth my father was a bullock feeder, working seven days a week, leaving home in the morning before it was light, and not returning in the evening until it was dark. He never saw his children, at this time, except for a little while on the Sunday, as they were always put to bed during the winter months before his return from work. At this time my father's wage had been reduced to 7s. [about $1.40] per week, and had it not been that my mother was able to add a little to her husband's wages by hand-loom weaving the family would have absolutely starved. I have known my mother to be at the loom sixteen hours of the twenty-four, and for those long hours she would not average more than 4s. [80¢] a week, and very often less than that.

The cottage in which the child was born was a miserable one of but two bedrooms, in which had to sleep father, mother, and six children. The family at this time was in abject poverty. When lying in bed with the infant the mother's only food was onion gruel. As a result of the bad food, or, properly speaking, the want of food, she was only able to feed the child at her breast for a week. After the first week he had to be fed on bread soaked in very poor skimmed milk. As soon as my mother was able to get about again, she had to take herself again to the loom. . . . Food rose to famine prices. . . . The only article which did not rise to such a proportionately high figure was meat, but that was an article of food which rarely entered a poor man's home, except a little piece of pork occasionally which would weigh about 1½ lb., and would have to last a family of nine for a week! At the time of the Crimean War meat never entered my father's house more than once or twice a year! . . .

In order to save the family from actual starvation, my father, night by night, took a few turnips from his master's field. My father used to keep our little boots in the best state of repair he could. My sister and I went to bed early on Saturday nights so that my mother might be able to wash and mend our clothes, and we have them clean and tidy for the Sunday. We had no change of clothes in those days. This work kept my mother up nearly all the Saturday night, but she would be up early on the Sunday morning to get our scanty breakfast ready in time for us to go to Sunday School.

This was the only schooling I ever had![1]

[1] From the autobiography of George Edwards (1850–1934), quoted in COLIN CLARK, *National Income and Outlay* (St. Martin's, New York, 1938), pp. 262–264.

Higher productivity gives us more product and more leisure:

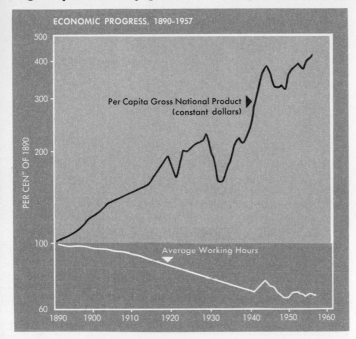

ECONOMIC PROGRESS, 1890-1957

Per Capita Gross National Product (constant dollars) ▶

PER CENT OF 1890

Average Working Hours ▼

Fig. 2. Technological improvements, better capital goods, and higher-skilled labor have raised production faster than the growth of population. (Note: this is a "ratio" or "semilog" chart; the vertical scale is arranged so that equal vertical distances depict equal percentage rather than equal absolute changes. Example: 400 is as much above 200 as 200 is above 100.)

TWO WORLDS?

Most of Asia and Africa are even today at lower levels of living than were the Western countries before the Industrial Revolution. Figure 2 shows how fortunate has been the United States growth in output. And a great economic statistician, Simon Kuznets of Johns Hopkins, has recently shown that the leading Western nations have for decades been averaging rapid rates of growth of output per head. How rapid growth? About 10 per cent per decade for France and England. About 16 per cent for Canada and the United States. And almost 30 per cent per decade for Sweden!

What about the progress of the poorer countries? We lack data to give firm answers. Professor Kuznets has made shrewd guesses and inclines to the view that their productivity growth has been lagging behind. He makes the important observation:

. . . the presently developed countries were already in advance of the "rest of the world" when modern industrialization began—and the latter only increased the disparity.[1]

[1] SIMON KUZNETS, "Quantitative Aspects of the Economic Growth of Nations: I," *Economic Development and Cultural Change,* vol. V, 1956, p. 25.

Income levels differ widely among the states:

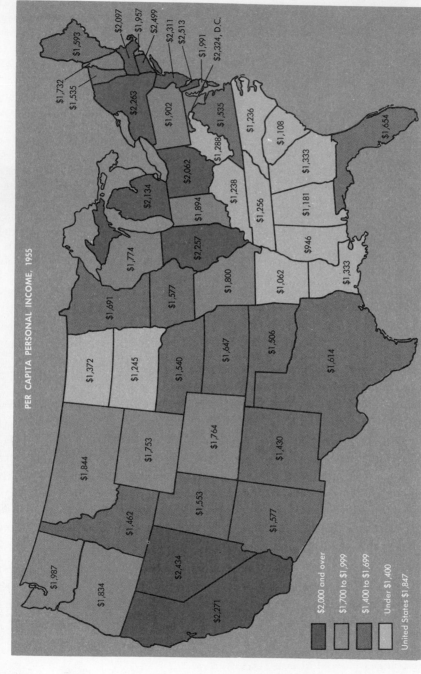

PER CAPITA PERSONAL INCOME, 1955

$1,987
$1,834
$1,844
$1,372
$1,245
$1,691
$1,774
$2,134
$1,593
$1,732
$1,535
$2,097
$1,957
$2,499
$2,311
$2,513
$1,991
$2,324, D.C.
$2,263
$1,902
$1,288
$1,535
$1,236
$1,108
$1,333
$1,654
$2,062
$1,894
$2,257
$1,238
$1,256
$1,181
$946
$1,577
$1,800
$1,062
$1,333
$1,462
$1,753
$1,540
$1,647
$1,506
$1,614
$1,553
$1,764
$1,430
$2,434
$1,577
$2,271

$2,000 and over
$1,700 to $1,999
$1,400 to $1,699
Under $1,400

United States $1,847

Fig. 3. State income differentials are narrowing as the South enjoys greater-than-average growth rates. Meanwhile in New England and some other high-level regions, per capita incomes grow at less-than-average rates, moving them down toward the nation's average. (Source: U.S. Department of Commerce.)

66

Americans enjoy highest standard of living in world:

Table 2. Per capita income of different countries, 1953. (Source: Center for International Studies, MIT. All estimates have been converted into U.S. dollars at exchange rates designed to reflect actual purchasing powers; but all figures should be regarded as rough approximations.)

United States	$1,908	USSR	441
Canada	1,318	Eire	416
Switzerland	995	European Satellites of USSR	369
United Kingdom	930	Argentina	366
Australia	921	Italy	307
Sweden	910	Mexico	207
Denmark	740	Japan	197
France	600	India	60
West Germany	482	China	60

Table 2 shows how great are recent geographical spreads of income per head. And the map in Fig. 3 shows that the United States itself is by no means an area of uniform income. The South has much lower incomes than do the Northeast and the West Coast. States like Mississippi have scarcely yet attained per capita incomes equal to those reached in Pennsylvania and New York back in 1890. But it is interesting to note that the regional differentials in income are gradually narrowing and changing. The South is pulling up, and regions like New England that have long been above the average are returning toward the average; other states, like California, grow faster than the average.

▶ HOW WE MEASURE INEQUALITY AMONG INCOME CLASSES

How great is the spread of incomes, and how shall we measure the degree of inequality of income distribution? From Table 1, we can say that roughly half of all Americans fall in the income range $2,500 to $6,500. This means that one-fourth fall below $2,500 and an equal number have incomes above $6,500. Of course, the fact that there are the same number of individuals and families in the above-$6,500 group as in the below-$2,500 group does not mean that they each receive the same percentage of the total income. Actually, the lowest fourth of the population receives much less than half the income received by the highest fourth.

This suggests how we can go about the task of getting a numerical measure of the degree of inequality of income distribution. We can ask: What per cent of all income goes to the lowest 10 per cent? What to the lowest 50 per cent? To the lowest 95 per cent? And so forth. Such data can be easily derived from the data of Table 1.

If incomes were absolutely uniformly distributed, the lowest 20 per cent of the population (which in this case would mean *any* 20 per cent) would receive exactly 20 per cent of the total income, the lowest 80 per cent would receive 80 per cent of the income, and the highest 20 per cent would also get only 20 per cent of the income.

This is typified by Fig. 4's picture of the so-called "Lorenz curve." This plots percentage of people on the horizontal axis and percentage of income on the vertical axis. From the second column of the table above Fig. 4 we get data for the diagonal straight line of absolute equality.

So much for the case of absolute equality. At the other extreme, we have the hypothetical case of absolute inequality, where everybody (say 99 out of 100 people) has no income, except for one person who has all the income. This is shown in the third column of the table above Fig. 4.

Why? Because the lowest 0, 20, 80, and 99 people have no income at all. But the lowest 100 include the last man, and all the people, of course, have all the income. The lowest curve on the Lorenz diagram—the black, right-angled line —represents the case of absolute inequality.

Any actual income distribution such as that of 1955, of course, falls in between these extremes. You can verify from columns (4) and (5) of Table 1 that its table of values is given roughly by the numbers in the fourth column of Fig. 4's table. Its Lorenz curve is given in Fig. 4 by the indicated intermediate curve, with the shaded area indicating the deviation from absolute equality, *i.e.,* the degree of inequality of income distribution.[1]

▶ **SOME FACTORS ASSOCIATED WITH INCOME DIFFERENCES**

What single profession seems to make the most money? Surprisingly enough, in recent years it has been the doctors. They have forged well ahead of lawyers; doctors have mean earnings of about $16,000 and median earnings of about $13,000; lawyers have mean and median earnings of $12,000 and $8,500. Why these high doctor earnings? Primarily because the costs of training doctors are so high, and the capacities of our medical schools are so low; as a result, we train not so many more doctors than we did in 1910 even though the demand has greatly increased.

---

[1] There are still other ways of measuring the degree of inequality of income. One of the most interesting of these we can mention but not discuss in detail here. The Italian-born Swiss professor of economics, Vilfredo Pareto, was often called, with somewhat questionable accuracy, the ideological precursor of fascism. By using a certain logarithmic chart called the "Pareto chart," he found that the "upper tail" of the income data of many different countries and many different times fell along straight lines of almost the same slopes. He came to believe this to be a fundamental natural law. According to Pareto's Law *there is an inevitable tendency for income to be distributed in the same way—regardless of social and political institutions and regardless of taxation.* In the past 50 years, more careful studies have refuted the universality of Pareto's Law, and its inevitability. Thus in Great Britain in the period following World War II, income taxation had gone so far as to leave only 70 people with incomes of more than $24,000 after taxes were paid!

Incomes are distributed with neither absolute equality nor absolute inequality:

Per cent of people	Per cent of income		
	Absolute equality	Absolute inequality	Actual 1955
0	0	0	0
20	20	0	5
40	40	0	16
60	60	0	33
80	80	0	55
100	100	100	100

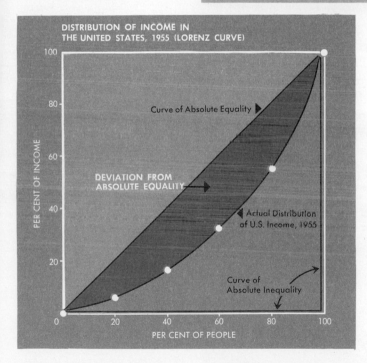

DISTRIBUTION OF INCOME IN THE UNITED STATES, 1955 (LORENZ CURVE)

Curve of Absolute Equality

DEVIATION FROM ABSOLUTE EQUALITY

Actual Distribution of U.S. Income, 1955

Curve of Absolute Inequality

PER CENT OF INCOME

PER CENT OF PEOPLE

Fig. 4. By plotting from the table above, we can see that the actual distribution-of-income curve lies between the two extremes of absolute equality and absolute inequality. The shaded area of this Lorenz chart measures relative inequality of income. (How would the curve have looked back in the roaring 1920's when inequality was greater?)

Dentists, engineers, and schoolteachers have median incomes of about $9,000, $8,000, and $4,000. College teachers as a class have a median salary of about $5,300 for a 9-month academic year ($6,300 if they also teach summer school, but only half have this opportunity). While teachers' salaries have been improving recently, it is ministers who are lowest paid of all professionals. Their median salary is still scarcely above $3,500! And even with special perquisites the final figure is unbelievably low.

Do incomes increase with age? Not in the lowest paid manual jobs. For such work, a man is at his best in the low twenties; after that he goes downhill. In the professions and in business executive jobs, earnings do increase with age: a doctor reaches his prime around fifty and so does a lawyer; both can hope to work beyond the normal retirement ages. A junior executive with an A.B. diploma will begin training at $450 a month; if very successful, he may retire as chairman of the board, earning say $70,000 a year and with stock bonuses and retirement provisions.

On the other hand, many corporations and institutions have been fixing inflexible retirement ages of sixty-five. With improvements in life expectancies, this poses the problem of long years of wasteful and unhappy retirement. The ultimate solution seems to be along the following lines: Let each man taper off slowly rather than discontinuously, with factors other than chronological age being given their full weight.

Finally, how do education and training affect income? Is the expense of a college training worth while? The evidence seems to be, Decidedly yes. Even if you have to borrow at 6 per cent interest, even if you have to put off years of gainful employment, even if you have to live away from home and pay for food and books, your lifetime earnings in the professions that are open only to college graduates will probably turn out to be more than compensatingly great. (Good grades help: a *Time* study showed "greasy grinds" end up with slightly higher pay than do "big men on campus"; both outearn the anonymous face in the college crowd.)

Figure 5 shows how professions differ in inequality of earnings. Can you

Self-employed lawyers and doctors show great income inequalities, professors and army officers less:

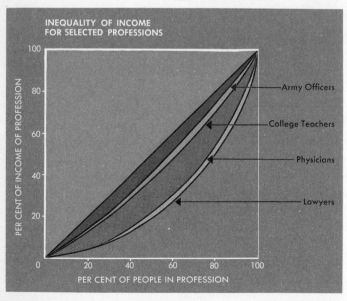

Fig. 5. Why would the curve for salaried doctors and lawyers fall in between our two sets of curves? Why would you expect dentists to have a curve just above doctors? (Source: G. J. Stigler, National Bureau of Economic Research, New York, 1956.)

Are abilities more normally distributed than market incomes?

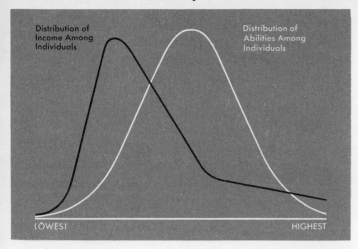

Distribution of
Income Among
Individuals

Distribution of
Abilities Among
Individuals

LOWEST   HIGHEST

Fig. 6. Heights, intelligence quotients, and many measured human traits seem to follow a so-called "normal" bell-shaped statistical distribution. Market incomes seem to be more skewed, highest incomes being more than a hundred times lowest.

guess why the order of inequality is lawyer, doctor, college teacher, and army officer?

▶ **DIFFERENCES IN ABILITY AND INCOMES**

In Part Four we shall study in detail the economic principles underlying the distribution of income. Our common sense enables us to anticipate part of that analysis and suggests that one factor helping to explain differences in income must be differences in people.

These differences in people may be physical, mental, temperamental, or even moral. They may be associated with biological inheritance through the genetic cells or with social and economic environment. They may be permanent—like being a blonde—or acquired, like educational advantage. These differences may even involve such artificial conventionalities as the possession or non-possession of a union card, and one's propensity to drop " (h) -aitches" in speaking or to pronounce "oil" with an "r" and "girl" without one.

These differences provide us with at least the beginning of an answer—but only a beginning. For we will find that most physical traits, such as height or hip girth, and most mental traits, such as intelligence quotient or tone perception, are not so different among people as are the differences in income distribution. Often, the scientist who measures these traits finds that they are "normally" distributed, with most people in the middle and fewer people at each end, as represented by Fig. 6's bell-shaped curve. Whereas incomes—even those from work rather than property—are distributed *askew,* as shown by the other curve with a very long tail off in the direction of the highest paid individuals.

One could go on speculating on these fundamental questions. Probably it would be more scientific and more fruitful at this point to reserve judgment until we have studied the principles determining pricing of goods and productive factors. However, it may be as well to mention at this point that a very careful study of wage inequalities in the Russian communistic economy[1] showed inequalities and dispersions between the best paid and the poorest paid workers that were surprisingly like those of our own society. Shostakovich and other top Soviet musicians probably make more than do Stravinsky and other American composers—maybe even including Irving Berlin!

Perhaps a warning is in order at this point against jumping to the conclusion that there is something *necessary* and *inevitable* about this dispersion of income. Within the framework of our free competitive society fundamental changes in education have already made significant changes in inequality. Moreover, as no one knows better than the man at the top, our system of progressive income taxation has already greatly changed the relative take-home and—what is more important—the "keep-at-home" of the high and low paid; and presumably this will continue to be an abiding feature of American life.

▶ **THE POSITION OF MINORITIES**

No discussion of the inequality of incomes would be complete without mention of the position of economic minorities. In a real sense this is the concern of everyone, because we all belong to some minority. Yes, even the Smiths or, for that matter, the Lodges and the Cabots.

Of course the economically most important minorities consist of Negroes, women, and old people. Careful, competent observers have asserted again and again that outright sexual discrimination in the sense of paying men higher rates for the same kind and volume of work is not a common practice. Similarly it has been asserted that racial discrimination in the sense of unequal pay for the same work is not prevailing practice.

How can we reconcile these statements with the economic inequalities which every sophisticated person knows prevail between the sexes and races and which are shown in Table 3? The answer to the paradox lies partly in the fact that discrimination usually takes the more subtle and more effective form of *not admitting men and women to the same jobs and barring Negroes from many of the higher paid jobs.*

Undoubtedly this explains much of the story. However, other competent

---

[1] ABRAM BERGSON, *The Structure of Soviet Wages* (Harvard University Press, Cambridge, Mass., 1944). The inequality of property incomes is, of course, less in a society hostile to private property. The inequality of political privilege among Soviet bureaucrats, military officers, Communist party members, and the Soviet public at large is not capable of precise numerical measurement.

Men still outearn women, whites still outearn Negroes:

	Male	Female
White	$4,458	$2,870
Negro	2,831	1,637

Table 3. Median wage incomes, 1955. (Source: Bureau of the Census.)

observers maintain that women and Negroes on exactly the same job do often receive less pay. Women grade-school teachers often receive lower pay than men. Where Negro and white dishwashers work side by side, sometimes the former get lower pay. In a large electrical-goods plant, job-evaluation experts divide all factory work into two parts: women's jobs and men's jobs. The pay of the lowest men begins about where the highest women's pay leaves off. Yet both management and the union will admit, off the record, that in many borderline jobs the productivity of women is greater than that of the men.

Now it cannot be denied that there are physical and temperamental differences between men and women. For example, a woman could not win the heavyweight wrestling championship or set a record for the 100-yard dash. On the other hand, the female sex is the stronger sex in the sense of life expectancy and also, perhaps, in being capable of sustained, painstaking effort. It is equally obvious that there are differences of skin color and hair texture between colored and white races.

Whatever one's views as to the biological and environmental differences between the races and sexes—and the views of the scientists who have studied the question most are very different from those of the man on the street—it is absolutely clear to any observer that there are numerous jobs which either sex or race can do equally well and is prevented from doing. This is shown by the experience of wartime and boom when the usual barriers are lowered.

Similarly the older worker in ordinary times finds himself at a disadvantage in our society. A man may be thrown on the scrap heap by the age of forty when many of his best years are still ahead. It is not true that an older worker is the first to be fired; usually his experience or seniority helps to protect him. But once he is fired, it is much harder for him to become reemployed. Paradoxically, the humanitarian measures adopted by corporations to aid older workers (retirement pension schemes, etc.) are one reason for corporations' refusing to hire older men, since it then becomes more expensive to hire them.

Again from the horror of war a few salutary lessons have been snatched. Women, Negroes, and older workers have shown that they are capable of holding down better jobs and earning more money than was thought possible before the war. The experience of the federal and state Fair Employment Practice Commissions has not been that prejudice can be legislated out of existence overnight, but that steady improvement is possible if the people really want it.

Nor can all of the blame be placed upon bigoted employers. Organized labor must incur some of the onus for Jim Crow legislation.

The war and postwar prosperity have improved the relative economic position of the Negro. From 1939 to 1955 nonwhite median wages more than quadrupled while white median wages tripled. But just as the Negro is the last to be hired, he is the first to be fired when depression comes. When jobs become scarce, whites invade even the fields of domestic service usually abandoned to the Negro.

Still once again we are faced with the challenge of providing full employment. For it is in the wake of layoffs and economic insecurity that the disruptive cry against minorities—against Negro, Jew, Catholic, "Okie"—gathers the force to cause our democratic institutions to tremble.

▶ ECONOMIC STRATIFICATION AND OPPORTUNITY

America has always been considered the land of opportunity where anyone with ability might get ahead in the world. The success legend of the Horatio Alger, Jr., "poor but proud" hero who worked his way to the top and married the boss's daughter—or vice versa—has no doubt been overdrawn. But it did have elements of truth as compared to the situation in older European countries, where an aristocratic tradition lingered on, and where free schooling beyond the primary grades was never established.

For example, the "old school tie" and, more important, the Oxford accent were until recently almost indispensable to political and social advancement in

Anyone can climb the ladder of success, but it helps to start high:

Table 4. Social origin of successful leaders in America. Though laborers far outnumber businessmen in the population at large, most successful businessmen had a businessman for a father. What trends do you make out in these tables? How would you explain them? (Source: F. W. Taussig and C. S. Joslyn, *American Business Leaders*, Macmillan, N.Y., 1932; *Fortune*.)

Occupation of father	Persons listed in *Who's Who*, 1912, per cent	American millionaires, living in 1925, per cent	American business leaders, 1928, per cent	American business leaders, 1952 per cent	American business leaders under 50, 1952 per cent
Businessman	35.3	75.0	60.0	61.8	67.8
Professional man	34.3	10.5	13.4	13.5	14.8
Farmer	23.4	7.3	12.4	12.7	11.1
Laborer	6.7	1.6	12.5	7.8	2.5
Other	0.3	5.6	1.7	4.2	3.8
Total	100.0	100.0	100.0	100.0	100.0

Britain; even with the free scholarship system, few members of the lower or middle class could jump this hurdle. In this country, few people outside the State Department even recognize a "prep school" accent and variations in speech are geographical rather than social. The American stenographer is almost indistinguishable in appearance from the blueblood debutante.

Moreover, ours has been rather a materialistic civilization in which success is interpreted in business terms. Because "money talks," it is easier for outsiders to break into the upper crust than it would be in a culture that puts greater emphasis upon tradition. The *nouveaux riches* of one generation, such as the Vanderbilts, become the social dictators of the next.

Nevertheless, careful questionnaire investigation of the social origins of successful businessmen, namely, the directors and officers of corporations, turns up some surprising facts. The typical American business executive does not come off a farm or out of a workingman's home, but more likely his father was also a businessman or possibly in one of the professions. Table 4 summarizes some typical research studies that have been made by Taussig and Joslyn and others.

Does this mean that American economic society is hardening along caste lines?[1] Taussig and Joslyn are not sure. They point out that two diametrically opposite explanations are possible: (1) In the past there was high social mobility in America: all the cream rose to the top, leaving naturally less gifted people at the bottom. (2) There are strong, and perhaps growing, barriers to circulation between the economic classes.

Taussig and Joslyn incline rather to the first view, feeling that "you can't keep a good man down." Most sociologists would disagree. They would emphasize the thousand and one subtle psychological, social, economic, and educational disadvantages of the children of less fortunate families; that equal ability is not always able to give rise to equal achievement; that

> Full many a flower is born to blush unseen,
> And waste its sweetness on the desert air.

Whichever view is right, the implications for policy are the same. Human beings are a nation's most important form of social capital—a form, moreover, in which we have invested too little in the past. Talent, wherever it may be, is worth being sought out and nurtured.

---

[1] When the first edition of this book was written, the author inclined toward the view that it was becoming increasingly difficult to go from the bottom to the top. Now he is not so sure. Recent careful studies of the origins of business leaders back before 1900 suggest that the present does not compare unfavorably with the good old days, which may not have been so good after all. Increasingly as organizations become bigger, the elements of nepotism and personal favoritism seem to become less important, and the increasing emphasis upon civil-servant-like quasi-objective tests of performance suggests greater mobility among the elite.

SUMMARY

1. Factual studies of the American distribution of income show that median incomes are lower than popularly believed. Even though incomes today are higher than in any other country or time, they are still not high in comparison with common notions as to what represents comfortable modern living.

2. The view that the poor are becoming poorer in modern industrial nations will not stand up under careful factual examination. Since the Industrial Revolution, average standards of life in Western Europe and America seem definitely to have been showing a rising secular trend, tending to outstrip the underdeveloped nations. Even within the United States, the differentials in living standards are very great. However, there is a trend toward narrowing the old differentials between North and South.

3. The Lorenz diagram is a convenient device for measuring the spreads or inequalities of income distribution. It shows what percentage of total income goes to the poorest 1 per cent of the population, to the poorest 10 per cent, to the poorest 50 per cent, to the poorest 95 per cent, etc. The modern distribution of American income appears to be less unequally distributed than in 1929, but it still shows a considerable measure of inequality. An interesting question is to relate the skew distributions of income with the differences in the mental and physical abilities of people.

4. Minority groups—such as the aged, women, Negroes, and various ethnic groups—pose important economic problems for any democracy. At the borders between economics and sociology, we run into the interesting questions concerning the "circulation of the elite." Such popular clichés as "shirt sleeves to shirt sleeves in three generations" appear to have a weak factual basis. There turns out to be a strong positive correlation between income and social status of a person's parents and grandparents and his own, but the exact direction of causation is hard to establish.

QUESTIONS FOR DISCUSSION

1. Let each member of the class write down on a slip of paper an estimate of his own family's income. From these, draw up a frequency table showing the distribution of incomes. What is the median income? The average income?

2. How much do you think it takes for a childless married couple to live comfortably in your community? How would the money be spent?

3. Were your parents better off than their parents? What does this suggest with respect to the advantages and disadvantages of capitalism?

4. Formulate some of your own ethical beliefs concerning how unequal incomes should be for people of different abilities and needs. How do you justify these beliefs? Would a nineteenth-century American agree? A Russian? A South Sea Islander?

5. The *Federal Reserve Bulletin* gives the following data on the 1956 inequality of distribution of liquid-asset holding by "spending units" (*i.e.,* members of a family living together and pooling their incomes) :

Percentage of spending units	0	20	40	60	80	100
Percentage of total liquid-asset holdings	0	0	1	4	18	100

Draw the Lorenz curve, and explain why the distribution of wealth is always so much more unequal than the distribution of income.

6. Review your understanding of the following concepts:

income distribution	*Lorenz curve*
mean, median, and modal income	*normal and skew distributions*
per capita incomes	*social stratification*

5 BUSINESS ORGANIZATION AND INCOME

The business of America is business.
CALVIN COOLIDGE

To understand our business civilization, we must first understand the organization and functioning of business enterprise. The first part of this chapter leads up to the analysis of the modern corporation, primarily by an extensive case study; the last half is concerned with the financial structure of corporations, particularly the modern large-scale or "giant" corporation.

In an appendix there is presented a brief introduction to the fundamentals of accounting, without a comprehension of which there can be no deep understanding of the economics of enterprise.

A THE FORMS OF BUSINESS ORGANIZATION

▶ THE POPULATION OF BUSINESS ENTERPRISES

There are over 4¼ million American business units in 1958. All except a very small fraction of these enterprises are very small-scale units owned by a single person. Most businesses are here today and gone tomorrow, the average life expectancy of a business being only 6 years. Some will terminate in bankruptcy; many more will be voluntarily brought to a close with sighs of regret for dashed hopes and an expensive lesson learned; still others will come to a joyous end when their "self-employed" owner finally lands a good, steady job or takes up a new line of endeavor.

As fast as old businesses die, others are born. The present population of business concerns grew up as a result of the cumulated excess of business births over business deaths during previous years. As the American economy grows, we may expect a steady further increase in the number of firms from a normal excess of business births over deaths.

During the war few old businesses failed, but few new businesses could be born. Since the end of the war there has been a spectacular growth of new businesses to make up for lost time. The causes are obvious: prosperity, increasing supplies of civilian goods, wartime cumulations of savings by would-be businessmen, easy credit conditions, and government help to veterans.

▶ BIG, SMALL, AND INFINITESIMAL BUSINESS

By number the tiny, transient, self-owned "individual proprietorship" is overwhelmingly the dominant form of American business. But in terms of dollar value, political and economic power, payrolls, and employment, some few hundred "giant corporations" occupy a strategically dominant position in the modern American economy.

Let us glance briefly at the role in our economy of "infinitesimal businesses." There are more than 340,000 grocery-store owners in the United States, all trying to make a living. There are over a quarter of a million automobile service stations; more than 54,000 drugstores; and so it goes.[1]

Some of these ventures are highly successful; but it is still true to say that most do not earn for their owners much more than they could get with less effort and risk by working for somebody else. Thus, chain stores do about 40 per cent of all the grocery business, the rest being divided among all the independents. Most of these independents consist of the so-called "Ma and Pa" stores, doing less than $100 of business every day. These are often started by people who have only a few thousand dollars of initial capital—less than half the amount necessary for an adequate grocery store to do the $150-a-day business necessary if the owner is to earn even minimum wages for his effort. Such small-scale efforts are doomed from their very beginning. When the owner's initial capital is used up, they are finished. They illustrate why one-third to one-half of all retail businesses are discontinued within 2 years.

Of course, fields differ in the amount of capital required. To build a modern service station costs more than $80,000 but to lease one from an oil company brings the initial capital down to around $5,000. Occupations with a

[1] Out of every 1,000 business establishments in the United States, approximately

110 are retail food stores	45 are beauty shops or barbershops
95 are contractors, etc.	40 are automobile dealers, repair shops, or garages
90 are wholesalers of various kinds	
90 are eating and drinking establishments	25 are appliance and home-furnishing stores
80 are in the real-estate, insurance, or finance fields	20 are laundries, etc.
55 are filling stations	20 are drug and liquor stores
45 are in transportation, communication, and other public utilities	15 are hotels, etc.
45 are clothing or general-merchandise stores	15 are hardware and farm-implement stores
	15 are manufacturers of lumber and basic timber products

high "rate of turnover of inventory"—like vegetable stores—obviously require less initial capital than drugstores, hardware, or jewelry stores where many items of stock will stay on the shelves for 3 to 5 years and where the average "turnover ratio" of annual sales to stock of inventory may be less than one.

Aside from the capital necessary to open a business, there is the tremendous amount of personal effort required. Self-employed farmers usually work from 55 to 65 hours per week as compared to about 45 for farm hands. Similarly, it has been estimated that the people who are their own bosses put in more hours per week than wage earners. Who, on his Sunday ride in the country, has not pitied some self-employed drudge, whose own efforts and those of all his family hardly suffice to cause him to break even?

Still, people will always want to start out on their own. *Theirs* may be the successful venture. Even if they never do succeed in earning more than a few thousand a year, there is something attractive about being able to make your own plans and doing the variety of tasks that a small enterpriser must tend to every day.

▶ THE SINGLE PROPRIETORSHIP

We may gain insight into the principal forms of business organization—the single proprietorship, the partnership, and the corporation—by following the history of a particular business venture as it grows from a small beginning into a good-sized corporation. In the last part of this chapter, we shall turn to the subject of the giant corporation and its modern economic role.

Let's suppose you decide to start a business to produce tooth paste. You may have hit upon a good preparation in your chemistry class; or perhaps you simply looked up an old formula in the *Encyclopaedia Britannica.* To be a single proprietor you need not get anybody's permission: you simply wake up one morning and say, "Today, I am in business!" And you are.

You can hire as few or as many men as you wish, borrow whatever capital you can. At the end of the month whatever is left over as profits—after all costs have been met!—is yours to do with as you like. And there is nothing to stop you from going to the cash register at any time, taking out $800 if you can find it there, and giving it to your wife to buy a fur coat or a Chippendale chair. (Of course as an individual you must pay personal income taxes on all earnings.)

The losses of the business are all yours too. If your sales fail to cover the costs you have incurred, your creditors can ask you to dig deep into your personal assets: the war bonds set aside for Junior's education, the old farmstead, and the rest. In legal terms an individual proprietor has "unlimited liability" for all debts contracted by the business. All his property, beyond a small minimum, is legally attachable to meet those debts.

▶ BUSINESS GROWTH AND THE NEED FOR SHORT-TERM CAPITAL

Let's suppose the business is prospering tremendously—perhaps because your low price has induced a chain of 5-and-10-cent stores to place a large order for tubes of paste to be marketed under its name. You are now making more money than you expected to; but you find yourself harder pressed for cash than ever before. Why? Because you are not paid in advance for your sales, whereas you must pay your workers and suppliers promptly on receipt of their services. For the moment you are putting out money and getting nothing for it, *i.e.*, nothing except the certainty of future payment on the sales orders which you have booked, nothing but a miscellaneous batch of "goods in process"—unfinished tooth paste, empty tubing, and so forth.

To some extent, the stringency of "working capital" can be relieved by your not paying for supplies until the end of the month or even longer. However, there is a limit to how far your suppliers will let you run up bills. Also letting your so-called "accounts payable liabilities" pile up is an expensive way of raising capital. This is because goods are often billed at 2 per cent discount if paid within 30 days; when you do not take advantage of such discounts, you are, in effect, paying a very high interest rate—24 per cent per year!

Where is such a single proprietor to borrow? A personal finance company will probably charge you something like 3 per cent per month or 40 per cent per year for a small personal loan; and even that company will prefer to lend to a man with a steady wage that can be legally "attached" or "garnisheed" in case of nonpayment. If you own a home without a mortgage, a loan at 6 per cent might be raised upon it. To borrow in this way is clearly to risk your family's future well-being, but probably if you are sufficiently convinced of your business future you might assume the risk.

Why can't the local banker be called upon for a commercial loan at 6 per cent? Ordinarily, a commercial bank will not provide "venture capital" for an unproven enterprise. The bank's president looks at your checking balance and finds it has always been near the vanishing point; this is natural, since as fast as payments have come in, you have had to write checks to stave off the everinsistent claims of your creditors. Ordinarily, the bank likes to make 3-month loans to be used for peak-season needs and to be canceled during the rest of the year. It is idle to pretend that 3 months from now your growing business will be more flooded with cash than now. At that time you will be applying for continuous renewal of the loan: you know it, and the banker knows it.

Even if the bank were emancipated from the older prejudice against "term loans" of some years' duration, it could not conscientiously provide the capital to a business like yours. No matter how certain and glorious the future of the business appears to you, to the banker you are only one of numerous would-be entrepreneurs: most, he knows, are destined for failure even in the best of times; and almost all would be wiped out if a really big depression came along. For the bank really to protect the sums entrusted to it by its depositors, it would have to charge you an extra risk premium, in addition to, say, 5 per cent interest, of perhaps 10 per cent or more.[1] Otherwise, the successful ventures would not be offsetting the losses of the unsuccessful.

There is one possibility of your getting a loan from the bank. The Small Business Administration (SBA) might join with the bank and make you a loan, thus coaxing the banker to make it. Or, in rare cases the SBA might directly make you a loan when no banker can be found to do so. And in some states, there are development commissions which have limited funds to help bring a business to town or keep it there.

Despite your makeshift attempts to raise capital, the business is still suffering from growing pains. You have exhausted all possibilities of raising further loan capital. Perhaps the time has come to look for a partner.

▶ THE PARTNERSHIP

Any two or more people can get together and form a partnership. Each agrees to provide some fraction of the work and capital, to share some percentage of the profits, and of course to share the losses or debts. A purely oral agreement will do; but it is more businesslike and makes for less misunderstanding if you have a lawyer draw up some sort of formal partnership agreement.

In the case of the tooth-paste business, let's suppose your brother-in-law is given a part ownership in the business in return for putting up $25,000 of capital. Like you, he is to work for the company, drawing let's say, $5,000 per year as compared to your $8,000. You are to receive two-thirds of all profits or losses computed after the partnership withdrawals are treated as costs; and he one-third.

Your partner has put up $25,000 in cold cash. What have you brought into the venture? In the first place, you have, of course, some unfinished barrels of tooth paste to contribute, along with some uncollected accounts receivable for goods already delivered. This doesn't seem like much.

Actually, what you bring to the partnership is an intangible but valuable asset: the profitable sales orders, the know-how, or what is called "good will." In short, you are bringing with you a potential profit-earning power over all costs and drawings of, say, $12,000 a year. You are letting your partner have

---

[1] Another alternative has been used extensively in Germany but not in the United States or Britain: German banks buy part ownership in business and share in the jack pot of profits. Such participation in ownership inevitably leads to management responsibilities by the banks and often to monopoly control of business by banking interests. For this reason, and others, such activity is legally forbidden to our banks.

a $5,000 a year job—which we shall assume is perhaps equal to what he can get elsewhere—and in addition for $25,000 he is purchasing a one-third slice of $12,000 every year.

To get this much per year from bond investments would cost him much more than $25,000. He would have to buy $100,000 worth of 4 per cent government bonds to get such a return, or $80,000 worth of 5 per cent private bonds. Aside from the risk element, your partner is getting a good buy for his $25,000, since he will yearly collect some 16 per cent on his investment. So your two-thirds share is justified by the good will that you supply.[1]

► "THIS IS THE WAY WE GROW"

And your business continues to prosper and grow. Each year, both partners agree to take out of the business only their stipulated drawings (which are like wages) and about a fifth of their share of profits, plowing back the rest of the profits into the business.

Why do you decide to take out any profits from the business at all? Because you need the cash to pay your federal personal income taxes, which are levied not only on your salaries but also *upon your respective shares of the partnership's earnings*. The government is a silent partner, sharing part of every extra dollar that your partnership earns for you.

Why does a business like yours grow? Here are some possible reasons: (1) Your tooth-paste sales have risen as a result of your trade name's becoming advertised and better known and as a result of your sending out more salesmen. (2) As more tooth paste is produced, economies of large-scale production are realized so that you are able to cut your price. (3) A new factor of growth results from "vertical integration." You decide to buy a chemical factory, to produce your own raw materials; and also you become your own wholesaler, thus operating three stages rather than only one "stage of production." (4) Too, the company begins to grow by "horizontal integration": you take advantage of a profitable opportunity to buy out a number of competitors who produce similar tooth pastes. (5) New "complementary products" such as soap and lipstick are added. You feel that bringing in the new lines under the same roof will help to spread the overhead expenses, and your salesmen feel that they might just as well get many orders as few when making a call. (6) Finally, your business may grow just because you are producing a better tooth paste.

► NEW NEEDS AND SOURCES FOR CAPITAL

Once again, the enterprise finds itself in a paradox: the more successful it is and the faster it grows, the harder up it is for capital! The $25,000 of new

[1] Good will and capitalized earning power are discussed in the accounting Appendix.

"equity capital" brought into the business did not long stay in the form of cash. It was quickly transformed into circulating assets such as goods in process and office supplies. In part it went to pay off the most pressing liabilities.

The remainder was used as a down payment on a factory building and equipment. The difference between the down payment and the purchase price of the factory was secured by a mortgage loan on the property. The mortgage money was advanced by a near-by life-insurance company and was to be amortized or paid off in installments over a period of 20 years along with $5\frac{1}{2}$ per cent interest per year on the actual principal still unpaid at any time. In case the loan should not be paid, the holder of the mortgage of course has the right to foreclose the mortgage, *i.e.*, to take over the ownership of the building and sell it for what it will bring. Since the down payment on the factory came to about one-fourth of its price, and since this price was a bargain price to begin with, and since each year the insurance company will be getting back part of its principal, the risk taken by the company is not very great. The only way it could lose would be if there were a disastrous real-estate crash within the first few years of the making of the contract.

Despite the continuous plowing of profits back into the business, the growth of the enterprise still leaves you needing more capital. But now, having established your reputation, so to speak, new avenues of borrowing are open to you. Your banker will be glad to lend you money to tide you over the busy pre-Christmas period. An industrial finance company, like the Commercial Credit Corporation, will lend you money on the basis of your safe, but as yet uncollected, "accounts receivable" (*i.e.*, the sums owed you for goods sold and delivered but not yet paid for). Finally, your bank, which before was leery of lending your business money for venture capital, now agrees to make a "term loan" for 5 years.

Suppose when all is said and done, you yet need more capital than you can raise by any kind of borrowing. The painful necessity arises of getting more "equity" capital by letting some new people share in the profits (and losses) of the business. (As a matter of fact, even if you could still find some institutions to borrow from, it would be unwise to do so. You have already superimposed too many liabilities and fixed charges on a narrow equity base. As long as things go well, it is lovely to earn 16 per cent profit on capital that costs you only 6. But if losses should occur, they will fall all the more heavily on your two partners, who are the residual owners.)

▶ **DISADVANTAGES OF THE PARTNERSHIP FORM**

One possibility of getting more ownership capital is to admit new partners. There is no limit to the number of partners that you can admit: there have been partnerships in the brokerage and banking fields involving more than

100 people. However, every time a new partner is admitted, or one dies or re-signs, a whole new partnership must be formed.[1]

Moreover, as the number of partners increases, there comes to the fore a factor that has been soft-pedaled in our discussion up to now. Each partner is liable *without limit* to the full extent of his personal fortune for all debts contracted by the partnership. If he owns 1 per cent of the partnership and the business fails, then he will be called upon to foot 1 per cent of the bills and the other partners will be assessed their 99 per cent. Suppose they can't pay any part of their assessment. Then the 1 per cent partner may be called upon to pay *for all,* even if it means selling his fine etchings at auction or his family home.

This feature of *unlimited liability* reveals why partnerships tend to be con-fined to small, homogeneous, personal enterprises. According to the doctrine of "mutual agency" involved in the law of partnerships, each partner has rather broad powers to act as an agent to commit the whole partnership. When it becomes a question of placing their personal fortunes in jeopardy, people are ordinarily very reluctant to put their capital into complex ventures over which they can exercise little control.

This explains why agriculture and retail trade are the only sectors of our economy where more than half of the business done is done by single pro-prietors and partnerships. In the field of investment banking, concerns like J. P. Morgan & Company used to advertise proudly "not incorporated" so that their creditors could have the extra assurance. But even these concerns have transmuted themselves into corporate entities.

The giant brokerage partnership of Merrill Lynch, Pierce, Fenner & Beane handles a sizable fraction of all stock-market trading in this country. It has many major partners and scores of junior partners. It illustrates that the bar-riers put up by the partnership form to running a large enterprise are not in-superable. But except in the brokerage field, such giant partnerships are rare. Undoubtedly, unlimited liability and the red tape needed to ensure conti-nuity are the main drawbacks to the partnership form.

---

[1] More weighty is the real disadvantage stemming from the fact that a partnership can be dissolved whenever any party finds the existing arrangement unsatisfactory and wishes to withdraw; and the law of partnerships makes it impossible for any partner to sell his share to a new party without the consent of his partners; if agreement cannot be secured, a costly liquidation of the assets of the partnership may be inevitable.

Perhaps the reader will remember how the novelist William Dean Howells has his famous title character, Silas Lapham, a rising self-made paint tycoon, present his partner with the ultimatum: "You buy me out or I'll buy you out." Silas' two excuses, that his were the real brains and energy responsible for the success of the business and that the proffered price ex-ceeded his partner's original investment, were cleverly seen through by Mrs. Lapham. She pointed out that, without the partner's money at the critical time, the business could never have succeeded and that Silas' offer to sell was premised upon the knowledge that his partner was not in a position to buy the whole of the business.

B THE MODERN CORPORATION

At this point, therefore—or even long before—you will probably decide to form a corporation rather than a partnership. Usually you will incorporate in the state in which you live and operate. However, if the corporation is of any size, you may prefer to establish token headquarters in some state like Delaware or New Jersey, which have put in very easy rules to attract firms.

Centuries ago, corporation charters were awarded by governments very rarely and only by special acts of the king and legislature. Parliament or Congress would graciously permit a public-utility enterprise or railroad to form a corporation to do specific things and perform specific functions. The East India Company was such a privileged corporation. The early railroads here and abroad often had to spend as much money in getting a charter through the legislature as in preparing their roadbeds. Gradually within the past century, this procedure began to seem unfair and it became the practice to pass general incorporation laws granting almost anyone the privilege of forming a corporation for almost any purpose, without having to get a special vote of approval from the state legislature or from Congress.

Today, for a small fee a lawyer will draw up the necessary papers and will write into the corporate charter almost as wide powers and purposes as you could wish. Automatically the state will grant the charter.

Let's see how the incorporating procedure works in the case of your toothpaste company. You decide to issue 20,000 shares of common stock in the corporation, 6,600 going to you, 3,300 to your partner, 100 to your wife, and the other 10,000 to be sold to outside interests. Although each share is to have an initial stated value of $10, your lawyer has advised you to make them no-par shares, since "par value" has no particular significance anyway.

The 10,000 shares to be sold to the public are to be marketed through a local *investment banking* firm. These firms are simply merchandisers of securities; and as with any merchant, their profit comes from the difference between their buying and selling prices. Because yours is such a small business, they must drive a hard bargain, especially since they can claim that the costs of selling the securities are likely to be high. Thus the investment brokers may offer you $10 per share and plan to resell at a price of $12.50 per share. Had you been a large company, you might have held out for as much as $12.40, or even in some cases $12.45, out of the $12.50 selling price, because of the eager competitive bidding of the different investment banking syndicates.

And, for a large company the investment banker would probably have agreed to *underwrite* the new issue of 10,000 shares. This means that he would have guaranteed the purchase of the full 10,000 shares at a set price. If the market then refused to buy all these shares from the investment banker at his announced price, he, not you, would have to absorb the loss. But he probably regards you as too small and untried a business to justify his assuming the underwriting risk. So he takes your issue on a "best effort" basis; and if he can't sell all the shares, you end up raising less capital.

Fortunately, all goes well and he pays you $100,000 in cash for the securities he has sold. Unlike the case of the partnership, you need not concern yourself with the people to whom he has sold the shares, or with the fact that they may resell their shares. The names of the owners of the shares are registered with the company just in case they get lost and so that you will know where to send the dividend checks or the announcements of stockholders' meetings.

Ordinarily, each share gives its owner one vote. He also has a share in the earnings of the corporation in direct proportion to the number of shares he owns. Those with 100 shares get 100 votes and correspondingly higher dividends.

The outside owners of 10,000 shares have paid in $100,000 of cash to the company. What have you and your partner paid in? Obviously not cash, but rather an equivalent amount of earning assets: plant, equipment, goods in process, and perhaps good will which is, as we have already seen, the capitalized value of the presumed "excess earning power" of the business, resulting from its trade-marks, patents, know-how, and so forth.

Back in the bad old days before 1929, you and your investment banker might have evaluated the good will pretty much as liberally as you wished, possibly giving yourself 20,000 rather than 10,000 shares. This practice has been called "watering the stock." But today, you would have to submit any sizable new issue to the SEC. They would have to satisfy themselves that there are no misleading claims before they would approve the new flotation. However, they do not pretend to pass judgment on or certify to the value of the stock. *Caveat emptor*—let the buyer beware—still prevails as a doctrine!

▶ ADVANTAGES AND DISADVANTAGES OF THE CORPORATE FORM

The corporation has solved most of the problems that bothered you about the partnership. It is an almost perfect device for the raising of large sums of capital. Of first importance, every stockholder now has *limited liability*. After paying $12.50 for a share of stock, the investor need not worry about his personal estate's being in jeopardy. If worse comes to worst and the business becomes bankrupt, the most that each shareholder could lose would be his original $12.50 per share. He cannot be assessed further.

Of secondary importance is the fact that the corporation is a fictitious legal person created by the state. It exists not by "natural right" but only at the pleasure of the state. The corporation, as distinct from its owners, can be sued in court and can sue. Any officer of the company, unlike any partner, is strictly limited in his legal ability to act as agent for the other owners and to commit them financially. Also, the corporation may have "perpetual succession" or existence, regardless of how many times the shares of stock change hands by sale or bequest, and regardless of whether there are 10,000 different stockholders. No group of shareholders can force any other group to sell or retain their holdings, and only a majority vote rather than unanimity is needed to reach usual business decisions. Normally the stockholders will be too numerous to meet for every decision; they will prefer to elect a board of directors consisting of a dozen or so members to represent them between annual meetings, in much the same way that democratic electorates select legislative representatives to act for them. As we shall see in a moment, the problem of keeping large corporations "truly democratic" is a hard one.

You will face one disadvantage to incorporation that has become increasingly serious in recent years. The federal government taxes corporate income. Thus, during the war a profitable corporation might have had to pay as much as 80 per cent of its income to the government in excess-profit taxation; the Korean war too brought an excess-profit tax. And in peace most corporations must pay 52 cents of each extra dollar of income. (This has nothing to do with the personal income tax that owners pay on dividends they get.[1])

A number of intelligent businessmen are coming to realize this is a rather high price for a small business to pay for limited liability and greater ease of raising capital; many are deciding to continue business in the partnership form. However, their decision is complicated by the existence of tax *advantages* offered by the corporate form. There is a loophole in our present law: *undistributed* corporate profits escape *personal* income taxes; only paid-out dividends are taxed by the personal-income-tax law. So a rich man, who is taxed about 85 cents of every dollar of personal income says: "Why should I pay such rates on partnership earnings? Let's incorporate, pay the 52 per cent corporate tax, and pay out practically no dividends."[2]

Another loophole used to avoid the disadvantages of double taxation under the corporate form is for the owners of a closely held corporation to vote most of its earnings to themselves and their relatives in the form of high salaries or perquisites. The Treasury Department tries to check up on such ways of avoiding taxes by puffing up expenses; but it is always hard to know whether a given second cousin is or is not worth $15,000 a year, and whether a trip to a lush convention is truly a business rather than a personal expense.

---

[1] Dividends received now give a personal-income-tax credit of 4 per cent.

[2] To some degree he is only putting off the evil day. For, unless his clever lawyer can work out a lightly taxed "capital-gains deal," his dividends later will be taxable when he receives them. But in any case the delay in tax payment is worth money to him.

▶ HOW A CORPORATION CAN RAISE CAPITAL

Let's suppose your corporation continues to grow as a result of vertical and horizontal combination, new products, economies of mass production, advertising promotion, and so forth. Besides borrowing on promissory notes or mortgages or buying on credit, what new forms of financing are available to you?

Bonds. First you may issue bonds. These are nothing but special kinds of promissory notes printed on gilt paper and issued in $100 or other denominations so as to be readily marketable for resale. A bond is a security promising to pay a certain number of dollars every 6 months for a number of years until it matures. At that time the borrowing company promises to pay off the principal of the bond at its face value. (Often the company has the right to call in the bond a few years before its maturity date by paying the bondholders some previously agreed upon price.) The dollar installments paid every 6 months, which represent the interest earnings of the bond, are usually called the "coupon" payments, because the owner of the bond cuts off a certain little corner of the bond each 6 months, and then mails it in to receive his interest payment.

Ordinarily, the coupons and principal must be paid on time regardless of whether the company has been making earnings or not. Otherwise the company is in default of its obligations and can be taken to court like any debtor.[1] Of course, there is no particular reason why a partnership could not borrow by the use of bonds; but ordinarily it would not be well enough known to succeed in interesting a lender. For that matter a small corporation can rarely raise capital by issuing bonds.

Common stocks. Issuing bonds and issuing common stocks are exactly opposite methods of financing. The common stockholder is providing "equity" capital. He shares in all profits and in control of business decisions, but he must also share in all losses. His is a more risky venture, because he can never receive any dividends until the fixed charges owed to the bondholder are paid off. The bondholder gets a nominally lower but steadier income. Unless the corporation is bankrupt or in danger of being so, the bondholder has ordinarily no legal control over the decisions of the business; but a wise management will take care to stay on good terms with all sources of future capital.

Preferred stocks. Intermediate between bonds and common stocks are so-called "preferred stocks." These are like bonds in that the buyer who puts up capital for them is limited in the percentage return that he can get from them—say, to a stipulated 4 per cent of the face value per share—no matter

---

[1] Income bonds, whose interest is payable only if there are large enough earnings, are not uncommon. Mortgage bonds, secured by property, are often met.

how profitable is the business in any year. However, he is more likely to get his dividend even when profit is small than is the common stockholder, because he legally stands next in line after the bondholder and before the common stockholder.

Often "cumulative" preferred stock is issued. This means that if for 5 years of depression there has not been enough in the way of earnings to pay any of the 4 per cent dividends on the preferred stock, then when good times come back again the "cumulated" $20 $(= 5 \times \$4)$ of unpaid preferred stock dividends must be made good before the common stockholders can begin to receive any dividends. Often, too, preferred stock is "callable" and is "convertible." The first term means that at some previously stated value, say $103, the company can buy back its outstanding preferred stock. The second term refers to the right given the preferred stockholder of converting each share into shares of common stock at some stipulated ratio.[1]

► ADVANTAGES OF DIFFERENT SECURITIES

From the standpoint of the investor, bonds, preferred stocks, and common stock usually form a sequence of increasing risk and decreasing security—balanced by an increased chance of making high earnings. Today, a "gilt-edge" bond may yield about 4 per cent, a good preferred stock about 5 per cent. Because common stocks may rise in value and give capital gains, they now often have a spread of dividend yields that begins even lower than bonds: some "growth stocks" like IBM yield much less than the safest government bonds! To test his understanding of these three forms of securities, the reader should make sure that he understands why common stocks are better investments in time of inflation than the other two.

It would be a mistake to leave the reader with the impression that bonds are perfectly safe investments. On the contrary, during depressions many companies have gone bankrupt and their bonds have gone into default, paying off only a few cents on the dollar. Often a company will undergo reorganization in which the stockholders may be squeezed out completely; the courts may appoint a "receiver" or trustee to run the business and the bondholders may be given bonds (or even stocks!) equal only to some fraction of their original investments. Moreover, certain bondholders may have prior claims over holders of other bonds. Many investors in railroad securities have learned of the above possibilities in the hard way.

From the corporation's view, bond debt creates low but inflexible fixed

---

[1] Also some preferred stocks are made more attractive by being made "participating." This means that once profit exceeds some agreed-upon figure, they share with the common stockholder in any further profits. But this form is rare.

charges. These may be embarrassing in bad times. Preferred stock is slightly better with respect to flexibility, equity capital best of all.[1]

► THE GIANT CORPORATION

We have now carried our successful tooth-paste enterprise far enough up the ladder of success. The rest of this chapter will be concerned with the economic position and power of the very large modern corporation, and the problems that they create for the American economy.

A list of the 200 largest nonfinancial corporations reads like an honor roll of American business, almost every name being a familiar household word. Among the industrial companies will be United States Steel, Bethlehem Steel, and the Aluminum Company of America; Standard Oil of New Jersey, of California, of Indiana; the Texas Company; General Motors, Chrysler, and Ford; Swift and Armour meat packing; American Tobacco (Luckies), R. J. Reynolds (Camels), and Liggett & Myers Tobacco (Chesterfields); The Great Atlantic & Pacific Tea Company, Sears Roebuck, Montgomery Ward, F. W. Woolworth, and J. C. Penney; National Dairy (Kraft's), Borden's, Procter & Gamble, Lever Brothers, and so forth.

Among the railroads are such old stand-bys as Pennsylvania, New York Central, Southern Pacific, and many others. The public-utility list is headed by American Tel. & Tel. If we go on to add the largest financial organizations, we bring in such giants as the Bank of America (California), First National City Bank (New York), the Chase Manhattan Bank, the Continental Illinois National Bank (Chicago), and the First National Bank of Boston; the Metropolitan Life Insurance Company, Prudential Life, Equitable Life, and so forth. Altogether there were in 1958 more than 70 companies whose assets had passed the billion dollar mark!

The tremendous concentration of economic power involved in these giant corporations may be gauged from the following facts: Alone they own 40 per cent of the total assets of all nonfinancial corporations, more than a third of all banking assets, and 85 per cent of all life-insurance assets. The largest 200 corporations hold between a fifth and a fourth of income-producing national wealth. They employ one out of every eight workers.

Their power did not grow overnight. After 1900, their percentage importance steadily mounted. Throughout the 1930's and up to World War II, they,

---

[1] Bond interest charges can also be deducted from the corporation earnings for tax purposes. There is an incentive, therefore, other things being equal, to use this method of financing rather than either kind of stock financing. However, other things have not been equal, and the trend in the past 20 years has been to grow by plowing back earnings, and to issue enough bonds to keep the debt-to-equity ratio about the same. New stock issues have not kept pace.

relatively speaking, just about held their own. During the war, the largest 200 corporations operated more than half of all new war-plant facilities and had a slightly higher profit to sales ratio than the next smaller group of 800 companies. But small concerns showed an even greater percentage of profitability and growth.

Large size breeds success and success breeds further success,[1] but there are also economic and political barriers to largeness. Recent economic research shows to be false the widespread view that the giants are gulping up more and more of modern industry. Statistics show that, relatively, the giants have probably lost a little ground since 50 years ago when the "trust movement" had not yet run afoul of the Sherman Antitrust Act (1890). And just as a hotel may be always full—but with different people—so do we find the list of biggest corporations to be a changing one. "Ashes to ashes; dust to dust" holds for fictitious legal persons as well as for real persons—but much more slowly!

▶ **DIVORCE OF OWNERSHIP AND CONTROL IN THE LARGE CORPORATION**

Let us begin to examine the internal workings of one of these giant corporations. *The most striking feature is the diversification of ownership among thousands and thousands of small stockholders.* In 1958 more than 1,500,000 different people had shares in A.T.&T. To be sure, half these people had less than 10 shares each; one-quarter of the shares were held in blocks of less than 100 shares; and no single owner had as much as 1 per cent of the total.

Berle and Means in a path-breaking study[2] pointed out that this wide diversification of stockholding has resulted in a *separation of ownership and control.* Recent studies show that in the typical giant corporation, all management together—officers and directors—hold only about 3 per cent of the outstanding common stock. The largest single minority ownership groups typically hold only about a fifth of all voting stock. Such a small fraction has been deemed more than enough to maintain "working control."[3]

▶ **AMPLIFICATION OF CONTROL BY THE PYRAMIDING OF HOLDING COMPANIES**

Even the figure of 5 to 1 amplification of the control exercised by minority stockholders is a gross understatement. In addition to the common stock out-

[1] The statistical evidence on profits suggests that profits increase with size but that the very biggest firms in an industry sometimes seem to show a slight dropping off of relative profits compared with the next to the largest. A larger percentage of small firms than of large firms falls in the class of firms making losses.

[2] A. A. BERLE, JR., and GARDNER C. MEANS, *The Modern Corporation and Private Property* (Commerce Clearing House, Inc., New York, 1932).

[3] See R. A. GORDON, *Business Leadership in the Large Corporation* (Brookings, Washington, D.C., 1945), Chap. II.

standing, the corporation may have the use of as much capital again in the form of bond borrowing or preferred-stock issues. Moreover, there grew up during the 1920's the practice of selling nonvoting common stock to the public while retaining control of the voting stock for the insiders. Therefore a figure of 10 to 1 of assets controlled to assets owned is often realistic.

Nor is this all. With $100,000 I can hope to control a million-dollar company. But what if the million-dollar corporation is a holding company whose sole function is to control a 10-million-dollar company through its ownership of 10 per cent of that company's stock? And the latter is a holding company controlling a 100-million-dollar company in a similar way? A small amount of money at the apex of the inverted pyramid can be given tremendous leverage of control simply by adding more layers to the structure—the result being 1,000 to 1 amplification of control, or even more.

This use of holding companies is not a mere theoretical possibility. During the 1920's, vast and complex public-utility empires were built up by their use. Just to chart the organizational structure of such corporations as the Associated Gas & Electric system would take a number of ordinary-sized book pages. The greatest losses to investors after the great 1929 stock-market crash came from such holding-company securities. The small and large investors who were eager to buy Middle Western Utilities from the respectable Chicago tycoon, Samuel Insull, lost every penny of their investments. For this and other reasons, Congress and the SEC have, by the Public Utility Holding Company Act (1935) passed a "death sentence" on such holding-company systems, and they are gradually dissolving themselves.

A less dramatic case of pyramiding of control may be mentioned. The du-Pont family owns most of the shares of a holding company, Christiana Securities Company. This company in turn owns about one-quarter of the voting stock of the great chemical concern E. I. duPont de Nemours, which in turn owns about one-quarter interest in General Motors. The Supreme Court, in an important 1957 decision, ruled that the duPonts must get rid of their GM holdings.

▶ **LEADERSHIP AND CONTROL OF THE LARGE CORPORATION**

The problem of keeping a large corporation truly democratic is a difficult one even to define. Until recent years, a dozen stockholders would turn up for the annual meeting. More recently, a few hundred have been attending such meetings, often drawn by free chicken salad and, it must be confessed, by the chance to heckle management.

Decisions at·the annual meeting are really settled by the use of "proxies." Each stockholder is asked to mail in a proxy permitting the management to exercise his votes. Some do not reply. But enough usually do to establish a quorum and a comfortable plurality for management. The SEC has tried to improve the democratic structure of corporations by insisting that motions to be decided at the annual meeting be indicated on the proxy statement so that stockholders can indicate their preferences; also rival groups must be permitted mailing access to the stockholders, and so forth.

Prior to recent years, most corporation managements could be said to be self-perpetuating. Whether the corporation runs well or poorly, whether the managers work efficiently or not, the typical small stockholder could do little about it. He could rubber-stamp approval; or relieve his feelings by not voting. In either case management went undisturbed.

Recently there has been a slight change. Thanks to the SEC rules, some challenging minority groups have attempted—and successfully attempted!—to oust the in-group and put themselves in as new managers. Thus, Robert Young ran a tremendous campaign—using all the devices of modern publicity —to oust the New York Central railroad officers. And he did succeed in winning majority support. Similar battles have taken place in connection with the New Haven railroad and Montgomery Ward. In a real sense, therefore, we can say that democratic control of corporations by owners has increased. But competent observers still insist that, under ordinary circumstances, management can count on remaining in office; and often the proxy battle is fought to determine which minority group shall control.

▶ A MANAGERIAL REVOLUTION?

Who do make corporate decisions? Primarily, the increasingly important class of *professional managers*. The old-time captain of industry, for all his creativeness and ability to calculate the risks necessary to build up a great enterprise, often had something of the buccaneer in his make-up and an irresponsible "the-public-be-damned" attitude. In company after company, the original founder has been replaced by a new type of executive, usually having a different surname; if he should be a completely self-made man, he will nevertheless probably have acquired special training and management skills. The new professional executive is more adept at public relations and in the handling of people. He is necessarily more the "bureaucrat," interested as much in preserving the *status quo* as in taking extreme risks.

Typically, the dominant man will be the president of the corporation. As he begins to feel his years, he may be made chairman of the board of directors. The chairman of the board is often an elder statesman, who, together with a small executive or steering committee of the board of directors, gives advice and approval to the actions of the president and his many vice-presidents.

The exact role of the board of directors varies from company to company, and from group to group. Some directors are simply well-known men selected to give prestige. Others possess special knowledge and take an active part in determining policy. On the whole, it would be going too far to say that most boards of directors act simply as rubber stamps to approve the decisions already taken by the officers of the company. But it is true that, so long as management possesses the confidence of the board, that body will usually not actively intervene to dictate specific policies. This is the same administrative procedure usually followed by the board of trustees of a philanthropic foundation or college, and is not too unlike the parliamentary system of ministerial responsibility.

Generally speaking, there will be no clash of goals between the management and stockholders. Both will be interested in maximizing the profits of the firm. However, in two important situations, there may be a divergence of interests, not infrequently settled in favor of management. First, insiders may legally or illegally vote themselves and their friends or relatives large salaries, expense accounts, bonuses, retirement pensions, and stock options at the stockholders' expense.

A second conflict of interest[1] may arise in connection with undistributed profits. The managers of every organization have an understandable tendency to try to make it grow and perpetuate itself. The psychological reasons are subtle and by no means always selfish. There is reason to question whether profits are not plowed back into a company in some cases when the same capital could better be invested by the stockholders elsewhere, or be spent upon consumption. Indeed, the case occasionally arises when a company would be well advised to wind itself up and pay back its capital. But a cynic might doubt that management is likely to vote itself out of existence and out of jobs.

▶ THE EVIL OF MONOPOLY

In view of all the above facts, it is not surprising to find that most important American industries are characterized by a few large corporations whose share of the output of that particular industry is vastly greater than their numerical importance would warrant. Figure 1 gives a list of large American industries and depicts their degree of concentration by showing the relative proportion of total industry employment controlled by the first four dominant corporations and by the next four.

In Part Three we shall analyze some of the problems raised by monopoly and imperfect competition. In the past 75 years, particularly since the 1890

---

[1] Other conflicts can involve outright cheating: executives may take bribes, throw business to their own companies, or violate SEC rules by using inside knowledge and spreading false rumors to make market profits on the company's stock.

Sherman Antitrust Act, there has been great concern over the breaking down of free competitive markets under the encroachment of large-scale enterprise.

From an economic point of view it does not much matter which of the following monopolistic devices cause price to be too high: (1) mergers of competing firms, (2) cooperative "pools" or "cartel agreements," (3) so-called "trusts" (involving selected "trustees" who "coordinate" pricing policy), (4) interlocking directorates, (5) "holding company" control, (6) tacit collusion and trade-association action, (7) government "fair price" legislation (Robinson-Patman Act, etc.) and government-sponsored "commodity agreements" (wheat, rubber, cotton, etc.). Too high a price, wastage of resources, and creation of monopoly profits are economic evils, however brought about and whatever the legal technicalities of the matter. This we shall study in Part Three.

▶ THE CURSE OF BIGNESS?

Is bigness itself a bad thing? Undoubtedly there is much popular hostility toward large corporations. Even if they could do so, General Motors or U.S. Steel would be most reluctant to swallow up competitors until they accounted for, say, nine-tenths of their respective industries. They would fear the effect on public opinion. Is this antagonism toward big business directed toward bigness itself? Or against the alleged evils of monopoly that are often supposed to be associated with bigness? What should public policy be toward a "benevolent, well-behaving, efficient" giant corporation?

The so-called "A & P" case provides an example. This chain of food

Some industries are dominated by a very few sellers:

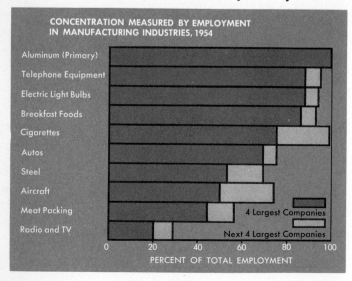

Fig. 1. In aluminum, autos, steel, and many other industries, a few firms get most of the business. This is in contrast to the notion of perfect competition among innumerable small sellers (e.g., farmers), each too small to affect the market price. But MIT's expert, M. A. Adelman, thinks concentration was probably even greater back in 1900. (Source: Federal Trade Commission.)

stores is noted for its low prices. Yet the Department of Justice prosecuted it under the antitrust acts. Leaving aside certain minor irregularities that the company may have engaged in, the basic issue was clearly posed: Shall it be a crime to grow large as a result of efficiency and continued maintenance of low, competitive prices? The federal courts seemed almost to answer, Yes.

Another example shows the policy problems are not easy. In the mid-fifties there has been a rash of mergers: *e.g.*, in the auto industry, Nash combined with Hudson, Studebaker with Packard, etc. Often there was a "tax angle" to the merger. But in some cases, firms merged in order to try to become more efficient so as to be able to compete with General Motors and Ford. Do such mergers—even though they undoubtedly increase the size of the merged units —really reduce competition rather than increase it? (Was Eisenhower's Attorney General wrong in forbidding a merger between Bethlehem and Youngstown steel companies?)

To produce an atomic bomb, the government turned to the duPont Company and gave it a cost-plus-one-dollar contract. The scientific know-how of General and Western Electric is invaluable for peace as well as war. In the words of a recent world-famous economist:[1]

The modern standard of life of the masses evolved during the period of relatively unfettered "big business." If we list the items that enter the modern workman's budget and from 1899 on observe the course of their prices not in terms of money but in terms of the hours of labor that will buy them—*i.e.*, each year's money prices divided by each year's hourly wage rates, we cannot fail to be struck by the rate of the advance which, considering the spectacular improvement in qualities, seems to have been greater and not smaller than it ever was before. . . . Nor is this all. As soon as we go into details and inquire into the individual items in which progress was most conspicuous, the trail leads not to the doors of those firms that work under conditions of comparatively free competition but precisely to the doors of the large concerns—which, as in the case of agricultural machinery, also account for much of the progress in the competitive sector —and a shocking suspicion dawns upon us that big business may have had more to do with creating that standard of life than keeping it down.

This suggests that the future problem may not be one of choosing between large monopolistic corporations and small-scale competitors, but rather that of devising ways to improve the social and economic performance of large corporate aggregates. To keep the tremendously creative abilities of the modern large-scale corporation working toward the public good—that may have to be the goal for the years ahead. We shall return to the problem of the maintenance of "effective and workable competition" after an analysis in Part Three of prices and cost under perfect and imperfect competition.

[1] J. A. SCHUMPETER, *Capitalism, Socialism, and Democracy* (Harper, New York, 1942).

Accounting is a great help to the understanding of economics, and its fundamental principles are presented briefly in the Appendix to this chapter.

SUMMARY

▶ **A. FORMS OF BUSINESS ORGANIZATION**

1. The present population of American businesses has grown up as a result of a cumulative excess of business births over business deaths. In the greater number it consists of infinitesimal single proprietorships, largely in retail and service establishments. Their turnover is rapid.

2. You should understand how an enterprise grows, its needs and avenues for short-term or long-term capital, and the advantages and disadvantages of the corporate form over the single proprietorship and partnership.

▶ **B. THE MODERN CORPORATION**

3. You should also be acquainted with the fundamental legal rights involved in the corporation, and with the general features of bonds, preferred- and common-stock corporate securities.

4. The problems created by the separation of ownership and control and by the great concentration of economic wealth and monopoly power in the modern giant corporation deserve serious study.

QUESTIONS FOR DISCUSSION

1. Imagine you are starting a business of your own. Write its case history.

2. Compare the advantages and disadvantages of (*a*) the single proprietorship, (*b*) the partnership, and (*c*) the corporate form of business organization.

3. What are the reasons underlying the growth of a business to large size?

4. List ways of raising capital for small, medium, and large businesses.

5. What are the advantages and disadvantages of different securities?

6. Discuss the structure of the modern large corporation.

7. What is meant by calling ours the age of the "Managerial or Bureaucratic Revolution"? Does this apply outside of government?

8. Give examples of divergent interests between stockholders and management. Of coincident interests.

9. Defend "bigness as such." Attack it. What evils might accompany bigness?

10. How might the economic evils of monopoly arise? Give examples.

11. Why do you think many corporate mergers are taking place? Do you approve? Give your reasons.

12. Review your understanding of the following concepts:

single proprietorship   *corporate and personal income tax*

partnership   *bonds, common and preferred*

corporation   *stocks*

liabilities and assets   *holding company and pyramiding*

vertical and horizontal growth   *proxy, minority control*

unlimited and limited liability   *director, executive*

investment banking   *forms of monopoly control*

SEC   *merger*

APPENDIX: ELEMENTS OF ACCOUNTING

Ours is the Age of the Machine. Also, it is the Age of Accounts. A little literacy in accounting has become a prime necessity.

The Balance Sheet

It is necessary for every student of economics to have some understanding of the two fundamental accounting statements: the Balance Sheet and the Statement of Profit and Loss (or the so-called Income Statement).

The balance sheet is presented in a report annually or oftener. It represents an instantaneous "still picture" of the condition of the enterprise as of some particular day, usually the last day of the year. Corresponding to the dollar value of every asset—tangible or intangible—there must necessarily be an exactly equal total amount of claims or ownership. The value of a $10,000 house is exactly matched by somebody's claim to its ownership consisting, for example, of $7,000 owed a creditor and $3,000 owned by its owner.

This is the fundamental identity underlying every balance sheet:

Value of assets = value of total claims or
                  ownership
             = value of liabilities (owed)
               + value of proprietorship (owned)

or

Assets = Liabilities + Net Worth

Let's illustrate this by considering a simple balance sheet as shown in Table 1: this lists Assets on the left and on the right Liabilities and Net Worth for a new company whose operations have just begun.

A blank space has been deliberately left next to the Common Stock Net Worth item because you should realize that the only correct entry compatible with our fundamental balance sheet truism is $200,-000. A balance sheet must always balance—because Net Worth, *i.e.*, ownership of the "residual claimants," always adjusts itself to make a balance.

To illustrate this, let's suppose a thief steals all the cash, and a fire burns up one-fourth the inventory. The accountant will

A balance sheet is a point-of-time picture showing that assets = liabilities + net worth:

ASSETS		LIABILITIES AND NET WORTH	
		Liabilities	
Current Assets:		Current Liabilities:	
Cash	$ 20,000	Accounts payable	$ 20,000
Inventory	80,000	Notes payable	30,000
Fixed Assets:		Long-term Liabilities:	
Equipment	130,000	SBA note	50,000
Buildings	170,000	Bonds payable	50,000
		Net Worth	
		Capital:	
		Preferred stock	50,000
		Common stock	_____
Total	$400,000	Total	$400,000

Table 1. Balance Sheet of Pepto-Glitter, Inc., as of December 31, 1963.

learn of this sad news without turning a hair. "Total Assets are down $40,000 all told. Liabilities remain unchanged. Very well, I must write down Net Worth by $40,000, to only $160,000." Such is the accountant's way of keeping score.

A number of interesting facts are revealed even by this simple balance sheet. First, it is customary to divide up assets according to whether they will be convertible into cash by normal operations within a year or not, the first category being called Current Assets and the second Fixed Assets. The liabilities can also be subdivided into Current and Long-term Liabilities depending upon whether they come due in less than a year.

Another thing to be noticed about our balance sheet is this: Although its two sides must balance *in total,* yet no single item on one side is matched by an item on the other side. Thus, the Bonds do not correspond in value to the Equipment or Buildings, nor do the Capital items correspond to the Cash. The only correct statement about a balance sheet is that the creditors have a general claim of a definite value against the enter-

prise, and the owners have a residual claim against the rest.

Most of the specific items listed are more or less self-explanatory. Cash consists of coins, currency, and money on deposit in the bank. Cash is the only asset whose value is exact rather than an estimate. All other valuations involve some guesswork, albeit careful guesswork. Moreover, all accounting valuations must be made relative to the actual intended purpose or use of the asset in question. If a business is a going concern and not in the process of liquidation, the accountant will be careful not to value the assets at the low figure that they would bring at a forced sale, but he will rather value them at their worth to the company in its normal operation.

Inventory, consisting in the case of our tooth-paste company of sugar, chemicals, tubing, raw materials, and other goods in process, can be valued in many different ways. Many conservative companies use original cost of the inventories or present market value, whichever is lower. Especially difficult problems arise when the prices of materials vary from month to month. Should we figure the chemical cost of the tooth paste at the original price of the ingredients actually used, which of course were bought some time ago when prices were different? Or should we figure, as our cost, the price that must *now* be paid for the chemicals to replace those being used up? An elementary discussion cannot go into these two possible methods of inventory valuation.[1] Obviously, it will make a great difference in stated profits during a time of inflation or deflation which of these two methods is used. It also will make a difference in income taxes. Therefore, the government is compelled to say, "Use whichever method you wish, but having made up your mind, stick to it." So much for inventories.

If we assume that the Equipment and Buildings items were just bought at the end of 1963, then their balance sheet values will be listed equal to their purchase price. This follows a fundamental accounting rule or convention: "At time of purchase a thing is presumed worth what the enterprise pays for it." However, as we shall see in connection with the income statement and the next year's balance sheet, tough problems are involved in deciding how to evaluate exactly equipment and buildings that have depreciated through use and age.

On the liability side, Accounts Payable are, as their name implies, the sums owed for goods bought and charged. Notes Payable are promissory notes owed to the banks or to a finance company. The SBA Note listed under the Long-term Liabilities is a 5-year loan advanced by, or guaranteed by, the federal Small Business Administration. The Bonds Payable are a long-term loan, floated at a 3 per cent coupon rate, and not due for 15 years.

Turning now to the Net Worth items, we find that 500 shares of $100, 4 per cent, cu-

mulative (nonparticipating) preferred stock have been issued. And finally 20,000 shares of no-par common stock were issued at $10 each.

This completes our first glance at a simple balance sheet.

The Statement of Profit and Loss, or Income Statement

Now let time march on. During the following months, the firm is profitably engaged in producing and selling tooth paste. To show its flow of income over the 12 months of the year, we must turn to its Income Statement, or, as many companies prefer to call it, the Statement of Profit and Loss.

This is a statement which reports the following: (1) Pepto-Glitter's income from sales in 1964, (2) the expenses to be charged against those sales, and (3) the profit remaining after expenses have been deducted. *I.e.*, total profit = total revenue minus total costs (the fundamental identity of the Income Statement). You will understand it better if at first you disregard the figures in the Manufacturing Cost of Goods Sold section (the indented figures) and look only at those in the right-hand column. Sales were $240,000; and the cost of manufacturing the goods sold came to $170,000. After deducting another $14,000 for selling and administrative costs, $56,000 remained in net operating profit. Out of this, a total of $19,000 in interest and taxes had to be paid, leaving $37,000 in net earnings. Dividends of $2,000 preferred and $5,000 common were paid, leaving $30,000 of net profit retained in the business.

Now turn to the indented Manufacturing Cost of Goods Sold section, which lists the costs incurred in this part of the business. The firm's outlays for materials, labor, and miscellaneous expenses are listed, together with an item for Depreciation. (Depreciation is worth a section to itself, and we shall consider it soon.) The sum of these four items, $175,000, is the Manufacturing Cost. Then follows what may seem a puzzling ad-

---

[1] Accounting texts refer to them as "First-in–first-out" (FIFO) and "Last-in–first-out" (LIFO) and analyze them in detail.

The flow of income over the year is shown by the income statement:

Net Sales (after all discounts and rebates)		$240,000
Less: Manufacturing cost of goods sold:		
Materials	$ 50,000	
Labor cost	100,000	
Depreciation charges	20,000	
Miscellaneous operating cost	5,000	
Total manufacturing cost	$175,000	
Add: Beginning inventory	80,000	
	$255,000	
Deduct: Closing inventory	85,000	
Equals: Manufacturing cost *of goods sold*	$170,000	170,000
Gross profit (or gross margin)		$ 70,000
Less: Selling and administrative costs		14,000
Net operating profit		$ 56,000
Less: Fixed interest charges and local taxes		6,000
Net earnings before income taxes		$ 50,000
Less: Corporation income taxes		13,000
Net earnings after taxes		$ 37,000
Less: Dividends on preferred stock		2,000
Net profits of common stockholders		$ 35,000
Less: Dividends paid on common stock		5,000
Addition to surplus		$ 30,000

Table 2. Income Statement of Pepto-Glitter, Inc., from January 1, 1964, to December 31, 1964.

justment. The value of the inventory on January 1 is added, and that of the year-end inventory is deducted. The result, which differs from Manufacturing Cost by $5,000, is the Manufacturing Cost *of Goods Sold.* What is the difference between these terms, and why is this inventory adjustment needed?

Pepto-Glitter began the year with an inventory of $80,000 in raw materials and finished goods. During the year, it built up its inventories by an extra $5,000. In such a case, it would be quite false to attribute all of the manufacturing costs to *the goods actually sold.* Some of these costs are really attributable to goods to be sold *in the future.* To neglect this fact would be to overstate the Manufacturing Cost of Goods Sold

in this year; it would be subtracting too much from this year's Net Sales; it would be understating this year's Profits.

If there had been no change in the amount of inventory, then all would be simple; Manufacturing Cost and Manufacturing Cost of Goods Sold would be one and the same.

On the other hand, what if we had had less Inventory on hand at the end of the year than at the beginning? Pretty clearly, we'll be fooling ourselves if we don't recognize that the cost of the goods we have sold this year ought really to be greater than the money we have paid out to labor and other firms. We'll have neglected the cost element of used-up and unreplaced inventory.

To summarize. To reach a valid figure for

Manufacturing Cost of Goods Sold, we must adjust the Manufacturing Cost figure as follows: If the year-end Inventory shows an increase over the beginning Inventory, deduct that increase; if the year-end Inventory has decreased, add that decrease.

Instead of subtracting $5,000 directly from the $175,000 total of manufacturing expense, the accountant does it in two steps. Rather than working with the difference between the two, he first adds the total beginning inventory, then subtracts the closing inventory. This procedure has the advantage of being standardized; it is the same whether inventory is up or down, whereas a single change-in-inventory figure would in some cases be a subtraction, in others an addition. And the accountant's method also reveals the change in inventory relative to the size of the total inventory.

Note that the items in Table 2 differ from those in Table 1's Balance Sheet. Income items refer to flows over time: moving-picture action. Balance Sheet items refer to stocks at an instant of time: still pictures.

Depreciation

At first, one may wonder why any Depreciation charges have been made for 1964. The buildings and equipment were newly bought at the beginning of the year, and surely they will not have been worn out already. (There will of course be need to spend money on men to maintain the equipment and keep the factories painted. But their wages are already included in Labor Cost or Miscellaneous Expense and are not included in Depreciation.)

Here is where the farseeing wisdom of the accountant comes to the fore. He points out that not a cent may have to be spent upon replacement of equipment for 10 years, at which time suddenly all the machines may have to be bought anew. It would be nonsense, he claims, to charge nothing to depreciation for 9 years and fool yourself into thinking you are making a nice profit and then suddenly in the tenth year to have to charge off all the value of the machines at once and think you have made a great loss in that year.

Actually, he points out, the equipment is being used up all the time. A truer, undistorted picture of net income or profit will be learned if the costs of the equipment are spread more evenly over its lifetime. The value of equipment declines as a result of age and use; it depreciates from its price when new to its final scrap value. In recognition of this, the accountant depreciates the value of fixed capital items by some *gradual* formula. We cannot go into the various methods that have been used. Here are two widely used ones.

The first is called "straight-line depreciation." Suppose that you have a truck whose cost when new is $10,100, and whose economic life is 10 years; after this its physical life may continue but its economic life will be over, because of its unreliability and maintenance costs. Suppose that its scrap value at the end of 10 years is $100. According to the straight-line method you will each year charge off to depreciation one-tenth of the lifetime decline in its total value, $10,-000 (new price minus scrap value). Thus, $1,000 will be charged in depreciation every year.

A second general method called the "service unit method"—or "unit of production method"—can be mentioned only briefly here. According to this we would estimate the number of miles, or loads, or service units that the truck will perform in its life. Thus, if the truck goes a million miles in 10 years and its loss of value during that time is $10,000, then each mile used up represents about 1 cent. This method has the virtue that during the first year of life of the truck, when presumably it will be used proportionately more than toward the end of its life, depreciation charges will be reckoned at perhaps $1,500 (for 150,000 miles) rather than at only $1,000 as in the straight-line method. Another advantage of this second method is that, during periods of depression when trucks are idle a good deal of the time, the calculated depreciation charges are less, and so the businessman may not be prevented from reducing prices by a misleading overestimate of his money costs.[1]

Although depreciation is usually figured by some apparently exact formula, every accountant knows the estimates are really very rough, being subject to large and unpredictable errors, and involving arbitrary corrections and assumptions. He comforts himself with two thoughts: (1) A rough method of depreciation, like an imperfect watch, is often better than none at all. (2) Mistakes in depreciation will ultimately "come out in the wash" anyway.

Let's see why a mistake in depreciation ultimately tends to correct itself. Suppose that the truck lasts 15 years rather than the predicted 10. We have been then overstating our depreciation *expenses* during the first 10 years. But in the eleventh and later years there will be no depreciation charged on the truck at all, since it has already been written down to its scrap value by the end of the tenth year. Our profits in these later years tend, therefore, to be overstated by about as much as they were understated in the earlier years. After 15 years, everything is pretty much the same after all.

Except for taxes. Different methods of depreciation result in a different apparent distribution of earnings over time, and therefore in a different pattern over time of corporation income taxes. Naturally a businessman prefers a method of depreciation that will make his income average out more

---

[1] Many accounting books also describe a third still different method that permits of greater depreciation when an asset is new than when it is old. This is the constant percentage depreciation method, whereby the truck would be depreciated a constant percentage of remaining value each year until it reached its final scrap value. During the first year, the depreciation charged would be largest because of the truck's high initial value; during the later years, a constant percentage of the greatly reduced remaining value would result in low annual depreciation charges. The 1954 tax law permits more rapid depreciation by this and related methods.

steadily over time—so as to keep his effective tax rate as low as possible and permit him to cancel off losses against profits; and he also likes a method that enables him to put off the evil day of taxes as far as possible.

This explains why so many corporations took advantage of the government's offer to let them amortize (or depreciate) their defense-time plants and equipment over 5 years. They were glad to be able, by charging high depreciation expenses, to reduce their stated profits during the defense emergency when their profits were enormous. They much preferred to take advantage of this "accelerated depreciation" plan so as to shift their profits from those emergency years to later years when corporation tax rates were hoped to be lower.

The Treasury will not let a corporation manipulate its depreciation charges so as to avoid taxes. The company may select any reasonable method; but having once made its choice, it must stick to it. Many people are today worried about the harmful effects of taxation on "venture capital." They argue we shall get more investment in new tools and create more jobs, if the Treasury is more liberal in letting companies depreciate their equipment more rapidly, thereby saving on their taxes. Today, therefore, the tax law lets you take two-thirds depreciation in one-half an asset's useful life.[2]

The Relation Between the Income Statement and the Balance Sheet

Now we must relate the description by the Income Statement of what has happened during the year to the Balance Sheets at the beginning and end of the year. Table 3 shows the Balance Sheet of our tooth-paste corporation at the end of its first year of operation. It has prospered. Net Worth, the difference between Total Assets and Total Liabilities, has increased between the begin-

---

[2] To play fair with investors, and to enable your managers to make correct decisions, you'll want to estimate true depreciation when the true figure and the tax-permitted figure differ widely.

After the year's operations, we get a new balance sheet:

Table 3. Balance Sheet of Pepto-Glitter, Inc., as of December 31, 1964.

ASSETS			LIABILITIES AND NET WORTH		
			Liabilities		
Current Assets:			**Current Liabilities:**		
Cash		$ 20,000	Accounts payable		$ 10,000
Inventory		85,000	Notes payable		17,000
Sinking Fund to Replace Equipment		5,000	Reserve for taxes		13,000
(U.S. government bonds)					
Fixed Assets:			**Long-term Liabilities:**		
Equipment	$130,000		SBA note		50,000
Less allowance (or reserve)			Bonds payable		50,000
for depreciation	15,000				
		115,000			
Buildings	$170,000		**Net Worth**		
Less allowance (or reserve)			**Capital:**		
for depreciation	5,000		Preferred stock		50,000
		165,000	Common stock		200,000
			Surplus		30,000
Intangible Assets:					
Patents		10,000			
Good will		20,000			
Total		$420,000	Total		$420,000

ning and end of the accounting period by $30,000—from $250,000 to $280,000. The amount of this increase, as seen by comparing balance sheets, just equals the earnings or profits *available* to the common stockholders but not paid out to them in dividends; or as we saw at the bottom of the Income Statement, just equal to $35,000 − $5,000, or $30,000 of undistributed profits.

Some Net Worth item must be written up by $30,000. It would clearly never do to increase the Preferred Stock Capital Account, because such stockholders are not the residual claimants to the profits of the corporation and no new stock has been sold. Conceivably, one could add the $30,000 to the Common Stock Capital Account. However, this is not done. Instead the Common Stock Capital Account is left at its original par or issued value.

It is more informative to create a new ac-

count called Surplus—or sometimes Earned Surplus or Earnings Retained in the Business—to show how much of the increase in "book value" or Net Worth has resulted from accumulated undistributed earnings plowed back through the years.

In many ways Surplus is a misleading word. It sounds like something extra or unnecessary; or too often like a nice spare chunk of cash which the company's workers or stockholders might hope to stage a raid against. Actually, Surplus is distinctly not an asset account, much less a pool of liquid cash. It simply indicates a part of the ownership—over and above liabilities to creditors and original subscribed capital ownership—in the polyglot assets of the corporation. A glance at Table 3 will convince us that the $30,000 of Surplus is not matched by an equivalent amount of cash on the asset side.

We must once again issue a warning

against trying to link up specific items on the two sides of the Balance Sheet. Only the totals correspond. That is all. It is not even possible to say exactly how the $30,000 plowed back into the business, or added to Surplus, has been used. An addition to surplus must be associated with an increase in Assets and/or a decrease in Liabilities— that's all we can say.

It would be an equal mistake to think that the profits of a corporation accrue in the form of cash; so that on the last day of the year, just before the board of directors decided upon its dividend rate, there was some $35,000 of cash on hand, available either for the stockholders or to be invested back in the business. In the case of our tooth-paste company, the very handsome profit earned was largely embodied in the form of new assets and lowered liabilities; not very much more than $5,000 could have been paid out as cash dividends without forcing serious changes in the financial decisions of the company—decisions such as to borrow more, to grow more slowly, to sell off some of the equipment and inventory at a loss, or to operate with a ludicrously low cash balance.

Summary of Elementary Accounting Relations
Before taking a last look at the new complexities introduced in the 1964 Balance Sheet over that of 1963, we may briefly summarize the relationship between balance sheets and income statements: (1) The Balance Sheet indicates an instantaneous financial picture: it's like a measure of the stock of water in a lake. (2) The Income Statement shows the flow of sales, cost, and revenue over the year or accounting period time: it measures the flow of water in and out of the lake. (3) The change in total Net Worth between the beginning and the end of the period—as shown by comparing the new and old balance sheets—is also to be understood from an examination of the changes in Surplus as shown at the end of most modern income statements: the change

in the lake's level over the year we can relate to the flows during the year. If new common stock is sold, that will be revealed by comparing the two Balance Sheets.

There do remain, however, certain shifts in the balance-sheet items from their previous levels in the earlier period to which the intervening Income Statement gives us no clue. A closer look at the December 31, 1964, Balance Sheet will therefore prove instructive, although enough has been said already to introduce the reader to the fundamentals of accounting.

Reserves and Funds
The new Balance Sheet looks much like the old for the most part; but some new items are present for the first time. The last of these new items, Surplus, we have already explained. Among the Liabilities there is a new item called Reserve for Taxes of $13,-000. It is not hard to understand. The taxes that the corporation will have to pay the government on March 15, 1965, and succeeding quarterly dates are as much short-term liabilities as the Accounts Payable or Notes Payable.

Taxes Payable might have been a better title, since the word "Reserve" suggests a pool of cash, which it decidedly is not. Instead the Reserve for Taxes is simply an earmarking of part of the total assets of the company for a special creditor—a reminder that the Net Worth of the owners is less by the amount of owed taxes. In a moment we'll see there are three main kinds of "reserves," and no one represents a pool of cash or liquid assets.

Let us turn to the Asset side for new items.[1] The first stranger, entitled "Sinking

---

[1] Neither this Balance Sheet nor the previous one contains a frequently met current asset item called Prepaid Expenses. Often an enterprise will pay its rent or buy some of its supplies a number of months in advance. Very properly, the enterprise is regarded as possessing on its Balance Sheet an equivalent asset.

Fund to Replace Equipment" is listed midway between the Current and Fixed Assets. It is an asset consisting of, say, 3 per cent government bonds which are to be held for the purpose of ultimately providing part of the money to buy new machines when the old ones are to be replaced. Although the corporation could change its mind and use the Sinking Fund bonds for some other purpose, it presumably will not choose to do so. The nature of this Sinking Fund is very understandable; it is simply a pool of liquid assets set aside for a specific future purpose.

Turning to the Fixed Assets, we find ourselves in for a surprise. From our previous discussion of the Depreciation charges of the Income Statement, we should have expected the Building and Equipment items to total $280,000. Why? Because at the beginning of the year they added up to $300,000, because no new equipment was bought during the year, and because the Income Statement told us that $20,000 of depreciation accrued during the period as part of the necessary costs of production.

Why then are these Fixed Assets carried on the new Balance Sheet at the old $130,-000 and $170,000 figure? Looking more closely we see that they really are not. From the $130,000 nominal Equipment valuation, there is subtracted an Allowance (or Reserve) for Depreciation, so that really only $115,000 is carried for Equipment. Similarly from the $170,000 original value of the Buildings, there is subtracted a $5,000 allowance for Depreciation. Our faith in the accountant's sanity is restored; but we may still wonder why he goes through this roundabout procedure of stating "two" as "four minus two" instead of simply as "two."

Actually, he has his good reasons. An honest accountant knows his depreciation charges are only the roughest of guesses. Were he simply to guess and put down the final figure of $115,000 for equipment, the public would not know how much reliance to place upon the figure. So he puts down $130,000 of original value, which is firmly

rooted in the solid fact of original cost; and he then carefully isolates his own guessed-at Allowance for Depreciation. Then the public is in a better position to evaluate the reliability of the final $115,000 figure. The roundabout procedure does no harm, and may do good.

Now we know the precise meaning of Depreciation Allowances or Reserves. They are not sums of money; they are not sinking funds of liquid assets that can be spent on replacement. They are simply *subtractions from overstated asset figures.* Thus, the Allowance for Depreciation of Buildings of $5,000 is simply an explicit correction to the original value of the Buildings, which would be an overstatement of the value left in them. This correction must be made to keep Assets and Net Worth from both being artificially inflated.

It must be made regardless of whether at the same time any money is or is not being set aside into sinking funds to replace the Depreciation asset. Note that there is no Sinking Fund for Buildings, and that the Sinking Fund for Equipment is only one-third as large as the estimated depreciation of equipment. As a matter of fact, American businesses rarely set aside any considerable sums of money in replacement Sinking Funds. This is because liquid gilt-edge bonds earn at most only a few per cent interest, whereas capital invested in the firm's own activities usually brings in much more.[1]

----

[1] Where then will the money be coming from to replace any particular machine or building if no sinking funds have been set aside? Ordinarily, the equipment can be purchased with sales dollars earned by other equipment that is not currently calling for replacement expenditure. The selling price of the output of such other equipment contains an accounting allowance for depreciation expense, and this sum of money is available for investment elsewhere in the business. Speaking somewhat loosely, we may say that each asset not needing replacement lends its depreciation charges to those which need replace-

We have met two kinds of reserves: (1) a Liability Reserve, like that for taxes, which is really simply a liability of fairly certain amount, and (2) an Asset Valuation Reserve like that for Depreciation (or allowance for estimated uncollectible bills), which is really simply a subtraction from an overstated asset. A third so-called "Surplus Reserve," which is also not to be confused with a sum of money, may be mentioned: Sometimes a firm takes part of its Surplus and sets it aside under a different name so the stockholders will not be tempted to lobby for higher dividend payments. For example, our tooth-paste company might earmark one-third of its $30,000 Surplus account into a Reserve for Research and Development. This $10,000 Reserve would no more consist of cash or liquid funds than does Surplus itself, or than does any other kind of Reserve. It should never be confused with a fund.[1]

We have now outlined the fundamentals of accounting, and the rest of the Appendix deals with some further developments.

Intangible Assets

Only one further new category of Assets can still be found on the December 31, 1964, Balance Sheet. To illustrate that an asset need not be a tangible commodity, a piece of equipment, or a sum of money, a patent has been introduced into the picture. Let us suppose that it is a patent on a profitable new chemical process, which gives us exclusive production rights for 17 years.

Such a patent is obviously worth money. Of course, as 5, 10, 12, and 16 years pass, the patent will be coming near to the end of

_____

ment, knowing that it too will be taken care of when the need arises.

[1] The problem of reserves becomes even more complicated in connection with contingencies that may or may not occur. Thus Reserve for Depression Contingencies or for Renegotiation would fall halfway between true Liability and Surplus Reserves.

its 17-year life and will be declining in value. Therefore, some depreciation formula will be applied to it just as if it were a truck.

Good Will and Monopoly Power

So much for the Patent as an illustration of an intangible asset. Let us suppose that, at the same time we bought the patent, we also took over a rival tooth-paste company. This horizontal combination will presumably add to our monopoly position and earning power. Therefore, we were willing to buy the company for more than its trifling assets —which happened to consist solely of a little inventory—were worth. Perhaps part of the purchase price went as profits to the promoters who engineered this little monopolistic merger.

An example of the capitalization of earning power is J. P. Morgan's formation of the giant United States Steel Company at the turn of the century. He bought out the Andrew Carnegie steel plants and combined them with half a dozen other holdings. But in economics, as in certain branches of atomic physics, the whole is equal to more than the sum of its parts. After Morgan had put the pieces together, he found himself with some 130 million dollars of extra capital value.

Who was hurt by this transaction? Certainly not Carnegie or Morgan. Even the people who bought the stock had no right to complain that it had been "watered," since for many years they got more than a fair return on their investments. To have sold them the stock for its actual cost (without water) would be (1) to make them a free gift of the enlarged profits of the concern, and (2) to give them the privilege of reselling the stock at the higher price that its earning power could earn for it in a competitive stock market. (In terms of standards at the time, there was nothing illegal or unethical about this merger.)

However, our practical-minded accountant is not concerned with such matters of public policy and political economy. He will tell our tooth-paste company or J. P. Morgan the same thing: "If you paid a certain sum of money for some assets, they must presumably be worth that much to you. If the assets don't exist, they must be created. 'Good Will' is their name." But since this term has come into bad repute in recent years, it is often lumped in with some other assets.

This explains our last intangible asset. Good Will is the difference between what a company pays in buying out another company and what it gets in the way of identifiable assets.

Conclusion

Finally, some interesting relations between economics and accounting can be briefly mentioned. (1) All balance sheets depend on valuation of assets, which is one of the basic questions of the capital and interest theory discussed in Part Four. (2) All our national income statistics are founded on the accounting data of sales, cost, etc.; this, too, is discussed in detail later. (3) As we shall see in a later discussion of how firms set price, accounting cost data play an important role in price determination.

The accountant deals with money magni-

tudes; the economist tries to probe deeper to the underlying real magnitudes. Especially in periods of great inflation or deflation, the accountant realizes that his ordinary methods may give strange results.

An example is the problem of changing price levels and depreciation. Suppose prices are rising sharply. If I sell my goods for enough to cover labor and other costs and also to cover depreciation, you might think I am breaking even. What would an accountant say who figured depreciation on the basis of the past low prices originally paid for my machines and building? He, too, would say I am breaking even. But in actuality I can be said to have been selling my goods at a *real* loss; for when my machines and buildings have worn out, I shall not have enough money to *reproduce them* at the new higher price level. The same is true of a merchant who sells off his inventory at a price lower than reproduction cost. So we must beware of fictitious money overstatements of real profits during rising prices and of fictitious understatements of profits during falling prices. (Later in national income statistics, you will note that profits are "adjusted" for inventory revaluations.)

SUMMARY TO APPENDIX

Instead of a lengthy recapitulation, this section presents only a check list of the accounting concepts that you should understand:

1. The fundamental balance sheet relationship between Assets, Liabilities, and Net Worth; and the breakdown of each of these categories into Current and Fixed Assets, Current and Long-term Liabilities, Capital and Surplus.

2. The character of the Income Statement (or Profit-and-loss Statement), and the relationship between its final undistributed prof-

its and the changes in Surplus on the new Balance Sheet.

3. The whole problem of Depreciation, both in its income statement aspect as a necessary expense, which need not be an expenditure, and in its balance sheet treatment as a deduction from a purposely overstated asset; also the logic of the two principal depreciation methods.

4. The difference between a Fund or a pool of liquid assets and the three kinds of so-called Reserves; also the meaning of such intangible assets as Patents or Good Will.

QUESTIONS FOR DISCUSSION

1. Describe the right-hand side of a balance sheet. Its left-hand side. What items must match as a result of the "fundamental identity"?

2. You are a banker deciding whether to lend money to the tooth-paste company. Why might you be especially interested in the current items?

3. Write out a list of as many different assets as you can, describing the nature of each in a few lines. Do the same for liabilities.

4. Is an income statement a "still picture" at an instant of time? Why not?

5. In 1964 a company has 10 million dollars of net sales and 9 million dollars of costs of all kinds (including taxes, interest, etc.). It rents its equipment, its inventory does not change in the year, and it has no preferred stock. It pays no dividends. Draw up its simplified income statement using at most half a dozen lines.

6. The same company as in (5) owes no money, having been completely equity-financed years ago. Fill in the year-end balance sheets at the bottom of the page.

7. Redo problems 5 and 6 making the following changes: In addition to the other expenses, its buildings depreciate by 2 million dollars; also its inventory has fallen off by 3 million dollars. Draw up an income statement showing its loss for the year, and adjust its 1964 balance sheet accordingly.

8. Describe two methods of calculating depreciation.

9. Differentiate between three different kinds of reserves. Which, if any, are also "funds"? Which cash? Give examples of intangible assets.

10. Guess how much you would pay for a business that is sure of yielding a net profit of $10,000 per year with little risk of principal. Suppose its total assets exclusive of Good Will were valued at $100,000. What would you guess for Good Will?

11. Review your understanding of the following concepts:

> *balance sheet identity*
> *income statement identity*
> *assets, liabilities and net worth*
> *current versus fixed or long-term*
> *earnings, dividends, surplus*
> *manufacturing cost of goods sold*
> *manufacturing cost, inventory change*
> *depreciation (as an expense and a reserve)*
> *intangible assets—patents and good will*
> *asset and liability reserves versus sinking fund*

ASSETS			LIABILITIES AND NET WORTH		
	1963	1964		1963	1964
			Liabilities	0	0
			Net Worth	$50 mil.	
Total	$50 mil.	____	Total	____	____

6 THE ECONOMIC ROLE OF GOVERNMENT: EXPENDITURE, REGULATION, AND FINANCE

Democracy is the recurrent suspicion that more than half the people are right more than half the time.

E. B. WHITE

The activities of the state are becoming an increasingly important part of the study of modern economics. This is reflected in the quantitative growth of government expenditure and in the great expansion of direct regulation of economic life. So in this chapter we survey government expenditure. In the next chapter we survey government taxation and local and state finance.

▶ THE GROWTH OF GOVERNMENT EXPENDITURE

Before World War I, federal, state, and local government expenditure amounted to little more than one-twelfth of our whole national income. During World War II, it became necessary for the government to consume about half of the nation's greatly expanded total output. Within the space of a third of a century, the cost of all government in the United States had risen from a paltry 3 billion dollars spent in 1913 to more than 115 billion dollars per year in the late 1950's.

If this remarkable contrast were the result of only a temporary wartime condition, it could be shrugged off as being of but passing significance. Actually, the exact reverse is the case. For more than a century, national income and production have been rising. At the same time, in almost all countries and cultures, the trend of governmental expenditure has been rising even faster. Each period of emergency—each war, each depression—expands the activity of government. After each emergency has passed, expenditures never seem to go back to their previous levels.

111

Nor is the end in sight. With the end of World War II, government expenditure receded from its wartime peak, but it did not drop down as far as those prewar levels which, a few short years ago, were considered alarmingly high. Before World War II, the annual federal budget never reached the 10-billion-dollar mark. In the years ahead, regardless of whether the Republican party or the Democratic party holds office, probably no man now alive will ever live to see the year when there is a federal budget of less than 50 billion dollars or a combined federal-state-local expenditure of much less than one-fifth of the national income.

Figure 1 indicates the historical trend of total government expenditure and federal debt relative to the growth of our national income. And Table 1 points up the fact that richer countries tend to spend more relatively on government than do poorer countries.

These are the hard, cold facts about public finance. Some may deplore them. Some may like them. But there they are. They make clear the increasingly important economic role of government. They explain why no modern economic textbook can relegate to an obscure corner the vitally important problems of public finance.

▶ **THE GROWTH OF GOVERNMENT CONTROLS AND REGULATION**

The increase in collective expenditure is only part of the story. Besides larger direct participation by government in national production, there has been a vast expansion in its laws and executive fiats regulating economic affairs.

Government expenditures show rising trend relative to growth in national income:

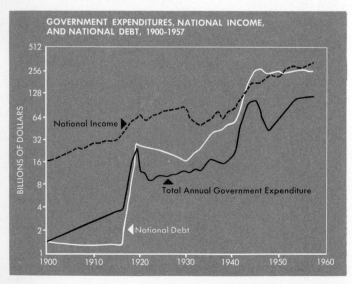

GOVERNMENT EXPENDITURES, NATIONAL INCOME, AND NATIONAL DEBT, 1900-1957

Fig. 1. Government expenditures include federal, state, and local annual expenditures. Note the relative trends. Also note that this is a "ratio" or "semilog" chart, with vertical distances arranged to reflect percentage changes. (Source: National Industrial Conference Board, Tax Foundation, Department of Commerce.)

Government share of national product is biggest in wealthy
developed countries:

Developed countries	Postwar average tax, per cent	Less developed countries	Postwar average tax, per cent
United Kingdom	35	Ceylon	19
France	31	Brazil	18
Canada	27	Puerto Rico	17
West Germany	27	Indonesia	15
United States	26	Colombia	10
Australia	25	Mexico	10
Japan	22	Pakistan	10
Italy	20	India	8

Table 1. Government receipts as percentage of national product. Poor, underdeveloped countries show a persistent tendency to tax less, relative to national product, than do more advanced countries. Government expenditure follows a similar pattern. (Source: H. T. Oshima, *American Economic Review,* 1957, pp. 282–3. Data includes all tax and nontax receipts. National product is actually gross domestic product.)

No longer does modern man seem to act as if he believed: "That government governs best which governs least." In a frontier society, when a man moved farther west as soon as he could hear the bark of his neighbor's dog, there was some validity to the view, "Let every man paddle his own canoe." But today, in our vast interdependent society, the waters are too crowded to make unadulterated "rugged individualism" tolerable. The emphasis is increasingly on "We're all in the same boat," "Don't rock the craft," "Don't spit into the wind," and "Don't disregard the traffic signals."

Perhaps nineteenth-century America came as close as any economy ever has to that state of *laissez faire* that Carlyle called "anarchy plus the constable." The result was a century of rapid material progress and an environment of individual freedom. Also there resulted periodic business crises, wasteful exhaustion of irreplaceable natural resources, extremes of poverty and wealth, corruption of government by vested interest groups, and at times the supplanting of self-regulating competition by monopoly.

Gradually, and in the face of continuing opposition, the methods of Alexander Hamilton began to be applied toward the objectives of Thomas Jefferson: the constitutional powers of central and local government were interpreted broadly and were used to "secure the public interest" and to "police" the economic system. Utilities and railroads were brought under state regulation; after 1887, the federal ICC (Interstate Commerce Commission) was set up to regulate rail traffic across state boundaries. The Sherman Antitrust Act and other laws were invoked after 1890 against monopolistic combinations in "restraint of trade." Regulation of banking became thoroughgoing; after 1913, the federal reserve system was set up to serve as a central bank, aiding and controlling member commercial banks; and since 1933 most bank deposits have been insured by the Federal Deposit Insurance Corporation.

Pure food and drug acts were passed following the revelations of the "muckraking era" of the early 1900's. Loan sharks came under regulation in many states. The abuses of high finance, before and after 1929, gave rise to ever more stringent regulation of the financial markets by the SEC and other bodies.

Humanitarian legislation to better factory conditions for children and women won at first only a grudging acceptance by the courts. But with the passage of time, the radical doctrines of one era became the accepted and even reactionary beliefs of a later era: state and federal legislation was expanded to include minimum-wage legislation, compulsory workmen's accident compensation insurance, compulsory unemployment insurance and old-age pensions, maximum-hour laws for children, women, and men, regulation of factory conditions of work, compulsory collective bargaining, fair labor relations acts, and so forth. (What new laws will *your* children take for granted?)

To understand this trend toward greater governmental authority one must maintain a sense of historical perspective. Each new step generated strong political feelings on both sides. Thus the "square deal" doctrines of the Republican Theodore Roosevelt, which today would cause no raising of eyebrows or fluttering of pulses, were considered dangerously radical in their time. Our republic cannot, and would not if it could, turn the clock back to the conditions of the nineteenth century as represented by Henry Ford's Greenfield Village and McGuffey's Reader. Still, it would be wrong to think these historical processes inevitable, to join Omar Khayyám in his mournful chant:

> The Moving Finger writes; and having writ,
> Moves on: nor all your Piety nor Wit
> Shall lure it back to cancel half a Line,
> Nor all your Tears wash out a word of it.

No immutable "wave of the future" washes us down "the road to serfdom," or to Utopia. Where the complex economic conditions of life necessitate social coordination, there can sensible men of good will be expected to invoke the authority and creative activity of government. But expansion of centralized power as a worthy end for its own sake is quite another matter—an end alien to the typical American citizen's credo.

Unfortunately, not until long after the event will history tell us—and perhaps not then—whether or not a given expansion of governmental authority was a good or bad policy; whether or not it should have the approval of all those genuinely interested in conserving and improving the good elements in our system. And in politics as elsewhere, it is only too true that the road to hell is paved with good intentions.

But this, past history does seem to suggest. Unyielding conservatism defeats its own purpose. Steel without "give" will rupture suddenly under strain. Brittle economic systems without the flexibility to accommodate themselves in an evolutionary manner to accumulating tensions and social changes—however strong such systems may appear in the short run—are in the greatest peril of extinction. For science and technology are constantly changing the natural lines of economic life. If the system is to continue to function well, our social institutions and beliefs must be capable of adjusting themselves to these changes. And without a sense of historical perspective neither radicals nor conservatives nor middle-of-the-roaders can effectively advance their own true long-run interests.

▶ FEDERAL, LOCAL, AND STATE FUNCTIONS

If we return now to the over-all figures of expenditure, we find that they become more meaningful when we break them down to see just what activities they represent and by which branch of government they are administered.

Primarily, each American is faced with three levels of government: federal, state, and local. It will surprise most people to learn that, of the three, the states have always been the least important with respect to government expenditure. This is still true, although, as we shall see, it is becoming less so.

Prior to World War I, local government was by far the most important of the three. The federal government did little more than pay for national defense, meet pensions and interest on past wars, finance a few public works, and pay the salaries of judges, congressmen, and other government officials. Almost all its tax collections came from liquor and tobacco excises and from tariff duties levied on imports. Life was simple in those days; local governments performed most functions and collected the most revenue, primarily from taxes on property owners.

In Fig. 2, we see how different everything has been since World War I. The federal government now leads in total expenditure. The states are still last but are now almost equal to the local governments.

▶ FEDERAL EXPENDITURE

The United States government is the biggest business on earth. It buys more typewriters and more cement, meets a bigger payroll, and handles more money than any other organization anywhere. Many a temporary "dollar-a-year" government executive, recruited from the top ranks of private industry, finds himself working harder and making bigger decisions than he ever dreamed of in private business life.

The numbers involved in federal finance are astronomical: not millions, or hundreds of millions, but literally billions (*i.e.*, thousands of millions). Obviously, such magnitudes convey no meaning to the human mind. We all know

Local and state spending has been rising faster than federal nondefense spending:

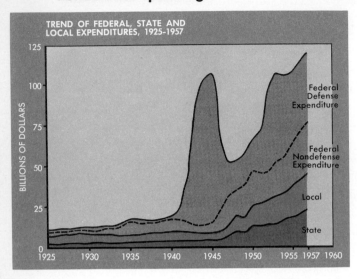

TREND OF FEDERAL, STATE AND
LOCAL EXPENDITURES, 1925-1957

Fig. 2. Federal expenditure rose sharply in the Great Depression, and even more during the war. Since the war, defense expenditure has remained high; but it is local and state expenditure on schools, sewers, and roads that shows the steepest civilian trends. (Source: National Industrial Conference Board and Tax Foundation.)

what it means to be a mile from home, but assertions that the sun is 93 million miles from the earth or that there are enough molecules in a glass of water to make a string of pearls from here to kingdom come always leave us unimpressed and somewhat cold. Perhaps public expenditure will have more meaning if we remember that each billion dollars amounts to about $6 per American man, woman, and child. A current federal annual budget of about 70 billion dollars would be equivalent, then, to about $420 per capita; it is as if almost 2 months of the year's income must go to the government.

Table 2 gives the estimated importance of different categories of federal expenditure in the fiscal year 1958, *i.e.,* from July 1, 1957, to June 30, 1958.

In the main, the first four items represent the costs of past and future wars. Together they account for four-fifths of all federal expenditure and for most of the increase in federal expenditure over prewar levels. Naturally, these are estimates—subject to change if international tension changes.

Much of the fifth item goes to the support of conservation programs, TVA, St. Lawrence Seaway project, etc. The various other items are mostly self-explanatory, representing aid to the farmer; welfare aid to the needy, aged, etc.; and expenditure on labor, education, and health. Highway and civil defense are included in the next to the last item.

The final category includes the costs of running Congress, the courts, and the general expenses of the executive branch of the government. In conclusion, it is to be emphasized that the bulk of current federal expenditure and debt is the consequence of war, not of depression or welfare programs.

▶ **EFFICIENCY AND WASTE IN GOVERNMENT**

The above estimates represent large sums of money. Undoubtedly, we should all be better off if the government were to increase its efficiency so as to give us the same services for lower costs or, what is equally important, if it were able to give us more and better services for the same dollar of expense.

Every effort should be made toward these ends. Having said this, one must go on to add: It is easier to preach economy than to practice it. It is easy to speak of cutting public expenditure to the bone. But when it becomes a matter of slashing aeronautical research, skimping on a veterans' hospital, denying aid to farmers, and so forth—do we know what we want to do? Even where government agencies overlap—where the same function is performed by two or more agencies—the reform is still difficult; for it must mean that some people lose their jobs—and those people have votes! The result: Our legislators are forced to talk one way and act another; to content themselves with occasional outbursts of penny wisdom mixed with dollar foolishness.

Every student of public administration and history knows that, if our government expenditures are too high, it is not primarily because of personal corruption or technical incompetence on the part of civil servants and legislators. As far as standards of intelligence, training, and personal financial accountability are concerned, the present federal government ranks far better than that of earlier times or than most of those at the state and local levels.

Nor is it enough to blame the cost of government on "pork-barrel" spending. Some government money *is* spent on dubious projects; but desirable though removal of this pork may be, it would not go to the root of the matter. The real issue goes much deeper. It lies within ourselves as citizens. We

Most federal expenditure goes to pay for defense and past wars:

	Estimate, billions	Percentage of total
National security	$43.3	61
Veterans services and benefits	5.0	7
Interest on public debt	7.4	10
International affairs and finance	2.4	3
Natural resources	1.5	2
Agriculture and agricultural services	5.0	7
Social security, welfare, and health	3.5	5
Commerce and housing	1.8	$2\frac{1}{2}$
Other, including general government	1.9	$2\frac{1}{2}$
Total expenditure	$71.8	100

Table 2. Estimated federal expenditure in fiscal year 1958. The first four items exceed 80 per cent of total expenditure. Hence, purely civilian expenditure for domestic peacetime purposes is less than one-fifth of the total! In the prewar era the proportions would have been reversed. What will they be if the cold war ever subsides and America becomes a richer nation? (Source: Bureau of the Budget)

want government economy, and at the same time we want the governmental services that cost money!

To put the matter in a more sophisticated way: Government expenditure is a way of utilizing national output so as to meet human wants and needs. When national income rises, people want more and better schooling and other forms of government services, just as they want to spend more on personal clothing, housing, and recreation. Our social conscience and humanitarian standards have completely changed, so that today we all insist upon providing certain minimum standards of existence for those who are unable to provide for themselves.

▶ THE CHANGING FUNCTIONS OF GOVERNMENT

The last quarter of a century has witnessed great political changes. Herbert Hoover's Republican administration was followed by the New Deal and Fair Deal regimes of Franklin Roosevelt and Harry Truman. Then Dwight Eisenhower brought the Republicans back to power. No doubt about it—the face of the country has changed. But how great have been the economic changes? How serious the departures from the traditional capitalistic system? We can tackle these questions by considering government activity under four headings:

1. *Direct controls.* As already noted, there has been a great increase in the amount of government *control.* Nevertheless, much of this body of regulation can hardly be dignified by the title of "planning," and despite its bulk we are still a long way from a planned state. Market prices still run most activities.

2. *Collective consumption.* As we have also seen, the increase in government expenditure means that as a nation we are consuming more of our national product *collectively* rather than individually through private money purchases. Rather than pay to ride on the public roads as we do to ride on railroads, we pay for such valuable services by taxes.

But note that such collectively consumed goods and services are still *largely produced by free private enterprise.* The government may pay for a hospital or a typewriter, but each of these items is produced by free private enterprise. And so it is with most government expenditure on productive goods. This is hardly what the socialists mean by socialism—"government ownership and operation of factories, etc."[1]

3. *Government ownership of production.* Next we must analyze the third kind of government activity, direct government production. We find that throughout recent decades there has been but little expansion in this direction. Historically, our government has performed certain direct economic production functions, and not others. The post office and parcel post have long

[1] See Chapter 38's discussion of socialism, communism, and fascism.

been a function of government, while private management has operated our telegraph service and railway express. Airports, but not railway terminal facilities, are usually governmentally owned. Municipalities now often provide water, gas, and electric utilities, but not telephone service.

The reasons for drawing the line at any one place rather than another are partly historical, partly arbitrary, and to some degree changing. The courts have held that, in the special case of "public utilities affected with public interest," there is limited possibility of effective competition among many independent producers, so they must be publicly regulated or owned; and one can decide which mode of operation would be the more successful only by a careful factual study that transcends the field of economics.

Whatever the merits of the arguments on each side, it is well to examine the facts to see how much government ownership of production has been introduced these last 25 years. Under the New Deal itself, there was only one direction in which such expansion took place—namely, the hydroelectric power field. (Examples: Tennessee Valley Authority, Bonneville Dam in the Northwest, Hoover Dam in the Southwest, and so forth.) Unlike Canada, or Sweden, or Britain, we have never had national ownership of railroads, coal mines, banks, or radio and television broadcasting.

If words are used in their traditional meanings, it was not incorrect of Eisenhower to call TVA "creeping socialism." The fact to note is how little of that sort of thing has, for better or worse, taken place in recent years.[1]

The atomic-energy program has been a post-New Deal development: It shows how poorly traditional "black-and-white" words and concepts are adapted to describe the gray territory of modern life. When the government pays General Electric a negligible fixed fee to start and run a vast nuclear industry, is this private or public enterprise? Private, in that the workers are GE employees and not civil servants. But the government puts up all the money, and certainly audits all major decisions. So the whole development of the atomic and hydrogen bombs could by some be called "galloping socialism." (Now that the problem of peacetime atomic energy has arisen, the government is relinquishing its monopoly. But decisions about secrecy, about fusionable and fissile materials, about patents, will necessarily keep nuclear energy "affected with public interest" and subject to public supervision.)

Before leaving this third category, which involves the use of human and other resources directly by the government, we should recognize that there has been a substantial rise of the federal payroll and in the number of government employees. Many of the latter are in the Washington executive offices, in regional laboratories, in the armed services, and so forth. Even if they are

---

[1] It is noteworthy that the war plants built by the government are, almost without exception, sold to private industry or shut down.

not directly producing private goods and services in competition with private industry, such resources are being used by the government; and it behooves us all as citizens that they be used wisely and in the right amounts relative to the importance of our different national needs.

4. *Welfare expenditures.* Finally, we turn to an activity of government that did expand tremendously in the 1930's and that will continue to loom large in the decades ahead: namely, government welfare expenditures, which transfer purchasing power to the needy or worthy without regard to their providing any service in return. Thus, payments are made to veterans, old people, blind and handicapped, orphans, and the unemployed. This fourth category of transfer expenditure deserves further detailed discussion. Indeed our modern governmental system is sometimes called the "welfare state."

▶ GOVERNMENT TRANSFER EXPENDITURES

A government check received by any such veteran or needy person differs economically from that received by a postal clerk or from that paid to a man who produces typewriters. It is important that we understand why, because our later discussion of national income will involve this same distinction between items that are "transfers" and items that we can truly count as parts of national production or income.

The payments to a postal clerk or typewriter producer are counted as parts of national income and output. Why? Because they do cover services rendered, they do use up resources and production, and they do provide collective direct or indirect consumption to the citizens of the United States. Whether they are financed by taxes, by the sale of postage stamps, or by any other means, the government uses the dollars it collects to provide services for the public. Such dollars are as much part of national income as the dollars used by a railroad company to provide transportation services for its customers.

A blind widow's pension is something else again. Socially, it may be one of our most desirable expenditures, but nevertheless it is not part of national output or national income. Why? Because the widow does not render any concurrent services to the government or its citizens in exchange for the pension. She does not provide any labor, land, or capital. The pension does increase her purchasing power, does permit her to live more adequately and to buy goods and services from other individuals. These goods and services that she buys are part of the national income and output; but they are *attributable* to the people and factories that have produced them, not to her.

Such transfer expenditures have grown greatly in recent years. They grew partly as a result of the depression, which made relief expenditures necessary, but mostly they grew because new minimum standards of health, nutrition, and security have been set up by the collective conscience of the American people. Society now rules that children shall not have rickets because of the bad luck or weakness of their parents, that poor people shall not die young because of insufficient money for operations and needed care, that the old shall be able to live out their years with some minimum of income.

Are such expenditures really anticapitalistic? We shall later see that "on the first round," these expenditures do not directly consume goods and services; but by swelling the purchasing power of their recipients, they do, "on the second round," create orders and jobs for free private enterprise. However, the thing to note is that *the production induced by this process is both privately produced and privately consumed.*

Unless these expenditures are financed by the printing of money or by government bond borrowing, larger taxes will have to be levied on the public, and it is for this reason that they are usually called "transfer expenditures." Often the more fortunate citizens are paying for the consumption of the less fortunate; and perhaps within reasonable limits, most people will feel that this is not improper.

Moreover to the extent that taxes come out of the income of the more well-to-do and thrifty and are used to make payments to the needy and ready-to-spend—to that extent the total of purchasing power is increased. In time of depression as we shall see, this may expand production and jobs. But in time of inflationary pressure, it may aggravate the upward spiral of prices and make shortages of goods worse.

▶ THREE WAYS TO FINANCE EXPENDITURE

Where does the money come from to meet government expenditures? Primarily from three sources: (1) taxes,[1] (2) the issue of non-interest-bearing currency, and (3) interest-paying loans. Normally, taxes are the most important of these. But during World War II borrowing was just as important, and during the Revolutionary War paper money was of greatest importance.

In Part Two we'll forge the tools to handle fiscal policy. Let's here examine the precise differences between the first two of these methods of finance, recognizing that this first survey but paves the way for Part Two's full analysis.

Suppose the government has spent or is about to spend an extra billion dollars on some project that the American people and their legislative representatives deem necessary and desirable. As a first alternative, the government can use its coercive powers and collect 1 billion dollars from its citizens in the form of one tax or another. Not all citizens would pay the same amount of

---

[1] Governments also receive some revenue from miscellaneous sources: sale of surplus equipment; sale of stamps, water, and gas; sale of public land; a few gifts; etc.

taxes. Not all citizens would have received the same benefit from the government's expenditure. Some will have received more benefit than they have paid for. Others will have received less benefit than they have paid for, but Congress will have felt that they can better afford the tax burden than other groups in the community.

The tax has provided the money for government expenditure. But it has done something else in addition, something that is especially important at a time when there are no idle men or factories. Superficially, the government needs only dollars for its expenditure program. Actually, and much more important, it needs land, capital, and labor resources to carry out its project. Where are these resources to come from if full employment is everywhere?

Here is where the taxes step in to perform a much more important function than mere provision of the necessary money. The individuals who are taxed find that their incomes are reduced. Because they cannot spend their receipted tax bills, they are no longer able to buy as much as previously of private consumption goods. These goods were being produced by land, labor, and capital. By contracting the production of such goods (or shifting goods directly to government use), we are releasing resources from the community's private consumption activities and shifting them to its collective governmental activities. Thus, *taxes shift resources from private to public uses.*

In a full-employment economy, scarcity and choice are all-prevailing. The more resources the people consume *collectively,* the less there is left for them to consume *individually,* and vice versa. They must choose carefully between the worth to the community of (1) more and better hospitals, post offices, agricultural laboratories; and (2) greater disposable family incomes to be spent individually on more and better clothing, food, shelter, tobacco, and recreation.

▶ **FINANCING GOVERNMENT EXPENDITURE BY NEW MONEY**

So much for the economic effects of tax finance under full employment. Still assuming full employment, let's look at the effects under the same conditions of full employment of the second method of financing our billion dollars of expenditure: printing new money. The government exercises its constitutional powers over the currency to print off one billion nice, new, crisp dollar bills. It finds that people are just as eager to work for these as for any other kind of money since they are all legal tender, interchangeable, and all the rest.

The American people have, therefore, succeeded in getting their billion-dollar collective project completed. The result has been completely painless, hasn't it? Why then ever levy taxes? Death may be inevitable, but why taxes?

The fallacy in these arguments applied to a full-employment economy should not be hard to isolate. And make no mistake about it, the arguments are then completely fallacious.

The government needs *resources* for its project—not primarily money. Where are the resources to come from in a full-employment world? Obviously only from the sacrifices of private persons. By printing enough bills, the government can outbid the present users of land, labor, and capital; it can suck resources into its own use. But in doing so, it bids up wages, rents, and prices.

Now we see who really foots the bill. Because the supply of goods available for individuals' use has been cut down, the cost of living will rise more than people's money incomes have increased. True, the government has not taken money away from them. But who can eat money or wear it on his back?

So such an increase in new-currency-financed government expenditure will in a full-employment world necessarily cause some degree of inflation. And inflation is a mighty tax collector—albeit an indirect and often unobserved one. The hidden tax of higher prices tends to fall most heavily on the old and on the relatively low-paid white-collar workers whose wages are sticky. There can be no doubt that inflation is a method of taxing, and a highly arbitrary and inequitable one, as we'll see when we later analyze the mechanics of spending and income determination.

► **FINANCING DEFICITS BY LOAN FINANCE OR BORROWING**

We have now noted the difference between tax financing and new-money financing in a full-employment world. There remains the intermediate case of loan financing by the sale of government bonds. The government uses the services of land, labor, and capital as before. But it does not pay by giving people receipted tax bills as in the first mode of finance. Nor does it simply present them with currency that they can then spend as they please. Instead it gives them I.O.U.'s, payable with interest in 1 or 25 years.

There is nothing compulsory about the process. People with savings are glad to subscribe for government bonds rather than hold their wealth all idle or in the form of private securities. Government bonds are an attractive investment because they can always be sold on the market or redeemed in case the need should arise. Equally important, there is never any possibility that the government—which has complete constitutional powers to issue new currency—would ever be unable to pay off the holders of government bonds in full. A European might hesitate to hold our bonds under some circumstances because he could be sure only of being paid off in *dollars* and he would be most concerned about francs or pounds. But an American, whose concern will naturally be with dollars, can rest easily even though his fortune is invested 99.9 per cent in government bonds: he knows the *dollar value* of his principal is perfectly safe. As we shall later see, he cannot be so sure that 5 or 20 years from now the dollars that he gets back will purchase as many goods as they do now. Still, that is a risk not peculiar to government bonds; the same would be true of money in the bank; and if he were to buy railroad bonds, he would still run such a risk, along with the additional risk that the principal of his bonds may go into default when collection day arrives.

We shall learn in Part Two how the government can sell bonds to the banking system and thereby enable it to manufacture bank money, *i.e.,* bank deposits. For this and other reasons, the economic effects of financing a deficit by loans may be more nearly like those resulting from the issue of new money than from taxation. We'll later show: Loan financing may not cause a significant curtailment of individual consumption and a subsequent release of resources for government use. At times of full employment, the result of such deficit financing is likely, therefore, to be inflationary. Prices are bid up by the government in order to win resources away from existing users.

▶ **THE BASIC ROLE OF TAXES**

Our conclusions concerning the different methods of finance can be summarized simply as they apply to a full-employment economy:

▶ Any additional government expenditure which the people think necessary and desirable should be financed by at least as much additional taxes. The primary purposes of taxation are to spread the "real" costs of collective governmental activity "fairly and equitably" among individuals and to prevent inflation.

▶ **FISCAL POLICY DURING BOOM AND DEPRESSION**

In concluding this chapter we can preview our later discussion of how fiscal policy can contribute to economic stability. We just saw that spending more than you tax increases inflationary pressure. Then what must be the effect of reversing the process? Taxing more than you spend should give us a mechanism for reducing inflationary pressure.

Actually this is what was done on a small scale in the postwar period, and many think *should* have been done even more intensively. Congress should have (1) cut down on government expenditure, and/or (2) raised taxes in order *to convert a deficit into a budgetary surplus.* The resulting excess of tax revenue over government expenditure could have been used to retire or pay off part of the public debt; but in any case the heavy tax collections would have reduced the excessive spending of the public and helped to moderate the inflationary pressures. However, it seems easier for us American people and our officials to vote increases in expenditure and cuts in taxes than vice versa.

The economic world as we used to know it in the last century and a half was not a stable system in full-employment equilibrium. Occasionally it ran an inflationary fever; often, and for long periods, it lay in the frozen torpor of unemployment and slump. Policies that are economically unsound in a full-employment world may be the height of wisdom in a period of deep and prolonged unemployment: levying taxes may be proper when we want people to release resources; but in time of depression, when we want to increase the number of both private and public jobs, increasing taxes may do harm. Similarly, policies that would wreck a normal world may be just what the doctor would order for an economy suffering from a runaway inflation.

No more than a warning to this effect need be sounded at this point. After the analysis of saving and investment in Part Two, the reader will be in a better position to understand the importance and the limitations of government fiscal policy. In Chapter 7, our discussion of public finance as it relates to the tax systems of the federal, state, and local governments will be continued. The expenditure of the states and localities and their coordination with the federal government will also be examined.

SUMMARY

1. The economic role of government has been a steadily expanding one. Not only are more and more activities in our complex, interdependent society coming under direct regulation and control, but also a larger fraction of the nation's output is being devoted to collective governmental consumption. And an increasing part of the national income is being "transferred" by taxation and government welfare expenditure from the relatively rich to the relatively poor. This trend has not yet been decisively reversed.

2. Since World War I, federal expenditure has far outstripped local and state expenditure. During the depression of the 1930's, expenditures on relief, public works, etc., lifted the federal budget to a level of almost 10 billion dollars. Our postwar budget remains many times prewar levels because of increased defense outlays, interest on the public debt, and aid to veterans. (NOTE: All this, without major need to spend to fight depression.)

3. Government expenditure is financed by three sources: taxes, interest-bearing loans, and issue of non-interest-bearing currency. In a full-employment world only the first method can be relied upon to secure an equitable distribution of the real costs of government. And in such a world, only the first will cause sufficient reduction in private individual consumption to release the necessary resources for governmental projects without inflation—that hidden tax collector. The proper fiscal policy for a period of unemployment and slump or for a period of inflation will be discussed later in Part Two.

QUESTIONS FOR DISCUSSION

1. What are some things that the government does today that it didn't formerly do?

2. Between now and 1970, how would you expect the government's share in the national income to develop? Why? What factors affect your answer?

3. How much does the increasing economic cost of government reflect decreasing efficiency? How would you go about making a scientific study of this?

4. "The radical doctrines of three decades ago' are the conservative doctrines of today." Is this ever true? Is it always true? Give favorable illustrations and exceptions.

5. "Government expenditure on goods and services represents collective consumption rather than individualistic consumption, but nevertheless it does represent consumption." Would you always agree? Give your qualifications.

6. "To bring back the federal budget to anywhere near the prewar, veterans' programs and defense will have to be the main items cut." Discuss.

7. What were some measures of the New Deal? Which no longer hold?

8. Define and give examples of a transfer payment.

9. Describe three ways of financing government expenditure. Contrast two.

10. Review your understanding of the following concepts:

government expenditure and taxes	*welfare state*
public debt and budget	*socialism*
laissez faire versus controls	*transfer expenditures*
TVA, ICC, SEC	*three methods of finance*
private versus collective consumption	*taxes and inflation*
	boom and depression fiscal policy

THE ECONOMIC ROLE OF GOVERNMENT: FEDERAL TAXATION AND LOCAL FINANCE

The power to tax . . . is not only the power to destroy but also the power to keep alive.

UNITED STATES SUPREME COURT

Our discussion of public finance continues in this chapter with a survey of the federal tax system, followed by a brief examination of expenditure and taxation at the state and local levels. It concludes with a short discussion of the problems of coordinating the activities of different levels of government.

► FEDERAL TAXATION

The great variety of present federal taxes is indicated by Table 1. Of these, the first two, personal income taxes and death (estate and gift) taxes, are sometimes called "equitable" in that they bear down "progressively"[1] more on those people with higher incomes. Payroll and sales taxes are relatively "regressive" in that they take a larger fraction of the poor man's income than they do of the rich man's. The corporation tax is intermediate in its effects; in one way, it is progressive, since most dividend dollars go to people of more than median income. Although it is true that many poor widows and orphans own some shares of stock, still the total that they own is not a large fraction of all stock shares. But to the extent that corporations can pass the tax on to the consumer in higher prices, a tax on business profits is regressive.

Our federal tax system is more progressive than it was 25 years ago or than are the tax systems of the states and localities today. A brief glance at the

---

[1] The word "progressive" can be misleading. A progressive tax is defined as one that takes a larger proportion of high incomes than of low. A regressive tax is one that takes a larger proportion of low incomes than of high. These are technical words, and we should be careful about giving them emotional meanings.

Personal and corporate income taxes are main federal revenue sources:

	Kind of tax		Receipts in millions
Progressive	Personal income taxes		$41.0
	Death and gift taxes		1.5
Intermediate	Corporation income taxes		22.0
Regressive	Employment or payroll taxes		8.5
	Sales or excise taxes		12.0
	Tobacco and liquor	$4.5	
	Manufacturing and retail excises	4.5	
	Customs duties	1.0	
	Miscellaneous	2.0	
	Other taxes and receipts		3.0
	Total tax collections		88.0
	Minus tax refunds		4.0
	Net total		$84.0

Table 1. Estimated tax receipts of federal government, fiscal year 1958. Three-fourths of federal tax revenues now come from personal and corporate income taxes. These respond quickly to changes in national income. Note that inheritance or death taxes do little these days to redistribute wealth and income. (Source: Bureau of the Budget.)

various taxes may be helpful.

Sales and excise taxes. In order of regressiveness, these would probably come first. So-called "liberals" usually oppose these taxes, while "conservatives" extol their virtues. As far as federal finance is concerned there has resulted a compromise: No general sales tax has been passed, but there are excise taxes on cigarettes, liquors, cosmetics, travel, and certain other goods.

Social security, payroll, and employment taxes. Most industries now come under the Social Security Act. Employees are eligible to receive old-age retirement benefits of so much per month, depending upon their previous earnings and not upon any humiliating demonstration of poverty. To help pay for these benefits, the employee and employer in 1958 each contribute 2¼ per cent of all wage income below $4,200 per year.

Taken by itself, the payroll tax is regressive in its impact upon the poor and middle classes. But combined with social security benefit payments, the degree of regressiveness is materially less.

Corporation income taxes. After a corporation has paid all its expenses and reckoned its annual income, it must pay part of its income to the federal government. In early 1958 a small corporation had to pay 30 cents of each dollar of its net income in taxes; but when its earnings got above $25,000 per year, it paid 52 cents of each extra dollar of earnings.[1]

Many people think the peacetime tax rate is too high, that corporations are

[1] In both world wars, this and other countries had an "excess-profits tax" on corporations in addition to the above ordinary income tax. In the 1951–1953 Korean emergency period, any corporation whose earnings had risen sharply relative to (1) its previous years' earnings

discouraged from venturing on worth-while (but risky!) job-making invest-ment projects. They argue that a small corporation would be able to grow more rapidly if it could plow back into the business what the government takes in taxes. Proponents of these views also say it is unfair "double taxation" for the government to tax corporate earnings and also to make the stockhold-ers pay personal income taxes on the dividends received from corporations. They advise: Cut corporate tax rates; or, alternatively, give the dividend re-ceiver some kind of tax credit for the taxes his corporation has paid. (In 1954 Congress made a token move in this direction, putting in a 4 per cent divi-dend-tax credit.)

On the other side there are a few who argue that corporations should be taxed heavily, with the bigger corporations taxed at progressively heavier rates. These people believe that, if the government must collect large sums of money and if further increases in the personal income tax are not feasible, then a tax on corporations is better than a sales tax or payroll tax. Moreover, they point out that corporations do not distribute all their earnings to the stockholders but save some to be plowed back in the business. The stockholder avoids personal income tax on these corporation savings by capital-gains loop-holes, as we'll see. According to these critics, a corporation tax will at least partially remedy the situation. The problem is too complex for us to attempt a final evaluation here.

▶ THE PROGRESSIVE INCOME TAX

Spring used to be an unhappy season. Along with the swallow's chirp, wails of anguish were heard throughout the land as people wrestled with their in-come-tax blanks. They used to have to pay taxes for the previous year's in-come—which often had already been spent.

Now things are better. All through the year our employers automatically *withhold* from each pay check most of what we shall have to pay to the gov-ernment. This puts us all on a pay-as-you-go basis, so by the end of the year we are more or less all paid up even if our pay checks have all been spent.

For some 30 million families, with incomes below $5,000 and no appreci-able property income, that's all there is to it. They simply turn in their with-holding-tax receipts at the end of the year, and the Treasury computes their tax and refunds them any excess they've paid. For still other millions of fam-ilies, who have moderate incomes and have not made extraordinary gifts to charity or incurred extraordinary medical expenses, there is a short form to fill out and rapidly compute one's taxes.

However, if you're lucky enough to have a sizable income, you'll have to fill

---

and (2) its invested capital had to pay a 30 per cent excess-profits tax on such additional earnings. Thus, such a company might pay in taxes 82 cents out of each *extra* dollar. (But no company had to pay more than 70 per cent of *all* its income.)

The income tax schedule climbs rapidly as income grows:

Table 2. Amount of federal income tax to be paid at different income levels by a childless couple, 1958.

Net income before exemptions (1)	Personal income tax (2)	Average tax rate, per cent (3) = (2) ÷ (1)	Marginal tax rate (= tax on extra dollar) (4)	Disposable income after taxes (5) = (1) − (2)
Below $ 1,200	$ 0	0	0	$ 1,200
3,000	360	12	20	2,640
5,000	760	15.2	20	4,240
8,000	1,416	17.7	22	6,584
10,000	1,888	18.9	26	8,112
20,000	4,870	24.4	34	15,130
50,000	19,600	39.2	59	30,400
100,000	52,800	52.8	72	47,200
200,000	134,000	67	87	66,000
500,000	404,000	80.8	91	96,000
1,000,000	859,000	85.9	91	141,000
Above $2,000,000	0.87 × Col. (1)	87	87	0.13 × Col. (1)

out the long form. That does involve some work; but no one should be graduated from high school who isn't able to do this.

First, you list your income from all sources. Then you can take a deduction or exemption for your spouse,[1] for each child, for other stipulated dependents, etc. You also deduct your state taxes paid, your interest expense on your home mortgage, your first $100 of dividends, your charitable gifts, etc. (Most people find they're ahead if they accept the "standard deduction" of 10 per cent of income or $1,000, whichever is lower.) There are numerous other deductions: e.g., excess of medical expenses above some percentage of your income, expenses for child care of a working wife or widower whose income is low enough, union dues and expenses to go to business conventions, etc. (If you're in business or a farmer, you must reckon depreciation and many other items that require an accountant's help.)

These are details. About how much does a typical person have to pay at each income level? Table 2 gives the approximate tax schedule as of 1957: (Rates are always changing, of course.) Column (2) shows about how much

[1] It certainly pays to be married. A bachelor with no major dependents would face a tax table much steeper than Table 2. Why? Because married couples can "split their incomes in two" and pay the tax at the lower-bracket *rate* of half their incomes. (NOTE: They pay taxes on all their incomes, but at the low rates of half their income. Table 2 was drawn up accordingly.) Quiz-whiz Charles Van Doren found his bride worth tens of thousands of dollars. Why? She made it possible for him to split his 1957 TV income for tax purposes!

taxes people would have to pay on each of the incomes listed in Column (1). Note that the tax starts at a low figure for poor people and rises very rapidly in relation to income. Indeed, when your income climbs up into the millions, up to 87 per cent will go to the government.

Column (3) shows just how progressive the personal income tax really is. A $10,000-a-year man is made to bear a relatively heavier burden than a $3,000-a-year man—19 rather than 12 per cent; and a millionaire is made to bear a still heavier relative burden. Column (4) shows an interesting fact: namely, the fraction of an *extra* dollar that taxes will take. Note this begins at the "normal rate" of 20 per cent and rises little until $10,000. This so-called "marginal (or extra) tax rate" finally reaches 91 per cent.

Column (5) shows the amount of disposable income left after taxes. Note that it always pays to get more income: even when the wealthy Doris Duke moves into a higher tax bracket, the move gives her more income to keep. As Column (4) shows, the government never takes more than 91 cents out of each *extra* dollar. At incomes around $35,000 it begins to take more than half of each *extra* dollar from a couple; a bachelor finds this happens to him at $17,500.

The income tax achieves its purpose of sharing the cost of government more "equitably" in relation to income. It tends somewhat to reduce the inequality of disposable income. Thus, in Fig. 1, the hypothetical effect of progressive taxes on the inequality of income is indicated in exaggerated form. Note how the area of inequality on the Lorenz diagram has been reduced; progressive taxation has shifted the solid line into the broken line, nearer to the 45° line.

Progressive taxes tend to equalize income distribution:

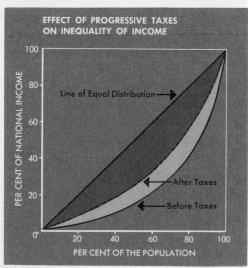

EFFECT OF PROGRESSIVE TAXES
ON INEQUALITY OF INCOME

PER CENT OF NATIONAL INCOME

Line of Equal Distribution ➤

After Taxes

Before Taxes

PER CENT OF THE POPULATION

Fig. 1. The black solid line represents the unequal distribution of income before taxes. The broken line shows how progressive (or "graduated") taxes result in a more equal distribution of "disposable" income after taxes. The effect is exaggerated for emphasis.

▶ THE BLACK ART OF TAXMANSHIP

Often, doubts are raised as to whether high income taxes do not discourage effort and risk taking. So far as effort is concerned, this is not an easy question to answer, since taxation will cause some people to work harder in order to make their million; many doctors, scientists, artists, and businessmen who enjoy their jobs and the sense of power or accomplishment that they bring, will work the same amount for $30,000 as for $100,000; still others may prefer more leisure to work as a result of progressive taxes. The net result is hard to be dogmatic about. We must content ourselves with posing the problem, returning to it in Part Four.

The effects of progressive taxes on risky investment are easier to appraise. They are probably adverse. In part the government says to the taxpayer "Heads I win, tails you lose." For example, suppose a man earns $200,000 in 1 year and nothing in the next 3 years, while his brother earns $50,000 in each of the 4 years. Their average earnings before taxes over the period are the same, but the venturesome brother pays over the period $134,000 in taxes, leaving him with a total income after taxes of $66,000 (see Table 2). On the other hand, the steady brother pays taxes of only $78,400 (= 4 × $19,600). He is left with total income after taxes of $121,600 for the period. In this example, the progression in the tax system has penalized the venturesome brother to the tune of leaving him only half as well off as his conservative brother.

Careful studies by the Harvard Business School, cited later in Part Four, seem to show that in fact there are sufficient perfectly respectable "loopholes" open to wealthy people so that they may typically pay but 50 per cent tax rates, not the 87 per cent shown in the table. They take risks and try for lightly taxed capital gains;[1] they invest in tax-exempt municipal bonds; they drill for oil, grow trees, or feed beef cattle—all of which are more lightly taxed.

Why do we go through the motions of high tax rates like 87 per cent, when all the revenue collected by more-than-50-per-cent rates is relatively small? A good question. We appease the prejudice for equality but often seem only to penalize the unimaginative folk who fail to use the tax-avoidance devices open to them.

Opposing any unfavorable effect of progressive taxes on investment and jobs, there is an opposite effect. To the extent that dollars are taken from frugal wealthy people rather than from poor ready spenders, progressive taxes may tend to keep purchasing power and jobs at a high level—at too high a level if inflation is threatening.

---

[1] When we remember the loopholes discussed in this study, we find that *high tax rates may encourage risk taking by those who seek capital gains* and who know that Uncle Sam finances up to 91 per cent of their deductible costs.

Thus no one can be sure whether the unfavorable effects of the personal income tax on investment offset the opposite effects in cutting down potentially excessive savings. In the last analysis, therefore, every voter must try to judge the costs and decide on ethical grounds whether he favors a more or less equalitarian society, greater or smaller rewards and incentives to individual initiative.

▶ STATE AND LOCAL EXPENDITURES

Let us now turn to public finance other than federal. Although quantitatively the federal government's multi-billion-dollar expenditures greatly exceed those of the states and localities, still these are very important in their own right.

To see what the states and localities spend their money on, turn to Figure 2. All these items are more or less self-explanatory. Note that expenditure on schools—mostly by localities—is the biggest single item by far.

Schools are the number one state and local expense:

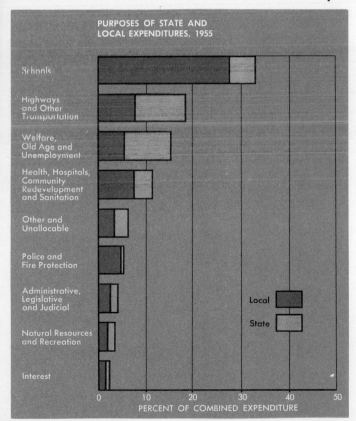

Fig. 2. The population outburst and move to the suburbs has put a strain on local and state finance, necessitating increased state and local debt issue. (Source: Bureau of the Census.)

▶ STATE AND LOCAL TAXES

To see the main sources of funds to finance such expenditure, turn to Fig. 3 and Table 3 which show the revenues of state and local governments. In terms of the previous discussion of kinds of taxes, it must be admitted that, on the whole, the principal taxes of the states and localities are "regressive taxes." Let's discuss some of the more important ones.

Property tax. Note that the property tax still accounts for almost half the total revenues of state and local finance. Figure 3 and Table 3 show it is the localities that primarily levy property taxes.

The property tax is levied primarily on real estate, land and buildings, but in some places also on personal property such as furniture and watches. Each locality sets an annual tax rate. Thus, in a large city $35 on each $1,000 of assessed valuation (3.5 per cent) might be it. This means I must pay $350 of property taxes if my house has been assessed as worth $10,000. However, in many places assessed valuations tend to be some fraction of true market value. My house and all like it may have a current market value of $15,000

The real-estate property tax still dominates local and state finance:

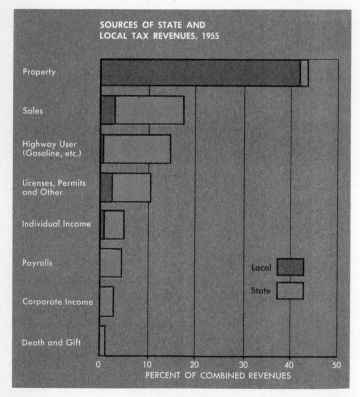

SOURCES OF STATE AND
LOCAL TAX REVENUES, 1955

Property

Sales

Highway User
(Gasoline, etc.)

Licenses, Permits
and Other

Individual Income

Payrolls   Local

     State

Corporate Income

Death and Gift

0   10   20   30   40   50
PERCENT OF COMBINED REVENUES

Fig. 3. Most local and state taxes are still of the regressive type, not easy to expand as needs grow. (Source: Bureau of the Census.)

but are assessed at about two-thirds that much. Therefore my true property tax rate is less than 3.5 per cent, really nearer to 2.4 per cent.

The property tax is rather inflexible. Rates and assessments tend to change slowly. In bad times when real-estate values fall, the tax is very burdensome and gives rise to bankruptcy, mortgage foreclosures, and forced sales. In the zooming postwar economy, property valuations and tax rates have been gradually moving up.

In colonial times, a man's total income and wealth may have been all connected with real estate; if so, then the effect of a tax on such property would have been roughly the same as a tax on income. Today, when so much of wealth and income is divorced from real estate, the property tax may be regressive relative to income—especially since small properties tend to be assessed relatively higher than large.

Highway user taxes. As the name suggests, these revenues come from two primary sources: from a tax of so many pennies per gallon of gasoline and from license fees on autos, trucks, and drivers. In many states, more is collected in this way than is spent on roads. The extra revenues are used for schools or old-age pensions, just as some colleges use profits from football games to buy fencing foils or even Greek manuscripts.

These highway taxes are usually justified on the grounds that the taxpayer is simply paying for the *benefit* of using the roads in much the same way as he pays for a railroad ticket or for his use of water and electricity.

Sales taxes. States are getting more and more revenue from general retail sales taxes. Each purchase at the department, drug, and grocery store pays a percentage tax. (Sometimes food and medicines are exempt.) Also states usually add liquor and tobacco excises onto the federal excises. (Some cities get in this act.) Most people—including many cigarette smokers and moderate drinkers—have a vague feeling that there is something immoral about tobacco and alcohol. They feel as though two birds are being killed with one stone when these articles are taxed: the state gets revenue, and vice is made more expensive.

The same rationalization is not possible for, say, a 5 per cent tax on everything that a consumer buys, whether a pair of shoes, a cake of soap, or a church candle. Rich and poor are taxed alike on each dollar spent; and since the poor are forced to spend a larger portion of their total dollars, it is easy to see that the sales tax on nonluxuries is a regressive tax; *i.e.,* it takes a larger portion of low than of high incomes.

Payroll and business taxes. States and localities often charge license fees for the privilege of acting as a corporation, running a tavern, and so forth. Some states tax the net income of a corporation as well, and collect miscellaneous other fees from business enterprises.

In addition, all states have been bribed by the federal government into col-

States receive federal grants-in-aid and also make grants to localities:

Source	State	Local
Taxes	$11.6	$11.9
Property	$ 0.4	$10.3
Other	11.2	1.6
Aid from federal government	2.8	0.4
Aid from state government		6.0
Fees and miscellaneous	5.1	5.9
Net total	$19.5	$24.2

Table 3. Taxes and other revenues of state and local government, 1955. (In billions). While state and local taxes are almost equal, note that the latter is made up mostly of property taxes. And note that the states give as grants to localities about twice what the federal government gives in grants to the states. (Source: Census Bureau)

lecting a wage tax equal to about 3 per cent of payrolls in occupations covered by social security. The proceeds are used to provide "unemployment compensation benefits or insurance" when workers become unemployed. The economics of social security as it concerns the individual and family will be discussed further in Chapter 9.

Personal income and inheritance taxes. More than half the states imitate the federal government, but on a much smaller scale, by taxing individuals according to the size of their incomes. Such a method of taxation has already been discussed in connection with federal finance. A few important states, such as Illinois, do not rely at all on this relatively progressive tax.

Inheritance taxes on individuals who inherit bequests of property upon death of a relative or friend are self-explanatory. They differ only in minor detail from estate taxes that are levied on the dead giver's estate and not on the receivers. Also, it will be obvious that gifts must be taxed, or else wealthy people would have every incentive to distribute before death all their wealth to their heirs, so as to escape taxation then.

Both the federal and the state governments share in estate and inheritance taxes. The federal government tries to act to prevent states like Florida from advertising to old folks, "Come here to die and avoid all inheritance taxes." The federal government gives up part of its revenues to any state that passes such a tax law: it accepts a state tax receipt in part payment of a citizen's taxes. However, states still differ widely.

The inheritance and estate tax is called a progressive tax. The poor widow's inheritance usually pays no tax at all because of liberal exemptions, while the rich man's estate pays at a progressive rate. Social reformers attach great importance to death taxes for the purpose of preventing the development in this country of a permanent moneyed caste, living not on its effort and intelligence, but on its property inherited from one generation to the next. As of 1958, the right to "split income," to make gifts, to set up complex "trusts," and to bequeath tax-free insurance policies—all these have reduced death-tax collections to a low level. (This is happening too in Great Britain.)

▶ INTERGOVERNMENTAL GRANTS-IN-AID AND DEBT-FINANCE

There are other miscellaneous revenues. Some localities sell natural gas and electricity. Some, especially in Nevada, tax slot machines and race-track betting. All collect some revenue from assessments on property owners who benefit from specific sewage and road improvements.

A much more important revenue source is the financial aid that states receive from the federal government and that localities receive from the states.

Having access to more revenue sources, the federal government has increasingly been making grants to the states, and in lesser degree to the localities. These were primarily for highways, public welfare assistance, and education (vocational and agricultural training, etc.). These help in part to offset the great regional differences in real incomes: *i.e.,* some of the grants are made to be more generous to the poorer states of the South.

Similarly, within the states there have been grants-in-aid to the localities—primarily for schools, highways, and public assistance (relief, old-age pensions, etc.) Only in this way can the poorer parts of each state maintain certain minimum standards of schooling, roads, and living. Only in this way can well-to-do suburbanites be prevented from running out completely upon their share of public responsibility.

Despite these grants-in-aid programs, there still remain sizable differentials in the ability of different regions of the country to provide minimum standards. It still matters where you are lucky enough to be born.

When all is counted in, it is yet not true that the total of state and local expenditures equals the total of their revenues. The difference represents new borrowing or debt repayment. The wartime prosperity swelled state tax revenues (despite the rationing of gasoline). At the same time it became impossible to build new schools and highways and unnecessary to support so many needy people on relief. As a result, in the war most states were able to run a surplus and retire part of their previously accumulated debt.

But since 1946 states and localities have again been increasing their debts. Their costs have risen, and many school and highway projects deferred during World War II have finally been undertaken. Veterans' bonuses, too, have added to state debts.

Between World War I and World War II, most state and local borrowing tended to behave perversely, so as to accentuate rather than damp down the business cycle. During the prosperous 1920's when the federal government was retiring part of its war debt, states and localities floated tremendous amounts of bonds, so as to build needed highways and schools at the high prices then prevailing. When the depression of the 1930's came, despite the publicity given to emergency borrowing of some cities, state and local governments on balance reduced their debts! They refused to build necessary public works even though costs were advantageous and jobs were desperately needed. Instead, they began to lean more and more on the federal government in this matter of public works as well as in connection with unemployment relief.

It is perhaps too much to ask the states and localities to take an active part in moderating the business cycle. But a minimum goal would be for them, if they cannot do good, at least to do no harm. If they are too weak to increase their outlay in depression, at least they should endeavor to withstand the temptation of increasing their expenditures in boom times. If they follow this advice, their dollars will go farther and the problem of unemployment will not be quite such a great and difficult one.

▶ CONCLUSION: THE THORNY PROBLEM OF TAX INCIDENCE

In ending this survey of taxes and other revenues, let's note a few warnings. Does "Who pays the taxes?" sound like an easy question? Well, it's not. You can't just assume that the person Congress says the tax is levied on will end up paying the tax. That person may be able to *shift* the tax: shift it "forward" on his customers, by raising his price as much as the tax; or shift it "backward" on the people he buys from, by being able to offer them less than he would have offered them had there been no tax.

Economists therefore say: We must study the final *incidence* of the tax. We must try to learn what the tax does to all prices. (Example: does a tax on wheat raise the price to the consumer by as much as itself, so that the incidence is on the consumer? Or does the tax raise the price by half itself, so that part of the incidence is on the producers? Does it change oats prices? And does the tax kill off all or much of wheat production, so that it is having incidence effects beyond those that show up in prices and wages and even beyond the burdens that you can allocate among the different citizens?)

Have economists yet learned how to measure the incidence of taxes accurately? Parts Three and Four will develop some of the important tools that you will need to begin to tackle this thorny problem. But, here and now, let's face this fact: economists are not yet in agreement on the final results. Some think the corporate income tax falls mostly on the consumer; some argue it falls mostly on stockholders or capitalists. Some split the difference between the two. Some toss a coin. And some throw up their hands in despair.

Figure 4 is a valiant statistical attempt to determine how progressive or regressive our tax system is. Its authors, Richard A. Musgrave and his collab-

Experts try to answer the question, "Who pays the taxes?":

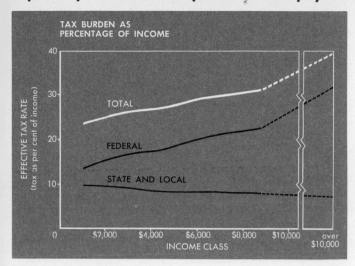

TAX BURDEN AS
PERCENTAGE OF INCOME

EFFECTIVE TAX RATE
(tax as per cent of income)

TOTAL

FEDERAL

STATE AND LOCAL

$2,000 $4,000 $6,000 $8,000 $10,000   over $10,000

INCOME CLASS

Fig. 4. Note the relatively regressive burden of state and local taxes. This is in contrast to the rising curve of mildly progressive federal taxes. (Source: R. A. Musgrave *et al.* in Nov. 9, 1957, compendium of Joint Committee on the Economic Report, p. 98.)

orators at the University of Michigan, have made their best effort to decide the approximate incidence of each tax. But Professor Musgrave is the first to insist that these are simply his best estimates of incidence. Though he's an expert in public finance, he isn't a magician capable of making a controlled experiment in which he (1) first measures things without taxes, and then (2) measures things with taxes, finally (3) determining tax incidence as the difference between these situations.

In any case, most experts agree that our state and local tax structure is more regressive than the federal tax structure, and Fig. 4 indicates this.

SUMMARY

1. About three-fourths of federal revenue comes from personal and corporation income taxes. The rest comes from so-called regressive taxes on payrolls and excises. The personal income tax is steeply progressive and tends to redistribute income between rich and poor.

2. State and local expenditures have been rising in the postwar period: the principal items are education, highways, public welfare, and the ordinary police and safety functions of government.

3. The property tax is still the most important source of local revenue. Sales taxes and excises are important at the state level. In the postwar period, states and localities have been spending more than they collect in taxation, thereby increasing their debts.

4. The problem of coordinating the federal, state, and local levels of government offers administrative difficulties. Increasingly the federal government gives grants of billions to the states, primarily for highways and matching grants-in-aid for social welfare. The states in turn are increasingly helping the localities in the fields of education, highways, and public assistance.

5. The incidence of a tax is its total effect on all prices and other economic magnitudes. Those upon whom a tax is levied may succeed in shifting part of its burden forward or backward. The economists' tools of Parts Three and Four will help tackle this difficult problem.

QUESTIONS FOR DISCUSSION

1. Make a list of different kinds of taxes in order of their progressiveness. What is each's importance at the (*a*) federal, (*b*) state, and (*c*) local level?

2. List different state and local expenditure categories in order of quantitative importance. Compare with federal expenditure categories as set out in Table 2, Chapter 6.

3. How do you think different government functions should be allocated among the three levels of government? How about revenues and grants-in-aid?

4. Should a citizen in Massachusetts be taxed to help a citizen in Arkansas? To help a citizen in Vermont? In Massachusetts? In Mexico?

5. "Since people don't change their smoking habits as a result of taxation, and since the poor smoke, a tax on cigarettes is really no different from a tax on bread." Do you agree? What would you conclude ought to be done if the above statement were true?

6. "No sane nation publicly spends more than 25 per cent of its income." Discuss.

7. Calculate from Table 2 the personal income tax paid by a typical doctor, lawyer, teacher, stenographer, mechanic, and carpenter.

8. "More kids and more cars mean local expenditure and borrowing." Explain what is meant by this.

9. Review your understanding of the following concepts:

progressive and regressive	*grants-in-aid, public debts, defi-*
incentive effects	*cits, and budget surpluses*
	tax incidence and shifting

8 LABOR AND INDUSTRIAL RELATIONS

MR. HENNESSEY: *But these open-shop min say they're f'r unions.*
MR. DOOLEY: *Shure, if properly conducted. No strikes, no rules, no contracts,
no scales, hardly iny wages an' dam few mimbers.*

FINLEY PETER DUNNE

America has become a "laboristic economy." This term, suggested by Sumner
Slichter, Harvard's eminent authority on labor economics, no doubt has an
element of exaggeration in it. Ours is still a "capitalistic economy," and it is
also a "mixed economy" in which the role of government is exceedingly important. But no one can deny that the huge growth of labor unions since 1933
has made them seats of economic and political power. A Walter Reuther is not
less important these days than a Henry Ford.

Unions are an important part of American life, and they are here to stay.
By law and custom, free trade-unions are recognized as legitimate institutions
in all democratic nations. In Hitler's Germany and Mussolini's Italy labor
unions as we know them were not permitted to exist. Nor are they allowed in
present-day Russia.

▶ WHO BELONGS TO UNIONS?

Almost 18 million Americans belong to a union. This means that about one-
third of the nonagricultural working force is made up of union men. If we
exclude white-collar workers, foremen, and executives, the proportion of union
men would be still higher. And if we examine certain important industries—
such as railway and water transportation, basic steel, automobiles, coal mining, and clothing—practically all eligible workers belong to unions. Few large
firms escape being organized by unions.

141

Figure 1 shows the prodigious growth of union memberships since 1900: the slow, steady advance up to World War 1, the upsurge during that war and immediately thereafter, and the rather sharp decline and slumping off during the 1920's. For the more recent period, Fig. 1 shows the explosive acquisition of new members during the New Deal recovery years after the Great Depression, the continued rapid growth during World War II, and finally the slower growth since the end of the war.

To what unions do workers belong? Figure 2 lists the largest ones. All but the United Mine Workers used to belong to the newly merged American Federation of Labor and Congress of Industrial Organizations—*i.e.,* the AFL-CIO. In late 1957, however, the Teamsters were expelled from the federation because of corruption disclosed by Congressional investigation.

Statistics of memberships understate the influence of unions. Many non-union people are covered by union agreements on wages, hours, and working conditions. If you took a solemn oath never to join a union or work under a union agreement, you would have to give up all hope of being a factory worker in many sectors of manufacturing industries. *In every single manufacturing industry,* at least 20 per cent of all wage earners are under union agreements—even if they are not actually union members. You'd have to give up a career in mining. In construction. In transportation. Where could you go? You could avoid unions on the farm, in government service, in finance, in wholesale and retail trade. White collar workers are generally tough targets for union organizers. Or go South: attempts to organize workers have met with strong resistance there; two-thirds of all union men now live in 10 industrial states.

Unionism spurted in the depression and during the war years, but since has leveled off:

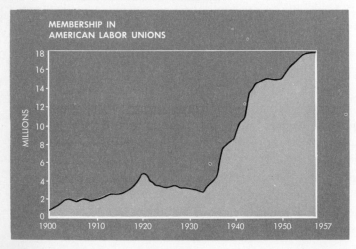

MEMBERSHIP IN
AMERICAN LABOR UNIONS

MILLIONS

Fig. 1. Thirty-five per cent of nonfarm workers today belong to unions, as against but 11.5 per cent in 1933. About 75 per cent of the 13 million production workers in the United States today belong to unions or are covered by union wage agreements. (Source: U.S. Department of Labor.)

▶ **NATIONAL AND LOCAL UNIONS**

There are three important layers in the structure of American unions: (1) the *local* union, (2) the *national* union,[1] and (3) the *federation* of national unions. To a union member, the *local* is the front line of unionism. He joins the local in his plant or town. He pays his dues to the local. Usually, the local union signs the collective bargaining agreement determining his wages and work conditions.

But the local is only one single chapter or lodge of the national union. Thus, a linotypist in Chicago belongs to the local union located there, but this is one of hundreds of local chapters of the International Typographical Union whose headquarters is in Indianapolis. Generally, part of the local dues—one-half or less, usually—must go to the national union; the bylaws and practice of the local cannot transcend the broad policies laid down at the national level. The president and other officers of the local will probably be local workers; but the important office of business agent is a full-time job, the salary for which is often paid by the national union. The trend is increasing for the national unions to lend a hand in local-union collective bargaining.

Altogether there are about 200 autonomous national unions. As we have seen, seven of these have over half a million members. Over half the national unions each have between 10,000 and 100,000 members, and a quarter of the national unions have less than 5,000 members.

The number of local union chapters or lodges is no less than 75,000. Some have as few as a dozen men. A few giant locals cover thousands of men. For

[1] Many unions in Fig. 2 have Canadian chapters and are called "international unions."

Unions, like corporations and government, these days come in giant sizes

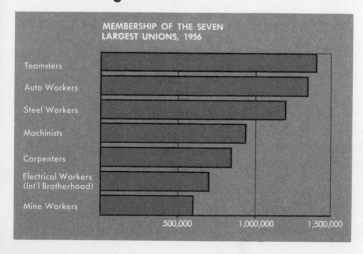

MEMBERSHIP OF THE SEVEN
LARGEST UNIONS, 1956

Teamsters

Auto Workers

Steel Workers

Machinists

Carpenters

Electrical Workers
(Int'l Brotherhood)

Mine Workers

500,000   1,000,000   1,500,000

Fig. 2. The combined dues-paying membership of these seven unions is 6⅔ million. Leaders of such large organizations must be regarded as among the most powerful men of our day.

example, the Ford local of the UAW is the largest of all. It alone has 33,000 members! The vast majority of locals fall in between in size, covering anywhere from 50 to 1,000 workers.

▶ NATIONAL UNIONS AND THE FEDERATION

The AFL-CIO is a loose federation made up primarily of national unions as members. The public thinks of this great federation as being the most important part of the labor movement. But it is not. It acts as spokesman for labor, but its own power is strictly limited. Thus Walter Reuther wields more real power in his capacity as head of the Auto Workers union than he does as vice-president of the AFL-CIO. Teamsters' boss, Dave Beck, had more to fear from government action than he did from criticisms of his financial peccadilloes by the AFL-CIO. As a federation the AFL-CIO strongly disapproves of union discrimination against Negroes, but it has no power to act against those few of its member unions which have restrictive rules written into their constitutions. When the CIO in 1949 and 1950 expelled the United Electrical Workers (UE) and 10 other left-wing unions held to have been Communist-infiltrated, this was considered quite a precedent-breaking action.

In the last 20 years the federation has increased in importance and power, but it remains a loose federation still. Later when we survey the history of the American labor movement, we shall see that federalism has been a characteristic feature of its evolution. And even today don't think that the word "federation" refers to the merger of the AFL and the CIO. Federation actually refers to the coming together into a loose organization of the national unions. The AFL-CIO is dependent upon these member national unions for financial support. Like the Big Five nations on the Security Council of the United Nations, the national unions have insisted upon their "sovereignty" and right of veto and their right to "exclusive jurisdiction" over workers in their area. Most of the headaches and fights come from such jurisdictional disputes.

Though merged together in 1955, the AFL and CIO still maintain some discernibly separate identity within the AFL-CIO. Both have become quite active in politics in recent decades. The Committee on Political Education of the AFL-CIO supports candidates favorable to labor. Nominally nonpartisan, organized labor has usually supported Democratic candidates; but there have been some notable exceptions. (*E.g.*, Republican Governor Knight of California got labor endorsement in 1954.) Moreover, a number of labor leaders, such as John L. Lewis and Dave Beck, have generally supported Republican presidential candidates.

Figure 3 gives an organization chart for the new AFL-CIO. The state and city federations shown thereon lobby at these levels of government and cooperate in producing radio programs, parades, and election or strike soli-

American labor finally reunited in the 1955 AFL-CIO merger:

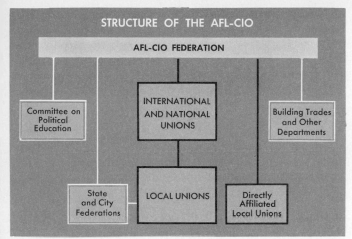

Fig. 3. The national and local unions remain the important units in our federated labor structure.

darity. The chart also reveals a few local unions attached directly to the federation rather than to any national union. Usually, these locals are in new fields just being organized or in fields that fall between jurisdiction and territories of the constituent national unions. The departments are coordinating bodies made up of unions in similar areas, such as building.

▶ HOW DOES COLLECTIVE BARGAINING WORK?

In the following pages we shall trace the historical genesis of the present American labor movement. But first let us examine how collective bargaining is carried on.[1] Suppose you work in a factory that has just been organized. An AFL union has petitioned the National Labor Relations Board (NLRB) for an election to determine the exclusive bargaining agent in this plant. You mark a secret ballot in favor of the union; it wins more votes than, let's say, an existing so-called "company union." A day is set for your union representatives to meet with representatives of management at the bargaining table.

Seated at the table will probably be a vice-president in charge of industrial relations; with him will be attorneys from a law firm that specializes in the labor field. On the union side will be the local business agent of the union and a small committee of union officers, and handling the negotiations will be an expert from union headquarters. Probably he is neither a lawyer nor a professional economist, but the economic research staff of the union has helped him to prepare an extensive brief backing up the union's demands.

[1] Chapter 28 includes a more analytical discussion of the collective bargaining process.

The union brief will analyze the company's profit position and published accounting records in great detail; it will present data showing that the president of the company receives $150,000 a year; etc. It will contain national figures on the changes in the cost of living and may even present local data to show that rents in that area have risen beyond the national average. The brief will also compare wages in that plant with those prevailing in other plants and other industries. It will bristle with theoretical arguments showing the necessity for higher wages to maintain workers' consumption and national full employment. The employer's brief will have carefully prepared rebuttals to each of these points. If this is an important industry, both union and management will be prepared with publicity releases to be given to the press.

Hourly wage rates will not be the only issue in bargaining. In addition the union may be asking for a dues "checkoff" (whereby union dues are automatically deducted from the payroll of union members). The union may be bargaining for a "union shop," requiring all employees to become union members. Pension and health-insurance demands may be discussed at the bargaining table. In many industries where piece rates prevail, the structure of rates will be an important subject for negotiation; the exact work load—how many looms each man will attend, etc.—may be discussed, and the general problem of how fast technological improvements shall be adopted will enter into the final contract. The seniority rights of workers and a grievance procedure for handling cases of discharge—these and many other problems will come into the collective bargaining.

Indeed, management has become worried over the inroads that organized labor has been trying to make into what it regards as its prerogatives. Many employers claim they can no longer run their business in the way that they feel is best. They find it hard to hire whom they will, fire for just cause, determine work methods, decide on the order in which people will be laid off, etc. They feel that every new decision occasions a meeting of a new committee; and time that could better be spent on producing output must be devoted to labor relations. They claim the worker acts as if he has a right to any job he has held for some time. Such critics complain that a good many unions oppose incentive wage schemes, insist upon rigid seniority, discourage efficient work methods, and seriously limit the autonomy of management. A recent casebook on collective bargaining devotes more space to issues arising out of workers' rights in jobs than to any other single subject!

But at last the contract, covering many pages of fine print, is signed. Everything is set down in black and white, including provisions for grievances that arise during the life of the contract; often, too, there will be provisions for *arbitration* over issues that arise under it, with each side agreeing in advance to accept the decision of an impartial outside arbitrator. The usual life of a contract may be a year, with provisions made for reopening negotiations for a new contract under specified conditions.

Collective bargaining is a complicated business—a matter of give and take.

▶ **BRIEF HISTORY OF THE AMERICAN LABOR MOVEMENT**

Although American labor was late in becoming organized, the beginnings go back well into post-Revolutionary War and pre-Civil War times. Local craft unions of highly skilled strategically placed workers (printers, etc.) were the first to be formed; and periodically, in boom times or in times of industrial unrest, these would combine in city and national federations for political and reform purposes. But not until the 1880's, when the AFL was formed, did the America labor movement assume its characteristic present-day form.

The Knights of Labor. In the last third of the nineteenth century, a "great upheaval" swept the land. Part of this populist revolt against the "big interests" was the formation of the Knights of Labor. At first this was a secret society which all but "lawyers, bankers, gamblers or liquor dealers, and Pinkerton detectives" could join. Later, secrecy was dropped; and by 1886, the high-water mark, the Knights had some 700,000 members. The Knights represented an attempt to form *one great labor union* to speak for all labor. But it was a heterogeneous collection, throwing together "craft unions" of skilled workers, "industrial unions" of all workers in a given plant or industry, and mixed assemblies of any who cared to join.

The Knights were very interested in political reform and agitation. Some officials were more interested in "uplift" and radical political changes than in day-to-day increases in hourly wages. After a few unsuccessful strikes, the Knights declined in membership as rapidly as they had grown. America was obviously not susceptible to such a political labor movement, and the organization of the Knights of Labor was too loose to give it any staying power.[1]

The American Federation of Labor. In 1881, and formally in 1886, the present-day labor movement took its form in the birth of the American Federation of Labor. For almost half a century, until his death in 1924, Samuel Gompers dominated this organization and gave the movement its characteristic pattern. Gompers himself was brought to this country as a child by immigrant parents. He was active in developing the Cigar Makers' Union and in founding the AFL as a rival organization to the Knights of Labor. Though

---

[1] Again, around the time of World War I, the IWW (Industrial Workers of the World, or "Wobblies") tried to organize the whole working class for the overthrow of capitalism. It had limited success in its efforts to organize unskilled migratory workers, loggers, and metal mine workers. It had greater success in inducing panic in Wilson's Attorney General Palmer, who in 1920 threw suspected radicals in jail in defiance of civil liberties. But nothing came of the IWW, and it soon faded away into complete ineffectiveness.

early interested in socialistic uplift movements, he soon realized that no movement opposed to capitalism would flourish on American soil.

His main principles were simple:

1. He insisted on "business unionism"—*i.e.,* unionism aiming at day-to-day higher wages and better work conditions. Forsaking pie in the sky, he instead asked for "more today than yesterday; more tomorrow than today." Labor was to get "more and still more" by evolution, not violent revolution.

2. He committed the AFL to the principle of *federalism,* with each national union having autonomous sovereignty and "exclusive jurisdiction" over its craft specialty. This meant that the AFL would not tolerate "dual unionism": two unions could not try to organize the same workers; and a group of workers could not break away from a recognized national union.

3. Finally he insisted on *voluntarism,* with the government not to interfere with collective bargaining, either in favor of or against labor. In politics he favored "rewarding labor's friends, punishing labor's enemies"; but he would not commit labor to any one political party.

Thus, the AFL was a polar opposite of the Knights of Labor in almost every respect. As the Knights dwindled in importance, the AFL grew. It has continued to grow. And you might say that the philosophy of the AFL turned out to be the dominant philosophy of the American labor movement.

The stagnant twenties. After World War I, the AFL had about 5 million members and seemed to be riding high. But during the 1920's, labor met determined opposition from the National Association of Manufacturers (NAM) and other business groups. The "open shop" was declared to be the "American plan." Moreover, the 1920's was a "new era" of eternal prosperity. As John J. Raskob, business executive and Democratic party leader, said, anyone could easily get rich by saving $15 a week and investing it in the stock market. (He added that not only was it possible for people to become rich—it was their *duty* to become rich as well.) Also, the 1920's was one of those rare high-employment periods when prices were not rising; so discontent over the cost of living was not operating to encourage unionization.

The AFL itself was rather stagnant. At Gompers' death, John L. Lewis and other strong men tried to get his job. So, William Green was elected as a compromise candidate and was president until his death in 1952. On the whole he voiced the viewpoint of "craft unions," made up of skilled workers of one occupation. Lewis, on the other hand, was associated with the "industrial unions," made up of all workers in a given industry or plant.

Recovery and the formation of the CIO. By the depths of the 1932 depression, the AFL had fallen to less than 3 million members. But with the recovery days, a new era for unionism was in the offing. The depression had soured the American public on many of the slogans of the 1920's and had excited class antagonisms. Moreover, even before the election of Franklin

Roosevelt, the electorate and the courts began to modify their opposition toward union activities.

But within the AFL itself, the old insistence on the exclusive jurisdiction of national unions stood in the way of organization of the great mass-production industries. For example, before Judge Gary of U.S. Steel crushed the great 1919 steel strike, an unwieldy committee of some two-score craft unions was set up to conduct the strike. To this day the Carpenters and Machinists unions have never been able to settle some of their differences.

Astute observers in 1933 saw the handwriting on the wall: industrial unions were to play an important part in the future. John L. Lewis of the UMW, the late Sidney Hillman of the Amalgamated Clothing Workers Union, and other leaders took matters in their own hands and in 1935 formed a committee to help organize the mass-production industries. For running counter to the exclusive jurisdiction principles of the AFL, they were later expelled from that organization, and so they formally organized the CIO, with Lewis as president. Helped by new government attitudes, legislation (especially the "Wagner Act of 1935"), and court decisions, a whirlwind campaign followed in which the important mass-production industries, such as automobiles, steel, rubber, and oil, were organized—despite the bitter opposition of the principal companies in these industries.

By this time the AFL had learned the important lesson of industrial unionism. It, too, began to organize on an industrial basis; but its craft unions remained dominant. Warfare between the AFL and CIO long continued, and some CIO unions such as David Dubinsky's Ladies' Garment Workers (ILGWU) returned to the AFL fold. In the end Lewis pulled his mine workers out of both federations.

Unions in the late 1950s. Finally, labor's dream of a united movement was realized after 1955. The AFL-CIO was formed, with AFL's George Meany its first president. And these days the union movement seems to have settled down. Few new industries are left to be organized; and in the South, the attempts to organize have met with limited success.

A new breed of man seems to be moving to the top. Back in the days when unions were being born and were fighting for their lives, colorful men like John L. Lewis, Philip Murray, and Dan Tobin were the leaders. As each of these dies off, their replacements are men who seem primarily *administrators*.

David McDonald, Murray's successor as head of the Steelworkers, even graduated from a business administration course! With millions of members and literally hundreds of millions of dollars in their welfare funds, the unions are in need of men who can administer.

The "managerial revolution" has hit labor as well as business. Are you ambitious to head a union? Then don't rush out onto a picket line. Instead pick a spot on the escalator and—funeral by funeral—work your way upward.

► COMMUNISM AND CORRUPTION IN UNIONS

Boring in by Communists was always something of a problem for the union movement. For example, in the 1920's Dubinsky led a successful effort to oust the communist influence from his union. During the 1930's the Communists attempted to influence policy in many unions. They provided zealous labor organizers, and Lewis himself in his factional disputes for a time tolerated their help. In the United Electrical Workers (until 1949 CIO), the National Maritime, and the longshoremen's unions, the struggles between the "Commies" and anti-Communists were especially severe; and in the International Fur and Leather Workers (CIO) the Communists did get control.

The Communists, who usually formed only a tiny percentage of membership, exercised an influence beyond their numbers because they acted as a unit, using Machiavellian tactics to achieve their goals. Those goals far transcended the day-to-day business unionism typical of American labor. Also, as was shown dramatically on the day Germany attacked Russia, the Communists followed the "Moscow party line" and suddenly ceased to attack Roosevelt as a "warmonger" interested only in promoting an "imperialistic war." Instead they hailed him as a great leader of the democratic fight against fascism.

For a long time the labor movement, in particular the CIO, had tolerated left-wing adherents provided they stood also for the same things that the unions stood for. But after 1949 there was a showdown. In addition to expelling the UEW and half a dozen other unions, the CIO in 1950 expelled Harry Bridges' West Coast longshoremen's union as a Communist-infiltrated union. In the mid-fifties, laws against Communists became stiffer and stiffer.

Except in a dozen or so unions, the Communists never attained any considerable power. Theirs was almost entirely a minority influence resting on their cleverness in strategy and in identifying themselves with popular labor causes. Whatever you think of the economic wisdom of its policies, American labor is red-white-and-blue, not red.

The role of gangsterism in the union movement is quantitatively less important than communism. After the repeal of prohibition, corrupt gunmen did work their way into a few urban unions (e.g., the longshoremen around New York). Such union officials were as ready to sell out labor for a bribe as to fight in labor's interests. Labor has been fairly successful in cleaning its own house; in cities where there is effective law enforcement, the evil of labor gangsterism is pretty well under control.

Only one trouble spot remains: fraud and mismanagement of the sizable union funds are not yet completely at an end. Teamster Dave Beck got rich speculating with union funds, and other misuses of union welfare funds have been turned up by congressional investigating committees. New laws, which will regulate such funds and yet not create needless red tape for honest men, are now being sought.

▶ HOW DEMOCRATIC ARE UNIONS?

Earlier we encountered the problems involved in democratic control by stock-holders of corporation management. A not dissimilar problem arises in connection with unions. It is true that union officials are elected to office, and all union members are given equal votes. But officers once elected often stay in power for a considerable time, and between annual conventions the union is usually run by a small executive board. A man like John L. Lewis is on the whole popular with his miners; but if a miner disagreed with the general policies laid down by Lewis, he would not get very far.

Like the average stockholder, but not to the same degree, the average union member does not participate very actively in policy formation. However, according to Sumner Slichter, who has made a study of this problem:

This does not mean the rank and file lack influence. Their influence is great, but influence is not participation. If democracy simply means strong rank and file influence, most unions are democratic. The typical situation in a union is similar to that found in most organizations, churches and clubs of all sorts. There is a minority which is sufficiently interested in the affairs of the organization to attend business meetings and to participate actively in discussing problems. In the case of unions this minority usually asks the officers to press for stiff demands—stiffer than employers would be willing to grant without a long fight, stiff enough to force many employers out of business. In order to avoid trouble, the great majority of the union would settle for much less than the active minority demand.

Quite naturally the professional leader feels on the spot. If he disappoints the active minority too deeply, his leadership will be challenged. If he gets the inactive majority into too much trouble, he may provoke revolt also. He compromises, as, of course, he must. Usually he is more interested in placating the active minority than the inactive majority because he knows that the support or opposition of the active members is more important than the support or opposition of the inactive members. The record shows that union officials lose their jobs, not for being too radical for the majority, but for being too conservative for the minority.[1]

▶ OPPOSITION TO UNIONS BY AMERICAN EMPLOYERS

In its struggles for higher wages and recognition of unions,

American labor has employed clubs, shotguns, and dynamite. It is the hardest-hitting and most violent unionism in all the world. The European mind has real difficulty in understanding that blood will be shed for the trifling object of putting a few more

[1] S. H. SLICHTER, *The Challenge of Industrial Relations* (Cornell University Press, Ithaca, N.Y., 1947), p. 111.

cents per hour into the pay envelope, . . . that over a million workers will be on strike at the same time, causing a creeping paralysis to spread over the economy, *without these strikers being the advance guard of revolution*.[1]

To understand this pattern of violence, we must record the fact that United States employers, like the employers in a few other Western nations, have been militantly antiunion. Historically, American management fought unions tooth and nail. Only as recently as the late 1930's, companies like Ford Motors and Republic Steel were spending literally millions of dollars on private detectives in a losing fight against unionization. Bullets were flying on the picket lines and killing a dozen men as recently as Memorial Day, 1937, years after the law of the land gave unions the unmistakable right to organize.

Much of this is past history now. Certainly today all the automobile companies, big and little, are engaged in relatively peaceful collective bargaining; the same is true of both Big Steel and Little Steel. But to understand the pattern of American labor history, this unfortunate record of last-ditch employer opposition must be taken into account.

The chief weapons used by employers to fight unions have been (1) *discriminatory discharge* of union members, (2) the *blacklist,* (3) the *lockout,* (4) the "yellow-dog" contract, (5) the labor spy, (6) the strikebreaker and armed guards, and (7) the "company union."[2] Also, employers have used the courts to fight against unions.

▶ **A CASE STUDY: HOW TO FIGHT A UNION**

To illustrate what all these terms mean, imagine that I am a business executive battling, back in the old days, against having my labor force unionized. I am not a cruel man; I am good to my family and I do not cheat my creditors; but to me war is war, and I feel it my duty to do battle in what I believe is a righteous cause. So, gory details omitted, here are some of the things that I might have been doing a score of years ago.

First, I ask the foremen, "Which men are the ringleaders of the new union?" Having learned their names, I fire them. More than that, I put their names on a blacklist so that all other employers are warned against hiring them. I help see to it that outside union organizers are tarred and feathered or run out of town on a rail; or at least they are warned to get out of town if they do not want to be arrested by the local constabulary for vagrancy and/or disturbing

---

[1] M. S. PITZELE, "Can American Labor Defeat the Communists?" *Atlantic Monthly*, March, 1947.

[2] *Violations of Free Speech and Rights of Labor,* Preliminary Report, Senate Report 46, 75th Congress, 15th Session (GPO, Washington, D.C., 1937). J. R. COMMONS' four-volume *History of American Labor* is a standard reference.

the peace. What influence I have is used to make sure that local schools and churches are not made available to the union for their meetings and rallies.

Before the union can call a strike, I beat them to the punch and call a lockout. I close my plant until the men come to their senses and drop out of the union. Any new men I hire must sign a so-called yellow-dog contract promising never to join a union. If they go back on this contract, I ask the courts to enforce it.

But in spite of my efforts, the union continues to make headway. So to protect myself against the union outsiders, I have to send away for outside help. There are a number of professional detective agencies who specialize in this kind of work; from them I can hire five men or five hundred. Of course, these men will not be liked by the violent union members, and so they must be armed in self-defense and in order to help protect private property from illegal violence. It may even be necessary to have some of them sworn in by the local sheriff as official deputies to help maintain order.

I tell these professionals not to use violent methods. And I really mean it. But they are only human, and their own lives are in jeopardy; so it is only natural that they should do whatever seems necessary to protect themselves from harm.

The unhappy day arrives when the union, losing all reason, calls a strike. I expect that only a few malcontents will walk out, but actually more than half the men get carried away by oratory and go out. They form a picket line outside the gates. They claim they are exercising their constitutional civil right of free speech, but their speech when they address my loyal employees reporting for work is hardly civil. "Scab" and "strikebreaker" are the politest of the words used. Even their women turn up in the picket line, shouting unladylike names such as "fink" and "goon" at my watchmen. Inevitably somebody gets carried away by the occasion and starts to throw stones at windows and at executives' cars. The crowd loses all reason and begins to tear down fences. In self-defense and to protect property from mob damage, some detective fires a shot. The next day the newspapers run headlines about labor massacres, and unfortunate public relations problems have been created.

In the end, I win the strike; the workers can hold out no longer. But faced with continued unrest and discontent after they have returned to work, I feel I must bow to the inevitable. If the men have to have a union, let them have one. But why must it be an uncooperative outside union rather than a reasonable one made up of men who have long been with the company and know its problems? So I encourage some of the born leaders among the men to form a "company union." I help pay for a barrel of beer for their initial get-together picnic; and to help the union treasury along, I let the boys sell soft drinks within the plant, the profits to go to the union treasury.

▶ NEW PATTERN OF INDUSTRIAL RELATIONS

The business executive caricatured above is now extinct. He has been retired, and a new generation of management has taken over. Why? In the first place, the unions did succeed anyway in organizing most large plants during the 1930's; and it was simply not good business, in terms of the net earnings of the corporation concerned, to continue the expensive war against unions. In the second place, what finally brought the unions in successfully was not a superiority in arms and violence. The real change came about from the changed attitude of government. After 1930 the dice of government became loaded toward rather than against the union movement. Misguided though they might think the New Deal labor policies to be, business leaders knew they could not fight the United States government. (We shall soon see how this historical shift in government's role began, and the recent turn it has taken.)

Also, many business leaders began to understand the wisdom underlying the statement by Cyrus S. Ching, formerly vice-president of United States Rubber Company and subsequently head of Federal Mediation and Conciliation:

Where we are dealing with organized labor, we are going to get about the type of leadership that we are ourselves.

And many businessmen began to recognize that there was at least a grain of realism in the statement by a labor leader:

Employers generally get the kind of labor relations they ask for. If the unions indulge in "excesses," then the employer as a rule has no one but himself to blame for it. For instance, if he engages the services of labor espionage agencies such as the Railway Audit, Pinkerton's or others, if he stocks up his plant with tear gas, hand grenades, submachine guns, blackjacks, rifles, and other implements of war, if he hires high-priced Wall Street lawyers to harass the union before the Labor Board and in the courts, if he distributes to his foremen anti-union literature and lets it be known to them that any harm they can do to the union would be forgiven by him, if he contributes to anti-labor organizations such as the notorious Johnstown Citizens' Committee, if he quibbles over words, if he refuses to consent to an election or to sign a contract when he knows the union has a majority, if after a contract has been forced from him he delays and hampers the settlements of grievances, if he continues to discriminate against union members, then labor will answer in kind and nine out of ten businessmen, viewing it from afar, will say, "Ah, another excess."[2]

So no observer of modern-day labor relations should get a false impression that all management has been antiunion. Violence makes the headlines while

[1] CYRUS S. CHING, "Problems in Collective Bargaining," *Journal of Business,* University of Chicago, 1938, Part 2, p. 40.

[2] P. MURRAY and M. L. COOKE, *Organized Labor and Production* (Harper, New York, 1940), pp. 259–260.

patient cooperation is unsensational and goes unnoticed. In most industries there has long been a successful pattern of fruitful cooperation between labor and management. To highlight this fact, the National Planning Association has published studies describing cases of successful labor relations. These reports describe "how historically hostile groups can co-exist on a basis of reasonable equality of position in the enterprise, and at the same time be participants in a common endeavor from which both seek security, opportunity, and sustenance."[1]

Thus, the West Coast pulp and paper industry, whose leading member is the Crown Zellerbach Corporation, has had 24 years of healthy labor relationships. The Dewey and Almy Chemical Company has a 19-year record of collective bargaining with its union, involving only three work stoppages. The Nashua Gummed and Coated Paper Company has maintained relationships with no less than seven AFL unions for 25 years without a strike. And the Hickey-Freeman Company, a men's-clothing manufacturer, has dealt with unions for 39 years without a strike; for 28 years no grievance has ever gone as far as arbitration.

These are not cases where peace has been maintained because the management or the union was soft. Hard bargaining on both sides is likely to accompany a good management-labor relationship: apathy on both sides or one-sided dominance would postpone solutions and ultimately lead to breakdown. In healthy cases, each side has a respect for the rights of the other. The two sides are not in love. But they are compatible.

▶ ROLE OF GOVERNMENT AGAINST LABOR

When modern unions first began in Britain a century and a half ago, they were held to be illegal. The old common-law doctrines against monopolistic conspiracy in restraint of trade were used to put unionists in jail. Subsequently Parliament passed laws explicitly making union organization legal. In this country, too, by a century ago the courts recognized that it was not illegal conspiracy for men to organize in a union to raise their wages, provided they used legitimate *means* to achieve this legitimate end.

In 1890 the Sherman Antitrust Act made monopolistic restraints of trade illegal. It didn't mention labor unions. But in the next 20 years, the Sherman Act was used increasingly by the courts to curb the activities of unions. If a union struck for ends which in a judge's opinion were undesirable, he would rule against it. And many traditional means used by unions were declared by judges to be illegal even if in pursuit of a legitimate end.

Criminal prosecutions against union men were not uncommon. Unions

[1] *Fundamentals of Labor Peace: A Final Report* Case Studies 14 (National Planning Association, Washington, D.C., 1953).

themselves, as well as their officers, were held liable for *damages: e.g.,* in the important Danbury Hatters Case (1908) every member of the union, as well as the officers, was held personally responsible for the damages caused by a *boycott;* a settlement of one-quarter of a million dollars ruined the union. Moreover, often unions were harassed by expensive damage suits that they could not afford to fight even if they were pretty sure to win. In addition to restrictions on the boycott, the courts often ruled against picketing in the absence of a strike and picketing in numbers, even if there was no mass picketing of a violent nature. The judges recognized the validity of the yellow-dog contract and made free use of court *injunction* against labor.

Samuel Gompers, though against labor's taking an active role in politics, was forced into the political arena by what he felt was government's stacking of the cards against labor. In 1914, labor was successful in getting the Clayton Antitrust Act passed. Although hailed as "labor's Magna Carta" and designed to remove labor from prosecution under the Sherman Act, this did not end legislative and judicial opposition to the labor movement.

▶ **GOVERNMENT IN DEFENSE OF LABOR**

But the tide was turning, and after 1930 the pendulum swung in support of union bargaining. In that year the Supreme Court upheld the constitutionality of the Railway Labor Act (1926) which accepted the basic premise of collective bargaining. In 1932 the Norris–La Guardia Act (1) explicitly ruled out federal enforcibility of the yellow-dog contract and (2) virtually wiped out injunctive interference by the courts in labor disputes, implicitly recognizing the validity of boycotting and group picketing in labor disputes.

Section 7 (*a*) of the National Industrial Recovery Act (NIRA), 1933, actively encouraged collective bargaining. Finally the important National Labor Relations (Wagner) Act, 1935, was passed. It stated bluntly: "Employees shall have the right to self-organization, to form, join, or assist labor organizations, to bargain collectively through representatives of their own choosing, and to engage in concerted activities, for the purpose of collective bargaining or other mutual aid or protection." (Sect. 7.) Moreover, it set up the National Labor Relations Board (NLRB) to make sure that employers do not engage in "unfair labor practices" against labor.[1] The NLRB also goes into plants and holds elections to see what organization is to be

---

[1] The term "unfair labor practices" as used in the Wagner Act was a broad one referring to employers' activities that interfere with employees' rights to self-organization. Examples of such employer practices are (1) firing men for joining a union, (2) refusing to hire men sympathetic to unions, (3) threatening to close an establishment if employees join a union, (4) interfering with or dominating the administration of a union, or (5) refusing to bargain with the employees' designated representatives. In the Taft-Hartley Act, these provisions were generally retained and a set of *"union* unfair labor practices" added.

regarded as the collective bargaining representative of workers. It can, and does, issue "cease and desist orders" against employers, enforceable after appeal by the courts. The Wagner Act, like the later Taft-Hartley Act, applies only to industries in interstate commerce, but many states also passed "little Wagner Acts," and the Supreme Court in upholding the constitutionality of the Wagner Act, has interpreted interstate commerce broadly.

▶ **REFORM LEGISLATION**

By 1940 the pendulum had swung still farther in favor of labor. The legislatures and the courts now recognized fully the right to collective bargaining, and heavy penalties were placed on the employer for his "unfair labor practices." But even this does not tell the full story. In the field of *protective* legislation, labor's tide was also running.

Back in the nineteenth century, when the first laws were passed regulating conditions of safety and health in factories, they were curiously enough passed by the Tory, or Conservative, party in England. The Whigs, or Liberals, who favored a policy of relative *laissez faire,* regarded such governmental fiats as interferences with natural rights and liberty; moreover, they argued that such interferences would do more harm than good, and under competition would gradually become unnecessary.

In this country, early attempts to pass laws setting minimum wages and working conditions for women and limiting child labor were bitterly opposed. Many such laws were declared unconstitutional by the courts. But gradually protective legislation for women and minors became widespread. Just before World War I, Workmen's Compensation Acts providing benefits in case of injury were passed. But even as late as 1930 the AFL went on record in opposition to social security in general and minimum-wage laws for men.

The Franklin Roosevelt administration introduced a number of such "welfare-state" devices. The Social Security Act (1935) was passed, providing unemployment insurance or compensation, contributory old-age and other benefits, noncontributory old-age assistance, and assistance to handicapped groups. The Walsh-Healy Public Contracts Act (1936) provided that prevailing minimum standard wage rates, as prescribed by the Secretary of Labor, were to be paid on government contracts.

In 1938, the federal government went all the way and passed the Fair Labor Standards Act. This set minimum wage rates for most privately employed nonagricultural workers engaged in interstate commerce (since 1956 at $1 per hour). Standards of 40 hours per week were set, with time and a half for hours in excess of this amount being mandatory in almost every case. Child labor in interstate commerce was finally barred. Many states, too, have minimum-wage and maximum-hours legislation.

▶ **TURNING OF THE LABOR TIDE: TAFT-HARTLEY ACT**

By the postwar period the pendulum went into reverse. Franklin Roosevelt was dead. The New Deal had lost its steam and some of its public following. The electorate was fed up with strikes and rising prices. Labor was no longer considered the underdog. Among congressmen there was a widespread feeling that the Wagner Act had been one-sided, that it favored labor and put all the penalties upon the employer. So in 1947 Congress passed the Labor-Management Relations (Taft-Hartley) Act.

This Act covers more than 20 pages of fine print. It has hundreds of detailed provisions that we need not try to understand. Primarily, its adherents aimed at a *two-edged* labor relations law that—unlike the Wagner Act—prescribes standards of conduct for unions as well as employers. The hand of the worker who does not want to join a union is also strengthened, as are rights of a member within the union as against the officers. Organized labor regards Taft-Hartley as a "slave labor act" and is bitterly opposed to it.

Some of the principal aims of the Taft-Hartley Act are briefly as follows:

1. *The closed shop is officially banned.* Employers do not have to hire union men. States are given a free hand to pass stronger laws against various union membership requirements. (And some states have since passed "right-to-work" laws that prohibit any compulsions forcing employees to belong to a union.)

2. *Strikes in essential industries may be temporarily banned by injunction.* While earlier legislation had aimed mostly at injunctions secured by private parties, now the United States Attorney General can ask for an 80-day court injunction in situations that would "imperil the national health or safety." (The powers and duties of the NLRB to secure court injunctions against unfair labor practices are also expanded.)

3. *Unfair labor practices on the part of unions* are defined for the first time. Unions can be sued, *e.g.*, for violation of a no-strike contract. Unions are now to be held responsible for acts of their agents. Their health and welfare funds are to be subject to strict supervision. Their exclusive right to handle grievances is curtailed. Their initiation fees cannot be unreasonable. They can't blatantly "featherbed" (*i.e.*, exact pay for services not performed). They must bargain collectively. Their right to an automatic checkoff of union dues is limited. So is their right to discipline members for other activities than non-payment of dues. Other curbs on unions could be listed. Employers, too, can be taken to court over violations of collective bargaining contracts.

4. *Unions are held accountable.* They must file data giving names of officers, their pay, their manner of election, etc. Officers must swear that they are not Communists. Financial data for the union must be reported.

5. Political activity and financial contributions by unions to federal election and primary campaigns are forbidden. The free-speech rights of the employer are

reaffirmed and strengthened as compared to the earlier Wagner Act provisions.

6. *Secondary* boycotts and *jurisdictional* strikes are made illegal.

7. Supervisors ("foremen") are given no protection to bargain collectively; an employer bargains with them collectively only if he wishes to.

8. A 60-day strikeless period is provided, requiring that much advance notice if a collective bargaining contract is not to be renewed. The penalty on workers who strike during this period is loss of their Wagner Act rights. Arbitration is not compulsory, but new mediation and conciliation machinery —removed from the Department of Labor—has been provided.

9. The NLRB is expanded in size from three to five members and given new duties. Subject to new restrictions, it becomes a quasi-judicial body.

▶ FUTURE STATUS OF LABOR MOVEMENT

How have things worked out in the dozen years since the Taft-Hartley Act? Despite dire predictions of labor leaders, the union movement has not been vitally crippled. Unions continue to bargain collectively; they continue to win NLRB elections as "exclusive bargaining agents." In certain trades, such as newspaper printing, although the closed shop has legally been abolished, all the operatives continue to be union men.

On the other hand, the hopes of the Act's supporters cannot be said to have been realized. The ensuing years were *not* particularly peaceful ones. And the relative quiet in the 1950's many observers explain by the relative stability of living costs and by the GM-type sliding-scale contracts that tie wages to moves in the index of living costs. As predicted, the Act hurts weak unions (*e.g.,* those trying for a foothold in the South) but leaves strong unions strong.

Even management is divided on the amendments in favor of labor pledged by the Eisenhower administration. Some think the Act should be strengthened, not weakened, by an amendment; and this group naturally favors the recent interpretations by the NLRB that now permit the employer to quiz workers as to union membership and that restore employers' right to speak freely to workers against unions.

In key industries, vital to the economic health and security of the nation, strikes are generally regarded by the public and the government as intolerable. Clearly such work stoppages do untold harm to the community at large. Back in 1919 Governor Calvin Coolidge achieved fame when he quashed the Boston police strike with the statement, "There is no right to strike against the public safety, by anybody, anywhere, any time." To a degree, this same doctrine is applied today in many vital industries. Whatever the legal theory, the government does not in practice permit strikes to go on in these vital areas. Presidents Truman and Eisenhower, both regretfully, found themselves forced to use the Taft-Hartley injunction machinery to end strikes in crucial areas.

▶ POSTWAR WAGE PATTERNS

During the war, the War Labor Board (WLB) set a general freeze on hourly wages. Payrolls rose sharply because hours worked went up; but labor felt its hourly rates did not keep up with living costs and productivity trends.

At the war's end, labor's pent-up frustrations exploded in widespread demand for a wage-rate boost; to keep total weekly take-home pay from being reduced as hours of overtime work were cut out, labor demanded a 30 per cent increase in wage rates. There followed a severe wave of strikes. In 1946 alone there were nation-wide strikes in coal, steel, meat-packing, and the railroad industries. Figure 4 tells the postwar work-stoppage story.

In the end, a national pattern of an 18½-cent-an-hour wage increase in a number of key industries was established and widely imitated. This was the so-called "first round" of wage increases, and it was followed by later rounds. Thus a new and somewhat disturbing postwar tendency developed: (1) wage bargains began to be made on a wider and wider scale; (2) there began to be a tendency for one great industry to imitate the pattern set by another key industry; (3) as each new round became widely imitated and began to raise costs and prices, it tended to be followed by another round; (4) after 1950, labor began to demand and win fringe benefits (pensions, insurance, vacations, free family medical care, etc.). Walter Reuther sought, and won, a modified "guaranteed annual wage" for the Auto Workers; and Reuther says he'll go on to seek a 32-hour week at 40 hours' pay.

Historically, our national productivity shows an average increase per year of something like 2 or 3 per cent. If money wages are to increase each year by an average of 10 per cent, what must be the result? There would certainly have to be an increase in costs and in the price level. Such an inflationary spiral might be self-perpetuating. Wages would chase prices and then push prices up

Work stoppages reached their peak just after the war:

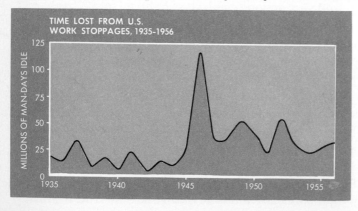

TIME LOST FROM U.S.
WORK STOPPAGES, 1935-1956

MILLIONS OF MAN-DAYS IDLE

125
100
75
50
25
0

1935   1940   1945   1950   1955

Fig. 4. While time lost from strikes is measured in millions of man-days, as a per cent of total labor-days worked it never has reached 1½ per cent, and has averaged less than ½ of 1 per cent. (Source: U.S. Department of Labor.)

still further. It is this problem that worried people in the years 1945–1947 and in 1950–1951. However, 1951–1955 turned out to be one of those periods in which, contrary to opinions of pessimistic economists, we had both high employment *and* stable consumer prices! As we face the 1960's, the peril of "wage costs pushing up prices" is again a popular topic.

▶ **CONCLUSION**

We shall study the general wage-price problem in later chapters. At this point a warning is in order: One must guard against exaggerating the universality of the postwar wage rounds; many industries and jobs did not share in the general increase. Also one must guard against assuming that the primary direction of causation was "Wage increases cause price rises" rather than "Price rises and inflationary money spending cause wage increases."[1]

Have unions really raised wages? Is collective bargaining consistent with the "laws of supply and demand"? What are some of the consequences if unions do succeed in their avowed purpose of raising wages?

These questions cannot be answered until after we have studied the basic principles governing national income, its distribution, prices, and production. Their final discussion must therefore be reserved for Parts Two, Three, and Four of this book and most particularly Chapter 28 on economics of wages.

SUMMARY

1. Labor unions have come to occupy an important role in the American economy, in terms both of membership and influence. Their present structure is in three layers: (*a*) local unions, (*b*) national unions, and (*c*) federation of unions (AFL-CIO) , the first two being the most important.

2. Once a union has been recognized by an NLRB election as the exclusive bargaining agent, management and labor representatives meet together to negotiate a contract fixing wage rates, work conditions, productivity standards, degree of union recognition, seniority rights, grievance procedures, etc.

3. By the 1880's, the typical American pattern of federated, nonpolitical, gradualistic business unionism had been established. Since 1933, the CIO and finally the AFL have modified the pattern in the direction of *industrial* unionization of whole mass-production industries rather than relying solely upon *craft unionization* of skilled workers.

---

[1] Many economists, by no means friendly to unions, believe the latter was true in the years after 1945. They think that the aftermath of World War II plus the cold war created a great excess of money-spending power; this pushed up prices of farm and factory products; and then wages followed. They think that without unions, prices and wages would still have risen. In my judgment there may be truth in both views of causation.

4. Right up until the middle 1930's there was bitter opposition to unions. But finally the pendulum of government swung in support of collective bargaining, and since the Wagner Act (1935) most manufacturing industries have become unionized. The result has been less violence, but still vigorous collective bargaining between the opposing groups. By 1947 Congress felt that the Wagner Act was one-sided in favor of labor and passed the Taft-Hartley Act to define illegal collective bargaining practices of unions.

5. A major postwar problem has been the relation of wage increases to the price level. If patterns are established of "successive rounds of general wage increases" that go far beyond the 2 or 3 per cent yearly increase in productivity, then the price level is almost sure to rise in an inflationary manner.

QUESTIONS FOR DISCUSSION

1. How extensive is union membership? When did unions grow most?

2. Describe the structure of America's organized labor. Describe the layers of the union movement. Which are the largest unions in your locality?

3. Historically, American unions have followed the principles associated with Samuel Gompers. What are these? How have they been modified since 1933 and the rise of the CIO? How do you explain the fact that American labor has not been more active in politics along the lines of European socialists?

4. Jot down tactics used by labor and management when in bitter opposition. Define briefly such terms as yellow-dog contract, scab, lockout, etc.

5. Give some contrasting examples of peaceful collective bargaining.

6. Describe the swing of the pendulum in the attitude of legislatures and courts toward organized labor before the Wagner Act and after.

7. Discuss the important provisions of the Taft-Hartley Act and recent laws.

8. What has been the history of "protective reform legislation"?

9. Should policemen have the right to strike? Postmen? Milkmen? Anyone?

10. "Wage rates tend to be sticky as far as downward moves are concerned." Why should this be increasingly true?

11. Review your understanding of the following concepts:

national and local union
AFL-CIO federation
UAW, UMW, NLRB
collective bargaining, arbitration
Knights, IWW
*business versus revolutionary
   unionism*
craft versus industrial unions

strike, lockout, work stoppage
boycott, injunction
Wagner and Taft-Hartley Acts
closed shop
wage "rounds"
wage-cost push on prices
productivity

9 PERSONAL FINANCE AND SOCIAL SECURITY

Flowers and kisses are all very well, but a diamond ring lasts forever.
ANITA LOOS, *Gentlemen Prefer Blondes*

Not everyone will come into first-hand contact with the workings of the gold standard or of federal reserve banking policy; but everyone will encounter, each day of his life, the problem of getting income, spending it upon consumption goods, and placing his savings so as to afford maximum protection against the vicissitudes of life.

▶ **BUDGETARY EXPENDITURE PATTERNS**

No two families spend their money in exactly the same way. But statistics show that there is a predictable regularity—on the average—in the way people allocate their expenditures on food, clothing, and other major items. Literally thousands of budgetary investigations have been made of the ways that people at different levels of income spend their money; and there is remarkable agreement on the general, qualitative patterns of behavior.[1] What are they?

Poor families must, of course, spend their incomes largely on the necessities of life: food, shelter, and in lesser degree, clothing. As income increases, expenditure on many food items goes up. People eat more and eat better. They shift away from the cheap, bulky carbohydrates to the more expensive meats and proteins—and to milk, fruit, and vegetables.

However, there are limits to the amount of extra money that people will spend on food when their incomes rise. Consequently, the percentage impor-

[1] These behavior patterns have been called "Engel's Laws," after the nineteenth-century Prussian statistician Ernst Engel (not to be confused with Marx's friend Friedrich Engels) who first observed them.

tance of food expenditure declines as income increases. (Actually, there are a few cheap, but filling, items such as potatoes whose consumption decreases absolutely with income increase. These are called "inferior goods.")

After you get out of the very poorest income class, your proportion of income spent on shelter is pretty constant for a wide range. This is expressed in a familiar rule of thumb: One week's salary should cover one month's expenditure on rent and house utilities. The other rule of thumb—that you should pay for a house less than 2 years' income—has a hollow ring these days.

Expenditure on clothing, recreation, and automobiles increases more than in proportion to income, until the very high incomes are reached. Of course, luxury items, by definition, increase in greater proportion than income; and in many ways, as we shall see in a moment, saving is the greatest luxury of all, particularly at very high incomes.

The above empirical generalizations are illustrated in Figures 1 and 2.

One warning: The average behavior of consumption expenditure does change fairly regularly with income. But averages do not tell all the story. Within the same income class there is considerable spreading out around the average. The Joneses are heavy eaters and live in a crowded apartment; the Smiths, with the same income, pay much more for rent but don't drive a car.

▶ REGIONAL DIFFERENCES IN THE COST OF LIVING

Of course, prices and living conditions vary throughout the United States. House rents are cheaper in the country than in the city, and they used to be cheaper on the West Coast than in the East. The postwar period has lessened

Family expenditures show regular income patterns:

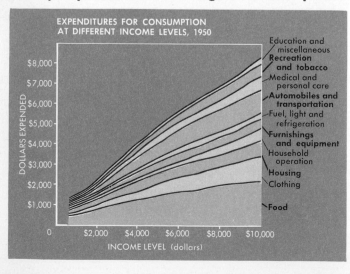

Fig. 1. Careful sampling of urban families verifies the importance of income as a determinant of consumption spending. (Source: Bureau of Labor Statistics, University of Pennsylvania Wharton School Consumption Study.)

The proportion spent on necessities falls as income grows, but on luxuries the proportion rises:

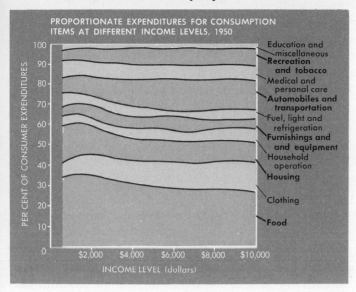

Fig. 2. Food and other necessities grow less than in proportion to income. Recreation and other luxuries grow greater than in proportion. (Source: Bureau of Labor Statistics, University of Pennsylvania Wharton School Consumption Study.)

the regional differentials in the cost of living, primarily by raising prices in the previously cheaper places more than in the large Northern cities.

However, even before the war people were prone to exaggerate the differences in the cost of living between North and South and between different cities. We can deduce from careful studies by the Labor Department that differences between the cost of living in large cities are now relatively minor.

Which do you think are the most expensive cities? New York? Philadelphia? You're wrong if you do. It turns out that San Francisco and Houston top the list. New York, along with Kansas City, is today a low-price city. The low cities are about 5 per cent below the average city, and the expensive cities are about the same above. So the price spread between top and bottom is 10 per cent at most.[1]

How are these cost-of-living measurements made? The statistical difficulties in constructing an index number of prices are considerable. First, a careful study must furnish accurate reports on actual price quotations. Then if *all* prices in Kansas City were exactly 91 per cent of all prices in San Francisco, we could assert with confidence that the cost of living in Kansas City was 91, as compared to San Francisco as a base of 100. But some prices in Kansas City are only 65 per cent of the corresponding San Francisco price, and a few will be 150 per cent. The statistician, therefore, must take *weighted* averages of the different price comparisons. The Bureau of Labor Statistics does this by care-

[1] Don't think the high-cost places pay compensatingly higher average wages. It turns out they don't. Statistics show many of the expensive places have lower-than-average money wages.

fully compiling a list of items necessary in each community for a given *equivalent standard of living,* and then reckoning the total cost of such goods.

Great care must be taken in doing this. For example, in the South, where the climate is warmer, a special allowance must be made in estimating heating and building costs. Even more difficult, and almost insoluble, problems arise from the fact that there are differences in taste between South and North: pork versus beef, and bourbon versus rye. However, as best he can, the statistician tries to measure the different costs of an equivalent standard of living.

This is where the man in the street may go wrong. He says to his wife, "Let's take that job teaching physics at Dixie Polytech. Of course, it only pays what we're now getting, but $6,000 there is like $10,000 here." It is true that people live on less in the rural South, but primarily because many live less well.

However, to the extent that we are worried about the problem of "keeping up with the Joneses," it is quite possible that a family in the South with $6,000 a year will feel happier than a comparable family in the North; because in the South there will be relatively fewer families with higher incomes. This helps to explain why farmers, small-town people, and Negroes are more thrifty at any given level of income than white city dwellers. A Negro with $9,000 a year income in Columbus, Ohio, may be as near the top of the income pyramid of his group as is a white person on Park Avenue in New York City with a $40,000 income, and both may save about the same percentage of their income. (Harvard's Duesenberry and bohemia's Veblen have stressed this point.)

▶ FAMILY DIFFERENCES IN THE COST OF LIVING

The same statistical budgetary data throw light on the age-old question: "Can two live as cheaply as one?" According to the Bureau of Labor Statistics the answer is, No. Even if one works in the home, it costs a married couple about $10\%_{70}$ times what it costs a single person to live, on the average. There are advantages, however; and this is still less than it costs two to live singly.

Each child in the family inevitably adds to the cost of living. Thus, if it costs 70 to live alone and 100 to live with a wife, it will cost about 130 with one child, 160 with two, and so forth, for each additional child. (Of course, as the number of children increase, some "economies of scale and spreading the overhead" set in.) Studies of poor families with many children turn up a surprising fact: large families spend a smaller fraction of their income on housing than do small families! Why? Because they must spend so much for food.

Canada,[1] England, France, Sweden, and other governments have begun to give "family allowances" every month, the amount varying with the number of children in the family. This is done both for humanitarian reasons and to try

---

[1] The Canadian government pays family allowances of $5 to $8 per month for each child, depending upon its age.

to stimulate population growth. It is easy to see why the government, rather than private industry, must make these payments; for if firms had to pay higher wages to men with large families, they might alter their hiring policy in favor of ancient bachelors and against the heads of large families.

▶ **THE BACKWARD ART OF SPENDING MONEY?**

In spending their money, people act with regularity but not always with rationality. For example, people with incomes of around $3,000 per year are known to spend less upon medical care than modern science and prudence would seem to suggest is necessary. Furthermore, what people consider to be absolute necessities consist to a large degree not of *physiological necessities,* but of *conventional social desirabilities.* Almost for a joke a tall American economist once calculated how much it would cost him to buy *most cheaply* a yearly diet with all the health ingredients (vitamins A, B, C, D, etc., iron, calcium, etc., etc.) recommended by the National Research Council. The cost per year (!) was $39 in 1939 and $57 in 1944. (In 1958, perhaps $75?) Of course the diet consisted of nothing so expensive as bread or potatoes, but rather of wheat flour, cabbage, lima beans, kidneys, and not much else. Most of us would bitterly resent such an unpalatable and monotonous diet—just as dogs, if conditioned to eat fish alone, will almost starve before touching the best steak.

A corporation buying a great quantity of a commodity tests carefully for quality and makes sure that it buys from the cheapest source. Not so the average consumer, who is an amateur when it comes to spending money. He pays 25 cents for 6 aspirin tablets when he could buy 100 equally good aspirin (monoaceticacidester of salicylic acid) tablets for 19 cents. Scarcely less money is spent on advertising the cigarettes he buys than is spent on their tobacco content. The cost of the ingredients in a $2 lipstick is exactly the same as that in a 25-cent one, and time and time again disinterested laboratory testers have been unable to detect any differences between them at all. A can of Campbell's soup sells for 17 cents in a chain grocery store and next door at a little "independent" for 20 cents. A large glass of Coca-Cola contains less than twice the amount of a small one. Until forbidden to by law, coffee companies would sell their "first-grade" coffees under a different label at lower prices; and a well-known brand-name tire used to be sold at a considerable reduction in price by a big mail-order and department store under its own brand name.

The consumer's health as well as his pocketbook is at stake. When Upton Sinclair published the novel, *The Jungle,* showing what conditions were like in the Chicago stockyards early in this century, many people stopped eating meat. Against the heavy opposition of business interests, Congress passed pure food and drug acts, but an American is still free to poison himself with hair dyes and to go to an early grave as a result of taking patent medicines and being his own doctor. The Federal Trade Commission prosecutes corporations indulging in extreme forms of misrepresentation in advertising, with the result that greater reliance is placed upon innuendo than upon direct statement. (For example, the label on a famous women's compound now says, "This preparation is recommended for those ailments to which it is adapted.")

A characteristic feature of our era is advertising. With our daily news and our Sunday pleasure rides, we are fed large doses of carefully selected descriptions of various products. A sizable amount of the nation's creative talent and of its paper and vacuum tubes are devoted to sales promotion.

Defenders of advertising claim for it many economic advantages. Useful information can be brought to the public; mass-production markets are created; and as a by-product of advertising expense we have a free press, a choice of many radio and television programs, and thick magazines. So the argument goes. On the other side, much advertising is self-canceling and adds little to the consumer's valid information. And for each minute of symphony music, there is half an hour of "soap opera." The situation would be the more debatable were it not for the surprising fact, turned up by the Gallup poll, that many people seem to like advertising. They don't believe all they hear, but they can't help remembering it just the same.

Actually, there are some signs that the American consumer is becoming pretty professional these days. Item: prodigious growth of cut-price supermarkets that sell us groceries at an extremely low markup. Item: marked growth of "discount houses" that sell durable appliances far below "list prices." Item: mushrooming of the "do-it-yourself" movement, whereby we quit work on Saturdays and paint our own rooms. Only observe a young couple about to buy a high-fidelity phonograph set. Note their hours of careful study and field work. What Arabian master of the art of buying and selling can match their professional competence? What laboratory scientist, their meticulous zeal?

▶ THE PROPENSITY TO SAVE AND PROPENSITY TO CONSUME

It is a matter of common observation that rich men save more than poor men, not only in absolute amounts but also in percentage amounts. The very poor are unable to save at all. Instead they "dissave"; *i.e.*, spend more every year than they earn, the difference being covered by going into debt or using up previously accumulated savings.

Table 1 gives data on saving and consumption that have been adapted from an official 1950 family study. Column (2) shows the net saving that accompanies each level of disposable income. The "break-even point," where the family neither saves nor dissaves, instead consuming all its income, falls at $4,000. Below this, as at $3,000 or $2,000, they actually consume more than their income. They dissave. (See the −$110 and −$170 data.) Above $4,000 they begin to do positive saving.

Most saving is done by families with incomes above the average:

Disposable income after taxes (1)	Net saving (+) or dissaving (−) (2)	Consumption (3)
$ 2,000	$ −170	$2,170
3,000	−110	3,110
4,000	0	4,000
5,000	+150	4,850
6,000	+400	5,600
7,000	+760	6,240
8,000	+1,170	6,830
9,000	+1,640	7,360
10,000	+2,150	7,850

Table 1. Postwar propensity of families to save and consume. The break-even point at which people cease to dissave and begin to do positive saving is here shown as $4,000. How much of each extra dollar do people around this income devote to extra consumption? How much to extra saving?

Column (3) shows the consumption pattern at each income level—the so-called "propensity to consume." Since each dollar of income is divided between the part consumed and the remaining part saved, Columns (3) and (2) are not independent: they must always exactly add up to Column (1). (Check that they do.)

In Part Two we'll find ourselves interested not simply in the total figures of saving and consumption, but in the *extra* saving and consumption that each *extra* dollar of income brings. Thus, as income goes from $4,000 to $5,000, the extra $1,000 of income is divided between $850 of extra consumption and $150 of extra saving—split up 85 and 15 per cent, so to speak. (Where did these numbers come from? You get them from $4,850 minus $4,000 and $150 minus $0. And verify that the division between consumption and saving of extra income dollars beyond $5,000 is respectively 75 and 25 per cent, 68 and 32 per cent, . . . etc. Does it seem reasonable to you that richer people will consume a little less of each extra income dollar than will poorer?[1])

Family propensity-to-save and propensity-to-consume patterns have been rather stable. Workers have long saved less than farmers and less than the self-employed. Later when we come to the discussion in Part Two of how saving and investment determine the level of national income and employment, we shall see how crucially important are (1) the propensity-to-save schedule relating saving and income, and its twin brother (2) the propensity-to-consume schedule relating consumption and income.

---

[1] Students at first find it hard to understand that, even when family income is below the break-even point and saving is negative, nonetheless each *extra* income dollar goes partly into positive extra saving and partly into positive extra consumption. Don't you believe it? To convince yourself, compare row 2 of Table 1 with row 1. Adding $1,000 to $2,000 of income gives $3,000. The extra income makes consumption go from $2,170 to $3,110, a gain of $940 with $60 of extra saving.

▶ THE WAR AND POSTWAR ACCUMULATION OF FAMILY ASSETS

The difference between your income and what you consume is your (algebraic) net saving. If you spend less than your income, your net saving is positive and you are adding to your assets and/or reducing your liabilities. *I.e.*, you are adding to your so-called "net worth." If you are spending more than your income, your net saving is negative. You are dissaving. You are reducing your net worth.

Let's investigate how you go about spending more than your income. You may of course spend out of previously hoarded cash. Or you may draw on your balance at the bank, either from a checking or savings account. Or you may cash in a government savings bond. Or, if you are among the relatively few with marketable bonds and stocks, you may ask your broker to sell enough of your securities to finance a trip to California or a new car.

As a result of the war, the American people accumulated more savings assets than ever before in our history. During the war years most families had abnormally high money incomes; but they were able to spend only at a normal rate on nondurable consumer goods, and at a very depressed rate on durable goods such as autos and radios. The difference between income and consumption piled up in the form of war bonds, savings accounts, insurance policies, the paying off of previous debts, and finally the holding of paper money and checking deposits. American individuals and businesses came out of the war with about 250 billion dollars (1/4 trillion!) of liquid wealth—almost half in government bonds, the rest in checking and savings accounts and currency.

This total of liquid wealth represents a threefold increase as compared to the prewar, so that Americans on the average now have a nest egg equal to about a year's income. This sum came into existence largely because of one factor—the great wartime increase in the federal government's public debt. (We'll see in Chapter 18 that these assets in the hands of the public are just the other side of the social balance sheet which shows the government's liability. If the public debt is a completely bad thing, then these family savings are essentially a bad thing; if these family savings are a good thing, then the public debt cannot be as completely black as it is often painted.) And as the postwar years have rolled by, average families have been doing more positive saving: they've added to their store of wealth; at the same time they've been shifting their assets away from government bonds and toward higher yielding assets.

In reality there is no such thing as the *average* family. The total of liquid assets is far from being divided equally among all families. Fortunately, we don't have to rely on guesses concerning the distribution of liquid wealth. At the request of the Federal Reserve Board, the Consumers' Survey Center at the University of Michigan makes careful statistical surveys of the distribution of savings. In the 1957 *Federal Reserve Bulletin*, their surveys showed that a quarter of all families (or "spending units") had no liquid savings at all: they had no savings accounts, no checking accounts, no government bonds. Over half the families had less than $500 of savings. On the other hand, the 10 per cent of families with the highest savings averaged more than $5,000 of liquid assets apiece and had two-thirds of the total liquid assets. The statistics did turn up one surprising result: Within any one income class, it appears that a small proportion of people tend to do much of the accumulating.

However, it still remains true as a broad generalization that the American people are better able to afford to make down payments on new houses and to buy new cars than ever before in history.

▶ HOW PEOPLE BORROW MONEY

Let's briefly explore the channels open to people who must borrow. Up until the last 20 years or so, poor people as a rule fell into the hands of unlicensed loan sharks; they still do, in some states which have not passed a uniform small-loan act. These loan sharks charge interest at anywhere from a low of 120 per cent per year to about 1,200 per cent per year! Not 12 per cent, 12 *hundred* per cent! It is not uncommon to hear of cases where a man borrowed $20 in 1939 because of illness, and then paid $2.25 every week until 1948, or $1,053 in all and at a rate of 600 per cent interest per year. The curse of the poor is their poverty. They go into debt because of a lack of money, and they cannot get out for the same reason. Moreover, the last thing that a loan shark wants is to have his loan paid back. He will occasionally use violence, but more often he blackmails his victim by threatening to tell his boss or wife. The borrower never realizes that legally he need only refuse to pay, and the loan shark will never dare bring the matter to court.

There is only one way to remedy this despicable situation. Paradoxically, it is by passing a small-loan act which *raises* the legal interest rate that can be charged to far above the 6 per cent maximum set by the old-time usury laws. For honest personal-finance companies cannot stay in business unless they can charge much higher rates than this on small loans. Such loans involve an element of risk and much costly red tape and supervision. A few states, primarily in the South and in the Rocky Mountain region, still have not adopted such sensible uniform small-loan legislation—primarily because of a campaign by the loan sharks of legislative bribing, blackmail, and demagogic appeal to protect the public against paying more than 6 per cent interest.

In the better regulated states, a person can borrow from a licensed personal finance company such a small sum as $250 and hope to pay it off in 12 installments at a cost of about 36 per cent interest per year, with no other fees. If the company he works for has a credit union, he can probably borrow there at about 12 per cent per annum. If he is willing to put up some article of jewelry, he can borrow about three-fourths of its auction sale value at a better pawn shop, paying about 40 per cent per year interest.

If his local bank will make him a small personal loan, repayable in installments, he will probably pay around 12 per cent per year for it, unless he is
known to be a very good risk. If he buys his automobile or furniture on installment credit from a reliable concern, he will probably pay something like 15
per cent interest per year. If he has a life-insurance policy with a paid-up
value, he can borrow on it from the insurance company at 5 or 6 per cent per
year. If he has listed securities or government bonds, he can make a collateral
loan on them at around 5 per cent.

These charges vary from region to region and from institution to institution, being generally lowest in Northeastern large cities and lowest for large
short-term loans. Thus, a dealer in New York City can obtain a large-scale loan
on *marketable* government bonds at around 3½ per cent per year.

All the above interest rates are expressed in terms of the average *unpaid*
balance. When a man thinks he is paying only 12 per cent per year on an installment loan, he is probably really paying 24 per cent, or twice as much.
Let's see why. Suppose he is to pay $112 per month for 10 installments to pay
off a $1,000 loan, the extra $12 being the monthly interest charge. Is he then
paying an interest charge of $12 per month on a principal of $1,000—only 1
per cent per month? The answer is, No, he is really paying about 2 per cent
per month or 24 per cent per year on his true *average unpaid balance*. The
average amount of his indebtedness during the period is not $1,000 but only
one-half that much, $500, because he is paying off the debt through the year.
Interest of $12 per month on $500 is about 24 per cent per year.

Few people realize this, and many are swindled by unethical dealers. Moreover, some people buy on installment credit, paying high rates of interest, at
the same time that they have bonds or money in the bank earning only 3 or 4
per cent per year. They do this either out of ignorance or because they wish
to make themselves save out of current income by having to make installment
payments. Good advice for most people who must borrow or buy on installments: First try a local bank or the credit union where you work.

The rise of consumer credit following World War II was tremendous. By
1958, it had grown to over 40 billion dollars (largely made up of installment
credit and charge accounts). This was a fivefold increase over the prewar.
Still, income too has risen—particularly income above the necessity level—
and people have assets to show for much of their debt. So it is not surprising
that few consumer loans turned sour during recent prosperous years.

▶ TO HOLD GOVERNMENT BONDS OR NOT TO HOLD?

Let's turn now to the more cheerful question of what people should do with
their accumulated savings. A few idiots, timid souls, or criminals hold their
money in the form of small bills kept in their stockings or rolled up in the
window shades. Some buy diamonds. More normal people ordinarily use

savings accounts: there they earn 2 or 3 per cent per year in commercial banks; and 3 or 4 per cent in federal savings and loan or building and loan societies.

Some people keep part of their past savings in United States savings bonds. These now earn $3\frac{1}{4}$ per cent interest per year. You can buy them directly out of your pay check under the payroll saving plan, or at any bank. They are issued in multiples of $25 and are registered in the name of one or two co-owners, or one owner and a beneficiary. As they are nontransferable, they can be neither sold nor borrowed upon. Each $25 face-value bond costs $18.75, and its face value is paid in full in just under 9 years. It is redeemable at any bank upon proper identification within 60 days after issue in accordance with a fixed scale of redemption values. These values are arranged so that the longer you hold the bonds the higher their yield; therefore, if you have to cash in part of your bonds prior to maturity, always cash in the *newest* ones first.

In the late 1950's people have been cashing in more bonds than they have been buying. "The ads say $3 will get you $4," they grumble. "What the ads don't say is that $4 buys a lot less today than $3 did 9 years ago. Those bonds are a swindle! Their *real* rate of interest in terms of *real purchasing power* is negative, not $3\frac{1}{4}$ per cent." A valid point? Yes, in part, in view of recent price rises. But don't forget that the same negative interest rate is what you've been getting on your bank accounts, your hoards of cash, and any other assets except common stocks and real estate.

▶ BUYING EQUITY SECURITIES OR COMMON STOCKS

People with sizable assets will not put all their eggs in one basket. They'll aim at a more diversified portfolio of securities such as the $100,000 holdings of a New England widow shown in Table 2.

What would an expert say? He'd admit 4.38 per cent is a good yield. These days he'd think that half in common stocks and half in bonds and preferred was not too daring. Should inflation strike, her common stocks would probably give her something of a hedge, since they'd probably rise in price. And perhaps she already has made capital gains on her portfolio: she can sell today for more than she originally paid. (American universities, which used to be afraid of common stocks, now put more than half their money in such equities; Wesleyan and Trinity have even dared put more than 80 per cent in commons.)

The expert would say the widow is banking on America's remaining prosperous. And unless she is quite expert, or has good guidance, should she be investing her own money? Shouldn't she (like millions of others these days) rather buy shares in an investment mutual fund—a so-called "open-end investment trust" that will let anyone at any time buy at current market value a proportionate share in its holdings of some 100 different securities? This will usually give her a stake in some "growth industries" as oil, gas, and chemicals. It will also give her a slightly lower return. Why? Because unless she's knowing

A balanced portfolio helps avoid putting all your eggs in one basket:

Table 2. Widow's $100,000 portfolio, 1957. Should more be put into fund?

Security	Value	1957 earnings	Yield, per cent
Government bonds, Series E	$ 10,000	$ 325	
General Telephone Corp. 4½ per cent (due in 1977)	10,000	450	
Consolidated Edison 4½ per cent (due in 1972)	10,000	450	
Total bonds	$ 30,000	$1,225	4.08
General Mills 5 per cent preferred	10,000	500	
Chesapeake and Ohio cumulative convertible 3½ per cent preferred	10,000	350	
Total Preferred	$ 20,000	$ 850	4.25
American Tel. & Tel. common	20,000	1,025	
Firestone Tire common	10,000	293	
General Motors common	10,000	475	
Pacific Gas & Electric common	5,000	245	
Tri Continental ("closed end" fund) common	5,000	272	
Total common stock	$ 50,000	$2,310	4.62
Portfolio total	$100,000	$4,385	4.385

enough to buy a "no-loading" fund, she will have to pay some 8 per cent load-ing charge as a salesman's commission. But note her investments will be run by experts (for which she'll be paying an additional, quite reasonable, annual charge of about ½ of 1 per cent of asset value).

Careful studies by the New York Stock Exchange and the Brookings Institu-tion reported that less than 9 million Americans own an appreciable amount of stocks. As people forget 1929 and realize that *over the long pull* stocks have done better than bonds or bank accounts, this may change.

▶ ECONOMICS OF HOME OWNERSHIP

The postwar period has witnessed a great building boom. During the depres-sion and war years a backlog of needed housing stored up. During and after the war, an unusually large number of marriages took place. With income and employment high, and in view of the difficulty in finding a rent-controlled house, many families wished to invest in home ownership. With labor and material costs high and in view of the limited technological advance in this backward industry, new and old homes tend to be priced today at more than twice their prewar price.[1]

[1] About an eighth of a home's cost goes for land (half this for improvements). The rest divides up almost evenly between labor and materials. To carry a $20,000 home, you'll need

Owning one's own home is not necessarily always a good investment, although it is usually an interesting hobby. Aside from the upkeep of a house, the most important costs are not the physical wearing out of the house but rather the deterioration and obsolescence of the neighborhood. These risks would not be so great were it not for the chance of a depression in real-estate values as a result of business slump, overspeculation, or overexpansion of building.

In decades of rising prices, these risks have been less. Because of higher incomes, larger families, and desire to move toward the suburbs, more than 60 per cent of our families now own (and owe on) their own homes. This has never been true in any other time or advanced economy.

▶ BUYING LIFE INSURANCE

Aside from government bonds, bank accounts, and homes, the only savings of most people are in the form of life insurance. This comes in three main forms: *group insurance* (provided, as the name implies, for a whole group of employees of institutions), so-called *industrial life insurance,* and finally so-called *ordinary life insurance.*

The first kind is gaining in popularity and usually represents an advantageous form of insurance, especially when the employer pays for all of it.

Industrial insurance refers to a special kind of insurance policy sold usually to relatively low-income families. Customarily an agent will sell you a nickel-a-week (or larger) policy without a medical health examination. He simply satisfies himself from observation and neighborhood reputation that you are not in bad health. Instead of mailing in premium payments once a year, you can pay small installments at the local insurance office; or your neighborhood agent will make regular calls at intervals, collecting a few nickels and dimes at each call. Just as you expect to pay more for milk delivered to your house, you naturally would expect to have to pay more for industrial insurance than for ordinary life insurance. Especially for the poor, who need insurance but who, experience shows, are not likely otherwise to buy it, industrial life insurance has a legitimate role to perform.

The type of insurance we shall primarily consider here is ordinary life insurance. This comes in a variety of different forms, the principal ones being (1) term insurance, (2) straight life, and (3) endowment plan.

Term insurance. Term insurance, which is not very popular in practice, is

---

at least a 20 per cent down payment; and your mortgage payments (6 per cent interest and 20-year amortization) plus taxes plus maintenance will run almost $200 per month. That doesn't count heat and light or phone. Does this seem high? Experts say you should have more than $10,000 income to carry this. Figure almost twice as much for a $40,000 house. (In borrowing to buy a house, these days you'll find it impossible to get a 4½ per cent Veterans Administration mortgage. Even a 5¼ per cent FHA mortgage will be hard to find. So you may have to pay 6 per cent, 7 per cent, or more—indeed, out West some have recently paid up to 25 per cent on second mortgages!)

the easiest to understand. Let's suppose that 100,000 men of age 35 each sign up for $1,000 of insurance for a term of 1 year. Mortality statistics show that a definite percentage of them will die within the year, say 1 per cent, or 1,000 men. The company will have to pay out to widows and beneficiaries, therefore, 1,000 × $1,000 or 1 million dollars. It must charge each thirty-five-year-old man, therefore, slightly more than $10 as his insurance premium. The next year it begins all over again, but of course as the men get older the cost of the insurance will gradually rise. Under term insurance, each year stands on its own legs, so to speak, and there is no need for the company to accumulate large saving reserves. In fact, buying term insurance involves no saving for the future at all. On the other hand, it gives you, while young and with a growing family, the maximum possible insurance protection in case of death.

Straight life insurance. Under straight life insurance, all the men who join at the age of 35 agree to pay a *constant* yearly premium until they die; this premium is naturally higher for people who join at 35 than for those joining at 34 or 30. This constant premium is set so that at first they are overpaying, on the average, for their insurance; *i.e.,* the company will begin by paying out to the whole group of thirty-five-year-olds less than it collects, the difference being invested at interest in bonds and mortgages. Late in life, the steady constant premium is less than the true insurance cost for the group, the difference coming out of the previously accumulated assets. By the time everyone in the group is 100 and dead, all the assets will have been used up.

Figure 3 compares renewable-term and straight life insurance for a man who joins at 35 and lives to be 80.

Endowment plan. Finally, an endowment plan policy provides a still larger element of saving than of insurance coverage. Under a 20-year endowment policy, the thirty-five-year-old man agrees to pay in a high constant premium for 20 years, after which time, at the age of 55, he will receive the whole face value of the policy even though he has not died. Thus endowment insurance is a combination of saving and insurance. Provided that it is not allowed to lapse prior to the end of the 20-year period, endowment insurance is a good thing for anyone who wants to make himself save regularly. Under it, he will not receive a higher rate of return than he could get for himself by doing what the insurance company primarily does anyway (*i.e.,* by placing his savings regularly in government bonds or other securities), but he'll be getting expert placement of his money.

For more details the student may be referred to his local agent. He will find that in practice each company's policy differs slightly in some provision from that of other companies, so that he will hardly know how to decide which is the best buy. The problem is complicated further by the fact that most "mutual" companies deliberately aim toward the side of overconservatism and "overcharge" their policyholders; then at the end of the year they pay back

Straight life insurance charges steady premiums, involving net saving in youth and net dissaving in old age:

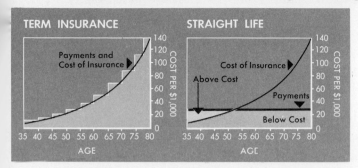

Fig. 3. Term insurance is on an actuarial pay-as-you-go basis, starting low but with annual cost rising sharply as you grow older and subject to higher current death risk. Straight life involves constant annual premiums which at first exceed current actuarial costs, the difference being invested at compound interest. Later, when actuarial costs exceed the premiums, the assets accumulated are gradually used up. (Source: *Public Affairs Pamphlet 62.*)

part of the overcharge in so-called "dividends." Still, according to the experts, policies of the various companies differ considerably in their true net cost, so that a little study of the problem and shopping around are worth while. Furthermore, in states like Massachusetts or New York, there are some advantages and disadvantages to buying Savings Bank Life Insurance at a bank. However, because life insurance is mostly "sold to people and not bought," the majority of the people will continue to buy from commercial companies. And the industry points out that insurance agents are sources of estate-planning advice that few amateurs can afford to do without.

► **SOCIAL SECURITY**

In 1937, the Social Security Act went into effect to help protect the American people against economic want resulting from old age or unemployment. Despite dire warnings at the time, the system has worked very well, and now both the Republican and the Democratic parties vie to extend it.

The system works simply and consists of three parts: (1) contributory old-age retirement and survivors' benefits insurance; (2) unemployment compensation insurance; and (3) old-age assistance and public welfare. Under the first two, people, as a matter of right, receive benefit payments when retired through old age or when unemployed. They don't have to go through a "needs test" to show whether they have money of their own.

Social security taxes are levied against payrolls as described in Chapter 7; so each person may be thought of as partially paying for his own benefits. However, social insurance or social security differs from private insurance in that a person may receive in benefits more than he is actuarially or mathematically entitled to on the basis of his payments. The difference is made up out of taxes and other people's contributions. The system is now placed pretty much on a pay-as-you-go basis, so that no actuarial reserves need pile up; in steps the payroll tax rates will rise to $8\frac{1}{2}$ per cent in all, as 1975 finds more people old and retired.

Under the unemployment compensation plans, set up by the states at the instigation of the federal government, payments are made into an unemployment reserve fund every week that a worker is employed. If he should be laid off, then by meeting certain requirements—such as being willing to accept any suitable job offered him by the Public Employment Exchange Office and having worked a minimum number of weeks in the period preceding his unemployment—he automatically receives a weekly unemployment compensation check whose magnitude depends upon his previous earnings and contributions. There is no humiliating "needs" test, nor are benefit payments set so high as to encourage people to remain idle. During prosperity, the unemployment reserve fund grows; during depression, when it is most needed, it is used to help support people and maintain general purchasing power.

The old-age assistance and public welfare part of the Social Security Act consists of grants-in-aid by the federal government to be used by the states to support the needy aged, blind, widowed and orphaned, physically and mentally handicapped, who themselves could not possibly contribute to their own support. The poor states receive larger relative grants than do the richer.

▶ GROWTH OF SOCIAL SECURITY

Not only is the social security system here to stay, but it is growing and being extended. Huge punch-card machines in Baltimore have made the administrative aspects of the program insignificant. Society today believes increasingly in the philosophy that the worst personal and social misfortunes result from contingencies over which the single individual has little control. In 1932 people walked the street without work; in 1929 and 1957 the same people had prosperous jobs; the answer is not wholly in them. Already annuities for widows and dependent children have been added to the social security benefits.

In 1950 the Democratic Truman Congress greatly extended the scope of social security. About 10 million new people began to be covered, and benefit payments were considerably increased. Farm labor, domestic help, and the self-employed were for the first time brought into the system, and employees of nonprofit organizations became eligible to join voluntarily.

The Republican Eisenhower administration further extended social security, bringing in 11 million more people. Among those included for the first time were self-employed farmers, ministers, and certain self-employed professionals. The rates of tax payment are now 2¼ per cent paid by employer and 2¼ per cent by employee, applied on the first $4,200 of annual wages. (The self-employed pay at a rate of 3⅜ per cent on the first $4,200 of earnings.)

Benefit payments have been raised so that their new range is $30 to $200 per month rather than the original $10 to $85. Retirement payments are made to a qualified man over sixty-five, and to his widow if she is over sixty-two or still has children under eighteen. Working women can now retire at sixty-two at 80 per cent benefits; and wives of qualified individuals become eligible for such benefits at sixty-two. Benefits for total disability have now been added; and there are various miscellaneous benefits and lump-sum payments paid when a worker dies. The exact formula for figuring retirement benefits is quite complicated, but its general nature is as follows: A worker's own benefit depends primarily upon his average monthly wage and is more generously reckoned on the first $110 of monthly wages; for each extra year that he has been covered there is a slight further increase in his primary benefits. After his benefit has been reckoned, his wife will receive, after age sixty-two, an extra 50 per cent of his benefits; his widow will receive, after sixty-two, 75 per cent; his surviving dependent children will receive a certain fraction too. A private insurance company would have to charge tens of thousands of dollars for such generous annuities and privileges.

It is one of the great advantages of a pay-as-you-go social security system that it rests on the general tax capacity of the nation; if hyperinflation wiped out all private insurance and savings, social security could nonetheless start all over again, little the poorer.

Will payments for sickness and disability and a comprehensive public health and hospital program be governmentally introduced in this next generation? There's no guessing; all this remains very controversial. But private health insurance is sure to grow. In 1931, many medical associations strongly disapproved and fought against the systems of private health and hospitalization insurance such as Blue Cross or Blue Shield. Today they are among the strongest supporters of these systems.

Other countries, such as Britain and Scandinavia, have gone much further in the direction of a so-called welfare state than has the United States. Thus, in Britain a program of "cradle to grave" social security provides aid to a child's family at his birth and family allowances while he is a minor, gives him virtually feeless medical and dental care all his life, and helps provide him with income when unemployed, ill, or retired. After he is dead, the state helps to defray his funeral expenses and support his survivors. Such programs have a great appeal to the electorate and are endorsed by Conservative as well as Labor governments. These programs are, of course, not costless, and the electorate must democratically decide how far it is worth while to push them in terms of their true costs.

SUMMARY

1. Patterns of family expenditure on different consumption items, such as food, clothing, shelter, and saving, are fairly regular and predictable after we make allowances for family size and regional differences in living costs.

2. The important propensity-to-consume and propensity-to-save schedules show how people spend on consumption more than their incomes at low incomes, the difference representing algebraically negative saving or dissaving. As income increases beyond the break-even point, some fraction of each extra dollar of disposable income goes into consumption and the rest into saving.

3. There are various ways in which a family can borrow, each involving widely differing rates of interest. Similarly, the ways in which a family can hold its wealth include bank accounts, government bonds, owning one's own home, marketable stocks and bonds, and the purchase of life insurance.

4. There are important differences between private and social insurance. Our social security program now provides the majority of our citizens, for the first time, a measure of protection against old age, unemployment, and physical handicaps. The program is still an expanding one.

QUESTIONS FOR DISCUSSION

1. Make up a budget for yourself or your family. What if your income were cut by 30 per cent or increased by that amount?

2. About what fraction of each extra dollar is consumed at the different income levels? Fill in a new column in Table 1.

3. Make certain assumptions about your own earnings and expenditures over the next 30 years. Draw up an investment program for yourself. Which investments would you buy if you thought that inflation was ahead? Deflation?

4. How would inflation affect private insurance? Social Security?

5. Review your understanding of the following concepts:

budget pattern

necessity and luxury

after-tax or disposable income

index number of cost of living

propensity to save

propensity to consume

fraction of extra dollars spent on consumption or on saving

net saving, dissaving, assets, liabilities, net worth

interest on unpaid balance

common stocks or equities

open-end mutual fund

industrial, ordinary, group insurance

straight life, endowment

level premium

social security or social insurance

unemployment compensation

old-age benefits

welfare payments

10 NATIONAL INCOME AND PRODUCT

The time has come, the Walrus said,
To speak of many things.
Of shoes, and ships, and sealing wax,
Of cabbages—and kings.

LEWIS CARROLL

We now turn to the chapter that is about the most important in any economics book, that on national income. "How can this be?" your father may ask. "Thirty years ago, when I was a sophomore, my text didn't even have the words 'national income' in the index. Much less a chapter."

That is true. Thirty years ago the United States government did not collect statistics on national income. We went into the Great Depression of the early 1930's having to guess from month to month where we stood.

Fortunately, as a result of the private efforts of the nonprofit National Bureau of Economic Research and a few scholars abroad, our government came around to realize the vital character of national-income statistics. Now the Department of Commerce provides us with valuable national-income figures each year, each quarter (*i.e.*, 3 months), and in some cases each month. On the day the new figures are released, the *Wall Street Journal* sells out. No well-informed observer of a country would neglect its national-income reports. That's why the United Nations tries hard to get all countries to collect such data.

▶ THE YARDSTICK OF AN ECONOMY'S PERFORMANCE

What is national income? It is the loose name we give for the money measure of the over-all annual flow of goods and services in an economy. Often we use instead of the name "national income" the equivalent name "national product" or "net national product (NNP) ."[1]

If you ask an economic historian just what the Great Depression really

[1] In a few pages we'll distinguish between net national product and gross national product, and in the Appendix we'll note the Commerce Department's peculiar use of the words "national income."

meant, his single best answer would be: "From a 1929 NNP of 95.8 billion dollars there was a drop to a 1933 NNP of 48.8 billion dollars. This halving of the money value of the flow of goods and services in the American economy caused hardship, bank failures, riots, and political turmoil."

In brief, national income or product is the final figure you arrive at when you apply the measuring rod of money to the diverse apples, oranges, and machines that any society produces.

▶ **TWO MEASURES OF NATIONAL PRODUCT: AS GOODS-FLOW OR AS EARNINGS-FLOW**

How do we measure the NNP? The general idea is simple. Figure 1 shows the circular flow of dollar spending in an economy which has no government and which has no accumulation of capital or net saving going on.

Flow-of-product approach. Each year the public consumes goods and services: goods like apples, oranges, and bread; services like manicures. The public spends dollars for these in the upper loop of Fig. 1. We add together all the dollars spent for these final goods to arrive at the total of NNP.

Thus, in our simple economy, you can easily calculate national income or product as the sum of the annual flow of goods and services: price of oranges × number of oranges + price of apples × number of apples + ··· etc.

Earnings or income approach. There is a second, equivalent way to calculate NNP in so simple an economy. Go to Fig. 1's lower loop. What is business

Net National Product is measured as flow of output or as equal flow of costs:

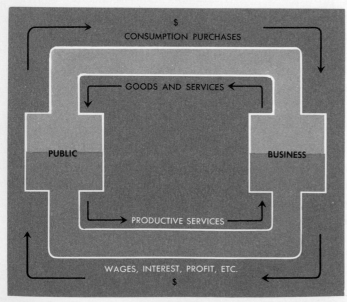

Fig. 1. In the upper loop, people spend their money on final goods: the total flow of these per year is one measure of NNP. The lower loop measures the annual flow of costs or of earnings that business pays out: with profit properly reckoned as a residual, the two measures of NNP must always be identical.

paying out there to the public? It is paying out wages, interest, rents, and profit. Why? Because these factor earnings are the *costs* of production of the flow of product.

The statistician can measure the annual flow of such factor earnings or income in the lower loop. This way he will again arrive at the NNP.

Now we have calculated NNP by the upper-loop flow-of-product approach and by the lower-loop earnings-flow approach. Which is bigger? Answer: They have to be *exactly* the same.

This identity is not obvious. Here is the reason for it, though. Do you remember that we included "profit" in the lower loop—along with wages, interest, and rents? Well, what exactly is profit? Profit is what you have left over from the sale of product (your oranges, apples, bread, and manicures) *after* you have paid off the other factor costs. *So profit automatically is the residual that takes on the size needed to make the lower-loop approach via earnings exactly match the upper-loop approach via flow of goods.*

Are you let down? Does this seem like a cheap trick, one that by virtue of its definition of profit achieves the stipulated equality between the product and earnings approaches? Well, it is a trick—the same trick that we earlier saw all accountants and bookkeepers use in getting the two sides of their accounts to balance. They call it "double-entry" bookkeeping.

And after you think about it, you'll be rather glad that the two approaches are really one: for, if the lower-loop earnings approach didn't accommodate itself to the upper-loop product approach (through the definition of profit as a residual), we could not sleep easy at night being perfectly sure that the two approaches would not some fine morning differ.

▶ To sum up: NNP or net national product is really measurable as the flow of product; but it is often convenient for the statistician to collect his statistics via the earnings approach in the lower loop. With the proper definition of profit, each approach must yield exactly the same NNP.

▶ **REAL VERSUS MONEY NATIONAL PRODUCT: USING A PRICE INDEX TO "DEFLATE"**

We see that NNP uses the measuring rod of money prices in the market to combine diverse apples, oranges, and other goods to a single total figure. But how would you like to measure with a rubber rather than a wooden yardstick —one that stretched in your hands from day to day? You wouldn't.

Well, that unfortunately is one of the problems we economists have to face when we use money as our measuring rod. We know that inflations and deflations do send most prices up or down. Or, as the economist puts it: "The value of money does change between years like 1929 and 1933."

What can be done about this? Most of the damage due to the changeability of our measuring rod we can repair by the use of an index number of prices.[1]

[1] Recall page 165's discussion of how you calculate an index number of prices.

A 1929–1933 comparison will illustrate the process by which we use a price index number to "deflate" a "current money NNP," converting it into a "real NNP in terms of dollars of unchanged 1929 purchasing power."

Table 1 gives the actual 1929 and 1933 NNP figures to the close approximations of 96 and 48 billion dollars. This shows a halving of money NNP. But the government estimates that prices of goods and services dropped on the average about 25 per cent in the depression. Using 1929 as a base of 100, the government says the 1933 price index was about 75. So our 48-billion-dollar 1933 NNP was really worth more than half of 1929's 96-billion-dollar NNP. How much more?

Table 1 divides through by the price index number to "deflate" and shows that *"real NNP" fell only to two-thirds the 1929 level:* in terms of dollars of 1929 purchasing power, it fell down to 64 billion dollars. Hence, part of the halving shown by the money NNP was due to the optical illusion of the changing price yardstick.

Figure 2 shows the history of money NNP (expressed in the actual dollars current in each historical year). For comparison, the real NNP expressed in 1956 dollars is shown. Note that part of the increase in NNP is spurious, being due to our money yardstick's price inflation of the last 25 years.

▶ **AVOIDING "DOUBLE COUNTING" OF INTERMEDIATE GOODS**

Returning to current money figures, we can go on to dispose of a problem that troubles many students. Did you wonder why the word "net" is put in the title "net national product"? Why not just use NP for "national product"?

Ignoring intermediate goods. The "net" is there to warn you against counting in bread *and also counting in the dough that goes to make the bread!* That would indeed be double counting, since the only reason we want the dough is to make the bread. Turn back to Fig. 1's two-loop diagram on page 182. You can see bread and manicures there. But you don't see any dough, or flour, or

We deflate by a price index to correct our rubber money yardstick:

Date	Money NNP (billions of current $) (1)	Index number of prices (2)	Real NNP (in billions of 1929 dollars) $(3) = \frac{(1)}{(2)} \times 100$
1929	96	100	$\frac{96}{100} \times 100 = 96$
1933	48	75	$\frac{48}{75} \times 100 = 64$

Table 1. Sample calculation of real NNP. Using column (2)'s price index, we deflate column (1) to get column (3)'s real NNP. (Riddle: can you show that 1929's real NNP was 72 billion dollars in terms of 1933 prices? Hint: with 1933 as a base, 1929's price index is $133\frac{1}{3}$.)

How rising prices spuriously inflated our Net National Product:

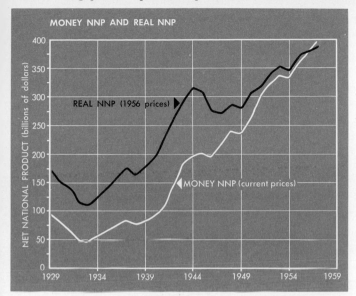

MONEY NNP AND REAL NNP

NET NATIONAL PRODUCT (billions of dollars)

REAL NNP (1956 prices)

MONEY NNP (current prices)

400
350
300
250
200
150
100
50
0

1929   1934   1939   1944   1949   1954   1959

Fig. 2. The real NNP lags in growth compared with money NNP because prices have been rising. Real NNP uses a 1956-based price index to "deflate" the money NNP to give a measure in dollars of 1956 purchasing power. (Source: U.S. Department of Commerce.)

wheat. Where are they? They are so-called intermediate products that are produced in all the stages leading up to the final bread product, and they are hidden in the block marked "business."

That is as it should be. We don't want such intermediate products to be double-counted along with final product. It was to indicate this emphasis on "net" that we use NNP and not NP.

Using "value added" to avoid double counting. Some students say, "All right. I can see that, if you are careful, your upper-loop approach to NNP will avoid including intermediate products. But I'm a little uncertain whether or not you won't find yourself in some difficulty when you use the lower-loop approach. After all, doesn't the Commerce Department gather income statements from the accounts of business firms? Won't it then be picking up what millers pay to farmers, what bakers pay to millers, and what grocers pay to bakers? Won't this result in double counting or even triple and quadruple counting of some items that go through several stages of production?"

This is a legitimate question. Fortunately we can give it a satisfactory answer. The statistician making lower-loop earnings or factor-cost measurements is always very careful to use what he calls the "value-added" approach. What does this mean?

The value-added approach refuses to include *all* the expenses shown on a business income statement into the lower-loop factor earnings. Which expenses are excluded? All purchases of materials and services from other business firms are excluded.

Example: Pepto-Glitter Co. buys electric power from the Edison Co. This expense on the Pepto income statement is *not* included in value added. Why should it be? It is not a wage payment, or an interest payment, or a rent payment, or a profit payment. In fact it is not a payment to any productive factor at all. So it never shows up in the lower loop at all. It stays inside the business block.

So it and all other such expenditures by a firm on intermediate goods are carefully subtracted from Pepto's receipts. What is left? Pepto's true value added—which is exactly the sum of its wage, interest, rent, and profit costs.[1]

Mind you, the electric power was produced by the Edison workers—and by the Edison interest, rent, and profit receivers. So don't worry that this electrical activity will get overlooked by the NNP statistician. It won't. He'll pick it up as the value added of the Edison Co. Which is as it should be: we want to count it in once, not twice or three times.

Table 2 illustrates with the several stages of a loaf of bread how careful adherence to the value-added approach will enable you to subtract the intermediate expenses that show up in the income statements of farmers, millers, bakers, and grocers—ending you up with the desired equality between (1) net value of final bread and (2) the lower-loop factor costs embodying the sum of all stages' value-added data.

All this can be summarized as follows:

▶ To avoid double counting, we take care to include in net national product only final goods, and not the intermediate goods that go to make the final goods. By resolutely sticking to the *value added* at each stage, taking care to subtract expenditures on the intermediate goods of other firms, the lower-loop earnings approach also avoids all double counting and records only wages, interest, rent, and profit.

This is not really hard to understand. Still, many monetary cranks have been unable to master it.[2]

▶ NET INVESTMENT OR CAPITAL FORMATION

So far we have banished all capital growth from our discussion. We talked of people as wanting to consume apples, oranges, bread, and manicures. Indeed the statistician lets them consume anything they want. He may think that cigarette smoking is bad for the consumers; but it is their income and if they

---

[1] Why the word "exactly"? Recall how Pepto's residual profit is calculated.

[2] Major Douglas, a retired engineer, started the Social Credit movement based upon his belief that the mysterious Type A and Type B payments of his system required recourse to printing new money. He still has followers in New Zealand; in Alberta and elsewhere the Social Credit party has won office, but after getting into office it has in practice toned down its monetary crankiness.

NNP is the sum of all stages' value added:

Stage of production	Sales receipts (1)	Cost of intermediate materials or goods (2)		Value added (wages, profit, etc.) (3) = (1) − (2)
Wheat	4	−	0 =	4
Flour	6	−	4 =	2
Baked dough	12	−	6 =	6
Delivered bread	20	−	12 =	8
	42	−	22 =	20
				sum of value added

Table 2. Bread receipts, costs, and value added (in cents per loaf). To avoid double counting, we carefully calculate value added at each stage, subtracting all the costs of materials and intermediate products not produced in that stage but bought from other business firms. Note that every intermediate product appears both in column (1) and with opposite sign in column (2); hence it is canceled out.

want to spend it on tobacco, he simply records the fact.[1]

Now it is a fact that people often want to devote part of their income to saving and investment. Instead of eating apples now, they may want to build new machines. In short, suppose that the final goals of people are to include investment or capital formation and not simply current consumption.

The national-income statistician has no choice: he bows to their will; if people are using part of society's production possibilities for capital formation rather than consumption, the statistician recognizes that he must include such output in his upper-loop flow of NNP. So really, we must modify our original definition to read:

▶ Net national product is the sum of consumption goods and services, and of net investment.

This net investment (or net capital formation) will include the net additions to our (1) stock of buildings, (2) equipment, and (3) inventories. Some case studies will illustrate the investment process.

Stationary society with zero net investment. If an economy is not growing, it will year after year have the same capital stock: the same buildings, equipment, and inventory. These capital items will be replaced just as they are used up, and no net additions will have been made to them. Society is then just *exactly consuming all its NNP* or national income—as shown in Fig. 3a.

Growing society with positive net investment. In the more usual case, society is adding to its capital. It is more than replacing its used-up buildings and machines; it is adding to them and also adding to its inventories of goods (leather, dough, wheat, etc.). Its net investment is thus positive; and hence its

---

[1] The statistician draws the line only at illegal expenditures, *e.g.*, opium consumption or prostitution. During the years when black-market operations were so important in Europe, the statistician found it necessary to supplement his official money statistics with estimates of black-market money transactons.

In an economy with *stationary* capital, Consumption just equals NNP:

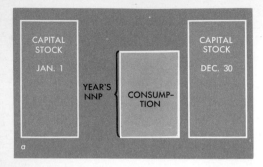

Fig. 3a. Capital is here being replaced as fast as it is used up or "depreciated."

NNP exceeds its Consumption. This is shown in Fig. 3*b*. (Note that the capital stock has grown by an amount equal to the year's net investment.)

Overconsuming society with negative net investment. Society may "live off its capital." Then its net investment is negative because it is not even replacing its worn-out capital goods. In national income terms, its consumption now exceeds its NNP.

How can this be, you'll ask—how can we eat what wasn't produced?

Of course, we can't eat what isn't there to eat. But we can eat—or drink—this year's corn and fail to set aside for next year our original seed; thus, we're consuming more than we have in this year produced net. A fanciful case? No. During the war most countries did just that—consumed more than their NNP, by failing to replace used-up capital goods. In 1944 were there hoards of canned goods that hungry soldiers and civilians could eat up? Is that what's meant by eating up your capital? Definitely not. Any air-raid warden will tell you that no society has much in the way of inventory of finished goods: most nations would starve in a month if that were the only way to live off capital.

What the economist means by the process of negative net investment is this: a nation consumes more than its net product *by shifting resources that nor-*

In an economy with *growing* capital, NNP exceeds Consumption by positive Net Investment:

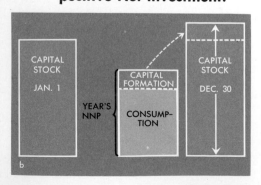

Fig. 3b. New capital formation exceeds depreciation of capital as people abstain from consuming all of today's income, instead saving for the future.

In an economy with *declining* capital, Consumption exceeds NNP:

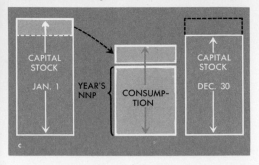

Fig. 3c. People can consume more than their net production by diverting resources from replacing depreciating capital to producing consumption goods.

mally replace capital goods over to the production of consumption goods. Figure *3c* shows what is happening to its stock of capital at the end of any year when it has done this.

▶ **NET INVESTMENT EQUALS GROSS INVESTMENT MINUS DEPRECIATION**

We've now given the income statistician no easy task. We've said: "Calculate all consumption flows. And then add to them net investment." Where can he get accurate figures on net investment?

He can't. He has to make estimates of inventories and of their changes. Worse still is his task of estimating net investment in buildings or equipment.

Why can't he just jot down all the buildings built and all the machines produced and add in inventory change to the total? He can, and does. But the resulting figure is too large—too gross. Recognizing this he gives a new name to the result—namely, "gross investment."

Why the word "gross"? The statistician uses this word to emphasize that he hasn't yet made any allowances for the using up of capital—*i.e.*, no allowance for capital depreciation.

You wouldn't think much of a statistician who estimated the change in a human population by ignoring deaths. If he just added up gross births, without subtracting off a good estimate for deaths, he would get an exaggerated notion of the net change in population. The same holds for equipment and buildings: net change is always gross births (of capital) minus deaths (or capital depreciation). This can be summed up in the definition:

▶ Net investment always equals gross investment minus depreciation.

Table 3 gives typical figures relating net and gross investment. They differ only by depreciation, and fortunately this is a sluggish item that won't change much over a period of a few years. That's why many forecasters, who really are interested in net investment, are satisfied to work with the gross investment figures, which are easier to find in the newspaper.

To get Net Investment, subtract Depreciation from Gross Investment:

Investment components	1929	1932	1956
New construction	$ 8.7	$ 1.9	$ 33.3
Producers' durable equipment	5.8	1.6	28.1
Change in business inventories	1.7	−2.6	4.5
Gross private domestic investment	$16.2	$ 0.9	$ 65.9
Allowances for depreciation or capital consumption (also = difference between GNP and NNP)	−8.6	−7.6	−34.3
Net private domestic investment	$ 7.6	$−6.7	$ 31.6
Net foreign investment	0.8	0.2	1.4
Net private investment	$ 8.4	$−6.5	$ 33.0

Table 3. Gross and Net Investment (in billions of dollars). Note that Gross Investment has three main components. After subtracting capital Depreciation we get net private domestic investment —to which net foreign investment can be added. (Source: U.S. Department of Commerce.)

▶ GROSS NATIONAL PRODUCT VERSUS NET NATIONAL PRODUCT

This unavailability of "net" figures is no joke. Even if you were lucky enough to get a copy of the *Wall Street Journal* on that day the new figures come out, I doubt that you would find NNP in it. Instead its headlines would blare out GNP—*i.e.*, gross national product rather than net national product.

What's the difference between the gross and net product figures—between GNP and NNP? The last section hints at the answer. The difference is simply this: gross national product contains gross investment (inclusive of depreciation!), while net national product has in it only net investment.

So GNP is bigger than NNP by the amount of depreciation. This is why the word "gross" is used; GNP is on purpose made to be a little too large, and the word "gross" is there to warn you of this fact. It's easy enough to get NNP from GNP if we know depreciation. We merely subtract depreciation from GNP to get NNP—as the depreciation row of Table 3 indicates. If you can't find depreciation in the newspaper, a little trick will help: NNP is usually about ten-elevenths of GNP, depreciation these days being about one-eleventh of GNP.

What are we paying the Washington civil servants for? Why don't they give us figures for NNP rather than GNP, if it is net figures we primarily want? A good question. They have this defense: "We do our best to estimate depreciation, but we aren't always too sure of how good our best estimates are. Businessmen's reported depreciation estimates need lots of adjustments, and no one is too sure of the final figure. So, having more confidence in the accuracy of GNP than NNP and since we actually first measure GNP, we along with other countries' statisticians make this our important published figure." And the hard-worked statistician goes on to say: "Besides, what are you kicking about? Using our depreciation estimate, you can with one subtraction get NNP for yourself. Or if you'll wait a while, we'll send you a full report with NNP and all."

Most economists will accept this reply. But we can't help wishing that a little more emphasis on the NNP, for all the difficulty of estimating it, were to be made in the future. Through the later chapters of this book, we shall usually speak of NNP, knowing that GNP and NNP change together for most practical purposes.

▶ BRIEF SUMMARY

Our task is almost done: we are almost ready to tackle the official 1956 national-product statistics. A pause for breath and consolidation is in order.

1. We now know how to measure NNP as an annual flow of goods and services. Or alternatively as an annual flow of factor earnings, being careful to avoid double counting by use of the value-added approach and being careful to define our residual profit so as to make the two measures equivalent.

2. We now know how to include net investment in NNP along with consumption. Realizing the difficulty of measuring net investment, we understand why the statisticians first estimate gross investment and then later try to make a good guess at the depreciation that should be subtracted off to get net investment. We realize that this is the reason they publish and talk so much about figures on gross national product rather than net national product. Since NNP differs from GNP only by depreciation, and since this last is only about one-eleventh of GNP and doesn't change too much during a short period of years when we are interested in observing and forecasting national incomes, we can pretty much use GNP or NNP interchangeably.

With these principles firmly in mind we can go on to see what complications come from government and elsewhere.

▶ GOVERNMENT EXPENDITURE ON GOODS AND SERVICES

Until now we have ignored government. We have talked about consumers but ignored the biggest consumer of all—namely, the federal, state, and local governments. NNP must somehow take into account the billions of dollars of product that a nation collectively consumes. How?

After some scratching of heads, the income statisticians of the United States and United Nations decided on using the simplest method of all. To the flow of (1) consumption product, and (2) net Investment product, they simply add (3) all government expenditure on goods and services. Again and again in the next few chapters, you will see $C + I + G$—which stands for these three components.

Here are some examples. Just as we include apple consumption and net investment in NNP, we include in it government expenditures on jet bombers. We include government expenditure on weathermen. Government expenditure on the services of judges, policemen, jet pilots, firemen, agriculture chemists. And just to complete the circle, we even include in NNP government expenditure on national-income statisticians in the Department of Commerce!

In short, all the government payroll expenditures on its employees plus the goods (typewriters, guns, airplanes, etc.) it buys from private industry are included in this third great category of flow-of-product labeled G and called "government expenditure on goods and services."

Exclusion of transfer payments. Does this mean that every dollar the government pays out is included in NNP? Definitely not. If I get an old-age pension from the government, that is called a "transfer payment" and is not treated as part of NNP. Why not? Because it is not a government expenditure on goods and services of this year. Or if your Aunt May receives a widow's assistance payment, that welfare expenditure is also a transfer item. Same for pensions to the blind and to Spanish War veterans.

Many other government transfer items[1] could be mentioned, but we can conclude with one big one: interest on the public debt. The interest paid on federal saving and other bonds years ago used to be included in NNP, but the fairly universal custom now is for countries to treat this as a transfer item. This is not included in G, on the argument that it is not a payment for current goods and services.[2] (Don't for a moment think that the Treasury's budget fails to take careful account of all transfer payments. The budgets back on page 117 did include these: the government surplus equals taxes minus sum-of-G-and-transfers. The official budget also includes certain purely bookkeeping expenses. But we must not confuse the budget with national income accounts; they are related but quite distinct.)

Treatment of taxes. In using the flow-of-product approach to compute NNP as $C + I + G$, we never have to worry about taxes or about how government finances itself. Whether the government taxes, issues interest-bearing I.O.U.'s,

[1] In Chapter 6, page 120, we saw that the name "transfer payment" is a little misleading. If you tax me to give a relief dole to my unemployed neighbor, that does sound like a "transfer." But suppose you print a new green 20-dollar bill to give him, or borrow by selling bonds to make relief payments. We still call the relief payments transfers—regardless of how they are financed—which might cause the dictionary maker to raise his eyebrows.

[2] How to treat government items in NNP is still controversial. Examples: (1) Some experts argue that G should be broken down into government current consumption and government net investment (increase in its buildings, equipment, and inventories) —just as private product is so broken up. And some nations do this. (2) Some experts say too that part of G is really "intermediate" rather than "final" product—much like dough rather than bread, in that it may merely contribute to final product that has already been counted in once. But few nations try to make estimates of how much such double counting may be in the G figures. (3) Some experts used to think the way government finances itself—by taxes, borrowing, or printing money—should affect the definition of G. Few today agree. An elementary text is not the place to go into these technical arguments among the experts.

NNP is sum of Consumption, Investment, and Government Expenditures:

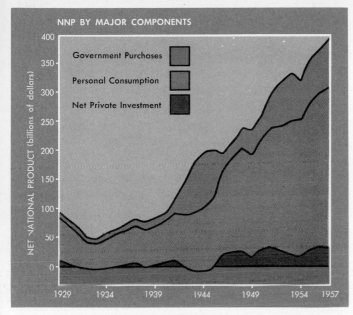

NNP BY MAJOR COMPONENTS

Government Purchases

Personal Consumption

Net Private Investment

Fig. 4. Though Consumption dominates NNP, note the war and postwar growth in Government Expenditure and In Investment (Source: U.S. Department of Commerce.)

or prints new noninterest I.O.U. greenbacks, the statistician computes G as the value of government expenditure on goods and services (evaluating these items at their actual cost to the government, without regard to where the money came from).

It is very well in the upper-loop flow-of-product approach to ignore taxes. But what about the lower-loop earnings or cost approach to NNP? In this lower loop, we indeed do have to take account of all taxes.

Take wages, for example. Part of what my employer pays me in wages I have to give to the government in the form of personal income taxes. So these direct taxes are definitely included in the wage component of the lower loop, and the same holds for direct taxes on interest, rent, and profit.

Or take the sales and other indirect taxes that manufacturers and retailers have to pay on a loaf of bread (or on the wheat, flour, and dough stages). Suppose these indirect taxes amount to 5 cents; and suppose wages, profit, and other value-added items added up in cost to the bread industry to 20 cents. (We don't care how much of this 20 cents goes to direct taxes.) What will the bread sell for in the upper loop? For 20 cents? Of course not. The bread will sell for 25 cents, equal to 20 cents of factor costs plus 5 cents of indirect taxes.[1]

---

[1] This is plainly so by definition of our residual profit. Admittedly this result involves a strained use of the word "cost" in that residual profit is treated as a cost; but this result definitely says *nothing at all* about whether the tax is passed forward to the consumer or backward to the factors, whose wages and other returns might have been higher had there been no taxes.

Hence we must always include taxes in the lower-loop cost approach to the NNP.

Disposable income: a disgression. Mention of taxes provides a good excuse to introduce the concept of disposable income, or income after taxes. Figure 5, along with GNP and NNP, shows the important magnitude disposable income (what people actually have to spend after they have paid their taxes).

Note that a considerable part of the NNP never gets to people at all. Why? Because so much of wages, rent, interest, and profit is directly taxed. Then too the government collects *indirect* business taxes (sales taxes, tariff duties on imports, excises, etc.). These are costs included in the value of NNP, but paid to the government, not to the public.

Still another reason why people don't have all the NNP to spend is the fact that corporations fail to pay out all *their* earnings in dividends: their undistributed corporate profits are thus subtracted out in the computation of disposable income.

One item goes a little way to offset these tax and undistributed-corporate profit subtractions involved in the computation of disposable income. The offsetting item that is added in is government transfer payments. Why add in transfers? Because pensions and government bond interests do come to families and are treated by them as part of their disposable income. The national-income statistician recognizes this, and—as shown in Fig. 6 of the Appendix —he does add in transfers into disposable income.

The different national income aggregates tend to move together:

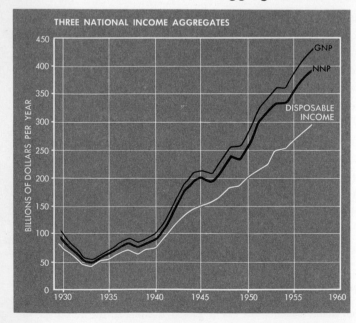

Fig. 5. NNP averages about ten-elevenths of GNP. Because of taxes and corporate saving, the Disposable Income of people is smaller still. (Source: U.S. Department of Commerce.)

Why is disposable income[1] important? We shall see in the next two chapters that it is the prime determiner of people's consumption spending and net personal saving. By habit and custom people show a propensity to spend their disposable incomes fairly regularly on consumption—as we shall see.

A pretty good rule to remember is that people save 7 to 8 per cent of their incomes on the average and spend on consumption 93 to 92 per cent of their disposable incomes.

We may summarize this section on the treatment of government as follows:

1. Along with consumption and net investment, the flow-of-product NNP must include government expenditure on goods and services (valued at their cost to the government and regardless of how financed).

2. Transfer expenditures by government on welfare or interest on public debt are not included in NNP (even though taken account of in the budget).

3. To keep the lower-loop cost approach to NNP in perfect equality with the upper-loop flow-of-product approach, we do have to take account of all taxes along with the usual value-added items.

▶ COMPLETE BIRD'S-EYE VIEW OF NATIONAL INCOME

No one thing learned about national income was hard. But there were so many things to learn that the subject can seem a little complicated. A look at the actual figures, therefore, will consolidate understanding and will show that once a person is properly prepared for national-income accounting it turns out not to be so hard.

Flow-of-product approach. Look first at the left side of Table 4 on the next page. It gives the upper-loop flow-of-product approach to NNP. Distinguishing between domestic and foreign investment, we have four components. Of these *C* and *G* and their obvious classifications require little comment.

And we can reserve for the Appendix and until Chapter 31 any more detailed study of foreign trade. It is enough to note here that our net foreign investment represents "the excess of what we currently export of all goods and services abroad over what we import of goods and services."

Net domestic private investment does require a little comment. Its net figure of 31.6 billion dollars was arrived at in the way already described: from the estimate of gross private domestic investment of 65.9, we subtracted the estimated value of depreciation of 34.3, just as we did in Table 3, page 190.

Adding up the four components on the left gives the important total NNP of 380.4 billion dollars. This is the harvest we have been working for: the money measure of the American economy's over-all performance for 1956.

---

[1] One wishes the government published monthly estimates of disposable income. It doesn't yet. But our Appendix shows that it publishes monthly a very similar concept which it calls "personal income": the other national-income concepts it publishes only quarterly.

The two ways of looking at NNP in actual numbers:

Table 4. Net National Product, 1956 (in millions of current dollars). The left side measures flow of product (at market prices). The right side measures flow of costs (factor earnings plus direct and indirect taxes). GNP, which includes Depreciation, is also shown. Be sure you understand the main items. (Source: U.S. Department of Commerce. The starred item includes the "statistical discrepancy" and arises from imperfect measurement of upper- and lower-loop data.)

FLOW OF PRODUCT APPROACH			EARNINGS AND COST APPROACH		
Personal consumption expenditure		$267.2	Wages and other employee supplements		$241.4
Durable goods	$ 33.9		Net interest		11.9
Nondurable goods	133.3		Rent income of persons		10.3
Services	99.9		Indirect business taxes and adjustments*		36.8
			Income of unincorporated enterprises (adjusted)		39.6
Government purchases of goods and services		80.2	Corporate profits before taxes (adjusted)		40.4
Net foreign investment		1.4	Dividends	$11.8	
Net private domestic investment		31.6	Undistributed profits	9.2	
			Corporate profits taxes	22.0	
			Reported profits (unadj.)	43.0	
			Inventory valuation adjustment	−2.6	
Net National Product		380.4	**Net National Product**		380.4
Depreciation (or capital consumption allowance)		34.3	Depreciation (or capital consumption allowance)		34.3
Gross National Product		$414.7	**Gross National Product**		$414.7

Finally, note that if we add depreciation back into the figures, we have the GNP of 414.7 billion dollars—which is bigger because it contains gross rather than net investment in its measure of product.

Lower-loop flow-of-cost approach. Now turn to the right-hand side of the table. Here we have all the value-added items plus taxes.

A few explanations are in order. Wages and other employee supplements include all take-home pay and fringe benefits, and they also have in them the withheld and other income or payroll taxes that wage earners have to pay.[1]

Net interest is a similar item. (Note only that interest on government bonds is not included in this. Remember that such interest is treated as a transfer, not as part of G or of NNP.)

Rent income of persons requires only one explanation. If you own your

---

[1] The late Sir Arthur Bowley of the London School of Economics noted how remarkably constant over almost a century is wage's share of national income. No one understands why this should be so. (And, to be sure, wage share does rise at the expense of profit during recession; moreover, in recent decades it seems to be growing more than Bowley's constancy hypothesis would indicate.)

own home, you are treated as paying rent to yourself. This is a so-called "imputed" item and makes sense if you really want to know what housing services the American people are enjoying and don't want the estimate changed everytime a tenant buys the house he's been living in. Admittedly, this imputed item has to be estimated, since we don't report rental receipts on our own homes.

Indirect business taxes we earlier saw do have to be included in the lower loop if we are to match the upper loop. What about direct taxes? Well, as we have just seen, any direct taxes on wages, interest, or rents are included in those items.

Lastly, we turn to profit. This should come last because it is the residual that is determined as what's left over after all the other items have been taken account of. There are two kinds of profits: profit of corporations, and profit of unincorporated enterprises (proprietorships and partnerships). Income of unincorporated enterprises (adjusted[1]) represents the latter. This includes much farmer income and much professional income: as we shall see in Chapter 30, really a good deal of this is a return to people for the labor, capital, and land they provide for their own businesses; but the statistician calls all of it profit.

Finally, corporate profit before taxes (adjusted) is shown. Its 40.4 billion dollars includes corporate profits taxes of 22.0. The remainder then goes to dividends or represents undistributed corporate profits: this last is what you leave or "plow back" in the business and is often called "net corporate saving."

Again, on the right side, the flow-of-cost approach gives us the same 380.4 billion dollars of NNP.[2] And for good measure the GNP figure is also shown, having been arrived at by adding back in the gross item of depreciation.

▶ EPILOGUE

Table 4 summarizes the main fundaments of national-income accounting. Understand it, and you are prepared to interpret the economic history of the

---

[1] The term "adjusted" refers to an inventory valuation adjustment of the following type: If money prices change *within* the year, our yardstick for measuring profits is faulty. Part of the reported profit is simply a markup (or markdown, if the price level is falling within the year) of inventory. The statistician uses within-the-year price changes to estimate how much such overreporting of profits has been. Thus, in 1956, prices were rising: so there had to be an inventory valuation adjustment of − 2.6 billion dollars that gets subtracted from reported corporate profits of 43.0 to give a more meaningful adjusted figure of 40.4. (In 1953, when prices fell, the adjustment was positive and added a billion to reported profits. Can you explain why?) A similar adjustment was made, but is not shown, for unincorporated incomes.

[2] Expert users of NNP and GNP data know that the Commerce Department tries to estimate the right and left sides independently. If their reports were perfect, the two would match perfectly. But their reports are only approximate. So there is usually what is called a "statistical discrepancy" between the two sides. So as not to confuse the beginner's understanding of principle, I have included the "statistical discrepancy" with the other "adjustments to indirect business taxes" such as business transfers and net government subsidies.

next few decades. And you are prepared to tackle Part Two's analysis of how the national income gets determined.

More information about national-income accounting and about the special definitions now in use by the United States government are given in this chapter's Appendix. Also given are some selected figures on the nation's recent economic history: the Federal Reserve Board's important production index, which comes out monthly; and data on employment and unemployment. These vital aggregates chart a nation's economic health.

SUMMARY

1. National income or NNP is most simply interpreted as a flow of product: the sum of consumption plus net investment (domestic and foreign) plus government expenditure on goods and services. That is, $NNP = C + I + G$.

2. By use of a price index, we can "deflate" NNP in current dollars to arrive at a more accurate measure of "real NNP, expressed in dollars of one base year's purchasing power." Use of such an average price index (of consumer-goods, investment-goods, and government-goods prices) is an approximate way of allowing for the rubber yardstick implied by changing money prices.

3. Because of the way we define residual profit, we can match the flow-of-product measurement of NNP by the lower-loop flow-of-cost measurement. This uses factor earnings, carefully computing values added to eliminate double counting of intermediate products. And after adding all wage, interest, rent, and profit income that people actually have disposable after paying taxes, it adds to this total all taxes: the direct taxes included in payroll reports, in interest, rent, and incorporated or unincorporated profits; and also indirect business taxes. (The lower-loop NNP definitely does *not* include transfer items such as receipt of interest on government bonds or receipt of welfare pensions.)

4. Net investment is positive when people are devoting part of society's resources to creating more buildings, equipment, and inventory than is currently being used up in the form of depreciation. Net investment equals gross investment minus depreciation. Since depreciation is hard to estimate, the statisticians have more confidence in their estimates of gross than net investment.

5. For the above reason, the official statistics put greatest stress on gross national product rather than net. $GNP = NNP + depreciation$, always. Since depreciation is sluggish and rarely goes much above one-eleventh of GNP (or one-tenth of NNP), we can use GNP and NNP interchangeably for most practical purposes.

QUESTIONS FOR DISCUSSION

1. America had a great depression from 1929 to 1933. In which charts can you read this story? In which charts, the wartime boom? The fairly sharp 1937–1938 recession in business activity? The mild 1948–1949 and 1953–1954 recessions? Trace these ups and downs carefully, referring to Table 5.

2. Compare Fig. 1's two-loop flow of money with Chapter 3's Fig. 1 on page 41. The latter shows the way a pricing system solves society's What, How, and For Whom problems. It deals with economics at the "micro" level. Show how Fig. 1's treatment of aggregate spending—the "macro" level—fits in with the earlier picture.

3. "You can't add apples and oranges." Show that money lets us do this.

4. The manicure example is there to point up the importance of *services* as well as material goods. Convince a skeptic that services do count—that we want most material goods for the consumption services they provide us.

5. Making a guess how prices have changed since 1956, test your knowledge of the deflating process by penciling in on Fig. 2 recent money NNP and recent real NNP. How might you deflate for population change? (Hint: Divide through to get per capita incomes.) If the United Kingdom has 1956 NNP of 16.5 billion pounds, and if £1 buys what $3 will buy, how would you express United Kingdom NNP in American 1956 dollars?

6. R. Crusoe produces upper-loop product of $1,000. He pays $750 in wages, $125 in interest, and $75 in rent. What *must* his profit be? Calculate NNP in the upper-loop and lower-loop way and show they must agree exactly.

7. Crusoe finds his manufacturing industry has bought $100 of materials from his agriculture department, and the latter's costs go half for wages and half for land rent. Calculate all value-added data. Avoid double counting and show that NNP is still $1,000 whether calculated from the flow-of-product or flow-of-factor-cost approach. (Hint: assume 2 industries and no depreciation.)

8. "Depreciation, or capital used up, is not always accurately measured in firms' income statements." If so, how does this affect net versus gross investment? NNP versus GNP? How does a nation disinvest?

9. From a recent *Federal Reserve Bulletin* or *Survey of Current Business* (Commerce Department), recalculate Table 4 for a later year than 1956. Explain the profit adjustments, and treatment of the corporation.

10. Distinguish between government transfer expenditure and the *G* that goes into NNP = *C* + *I* + *G*. Why must you remove all taxes from NNP and add in transfers to get disposable income?

11. Review your understanding of the following concepts:

NNP

1960 money NNP in current dollars and 1960 real NNP in 1956 dollars

intermediate goods, double counting, value added

gross investment − depreciation = net investment

GNP − depreciation = NNP

NNP = C + I + G

government transfers, indirect and direct taxes, disposable income

net foreign investment = all current exports − all current imports

undistributed profit

income of unincorporated enterprise

APPENDIX: THE OFFICIAL NATIONAL INCOME DATA

The main chapter has expounded the basic principles of national income. Here a few special points are elaborated (*e.g.*, international aspects), and an explanation is given of the official statistical concepts reported by the United States government and by many UN members.

A Few Brain Teasers

Some readers like to worry about fine points. Here are a few sample cases.

1. Services of a housewife never get counted in the NNP. So if a man marries his housekeeper, the NNP may go down! Or if my wife should arrange with our neighbor for each to clean the other's house in return for $4,000 a year, then the NNP would go up by $8,000!

Is all this logical? Not particularly. It is done, though, because it would be hard to get accurate estimates of the money value of a wife's services. Who would dare make the estimate? And anyway, so long as the number of women working at home doesn't change much in relative importance, the ups and downs of NNP will be about the

same whether or not we include this item.[1]

All this illustrates an important rule of approximate measurement in economics: Often it doesn't matter which definition of measurement you use, so long as you consistently stick to one definition.

2. For many items it is hard to know whether to put them in the intermediate or final class. Examples: A carpenter's hammer is certainly not to be charged as a final consumption item. Like bread dough, it is an intermediate expense item that has already been counted in as part of the fine tables and homes he builds.

What about his overalls? His carfare from one job to another? His carfare from home to work? The beer he buys a prospective customer? The beer he himself then drinks? The ball game he takes that prospective customer to, in his campaign to get more business? Would you treat the last two differently if the carpenter himself likes beer and baseball?

Each of these items can raise an argument.

[1] Similar problem: home-grown vegetables; do-it-yourself activity.

Each has an element of intermediate business expense in it, and each an element of consumption. The tax collector and the national-income statistician don't always agree on the treatment of these, and we can raise questions about each one's decisions. (Example: The tax collector won't let anyone deduct his commuting costs to work *in town;* but out of town he may be able to. The hammer is clearly deductible from taxable income and from NNP; but the overalls are not if it can be shown that wearing them saved an ordinary suit's wearing out. So it goes. Close decisions and arbitrary ones.)

3. Gifts that are not disguised payments for work done or for goods and services are not included in NNP. They are like government transfers that we have already discussed. Same goes for the allowance a father gives his son. But what about the fee he pays the son for mowing the lawn? In logic it should be in NNP, but I doubt that it often gets reported.

4. If I buy an old painting, a corner lot, or a used car from someone else, that transaction is not a final transaction to be put into NNP. He and I have just exchanged assets: money for picture, etc. Nothing has been produced.[1] So this is more in the nature of a special kind of transfer.[2] It illustrates an important fact: the total dollar volume of all intermediate transactions greatly exceeds the dollar volume of the final transactions that we call national income or product. The loops of Fig. 1 include only a minority of the transactions that are taking place within and between the business and public blocks of that diagram.

Note too that we try not to let capital gains due to mere price changes enter into NNP. If Wall Street bids up my Ford stock, I may feel rich and go out to a night club.

[1] If a broker earns a fee for arranging the deal, that fee is counted as part of NNP. Just as some men produce satisfactions in the form of bread, brokers and salesmen produce satisfactions in the form of bringing transactors together.

[2] Don't confuse this kind of transfer with the government transfers we've talked about.

But that windfall gain is not like a permanent addition to my monthly income, and the statistician tries to keep it out. That's why he makes the inventory valuation adjustment in corporate profits.

5. I could go on giving borderline cases but will conclude with a last one. In measuring NNP we are not interested in consumption and investment goods merely for their money value: money is the measuring rod we use to give some kind of an approximate figure to the underlying "satisfactions" or "benefits" or "psychic income" that comes from goods. Strictly speaking then, each time I play a phonograph record, shouldn't that get into the NNP at its fair market value? In principle, Yes. And if I have put a dime in a juke box, it may in fact get directly in the NNP. But playing it at home won't directly get it into the NNP.

Indirectly this enjoyment of a psychic pleasure does tend to get in the NNP to the extent that I wear out the record by playing it. Hence, as I replace my records my consumption purchases at the store give a rough money measure of my enjoyments. But only a rough measure.

The statistician admits this, defending his practice by saying that a man's house is his castle and no accountant dare enter into his abode to measure his actual current consumptions, instead treating a thing as consumed when it enters his abode. Which works well enough except in one case.

More and more these days we spend our consumption dollar on durable consumer goods. (This will be seen in Table 4's breakdown of consumption into services, durable goods, and nondurable goods.) Actually then, in the years that we are building up our home inventories of such durable goods, our true psychic consumption is being overstated by our retail purchases; and vice versa in the years when we run down our home inventories.

Some purists say: "In NNP, let's try to estimate actual home consumption of durables and put that in *C*, not the mere retail purchases of the year." The Commerce Department thinks this too hard a job to do, but for special purposes economists have tried to get (from gas and mileage records, for example) more accurate estimates of auto consumption than is provided by new car sales.[1]

Fortunately, in the long run, the two methods tend to come to the same thing— most particularly if the society is not growing too fast.

International Aspects of Income

Here is the place to give a few details on how net foreign investment was arrived at.

From the beginning we agree to mean by United States national income the income or product accruing to all "permanent residents" of the United States. This includes American citizens temporarily abroad and also unnaturalized immigrants who live permanently in the United States.

Note that, if an Englishman owns an acre of land in this country, his income therefrom is to be included in the United Kingdom national income and not in the United States national income. Similarly, if Americans receive dividends from British companies, this is part of the American income and not the British, being treated as payment for a property service that we have exported.

The previous paragraph shows that it is a considerable task to allow for international aspects of income. We must take account of exports, imports, dividends paid in and out of a country, etc. As we shall see in Part Five's discussion of international finance, a balance of international payments between the United States and the rest of the world can be drawn up of all such items. There is

no need at this point of our national-income discussion to anticipate all the details of Part Five's discussion. We are interested only in the bare logic of the task of finding out the magnitude of net foreign investment, which must be combined with net private domestic investment to give us the third or investment component of NNP. (Turn back to Table 3.)

To get our net foreign investment we must calculate the surplus of all the goods and services we provide to foreigners over what they provide to us. Thus calculate A, the total of our exports to them (automobiles, shipping, etc.) plus our earnings from factors of production we own abroad (dividends and interest payable to us). Also calculate B, the total of what we import from them and must pay them for their ownership of productive factors located in this country. If A exceeds B, foreigners must be going into our debt; the surplus of A over B represents our net foreign investment. But note that B might exceed A in some years. What then? We are then buying more abroad than we are earning abroad, going into debt for the difference. Now our net foreign investment is negative, representing net foreign disinvestment for us.[2]

The Official Statistics

Figure 6 summarizes the relations of the different United States government statistics on national income or product. It shows GNP, NNP, and disposable income. It also shows the very special concept that the Department of Commerce chooses to name "national income."

Many economists—I am one—prefer to use the term "national income" to refer to the whole subject—to NNP, GNP, and all

---

[1] It is interesting that in the case of a house, the most durable consumers' good of all, the officials do actually follow this principle: they don't take expenditures on houses as its C, but estimate the house use separately. Yet where cars and other consumer durables are concerned, the officials do not keep capital accounts on them but are content to use retail purchases as an approximate measure.

[2] Warning to the advanced reader: Our government's aid to foreigners is included in government purchases and not in net foreign investment. On the other hand, when the government's Export-Import Bank makes a loan to a foreign government, that is included in net foreign investment. Chapter 31 discusses all this and also the role of gold flows.

How to picture the relations among official national income data:

Fig. 6. Here for the first time is shown what the Commerce Department chooses to call "national income." To help you master these official statistics, pencil in actual numbers from Table 6 or later years on these blocks.

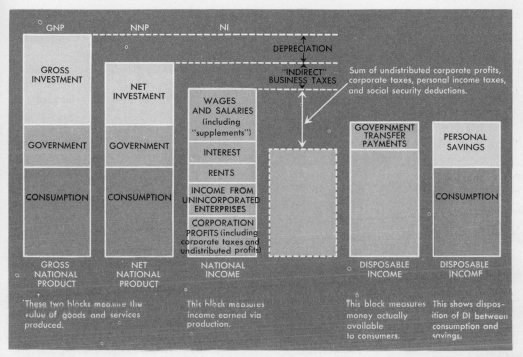

the rest. If we had to pin national income down to a single one of these concepts, we'd plump for net national product—using the terms interchangeably.

This the Department of Commerce definitely doesn't do. For historical reasons not worth going into here, it uses the term "national income" to cover what we should call "NNP with indirect business taxes taken out." (See the third block of NI in the figure.) [1]

-----

[1] It defends itself with the argument that you strain the dictionary meaning of "income" if you use it to cover the taxes that are paid by business even before the public gets its factor earnings. True enough. But if that really bothers you, why stop there? Why include in a stockowner's income the taxes his corporation has already paid? And why kid yourself by treating

There is but one way to grasp Fig. 6's content: Study it. And relate it to Table 6, where such official statistics as personal income are also shown.

Table 5, along with national-income data,

-----

your wage income as including the direct taxes that were withheld before you ever got your take-home pay? If the Commerce statisticians insist on using the word "income" for what factors can actually spend, it should call disposable income "national income" and not use that name for its halfway hybrid term. (Prior to 1947, it used still another concept.)

The beginner need not worry about still another Commerce concept: so-called "personal income." This is more like "disposable income with most personal taxes left in," and it is important only because available monthly rather than quarterly like all the other measures.

These aggregates chart the nation's economic health:

Table 5. Principal economic aggregates. Forecasters like to use the production index because it moves more sensitively than income data. Statesmen worry about unemployment. (Source: U.S. Department of Commerce; Federal Reserve; *Economic Report of the President.*)

Year	Gross national product	Net national product	National income	Disposable income	Net saving as per cent of disposable income	Gov. expenditure on goods and services as per cent of GNP	Federal Reserve Board index of industrial production	Civilian labor force	Unemployment as per cent of civilian labor force
1929	104.4	95.8	87.8	83.1	5.0	8.1	59	49,180	3.2
1930	91.1	82.6	75.7	74.4	4.6	10.1	49	49,820	8.7
1931	76.3	68.1	59.7	63.8	3.9	12.1	40	50,420	15.9
1932	58.5	50.9	42.5	48.7	−1.3	13.8	31	51,000	23.6
1933	56.0	48.8	40.2	45.7	−1.4	14.4	37	51,590	24.9
1934	65.0	57.9	49.0	52.0	0.2	15.0	40	52,230	21.7
1935	72.5	65.3	57.1	58.3	3.5	13.8	47	52,870	20.1
1936	82.7	75.2	64.9	66.2	5.4	14.3	56	53,440	16.9
1937	90.8	83.0	73.6	71.0	5.3	12.9	61	54,000	14.3
1938	85.2	77.4	67.6	65.7	1.6	15.0	48	54,610	19.0
1939	91.1	83.3	72.8	70.4	4.1	14.6	58	55,230	17.2
1940	100.6	92.5	81.6	76.1	5.5	14.0	67	55,640	14.6
1941	125.8	116.8	104.7	93.0	11.9	19.7	87	55,910	9.9
1942	159.1	149.0	137.7	117.5	23.6	37.5	106	56,410	4.7
1943	192.5	181.6	170.3	133.5	24.7	46.0	127	55,540	1.9
1944	211.4	199.4	182.6	146.8	25.2	45.7	125	54,630	1.2
1945	214.6	201.0	181.2	150.4	19.1	38.8	107	53,860	1.9
1946	209.2	197.6	179.6	159.0	7.9	14.8	90	57,520	3.9
1947	232.2	218.1	197.2	169.0	2.4	12.3	100	60,168	3.6
1948	257.3	240.8	221.6	187.6	5.3	14.2	104	61,442	3.4
1949	257.3	238.9	216.2	188.2	4.0	17.0	97	62,105	5.5
1950	285.1	264.6	240.0	206.1	5.9	14.7	112	63,099	5.0
1951	328.2	304.8	277.0	226.1	7.8	19.1	120	62,844	3.0
1952	345.4	321.6	290.2	237.4	8.0	22.4	124	62,966	2.7
1953	363.2	336.7	302.1	250.2	7.9	23.2	134	63,815	2.5
1954	361.2	332.2	299.0	254.5	7.0	21.2	125	64,468	5.0
1955	391.7	360.1	324.1	270.2	5.8	19.7	139	65,848	4.0
1956	414.7	380.4	343.6	287.2	7.0	19.3	143	67,530	3.8
1957	433.9	396.8	358.5	300.0	6.5	20.0	143	67,946	4.3

How the official statistics of national income are interrelated:

Table 6. Gross and net national product, national income, personal income, and disposable income (in billions of dollars). Read this together with Fig. 6 to understand the official data most easily. (Source: U.S. Department of Commerce; *Economic Report of the President;* note that detail may not add to totals because of rounding.)

Items	1929	1933	1939	1945	1953	1954	1955	1956	1957
Gross National Product	104.4	56.0	91.1	213.6	363.2	361.2	391.7	414.7	433.9
Less: Capital consumption (Depreciation)	8.6	7.2	7.8	12.5	26.5	28.9	31.6	34.3	37.1
Equals: **Net national product**	95.8	48.8	83.3	201.0	336.7	332.2	360.1	380.4	396.8
Less: Indirect business taxes	7.0	7.1	9.4	15.5	30.2	30.1	32.9	35.0	36.9
Business transfer payments	0.6	0.7	0.5	0.5	1.4	1.3	1.3	1.3	1.3
Statistical discrepancy	0.3	0.9	1.2	4.5	2.6	1.7	2.1	1.6	1.7
Plus: Subsidies less current surplus of gov. enterprises	−0.1	0.0	0.5	0.8	−0.4	−0.2	0.2	1.1	1.6
Equals: **National income**	87.8	40.2	72.8	181.2	302.1	299.0	324.1	343.6	358.5
Less: Corporate profits and inventory valuation adjustment	10.1	−2.0	5.7	18.4	36.0	33.1	40.7	40.4	40.6
Contributions for soc. insurance	0.2	0.3	2.1	6.1	8.7	9.7	11.0	12.4	14.4
Excess of wage accruals over disbursements	0.0	0.0	0.0	0.0	−0.1	0.0	0.0	0.0	0.0
Plus: Gov. transfer payments	0.9	1.5	2.5	5.6	12.9	15.0	16.1	17.2	19.9
Net interest paid by government	1.0	1.2	1.2	3.7	5.0	5.2	5.2	5.7	6.0
Dividends	5.8	2.1	3.8	4.7	9.3	9.9	11.0	11.9	12.3
Business transfer payments	0.6	0.7	0.5	0.5	1.4	1.3	1.3	1.3	1.3
Equals: **Personal income**	85.8	47.2	72.9	171.2	286.0	287.4	305.9	326.9	342.9
Less: Personal taxes	2.6	1.5	2.4	20.9	35.8	33.0	35.8	39.7	43.0
(Federal)	1.3	0.5	1.2	19.4	32.4	29.2	31.5	35.1	37.8
(State and local)	1.4	1.0	1.2	1.5	3.4	3.8	4.2	4.6	5.2
Equals: **Disposable personal income**	83.1	45.7	70.4	150.4	250.2	254.5	270.2	287.2	300.0
Less: Consumption expenditures	79.0	46.4	67.6	121.7	230.5	236.6	254.4	267.2	280.4
Equals: Personal saving	4.2	−0.6	2.9	28.7	19.7	17.9	15.8	20.0	19.6

gives the other principal aggregates which businessmen and public officials closely watch.

The Identity of Measured Saving and Investment

To pave the way for Chapter 12's discussion of intersecting saving and investment schedules, we can here show that the national-income statistician defines the saving he measures as exactly the same thing as the investment he measures. This equality of measured saving and measured investment is an identity of double-entry bookkeeping and holds by definition.

What is the measure of investment? Forgetting government, we know I is the output in the upper loop that is not C, *i.e.,* not consumed. What is the measure of saving, S? Again forgetting government and corporate saving, we know that S is that part of the lower-loop disposable income or NNP that is not spent on C. To summarize:

$$I = \text{upper-loop NNP minus } C$$
$$S = \text{lower-loop NNP minus } C$$

But we know that the two loops must give the same measure of NNP. So $I \equiv S$: the identity between measured saving and investment.

Our task will be done once we bring the corporation and government into the picture. Investment is just as before. But now saving S must be split into three different terms: (1) net personal saving, which people do out of their disposable incomes; (2) net corporate saving, that part of their incomes which corporations fail to pay out as dividends; finally (3), net government surplus (or "saving"), which represents the excess of its tax revenues over its expenditure on goods and services *and* on transfers.

Our identity of measured S and I now has to be written in terms of the three components of total S.[1]

$$I \equiv NPS + NCS + NGS$$

[1] The eager reader can test his grasp of this fundamental identity (which must hold at all times whether or not an economy is in equilibrium or is galloping to or from an equilibrium) by going back to page 194's discussion of how disposable income is defined in terms of NNP − taxes − NCS + transfers, and how $NPS = DI - C$. These relations combined with the $C + I + G$ breakdown of NNP can be used to give an algebraic demonstration of our identity.

part

2

DETERMINATION OF

NATIONAL INCOME

AND ITS FLUCTUATIONS

11 SAVING, CONSUMPTION, AND INVESTMENT

Micawber's equation. Income 20 pounds a year:expenditure 19 pounds, 19 shillings and sixpence = HAPPINESS. Income 20 pounds:expenditure 20 pounds and sixpence = MISERY.

CHARLES DICKENS

In Part One the groundwork was laid for an understanding of the concept of national income. Now we can go beyond the anatomy of the problem to its physiology. What causes national income to rise? To fall? To be what it is at any time rather than something larger or smaller?

This chapter provides an introduction to what is called the "modern theory of income analysis." The principal stress is upon the *level of total spending as determined by the interplay of the monetary forces of saving and investment.*

Although much of this analysis is due to an English economist, John Maynard Keynes (later made Lord Keynes, before his death in 1946), today its broad fundamentals are increasingly accepted by economists of all schools of thought, including, it is important to notice, many who do not share Keynes' particular policy views and who differ on technical details of analysis.[1]

The income analysis here described is itself neutral: it can be used as well to defend private enterprise as to limit it, as well to attack as to defend government fiscal intervention. When business organizations such as the United States Chamber of Commerce, the Committee for Economic Development, or the First National City Bank use the terminology of saving and investment, it is absurd to think that this implies that they are "Keynesian" in the sense of belonging to that narrow band of zealots associated with some of the policy programs that Keynes himself espoused during the Great Depression.

In recent years 90 per cent of American economists have stopped being "Keynesian economists" or "anti-Keynesian economists." Instead they have

[1] Keynes himself was a many-sided genius who won eminence in the field of mathematics and philosophy and in the literary field. In addition he found time to run a large insurance company, to advise the British Treasury, to help govern the Bank of England, to edit a world-famous economic journal, and to sponsor ballet and drama. He was also an economist who knew how to make money, both for himself and for King's College, Cambridge. His 1936 book, *The General Theory of Employment, Interest and Money,* created the greatest stir in economic thinking of the century and is likely to live long as a classic.

worked toward a synthesis of whatever is valuable in older economics and in modern theories of income determination. The result might be called "neo-classical economics" and is accepted in its broad outlines by all but about 5 per cent of extreme left-wing and right-wing writers.

▶ **THE CLEAVAGE BETWEEN SAVING AND INVESTMENT**

The most important single fact about saving and investment is that in our in-dustrial society they are generally done by different people and for different reasons.

This was not always so; even today, when a farmer devotes his time to drain-ing a field instead of to planting and harvesting a crop, he is saving and at the same time investing. He is saving because he is abstaining from present con-sumption in order to provide for larger consumption in the future, the amount of his saving being measured by the difference between his net real income and his consumption. But he is also investing; *i.e.,* he is undertaking net capital formation, improving the productive capacity of his farm.

Not only are saving and investment the same things for a primitive farmer, but his reasons for undertaking them are the same. He abstains from present consumption (saves) only because he wants to drain the field (to invest). If there were no investment opportunity, it would never occur to him to save; nor would there be any way for him to save should he be so foolish as to wish to.

In our modern economy, net capital formation or investment is carried on by business enterprises, especially corporations. When a corporation or a small business has great investment opportunities, its owners will be tempted to plow back much of its earnings into the business. To an important degree, therefore, business saving does depend directly upon business investment.

Nevertheless, saving is also done by an entirely different group: by indi-viduals, by families, by households. An individual may wish to save for a great variety of reasons: because he wishes to provide for his old age or for a future expenditure (a vacation or an automobile). Or he may feel insecure and wish to guard against a rainy day. Or he may wish to leave an estate to his children or to his children's children. Or he may be an eighty-year-old miser with no heirs who enjoys the act of accumulating for its own sake. Or he may already have signed himself up to a savings program because an insurance salesman overcame his resistance. Or he may desire the power that greater wealth brings. Or thrift may simply be a habit, a conditioned reflex whose origin he himself does not know. And so forth.

Whatever the individual's motivation to save, it has often little to do with investment opportunities. This truth is obscured by the fact that in everyday language "investment" does not always have the same meaning as in economic discussions. We have defined "net investment" or capital formation to be the net increase in the community's real capital (equipment, buildings, inventories, etc.). But the man on the street speaks of "investing" when he buys a piece of land, an old security, or any title to property. For economists these are clearly *transfer* items. What one man is investing, someone else is disinvesting. There is net investment only when new real capital is created.

In short, even if there are no real investment opportunities that seem profitable, an individual will often still wish to save. He can always buy an existing security or asset. If necessary, he can accumulate, or try to accumulate, cash.

▶ THE VARIABILITY OF INVESTMENT

Thus, we are left with our proposition: *Saving and investing are often done by different individuals and for independent reasons.* Net capital formation takes place largely in business enterprise. Its amount is highly variable from year to year and decade to decade. This capricious, volatile behavior is understandable when we come to realize that investment opportunities depend on *new* discoveries, *new* products, *new* territories and frontiers, *new* resources, *new* population, *higher* production and income. Note the emphasis on "new" and on "higher." Investment depends on the *dynamic* and relatively unpredictable elements of *growth* in the system, on elements outside the economic system itself: technology, politics, optimistic and pessimistic expectations, governmental tax and expenditure, legislative policies, etc.

This extreme variability of investment is the next important fact to be emphasized. We shall see that an industrial system such as our own can do many wonderful things. It can mobilize men, tools, and know-how to respond to any given demand for goods. Over time it can improve upon its own response.

But there is one thing it cannot do. Unless proper policies are pursued, it cannot guarantee that there will be just exactly the required amount of investment to ensure full employment: not too little so as to cause unemployment, nor too much so as to cause inflation. As far as total investment or money-spending power is concerned, the laissez-faire system is without any thermostat. For decades there might tend to be too much investment, leading to periods of chronic inflation. For other years or decades, there might tend to be too little investment, leading to deflation, losses, excess capacity, unemployment, and destitution.

Nor is there an "invisible hand" guaranteeing that the good years will equal the bad, or guaranteeing that scientists will discover just in the nick of time precisely sufficient new products and processes to keep the system on an even keel. From the 1850's to the 1870's railroads were built all over the world. In the next two decades nothing quite took their place. The automobile and public utilities produced a similar revolution in the 1920's. In the 1930's plastics and radio had no comparable effect on total net investment.[1] And in the 1950's we most of the time were plagued by too much investment spending.

Nor are the instabilities all on the downward side. Economic history is a history of inflations. Anyone who comes of age in 1958 has seen prices more than double in his own lifetime. Unless proper policies are followed, he can look forward to gyrating prices for the rest of his life.

This then is one of our most important economic lessons. Where total investment is concerned, the system is in the lap of the gods. We may be lucky or unlucky; and the only thing you can say about luck is, It is going to change.

Fortunately, things need not be left to luck. We shall see that perfectly sensible public and private policies can be followed that will greatly enhance the stability and productive growth of our economic system. They cannot expect to wipe out business fluctuations 100 per cent. We wouldn't want them to even if they could. But they can try to reduce the range of wild fluctuations in prices and employment—as the following chapters discuss.

The next chapter will show how investment and saving determine the equilibrium level of national income. First, we must understand the important graphical curves relating consumption, saving, and income.

▶ THE PROPENSITY-TO-CONSUME SCHEDULE

Income is the single most important determinant of consumption and saving. Poor families spend much of their income on the necessities of life—food, shelter, and, in lesser degree, clothing. By and large, rich men can, and do, save more than poor men, not only absolutely, but as a percentage of their income.

In Chapter 9, we saw how people with different-sized budgets spend their incomes on the various consumption items and on saving. Turn to Table 1, where the 1950 family data given in Chapter 9, page 169, have been rearranged. For the moment disregard Columns (3) to (5) of this table and notice how consumption expenditure goes up at each higher level of income.

This same relation can be shown even more vividly in diagrammatic form. In Fig. 1, the total of consumption expenditure in Column (2) is plotted against family disposable income of Column (1); through the resulting circles, *A, B, C, D, E, F, G,* and *H,* a smooth curve has been drawn.

This is called the consumption schedule, or propensity-to-consume schedule, or often simply the propensity to consume. The consumption schedule is a basic, important concept whose general properties we must study.

---

[1] Scientific progress was going on in the 1930's. Our wartime production shows that clearly. But some scientific discoveries can have a harmful effect on employment and purchasing power, both in the long run and in the short run, but especially in the latter. Again, there is no automatic principle of compensation which guarantees that technological change will produce a *sufficiently* favorable effect on purchasing power, or even any favorable effect. See Chapter 35 on automation for further discussion.

How we depict important consumption-income patterns:

1st, A table presents the propensity-to-consume schedule

Table 1. Propensity to consume and propensity to save. Each dollar of income not consumed is saved. And each extra dollar of income goes into extra consumption or extra saving —giving us two important concepts we are to study: The MPC and MPS. (Source: Table 1, Chap. 9, p. 169.)

	Disposable income (after taxes) (1)	Consumption expenditure (2)	Marginal propensity to consume (MPC) (3)	Net saving (1) − (2) (4)	Marginal propensity to save (MPS) (5)
A.	$ 3,000	$3,110		−$ 110	
			$\frac{890}{1000} = .89$		$\frac{110}{1000} = .11$
B.	4,000	4,000		0	
			$\frac{850}{1000} = .85$		$\frac{150}{1000} = .15$
C.	5,000	4,850		+150	
			$\frac{750}{1000} = .75$		$\frac{250}{1000} = .25$
D.	6,000	5,600		+400	
			$\frac{640}{1000} = .64$		$\frac{360}{1000} = .36$
E.	7,000	6,240		+760	
			$\frac{590}{1000} = .59$		$\frac{410}{1000} = .41$
F.	8,000	6,830		+1,170	
			$\frac{530}{1000} = .53$		$\frac{470}{1000} = .47$
G.	9,000	7,360		+1,640	
			$\frac{490}{1000} = .49$		$\frac{510}{1000} = .51$
H.	10,000	7,850		+2,150	

It will help you to understand its properties if first you look at the 45° line also shown in Fig. 1. Inasmuch as the vertical axis of consumption has been drawn to the same scale as the horizontal axis of income, any point lying on the 45° helping line has the following simple property: Its indicated consumption expenditure—measured by the vertical distance of the point from the horizontal axis—is exactly equal to 100 per cent of its indicated level of disposable income—measured by the horizontal distance of the point from the vertical axis. (Use your eye to verify that any point *not* on the 45° line cannot possibly be equidistant from the two axes.)

The "break-even" point. The 45° line will tell us right away, therefore, whether consumption spending is equal to, greater than, or less than the level of income. The point on the consumption schedule where it intersects the 45°

2d, A schedule graphs the propensity to consume

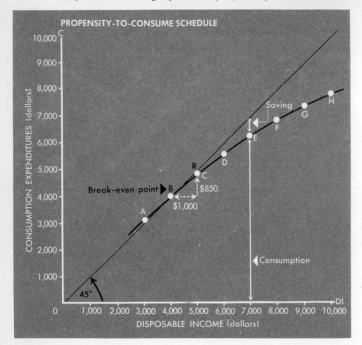

PROPENSITY-TO-CONSUME SCHEDULE

Fig. 1. The curve through *A, B, . . . , H* is the consumption schedule or the propensity to consume. Its slope at any point—as measured by forming a little triangle and relating altitude to base—is the MPC, the marginal propensity to consume. The 45° line helps locate the break-even point and helps our eye measure net saving. Can you see how? (Source: Table 1.)

line shows us the level of disposable income at which families just break even. This break-even point is at *B*; here, consumption expenditure is exactly equal to disposable income; the family is borrowing nothing and on balance saving nothing. Similarly, *anywhere else* on the propensity-to-consume curve, the family cannot be just breaking even. To the right of point *B*, the curve lies below the 45° line; the arrows in Fig. 1 show that the vertical distance (consumption expenditure) is less than the horizontal distance (disposable income). If the family is not spending all its income, then it must be saving the remainder. The 45° line tells us more than that; it enables us to find *how much* the family is saving. Net saving is measured by the distance from the propensity-to-consume curve up to the 45° line, as shown by the appropriate arrows.

Similarly, to the left of point *B,* our 45° helping line tells us that the family is for the moment somehow spending more than the income it receives. The excess of consumption over income is its "net dissaving" and is measured by the vertical distance between the two curves.

To review: When the propensity-to-consume schedule lies above the 45° line, the family is dissaving. Where the two curves meet, the family is just breaking even. Where the propensity to consume lies below the 45° line, the family is performing net positive saving. And the amount of dissaving or saving is always measured by the distance between the two curves.

3d, The saving schedule is the exact twin of the consumption schedule

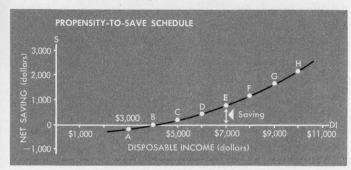

Fig. 2. This saving schedule comes from subtracting consumption from income. (Graphically, we vertically subtracted the consumption schedule from the 45° helping line.) Note the break-even point B is at same $4,000 level as in Fig. 1. Why? Measure MPS by the curve's slope at any point. Does MPS + MPC = 1 everywhere? (It had better!)

The "propensity-to-save schedule." This means that we can easily derive from the consumption schedule in Fig. 1 a new schedule: the propensity to save, or as it is sometimes called, the "saving schedule."

Graphically, this is shown in Fig. 2. Again we show disposable income on the horizontal axis; vertically we now show what the family *does not* spend; *i.e.*, we show its net saving, whether negative or positive in amount.

This propensity-to-save curve comes directly from Fig. 1. It is simply the distance between the 45° line and the propensity-to-consume schedule. At a point such as *A* in Fig. 1, the fact that the family's savings were negative was indicated by the propensity-to-consume schedule lying above the helping line. Fig. 2 shows this fact directly, and similarly for the positive savings that begin when family income pushes past point *B*.

▶ **THE MARGINAL PROPENSITY TO CONSUME**

In the next chapter, we shall be attaching much importance to the *extra* amount that people will want to spend on consumption if given an *extra* dollar of income. Economists are so interested in this concept that they have given it a special name: the marginal propensity to consume, or MPC. (The word "marginal" is used by the economist to mean "extra"; thus, marginal cost is later defined as extra cost of producing an extra unit of product, marginal utility as extra utility, marginal revenue as extra revenue, etc.)

Column (3) of Table 1 shows how we compute the marginal propensity to consume. Between *B* and *C*, income rises by $1,000, going from $4,000 to $5,000. By how much does consumption rise? Consumption grows from $4,000 to $4,850, or by $850. The extra consumption is, therefore, .85 of the extra income. Out of each extra dollar of income, 85 cents goes to consumption and 15 cents goes to saving. We therefore can say that the marginal propensity to consume is .85 between *B* and *C*, which agrees with Column (3) of Table 1.

You can easily compute the MPC between other income levels. In Table 1, the MPC begins at .89 for poor people and finally falls to .49 at higher incomes.

Why is the MPC so important? Because it helps us know what people will do with the *extra* money they get. Example: Suppose you transfer a dollar from a $10,000-a-year man to a $3,000-a-year poor man. If all other things remain constant, the poor man will up his consumption by what? With his MPC = .89, by 89 cents. And the rich man will cut his consumption by his MPC of 49 cents. Result of the redistribution: an extra 40 cents of consumption spending.[1]

Now we know how to compute the MPC numerically. What is its geometric meaning? It is a numerical measure of the steepness of slope of the consumption schedule.[2] Look again at Fig. 1. Below points *B* and *C* is drawn a little triangle. As we move to the right from *B* by $1,000, in order to stay on the schedule, we must go up by $850; this gives a numerical slope $850/$1,000, or .85. NOTE: If higher incomes have a lower MPC, the family consumption schedule will look slightly bowed or convex (from above).

▶ **THE MARGINAL PROPENSITY TO SAVE**

Along with the marginal propensity to consume goes a Siamese-twin concept, the *marginal propensity to save, or MPS.* This is defined as *the fraction of each extra dollar that goes to saving instead of to consumption.*

Why are MPC and MPS joined like Siamese twins? Since each extra dollar of income must be divided between extra consumption and extra saving, it is obvious that, if MPC is .85, then MPS must be .15. (What would MPS be if MPC were .6? Or .99?) A comparison of Columns (3) and (5) of Table 1 confirms our common-sense feeling that at any income level, MPC and MPS must always add up to exactly 1, no more and no less.[3]

---

[1] But an important warning is in order: Careful study of budget statistics shows that the difference between the MPC of rich and poor is not so great as the man in the street might guess from his knowledge that the poor do little *total* saving and the rich do much. And before drawing any final conclusions on the effects of redistributive taxes on aggregate spending, we should have to take into account any adverse effects of the taxation upon investment.

[2] By the numerical slope of the line *XY*, we always mean the numerical ratio of the length *ZY* to the length *XZ*.

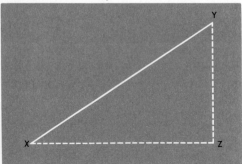

[3] You can also verify from Fig. 2 that the numerical steepness of slope of the propensity-to-save schedule is the geometric expression of MPS. This shows: The savings schedule will always have the opposite curvature to that of the consumption schedule; as MPC falls, MPS must rise. And since every extra dollar must divide up between extra consumption and extra saving, it follows that neither the consumption nor the savings schedule can *anywhere* have a slope as steep as the 45° line, which by definition has a slope of 1. (Remember, we are here discussing *marginal* propensities. Thus, at point *A* the family is spending more than its income; but that doesn't alter the fact that, at *A*, its *marginal* propensity to consume *extra* income is less than 1.)

▶ **BRIEF REVIEW OF DEFINITIONS**

For the record let's jot down the main definitions now learned.

1. The propensity-to-consume schedule or consumption schedule relates in a table or a curve the level of consumption to the level of income.

2. The propensity-to-save schedule or saving schedule relates saving to income. Since what is saved is the same thing as what is nonconsumed, saving and consumption schedules are Siamese twins in the sense that

$$\text{Saving} + \text{consumption} = \text{disposable income}$$

3. The "break-even point" is the income level where net saving is zero. Below it, there is dissaving or negative saving; above it, positive net saving. Graphically, the break-even point is where the 45° helping line intersects the consumption schedule; or it is where the saving schedule intersects the horizontal axis.

4. The marginal propensity to consume (MPC) is the amount of *extra* consumption generated by an *extra* dollar of income. Graphically, it is given by the slope of the consumption schedule—a steep slope meaning a high MPC and a flat one meaning a low MPC.

5. The marginal propensity to save (MPS) is the *extra* saving generated by an *extra* dollar of income—or the slope of the saving schedule. Because the part of each dollar that is not consumed is necessarily saved, MPS = 1 − MPC always. Hence, rising family income that lowers MPC must raise MPS, implying a convex-from-above consumption schedule and a concave saving schedule.

▶ **THE COMMUNITY'S OVER-ALL CONSUMPTION SCHEDULE**

So far we have been talking about the consumption patterns shown by families of different incomes. To study what determines national income, we are interested in a propensity-to-consume schedule slightly different from the family budget schedule. We are interested in the so-called national propensity-to-consume schedule, relating total consumption to total "disposable income."[1] This is because we are interested in how the total of *all* consumption spending in the United States changes as the total of our national income rises.

While aggregate income is not the only factor determining aggregate consumption, common sense and statistical experience tell us that it is one of the most important factors. Note in Fig. 3 how closely consumption follows yearly disposable income; the only exceptional period is that of the war, when goods were scarce and rationed and people were urged to save.

Figure 4 shows this relationship between consumption and disposable income in the form of a "scatter diagram" for the years 1929 to 1957. Each dot indicates the magnitude for each year. The resulting scatter of points

---
[1] Remember disposable income is people's income *after* they've paid their taxes.

4th, National consumption did move with national income

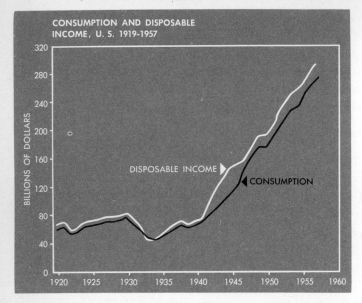

CONSUMPTION AND DISPOSABLE
INCOME, U. S. 1919-1957

DISPOSABLE INCOME

CONSUMPTION

BILLIONS OF DOLLARS

Fig. 3. Can you see how great saving became during wartime goods shortage and rationing? (Source: U.S. Department of Commerce.)

shows no particular curvature, so a straight-line consumption schedule was drawn in. Note how the actual data fall near, but not exactly on, the "fitted" consumption schedule,[1] reminding us that economics is not, like physics, an exact science.

▶ **QUALIFICATIONS**

We are now prepared for the theory of income determination. We have introduced the crucially important concepts of consumption and saving schedules that will be used in the next chapter. But warnings are in order.

The national consumption schedule must be in some sense an aggregation of the family schedules. Yet even if we knew that the family schedules were perfectly reliable, we should still have to know something about the distribution of income before we could get the national schedule. Thus, if the Lorenz curve of income distribution were to shift toward greater inequality, we should expect the national saving schedule to shift upward and the national consumption schedule to shift downward. (Why?) On the other hand, if the national income rises and this rise is associated with the usual shift in the Lorenz curve, then we will be moving along on our unshifted national consumption schedule.

Aside from the distribution of income, there is a second factor that must be

---

[1] So that no reader may think there is great accuracy in this line, let me explain that I fitted it in 1950 by stretching a black thread through the peacetime data at what appeared a reasonable position. The 1950 line luckily gave a pretty good fit to the 1957 data!

5th, The national consumption schedule in statistical form

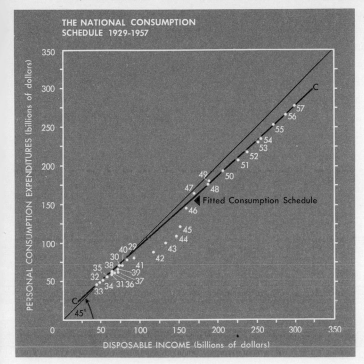

Fig. 4. The curve CC approximately fits the peacetime statistical points. Can you verify its break-even point of about $60 billion and MPC of about .92? (Source: Figure 3.)

taken into account in any attempt to relate the family and national patterns. Suppose my income were to go from $5,000 a year to $40,000 a year. Would I spend and save my money in the same way that the budget studies showed $40,000-a-year people spend their money? Not necessarily. Especially at the beginning, I would be *nouveau riche* and have different patterns of behavior.

A third reason why it is difficult to go from the family to the national consumption schedule is suggested by the expression "keeping up with the Joneses." Fifty years ago if your family had $2,000 worth of purchasing power, you would have been quite well off and above the break-even point of zero saving. But today many people have incomes above that level. Because man is a social animal, what he regards as necessary comforts of life depends on what he sees others consuming. So today with $2,000 of income, you would be desperately poor and unable to make ends meet. This fact that one man's consumption depends upon the incomes and consumption of others means that we cannot expect the final national pattern to be the simple sum of the separate family patterns. It also means that we must expect the consumption schedule to be shifting upward each decade as living standards rise.

A number of other important qualifications will occur to the reader.[1] The national consumption schedule will shift every time that prices change and total population grows. Statisticians sometimes try to allow for this by working with per capita consumption and per capita income, expressed in real terms by means of a deflating price index of the sort discussed in the last chapter.

We can think of still other reasons why the propensity-to-consume schedule might shift around. Thus, at the end of World War II, many economists made a famous wrong prediction. They neglected the fact that people came out of the war with greatly increased amounts of liquid assets; for this and other reasons, the consumption schedule turned out to be at a higher level than many pessimistic predictions had indicated.

Again we are reminded that no social science can have great exactitude. We shall have to use tools, like the propensity-to-consume curve—or later, in Part Three, curves of supply and demand—which we know are subject to error and which tend to shift through time rather than remain stable.

SUMMARY

1. Income is one of the most important determinants of consumption and saving. The propensity to consume is the schedule relating consumption and income. Because any dollar of income is either saved or consumed, the propensity-to-save schedule is the other side of the propensity-to-consume picture.

2. The consumption schedules rises with income. Below some break-even point people consume more than their income. The break-even point is depicted graphically at the point where the consumption schedule intersects a helping 45° line. To the right of the break-even point, net saving is positive and can be read from Fig. 1 by measuring the vertical distance that the consumption schedule lies below the 45° line.

3. The saving schedule is almost the mirror image or Siamese twin of the consumption schedule. It, too, rises with income but usually at a much slower rate. Its indicated break-even point must, of course, be at the same income level as in Fig. 1, but graphically this is recognized in Fig. 2 as the point where the saving schedule intersects the horizontal axis and passes from being negative to being positive.

4. The marginal propensities to consume and to save, MPC and MPS, represent the fractions of each extra dollar of income that are, respectively, consumed and saved. Their sum is unity: $MPC + MPS = 1$. Geometrically they are shown by the numerical steepness of the slopes of the consumption and saving schedules. Typically, there is an empirical tendency for the MPC to decline as people become richer and for the MPS to rise; this means that the

---

[1] Here's one: if people look forward to *variable* incomes, they'll tend to save more. So *part* of the higher saving rate of the rich may be due to the temporary nature of their high incomes. Part but, I suspect, not all.

consumption schedule has a slight convex curvature while the saving schedule has an opposite and equal concave curvature. It also means that redistributing incomes from higher to lower incomes has a slight tendency to increase the total spent on consumption out of any given income.

5. (a) If we knew the distribution of income for each level of disposable income, (b) if families always stuck to the same consumption-income patterns, (c) if we could forget the fact that one man's consumption is influenced by the income levels of his neighbors, and (d) if price levels, population, corporate saving, and taxes could be neglected, then we could aggregate the family consumption schedules to get the national propensity-to-consume schedule. The statistical data suggest that total consumption expenditure follows rather closely the changes in total disposable income. But in using the propensity-to-consume concept in the next chapter's discussion of income determination, we must beware of forming an exaggerated notion of the accuracy and empirical stability of such a theoretical concept.

QUESTIONS FOR DISCUSSION

1. What are some of the reasons why people save? What are some of the forms in which they keep their assets?

2. Exactly how in Table 1 were the MPC and MPS computed? Illustrate between *A* and *B*. Is "marginal" a good name for "extra"? Explain why it must always be true that MPC + MPS = 1.

3. I consume *all* my income. Draw my consumption and saving schedules.

4. Do you think the break-even point is the same in New York and in Mississippi? What do you think is the current break-even point in your community? List a number of ways a person can incur negative net saving for a while.

5. "Along the consumption schedule, income changes more than does consumption." Why? Show that this is even more true on the saving schedule.

6. What factors must be taken into consideration if we want to aggregate family budgetary propensity-to-consume schedules to arrive at a national propensity-to-consume schedule? What would happen to the amount consumed out of $400 billion of NI if the degree of inequality of income were increased? To the amount saved? What if total taxes out of the $400 billion were to increase? If people were to have more government bonds and bank deposits, how would that affect saving out of $400 billion of national income?

7. Review your understanding of the following concepts:

net investment and transfers	*MPC and MPS*
saving motives and volatile investment decisions	*break-even point and 45° line*
	after-tax or disposable income
propensity to consume or save, consumption and saving schedules	*national consumption schedule versus family schedule*

THE THEORY OF INCOME DETERMINATION

Given the propensity to consume and the rate of new investment, there will be only one level of employment consistent with equilibrium.

J. M. KEYNES (1936)

All modern economists are agreed that the important factor in causing income and employment to fluctuate is investment. Whether we are to face a situation of inflationary bidding up of prices or shall live in a frigid state of mass unemployment depends, we shall see, upon the level of investment.

There is no need to emphasize the importance of the problem of income determination. For the last decade, nations everywhere have been plagued by problems connected with too high general money demand, shortages, and price increases. But memories are short, and there is danger that we shall forget the tremendous costs that were associated with the mass unemployment of the prewar Great Depression. Figure 1 reminds us that the cost of that depression—as measured in terms of the value of production wasted through unemployment of men and machines—ran to more than half a trillion postwar dollars! It is scarcely an exaggeration to say that the economic costs of that depression were of the same general magnitude as the costs of all the economic resources which had to be used up in World War II itself.

A DETERMINATION OF THE EQUILIBRIUM LEVEL OF INCOME

Figure 2, page 224, gives a simplified picture of the propensity-to-consume and propensity-to-save schedules for the community. As discussed in the preceding chapter, they are drawn up on the basis of our knowledge of the thriftiness of different families, the distribution of incomes between families, and so forth.

222

Cost of the Great Depression rivals that of war:

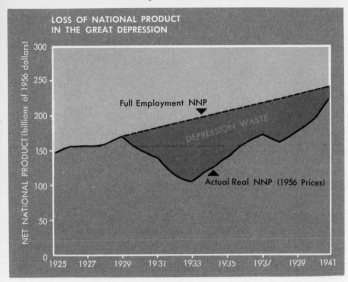

LOSS OF NATIONAL PRODUCT
IN THE GREAT DEPRESSION

Full Employment NNP

DEPRESSION WASTE

Actual Real NNP (1956 Prices)

NET NATIONAL PRODUCT (billions of 1956 dollars)

300
250
200
150
100
50
0

1925 1927 1929 1931 1933 1935 1937 1939 1941

Fig. 1. The shaded area shows the gap between what we actually produced in the 1930's and what our economic system was capable of producing. In postwar dollars, this waste exceeds half a trillion dollars.

(At the beginning, we shall make the further simplifying assumptions that there are no taxes or undistributed corporate profits to worry about; hence, we do not have to worry about any distinction between net national product and disposable income, and we can use the word "income" to refer to either. Also, we shall initially neglect any changes in the price level.)

To summarize: each point on the consumption schedule shows how much the community will *want to continue to consume* at that level of disposable income. Each point on the saving schedule shows what it will want to continue to save at that income level. The two schedules are clearly related: since $C + S =$ income always, the CC and SS curves are Siamese twins that would add up always to the 45° line.

> ### ► HOW INCOME IS DETERMINED AT THE LEVEL WHERE SAVING AND INVESTMENT SCHEDULES INTERSECT

We have seen that saving and investment are dependent on quite different factors: Saving tends to depend in a "passive" way upon income, while volatile investment depends upon "autonomous" factors of dynamic growth. (Reread page 211 if this is not clear.)

For simplicity, let's first suppose investment opportunities are such that net investment would be exactly 10 billion dollars per year regardless of the level of NNP. This means that, if we now draw a schedule of investment against NNP, it will have to be a *horizontal* line—always the same distance above the

Society's national income determines its consumption and saving:

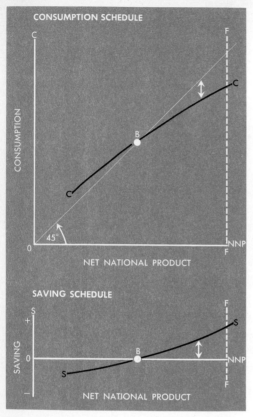

Fig. 2. CC is the propensity-to-consume and SS is the propensity-to-save schedules for the community. Note that these are closely related: the break-even point B is shown on the upper diagram where CC intersects the 45-degree line, and on the lower diagram where SS intersects the horizontal axis. Can you explain why the vertically aligned white arrows *must* be equal? The broken line F depicts the full-employment NNP. What would consumption and saving be at that level?

horizontal axis. In Fig. 3, this investment schedule is labeled *II* to distinguish it from the *SS* saving schedule.

The saving and investment schedules intersect at *E,* which corresponds to a level of NNP equal to the distance *OM.*

▶ This intersection of the *saving and investment schedules is the equilibrium toward which national income will gravitate.* Under our assumed conditions, no other level of income can perpetuate itself. The remaining pages of Section A of this chapter are devoted to the single task of explaining this important truth.

Let us see why the equilibrium income must eventually be at *E,* the point of intersection between the investment and saving schedules. We consider three cases to show this.

The first case is that in which the system is *at E* itself, where the *II* schedule of what business firms want to invest just intersects the *SS* schedule of what families want to save. Consequently everyone will be content to go on doing just what he has been doing. Firms will not find inventories piling up on their shelves, nor will they find sales so brisk as to force them to produce more goods. So production, employment, and income spending will remain the same. NNP in this first case does truly stay at the point *E;* and we can rightly call that "equilibrium."

The second case is where the system starts out with an NNP *higher* than at *E,* so that it is east of *E,* at an income level where the *SS* schedule is higher than the *II* schedule. Why can't the system stay there? Because at such an income level, families are saving—are refraining from spending on consumption— *more* than business firms will be willing to go on investing. Firms will thus find too few customers and will find their inventories piling up against their wishes; and they won't want to go on being forced into such undesired inventory investment. Well, what can they do about it? They can certainly cut back production and lay off workers. This moves our NNP downward, which means westward in Fig. 3. Where does the system stop being in such disequilibrium? Only when it gets back to *E,* the equilibrium intersection point. There the tendency to change has disappeared.

The third case should be mastered by you, the reader. You should show that if NNP were *below* its equilibrium level, strong forces would be set up to move it eastward back to *E.* (Hint: At any NNP level where families intended saving falls short of business firms' intended investment, there will · result consumption of more goods than are being currently produced. What does this mean? It means that business will find itself having to sell inventory off its shelves faster than its production line is producing such goods. Once businessmen notice that they are being forced into less investment—*i.e.,* into more inventory *dis*investment—than the *II* curve shows they want, what will they do? You should show that they will then begin to expand production and hire more men. And this will complete your demonstration that the system does move back eastward until it gets to *E.*)

All three cases then lead to the same summary:

We can show equilibrium determination of national income in the following equivalent ways:

1st, by intersection of saving and investment schedules:

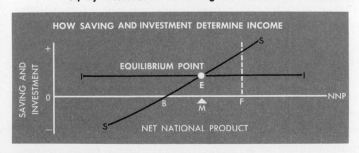

HOW SAVING AND INVESTMENT DETERMINE INCOME

Fig. 3. *E* marks the spot where investment and saving curves intersect. Equilibrium is there because at no other level of NNP could the desired saving of families match the desired investment of business.

▶ The only equilibrium of national income is at *E*, where the saving and investment schedules intersect. At any other point, the desired saving of families will not match the desired investment of business, and this discrepancy will cause businessmen to change their production and employment levels—in such a way as to return the system to the equilibrium intersection.

Before we go on, a warning is in order. An equilibrium level like *E* is a point where the system tends to stay. But don't think that there is something heavenly about every equilibrium point. There isn't. Note the vertical dotted line *F* in Fig. 3 that depicts full-employment income. Be sure you grasp the fact that the shown *E* equilibrium is at a level of NNP lower than that corresponding to *F*'s full employment.

During a great depression, a capitalistic system may be firmly stuck at a point of very great unemployment. It is then at the *E* given by its low *II* schedule. But no one would make the mistake of thinking that such a deep-unemployment equilibrium point is in any sense a good thing. Instead we would try to help the economic system get its curves shifted until a new equilibrium point, *E'*, ends up at a desirable level.

▶ **INCOME DETERMINATION BY CONSUMPTION AND INVESTMENT**

There is a second way of showing how income is determined, other than by the intersection of the saving and investment schedules. The final result is exactly the same, but our understanding and confidence in the theory of income determination will be increased if we work through this second approach.

This second approach is called the consumption-plus-investment rather than the saving-investment approach. The *C* + *I* approach takes advantage of the Siamese-twins property of the saving and consumption schedules. Thus it must always lead to exactly the same equilibrium income as does the saving-and-investment approach. This is shown by the fact that when you carefully line up Fig. 4 vertically under Fig. 3, you always find that *E* falls in both charts at exactly the same NNP equilibrium.

The *C* + *I* approach has the advantage of concentrating on *total spending:* on all the spending for consumption goods plus all the spending on investment goods. The *C* + *I* approach adds the *CC* consumption schedule of families' desired consumption spending to the *II* schedule of business firms' desired investment.

Only where the two desired amounts of spending add up to equality with the value of NNP being produced will there be equilibrium.

With what must the combined *C* + *I* schedule intersect to depict this equilibrium? Figure 4 introduces a very useful 45° line to provide our looked-for intersection point. The 45° line, we have earlier seen, has the nice property that it lays off in the vertical direction a distance always exactly equal to the

2d, by intersection of C + I schedule with 45-degree line:

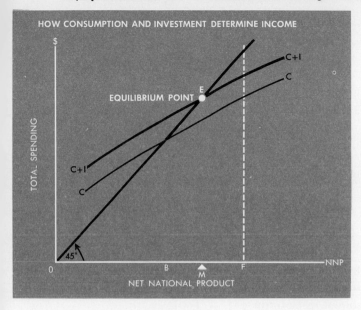

HOW CONSUMPTION AND INVESTMENT DETERMINE INCOME

Fig. 4. Adding *II* to *CC* gives the C + I curve of total spending. At E, where it intersects the 45-degree line, we get the same equilibrium as in the saving and investment diagram. (Note the similarities between this figure and Fig. 3: the investment added to CC is the same as Fig. 3's *II*: B and F each come at the same place on the two diagrams, *and so must the E intersection*.)

income shown on the horizontal axis. So the 45° line is admirably designed to depict the expense that firms are incurring for the productive factors needed to produce national output, and which they must be getting back if they are to stay content to go on hiring the same number of men and producing the same level of NNP.[1]

We can summarize the *C + I* method of income determination thus:

▶ The equilibrium level of national income is at the intersection of the *C + I* schedule of desired total spending with the 45° line depicting value of total output. This equilibrium *E* corresponds exactly to the saving-and-investment equilibrium because of the Siamese-twins relation between the consumption and the saving schedules.

We'll see in Section C that the *C + I* approach has great advantages in helping to analyze government expenditure and fiscal policy. It easily turns itself into an exactly similar *C + I + G* approach.

[1] As the intermediate texts would put it: If the system is not at this intersection, there will be *unintended* inventory investment or disinvestment and/or *unforseen windfall* profits or losses. As a result, there cannot be equilibrium, but rather there will be set up a chain of new decisions to expand or contract output, and possibly to raise or lower prices. So the system will move in disequilibrium until it ends up at the intersection point of equilibrium. Those same intermediate texts point out that *measured S* and measured *I* stay identical even during the worst disequilibrium—by virtue of some people's experiencing unintended losses or gains and/or experiencing unintended investment or saving.

▶ ARITHMETIC DEMONSTRATION OF INCOME DETERMINATION: A THIRD RESTATEMENT

A thoughtful reader may still not be satisfied with his comprehension of *why* the equilibrium level of income will have to be at the intersection of the saving and investment schedules. What forces push income to that level and no other?

An arithmetic example may help to clinch your grasp of this important matter. In Table 1, an especially simple pattern of the propensity to save against national income has been recorded. The break-even level of income where the nation is too poor to do any net saving on balance is assumed to be 240 billion dollars. Each change of national income of 30 billion dollars is assumed to lead to a 10-billion-dollar change in saving and a 20-billion-dollar change in consumption; in other words, MPC is assumed to be constant and exactly equal to $2/3$ with $MPS = 1/3$. For this reason, the saving propensity schedule, *SS*, in Fig. 5 takes 'on the especially simple form of a perfectly straight line.

What shall we assume about investment? For simplicity, let us suppose again that the only level of investment that can be maintained indefinitely is exactly 20 billion dollars, as shown in Column (4) of Table 1.

Now, Columns (5) and (6) are the crucial ones. Column (5) shows how much expense business firms undergo at each level of national production for wages, interest, profit, etc. This is nothing but NNP of Column (1) copied

3d, the tendency toward equilibrium is shown by an arithmetic table:

Table I. National income determination by saving and investment (billions of dollars). The unshaded row depicts the equilibrium NNP, where the 20 billion dollars that businessmen will continue to invest is just matched by families' intended saving. (In higher rows, firms will be forced into unintended inventory investment and will respond by cutting production and NNP back to equilibrium. You interpret the lower rows' expansion arrows.)

Possible levels of NNP (1)	Scheduled con- sumption (2)	Scheduled saving (3)=(1)−(2)	Scheduled level of main- tainable invest- ment (4)	Expense in- curred by business to produce NNP (5)=(1)	Scheduled spending that would be received back by businesses (6)=(2)+(4)	Resulting tendency of income (7)
$360	$320	$40	$20	$360	>	$340	Contraction
330	300	30	20	330	>	320	Contraction
300	280	20	20	300	=	300	Equilibrium
270	260	10	20	270	<	280	Expansion
240	240	0	20	240	<	260	Expansion
210	220	−10	20	210	<	240	Expansion

4th, a graph of the table shows national income determination:

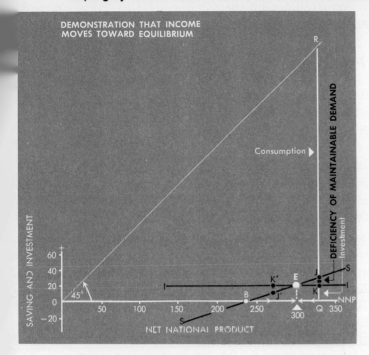

Fig. 5. Only at *E* is there no gap between scheduled saving and investment. A gap like that shown at *JK* will cause firms to cut their production, which explains the westward arrow pushing NNP back to *E*'s equilibrium level. (You show that the opposite gap at *J'K'* will mean firms find their sales so great as to deplete their inventories. And interpret the eastward arrow showing that firms expand production so that NNP goes back to *E*. (Source: Table 1.)

once again into Column (5), because our repeated discussions of Chapter 10 showed that upper- and lower-loop representations are the same.

Column (6), on the other hand, shows what business firms would be *getting back* in the form of scheduled consumption spending plus scheduled investment.

When business firms as a whole are temporarily producing at an expense greater than what they can recover, they will want to contract their operations and NNP will tend to fall. When they are getting back more than their current expense for production, they will increase their production, and NNP will rise.

Only when Column (3)'s level of scheduled saving is exactly equal to Column (4)'s scheduled investment will business firms continue to be in aggregative equilibrium. Their sales will then be just enough to justify continuing their current level of aggregate output, so national income will neither expand nor contract.

This same story is shown in Fig. 5. NNP can be read in either of two ways: on the horizontal axis, or (from the nature of a 45° line) as the equivalent vertical distance from that axis up to the helping 45° line. The line *SS* represents the saving schedule; the line *II* represents the scheduled level of investment that can be maintained over time. Consumption can also be seen in the figure. Since income not saved is consumed, consumption is always the vertical distance between the saving schedule and the 45° line.

Now we can use Fig. 5 to confirm what has just been shown by the arithmetic of Table 1. No level of income can *long persist* if it is higher than the equilibrium level given by the saving and investment intersection at 300 billion dollars. To the right of the intersection point *E*, the expense incurred by businesses would exceed the *amount received back* by businesses in the form of consumption plus investment.

Graphically this is shown by the following: The amount continuously paid out by business is the whole distance up to the 45° line, *e.g.*, from *Q* to *R*; but the amount that would continuously be received back by business would be only the sum of investment *QK* and consumption *JR*. There is a gap of *JK*. Businesses face a real dilemma. For a while they could keep their prices high and let unsold goods pile up on their shelves, but that would not represent an equilibrium situation and could not persist. Or for a while they could lower prices on their goods and sell below cost; but that, too, could not last.

Thus, it is completely clear that income cannot permanently be maintained higher than the equilibrium level—*the level where the amount of saving that people want to do is matched by the amount of investment businessmen are willing to maintain.* A persistent gap of the *JK* type must, through attempts to cut down losses and excessive inventories, result in a contraction of employment and net national product back toward the equilibrium point where there is no gap. Therefore, the arrow near *Q* points leftward back toward the equilibrium level.

You should go through a similar argument to show why income will tend to rise from any place to the left of the equilibrium-intersection level. Indicate on the diagram the relation between business expense and what business receives back. Show that there will be a favorable gap (as at *J'K'*): Business will either be selling so much as to be depleting inventories on their shelves, or they will be temporarily raising their prices and earning extra profits. In either case, they will be tempted to expand their employment and production. And when they do, the result will be a rise in income back toward the equilibrium level.[1]

---

[1] Do the recorded income statistics ever show the gap depicted in *JK* and by Column (6) minus Column (5)? No. Why not? Because these are gaps in people's *scheduled* quantities. They show levels that cannot continue to persist. On the other hand, the *measurable* statistics of saving and investment are definitionally equal no matter what income is doing: thus, when inventory is involuntarily piling up, the Commerce Department cares not that its identity of investment and saving is the result of unintended investment. Why should it? It never goes beyond the anatomy of the problem. But we—interested in dynamic physiology of income determination—are vitally interested in schedules. (NOTE: In Part Three's supply and demand schedules, the same problem will recur; the wheat bought is always numerically identical with the wheat sold, but only at equilibrium market price do the *scheduled* amounts intersect.)

▶ **THE SIMPLE THEORY OF INCOME DETERMINATION RESTATED**

Figure 6 pulls together in a simplified way the main elements of income determination. Without saving and investment, there would be a circular flow of income between business and the public: business pays out (in the upper pipe) wages, interest, rents, and profits to the public in return for the services of labor and property; and in the lower pipe the public pays consumption funds to business in return for goods and services.

Realistically, we must recognize that the public will wish to save some of its income, as shown at the spigot Z. Hence, businesses cannot expect their consumption sales to be as large as the total of wages, interest, rents, and profits. Why not? Because dollars saved can't come back *as consumption sales*.

Some monetary cranks think that this saving necessarily means unemployment and depression. Such a view is simply incorrect. If there happen to be profitable investment opportunities, business firms will be paying out wages, interest, and other costs in part for new investment goods rather than 100 per cent for consumption goods. Hence, to continue to be happy, business needs to receive back in consumption sales only *part* of the total income paid out to the public—only that part which involves the cost of current consumption goods. The saving of the public will do no harm to national income so long as it is not greater than what business can profitably invest.

In Fig. 6, investment is shown being pumped into the income stream at A. The handle of the pump is being moved by (1) technological invention, (2) population growth, and (3) other dynamic factors. When the investment pump is going at a rapid pace, national income is high and reaches its maintainable equilibrium rate when saving at Z just balances investment at A.

This demonstrates that the pessimistic monetary cranks who think that

Dynamic investment pumps national income up and down:

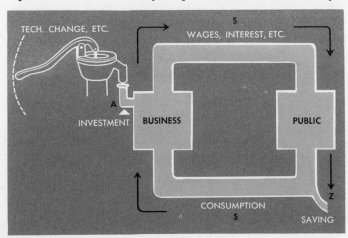

Fig. 6. Technological change, population growth, and other dynamic factors keep the investment pump handle going. Income rises and falls with changes in investment, its equilibrium level, at any time, being realized only when intended saving at Z matches intended investment at A.

saving is always disastrous are plain wrong. But there is also a second school of monetary cranks: they go to the opposite extreme and insist that saving and investment can never cause income to be too high or too low. They make the fatal error of rigidly connecting up the pipe at Z with the pipe at A. Roomfuls of books have been written on this subject, but it is only in the last few decades that economists have learned how to separate the truth and falsity of both extreme viewpoints. The next 100 pages deal with this important question, in its relation to income, banking, and business-cycle policy.

B INVESTMENT AND INCOME

▶ THE "MULTIPLIER"

We have now completed the essentials of the modern theory of income determination. Naturally, we must go on to discuss a number of important qualifications (*e.g.,* the effect of government finance on income analysis). But refinements can wait. In Section B let's explore the relations between investment movements and income.

Let's first show how *an increase in private investment will cause income to expand,* and how *a decrease in investment will cause it to contract.*

This is not a very surprising result. After all, we have learned that investment is one part of net national product; when one of the parts increases in value, we should naturally expect the whole to increase in value.

That's only part of the story. Our theory of income determination gives us a much more striking result. Modern income analysis shows that an increase in net investment will increase national income by a multiplied amount—by an amount greater than itself! Investment dollars are high-powered, double-duty dollars, so to speak.

This amplified effect of investment on income is called the "multiplier" doctrine; the word "multiplier" itself is used for *the numerical coefficient showing how great an increase in income results from each increase in investment.*

Some examples will make this terminology clear. If an increase of investment of 5 billion dollars causes an increase of income of 15 billion dollars, then the multiplier is 3. If the increase in income were 20 billion dollars, then the multiplier would be 4. The multiplier is the number by which the change in investment must be multiplied in order to present us with the resulting change in income.

No proof has yet been presented to show that the multiplier will be greater than 1. But using ordinary common sense, can you begin to see why, when I hire unemployed resources to build a $1,000 garage, there will be a secondary expansion of national income and production, over and above my primary investment?

My carpenters and lumber producers will get an extra $1,000 of income. But that is not the end of the story. If they all have a marginal propensity to consume of ⅔, they will now spend $666.67 on new consumption goods. The producers of these goods will now have an extra income of $666.67. If their MPC is also ⅔, they in turn will spend $444.44, or ⅔ of $666.67 (or ⅔ of ⅔ of $1,000). So the process will go on, with each new round of spending being ⅔ of the previous round.

Thus a whole endless chain of secondary consumption respending is set up by my primary $1,000 of investment spending. But it is a dwindling chain, and it all adds up to a finite amount. By either grade-school arithmetic or high-school geometric progression,[1] we get

$$
\left.
\begin{array}{c}
\$1,000.00 \\
+ \\
666.67 \\
+ \\
444.44 \\
+ \\
296.30 \\
+ \\
197.53 \\
+ \\
\dots
\end{array}
\right\}
=
\left\{
\begin{array}{c}
1 \times \$1,000 \\
+ \\
\dfrac{2}{3} \times \$1,000 \\
+ \\
\left(\dfrac{2}{3}\right)^2 \times \$1,000 \\
+ \\
\left(\dfrac{2}{3}\right)^3 \times \$1,000 \\
+ \\
\left(\dfrac{2}{3}\right)^4 \times \$1,000 \\
+ \\
\dots
\end{array}
\right.
$$

$$
\begin{array}{cc}
\dfrac{\$2,999.9999}{\text{or}} & \dfrac{1}{1 - \tfrac{2}{3}} \times \$1,000 \text{ or } 3 \times \$1,000 \\
\$3,000 &
\end{array}
$$

This shows that, with an MPC of ⅔, the multiplier is 3, consisting of the 1 of primary investment plus 2 extra of secondary consumption respending.

The same arithmetic would give a multiplier of 4 if the MPC were ¾. (Hint: What does $1 + ¾ + (¾)^2 + (¾)^3 + \dots$ finally add up to?) If the MPC were ½, the multiplier would be 2. The size of the multiplier is seen to depend upon how large the MPC is. Or it can be expressed in terms of the twin concept, the MPS. If the MPS were ¼, the MPC would be ¾, and the

---

[1] High school algebra says the formula for an infinite geometric progression is:

$$ 1 + r + r^2 + r^3 + \dots + r^n + \dots = \frac{1}{1-r} $$

as long as r is less than 1 in absolute value.

multiplier would be 4. If the MPS were $\frac{1}{3}$, the multiplier would be 3. If the MPS were $1/X$, the multiplier would be X.

By this time the reader will guess that the multiplier is always the upside-down or "reciprocal" of the marginal propensity to save. Our general multiplier formula is always

$$\text{Change in income} = \frac{1}{\text{MPS}} \times \text{change in investment}$$

$$= \frac{1}{1 - \text{MPC}} \times \text{change in investment}$$

In other words, the greater the extra consumption spending, the greater the multiplier. The greater the "leakage" into extra saving at each round of spending, the smaller the final multiplier.

▶ GRAPHICAL PICTURE OF THE MULTIPLIER

Up to this point, we have discussed the multiplier in terms of common sense and arithmetic. Will our saving-investment analysis of income give us the same result? The answer must, of course, be, Yes. Suppose, as in Table 1, the MPS is $\frac{1}{3}$ and now a new series of inventions comes along and gives rise to an extra 10 billion dollars of continuing investment opportunities, over and above our previous 20 billion dollars. Then the increase in investment should raise equilibrium NNP from 300 billion to 330 billion dollars if the multiplier is correctly given by our previous analysis.

Figure 7 confirms this result. Our old investment schedule II is shifted upward by 10 billion dollars to the new level $I'I'$. The new intersection point is E'. Lo, the increase in income is exactly three times as much as the increase in investment! This is because an MPS of only $\frac{1}{3}$ means a relatively flat SS saving schedule. As the white arrows show, the horizontal income distance is three times as great as the "primary" vertical saving-investment distance, the discrepancy being equal to the secondary "consumption responding."

In short, income must rise enough to bring out a volume of voluntary saving equal to the new investment. With an MPS of $\frac{1}{3}$, income has to rise by how much in order to bring out 10 billion dollars of new saving?[1] By exactly 30 billion dollars.

▶ HOW THRIFTINESS OR SHIFTS IN THE CONSUMPTION SCHEDULE AFFECT INCOME

We've seen that investment affects incomes. Let's now consider changes in thriftiness. Won't an increase in thriftiness shift upward the SS saving sched-

---

[1] Table 1 will also verify this answer. In Column (4), we now have 30 billion dollars instead of 20 billion dollars of investment. The new equilibrium level of income now shifts one row up from the old unshaded equilibrium row.

The saving and investment diagram has many applications.
It shows how:

1st, each dollar of investment can be "multiplied" into three dollars of income:

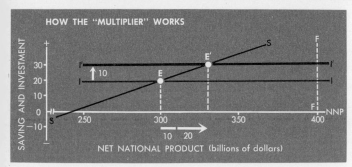

Fig. 7. New investment shifts *II* up to *I'I'. E'* gives the new equilibrium income, with income increasing 3 for each 1 increase in investment. (Note that the broken horizontal white arrow is 3 times the length of the vertical arrow that shows the shift in investment, and is broken to show 2 of consumption responding for each 1 of investment.)

ule? And won't the new *S'S'* schedule intersect an unchanged *II* schedule in a new equilibrium *E'*? And won't this correspond to lower national income?

The answers to these three questions are, Yes, yes, and yes. Figure 8 shows that an upward shift in the saving schedule—and, what is the same thing, an equivalent downward shift in the consumption schedule—will tend in the absence of any change in the investment schedule *to lower the equilibrium level of income.*

Common sense tells us why. If people consume less out of their incomes and if business won't willingly invest more, sales will fall and production will have to be cut. How far cut? Until so much national income has been destroyed as to make people feel poor enough that they will finally agree not to try to save more than business will go on investing.

Perhaps this seems an obvious point. But Fig. 8 tells us something much more surprising. It shows that a $1 upward shift in the saving schedule will kill off $3 of income. Contrariwise, a $1 downward shift in the saving schedule, which means a $1 upward shift in the consumption schedule, will produce

2d, changes in thriftiness—or a shift in CC—will change income:

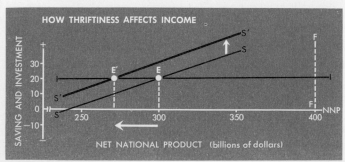

Fig. 8. A desire to consume less at every income level will shift the saving schedule upward. With *II* unchanged, equilibrium drops to the *E'* intersection. Why? Because income has to fall until people feel poor enough to again want to save what the system can invest.

a similar "multiplier" $3 increase in income. In short, just as investment dollars are "high-powered dollars" that have multiplier effects on income, high-powered too are those consumption dollars that represent a genuine shift in the propensity to consume.

We shall see many examples of this. Thus, in Section C we'll see how reducing taxes can increase consumption and thereby expand income by more than that consumption shift. Or, for a second example, take the case of a famous Harvard economics professor of a past generation, Frank W. Taussig. During the Great Depression he went on the radio to urge everyone to save less, to spend more on consumption. What did he have in mind? That was before the modern theory of income determination was known, but he must have meant that such spending would on the first round give jobs and incomes to people; that their respending on consumption would create second-round jobs and income; and that so it would go in a multiplier chain.

A last example will arise in connection with the next section's so-called "paradox of thrift." The following summary paves the way for it.

>   Other things being equal, an upward shift in the saving schedule—which means an equal downward shift in the consumption schedule—will kill off national income until income falls low enough to bring people's desired saving into equality with investment opportunities. Thus an attempt to save may not lead to more saving, but instead may simply reduce national income.

> **INDUCED INVESTMENT AND THE PARADOX OF THRIFT**

Until now we have always treated net investment as an autonomous element, absolutely independent of national income. All our investment schedules have been drawn as horizontal lines, their level being always the same regardless of income. This simplification can now be relaxed.

Any practical businessman will tell you that he is more likely to add to his plant or equipment if his sales are high relative to his plant capacity. In the short run (before businessmen have had time to adjust their capital stock to a changed plateau of income), it is reasonable for us to draw the *II* schedule in Fig. 9 as a rising curve. *An increase in national income may induce a higher level of net investment.*

As before, the equilibrium level of (maintainable) national income is given by the intersection of the investment and saving schedules; or by *E* in Fig. 9. So long as the *SS* curve always cuts the *II* curve from below, businessmen's action must bring the economy back to the equilibrium level.[1]

---

[1] If the two curves crossed in the opposite way, we should have unstable equilibrium, and the economy would rush away—in either direction—from the intersection neighborhood. A physical analogy may be suggestive: An egg on its side is in stable equilibrium; when given a slight disturbance, it returns to equilibrium. An egg on its tip is in unstable equilibrium; a light touch and it topples.

3d, higher income will induce businessmen to want higher investment:

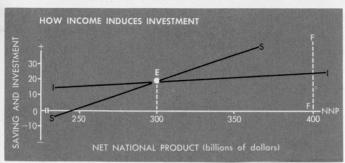

HOW INCOME INDUCES INVESTMENT

SAVING AND INVESTMENT

NET NATIONAL PRODUCT (billions of dollars)

Fig. 9. Now we drop the assumption of a horizontal *II* schedule. Now *II* slopes upward, showing intended investment less than $20 billion at low NNP and more than $20 billion at high NNP. Equilibrium is still at *E* where *SS* intersects *II* from below.

Induced investment means that anything increasing national income is likely to be good for the capital-goods industries; anything hurting national income is likely to be bad for those industries.

This throws a new spotlight on the age-old question of thrift versus consumption. It shows that an increased desire to consume—which is another way of looking at a decreased desire to save—is likely to boost business sales and increase investment. An increase in thriftiness, on the other hand, is likely to reduce inflationary pressure in times of booming incomes; but in time of depression, it is likely to make the depression worse and reduce the amount of actual net capital formation in the community. *High consumption and high investment then go hand in hand rather than being competing.*

This surprising result is sometimes called the "paradox of thrift." It is a paradox because in kindergarten we are all taught that thrift is *always* a good thing. Benjamin Franklin's *Poor Richard's Almanac* never tired of preaching the doctrine of saving. And now along comes a new generation of alleged financial experts who seem to be telling us that black is white and white is black, and that the old virtues may be modern sins.

Let us for the moment leave our cherished beliefs to the side, and try to disentangle the paradox in a dispassionate, scientific manner. Two considerations will help to clarify the whole matter.

The first is this. In economics, we must always be on guard against the logical fallacy of composition. What is good for each person separately need not be good for all; under some circumstances, private prudence may be social folly. Specifically, this means that the *attempt* of each and every person to increase his saving may—under the conditions to be described—result in a reduction in *actual* saving by all the people in the community. Note the italicized words "attempt" and "actual"; between them there may be a world of difference if people find themselves thrown out of jobs and with lowered incomes.

The second clue to the paradox of thrift lies in the question of whether or not national income is at a depression level. If we were at full employ-ment, then obviously the more of our national product that we devoted to current consumption, the less would be available for capital formation. If out-put could be assumed to be always at its maximum, then the old-fashioned doctrine of thrift would be absolutely correct—correct, be it noted, from both the individual and the social standpoints. In primitive agricultural communi-ties, such as the American colonies of Franklin's day, there was truth in Franklin's prescription. The same was true during World Wars I and II, and it becomes true during periods of inflation and boom: if people will become more thrifty, then less consumption will mean more investment.

But according to the statistical records, full employment and inflationary conditions have occurred only at intervals in our nation's history. Much of the time there was some wastage of resources, some unemployment, some in-sufficiency of demand, investment, and purchasing power. When this is the case, everything goes into reverse. What once was a social virtue may then become a social vice. What is true for the individual—that extra thriftiness means increased saving and wealth—may then become completely untrue for the community as a whole.

Under conditions of unemployment, the *attempt to save* may result in *less,* not more, saving. The individual who saves cuts down on his consumption. He passes on less purchasing power than before. Therefore, someone else's income is reduced. For one man's outgo is another man's income. If one man succeeds in saving more, it is because someone else is forced to dissave. If one man succeeds in hoarding more money, someone else must do without. If all individuals try to hoard, they cannot all succeed in doing so, but they can force down the velocity of circulation of money—and national income.

Thus, when there is unemployment, consumption and investment are com-plementary, not competitive. What helps one helps the other. The attempt to cut down on consumption (to save) only results in a reduction of income until everyone feels poor enough to try no longer to save more than can be invested. Moreover, at lower levels of income, less and not more capital goods will be needed. Therefore, *investment will actually be less.*

Let's clinch our common-sense understanding of this paradox by combining Figs. 8 and 9 into Fig. 10. An increase in thriftiness or the desire to save will shift the *SS* curve upward to *S'S'*. Note that the new intersection, *E'*, is now at a lower level of income. Because of induced *dis*investment, the drop in income will also mean lower investment. Thus both income and investment have actually decreased. The attempt to save more in depression times has resulted in less actual saving![1]

[1] At the end of page 236's summary, pencil in the words: "Sometimes the attempt to save may even reduce actual saving!"

4th, an attempt to save more could result in less actual saving and investment:

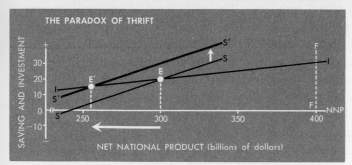

THE PARADOX OF THRIFT

Fig. 10. The shift of SS upward to S'S' depresses income. And the drop of income kills off some investment, moving you southwest along the sloping II schedule. (If the system were straining at the full-employment level of F, what would be the effect of increased thriftiness?)

If true, this is an important lesson. Never again can men be urged in time of depression to tighten their belts, to save more in order to restore prosperity. The result will be the reverse—a worsening of the vicious deflationary spiral.

What becomes of the argument that wealthy people are needed to provide saving, that inequality of the distribution of income is needed to push up the saving schedule? We see it then go into reverse. An economic lobbyist of the capital-goods industries would, if he has their selfish interests at heart, advocate less thriftiness in depressed times, so that the consumption schedule will be pushed upward, and so that attempts to save—which then really lead only to decreases in income—will be discouraged. For only then will investment and sales of heavy capital goods flourish.[1]

Later, we shall see that the modern neoclassical synthesis can rob the paradox of thrift of its terrors.

▶ **THE DEFLATIONARY GAP**

The multiplier is a two-edged sword. It will cut for you or against you. It will amplify new investment, as we have seen. But it will also amplify downward any decrease in investment. Thus, if investment opportunities drop by 10 billion dollars in our earlier examples, then national income will have to fall by three times as much—by 30 billion dollars. If net investment drops away to zero, income will have to fall down to the break-even point where the community is made poor enough to stop all net savings.

This reminds us once again that there may be nothing particularly good about what we have called the equilibrium level of national income. If in-

[1] We have seen that this line of argument does not apply in conditions of full employment. It also requires some slight modifications to allow for the fact that thriftiness, by lowering income, may also lower interest rates and promote investment, or it may depress wages and prices and thereby increase the real purchasing power of people's money holdings enough to destroy their initial thriftiness. These qualifications are discussed at length later; in my opinion they are rather unimportant in time of deep depression.

vestment is low, the equilibrium level of income will involve much unemployment and wastage of national resources. The only level of national income
that we are entitled to regard as a desirable goal is that near to full employment. But we shall end up at such a level of high employment only if investment opportunities happen to be as large as full-employment saving.

Unless this full-employment saving is "offset" by private investment (or by
public policies), the nation cannot continue to enjoy full employment. There
is then said to be a "deflationary gap," its size being measured by the deficiency of investment compared with full-employment saving.

We can picture the deflationary gap in Fig. 3 as the vertical distance between the saving and investment schedules at the full-employment level of
income, *F*. Or, as in Fig. 11, we can picture the deflationary gap on a consumption-plus-investment graph. Suppose that 400 billion dollars represents
the full-employment income. Suppose that, at this income, the scheduled total
of *C* + *I* adds up only to 380 billion dollars, as shown at *G*. *This leaves a
20-billion-dollar deflationary gap between* G *and* F. Since we obviously cannot
then remain at full employment, what will happen? Will income drop by
only 20 billion dollars? Clearly not. It must drop by some greater multiple of

When the C + I spending that would be generated at full employ-
ment differs from the full-employment NNP, we call:

1st, any spending deficiency, a "deflationary" gap:

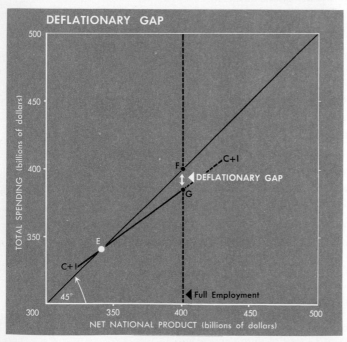

Fig. 11. The deflationary gap is
always measured at the full-employment NNP level. It is the
vertical distance there between
the 45-degree line and the *C* + *I*
schedule, i.e., *FG*. Such a deflationary gap will depress income
in a multiplied way.

2nd, any spending excess, an "inflationary" gap:

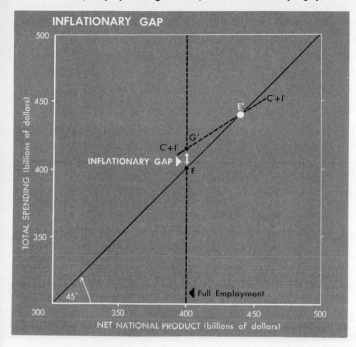

Fig. 12. *FG'* measures the Inflationary gap. People are trying to buy more than can be produced and thereby they are inflating the price level. (With all prices changing, the spending schedules are likely to shift upward, so it would be a mistake to regard *E'* as a simply attainable equilibrium point.)

the original deflationary gap. If each dollar of reduced income results in a cut of $2/3 in consumption spending, income will have to fall until it has dropped three times as much as the original deflationary gap. (See Fig. 11's point *E*.) [1]

▶ **THE PROCESS OF PRICE INFLATION**

Instead of a deflationary gap, we may have an inflationary gap. If investment tends to be greater than full-employment saving, then more goods will be demanded of business than it can produce and prices will begin to rise. Figure 12 shows how we measure the inflationary gap as a vertical distance: The new *C' + I'* curve lies *above* the 45° line at the full-employment level by the distance *FG'*, giving us an inflationary gap of 15 billion dollars.

Now what will happen? Can production rise by 45 billion dollars to give us a new equilibrium at *E'*? Obviously not. Already everyone is fully employed and factories are producing at their practical capacity points. The region to

[1] What can be done about this? If we continue to leave the government out of the picture, we must have either an increase in investment or an increase in consumption. By how much must the level of investment or of the consumption schedule shift upward if full employment is to be restored? By the full 60 billion dollars of needed income? Surely not. Because of the multiplier, to wipe out a deflationary gap, the *C + I* schedule need shift upward only by the amount of the gap itself, and not by any multiple of the gap.

the right of the vertical full-employment line through F is a never-never land. It shows us what we should like to be able to produce, but not what we are actually able to produce. Although an inflationary gap is the opposite of a deflationary gap, its effects upon employment and production are of a slightly different qualitative nature. A deflationary gap can move production leftward, down to three-quarters or even one-half of a full-employment level. But an inflationary gap cannot possibly move employment rightward to 150 per cent of full or maximum employment. The economic system cannot move in real terms very far to the right of the broken full-employment line.

The excess in purchasing power can result only in price increases and an inflationary spiral; money national income will rise because of "paper" price changes, but real national product cannot go above its maximum full-employment level. Unfortunately, the upward movement of prices will continue for as long as there is an inflationary gap,[1] *i.e.,* until we are lucky enough for investment or consumption demand to fall off, or smart enough as a nation to adopt corrective policies that will wipe out the inflationary gap.

Far from being "depression economics," modern income analysis has many of its most important applications in connection with the process of inflation and what can be done about it. During and after World War II, the concept of the inflationary gap was indispensable in indicating the quantitative magnitude of taxation needed to keep decontrolled prices from rising; and without understanding the rudiments of income analysis, we cannot follow the important economic issues discussed in Congress and the public press.[2]

C FISCAL POLICY IN INCOME DETERMINATION

When there is a large inflationary or deflationary gap, the government is called upon to do something about the price rise or the widespread unemployment. Tax and government expenditure policies will change the equilibrium level of income. So we must explicitly introduce government fiscal policy into the picture to see exactly how income determination is affected. As you might guess, we now consider a $C + I + G$ spending schedule to show the equilibrium with government in the picture.

It will simplify our task if in the beginning we analyze the effects of government expenditure with taxes held constant. With taxes in the picture, no

---

[1] The process does not end with higher prices. The new higher price level will not equilibrate total supply and demand once and for all. On the contrary, since the higher prices received by businesses become in turn somebody's income—that of worker or property owner—demand again shifts upward and prices must continue to rise. Attempts of labor to secure higher wages as compensation for the soaring cost of living may only cause the inflationary spiral to zoom at a dizzier speed.

[2] See Chapters 17 and 18, and Chapter 36's discussion of war finance for further applications.

Government expenditures act like consumption and investment in determining national income:

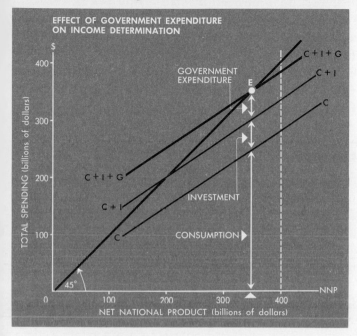

EFFECT OF GOVERNMENT EXPENDITURE
ON INCOME DETERMINATION

Fig. 13. On top of consumption spending and investment spending, we now add government spending on goods and services. This gives us the $C + I + G$ schedule. At E, where this intersects the 45-degree line, is equilibrium. (What if G increased or decreased? Can you show the multiplied changes in income?)

longer can we ignore the distinction between disposable income and net national product. But with taxes first held constant, they will differ always by the same amount; and taking account of taxes, we can plot the CC consumption schedule against NNP rather than against DI.

In Chapter 10 we learned that net national product consists of three, rather than two, parts; namely,

NNP = consumption expenditure + private net investment + government expenditure on goods and services
$$= C + I + G$$

Therefore, on our 45°-line diagram in Fig. 13 we must superimpose upon the consumption schedule not only private investment but also government expenditure G. This is because public road building is financially no different from private railroad building and collective consumption expenditure involved in maintaining a free public library has the same effect upon jobs as private consumption expenditure for movies or rental libraries.

We end up with the $C + I + G$ schedule showing the amount of total spending forthcoming at each level of NNP. We now must go to the intersection with the 45° line to read off the equilibrium level of national product. At this equilibrium NNP level, the total the nation wants to spend on all goods is just equal in value to the full costs of production of these goods.

Figure 13 shows that government expenditure, taken by itself and disregarding taxes, has a multiplier effect upon income just like that of private investment. The reason is, of course, that a chain of consumption respending is set into motion by the road builders, librarians, and other people who receive primary income from the government.[1]

To show the effects of an extra 10 billion dollars of G, shift $C + I + G$ in Fig. 13 up to $C + I + G'$ and show that the new E' will record a multiplier response of NNP to the government spending.

▶ TAXATION AND EQUILIBRIUM INCOME

Now let us turn to the depressing effects of taxes on the equilibrium NNP level. Without graphs, our common sense tells us what must happen when the government (1) takes away more from us in taxes while (2) at the same time holding its expenditure constant. Extra taxes will mean we have lower real disposable incomes, and lower disposable incomes mean we shall cut down on our consumption spending. Obviously, if investment and government expenditure remain the same, a reduction in consumption spending will then reduce net national product and employment; or if we already were having an inflationary gap, the new taxes will help close the gap and wipe out excessive inflationary price increases.

Our graphs confirm this reasoning: $I + G$ is unchanged, and the increase in taxes will lower disposable income, thereby shifting the consumption schedule downward; so in all, the $C + I + G$ schedule will shift downward, and its new intersection with the crucial 45° line must definitely be at a lower equilibrium level of NNP.

Figure 14 shows how tax receipts shift the CC schedule downward.[2] Suppose people have an MPC of about ⅔; new taxes of 30 billion dollars now cause their disposable income to fall 30 billion dollars below NNP. Will consump-

___

[1] Our saving-investment diagram will give the same answer as the 45°-line diagram. The increase in government expenditure means an equivalent increase in the government deficit if taxes have not been increased. Net saving must always equal private investment + government deficit. Therefore, we add the deficit on top of the II curve and get our new greater equilibrium level of national income at the intersection with the SS curve. In more advanced discussions, we could employ Fig. 13 to show how induced investment or government expenditure (*i.e.,* induced by a changed level of income) will enter into the multiplier. The final change in income resulting from a unit upward shift in the $C + I + G$ schedule will always turn out to be $1 \div (1 - K)$ where K is the slope of the $C + I + G$ schedule and might be called the "marginal propensity to spend."

[2] The shift of CC in Fig. 14 can be regarded either as a fall or as a movement to the right. The rightward movement equals the full amount of the tax. Why? Because we must subtract the full tax from the NNP at V to get its associated disposable income and consumption, as shown at U. Advanced texts develop and qualify all this.

Higher taxes will cut disposable income and consumption:

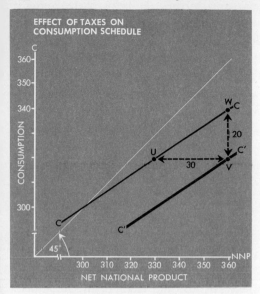

EFFECT OF TAXES ON
CONSUMPTION SCHEDULE

Fig. 14. A tax increase lowers the CC schedule. By how much? Because a $30 billion tax will cut saving $10 billion and consumption $20 billion (with MPC = ⅔), the tax will shift the consumption schedule $30 billion rightward and $20 billion downward, (I.e., $UV = 30$ and $VW = 20$).

tion fall by 30 billion? No. With an MPC of ⅔, consumption will fall by only 20 billion dollars; personal saving will fall the remaining 10 billion.

[Remark: Now we know something that common sense did not immediately tell us. To offset a 20-billion-dollar upward shift in $I + G$, we must increase tax collections by *more* than 20 billion dollars. This means that (1) when increased government defense spending is added onto a full-employment economy with a balanced budget, then (2) taxes will probably have to be increased by *more than enough to balance the budget* if we are determined to avoid an inflationary gap.]

We can easily reverse the above analysis to explain why tax reductions help to fight a bad depression. Each dollar of tax reduction leads to an increase in people's disposable income by a dollar and leads to almost a dollar increase in initial consumption spending. Hence, dollars of tax reduction are almost as powerful a weapon against mass unemployment as are increases in dollars of government expenditure. Such a program may involve a larger deficit than would an expenditure program. But it also means that there is no expansion of the government's sector of the economic system.

► QUALIFICATIONS TO SAVING AND INVESTMENT ANALYSIS

The theory of income determination sketched in this chapter is a powerful tool.[1] It helps us to understand the ups and downs of the business cycle. It

───────────

[1] Advanced discussions show corporate saving can be handled graphically much like taxes.

helps us to understand how foreign lending (which is one part of total net investment) affects domestic employment and income. It helps us to understand how governmental fiscal policy can be used to fight inflation and unemployment. All these topics are developed in later chapters.

But it would be a mistake to think that an economist can be made out of a parrot, simply by teaching him the magic words "saving" and "investment." Behind the scenes of these schedules a great deal is taking place. After the next chapter's survey of our business-cycle history, the following chapters discuss money and banking, to show how interest rate and credit changes may cause the investment schedule to shift.

Also, an increase in the public's holding of government bonds and other wealth may shift the consumption schedule upward. Or rising living standards (resulting from advertising and the invention of new products) may shift the consumption schedule up just as it has in the past.

In short, it is an oversimplification to regard investment as always an autonomous factor, and consumption always a passive factor depending upon income. True, this is a fruitful oversimplification. But as we have already seen, some of net investment may be "induced" by income changes in the short run. Likewise, consumption will sometimes shift autonomously even though income has remained constant. And, as the reader can verify by experimenting with the saving-investment and the 45°-line diagrams, such shifts in the consumption or saving schedules have multiplier effects upon national income—just like the multiplier effects of changes in investment.

SUMMARY

▶ A. INCOME DETERMINATION

1. The motives that make people save are often different from those that make businesses invest. Net investment tends to depend on such autonomous elements as new population, new territory, new inventions, new tastes, and other growth elements; consumption and saving tend to behave along passive schedules plotted against national income.

2. People's wishes to save and the willingness of businesses to invest are brought into line with each other by means of changes in income. The equilibrium level of national income must be at the intersection of the saving and investment schedules; or what is exactly the same thing, at the intersection of the consumption plus investment schedule with the 45° line of total income.

3. If incomes were to be temporarily above the equilibrium level, business would find itself unable to sell all it is producing at prices that fully cover all costs of production. For a short time inventories might pile up or sales at a loss might take place, but eventually employment and production would be cut back toward the equilibrium level. The only plateau of income that can be maintained is at the income level where families will voluntarily continue to save exactly as much as business will voluntarily continue to invest.

4. To sum up the matter most simply: Investment calls the tune; investment causes income to rise or fall until voluntary saving has adjusted itself to the level of maintainable investment.[1] The simplest sequence is:

B. INVESTMENT AND INCOME

5. Investment has a multiplier effect on income. When investment changes, there is an equal *primary* change in national income. But as these primary income receivers in the capital goods industries get more earned income, they set into motion a whole chain of additional *secondary* consumption spending. If people always spend about ⅔ of each extra dollar of income upon consumption, the total of the multiplier chain will be

$$1 + \tfrac{2}{3} + (\tfrac{2}{3})^2 + \cdots = \frac{1}{1 - \tfrac{2}{3}} = 3$$

The multiplier works forward or backward, amplifying either increases or decreases in investment. The multiplier is numerically equal to the reciprocal of the MPS; this is because it always takes more than a dollar's change in income to bring forth a dollar's change in saving.

6. The *attempt* to save more is quite different from the achievement of increased saving for society as a whole. The paradox of thrift shows how an increase in thriftiness may reduce already depressed income and, through induced effects on investment, actually result in less net investment. Only when employment always remains full are consumption and investment necessarily competing; only then are private virtues always social virtues.

The moral is not for each individual to squander his money during a depression, trying to be patriotic. Instead, through proper national policies, we must recreate a high-employment environment in which private virtues are no longer social follies.

7. In short, we must avoid both inflationary and deflationary gaps, so that

[1] The equality of the saving that people are willing to maintain with the investment that business firms are willing to maintain is the equilibrium condition that permits national income to remain steady. This equality should not be confused with the definitional identity of measured saving and investment at *every* income level discussed in Chap. 10's Appendix.

full-employment saving and investment just match without inflation. We measure the size of the deflationary or inflationary gap as the vertical discrepancy at full-employment income between (a) the saving and investment schedules or, what is exactly the same thing, by (b) the vertical distance between the $C + I$ schedule and the 45° line.

▶ **C. FISCAL POLICY AND INCOME DETERMINATION**

8. An increase in government expenditure—taken by itself with taxes and investment unchanged—has expansionary effects on national product much like those of net investment. The schedule of $C + I + G$ shifts upward to a higher equilibrium intersection with the 45° line.

9. An increase in taxes—taken by itself with investment and government expenditure unchanged—depresses the equilibrium level of national product. The schedule of consumption plotted against NNP is shifted downward by taxes; but since extra dollars go partly into saving, the dollar drop in consumption will not be quite so great as the dollars of new taxes. Therefore, to combat an inflationary or deflationary gap, we may require an even larger change in taxation.

10. The art of economics consists of recognizing both the core of truth in the simple theory of income determination and also its needed qualifications. In later chapters we shall see how interest rates and other factors may cause shifts in the schedules that determine levels of national income.

We must leave to Chapters 17 and 18 the analysis of government monetary and fiscal policy. To the intervening chapters we turn for an analysis of the wild dance of the business cycle, of money, banking policy and interest.

QUESTIONS FOR DISCUSSION

1. The saving and investment diagram and the 45°-line (or $C + I$) diagram are two different ways of showing how national income is determined. Describe each. Show that they are equivalent. Which do you prefer?

2. Reconstruct Table 1 assuming that net investment is equal to (a) 40 billion dollars, (b) 50 billion dollars. What is the resulting difference in national income? Is this greater or smaller than the change in investment? Why?

3. Describe in a few paragraphs (a) the common sense, (b) the arithmetic, and (c) the geometry of the multiplier. What are the various multipliers when $MPC = 0.9$? 0.8? 0.5?

4. In Fig. 3, how would you measure the deflationary gap? In Figs. 4 and 5? in Table 1? How would you change the figures to show an inflationary gap?

5. Give arguments for and against thriftiness. Contrast carefully (*a*) the individual and the community viewpoint, and (*b*) boom and depression.

6. Describe briefly the effects upon income of (*a*) government expenditure, (*b*) taxes, (*c*) our sale of less goods and services to foreigners than we buy from them.

7. "The purpose of fiscal policy is to help wipe out inflationary or deflationary gaps. Thus, if $C + I + G$ is too high we have an inflationary gap; and we raise taxes to shift the new $C' + I' + G'$ schedule downward, thereby wiping out the inflationary gap." Explain. Show what you would do to taxes to fight a deflationary gap. To government expenditure?

8. Review your understanding of the following concepts:

investment, saving, and consumption schedules, 45° lines

equilibrium intersection and forces moving you when you're not in equilibrium

multiplier impacts of investment

multiplier effects on income of saving or consumption shifts

induced investment

paradox of thrift

$C + I + G$ *schedule*

tax effect on CC *and* E

inflationary and deflationary gaps

cumulative inflation

qualifications to the analysis

13 BUSINESS CYCLES AND FORECASTING

The fault, dear Brutus, is not in our stars—but in ourselves.

WILLIAM SHAKESPEARE

We have now examined the economic forces operating to determine the level of national income—the balance of saving and investment. We now turn to the problem of how and why the level of national income fluctuates, and how economists try to forecast the future.

In the next chapter, we bring in the problems of fiscal policy, showing how fiscal and monetary policies must interact to achieve a prosperous and stable economy.

▶ **PROSPERITY AND DEPRESSION**

Business conditions never stand still. Prosperity is followed by a panic or a crash. National income, employment, and production fall. Prices and profits decline and men are thrown out of work. Eventually the bottom is reached,

Are business cycles calming down?

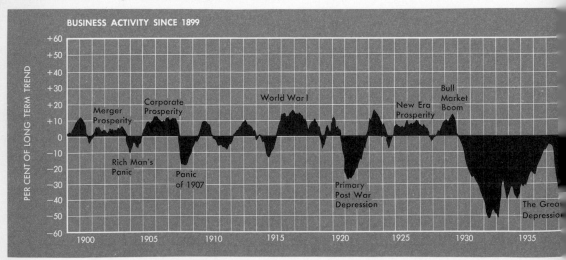

BUSINESS ACTIVITY SINCE 1899

and revival begins. The recovery may be slow or fast. It may be incomplete, or it may be so strong as to lead to a new boom. The new prosperity may represent a long, sustained plateau of brisk demand, plentiful jobs, buoyant prices, and increased living standards. Or it may represent a quick, inflationary flaring up of prices and speculation, to be followed by another disastrous slump.

Such in brief is the so-called "business cycle" that has characterized the industrialized nations of the world for the last century and a half at least, ever since an elaborate, interdependent *money economy* began to replace a relatively self-sufficient precommercial society.

No two business cycles are quite the same; yet they all have much in common. They are not identical twins, but they are recognizable as belonging to the same family. No exact formula, such as might apply to the motions of the moon or of a simple pendulum, can be used to predict the timing of future (or past) business cycles. Rather do they resemble, in their rough appearance and irregularities, the fluctuations of disease epidemics, the vagaries of the weather, or the variations in a child's temperature.

From these introductory remarks, it will be clear that the business cycle is simply one further aspect of the economic problem of achieving and maintaining high levels of jobs and production, and a progressive economy.

▶ **MEASURING AND FORECASTING THE BUSINESS CYCLE**

Figure 1 shows how the economic system has been plagued with the business cycle throughout our history as a nation, although never with so sustained and costly a slump as in the post-1929 Great Depression. The same pattern of cyclical fluctuations is repeated in England, Germany, and other foreign nations with surprisingly few variations. But it is a strange fact that the United

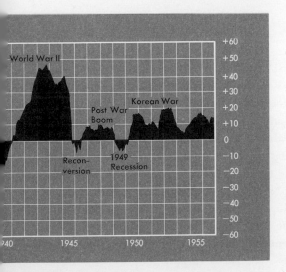

Fig. 1. For 20 years now, we've had no significant depressions. But 'twas not always so in our history. (Source: Cleveland Trust Co.)

Most economic activities move up and down together:

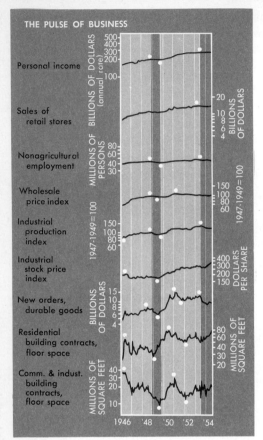

THE PULSE OF BUSINESS

Personal income

Sales of retail stores

Nonagricultural employment

Wholesale price index

Industrial production index

Industrial stock price index

New orders, durable goods

Residential building contracts, floor space

Comm. & indust. building contracts, floor space

1946   '48   '50   '52   '54

Fig. 2. The dark stretches show periods of contraction; the light stretches show expansions. Note that the lower curves, which are more akin to investment, do show greater fluctuations. Can you spot any "early turners"?

After mid-1954, recovery set in. But by 1957, the dark stationery again became necessary as the Second Eisenhower Recession got under way. (Source: National Bureau of Economic Research.)

States, supposedly one of the youngest and most vigorous of nations, tends always to have greater average amounts of unemployment and greater variation in unemployment than any other country. Not only was this true in 1933, when our percentage of unemployment surpassed even that of Germany, but it appears to have been the case for almost as far back as we have any records or indications. Only in the last 15 years have we kept unemployment low.

Figure 2 shows a number of diverse recent economic "time series," presented next to each other for comparison. Note the all-pervasive common pulse of the business cycle: in production, in employment, in incomes, and even in such particular series as stockmarket prices and building. Moreover, if data had been included on such noneconomic matters as marriages, births, and malnutrition, we should also be able to see in them the heavy hand of the business cycle. Even political party elections follow the business cycle; in depressions, the ins often go out.

Of course, as economists and citizens, we are primarily interested in the fluctuations in total jobs, total production, and total (real) national income. But for many countries and for many earlier decades, such data are very hard to come by. Moreover, certain specialists are often interested in various secondary series: in stock prices, in wholesale prices, in profits, in steel production, and so forth. Often, therefore, statisticians use such a time series as pig-iron production as an index of the business cycle. Or better still, they may take some sort of weighted average of many series—such as freight-car loadings, electric-power production, or bank clearings (value of checks cashed)—and combine them into a barometer of the business cycle. Figure 1 illustrated such an index of business activity.

Many grown men, who should perhaps know better, ruin their eyesight peering at charts like those shown in Fig. 2, in the hope of finding a magic forecaster which always moves up or down a few months *before* business conditions, and by its movements signals the coming trend of events.[1] Alas, they thus far have met with only limited success. For example, in 1937 the stock market began to turn down early in the year as though in anticipation of the sharp mid-year recession of 1937–1938. But if we go back to 1929, we find that the stock market continued to boom until well into autumn, whereas business conditions—we now know!—began to turn down some months earlier. Many brave souls have been led to believe in one system or another for "calling the turns" of the cycle, but usually the next boom or depression kills off their hopes and—it may be added—their clients.

Let's for the moment, therefore, stick to the facts and statistics. Later we shall attempt to devise hypotheses and explanatory theories to account for the broad factual patterns, but not for the month-to-month happenings.

▶ STATISTICAL CORRECTION FOR SEASONAL VARIATION AND FOR TRENDS

First, of course, we must remove from our statistical data irrelevant, disturbing factors such as seasonal patterns, and also certain so-called long-term "trends." If Sears Roebuck's sales go up from November to December, 1953, we cannot conclude from this that Fig. 2's 1953 recession doesn't exist. Retail trade goes up every Christmas, just as New Hampshire hotels tend to be

---

[1] The Harvard Economic Society's A, B, and C barometers did badly in 1929. Recently, the National Bureau suggested the following as "leaders": new incorporations, average weekly hours, residential and nonresidential building, commodity and stock prices, and failure liabilities (inverted). How regular will they be? Are they prone to "cry wolf"? *E.g.*, in 1952 they called for a recession that didn't develop on schedule.

crowded in summer. The statistician attempts to remove the "seasonal influence" by carefully studying previous yearly patterns. If he finds that every December tends to involve about 150 per cent as much business as the average month of the year, and every January only 90 per cent, then he will take the actual raw monthly data and divide all the December figures by 1.5 and all the January figures by 0.9, and so forth, for each month. After this has been done, the statistician will end up with a time series of monthly department-store sales which have been "seasonally adjusted." These will show what we expected all along, that business was really still declining throughout all the last months of 1953, because December's increase of business over November's was less than the seasonal normal.

A similar problem arises when we examine the fluctuations over time of such a rapidly growing time series as electric-power consumption. Electric-power production did not decline much in the depression. But the depression is to be seen in that series, nevertheless. It rears its ugly head in the form of a *slowing down of the rate of growth* of the time series as compared to its normal or long-term "secular trend." If we draw a smooth trend line or curve, either by eye or by some statistical formula, through the *electric-power production* chart, we shall discover the business cycle in the twistings of the data above and below the trend line. If we measure the vertical deviations up and down from the trend line and plot them on a separate diagram, we shall get a pretty clear picture of the business cycle.[1] Let's take a look at it.

▶ **THE FOUR PHASES OF THE CYCLE**

Early writers on the business cycle, possessing little quantitative information, tended to attach disproportionate attention to *panics* and *crises* such as the collapse of the South Sea Bubble in 1720, the panic of 1837, the Jay Cooke panic of 1873, the Cleveland panic of 1893, the "rich man's panic" of 1907, and of course, the superduper stock-market crash of "black Tuesday," October 29, 1929. Later writers began soon to speak of two phases of business: prosperity and depression, or boom and slump—with peaks and troughs marking the turning points in between.

Today, it is recognized that not every period of improving business need necessarily take us all the way to full employment. For example, throughout the decade of the 1930's there was a measure of recovery from the 1932–1933 trough levels, but we could by no means speak of the period as being one of true prosperity. The prevailing fashion, therefore, is to follow the terminology

---

[1] The reader may be referred to any standard textbook on statistics for these technical procedures. However, cautious judgment must be exercised in using the mechanical tools of statistics. A beginner, carelessly "eliminating a trend," may throw out the baby along with the bath water if not careful, or at least distort the true appearance of the infant.

The business cycle, like the year, has its seasons:

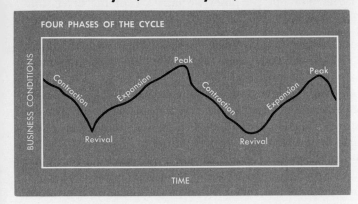

FOUR PHASES OF THE CYCLE

BUSINESS CONDITIONS

Contraction
Expansion
Peak
Revival
Contraction
Expansion
Peak
Revival

TIME

Fig. 3. Cyclical expansions follow contractions, with turning points in between. The National Bureau of Economic Research has dated these phases for America's history and for many other countries.

of the late Wesley C. Mitchell, long-time director of the nonprofit National Bureau of Economic Research and assiduous student of business cycles.[1]

The cycle is broken up by Mitchell and many other economists into four phases, the two most important ones being called the periods of "expansion" and "contraction." The expansion phase comes to an end and goes into the contraction phase at the so-called upper turning point or "peak." Similarly, the contraction phase gives way to that of expansion at the lower turning point (trough) or "revival." Thus, the four phases keep repeating themselves in the oversimplified picture as shown in Fig. 3. Note that the emphasis now is not so much on *high* or *low* business activity, but on the dynamic aspects of *rising* or *falling* business activity.

Each phase of the cycle passes into the next. Each is characterized by different economic conditions[2] and requires special explanatory principles. But let's continue with more facts before attempting analysis and theorizing.

How long are the usual economic cycles? This depends upon how many minor cycles you wish to count. Most observers have no trouble in agreeing on the major cycles, which run around 8 to 10 years in length. Everyone agrees that the late 1920's represent a period of prosperity and the early 1930's one of depression, and similarly with past major business cycles. But not all economists attach importance to the shorter minor cycles that are to be seen in economic charts. In 1924 and 1927, there were small dips in business activity. Shall we call the 1920's therefore, three different (minor) cycles or one major prosperity period? In 1948–1949, and again in 1953–1954, we suffered mild recessions. Should these count as cycles?

[1] W. C. MITCHELL, *Business Cycles: The Problem and Its Setting* (National Bureau of Economic Research, New York, 1927). "Peak" has replaced his term, "recession."

[2] For example, during expansion, we find that employment, production, prices, money, wages, interest rates, and profits are usually rising, with the reverse true in contraction.

In an elementary introduction of this type, it is perhaps best to stick primarily to major business cycles. For our purposes we may accept the brief summary of Harvard's Alvin Hansen:[1]

The American experience indicates that the major business cycle has had an average duration of a little over eight years. Thus, from 1795 to 1937 there were seventeen cycles of an average duration of 8.35 years. . . .

Since one to two minor peaks regularly occur between the major peaks, it is clear that the minor cycle is something less than half the duration of the major cycle. In the one hundred and thirty-year period 1807 to 1937 there were thirty-seven minor cycles with an average duration of 3.51 years.

. . . it appears that the building cycle averages somewhere between seventeen and eighteen years in length, or almost twice the length of the major business cycle. . . .

. . . American experience indicates that with a high degree of regularity every other major business boom coincides roughly with a boom in building construction, while the succeeding major cycle recovery is forced to buck up against a building slump. . . . the depressions which have fallen in the interval of the construction downswing are typically deep and long. And the succeeding recovery is held back and retarded by the unfavorable depressional influence from the slump in the building industry.

▶ LONG WAVES?

Some economists, taking a broad historical view, like to speak of very "long waves," whose complete cycle length is about half a century. Thus from the end of the Napoleonic Wars in 1815 to the middle of the nineteenth century, prices tended to fall and times tended to be unusually hard, on the average. After the Californian and Australian gold discoveries following 1850, and as a partial result of the Civil and Crimean Wars, prices tended to rise. A new long cycle of falling prices followed the 1873 depression, lasting until the 1890's when there was a great increase in gold production following the African and Alaskan gold discoveries. McKinley and the Republican party swam to prosperity and power on the crest of the new long wave.

Whether these long waves are simply historical accidents due to chance gold discoveries, political wars, and chance inventions, it is still too soon to say.[2]

▶ A FIRST CLUE TO THE BUSINESS CYCLE: CAPITAL FORMATION

Hansen's emphasis on construction gives us our first clues as to the causation of the business cycle. Certain economic variables always show greater fluctuations than others in the business cycle. Thus, if we plot pig-iron production and anthracite-coal consumption side by side, we hardly see the business cycle

---

[1] ALVIN H. HANSEN, *Fiscal Policy and Business Cycles* (Norton, New York, 1941), pp. 18–24.

[2] The interested reader may be referred to J. A. Schumpeter, *Business Cycles* (McGraw-Hill, New York, 1939), Chaps. 6, 7, where long cycles are called "Kondratieffs."

in the latter. But in the pig-iron series there is little else to see but the business cycle. Why? Because anthracite is used largely for heating people's houses, and in both good and bad times most people are going to manage to keep reasonably warm. Pig iron, on the other hand, is one of the principal ingredients of capital and durable goods of all kinds: of plant equipment and durable machinery, of industrial and residential construction, of automobiles, washing machines, and other durable consumers' goods.

By their nature, such durable goods are subject to violently erratic patterns of demand. In bad times their new purchase can be indefinitely postponed; in a good year, everyone may suddenly decide to stock up on a 10-year supply of the services of such durable goods. *Our first clue to the nature of the business cycle lies then in the fact that it is the durable or capital goods sector of the economy which shows by far the greatest cyclical fluctuations.*[1]

If you will turn back a few pages to Fig. 2, you will see the contrast between capital- and nondurable-goods fluctuations clearly brought out. The last few times series all represent various categories of durable- or capital-goods formation. Note how wide their swings all are, as compared to those of the second time series which represents primarily consumers' goods. Except for a few short, choppy surface disturbances in this latter series, it will be seen to follow the general flow of income in a rather passive fashion. Ordinarily, consumption movements seem the effect rather than cause of the business cycle, while there is good reason to believe that the movements of durable goods represent key causes in a more fundamental sense.

It is comforting to find that statistical analysis supports the emphasis in previous chapters on the crucial importance of the capital investment process.

▶ A FEW THEORIES OF THE BUSINESS CYCLE

An industrious student could easily compile a list of separate theories of the business cycle that would run into the dozens.[2] Each theory seems to be quite

---

[1] Lord Beveridge in his *Full Employment in a Free Society* (Norton, New York, 1945) made a careful calculation of the degree of variability of the capital-goods industries in Great Britain ever since 1785 and found it to be twice as great as for other industries.

[2] We may just mention a few of the better known theories: (1) the *monetary* theory—attributes the cycle to the expansion and contraction of bank credit (Hawtrey, *et al.*) ; (2) the *innovation* theory—attributes the cycle to the clustering of important inventions such as the railroad (Schumpeter, Hansen, *et al.*) ; (3) the *psychological* theory—treats the cycle as a case of people's infecting each other with pessimistic and optimistic expectations (Pigou, Bagehot, *et al.*) ; (4) the *underconsumption* theory—claims too much income goes to wealthy or thrifty people compared to what can be invested (Hobson, Foster and Catchings, *et al.*) ; (5) the *overinvestment* theory—claims too much rather than too little investment causes recessions (Hayek, Mises, *et al.*) ; (6) the *sunspot-weather-crop* theories (Jevons, Moore) . The interested reader should consult G. Haberler, *Prosperity and Depression* (League of Nations, 1944, 3d ed.) or other business-cycles texts for further information.

different; but when we examine them closely and throw out those which obviously contradict the facts or the rules of logic, or which just appear to be conveying an explanation when really they are not saying anything at all—when we do all this, we are left with a relatively few different explanations. Most of them differ from each other only in emphasis. One man believes the cycle to be primarily the result of fluctuations in total net investment, while another prefers to attribute the cycle to fluctuations in the rate of technological inventions and innovations, which act on business *through* net investment. A third man says that the root of the cycle is to be found in the fact that the creation of deposit money by our banking system causes investment spending to expand and contract so as to create boom and bust.

These sound like three different theories, and in most advanced textbooks they might be given the names of three different writers, but from our standpoint they are but three different aspects of the same process. This doesn't mean there is perfect agreement among all theories of the cycle or that there are not some important differences in emphasis among different writers.

To classify the different theories, we may first divide them into the two categories of primarily *external* and primarily *internal* theories.

The external theories find the root cause of the business cycle in the fluctuations of something *outside* the economic system—in sunspot cycles, in wars, revolutions, and political events, in gold discoveries, in rates of growth of population and migrations, in discoveries of new lands and resources, and finally in scientific and technological discoveries and innovations.

The internal theories look for mechanisms *within* the economic system itself which will give rise to self-generating business cycles, so that every expansion will breed recession and contraction, and every contraction will in turn breed revival and expansion, in a quasi-regular, repeating, never-ending chain.

If you believe in the sunspot theory of the business cycle, then the distinction between external and internal is rather easy to draw; although even here, when you come to explain how and why disturbances on the surface of the sun give rise to the business cycle, you begin to get involved in the internal nature of the economic system. But at least no one can seriously argue that the direction of causation is in doubt, or that the economic system causes the sunspots to fluctuate, instead of vice versa. However, when it comes to such other external factors as wars and politics, or even births and gold discoveries, there is always some doubt as to whether the economic system does not at least react back on the so-called "external" factors, making the distinction between external and internal not such a hard and fast one. Still, no one will deny that any such "feedback" effects take us outside the traditional boundaries of economics, and this is our justification for distinguishing between external and internal theories.

▶ SUNSPOTS AND RELATED PURELY EXTERNAL THEORIES

Few professional economists today put much stock in these physical theories. Not infrequently an amateur economist, often a scientist in some other field, will argue that sunspots, which have an average periodicity of some 11 to 13 years, have important effects upon the weather. This affects crops. Good crops cause low incomes and bad business. Or else it is the other way round, and good crops are supposed to mean prosperity. The sunspot theorists cannot always make up their minds just which! In other versions, it is said that sunspots affect the intensity of solar radiation. Everyone knows that vitamin D depends on sunshine, and that people near the North Pole become despondent during the long winter nights. Hence, sunspots affect business by affecting pessimism, optimism, or health in general. One ingenious writer, dropping sunspots because they did not give an 8-year cycle, set forth the belief that whenever the planet Venus came between the sun and the earth, this caused magnetic absorptions and an 8-year business cycle.

Unfortunately, the field of economics has not the classic simplicity of physics or mathematics. In those fields a crank who thinks he can square the circle or build a perpetual-motion machine can be shown up, if not to his own satisfaction, at least to that of every competent observer. In economics, it is not quite so easy to demonstrate that sunspot theories of the cycle are all moonshine, especially if their proponents are willing to spend a lifetime manipulating statistics until they produce agreement. This sad fact is important not because we find it difficult to disprove the sunspot theory—no one really cares much today about sunspot theories—but rather because our cockiness about what we think are better and truer theories must always be subject to liberal reservations in view of the complexity of economic observations and data that makes it so difficult to disprove a bad theory or verify a good one.

▶ PURELY INTERNAL THEORIES

As against the crude external sunspot theory, we may describe a simple example of a possible crude internal theory. If machinery and other durable goods all had the same length of life, say 8 or 10 years, then we might try to explain a business cycle of the same length by this fact. If once a boom got started —never mind how—then there would be a bunching of new capital goods all of the same age. A few years later before these goods had worn out, there would be little need for replacement. This would cause a depression.

But after 8 or 10 years all the capital equipment would suddenly wear out and would all have to be replaced, giving rise to an inflationary boom. This in turn would give rise to another complete cycle, with a new cycle of depression and boom every decade. Thus, as a result of self-generating "replacement waves," we might have a purely internal business-cycle theory.

Actually, not all equipment has the same length of life; and not even all identical automobiles produced on the same day are in need of being replaced at the same time. Therefore, any bunching of equipment expenditures will tend over time to spread itself out, at most giving rise to weaker and weaker replacement peaks. Twenty-five years after the Civil War one might have observed a deficit of births because of that conflict. But another generation later and the dip would be hardly noticeable, while today it is just as if there had never been that particular violent disturbance of population. Replacement waves, therefore, are like a plucked violin string. They tend to dampen down and die away unless there is a new disturbance.

The laws of physics guarantee that friction will lessen any purely autonomous physical fluctuations. In social science, there is no law like that of the conservation of energy preventing the creation of purchasing power. Therefore, a much better example than replacement waves of a self-generating cycle would be the case where people became alternately optimistic and pessimistic, each stage leading as inevitably into the next just as the manic stage of an insane person leads eventually to the depressive stage. We cannot rule out such an internal theory. But neither can we be satisfied with it as it stands, for it does not say much or explain a great deal.

▶ COMBINING EXTERNAL AND INTERNAL ELEMENTS INTO A SYNTHESIS

Everyone has observed how a window or a tuning fork may be brought into pronounced vibration when a certain note is sounded. Is this vibration externally or internally caused? The answer is, Both. The sounded note is certainly an external cause. But the window or tuning fork responds according to its own internal nature, coming into strong resonance not with any sounded note but only with one of a certain definite pitch. It takes the right kind of trumpets to bring down the walls of Jericho.

Likewise we may look upon the business cycle as not unlike a toy rocking horse that is subjected to occasional outside pushes. The pushes need not be regular; great technical inventions never are. But just as the horse rocks with a frequency and amplitude that depend partly upon its internal nature (its size and weight), so too will the economic system according to its *internal* nature respond to fluctuations in external factors. Both external and internal factors are important, then, in explaining the business cycle.

Most economists today believe in a synthesis or combination of external and internal theories. In explaining the major cycles, they place crucial emphasis on fluctuations in *investment* or *capital* goods. Primary causes of these capricious and volatile investment fluctuations are to be found in such external factors as (1) technological innovation, and (2) dynamic growth of population and of territory. With these external factors, we must combine the internal factors that cause any initial change in investment to be amplified in a cumulative, multiplied fashion—as people who are given work in the capital-goods industries respend part of their new income on consumption goods and as an air of optimism begins to pervade the business community, causing firms to go to the banks and the securities market for new credit accommodation.

Also, it is necessary to point out that the general business situation definitely reacts back on investment. If high consumption sales make businessmen optimistic, they are more likely to embark upon venturesome investment programs. Inventions or scientific discoveries may occur independently of the business cycle, but their economic introduction will most certainly depend on business conditions. When national income moved to a new postwar plateau some 50 per cent higher than prewar, it was reasonable to expect that a considerable volume of capital formation (new machines, added inventories, construction) would be induced. Therefore, especially in the short run, investment may be in part an *effect* as well as a cause of the level of income.

In the longer run, no matter how high a plateau of income is maintained, the stock of capital goods will become adjusted at a higher level and new net investment will drop off to zero unless there is (1) a growth of income, (2) a continuing improvement of technology, or (3) a never-ending reduction in interest rates. The first of these processes, showing how investment demand may be induced by *growth* of sales and income, has been given a rather high-sounding name—the "acceleration principle." Almost all writers bring it in as one strand in their final business-cycle theories. Let us examine how this internal cyclical mechanism works itself out and interacts with other factors.

▶ THE ACCELERATION PRINCIPLE

According to this law, society's needed stock of capital, whether inventory or equipment, depends primarily upon the level of income or production. Additions to the stock of capital, or what we customarily call *net* investment, will take place only when income is growing. As a result, a prosperity period may come to an end—not simply because consumption sales have gone down—but simply because sales have *leveled off* at a high level or have continued to grow but at a lower rate than previously.

A simplified arithmetical example will make this clear. Imagine a typical textile-manufacturing firm whose stock of capital equipment is always kept equal to about ten times the value of its yearly sales of cloth.[1] Thus, when its sales have remained at 6 million dollars per year for some time, its balance sheet will show 60 million dollars of capital equipment, consisting of perhaps

---

[1] To keep the discussion simple, we use the exaggerated ratio 10:1 and ignore changes in interest rates or degree of utilization of capacity. The reader can include inventory change as well as equipment change in the analysis.

20 machines of different ages with one wearing out each year and being re-placed. Because replacement just balances depreciation, there is no *net* invest-ment or saving being done by the corporation. *Gross* investment is taking place at the rate of 3 million dollars per year, representing the yearly replace-ment of one machine. (The other 3 million dollars of sales may be assumed to go for wages and dividends.) The first phase of Table 1 shows this.

Now let's suppose that, in the fourth year, sales rise by 50 per cent—from 6 to 9 million dollars. Then the number of machines must also rise by 50 per cent, or from 20 to 30 machines. In the fourth year, 11 machines must be bought, 10 new ones in addition to the replacement of the worn-out one.

Sales have gone up by 50 per cent. How much has machine production gone up? By 1,000 per cent! It is this accelerated effect of a change in consumption on investment levels that gives the acceleration principle its name.

If sales continue to rise in both the fifth and the sixth years by 3 million dollars, then we shall continue to have 11 new machines ordered in every year.

So far, the acceleration principle has given us no trouble. On the contrary, it has given us a tremendous increase in investment spending as a result of a moderate increase in consumption sales. But now we are riding a tiger. Con-sumption has to keep increasing in order for investment to stand still! If con-sumption should stop growing at so rapid a rate—if it should level off in the seventh year even at the high level of 15 million dollars per year—then net

The acceleration principle shows how variations in a system's growth rate will induce variations in its level of investment:

Table. 1. Illustration of the acceleration principle (in millions of dollars).

Time	Yearly sales	Stock of capital	Net in-vestment, NI	Gross investment, GI (NI + replacement)
First phase				
First year	$ 6	$ 60	$ 0	1 machine at $3 = $3
Second year	6	60	0	1 machine at $3 = $3
Third year	6	60	0	1 machine at $3 = $3
Second phase				
Fourth year	$ 9	$ 90	$30	(1 + 10) machines at $3 = $33
Fifth year	12	120	30	(1 + 10) machines at $3 = $33
Sixth year	15	150	30	(1 + 10) machines at $3 = $33
Third phase				
Seventh year	$15	$150	$ 0	1 machine at $3 = $3
Fourth phase (to be filled in by reader)				
Eighth year	$14.7	$___	−$ 3	_ machines at $3 = $__

investment will fall away to zero, and gross investment will fall back to 1 machine (see the table). In other words, a drop of zero per cent in sales has resulted in a 90 per cent drop in gross investment and a 100 per cent drop in net investment! (See Table 1's third phase, and fill in the fourth phase.)

The Lord giveth and the Lord taketh away. The acceleration principle is a two-edged sword. If sales should drop below 15 million dollars, gross investment would drop away to nothing; in fact, the firm would want to disinvest by selling off some machinery on the used-equipment market.

It is now clear that a depression can set in just because consumption has stopped growing so rapidly, even if it has not dropped off absolutely, but only leveled off at a high level.

Needless to say, the curtailment of production in the machine-producing industries will cause them to shut down, will curtail their income and spending on food and clothing, and lead to still further "multiplier" changes in spending. This might ultimately cause textile sales to stop growing altogether, or even to decline. This will cause a further accelerated drop in net investment. Thus, we may be in a vicious circle whereby the acceleration principle and the multiplier interact so as to produce a cumulative deflationary (or inflationary) spiral.

Our example used machines. Does that mean the acceleration principle is not involved in the inventory "recessions" (such as 1920–1921, 1937–1938, 1948–1949, 1953–1954) that have been so important recently? Not at all. The same principle—that stocks of capital goods try to hold in some proportion to sales per unit time—is also used to explain short inventory cycles.

It is easy to see that in the acceleration principle we have a powerful factor making for economic instability. We have all heard of situations where people have to keep running in order to stand still. In the economic world, matters may be still worse: the system may have to keep running at an ever-faster pace just in order to stand still!

If business sales go up and down, the acceleration principle can intensify their fluctuation. It induces net investment on the upswing but causes about the same amount of net *disinvestment* on the downswing. In the long run, if the system is growing because of population increase or higher real incomes, then the acceleration principle works primarily as a stimulating factor: growing national income causes extensive growth of capital, which in turn means brisk investment demand and relatively low unemployment.

▶ **FORECASTING THE FUTURE OF BUSINESS ACTIVITY**

Businessmen have to make guesses about the future in making their investment and production decisions. If they thought next year would bring a depression, they might want to reduce inventory now. If, to the contrary, they expected prices to rise greatly four months from now, they might hasten today to buy goods forward and to add to equipment and plant.

Similarly speculators would like to know the future so as to be able to buy or sell common stocks and make a profit. And more important to us, policy makers in Washington would like to have a peek at next year's national income accounts so as to be able to take remedial fiscal and monetary actions right now.

Statisticians and economists can't yet make accurate forecasts. Their guesses sometimes turn out to be quite wrong. Nonetheless, their bosses insist on their doing their best. Why? Because refusal to make a forecast usually itself involves an *implicit* forecast. And it turns out that noneconomists have even a worse long-run batting average at making forecasts than do trained statistical economists.

What methods do the best forecasters—those who bat .570 rather than .336 —use? No simple description can be given, but here are a few of the most common practices.

1. They follow all the national income accounts very closely. GNP every quarter; personal income every month; new construction; equipment spending; the important short-run behavior of inventory change; estimates of coming government expenditures and taxes. They also watch prices and the Federal Reserve Board monthly index of production.

In addition they watch many, many statistics as they become available. Department-store sales each week. Chain-store sales (Woolworth, J. C. Penney, etc.) and mail-order sales (Sears, Ward's, etc.) each month. New orders and inventory changes of manufacturing and trade each month.

2. Since the war, the forecaster can study various surveys of future events: the McGraw-Hill questionnaire of business intentions to invest and the SEC-Commerce official questionnaires on the same subject are the most important fixed investment clues. The intentions reported by purchasing agents are most important for inventories.

For consumers, the monumental random samples that the Federal Reserve commissions the University of Michigan Group Survey Center to take give information on whether or not the consumer is in a buying mood and what are his spending intentions.

For businessmen generally, Dun & Bradstreet and *Fortune* take frequent polls of opinions about the future and present intentions. In Europe this polling technique has also made great progress.

3. Many forecasters then try to draw up "C + I + G-type models" to make *approximate guesses* about future changes. They try to come out with a range of probable answers, not with a single answer accurate to four decimals.

4. Some reinforce these guesses by considering whether most diverse time

series—like those in Fig. 2—are going up or down. Are certain "leaders" or "early turners" such as hours worked per week, or new orders, or stock prices, or construction, or failures (inverted) beginning to show a change from all rising to all falling?

When all is said and done, the president of a large company feels that his forecasters do help him in making his decisions. He knows that the forecasters don't do a great deal better than would a parrot who always forecasted: "Next year the same as this year." But it's that little bit better that makes the economics department a profitable operation for the company.

And the same holds for the various branches of the government. Its economists have done remarkably well these last dozen years in calling future trends. No one can expect more than that from so inexact a science as economics.

SUMMARY

1. The business cycle is a pulse common to almost all sectors of economic life and to all capitalistic countries. Movements in national income, unemployment, production, prices, and profits are not so regular and predictable as the orbits of the planets or the oscillations of a pendulum, and there is no magical method of forecasting the turns of business activity.

2. However, the four phases of expansion-peak-contraction-revival can be separated out for analysis and can be distinguished from seasonal fluctuations or long-term trends. The resulting pattern of 8- to 10-year major cycles, shorter minor cycles, and longer construction cycles has been carefully described by economists, statisticians, and historians.

3. When it comes to theories to explain the cycle, our first clue is to be found in the greater amplitude of fluctuations of investment or durable capital-goods formation. Although most economists agree on this fact, they differ in their emphasis upon external or internal factors. Increasingly the experts are tending toward a synthesis of external and internal factors, where on the one hand importance is attached to fluctuations in inventions, in population and territorial growth, in gold discoveries and political warfare. On the other hand, economists stress also the way that these external changes in investment opportunities are modified by the multiplier reactions of the economic system, the credit practices of banks, waves of optimism and pessimism, replacement cycles, the acceleration principle which brings in dynamic rates of change as well as levels, and still other feedback effects of income upon investment.

4. Forecasting is still inexact. Those with the best long-run batting averages follow national income and related statistics very closely. They rely heavily on surveys of government, consumer, and business intentions. They reinforce their $C + I + G$ guesses with the study of "early turners."

In the next three chapters we turn to study the effects of money on national income. Then the last two chapters of Part Two deal with what can be done to moderate the wild contortions of the cycle, not only to calm it down, but to do so at a level of high employment and long-term growth. This is the challenge to monetary and fiscal policy.

QUESTIONS FOR DISCUSSION

1. What is meant by the business cycle? How would you measure it?

2. Describe the history of business cycles in this country.

3. Describe the different phases of the cycle. In what one are you now?

4. Which theory or theories of the cycle do you like best? Why?

5. Write a two-page explanation of the acceleration principle. Can you guess how it interacts with the multiplier?

6. Why is it important to be able to forecast the future of business activity? Illustrate with examples of typical businesses. How would you forecast? With what confidence?

7. Review your understanding of the following concepts:

business cycle, crisis, recession,
  turning point, phase
seasonal and trend corrections
"early turners"

internal and external theories
replacement waves, sunspots
acceleration principle
forecasting methods and batting
  averages

PRICES AND MONEY

Only one fellow in ten thousand understands the currency question, and we meet him every day.

KIN HUBBARD

The last chapters show how the modern economist finds it convenient to analyze the forces making for expanding or contracting money income in terms of saving and investment schedules—or, what is the same thing, in terms of the components of consumption, investment, and government spending.

As these change, employment and production change. But once full employment is reached and all plants are used up to capacity, further expansions in spending must primarily result in a bidding up of prices. The multiplier process still operates, but it operates to produce inflationary gaps and to produce secondary chains of inflationary price rises.

The first part of this chapter will describe the historical behavior of prices. It will analyze the various good and bad effects of inflationary price rises, contrasting these with the good and bad effects of deflationary price falls.

That completes the first part of the chapter. Then in its last part, this chapter goes into the problem of how much money the community has: how much coin, currency, and bank money ("demand or checking deposits").

▶ THE ATTRACTIVE, BUT OVERLY SIMPLE, "QUANTITY THEORY"

You may well ask: Why put the two different subjects of prices and money in the same chapter? Our answer must be: Tradition. Before the modern saving-investment theory of income determination was developed, economists framed an exceedingly simple theory of general prices. They framed what was called the "quantity theory of money and prices" which said:

▶ Doubling the nation's stock of money M will tend to exactly double its price level P. Or halving M will halve P. So to stabilize the price level, all you have to do is to stabilize the money supply M.

Isn't that a simple theory? You can memorize it in ten minutes, and teach it to your little sister in twenty.

Well, as we'll see (particularly in the Appendix) the quantity theory is overly simple. It won't fit the facts. It has to be modified so as to take into account investment spending decisions. And consumption decisions. And interest rates. And many other things.

After it has been modified and qualified, you may not be able to write it down on a postage stamp or teach it to a parrot. But you'll then find it a more useful tool to work with.

For make no mistake about it: what banks and governments do about the supply of money *does* have important effects on our saving-investment schedules. Particularly in the postwar years, economists have come to learn how necessary it is to combine (1) their income analysis and their analysis of fiscal policy with (2) their analysis of money and bank credit, and to show how these can be affected by the government's Federal Reserve policies.

▶ **INFLATION, DEFLATION, AND REDISTRIBUTION OF INCOME AMONG GROUPS**

By inflation we mean a time of generally rising prices. By deflation we mean a time when most prices are falling. The cause of inflation and deflation is usually taken to be a change in total dollar *spending* relative to the flow of goods offered for sale. If the total flow of purchasing power coming on the market is not matched by a sufficient flow of goods, prices will tend to rise. On the other hand, when total spending goes down, prices and production tend to fall.

Neither in inflation nor in deflation do prices move all in the same direction or in exactly the same proportion. As a result of changes in *relative* prices and in total spending, the two processes of inflation and deflation cause definite and characteristic changes in (1) the distribution of income among economic classes, and in (2) total output.

Inflation tends to favor debtors and profit receivers at the expense of creditors and fixed-income receivers. Deflation has the opposite effect. Here's why.

Suppose you lend $1,000 today and are paid back one year from now. If in the meantime prices have doubled, then your debtor will be paying back only one-half as much real purchasing power as you gave him. If prices were to increase a trillion-fold, as they did in the German inflation of 1920–1923, then the wealth of creditors would be completely wiped out. This actually happened to German university endowments and life-insurance assets.

After World War II an American who earned 5 per cent yearly on a mortgage found that he was not even holding his own as far as the *real purchasing power* of the dollar was concerned. United States government savings bonds bought for $75 in 1948 paid off $100 in 1958. But one hundred 1958 dollars had a lower purchasing power than did seventy-five 1948 dollars. During and after World War I, American prices were still more inadequately controlled; so white-collar workers like teachers, postmen, and bookkeepers found their relatively fixed incomes inadequate to maintain living standards in the face of the rising cost of living.

Widows living on fixed pensions, on life-insurance annuities, or on interest find themselves in the same difficult straits because today's dollar buys less than a prewar 50-cent piece. Some workers in highly organized occupations may, by militant collective bargaining, be able to keep up with the high cost of living; but many find their real wages shrinking.

On the other hand, one who invests his money in real estate, in common stocks, or in sacks of flour makes a great money profit during inflation. The volume of business sales shoots up. Prices rise between the time that businessmen buy and sell their merchandise. Fixed or overhead costs remain the same; other costs rise but not so rapidly as prices. For all these reasons profits increase—often faster than does the cost of living. In such periods of great inflation, every reckless fool can become a great financier.

In time of deflation, the shoe is on the other foot. Creditors and fixed-income receivers tend to gain at the expense of debtors and profit receivers. If prices fall between the time that a creditor lends money and is repaid, then he gets back more purchasing power than he lent. Between the time that a merchant buys and sells goods, he will have to take a loss.

The schoolteacher who keeps her job and whose pay is not cut too deeply finds that her real income has increased. The widow who withstood the temptation to buy common stock during the boom and instead put all her money into gilt-edge government bonds finds herself better off. At the same time the government finds the real burden of its public debt goes up relative to tax collections and national income. A hoarder who earns no money interest on his mattress cache finds the real value of his wealth increasing every day as prices fall. If prices fall at the rate of 10 per cent per year, he is being rewarded for his antisocial act of hoarding at a 10 per cent rate of interest in real terms, while the businessman who is foolish enough to give someone a job may find that he can't even get back his original outlay, much less earn a profit.

▶ **EFFECTS OF CHANGING PRICES ON OUTPUT AND EMPLOYMENT**

An increase in prices is usually associated with high employment. In mild inflation the wheels of industry are well lubricated and output is near capacity. Private investment is brisk, and jobs are plentiful. Thus a little inflation is usually to be preferred to a little deflation. The losses to fixed-income groups are usually less than the gains to the rest of the community. Even workers with relatively fixed wages are often better off because of improved employment opportunities and greater take-home pay; and a rise in interest rates on new securities may partly make up any losses to creditors.

In deflation, on the other hand, the growing unemployment of labor and capital causes the community's total well-being to be less; so the gainers get less than the losers lose. As a matter of fact, in deep depression, almost everyone—including the creditor who is left with uncollectible debts—suffers.

The above remarks show conclusively why an increase in consumption or investment spending is a good thing in times of unemployment, even if there is some upward pressure on prices. When the economic system is suffering from acute deflation, it makes little sense to criticize private or public spending on the ground that this might be inflationary. Actually most of the increased spending will then go to increase production and create jobs.

But the same reasoning shows that once full employment and full plant capacity have been reached any further increases in spending must necessarily be completely wasted in "paper" price increases.

▶ GALLOPING INFLATION

If price increases could be held down to, say, 2 per cent per year, such a mild steady inflation need not cause too great alarm. But if each increase in prices becomes the signal for an increase in wages and costs, which again sends prices up still further, we may be in the midst of a malignant, galloping hyperinflation. Nothing good can be said for a rapid rise of prices such as took place in Germany in 1920–1923 and more recently in China and Hungary. Production and even the social order are then disorganized. The total wealth of large groups of the population is wiped out as money becomes worthless. Debtors ruthlessly pursue creditors in order to pay off their obligations in valueless money. Speculators profiteer. Housewives rush to spend their husbands' pay checks before prices rise still further, but in doing so they only bid prices up even faster. As a Southerner said during the Confederate inflation,

> We used to go to the stores with money in our pockets and come back with food in our baskets. Now we go with money in baskets and return with food in our pockets. Everything is scarce except money! Prices are chaotic and production disorganized. A meal that used to cost the same amount as an opera ticket now costs twenty times as much. Business is often at a standstill because no one knows how much to charge. As a result, everybody tends to hoard "things" and to try to get rid of the "bad" paper money, which drives the "good" metal money out of circulation. A partial return to barter—with all its inconveniences—is the result.

Fortunately, there are few cases of hyperinflation except during war or in the backwash of war and revolution. There are economists, however, who fear that our system is becoming jittery with a tendency to go into an explosive price rise whenever full employment comes in view. If workers, farmers, and businessmen become aware that their welfare depends as much on what their

Wars bring sharpest price rises:

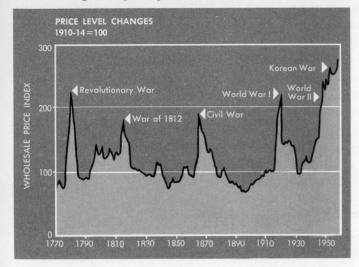

PRICE LEVEL CHANGES
1910-14 = 100

Fig. 1. In each postwar period since the beginning there has been slightly less of a price drop. Indeed, after the last war, there was no significant drop. For 60 years the price trend has seemed definitely upward.

money can buy as on their money earnings, perhaps this awareness might cause them in the future to moderate their demands for higher prices and money wages. This would tend to have a favorable result: for then all increases in purchasing power would go to create increases in employment and real output, rather than dissipate themselves in higher prices.

In the first postwar years, the rapid rise in prices drove some economists to the gloomy view: "We can never get near full employment without having rising wages and prices; only a price-fixing board can make full employment and price stability compatible." The 1936–1937, 1945–1948, and 1956–1957 experiences did give this view some plausibility. However, 1951–1955 were mostly years of low unemployment and also years of falling wholesale prices and steady living costs. So it is not clear that we who value freedom of enterprise and dislike authoritarian government controls need yet despair over the compatibility of full employment with efficiency and freedom. (In later chapters, we return to this problem.)

▶ PAST BEHAVIOR OF PRICES

Figure 1 shows the historical ups and downs of wholesale prices.[1] Each war is clearly marked by a peak. At first glance there seem to be no general upward or downward trends. But look carefully at the chart or at this book's opening

[1] We saw on Chapter 9's page 165 the many statistical and theoretical problems in computing an average index number of prices. Not only is it difficult to get accurate price quotations for all commodities, but there is also the question of how to weight the different prices. The cost of living for a rich man may change differently from that for a poor man, just as the cost of living of a vegetarian may change differently from that of a steak addict. In view of these difficulties, it is surprising how alike are the changes of different kinds of index numbers.

flyleaf to see what has happened in the twentieth century. The trend of prices has been generally upward; the value of the dollar—as measured by its purchasing power, by what it can buy—has been cut in half since today's college student was born.

As an omen for the future, note one terribly significant fact: After World War II there was no decline in prices at all comparable to what followed previous wars. Wages and prices seem to have become sticky as far as downward movements are concerned; also government has become quick to act to stem any depression that is beginning to get under way. If prices rise in good times and don't fall much in bad times, what is the long-term outlook for prices? The question answers itself.

▶ DEMAND-PULL OR WAGE-PUSH?

Just as some try to explain prices by the stock of money alone, others try to explain a long-run upward trend in prices by the push of money wages alone. "It's not," they claim, "the pull of demand that is raising prices. It's the remorseless push upward on prices from the unions. Their leaders force up wages by strike threats; and with no commensurate increases in productivity, the result must be a rise in unit costs of production and in prices."

We can't pretend to judge this debate until later chapters. But we should list the rebuttal of the demand theorists. "Would labor succeed in raising money wages if monetary demand were not permissive? Actually, we claim it's the strong upward pull of demand on prices that *permits* the unions to get their money wage increase. If the demand weren't there, any increase in money wages would result in pricing goods so high that production and employment would have to fall."

We'll see in Chapter 17 that a theory that combines wage push with demand pull may be the most realistic one to explain recent economic history.

▶ GOALS OF LONG-TERM PRICE BEHAVIOR

Ideally, we all want a progressive full-employment economy in which the excesses of the business cycle are moderated. We want to control the "mad dance of the dollar" as the business cycle passes from boom to crisis and slump. But as far as the long-run trend of prices is concerned, there are three possible programs espoused by different economists:

1. *Prices—on the average—are to be stable.* As output increases over time owing to population increase and technological progress, the total of spending rises. Money wages and real wages also rise as a result of increases in productivity over time.

2. *Prices are to be gently rising.* Because full-employment output is also in-

creasing with productivity and growth, total spending rises even faster than
prices. Money wages also rise steadily; but the increase in real wages is not
quite so great, because of the upward trend in the cost of living.

3. *Prices are to be falling steadily.* The total of money wages and property
income remains almost constant. But the increase in output resulting from
improved technological productivity is passed on to all consumers in lower
prices. Real wages rise even though money wages may remain constant. Such
a fall in prices need not depress business activity unduly, provided that it
results from previous reductions in cost.

All three solutions are tolerable if unemployment is kept at a low figure.
But economic history and analysis suggest that high employment is least likely
to be maintained under the third possibility, and the real burden of the public debt would be heaviest. Most of the vigorous periods of healthy capitalist
development have been during periods of stable or gently rising prices. Capitalism, itself, developed during the centuries when Spanish New World gold
was raising prices—not because anyone planned it that way, but simply because our monetary system used to consist of precious metals, and Columbus
accidentally discovered the New World. The life expectancy of free private
enterprise may well be lowered if there are to be deflation and falling prices
in the decades ahead.

Suppose we do agree that there is nothing alarming in a gently rising trend
of prices. Can such a gentle rise remain gentle? Or will it more likely snowball into a rapid rate of increase, thereby creating grave problems for fixed-
income groups and older people who had hoped to retire on their savings?
Those who believe "it can't happen here" need only look to the historical experience of a country like Brazil; there prices have steadily risen for more than
a century! If you lived in Brazil, how would you feel about holding idle cash
as its purchasing power melted away?

► **IMPORTANCE OF MONEY**[1]

The behavior of prices is intimately related to the balance of saving and investment expenditure. We have already seen, and we shall later see further,
that the policy maker can change the equilibrium flow of income by direct
operation on the flow of government expenditure and the flow of taxation.
The supply of money and of liquid assets such as government bonds can also
have effects upon the level of the investment and saving schedules. The government, through the federal reserve system, has a responsibility to use monetary policy to help curb inflation and fight depressions.

[1] Chapter 3 gave an introductory description of the superiority of money over barter in
facilitating exchange and division of labor; the reader may turn back to p. 54 for a discussion
of the functioning of money as a unit of account and a medium of exchange.

But, as we mentioned in this chapter's beginning, economists used to think that the important explanation of price behavior could be found in the stock of money, *M*, alone. The Appendix discusses just what the quantity theory of money and prices had in mind, and what some of the objections to it are.

Even if we deem the quantity theory overly simple, we recognize the importance of money and credit. The way is now clear to take up the last topic of this chapter: namely, the basic facts about our supply of money.

▶ THE THREE KINDS OF MONEY: SMALL COINS, PAPER CURRENCY, AND BANK DEPOSITS

Let's list the main categories of money that we all have daily contact with: small change, paper currency, and bank-deposit money.

First, there is small change: copper pennies, nickel five-cent pieces, silver dimes, quarters, half dollars, and (in the Far West) silver dollars. These constitute our so-called "fractional currency." In total they do not add up to very much—in fact, to much less than one-fifteenth of the community's cash. Because the metal in all these coins is worth far less than their face value, they are termed "token money." Obviously, these coins are valued far beyond their metallic worth only because they can be readily converted into other kinds of money—20 nickels to the dollar, etc. They are not forced upon anybody; their quantity is limited by the public's demand for them to buy cigarettes, newspapers, and so forth.

Far more important is the second kind of money: "folding money" or paper currency. Most of us know little more about a one-dollar or five-dollar bill than that each is inscribed with the picture of some American statesman, that each contains the signature of one or another government official, and—most important of all—each bears a number showing its face value.

If you look at a one-dollar bill more closely, you find it contains the words "Silver Certificate." This means the United States Treasury is holding on deposit a silver dollar for you to claim if you wish. But as already mentioned, a silver dollar contains considerably less than a dollar's worth of silver. So, if you really want silver, you will do much better to buy it on the open market with your paper dollar, rather than go to the Treasury. Anyone who knows much about American politics and history realizes that some paper currency is called "silver" certificates only because a few Western senators from mining states could persuade Congress to give silver mining a continuing subsidy by buying up quantities of silver for monetary use. Otherwise, silver has absolutely no monetary significance; many countries are abandoning it even for small coins, and it is even losing its hold on the Orient.

Examine a ten-dollar bill or some other paper bill. You probably find it says

"Federal Reserve Note."[1] Like the dollar bill, this announces itself as "legal tender for all debts, public and private," but it contains the further, and non-sensical, statement that it "is redeemable in *lawful money* at the United States Treasury or at any Federal Reserve Bank." Why italicize "lawful money"? Because there is no such thing other than "legal tender" bills under discussion, namely, federal reserve notes, silver certificates, etc. In short, your old wrinkled ten-dollar bill is redeemable into a crisp new bill, into two fives, or into ten ones if your prefer! But that is all.[2]

Today, all American money is essentially "fiat" money. It is money because the government decrees it is money; and because we all accept it.

Back before 1933, it was not uncommon for good little boys and girls to be presented on their birthdays with five- or ten-dollar gold pieces. And gold certificates were often seen in circulation. These certificates were warehouse receipts promising the bearer redemption in gold upon application to the United States Treasury. But in 1933, when Congress raised the buying prices of gold from about $21 to $35 an ounce, all gold—except that tied up in wedding rings and dental fillings—was called in. This was done so that holders or hoarders of gold could not make a 67 per cent profit as a result of the devaluation of the dollar. At the same time, all gold certificates were called in. Congress ruled that these certificates were not to be exchanged for gold upon being called in, but simply for ordinary paper dollars. A few absent-minded people still have not turned in their gold certificates, but once these are brought to a bank, they will be retired from circulation forever and replaced by other bills.[3]

From the standpoint of understanding the nature of money, it is a good thing these gold certificates no longer exist. The modern student need not be misled, as were earlier generations of students, by some mystical belief that "gold backing" is what gives money its value. Certainly gold has little to do with the problem. Every expert knows that the popular conception "money has more value if it is exchangeable into gold" exactly reverses the true relation. If it were not that gold has some monetary uses, its value as a metal

---

[1] Two-dollar bills, considered to be bad luck in most parts of the country other than New England, are so-called United States Notes—remnants of the greenbacks used to finance the Civil War. So are many five-dollar bills. Occasionally you may run into a bill that says "Federal Reserve Bank Note" or even a "National Bank Note" containing the name of some near-by national bank; these are being gradually retired from circulation.

[2] A Cleveland businessman not long ago wrote to the Treasury asking for some "lawful money" in return for a ten-dollar bill. He received two polite letters, but no satisfaction.

[3] The courts also upheld a statute that invalidated contracts calling for payment in gold; only payment in terms of dollars was permitted. Otherwise, creditors would have made a 67 per cent profit on the revaluation and debtors would have lost 67 per cent. As we shall see in Chapter 16 the 12 Federal Reserve Banks hold special-type gold certificates.

would be much less than it is today. We should have cheaper inlays and wedding rings, and South African miners would be poorer than they are.

We shall later see that, when a government requires itself to hold some fraction of gold reserves against its paper money, the gold affects prices only through its ability to *limit or to expand the volume of paper money and total spending.* This was overlooked by foolish European chancellors of the exchequer who, after World War I, tried to stop inflation by accumulating new gold reserves through the purchase of gold on the open market with newly printed money. Of course, the effect was just the opposite. Only after they had reversed the process and used their gold to buy up and burn outstanding paper money did they enjoy any success.

▶ WHY CHECKING DEPOSITS ARE CONSIDERED TO BE MONEY

There is also a third category of what economists call money, in addition to metallic small change and paper currency. This is so-called "bank money"— made up of bank deposits subject to checking on demand. If I have $1,000 in my checking account at the Cambridge Trust Company, that deposit can be regarded as money. Why? Because I can pay for purchases with checks drawn on it. The deposit is like any other medium of exchange and, being payable on demand, it serves as a "standard of value" or "unit of account" in the same sense as $1,000 worth of silver quarters, *i.e.,* both the deposit and the quarters are convertible into standard money or cash at fixed terms, dollar for dollar.

Possessing the essential properties of money, bank demand deposits might just as well be counted as money. And they are.[1]

Actually, as was noted in the discussion of money in Chapter 3, bank money is quantitatively more important than currency because most transactions are made by check. The convenience of checks for mailing, for paying the exact sum of money due, for providing a receipt in the form of the canceled check voucher, for protecting against loss when stolen or misplaced (while unendorsed or, for that matter, endorsed) —all these advantages are obvious and explain the widespread use of bank money.

Table 1 illustrates the quantitative importance of the three kinds of money.

▶ LIQUID WEALTH OR "NEAR-MONEY"

Along with the total of money, Table 1 also shows the total of "near-money." What is meant by this concept? Different economists define the term differ-

---

[1] My balance on deposit in the bank is usually considered to be money—not the checks I write. These represent only the spending or transfer of money; the money itself, quantitatively, is the deposit.

Demand deposits form three-fourths of our total money supply:

Kinds of money	March, 1939	March, 1957
Small change (outside of banks):		
Minor coins (pennies & nickels)	$0.2	$ 0.4
Silver coins	0.4	1.3
	$ 0.6	$ 1.7
Paper currency (outside of banks):		
Federal reserve notes	$4.3	$23.3
Silver certificates and U.S. notes	1.6	2.1
Other currency (largely in process of being retired)	0.3	0.2
	$ 6.2	$ 25.6
Bank money		
Demand deposits of all banks (adjusted to exclude government deposits, etc.)	26.1	105.2
Total money	**$32.9**	**$132.5**
"Near-money" (estimated):		
Time or savings deposits (includes mutual savings banks, postal savings, and savings and loan agencies)	$30.0	$122.9
U.S. government bonds held by individuals and business (excluding banks, insurance companies, etc.)	12.0	86.7
Total "near-money"	**$42.0**	**$209.6**

Table 1. Total quantity United States money and "near-money" (in billions). (Source: *Federal Reserve Bulletin*.)

ently. Table 1 includes in near-money the total of savings deposits which any person could quickly cash in and the total of government bonds which anyone could present for redemption or sell for cash in the open market.

These liquid-wealth items have many of the properties of money. True, I do not pay my monthly expenses directly with government bonds, and so I hesitate to call such an item "money." Still, the fact that I have such an easily cashable asset means that my current spending habits are probably affected in much the same way as they would be if I owned a bank deposit instead of the government bonds. Similarly, if I have $10,000 on demand deposit and my brother has $5,000 on time deposit and $5,000 on demand deposit, will our saving and consumption schedules be very different ones? At equal incomes, is he likely to save a much larger percentage than I am?

No dogmatic answers can be given to these questions. But this much is clear:

Government bonds and savings accounts have many of the same effects as currency and demand deposits; and hence economists often choose to call such liquid assets "near-money."[1]

▶ CONCLUSION

Part of the buoyant postwar balance between saving and investment is explained by the tremendous wartime growth, shown in Table 1, of our total liquid wealth. How were 80 billion dollars of demand deposits created in the last 20 years? The next chapter will show how our banking system can create deposits.

SUMMARY

1. Prices and money are related because the stock of money can influence the saving-investment or $C + I + G$ schedules of spending. Older economists oversimplified this relation in the form of the "quantity theory of prices and money." In its strongest form, this theory says that P is directly proportional to M, so that a policy that stabilizes M will stabilize prices—a doctrine that the Appendix shows to be overly simple.

2. When prices change in periods of inflation or deflation, they do not all change in exactly the same degree. Instead of being neutral, such price changes have definite real effects on the economic system. In times of inflation, debtors and profit receivers benefit at the expense of creditors and fixed-income groups. Deflation has opposite effects upon the distribution of income between economic classes.

3. Aside from causing transfers between economic groups, deflation acts to reduce the total of national production and employment. Until it becomes excessive, inflation tends to expand employment and output, because any resulting lag of costs behind prices will stimulate industrial expansion.

4. Desirable long-term goals are stable prices or slowly rising prices, with money wages rising even more rapidly as the growth of productivity makes higher real wages possible. We must recognize that there is a serious long-term problem of keeping prices from showing a too strong upward trend.

5. There are three kinds of modern money: small token coins (or small change), fiat paper currency issued by the government and its federal reserve system, and demand bank deposits subject to check. Being convertible into

---

[1] It would not be illogical to subtract out from people's liquid assets their current liabilities (charge accounts, installment loans, etc.). Along with income, perhaps their "net worth" would be the single most important determinant of their spending.

each other at par, all these have the same value unit for unit, independently of the trifling paper, ink, and metal costs involved in each.

6. "Near-money" is defined as those liquid assets which a person can easily and quickly convert into cash and which therefore have many of the same effects on the propensity to consume as does money itself. According to this definition, savings accounts and government bonds are near-money.

7. Since 1939 the money supply has more than quadrupled, while near-money has increased almost fivefold.

QUESTIONS FOR DISCUSSION

1. If we printed and spent 100 billion new greenbacks, what do you think would happen to prices? Is there some truth then to the quantity theory?

2. If sure of inflation ahead, what might you do to protect yourself? List some of the dramatic happenings that go with galloping hyperinflation.

3. "Because labor's share of NNP never changes much, real wages can rise only with rises in labor productivity. So any increase in money *W* faster than productivity increases must push up money *P*." Use this formulation to show how *P* and *W* change in page 272's three cases.

4. Sometimes wages or loan contracts are expressed in terms of a sliding scale rather than in terms of fixed money. How did General Motors use an index of the cost of living to protect workers against a change in real wages due to price-level changes? How would you do the same thing with respect to an I.O.U.?

5. Take inventory of the different kinds of money in the pockets of the class members. Make up a table. What about checking deposits?

6. Why are checks used as often as they are? Why not more often? Trace the history of a check sent to your broker when you buy a share of A.T. & T. stock at $170 per share. Suppose your broker is 1,000 miles away.

7. Explain what is meant by "near-money" and how it got its name.

8. Two identical twins have identical incomes and wealth. One has half of his wealth in cash and half in liquid government bonds. The other has nine-tenths in cash and one-tenth in bonds. Will their propensities to consume be significantly different?

9. Review your understanding of the following concepts:

quantity theory	*fractional coinage or token*
inflation, deflation, hyperinfla-	*money, forms of currency,*
tion	*demand versus time deposits*
technological cost-price reduc-	*near-money*
tion	*net worth*
wage push versus demand pull	*real versus money wage*

APPENDIX: **THE "QUANTITY THEORY" AND THE LIQUIDITY-DEMAND FOR MONEY**

The next few chapters will show the steps by which the Central Bank can affect the commercial banks, causing a change in the quantity of money, and will show how that change of money may affect money spending and prices. Years ago, many economists omitted some of the detailed steps of this process. Instead they shortened the argument: they relied on the so-called "quantity theory," or what might more exactly be called "the theory that the level of money spending and of prices *is directly proportional* to the quantity of money in existence."

Few, if any, economists hold rigidly to the quantity theory today. But it still has much popular appeal; and in analyzing its limitations—*e.g.*, in the "liquidity-preference" discussion at the close of this Appendix—our understanding of monetary policy will be furthered, and we shall be better equipped for the next chapters' discussions of the federal reserve system.

The Quantity Theory of Money
In its simplest form, the argument goes something like the following:

As long as any commodity is scarce, its value will be high. If you increase the supply of wheat, its price will fall. Money is no exception. Even though the paper in a particular nation's money is worthless, yet fiat money will have value as long as (1) people are accustomed to using the money in question in making their exchanges, and (2) the total supply of money is kept *limited in amount*. Of course, if the printing presses spit out billions and billions of units of money, then prices will rise indefinitely high and money will become worthless.

But money differs from wheat and other commodities in an important respect: Money is useful only for what it will buy. The demand for money, therefore, has a very special form: *Double the value of money or halve the price level and you will exactly halve the amount of money that people will wish to hold.*

Why? Because if everything now costs only one-half as much, people's cash requirements will be only half as great. In fact, when the prices of absolutely everything change in exactly the same proportion, money is the *only* commodity whose demand is changed—because as far as all *real* magnitudes are concerned, nothing has changed.

Consequently, these theorists arrive at the important conclusion: Other things being equal, the *price level is directly proportional to the amount of money in existence; conversely, the amount of money that people will hold is directly proportional to the price level.* If the total amount of all kinds of money is M and the price level is P, then according to the simplified quantity theory,

$$M = kP \qquad \text{or} \qquad P = \frac{1}{k} M$$

where k is a factor of proportionality that remains constant if "other things are equal."

In bare essentials, this is the quantity theory. How valid is it? How useful? As stated, it is obviously a highly simplified theory, and most economists today would say it is a highly *over*simplified theory. The "other things" do not always—or often—remain equal in real life, and so the simple quantity theory breaks down. At the very least, in these days when near-money is so important, M should have added to it some allowance for the size of time deposits and for government bonds held by the public.

The fact, however, that the quantity theory is a simplification of the truth and does not always hold with great precision should not be used to damn it utterly. If at least it indicates the general direction of economic behavior, that would be a great deal to be said in its favor. Unfortunately, even this limited claim cannot always be made for the quantity theory. Some of the reasons for this we shall see presently.

But first, mention should be made of some of its more valid applications. In times of great inflation when the printing presses are pouring out floods of paper money, the general direction of causation is so simple that even a simplified theory can throw much light on the facts. During the hyperinflations characteristic of some wars or periods of postwar breakdown, the quantity theory could aid in the interpretation of economic events. The postwar Chinese and Hungarian inflations provide such examples; and so does the 1920–1923 German inflation. Still earlier examples occur in American history during the Revolutionary War and at the time when the Southern Confederacy was forced to issue tremendous amounts of paper money.[1]

The simple quantity theory may also have a limited validity in interpreting some of the historical long swings in the price level: the rise in prices following the Spanish discovery of New World gold, the rise in prices after the Californian and Australian gold discoveries of the middle of the nineteenth century, the rise in prices around the turn of the century as a result of South African and Alaskan gold production, and our postwar doubling of prices following upon the wartime expansion of money.

The truth of the quantity theory of prices depends upon two propositions, neither of which is universally valid: (1) *Prices* must be proportional to *total spending,* and (2) *total spending* must be proportional to the amount of *total money* in existence. It would then follow that prices are proportional to the total quantity of money. If either or both (1) and (2) fail to be true, the quantity theory fails as a correct explanation of prices.[2]

---

[1] Even in such times, the painstaking observer will be left with the feeling that the quantity theory does not get down to the fundamental reasons why money is being created at the rate it is being created. The true direction of causation is by no means in the one-way direction from M to P.

[2] There is a third serious drawback to the quantity theory which cannot be discussed in an elementary treatment of the subject. Even if it were valid, the quantity theory would be of

Inadequacies of the Quantity Theory: (1) Prices Not Proportional to Total Spending

That prices are not always proportional to total spending is clearly seen if we examine an upswing of business activity from a time of deep depression. If the output of goods increases along with the total of spending, *i.e.,* so long as there is still unemployment of labor and factories, there is no need for prices to increase much. In fact, economies of mass production may permit prices to fall as demand increases. Only if we were to make the highly unrealistic assumption of full employment and constant total output —only then would an increase in the total of spending always send prices up proportionately. But if, on the contrary, total output should double, then spending could double without having *any* effect on prices!

In most cycles of business activity, the truth lies somewhere in between: An increase from depression levels in total spending causes a considerable increase in output and a less than proportionate increase in average prices; during a recession of business, the drop in spending results in a drop in output and employment with less than a proportionate fall in prices.

One further example shows how unjustified is the assumption that output will always remain constant in such a way as to keep total spending and prices in direct proportion to each other. Suppose trade-unions succeed in getting fantastic wage increases, so that competitive costs and prices both double. You need not assert that this must *necessarily* cause a reduction in employment and production. But certainly no one—least of all a believer in the quantity theory—will deny that there might follow, under some assumptions about banking policy, a cut in production as a result of such a vast increase in prices. It then follows that total spending will less than double when prices double.

---

limited usefulness to the extent that the quantity theorists have no theory—except an inadequate and superficial one—of what determines changes in the quantity of money.

Inadequacies of the Quantity Theory: (2) Total Spending Not Proportional to the Stock of Money

The quantity of money is a stock. Like any asset, it exists at an instant of time. An instantaneous "still photo," or balance sheet, would record its amount. Total spending, excluding all "transfer" transactions, is the sum of the values of all output, *e.g.*, the price of oranges times the number of oranges produced plus the price of apples times the number of apples produced, and so forth for all goods and services. Total spending represents a *flow of income over time,* a rate of dollars per day, per month, or per year. Dimensionally speaking, spending bears the same relationship to the stock of money that a flow of water through a lake bears to the lake itself.

What is the factor relating the flow of income spending to the stock of money? It is easy to give a name to this factor; but, as we shall see, it is not very helpful to do so. In fact, scientists must constantly guard against a universal human weakness that makes us impute life and importance to a concept just because it has received a name and has been called to our attention.

The factor relating the volume of spending per unit time to the total stock of money is the *income velocity of circulation of money.* The total stock of money in the United States in 1957 was about 133 billion dollars. (This includes coins, paper currency outside the banks, and checking deposits.) Total volume of spending on final products (including net capital formation) was, of course, equal to net national product or to about 400 billion dollars. Consequently, we can say that the average income velocity of money was about 3 per year or about 0.25 per month. This means that, although some coins, bills, and deposits were used many times during that year, other units of money were not used even once.[1] On the average,

money turned over once in every 4 months.

We may summarize the definition of the average income velocity of circulation of money, V, as follows:

$$\text{Average income velocity per year} = \frac{\text{rate of income spending per year}}{\text{total volume of money}}$$

or in symbols:

$$V = \frac{NNP}{M} = \frac{p_1 q_1 + p_2 q_2 + \cdots}{M}$$

$$= \frac{\text{sum } pq}{M} = \frac{PQ}{M}$$

where M = total volume of all money
$p_1 q_1$ = amount spent on the first good or service (*e.g.*, oranges)
$p_2 q_2$ = amount spent on second good or service (*e.g.*, apples)
P = average price level of output
Q = total quantity of output per unit time

Note that this equation is simply a definition of the velocity of circulation of money —nothing more and nothing less.

So much for the definition of the velocity of money. What good does it do us to have introduced the concept? The older economists, who were good quantity theorists through thick and thin, thought it did lots of good. Today, those of their ranks who are still alive are not so sure; and the new generation of economists tends to believe that the concept of velocity is of limited usefulness and that in most circumstances of boom and depression, it may do harm as well as good.

---

[1] Of course, most transactions are not for final goods and services, but rather are transfers; *e.g.*, when a baker pays a miller for flour, when an investor buys a stock or shares or real estate, etc. According to recent statistics of bank debits

(checking transactions), urban bank deposits turn over some 23 times a year outside of New York City and 47 times a year in New York City. This velocity of circulation for all transaction purposes must be contrasted with the 3 income velocity rate of turnover against final goods and services. It may be of interest to mention that all these velocity figures have been changed in the four editions of this book. Far from remaining constant, they've been steadily rising for a dozen years now!

It puts off answering a question by asking another question. Thus, one of the reasons given for the Great Depression of the 1930's was the reduced velocity of circulation of money. But why was velocity reduced? To know that is already to know the answer to the riddle of the slump. Similarly, those who thought recovery could be ensured by increasing the quantity of money were disappointed by the unexpected decline in the velocity of the new money, and the years since 1955 have here and abroad thwarted the naïve quantity theorist. Though M changed little, V in Canada, Britain, and the United States rose considerably!

This takes us back to the heading of the present section; or to the fact that the quantity theory is invalidated by the failure of total spending to be proportional to the quantity of money. In terms of our new concept, this failure may be explained as follows: *the velocity of circulation of money is not even approximately constant.* It changes in boom and depression in a way that cannot be predicted except from fundamental factors such as savings and investment, trade-union policy, technological innovations, the total quantity of money, the composition of that quantity of money, the way that money came into existence, the amount of near-money, and finally—to bring the list to an end—the movement and structure of interest rates and security prices.[1]

---

[1] If correct, these statements illustrate the relative sterility of the so-called "quantity equation of exchange," according to which

$$MV = PQ \quad \text{or} \quad P = \frac{V}{Q} M$$

This is a truism based, as we have just seen, on the definition of V, and it should not be confused with the quantity theory, which had the merit of attempting to set up an explanatory hypothesis to fit facts. If, as the older writers thought, V were a constant, or if the movements of Q were such as to offset the movements of V, thereby leaving V/Q a constant, then the equation of exchange might be a useful truism. But if, as has been argued, V is a catchall almost as hard to understand as the business cycle itself, then the equation of exchange is a blind alley or possibly a red herring. Instead of setting out the important questions in a useful way, it diverts

Active and Inactive Money

One bitter lesson we have learned since 1929: There is no inherent tendency for money to be spent for goods at a constant velocity. If my current income is low, and if my expectations are pessimistic concerning real investment projects, then I may hold large sums of cash from 1930 to 1940 without at all increasing my spending. Call this hoarding if you like; but if interest rates are low, and if I am pessimistic concerning the future values of securities and real estate, then to hold cash is the most sensible speculation that I can make.

There are many ways that we might split up the demand for money. One convenient breakdown is to split money up into two parts. (1) There is a *transaction demand for money* to facilitate our ordinary purchases of goods and services. (2) There is what I might call a *liquidity-demand for money,* in order to hold part of our wealth in a form whose cash value is safe and which will be readily available against unforeseen contingencies.[2]

---

attention from the really interesting and important problems. The better economists of a generation ago often used their common sense to arrive at correct judgments of how spending and prices would behave; then later they translated these judgments into the language of V and other variables in the equation of exchange.

More important than the tautological equation of exchange is the quantity-theory hypothesis. Economists repeatedly kill it off. But it keeps coming back to life! This is not, I believe, an accident. For, so long as paper money is valued only for the exchanges it helps make, doubling M can result in exactly the same "real" equilibrium but with *all P's* doubled. Hence, a new long-run equilibrium consistent with the quantity theory is possible; and, indeed, if but one equilibrium configuration existed, this would be the only possible long-run outcome.

[2] Often the demand for money is broken up into three components, but in this discussion the author found it convenient to lump into the liquidity demand for money all those elements which do not depend directly upon the level of money income (the so-called "speculative motive" and part at least of the so-called "precautionary motive") .

Now we can see why the quantity theorists went wrong in believing in the constancy of V: They forgot about the second liquidity-demand for money and concentrated only on the first transaction demand. If the transaction demand were the only one, then the total of M might indeed tend to be in fairly close proportion to the level of total money spending. We could then speak of all money as "active money" with a fairly constant and quite large velocity of circulation. If the experience of the decades before 1929 could be trusted, then active money could be expected to have a velocity of at least four times per year. Less money would today be needed in the community to finance national incomes of the present magnitude. What would happen to the present excess money if it all had to be active? Some used to think it would all have to be spent for consumption, thereby bidding up the prices of goods and services. Prices would have to rise to an equilibrium level just high enough to keep all the money in existence circulating "actively."

For 25 years any such simple concept of all money as being active money has been false to the facts. Thus, in the depression the transaction demand declined with the decline in incomes; people were very much on edge and increased their precautionary balances; more important, with interest rates so low, people had little inducement to buy securities rather than to hold nonearning cash. They were apprehensive over the future losses they might experience in securities; so they increased their money holdings.

In short, the facts suggested that we split money up into our two categories: active (transactions) money, which depends primarily on the flow of income, and inactive (liquidity) money, which depends on the lowness of interest rates and the uncertainty of the future. Even this is an oversimplified picture, since the shifts in the demand for inactive money (for precautionary and speculative reasons) can be very rapid and unpredictable. But at least it helps us recognize the worst shortcomings of an oversimplified monetary approach.

Figure 2 shows that the total of inactive money increased with the lowness of the interest rates. On the basis of past experience concerning the minimum amount of money needed for transaction purposes, we can make rough estimates of the amount of active

High interest speeds up M's velocity, kills off inactive M:

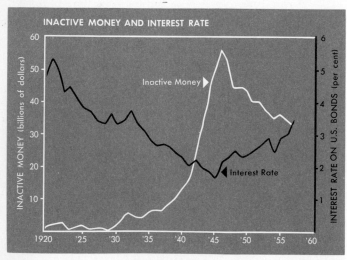

Fig. 2. From total M has been subtracted "active money" (defined to bear same proportion to income transactions as held before the depression). The resulting "inactive money" goes down as interest rate rises. Why? Because high interest means you forego a good yield when you hold zero-earning cash.

Increasing M will lower interest rates:

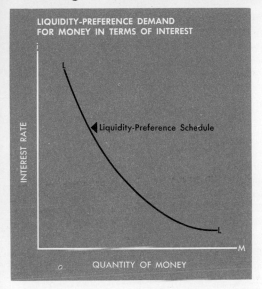

LIQUIDITY-PREFERENCE DEMAND
FOR MONEY IN TERMS OF INTEREST

i

L

◀ Liquidity-Preference Schedule

INTEREST RATE

L

M

QUANTITY OF MONEY

o

Fig. 3. If the government or Central Bank increases the supply of money, security prices will be bid up and interest rates bid down until people are willing to hold all the new M. They hold less M at high interest rates because holding M means foregoing the interest yield on securities.

money needed at any time to take care of transactions. Subtracting the calculated total of active money from the total of all money, we arrive at the total of inactive money. The resulting data show that *V* depends on the interest rate, rising when interest rises and falling when interest falls and definitely failing to stay constant.

Money and the Determination of Interest Rates

This discussion gives us one clue to the determination of the interest rate, or the structure of interest rates. From one point of view, interest can be thought of as the "price of money." (More precisely, it is the price or rental of the *use* of money.)

The late Lord Keynes showed how a large supply of money will—other things being equal—tend to depress interest rates. Suppose gold mines or printing presses or the banking system have created a large amount of money some time in the past. This money has to be held by someone. If more money is given to people than they find convenient or necessary for their level of income and expenditure, what will they do?

The simple quantity theory held that they would spend it on consumers' goods. But this would pass the money to someone else; and he, also being unwilling to hold the "hot brick," will spend it on consumers' goods. In the end, the prices of goods will be bid so high that people will finally need all the existing money just for transaction purposes. So argued the quantity theorists.

Keynes argued that people's consumption spending depends primarily on their income and total wealth, and only secondarily upon the composition of their wealth between cash and less liquid assets. Therefore, if the amount of total *M* tends to be too large, people and banks will try to use the excess to buy securities—not consumers' goods. This will gradually raise the price of stocks and bonds, or what is the same thing, reduce interest rates.

How long will this process go on? At first, one might be tempted to say until all the extra money is used up. But this would be wrong, since money cannot be used up in this way. For every buyer of a bond, there is a seller, and the money appears in his pockets. The only true end will be as follows:

> *An increase in total money tends—other things being equal—to lower the rate of interest, until finally the yield of stocks and bonds is so low that they cease any longer to be attractive alternatives to the holding of cash. At a low enough rate of interest, people will finally develop a strong enough liquidity motive for holding all the existing amount of money. (See Figure 3.)*

This is an important clue to the determination of interest. It is often called the "liquidity-preference theory of interest." Later, Chapter 29 will show that it is only one clue among a number.[1] The "net pro-

---

[1] We must not forget the qualifying expression, "other things being equal." Other things do not remain perfectly equal: people's expectations about the future profitability of noncash assets may change, which can affect interest, even though M does not change. And P can partially change.

Interest-rate theory is one of the most difficult parts of economics, and an elementary treatment can only hope to raise the important issues. Later, in Chapter 29, the role of real factors in

ductivity of capital goods" will also be shown to have a vital bearing on interest—particularly on the long-run rate of interest of any economic system that retains full employment at stable prices.

---

determining the rate of interest is synthesized with the role played by money. For those interested in refinements of economic theory, it can be said that recent discussions have greatly reduced the area of disagreement between the various differing theories. In particular it has become recognized that (1) if all wages and prices can fall flexibly downward, (2) if the total of money and near-money does not at the same time shrink as much as prices do, and (3) if too perverse expectations are not generated by the *falling* of prices—if all these conditions are realized—then the real value of money and near-money may finally be raised enough to shift the saving schedule downward far enough to wipe out the deflationary gap and restore full employment. However, few economists have recommended such a deflationary process as the best way of getting money to be "active"; it is usually thought better to follow alternative expansionary monetary and fiscal policies. A. C. Pigou, long-time professor of economics at Cambridge, has helped clarify these theoretical issues.

SUMMARY TO APPENDIX

1. In its simplest and most interesting form, the quantity theory says prices tend to be proportional to quantity of money.

2. This is regarded as an oversimplification because its two implicit assumptions are not factually true: (*a*) There is very far from a direct proportionate relationship between prices and total spending; the total of output is an important variable rather than a constant. (*b*) There is very far from a directly proportionate relationship between the flow of total spending and the stock of total money. The velocity of circulation of money is an important variable and not a constant. The velocity varies with changes in interest rates, expectations, saving and investment schedules, and other variables.

3. At the least, we must split the total demand for money into two components: the active-money *transaction demand* that is largely dependent upon the level of money income; and the more volatile inactive-money *liquidity-demand* that depends upon the lowness of interest rates, people's expectations concerning the future prices of assets other than money, and the precautions they feel are necessary against contingencies.

4. We can if we wish describe the process by which monetary policy produces a lower interest rate in terms of the liquidity-preference theory of interest. An increase in the stock of M will result in a new equilibrium level of interest rates just low enough to induce people to be willing to hold all new M.

15 THE BANKING SYSTEM AND DEPOSIT CREATION

> . . . one rule which woe betides the banker who fails to heed it,
> . . . never lend any money to anybody unless they don't need it.
>
> OGDEN NASH

The outstanding importance of bank deposits as part of the community's money supply has already been discussed. This chapter continues the discussion in two distinct parts. In the first, we must examine briefly the important facts and functionings of the modern banking system, showing how the present-day commercial bank gradually began to keep only "fractional cash reserves" against its deposits; in the second part, an attempt is made to describe simply and clearly how the banking system "manufactures" bank deposits—the most important component of our money supply.

A NATURE AND FUNCTIONING OF THE MODERN BANKING SYSTEM

▶ THE PRESENT STATUS OF BANKING

Today there are over 13,000 banks in the United States that accept checking deposits. Only about a third of these banks are national banks, the rest being under state supervision. All national banks are automatically members of the federal reserve system, and in addition most of the larger state institutions are federal reserve members. Although this still leaves more than half of all the banks not members of the federal reserve system, they are sufficiently small in size so that their deposits are only about one-seventh of the total.[1] Moreover, since 1933 almost all commercial banks, state or national, have had their deposits insured by the FDIC (Federal Deposit Insurance Corporation). The FDIC insures each deposit up to the sum of $10,000.

Unlike England or Canada where a few large banks with hundreds of branches are dominant, the United States has tended to rely upon many independent, relatively small, localized units.[2] Until fairly recently, almost anyone could open a bank with relatively limited capital. It is not surprising, therefore, that the American history of bank failures and losses to depositors has been a grievous one. Indeed, only about one-half the banks in existence in 1915 are still solvent; even in prosperous 1929, long before the Great Depression, no less than 659 banks with estimated total deposits of 200 million dollars failed. Since the FDIC, things have changed; today a bank failure is a great rarity.

The primary economic function of commercial banks is to *receive demand deposits and to honor checks drawn upon them*. A second important function is to lend money to local merchants, farmers, and industrialists.

Banks also perform a variety of other functions in competition with other financial institutions. Thus, they usually accept savings or time deposits—theoretically withdrawable only after 30 days' notice—but in fact usually withdrawn (by their owners) on demand. In taking on such a function, the commercial banks are, in parts of the country, competing with the so-called "mutual savings banks," which accept only time deposits; almost anywhere in the country they are competing with cooperative building and loan societies and federal saving societies. In selling money orders or travelers' checks, the banks are competing with the post office and with Western Union. In handling "trusts" and estates, they overlap with investment counselors, executors, and other fiduciaries.

Even in lending money to individuals and businessmen, the banks are competing with finance companies, and with so-called "factors," who provide corporations with working capital. In buying bonds, mortgages, and securities, the banks compete with insurance companies and other investors.[3]

The commercial banks are by no means, therefore, our only financial institutions. But, by definition, they are the only organizations able to provide "bank money," *i.e.*, checkable demand deposits that can be conveniently used as a medium of exchange. Therein lies their primary importance and chief economic interest.

[1] Many state banks that are not full-fledged members nevertheless do belong to the federal reserve clearinghouse system and can use this service in handling checks on other banks.

[2] In California, the Bank of America has numerous branches all over the state, just as the Chase National Bank has branches all over New York City, and just as a few holding companies control many banks in Minnesota and Wisconsin. But by and large, the old American distrust of "big finance" has caused legislatures to restrict multiple-branch banking.

[3] Massachusetts, Connecticut, and New York savings banks even sell life insurance.

The second main function of banks worth remembering is the following credit function: They provide short-term credit to businesses and families; they make long-term mortgage loans; and despite the old-fashioned view that banks should only lend seasonally, they increasingly provide intermediate-term credit through "term loans" of more than a year's duration.

▶ CREATION OF THE FEDERAL RESERVE SYSTEM

In 1913, the Federal Reserve Act was passed by Congress and signed by President Wilson. The panic of 1907, with its more than usual epidemic of bank failures, was the straw that broke the camel's back: the country was fed up once and for all with the anarchy of unstable private banking. After half a dozen years' agitation and discussion by both the Republican and Democratic parties, the federal reserve system was formed—in face of the opposition of the large banks and of bankers' associations.

The country was cut into 12 federal reserve districts, each with its own Federal Reserve Bank. Their initial capital was subscribed by the commercial bank members of the federal reserve system; and so *nominally* each Federal Reserve Bank is a corporation owned by the "Member Banks." All are co-ordinated by the seven-member Board of Governors of the federal reserve system in Washington—the so-called "Federal Reserve Board."[1]

When the system was first established, numerous petty "checks and balances" were written into the law, largely on the basis of a number of now obsolete theories about money and because of the then prevailing fear of centralized banking authority. It was another example of what is so common in our history: the desire of the American people to go swimming without going near the water. We wanted, we desperately needed, a Central Bank; yet we were afraid of the concept. Therefore, a compromise bill was passed—dividing the country up into 12 separate districts; providing for six directors of each bank to be appointed by the vote of the Member Banks and three to be appointed by the Board of Governors; requiring three of the local six directors to be bankers and the other three to represent business, industry, and agriculture, respectively; providing 14-year terms for governors; limiting the 12 Reserve Banks to certain special types of loans, and preventing them from buying bonds directly from the government; etc.

Today none of these restrictions is of primary importance. Again and again Congress has modified the original act whenever one of these restrictions stood in the way of the needs of the time. Let us summarize, therefore, the effective realities and present status of the federal reserve system.

---

[1] There is also a 12-man Federal Open Market Committee, consisting of five representatives of the 12 districts as well as the seven-man Board of Governors. In addition a Federal Advisory Council, consisting of a representative selected by each of the 12 banks, can make suggestions but is without legal powers.

It consists of a Federal Reserve Board with wide powers. Responsible only to Congress, the Board usually works very closely with the President and the Treasury, and has in effect 12 branch offices throughout the land (of which the New York Federal Reserve Bank is by far the most influential).

Although the Member Banks nominally own the Reserve Banks, in fact no profits over 6 per cent of the original capital may be paid out to Member Banks; and all excess earnings are voluntarily paid into the United States Treasury. While the Reserve Banks have been enormously profitable, the public interest and not profit is their goal; and many of their most important acts are deliberately done in the full knowledge they will involve losses.[1]

The detailed functionings of the Federal Reserve Banks are reserved for discussion in the next chapters. Here it is only necessary to know that they are banks for bankers and for the government. Most of the federal taxes and expenditures pass through the Reserve Banks. The Member Banks hold their cash reserves on deposit in the nearest Reserve Bank, and look to it for help in time of crisis and for leadership at all times.

▶ BANKING AS A BUSINESS

The commercial bank is a relatively simple business concern. Banking is a business much like any other business. A bank provides certain services for its customers (depositors and borrowers) and in return receives payments from them in one form or another. It tries to earn a profit for its stock owners.

A bank's balance sheet shows certain assets, certain liabilities, and certain capital ownership. Except for minor rearrangements, the bank's published balance sheet looks, on the whole, much like the balance sheet of any other business, and rather simpler than most.

The only peculiar feature about the consolidated bank balance sheet shown in Table 1 is the fact that such a large portion of the banks' liabilities are payable on demand; i.e., they are deposits subject to checking.

This fact is intriguing to the economist because he chooses to call such demand liabilities money; but to the banker it is a familiar condition which has long since been taken for granted. He knows full well that, although it would be possible for every depositor suddenly to decide to withdraw all his money from the bank on the same day, nevertheless the probability of this happening is infinitely remote. Each day as some people are withdrawing

---

[1] That the details of ownership of a Central Bank are not vital is indicated by the history of the Bank of England. For two and a half centuries prior to its being nationalized by the postwar Labor government, it was a private corporation; but for the last century it acted (except for a few slips) pretty much the same as it would have if officially part of the government.

Demand deposits form the bulk of our money supply:

ASSETS		LIABILITIES AND NET WORTH	
Vault cash	$ 2.5	Capital accounts	$ 13.7
Reserve balances with Federal Reserve Banks	18.7	Demand deposits	127.0
		Time deposits	40.9
Loans and discounts	78.0	Other liabilities	3.3
U.S. government securities	47.6		
Other securities	13.2		
Other assets	24.9		
Total	$184.9	Total	$184.9

Table 1. Consolidated balance sheet of all Member Banks, Jan. 1, 1957 (in billions). Reserve balances kept with the Federal Reserve and demand deposits are the two key items of interest to our later economic analysis. (Source: *Federal Reserve Bulletin*.)

their money, others are normally making deposits that tend to cancel the withdrawals. Actually, in a growing economy new deposits more than offset the withdrawals.

This, however, need not be strictly true at any one moment, in any one day, or in any one week. By chance alone the amount of withdrawals might exceed deposits for some period of time—just as a coin may land with heads turned up rather than tails for a consecutive number of tosses. For this reason, the banker keeps a little cash handy in his cash vaults and a "reserve deposit" at the near-by Federal Reserve Bank. *Normally the till money in the bank's own vaults and its reserves at the Reserve Bank need be only a small fraction of the bank's total deposits;* and the same mathematical law of large numbers that makes life insurance possible assures the banker that the larger his bank and the more numerous his independent depositors, the smaller need this fraction be.

▶ **HOW BANKS DEVELOPED OUT OF GOLDSMITH ESTABLISHMENTS**

All these facts are so much taken for granted by every modern banker that he is hardly aware of them. But it was not always so. Commercial banking is usually assumed to have begun with the ancient goldsmiths who developed the practice of storing people's gold and valuables for safekeeping. At first such establishments were simply like parcel checkrooms or warehouses. The depositor left his gold for safekeeping, was given a receipt, later presented that receipt, paid a small fee for safekeeping, and got back his gold.

Quite obviously, however, money is wanted only for what it will buy, not for its own sake. Money has an anonymous quality, so that one dollar is just as good as another, and one piece of pure gold as good as another. The goldsmiths soon found it more convenient *not* to have to tag the gold belonging to any one individual so as to be able to give to him upon request exactly the same piece of gold that he had left. Instead, the customer was quite willing to accept a receipt for an amount of gold or money *of a given value,* even though it was not the identical particle of matter that he actually left.

This is important. Therein lies a significant difference between today's bank and a checkroom or warehouse. If I check my bag at Grand Central Station and later see someone walking down the street with that same suitcase, there is nothing for me to do but call my lawyer and sue the railroad company. If I mark my initials on a $10 bill, deposit it in my bank account, and later notice it in the hands of a stranger, I have no grievance against the bank management. They have agreed only to pay me on demand any old $10 of legal tender.

But let us return to the goldsmith establishments which are supposed to typify the first embryonic commercial banks. What would balance sheets of a typical establishment look like? Perhaps like Table 2.

We have assumed that the company has long since dropped its activities as a smith and is principally occupied with storing people's money for safekeeping. Over past time, 1 million dollars has been deposited in its vaults, and this whole sum it holds as a cash asset. To balance this asset, there is a current deposit liability of the same amount. Actually such a business need have no other assets (except the negligible value of its office space and vaults). But there is no reason why its owners should not have—on the side, so to speak— subscribed $50,000 of capital to be lent out at interest or to buy securities such as stocks or bonds. On the asset side this amount is shown under the heading Loans and Investments; this is balanced on the right-hand side by a similar sum in the Capital account.

At this primitive stage, the bank would be of no particular interest to the economist. The investment and capital items have nothing to do with the bank's deposits; if all the loans and investments should go sour and become worthless, the loss would fall completely on the stockholders who have agreed to take that risk in the hope of making a profit. Every depositor could still be paid off in full out of the 100 per cent cash reserves held by the bank. The

The first Goldsmith bank held 100 per cent cash
against its demand deposits:

ASSETS		LIABILITIES AND NET WORTH	
Cash	$1,000,000	Capital and surplus	$ 50,000
Loans and investments	50,000	Demand deposit liability	1,000,000
Total	$1,050,000	Total	$1,050,000

Table 2. Balance sheet of early bank.

bank would still cover its overhead and clerical expenses by making its customers pay storage charges. These would presumably vary with the length of time the customer left his money for safekeeping, the average amount of his money that required safekeeping, and the number of times the turnover of his account made a clerk wait on him and keep records.

The economist would have little interest in such a bank's operations. The bank money[1]—the demand deposits created jointly by the bank's willingness to accept a demand obligation and the customer's willingness to hold a deposit—would just offset the amount of ordinary money (currency or coin) placed in the bank's safe and withdrawn from active circulation. The whole process would be of no more interest than if the public decided to convert some of its dollar bills into an equivalent amount of dimes. In fancy language, we would say that the banking system is having a *neutral* effect on spending and prices—neither adding nor subtracting from total ("active") money.

Before leaving this simple first stage of banking, we must point out that there is a small group of economic experts who today advocate as a thorough-going reform of our banking system the return to a system of 100 per cent cash reserves against all demand deposits. This, they say, is the only safe system of banking, in which depositors can really all get their money out of the bank any time they all want it together. It is the only honest system of banking, in which the banks are not "creating" new money for their own profit, and in so doing usurping the constitutional monetary prerogatives of the government. Finally, it is the only system of banking in which the banking system is neutral, neither creating money in time of boom and thereby adding to inflation, nor contracting the money supply in times of panic and depression and thereby adding to deflation, bankruptcy, and unemployment.

We cannot appraise the value of this reform until we have examined the nature of modern banks operating with only fractional legal reserve ratios.

▶ MODERN FRACTIONAL RESERVE BANKING

Let us return to our early goldsmith-banker to see how modern banks gradually evolved. If he were an alert fellow, he would soon notice that, although his deposits are payable on demand, they are not all withdrawn together. He would soon learn that, although 100 per cent reserves are necessary if the bank is to be liquidated and all depositors to be paid off in full, they are not at all necessary if his bank is a "going concern." New deposits tend to balance

[1] The economist would consider the demand deposit as money just as soon as the custom grew up for depositors to pay for the goods they bought by giving the storekeeper a little note to the bank saying, "Mr. Goldsmith, pay to the order of Sears, Roebuck $2.99, (signed) John Q. Doe." In other words, as soon as the use of checks became customary.

withdrawals. Only a little till money, perhaps less than 2 per cent, seems normally needed in the form of vault cash.[1]

At first he probably thought this discovery too good to be true. Then perhaps he recalled the story of a rival bank whose dishonest clerk ran off with 95 per cent of its cash reserve—which was never discovered for 50 years. No one ever had occasion to go to the back rooms of the vault because all withdrawals were financed by recently deposited money held in the front vaults!

We can imagine our intelligent banker—at first cautiously—beginning to acquire bonds and other earning assets with some of the cash entrusted to his care. Everything works out all right; depositors are still paid off on demand, and the bank has made some extra earnings. Gradually the banker no longer feels it necessary to conceal from his depositors what he is doing. If a depositor complains, the banker retorts, "Your money is safe. If you don't like my way of doing business, you are at liberty to withdraw your funds. Besides, haven't you noticed that the new method of fractional cash reserves has enabled me to lower my service charges to you? Also, it has enabled me to give a helping hand to our local businessmen who need more capital to buy new tools, buildings, and inventories. Such capital formation benefits consumers because they get better goods for lower prices. It also creates jobs for workers."

Little wonder, therefore, that all banks should have begun to invest most of the money deposited with them in earning assets and to keep only fractional cash reserves against deposits. Indeed, as long as business confidence remains high, and provided the managers of the bank are judicious in their choice of loans and investments, *there is no reason why the bank should keep much more than 2 per cent cash reserves against deposits.*

What if the banker makes a mistake in his investments? Since nobody's judgment is perfect and all investments involve some element of speculative risk, this is certainly a possibility that must be reckoned with. To lessen the chance of extreme losses, the banker can try to diversify his investments, not putting all his eggs in one basket. More than that, a conservative bank will have a considerable amount of capital put up by the stockholders. For example, capital stock may have been issued equal to 10 per cent of demand deposits. Then, even if all the bank's assets are in earning investments rather than in nonearning cash, the depositors are protected against all capital losses that do not exceed 10 per cent of the bank's investment portfolio. Ordinarily, this

---

[1] If the bank could pay off its depositors with one of its own checks (or as in former times with one of its paper bank notes), it might not have to keep any till money at all! By judiciously limiting the rate at which it was making loans and investments, the bank could ensure that the checks it received from other banks plus cash deposited were just matched by its outpayments. An occasional, temporary outward drain of funds could be met by permitting the bank to pay by check what it owed to other banks for the few hours or days until some part of its asset portfolio was able to be liquidated or until it contracted its operations so as to get in a surplus of inpayments over outpayments.

would be quite sufficient so long as the bank keeps to high-grade bonds, mort-gages, and conservative business loans.

There is only one last requirement the bank must meet if we are to give it an A+ in deportment. The management must watch the general trend in the growth of its deposits to make sure that the city where it is located is not becoming a "ghost town" and that the bank is not losing deposits steadily over time. Were that the case, the bank's investment portfolio would have to be ar-ranged to consist of securities and loans that could be gradually liquidated and converted into cash to meet depositors' withdrawals.

Even if the bank is not a declining business, prudent managers must still protect themselves against a temporary surge of withdrawals. To hold cash against such a contingency would be costly, since cash earns no yield. They will usually decide, therefore, to hold in their portfolios as secondary reserves some securities that always have a ready market and can be liquidated at short notice. Government bonds serve this purpose admirably. Short-term bonds (called "notes," "bills," or "certificates") vary little in value and can be liquidated simply by not buying news ones as the old ones come due every 90 days or 12 months. But even long-term government bonds, with 30 years of life before they mature, can serve as secondary reserves in normal times, because they can always be transferred[1] to some other buyer at some quoted market price—albeit a varying price. The important thing in this connection is not the *date of maturity* of the bond or loan, but rather how "shiftable" the asset is to some other investment institution. Thus, a 90-day loan to a local merchant, which is nonshiftable, is intrinsically less appropriate as secondary reserves than a 90-year gilt-edge bond traded on a securities exchange.

▶ LEGAL RESERVE REQUIREMENTS

The above precepts of sound banking practice are quite simple and under-standable. They are a little harder to carry out in practice than to state in principle; but the same is true of most prescriptions for wise living.

If we compare a "going and growing" bank with any corporation, the surprising thing is not how little cash reserves the banks keep, but that they keep any at all (in excess of till-money requirements). *As long as financial skies are sunny, the same logic that compels the abandonment of a system of 100 per cent reserves argues in favor of negligible reserves!*

Yet, if we turn to the facts, we find that a modern prudent bank is expected—and required by law!—to keep a substantial portion of its assets in nonearning cash. These "legal reserves" are in addition to the till money in the bank's vaults and are kept on deposit with the local Federal Reserve Bank. They are never to be used up so long as the bank is solvent. At the

[1] There is a saying "You can sell government bonds even on Sunday."

Reserve requirements vary, depending on the location of the bank:

Kind of bank	Reserve rates required	
	against demand deposits, per cent	against time deposits, per cent
Central Reserve City Banks (New York and Chicago)	20	5
Reserve City Banks (large and medium cities)	18	5
Other Member Banks (small town or country)	12	5

Table 3. Legal reserve rates for Federal Reserve member banks, January 1958. Before 1936, reserve requirements were for a long time at 13, 10, and 7 per cent against demand deposits and 3 per cent against time deposits. Subsequently, Congress gave the Federal Reserve Board authority to raise these rates, at its discretion, up to double these figures, or to 26, 20, 14, and 6 per cent, respectively—authority it often used.

present time commercial Member Banks belonging to the federal reserve system are, on the average, legally required to keep in the form of nonearning cash reserves deposited with the Federal Reserve Bank a little less than 20 per cent of their demand deposits.[1] More precisely, Table 3 gives the present-day legal reserve requirements of all federal reserve Member Banks.

These legal reserve requirements need to be explained. They are an important part of the mechanism by which the Federal Reserve Board controls bank money.

Archaic geographical requirements. First, why should the size of a town affect the legal reserve requirement? Before the federal reserve was created, the New York and Chicago banks used to hold the safety reserves of smaller town banks. When a crisis came, the smaller banks tried to withdraw cash from the city banks. So it then seemed logical to make New York and Chicago banks hold higher reserve requirements.

Those days are past. Now it is the Federal Reserve Banks, not the big city banks, that hold the reserves of the smaller Member Banks. Most experts, therefore, say: "The time has come to get rid of the different reserve requirements based upon geography and size of city. There should be one uniform rate for all Member Banks."[2]

Some day we shall see geographically uniform legal reserve requirements. In any case, it will keep our arithmetic simple if we always speak of a single rate—say 20 per cent—in the discussions that follow.

Legal reserve requirements too high? Second, many bankers think wist-

[1] English banks, by force of custom rather than law, keep about 8 to 10 per cent cash reserves, and, if possible, another 20 per cent in the secondary form of short-term government and private "bills" (highly endorsed, and negotiable, short-term promissory notes).

[2] When you learn that Providence, Rhode Island, is a country town and Waco, Texas, a Reserve City, you realize how long overdue is this reform.

fully about how much they could earn on loans or bonds if they were free to use part of the money they are forced to keep on deposit with the nearest Reserve Bank as legal reserves against their own deposits. They argue: "Money we are required to keep as legal reserves doesn't earn us one red cent. So why do we have to keep such high legal reserves? One-fifth of our deposits is more than is really needed for safety. For, after all, our withdrawals never bunch up much; the laws of statistics take care of that. And we do keep 2 per cent vault cash anyway. Besides, were we ever to need more, we could sell off some government bills or could turn to the 'Fed' (i.e., the Federal Reserve) for help or could borrow temporarily from some other bank. We bankers think that legal reserves of as little as 10 per cent—some of us would say 5 per cent!— is all that prudence requires in this age of insured deposits."

In part the bankers are right. Years ago the legal reserve requirements for the three types of banks were lower: they were 13, 10, and 7 per cent against demand deposits and 3 per cent against time deposits. After the mid-thirties Congress gave the Reserve Board the right to double these ratios and the Board used its discretion to do this in a number of gradual steps.

But why did the Board raise the legal requirements? And why did it later ask Congress to give it authority to raise them still further? Because of the belief that such high legal ratios are needed to assure depositors of being able to withdraw their money when they want to?

No. Definitely no. The main purpose of legal reserve requirements is *not* to make deposits safe and liquid, payable on demand.

What then is the function of legal reserve requirements?

Their vital function is to enable the Federal Reserve Authorities to be able to control the amount of demand deposits—or bank money—that the Member Banks can create. By imposing fixed reserve requirements, the Fed can limit the growth of bank deposits. Just how this all works, we'll learn in the second half of this chapter and in Chapter 16.

▶ **THE GOVERNMENT STANDS BEHIND THE BANKS**

Banks are much safer than they used to be before the depression. If this has little to do with legal reserve requirements, what is it due to?

▶ Our banks are today safe because we now realize that it is a vital function of the government to stand behind them if ever there should be another depression and another avalanche of panicky "runs" on the banking system.

No banking system with fractional reserves—*i.e.*, none which keeps less than 100 per cent of its deposits in cash—can ever turn all its deposits into cash on a moment's notice. So every fractional reserve system would be a "fair-weather system" if government didn't stand ready to back it up. If panic ever again came, Congress, the President, the Secretary of the Treasury, and the Federal Reserve Board chairman would all act. They'd say: "If the panicky American people all insist on taking their money out of the banks, we'll print as much money as is needed to meet the emergency."

Had this been said and done back in the black days of the early 1930's, history would have been different. Our country would have been spared the epidemic of bank failures[1] that created fear and crisis and that almost brought the capitalistic system to an end.

Fortunately, now that the American people of both political parties realize that the government stands behind the banking system, it is highly improbable that a panic could ever get started. Here is a case where being prepared to act heroically makes it unnecessary for you to act at all!

▶ KEEPING EACH BANK SAFE

Just because the peril of a nationwide bank run has been conquered doesn't mean that each banker can stop worrying about *his* bank's safety. There are numerous important reforms that have been introduced in recent decades to increase the safety of the individual bank's deposits. The successive steps taken by government to modify the instability of laissez-faire banking can be briefly described:

1. *Regulation of bank formation and activity.* For decades, either state or federal authorities have set down conditions under which banks could be formed—the minimum amount of capital they must have, etc. Bank examiners periodically scrutinize bank assets and pass on the bank's solvency, always keeping in mind that an ounce of prevention is worth a pound of cure.

2. *Formation of federal reserve system.* The next great forward step was the establishment of Central Banks, whose primary function is to stand as a Rock of Gibraltar in time of panic, to be ready to use the full monetary powers of the government to stem collapse of the banking system. The other important functions of a Central Bank will be discussed later.

3. *Government insurance of bank deposits.* One of the most important government bank reforms is also one of the most recent. Following the bank crisis of 1933, the FDIC was set up to insure the safety of all bank deposits.[2] All banks which are members of the federal reserve system *must* belong, and

---

[1] Some 8,000 banks with 5 billion dollars of deposits became insolvent in 1930–1933. To keep all banks from collapse, Franklin Roosevelt's first act was to close them up, declaring a "bank holiday" until confidence was restored.

[2] In 1958, there were more than 100 million depositors in FDIC banks; the $10,000 limit insured about 95 per cent of all depositors. On a $\frac{1}{12}$ of 1 per cent annual premium charged on all deposits, FDIC has accumulated almost two billion dollars of surplus.

most state banks do also belong. In return for a yearly payment by the banks, which varies with their total deposits, all their customers are completely protected against any loss (up to $10,000) even if the bank should go bankrupt.

The importance of this measure can hardly be exaggerated. From now on banks will be closed up by bank examiners and government authorities, and not by the panicky behavior of depositors whose fears bring on the very contingency they are most afraid of. A single bank need no longer fear that its reputation, like that of a good woman, is compromised simply by being brought into question.

B THE CREATION OF BANK DEPOSITS

► CAN BANKS REALLY CREATE MONEY?

We now turn to one of the most interesting aspects of money and credit, the process called "multiple expansion of bank deposits." This is little understood. Most people have heard that in some mysterious manner banks can create money out of thin air, but few really understand how the process works.

Actually, there is nothing magical or incomprehensible about the creation of bank deposits. At every step of the way, any intelligent person can follow what is happening to the banks' accounts. The true explanation of deposit creation is simple. What is hard to grasp are the false explanations that still circulate.

According to these false explanations, the managers of an ordinary bank are able, by some use of their fountain pens, to lend several dollars for each dollar deposited with them. No wonder practical bankers see red when such power is attributed to them. They only wish they could do so! As every banker knows, he cannot invest money that he does not have; and money that he invests in buying a security or making a loan soon leaves his bank.

Bankers, therefore, often go to the opposite extreme. They sometimes argue that the banking system cannot (and does not) create money. "After all," they say, "we can invest only what is left with us. We don't create anything. We only put the community's savings to work." Bankers who argue in this way are quite wrong. They have become enmeshed in our old friend, the fallacy of composition: what is true for each is not true for all. The banking system as a whole can do what each small bank cannot do: it can expand its loans and investments many times the cash given it, but all the time each small bank is lending out only a fraction of its deposits.

Our answer then to the basic question is in the affirmative. Yes, the banking system and the public do, between them, create about $5 of bank deposits for every dollar taken out of circulation and left in the banks. Let's see how.

▶ HOW DEPOSITS ARE CREATED: THE FIRST-BANK STAGE

We begin with a brand-new deposit of $1,000 which is brought to a bank.[1] Now, if banks were to keep 100 per cent cash reserve balances, like the old goldsmiths, they could not create any extra money out of a new deposit of $1,000 left with them. The depositor would be simply giving up $1,000 of currency for a $1,000 checking deposit when bringing money to the bank.

The change in the bank's balance sheet, as far as the new demand deposit is concerned, would be as shown in Table 4a.[2]

1st, a new deposit is added to the original bank's balance sheet:

ASSETS		LIABILITIES	
Cash reserve		Deposits	+$1,000
balances	+$1,000		
Total	+$1,000	Total	+$1,000

Table 4a. Original bank in initial position.

The bank has not created this deposit *alone*. The customer had to be willing to make the deposit. Once he took the initiative, the bank was also willing to accept his checking account. Together the bank and the public "created" $1,000 of bank money or deposit. But there is no multiple expansion, no 5 for 1 or anything else. So long as the banks keep 100 per cent reserves, the growth of bank money is just offset by the decline of currency in circulation.

Suppose now that the bank does not have to keep 100 per cent reserves. Suppose that the law requires it to keep only 20 per cent legal reserves. (It can always keep larger reserves if it wishes to; but if there are many outstanding, relatively safe, interest-yielding government bonds or numerous profitable lending opportunities, the bank will not find it profitable to keep much more reserves than the law requires.)

What can the bank now do? Can it expand its loans and investments by $4,000 so that the change in its balance sheet looks as shown in Table 4b? The answer is definitely "no." Why not? Total assets equal total liabilities. Cash reserves meet the legal requirement of being 20 per cent of total deposits.

True enough. But how did the bank pay for the investments or earning assets that it bought? Like everyone else it had to write out a check to the man who sold the bond or signed the promissory note. If all such people would promise not to cash the bank's check—or what is the same thing, to hold all

---

[1] It is simplest to think of the original depositor as having made a decision to increase permanently his average bank balance at the expense of his cash held at home or abroad.

[2] For simplicity all our tables will show only the *changes* in balance-sheet items. To simplify the arithmetic, we use reserve ratios of 20 per cent, which are a little larger than the legal rates of Table 3. The tables' cash reserve balances disregard "till money" and are held at the nearest of the 12 Reserve Banks.

Important note: bankers refer to their loans and "investments." By "investments" they mean their holdings of securities. They don't mean what we mean by I in $C + I + G$.

2d, of course the bank cannot then loan out four times the amount of the deposit:

ASSETS		LIABILITIES	
Cash reserve		Deposits	+$5,000
balances	+$1,000		
Loans and			
investments	+ 4,000		
Total	+$5,000	Total	+$5,000

Table 4b. Impossible situation for single small bank.

such money frozen on deposit in the bank—then, of course, the bank could buy all it wants to without losing any cash.

But, in fact, no one will borrow money at 6 per cent just to hold it all in the bank. The borrower spends the money on labor, on materials, or perhaps on an automobile. The money will *very soon*, therefore, have to be paid out of the bank. And if the bank is but one of the many banks serving that city, county, state, and country, only a fraction of the sums withdrawn will ever come back to the original bank in another customer's deposit.

This loss of cash by a bank expanding its investments is even more clearly seen if the bank buys a bond rather than makes a local loan. When my Boston bank buys a government bond, what are the chances that the man who sells the bond will happen to have an account with it? The likelihood is negligible. Probably he lives in New York City. Or Ames, Iowa. So my bank knows it will soon have to pay out *all* the money it places in bonds.

A bank cannot eat its cake and have it too. The New England bank cannot buy a bond and keep its cash at the same time. Table 4b gives, therefore, a completely false picture of what an individual bank can do.

Does this mean that Table 4a tells the end of the story? Must the bank, therefore, behave like the 100 per cent reserve goldsmith bankers?

Of course not. Although the bank cannot jack its deposits up to five times its cash reserve, it certainly can *reduce its cash down* to one-fifth of its deposits. Nothing is easier. For, as we have just seen, all it has to do is acquire $800 worth of earning assets—bonds, loans, or mortgages. In a day or so it will lose practically all this cash as its checks come back for payment. Now its balance sheet will be as shown in Table 4c.

3d, but what it can do is loan out four-fifths of the deposit:

ASSETS		LIABILITIES	
Cash reserve		Deposits	+$1,000
balances	+$ 200		
Loans and			
investments	+ 800		
Total	+$1,000	Total	+$1,000

Table 4c. Original bank in final position.

As far as this first bank is concerned, we are through. Its legal reserves are just enough to match its deposits. There is nothing more it can do until the public decides to bring in some more money on deposit.

Before leaving the single small bank, note this important fact: It has created money! How? Clearly it retains from the public only $200 of cash. And it has added $1,000 of bank money (or deposits) to the public's total.[1] Thus, its activity has created a net increase of $800 in the money supply.

▶ CHAIN REPERCUSSIONS ON THE OTHER BANKS

But the banking system as a whole cannot yet settle down. The people who sold the bonds or borrowed from the bank will presumably deposit the proceeds in some other bank or will pay them out to someone else who will make such a deposit. Our original bank has thus lost $800 *to some other banks* in the system. If we lump these other banks all together and call them "second-generation banks," their balance sheets now appear as shown in Table 4d.

4th, the money loaned out by the original bank is soon deposited in other banks:

ASSETS		LIABILITIES	
Cash reserve		Deposits	+$800
balances	+$800		
Total	+$800	Total	+$800

Table 4d. Second-generation banks in initial position.

Of course, these banks are scattered all over the country. (Our original bank might even constitute a small part of the second generation as a few of its checks fell into the hands of its own depositors.) To these banks the dollars deposited are just like any other dollars, *just like our original deposit;* these banks don't know, and don't care, that they are second in a chain of deposits. They do know, and they do care, that they are now holding too much nonearning cash. Only one-fifth of $800, or $160, is legally needed against $800 deposits. Therefore, they can, and will, use the other four-fifths to buy $640 worth of loans and investments; so that in a few days, their balance sheet will have reached equilibrium as shown in Table 4e.

So much for the second-generation banks. They too have created money. Thus far, the original $1,000 taken out of hand-to-hand circulation and put

---

[1] Many economists—and even the official federal reserve handbook!—miss this point. Such economists say: "Bankers are wrong to think the whole banking system cannot create money. *Their view is right as applied to a single bank:* but all the banks together can do what no small single bank can separately do." The italicized words are wrong. We have seen that the single bank *does* create 5:1 money (or, more precisely, $1:\frac{1}{5}$). But it doesn't do so by the impossible act of lending out five times what it has. It does so by investing four-fifths of the original new cash left with it: and after it has lost that four-fifths, *its remaining one-fifth of cash reserves* is enough to support five times itself in checkable deposits. (NOTE: This footnote is entirely consistent with the discussion comparing Tables 4i and 4b.)

5th, four-fifths of this new deposit will be loaned out by the second-generation bank:

ASSETS		LIABILITIES	
Cash reserve		Deposits	+$800
balances	+$160		
Loans and			
investments	+ 640		
Total	+$800	Total	+$800

Table 4e. Final position of second-generation banks.

into the banking system has given rise to $1,000 (first-generation deposits) plus $800 (second-generation deposits). The total of money has increased. And the end is not yet in sight. Here's the reason.

The $640 spent by the second-generation banks in acquiring loans and investments will go to a new set of banks called the "third-generation banks." You, the reader, should by now be able to fill in their balance sheets as they look initially (see Table 4f). Evidently the third-generation banks will at first have *excess* cash *reserves* of an amount equal to four-fifths of $640, or $512. After this has been spent on loans and investments—and only then—the third-generation banks will reach the equilibrium of Table 4g.

6th, and similarly in third-generation banks:

ASSETS		LIABILITIES	
Cash reserve		Deposits	+ ____
balances	+ ____		
Loans and			
investments	____		
Total	+ ____	Total	+$640

Table 4f. Initial position of third-generation banks.

ASSETS		LIABILITIES	
Cash reserve		Deposits	+$640
balances	+$128		
Loans and			
investments	+ 512		
Total	+$640	Total	+$640

Table 4g. Final equilibrium of third-generation banks.

The total of bank deposit money is now $1,000 plus $800 plus $640, or $2,440. This is already almost $2\frac{1}{2}$:1 expansion of the original cash deposit. But a fourth generation of banks will clearly end up with four-fifths of $640 in deposits, or $512; and the fifth generation will get four-fifths of $512, or $409.60; and the sixth generation four-fifths of $409.60; and so on; until finally by the twenty-fifth round, we shall have all but $1 of the total sum of the infinitely many generations.

What will be the final sum: $1,000 + $800 + $640 + $512 + $409.60 + · · · ? If we patiently do out the sum by arithmetic, we shall find that it gets to $4999.999 . . . and "finally" to $5,000. Table 4h shows the complete effects of the chain of deposit creation and we can also get the same answer in two other ways—by common sense and by elementary algebra.[1]

7th, through this chain process the banking system eventually creates total deposits equal to five times the original new reserves:

Position of bank	New deposits	New loans and investments	Cash reserve balances
Original banks	$1,000.00	$ 800.00	$ 200.00
2nd-generation banks	800.00	640.00	160.00
3rd-generation banks	640.00	512.00	128.00
4th-generation banks	512.00	409.60	102.40
5th-generation banks	409.60	327.68	81.92
6th-generation banks	327.68	262.14	65.54
7th-generation banks	262.14	209.72	52.42
8th-generation banks	209.72	167.77	41.95
9th-generation banks	167.77	134.22	33.55
10th-generation banks	134.22	107.37	26.85
Sum of first 10 generation banks	$4,463.13	$3,570.50	$ 892.63
Sum of remaining generation banks	536.87	429.50	107.37
Total for banking system as a whole	$5,000.00	$4,000.00	$1,000.00

Table 4h. Multiple expansion of bank deposits through the banking system. (From the 7th generation on all data have been been rounded off to two decimal places.) Note that in every generation each *small* bank has "created" new money in the following sense: It ends up with final bank deposit 5 times *the cash it finally retains* from the rest of the economy.

Common sense tells us the process of deposit creation must come to an end only when no bank *anywhere in the system* has cash reserves in excess of the 20 per cent reserve ratio to deposits. In all our previous examples no cash has ever leaked out of the banking system, but has simply gone, as a result of security purchases, from one set of banks into another set of banks' vaults. Everyone will be at equilibrium only when a consolidated balance sheet for all the banks together—for the first, second, and hundredth generation— would look as shown in Table 4i. For if total new deposits were less than $5,000, the 20 per cent ratio would not yet be reached and equilibrium would not yet have been everywhere reached.

If the reader will compare Table 4i with Table 4b previously marked "im-

[1] This can be proved by algebra as follows:
$$\$1,000 + \$800 + \$640 + · · · = \$1,000[1 + \tfrac{4}{5} + (\tfrac{4}{5})^2 + (\tfrac{4}{5})^3 + · · ·]$$
$$= \$1,000 \left(\frac{1}{1 - \tfrac{4}{5}}\right) = \$1,000 \ (5) = \$5,000$$

8th, now we can see that all banks together can do what was
   impossible for one bank alone:

ASSETS		LIABILITIES	
Cash reserve		Deposits	+$5,000
balances	+$1,000		
Loans and			
investments	+ 4,000		
Total	+$5,000	Total	+$5,000

Table 4i. Consolidated balance sheet showing final position of all banks together.

possible," he will see that the whole banking system can do what no one bank can do by itself. It can expand its deposits to five times the *initial* new deposit. *Bank money has been created 5 for 1—and all the while each bank has invested and lent only a fraction of what it has received as deposits!*[1]

Who creates the multiple expansion[2] of deposits? Three parties do so jointly: the public by always keeping its money in the bank on deposit; the banks by keeping only a fraction of their deposits in the form of cash; the public and private borrowers who make it possible for the banks to find loans and attractive earning assets to buy with their excess cash. (There is also a fourth party, the Central Bank, which by its activities makes it possible for new reserves to come to the banking system: it will be the task of the next chapters to survey and explain this process.)

Before leaving this section, test your knowledge of credit creation by tracing through in detail what happens when a nervous widow permanently *withdraws* $1,000 from a single bank and hides it in her attic. (1) The bank loses $1,000 of cash and $1,000 of deposits. But it previously held only 20 per cent cash reserves or $200 against her deposit. Clearly it must have given up to her some of its legally necessary cash reserves held against its other demand deposits. Show that its total reserves are now below the legal minimum. (2) Therefore, it must sell $800 worth of investments or call in that many loans. The first-generation bank will be in equilibrium only when its balance sheet finally looks as shown in Table 5a.

But in selling its securities, our original bank has drained $800 from a second generation of banks; and they in turn by liquidating securities, drain reserves from a third generation. And so it goes—until the widow's withdrawal of $1,000 has produced a chain "killing off" $5,000 worth of deposits

[1] Note that each small bank *has* created money on a 1:⅕ basis!

[2] There is nothing paradoxical in the fact that total bank deposits are several times as great as the amount of paper cash in existence anywhere; the same is true of the total of government bonds and real-estate values. Deposits are something that banks *owe* their customers; cash is *left* in a bank, but it does not *remain* in that bank. Throughout its lifetime a dollar may have been *left* in many banks, just as it may be used over a long period of time to buy hundreds of dollars of merchandise. The one thing to keep firmly in mind is that bank deposits are one of the three forms of modern money, and quantitatively the most important.

9th, when a deposit is drawn out, a multiple contraction begins to take place:

ASSETS		LIABILITIES	
Cash reserve		Deposits	−$1,000
balances	−$ 200		
Loans and			
investments	− 800		
Total	−$1,000	Total	−$1,000

Table 5a. Equilibrium position of original bank losing a deposit.

throughout the whole system and $4,000 of bank-earning assets. The student should trace through each stage: Table 5b, Table 5c, . . . , etc.

You should also be able to show how an initial deposit of $1,000 can result in $10,000 of bank deposits if banks keep only 10 per cent reserve ratios, as they used to in the 1920's. And since Table 3's reserve ratios average below 20 per cent, you might show that 6:1 is a more accurate figure than 5:1.

▶ A "MONOPOLY BANK"

In all of the above processes, it was assumed that no cash leaked out of the banking system into someone's mattress or into permanent hand-to-hand circulation. The banking system was then in the enviable position of finding that its checks were always deposited somewhere within itself.

This being so, it is easy to see that a single "monopoly bank" (with many branches), serving the whole nation, would be able to do at once what we have said each small bank cannot do. Its balance sheet could quickly go to the condition shown in Table 4b or 4i. It could write checks freely to pay for securities or loans, knowing that the people to whom they are paid would always deposit their proceeds back in the one and only monopoly bank.[1]

▶ SIMULTANEOUS EXPANSION OR CONTRACTION BY ALL BANKS

In the previous section we have seen how the banking system can reach the limits of its expansion through many successive rounds or generations. If we allow half a week for checks to clear at each stage and for decisions to be made, then 5 to 8 weeks would be required for the process to have substantially worked itself out through more than a dozen rounds.

As a practical matter, it is usually not necessary to follow the chain of each dollar deposited through its successive rounds. Here's why. A decrease in

---

[1] In countries like England, where there is a "big 5" group of branch banks, or like Canada where there are a few large banks, or in states like California where there are a few great multiple-branch banks—in such cases a bank may be able to lend out more than its legal excess reserves, knowing that part of the money will come back to itself in later "generations." However, these so-called "derivative" or "self-returning" deposits are not important for the United States, and calling attention to them could only confuse the beginning student.

hoarding by the public will affect almost all the banks at the same time. They will all receive some new deposits at pretty much the same time. They will all have excess reserves in the first instance, and so they will all together begin to buy securities or make loans.

When a single small bank, all by itself, writes checks to acquire securities, these checks go to other banks and it loses cash. But when all are writing checks simultaneously and in balance, there will tend to be a cancellation of new checks deposited in each bank against those paid out. No one bank need lose cash reserves. Consequently, without going through the successive generations of the previous section, all banks together can simply and blithely expand their loans and investments—so long as each does not jeopardize its reserve position—until deposits are finally brought into a 5:1 relation to cash. When this state has been reached, the banking system has reached the limit of its ability to create money.

The reader might work through the similar process by which all banks simultaneously contract money 5:1 for each dollar of reserve withdrawn from the banking system, and also show how a monopoly bank would contract.

▶ THREE QUALIFICATIONS

Finally, three qualifications must be made. We have shown that $1,000 taken out of hand-to-hand circulation and put into a bank can result in an increase of $5,000 of bank deposits. This assumed that all the new money remained somewhere in the banking system, in one bank or another at every stage, and that all banks were able to keep "loaned up" with no "excess reserves."

1. *Leakage into hand-to-hand circulation.* It is quite possible, however, and even likely, that somewhere along the chain of deposit expansion some individual who receives a check will not leave the proceeds in a bank, but will withdraw it into circulation or into hoarding outside the banking system. As a matter of fact, in boom times when bank deposits are expanding, there is usually at the same time an increased need for pennies, dimes, and paper currency to transact the increased volume of petty transactions.

The effects of such withdrawals on our analysis are simple. When $1,000 stayed in the banking system, $5,000 of new deposits were created. If $200 were to leak out into circulation outside the banks, and only $800 of new reserves were to remain in the banking system, then the new deposits created would be $4,000 ($800 × 5). *The banking system can always amplify in a 5:1 ratio whatever amount of new reserves is permanently left with it.*

2. *Leakage into bank vault cash.* Similar to the leakage of cash into circulation outside the banks is the fact that banks will have to keep some of their new cash in the form of till money, *i.e.,* vault cash. This is in addition to their legally required 20 per cent reserves left on deposit with the local Federal

Reserve Bank. Such cash cannot be counted as part of the bank's 20 per cent legal reserve because all legal reserves must be on deposit with the Federal Reserve Bank in the bank's district. In 1958, 2 per cent of their deposits were kept by banks as till money. An increase of such vault cash acts rather like a leakage of cash into hand-to-hand circulation. Instead of having new deposits equal to $5 \times \$1,000$, we have them equal to about $5 \times (\$1,000 - \$100)$ or $\$4,500$. This is because $\$100$—more or less 2 per cent of $\$5,000$—is the amount of vault cash which the bank cannot use as its legal reserve.[1]

3. *Possible excess reserves.* Our description of multiple deposit creation has proceeded on the assumption that the commercial banks stick fairly closely to their legal reserve ratios. Of course there is no reason why a bank cannot choose to keep more than the legally required amount of reserves. Thus, suppose the original bank receiving a new $\$1,000$ deposit had been satisfied to hold $\$800$ of it in excess reserves. Then the whole process would have ended right there, with no multiple expansion of deposits. Or if banks were always to keep 5 per cent excess reserves, in addition to the 20 per cent legal requirement, we should have a chain of expansion of deposits of the form $[1 + \frac{3}{4} + (\frac{3}{4})^2 + \cdot \cdot \cdot]$ rather than $[1 + \frac{4}{5} + (\frac{4}{5})^2 + \cdot \cdot \cdot]$, with only a 4:1 rather than a 5:1 expansion of deposits.

Hence there is nothing automatic about deposit creation. Four factors are necessary: The banks must somehow receive new reserves; they must be willing to make loans or buy securities; someone must be willing to borrow or to sell securities; and finally, the public must choose to leave its money on deposit with the banks.

SUMMARY

▶ A. THE MODERN BANKING SYSTEM

1. The American banking system consists primarily of relatively small-scale unit banks, chartered by the national government or by the states. Although less than half are members of the federal reserve system, member demand deposits include six-sevenths of the total of all deposits.

2. The functions of commercial banks are numerous and overlap with

---

[1] Another way of expressing this relation, and one that is slightly more exact, is as follows: The new $\$1,000$ will give rise not to

$$\$1,000 \times \frac{1}{0.20} \qquad \text{but to} \qquad \$1,000 \times \frac{1}{(0.20 + 0.02)}$$

This gives $\$4,545.45$ of new deposits. Advanced texts show you can handle excess reserves and the cash leakage to the public in the same way: along with adding the vault-cash ratio to the legal ratio, also add the fractions-to-deposits going respectively into excess reserves and to hand-to-hand circulation.

those of such other financial institutions as mutual savings banks, cooperative building and loan societies, finance companies, and insurance companies. But in their function of collecting and honoring bank checks, the commercial banks perform a unique and important economic role. Their demand deposits constitute the single most important component of our money supply or medium of exchange. And they are important sources for credit.

3. The federal reserve system consists primarily of (a) Member Banks, (b) the 12 Federal Reserve Banks spread over the country, (c) the Federal Reserve Board in Washington.

Although nominally corporations owned by the Member Banks, the Federal Reserve Banks are, in fact, almost branches of the federal government, possessing wide powers and being concerned with the public interest rather than with bank profits. Responsible to Congress, in practice their activities are not independent of Treasury and Administration policy. It is the primary responsibility of the Reserve Banks to use their powers in time of panic to prevent a collapse of the banking system, and at all times to contribute toward full employment with stable prices.

4. Modern banks gradually evolved from the old goldsmith establishments in which money and valuables were stored. The practice finally became general of holding far less than 100 per cent reserves against deposits, the rest being invested in securities and loans for an interest yield.

5. If the government did not stand ready to use its emergency powers to protect the banking system, an attempt by all depositors at the same time to withdraw their money would ruin any fractional-reserve banking system. But knowing the government is ready to act, people will never put it to the test.

The Member Banks are required to keep legal reserves on deposit with their regional Reserve Bank in proportion to their deposits. (The geographical differences in requirements are archaic and will someday disappear.) These legal reserve requirements are *not* primarily to protect deposits. Their function is rather to permit the Federal Reserve to control the volume of bank deposits.

6. Without government regulation and examination, the federal reserve system, and the guaranteeing of bank deposits by the FDIC, our system of small-unit banking would be intolerable. These reforms have greatly improved the safety of individual banks.

▶ B. THE CREATION OF BANK DEPOSITS

7. Bank demand deposits serve as a medium of exchange and a store of value; they are considered, therefore, to be money.

8. If banks kept 100 per cent cash reserves against all deposits, there would be no creation of money when currency was taken out of circulation and

deposited in the banking system. There would be only a 1:1 exchange of one kind of money for another kind of money.

9. Modern banks do not keep 100 per cent cash reserves against deposits. In 1958 members of the federal reserve system are required to keep, on deposit with the regional Federal Reserve Bank, legal reserves equal to 20, 18, or 12 per cent of demand deposits, depending on city size.

Consequently, the banking system as a whole—together with public or private borrowers and the depositing public—does create deposit money almost 5:1 for each new dollar taken out of circulation and left on deposit somewhere in the system.

10. Each small bank is limited in its ability to expand its loans and investments. It cannot lend or invest more than it has received from depositors; it can lend only about four-fifths as much. Its deposits are five times its cash, only because its cash decreases and not because its deposits increase. But it does create 1 of bank money for the $\frac{1}{5}$ of reserves it retains.

11. The system as a whole can expand at once as each small bank cannot. This can be seen if we examine a monopoly bank in a closed community. The checks written by such a bank always come back to it; therefore the only restriction upon its ability to expand its investments and deposits (its assets *and* its liabilities in double-entry bookkeeping) is the requirement that it keep one-fifth cash reserve ratios against deposits. When deposits have expanded until they are five times the increase of reserves, the monopoly bank is "loaned up" and can create no further deposits until given more cash reserves.

12. In present-day America, there is no monopoly bank. Nevertheless, the same 5:1 expansion of bank deposits takes place. The first individual bank receiving a new $1,000 of deposits spends four-fifths of its newly acquired cash on loans and investments. This gives a second group of banks four-fifths of $1,000 in new deposits. They, in turn, keep one-fifth in cash and spend the other four-fifths for new earning assets; this causes them to lose cash to a third set of banks, whose deposits have gone up by four-fifths of four-fifths of $1,000. Obviously, if we follow through the successive groups of banks in the dwindling, never-ending chain, we find for the system as a whole that new deposits created are

$$\$1,000 + \$800 + \$640 + \$512 + \cdots$$
$$= \$1,000 \times \left[1 + \frac{4}{5} + \left(\frac{4}{5}\right)^2 + \left(\frac{4}{5}\right)^3 + \cdots \right]$$
$$= \$1,000 \left(\frac{1}{1 - \frac{4}{5}} \right) = \$1,000 \left(\frac{1}{\frac{1}{5}} \right) = \$5,000$$

Only when every one of the $1,000 of new reserves supports $5 of deposits somewhere in the system, will the limits to deposit expansion be reached. Then the system is loaned up; it can create no further deposits until it is given more reserves.

13. In practice, it is not necessary to wait for the successive rounds in the chain of $1,000, $800, $640, etc., to work themselves out. Usually, many banks tend to get new reserves at about the same time. If they all expand their loans and investments pretty much in balance, their outpayments will tend to cancel each other. Consequently, each will not lose cash. And so, all together can rather quickly expand their earning assets and deposits to the 5:1 limit.

14. As a minor qualification to the above discussion, we must admit that there will be some leakage of the new cash reserves of the banking system into circulation outside the banks. Therefore, instead of $5,000 of new deposits created as in the previous examples, we may have something less than that— the difference being due to what is withdrawn out of the system.

A second minor qualification must take account of the need of banks to use a little of their new reserves for vault cash or till money. Recently this has been about 2 per cent of deposits. This reduces our true ratio of expansion from about 5:1 to about 4.5:1, or more exactly 1: (0.20 + 0.02).

A third and more important qualification results from the fact that a bank may keep *excess reserves* in addition to legally required reserves.

In this chapter we have seen how bank deposits are kept at about five times the legal reserves of the banking system. In Chapter 16 we shall learn how the Federal Reserve Banks cause bank reserves to go up when an expansion of the total money supply is desired. When a contraction of the quantity of money is in order, the Federal Reserve authorities pull the brakes. Instead of pumping new reserves into the banking system, they kill off some of the reserves. We shall see that in so doing they are able to reduce the quantity of money, not 1 for 1, but (as just shown) almost 5 for 1.

QUESTIONS FOR DISCUSSION

1. Describe the banking setup in your area. Make a list of the services rendered by banks. Who else renders such services? Examine the balance sheets of local banks. Interpret the different items. Can you find out how local checks are cleared?

2. Suppose that all banks kept 100 per cent reserves. How different would they be? What function do legal reserves perform?

3. Assume a 10 per cent reserve ratio. Trace through the process of multiple bank expansion, duplicating Tables 4a through 4i. Reverse the process.

4. Do bankers create deposits? Who does? If a banker receives a new deposit and new reserves, is he always able to find borrowers? Can he always expand his holdings of government securities? How does he go about it?

5. How would you manage a bank? Give a typical asset portfolio.

6. How would your answer to Question 3 be changed if banks always kept 2 per cent of their deposits in the form of vault cash?

7. "Banks borrow from their depositors at zero or low interest rates and invest most of the proceeds in higher yielding loans and investments. They use the difference to pay their expenses, to provide us with low-cost mediums for monetary transactions, and to reward their stockholders for taking on the risks of declines in earning-assets' values. They represent an efficient way of allocating out the saving of the community to worthy local enterprises. One can scarcely imagine a better system than this, particularly with the recent reforms that insure depositors from loss and make psychological bank runs improbable." Discuss critically but fairly.

8. Review your understanding of the following concepts:

national and state banks, Member Banks, insured banks	*legal reserve requirements*
	FDIC
Board of Governors, 12 Federal Reserve Banks	*deposit creation for a monopoly bank or for a system of many small banks*
bank balance sheet	
goldsmith and fractional-reserve banking	*qualifications to multiple deposit creation*

16 FEDERAL RESERVE AND CENTRAL BANK MONETARY POLICY

> *There have been three great inventions since the beginning of time: Fire, the Wheel, and Central Banking.*
>
> WILL ROGERS

The Federal Reserve is a Central Bank. Like the Bank of England or the Bank of France, it is a bank for bankers. In this chapter we'll see that a Central Bank does not have for its goal the making of profit. It is a public institution, whether owned outright by the government or not.

Every Central Bank has one prime function: *It operates to control the economy's supply of money and credit.* If business is getting worse and jobs are getting scarce, the Federal Reserve Board will try to expand money and credit. But if spending threatens to become excessive, so that prices are rising and there are many job vacancies, then the Federal Reserve Authorities (called the "Fed" by bankers and the financial press) will do all possible to step on the brakes and contract money and credit. As Board Chairman William McChesney Martin, Jr., would say: "We at the Fed have the task of leaning against the prevailing economic winds."

In a nutshell that's the gist of Central Banking. Here in this chapter we survey the actual weapons that the Fed uses to expand or contract money and credit.

▶ **HOW MONETARY POLICY WORKS TO CONTROL SPENDING**

What are the exact steps by which the Reserve Authorities affect general spending? Here are five steps of the process.

1. The last chapter showed that commercial or Member Banks must have

313

reserves to support their assets and deposits. (So important are these "reserves" that we'll capitalize the word for the rest of this chapter.)

The first step of the Fed, therefore, when it wants to put on the monetary brakes, is to take action to cut down on bank Reserves.

2. *Each dollar contraction in bank Reserves forces a 5:1 contraction in total bank money* (i.e., in *total demand deposits*). That we saw in last chapter's discussion of multiple deposit creation in a fractional-reserve banking system.

3. *The contraction in total money makes credit generally "tight," which means both dearer and less available.* Less *M* will raise interest rates.[1] Equally important, less *M* will make credit less available to people.

Interest rates will rise to mortgage borrowers: to city governments building schools and roads; and to businessmen anxious to build plants, buy new equipment, or add to inventory.

Reinforcing higher interest cost is credit's lessened availability. Thus if you want to build a house, it matters to you that the interest rate has risen from 5 to 6 per cent. But if you are like most families, it matters even more to you that you may now find it hard to get a low-down-payment mortgage. You may find your banker's manner a shade cooler; and he may discourage you from buying the $25,000 house that you really prefer to the $18,000 one you've been considering.

4. *With credit expensive and hard to get, private and public investment will tend to fall.* Why this downward shift in the *I + G* schedule?

Because people's decisions as to whether to build a new house or plant, to order a new machine, and to hold more inventory usually depend upon how they can finance such investment spending. If they have to pay a high interest rate for loans or find it very hard to get loans, they often scale down their investment plans. And the same holds for state and local governments. The old road gets patched up and that new road postponed when the town finds it can't float its bonds at any reasonable interest rate. The gymnasium and library are cut out of the new school plans when the citizens learn their tax rate is going up because it now costs 4 per cent to borrow where it used to cost 3 or 2½ per cent.

5. *Finally, the pressure on credit and on investment spending will, through the downward shift in the I + G schedule, have a downward effect on income and on jobs.* The multiplier analysis of Chapter 12 showed us how such a drop in investment will tend to depress income spending sharply.

And, if the Fed has been right in its diagnosis of inflationary conditions, the drop in money income will be just what the doctor ordered to help the

---

[1] With *M* scarce and credit tight, you can show that bonds and other securities will slump in price both on Wall Street and Main Street. Now the bond that pays you $5 a year may cost you only $80 rather than $100: so your interest yield will rise from 5 to better than 6 per cent. The same holds for most securities.

situation. The Fed's action will then have succeeded in reducing the size of the inflationary gap. Deep within the great white marble palace of the Federal Reserve Board, the seven Governors can then clap each other on the back and congratulate themselves on their wise actions—and on their good luck!

▶ RECAPITULATION

This five-step sequence—from induced changes in the commercial banks' Reserves, to 5:1 changes in total M, to changes in credit's cost and availability, to changes in private and public investment spending, and finally to multiplied changes in money income—is vital. By rereading the italicized parts of the previous section, you can consolidate your understanding of it.

Better still, psychologists tell us we learn a thing fastest by ourselves participating. The previous section has been explained in terms of a time when the Fed wants to *contract* business activity. It's left to you to tackle the problem of how things proceed when the Fed wants to *expand* business activity.

Suppose you were Chairman Martin at a time when the economy is mildly depressed. Suppose you were called to testify before a congressional committee —as Martin so often is—and suppose you had to explain to a tobacco-chewing senator just how your *expansionary* acts would operate. Could you trace the detailed steps?

▶ THE CENTRAL BANK AS AN OMNIPOTENT AND BENEVOLENT COUNTERFEITER

Now that we have surveyed the process of monetary policy with a telescope, we can study the mechanism in some detail. We won't pretend to put Federal Reserve policy under a microscope, since that is the job of an intermediate course in money and banking. But we do want to get a general view of exactly what weapons the Fed can use to affect bank Reserves.

But before we proceed, let's make clear that the Fed is not alone in its ability to affect Reserves. There is nothing magic about its powers. You too can affect bank Reserves. Every time you change your habits about how much money you hold in the form of currency rather than in the form of a checking account, you are affecting bank Reserves. (Remember how, back in the last chapter, the whole process of 5:1 deposit contraction started when a widow started keeping her money at home?)

Admittedly, your few dollars won't affect things much. But suppose that Congress gave you, like the Fed, the right to be a legal counterfeiter—to print off new currency. Suppose banks would take your checks the way they will the Fed's and would keep their money with you. Then you wouldn't find it a bit mysterious that you could powerfully affect credit, investment, and income spending.

A Central Bank is just such a legal counterfeiter. Its power comes from its ability to expand its liabilities—its notes and deposits. These liabilities are the assets of the public and the banks. The history, therefore, of the Fed is to be found in the history of its changing balance sheet.

The Fed is a free will. Its own actions form its balance sheet and cause changes in bank Reserves. These acts we shall study—for they form its principal monetary weapons.

▶ FOREIGN GOLD MOVEMENTS: A DIGRESSION

But there is one source outside the Fed which does have a significant effect on bank Reserves. This is the export and import of gold—the international medium of exchange. Domestic widows may not often bring new Reserves to the banks, but foreign traders (and in lesser degree gold miners) are very likely to do so. Or foreigners may withdraw money from our banks. Thus, the Fed does have to watch carefully our international exports and imports.

International economics is studied in Part Five. Here we need simply relate the process to the banking mechanism.

The old gold standard. Back before 1933 the analysis was simple. We Americans had gold coins, just as England did before 1914. And, since coins are not very handy to do business with, we had gold certificates. These were nicely printed gold-and-black bills that were warehouse receipts issued by the Treasury and gave you the right to $10 or $20 worth of gold.

What happened back before 1933 when the United States sold more exports than the imports she bought, paying the difference by importing gold bars? These bars of gold were exchanged at the nearest Treasury office for gold coin or for gold certificates. The exporter then took these to his commercial bank. And then could begin one of our familiar multiple expansions of deposits: 10:1 rather than 5:1, because before 1936 Member Banks only had to maintain a legal reserve ratio of about one-tenth their deposits. (You should be able to show how deposits had to contract in a 10:1 fashion when America exported gold to pay for the surplus of our imports over exports.)

Since 1933. Today things are not so much different. When the New Deal Congress decided to raise the price of gold from about $21 an ounce to $35 an ounce, it called in all the gold and all the gold certificates. (The Supreme Court did approve the constitutionality of this use of congressional power over the currency.) Congress called in the gold at $21 an ounce so that those who held it would not make a profit from the revaluation of gold. And just in case any future Congress should raise gold's price again and face the same problem, a law was passed forbidding Americans to hold gold—except in jewelry, dental fillings, old coins, etc.

But it still is true that whenever we export more than we import and get paid in gold, the Treasury will convert that gold into new money. But now it doesn't convert it into gold coins that you can hold, or into gold certificates that private people can hold. What the Treasury now does is to use the Federal Reserve Banks to accomplish this same result.

In essence, here's how the process works. Any gold you've earned by exporting goods (or mining with pan and pick) you sell to the Federal Reserve Bank of New York. It gives you $35 an ounce for the gold. It gives you this in cash—not in gold certificates but in ordinary federal reserve notes. You can put this cash in your sock or in the bank. And, like the pre-1933 case, this new currency created by the gold can start a multiple deposit expansion.

What does the Federal Reserve do with the gold? It could hold it, but the practice is to give it to the Treasury to put into Fort Knox, Kentucky, in exchange for gold certificates of equal value. The Federal Reserve Banks are the only ones in our system who can today hold gold or gold certificates.

In short, new gold tends to expand the Reserves of the banking system and loss of gold tends to contract bank Reserves. So unless the Central Bank does something about it, gold would be a disturbing factor causing 5:1 ups and downs in our total money supply. But as we'll see, the Fed does act to stabilize this and other disturbances.

▶ BALANCE SHEET OF THE FEDERAL RESERVE BANKS

Table 1 lists the consolidated balance sheet of the 12 Federal Reserve Banks. Not quite half its total assets are gold certificates. Most of the rest are its holdings of government securities. Then there is the smaller item: discounts, loans, and acceptances. These are primarily loans or advances made to Member Banks; the charge the Fed makes for such loans or "discounts" is called the "Discount Rate," which usually is the same rate in all 12 Reserve Districts.

Federal reserve notes and deposits underlie our money supply:

Table 1. Combined balance sheet of 12 Federal Reserve Banks May 31, 1957 (in billions). By (a) controlling its earning assets (government securities and discounts) the Fed (b) controls its liabilities (deposits and federal reserve notes)—thereby (c) controlling the economy's money supply (currency and demand deposits).

ASSETS		LIABILITIES AND NET WORTH	
Gold certificates and other cash	$22.6	Capital accounts	$ 1.3
U.S. government securities	23.1	Federal reserve notes	26.5
Discounts, loans and acceptances	1.2	Deposits:	
Miscellaneous other assets		Member Bank reserves	19.0
(primarily "uncollected		U.S. Treasury	0.6
items")	4.7	Foreign and other	0.6
		Miscellaneous liabilities	3.6
Total	$51.6	Total	$51.6

The right-hand side lists the usual capital accounts: original capital subscribed by the Member Banks plus accumulated surplus. This would be much greater for so profitable a business were it not for the mentioned fact that the Federal Reserve gives back to the Treasury all its excess profits.

Federal reserve notes are its principal liabilities. These are the five- and ten-dollar bills we all carry in our wallets. They cost the Fed no interest and it is highly privileged to have been granted by Congress this power to issue currency.

Little comment is needed on several of its deposit liabilities: United States government deposits, foreign central bank deposits, and miscellaneous.

Of vital importance, though, are the Member Banks' reserve balances kept by them on deposit with the Federal Reserve Banks. These are the Reserves we have been talking about, which provide the basis for multiple deposit creation by the Member Banks.

We now can study what the Fed can do to alter its holding of government securities and discount assets in order to cause changes in the Reserves of the commercial banks—thereby setting off our earlier-mentioned five-step sequence. Its government securities plus discounts are often called "Reserve Bank credit"; and observers watch carefully, in weekly newspaper reports, the moves in this important magnitude which reflect the desire of the Fed to expand or contract credit. (Later, Fig. 2 will show how these important balance-sheet items have changed in recent years.)

▶ DISCRETIONARY MONETARY POLICIES BY THE FEDERAL RESERVE

We have seen that foreign trade can affect bank Reserves and credit tightness. So long as the Fed simply let gold shipments from abroad have their effects on its gold certificates and on the banks' Reserves, it would be doing nothing positive. It would simply be neutral.

These days you can't expect the money authorities to sit quietly while events abroad are causing our investment and income to rise or fall. These days the Fed will take a positive role, trying to offset any destabilizing forces impinging on us from abroad—or any destabilizing forces arising at home.

To initiate its five-step stabilization sequence, the Federal Reserve has three main weapons, which are listed in order of their importance: (1) open-market operations; (2) Discount Rate policy; (3) changing the legal reserve requirements of the Member Banks.

The Fed has at one time or another had four further minor weapons: (4) use of *"moral suasion"*; (5) selective controls over "margin requirements" for loans made to buy stocks; (6) selective credit controls over installment contracts and other forms of consumer credit; (7) selective controls over the terms of housing mortgage contracts. The last two powers Congress let lapse in 1952 and 1953.

Let's examine each weapon in turn, starting with the three major ones.

► OPEN-MARKET OPERATIONS

By selling or buying government bonds in the open market (mostly in New York City), the Reserve Authorities can tighten Member Bank Reserves or loosen them. These so-called "open-market operations" are the Fed's most important stabilizing weapon. Right today, as you read this book, the Open Market Committee is meeting to decide whether to pump more Reserves into the banking system by buying government bills (*i.e.*, short-term bonds) or whether to tighten things up a little by selling bills. It is a never-ending job.

To see how an open-market operation changes Reserves, let's suppose the Fed thinks the economic winds are blowing up a little inflation. Its Open Market Committee holds the usual secret meeting. The Washington and New York members are listened to most. They say: "Let's sell 1 billion dollars of government bonds from our portfolio to contract credit." The motion is unanimously carried.

The New York Bank representative gets up and says: "How about our selling some long-term 3 per cent coupon government bonds, which have 38 years still to go. Our order to sell will depress their price—say from 90 to 88. This will directly represent a higher interest yield on such bonds, and the higher interest rates will spread to all securities. That will discourage real investment, which is just what we want to accomplish."

The Washington Board members will protest. It's an old quarrel between New York and Washington. The latter will say: "No, since 1953 we've agreed to conduct our open-market operations in terms of short-term governments— namely, in terms of government bills. That way we'll leave to the free market the determination of the spread between long and short interest rates."

When Washington and New York disagree, who wins these days? You can bet the open-market sale will end up being made in terms of bills (90-day government bonds). To whom were the bills sold? No one knows. The dealers in government bonds—there are about half a dozen big ones—won't reveal the names of the buyers. But you can guess that they are primarily insurance companies, big business firms, and commercial banks. Not many ribbon clerks deal in bills!

The buyers will most likely pay for the bills by check. But you'll find the process easier to understand if you first suppose that they pay in cash—in the ordinary five- and ten-dollar federal reserve notes that we all carry in our wallets. Table 2 shows the final effect on the Federal Reserve balance sheet. The

Open market sale of government bonds cuts down the currency:

F.R. ASSETS		F.R. LIABILITIES	
U.S. securities	−$1.0	Federal Reserve Notes	−$1.0
Total	−$1.0	Total	−$1.0

Table 2. Change in federal reserve balance sheet. The public now has $1 billion extra bonds, paid for by giving up $1 billion of currency.

open-market sale has cut down the community's total money and has cut down on the Fed's assets and liabilities.

Actually, this understates the potency of open-market sales. In all likelihood the 1-billion-dollar sale of bills will result in a 5:1 cut in the community's money supply. Why? Because the buyers will not use currency to pay, thereby cutting down on the currency in circulation. More likely, they'll pay by checks. As they do, their commercial banks will have to honor those checks and will have to honor them out of the commercial banks' Reserve balances on deposit with the Fed. Result: Reserves go down by 1 billion dollars; and, as we've seen, that tends to set off a 5:1 chain of contracting deposits. Table 3 shows the process when Reserve deposits rather than currency have been extinguished by the open-market operation. In this more usual case, the Fed's open-market sale has put 5:1 contractionary pressure on bank deposits.

You can't be sure you really understand open-market operations until you test yourself on the reverse process. Suppose incomes are too low. What will the Open Market Committee want to do? How will it do it? What will the result be? Trace all the steps, using balance sheets if that helps.

Open market sale cuts Reserves and cuts deposits 5:1:

first, producing this change in the Federal Reserve Banks' balance sheet

F.R. ASSETS		F.R. LIABILITIES	
U.S. securities	−$1.0	Member Bank reserves	−$1.0
Total	−$1.0	Total	−$1.0

finally, producing this change in the Member Banks' balance sheet

MEMBER BANK ASSETS		MEMBER BANK LIABILITIES	
Reserves	−$1.0	Demand deposits	−$5.0
Loans and investments	− 4.0		
Total	−$5.0	Total	−$5.0

Table 3. Change in federal reserve and in Member Bank balance sheets (in billions). When an open market sale kills off $1 billion of Reserves, it induces a $5 billion drop in total demand deposits. The Member Banks must call in loans and sell off their "investments" (i.e., their securities).

▶ DISCOUNT RATE POLICY

The Federal Reserve Banks also make loans to the Member Banks. These we can call advances, rediscounts, or (best for our purposes) simply "discounts." When its discounts are growing, the Fed is helping bank Reserves to grow; when its discounts are dropping, it is helping bank Reserves to contract.[1]

Unfortunately, the Fed is not free to pursue a discount policy just exactly the way it wants to. It can't send salesmen out to drum up more discounts whenever it wants to expand them. All it can do is wait for banks to come to it. All it can do is name the "Discount Rate" which gives the interest charge it will make in each of the twelve Regions for such discounts.

True, it can sometimes get more business by lowering the Discount Rate or can discourage the volume of its discounts by raising the Discount Rate. But as far as discount policy is concerned, the Fed must play the woman's role. It can say, No. It can sit and wait. It can make its rate attractive. But it certainly cannot set its amount of *discounts* at precisely the figure it wants to. Only in its open-market operations can it take the active male role. But never underestimate the power of a woman! By being able to say No, the Fed has strong powers to put contractionary pressure on its discounts.

Changing the Discount Rate. On New York's Wall Street, Chicago's LaSalle Street, and Boston's State Street, everyone is keeping careful watch on the Discount Rate that the Fed charges for its discounts. Thus, on the Thursday in August, 1957, when the Discount Rate was raised from 3 to 3½ per cent, stocks and bonds fell in price. Even London and Paris find their interest rates and investment spending influenced by changes in our Discount Rate.

The Discount Rate is usually set to *follow* the market. After open-market sales have been forcing interest rates up, banks will more and more try to borrow from the Fed at the not-yet-raised Discount Rate. To discourage such a growth in its discounts and advances, the Fed will eventually have to raise

[1] When the federal reserve system was started, it was thought that discount policy would be most important of all. The idea was to have Member Banks "rediscount" their customers' promissory notes, sending them over to the Reserve Banks in return for new cash. That way the neighborhood banks would never run out of money to accommodate worthy farm and business borrowers.

It didn't work out that way, for two reasons. First and most important, today we realize that the last thing a healthy economy wants is an *elastic* money supply that will *automatically* expand when business is good and contract when it is bad. That way lies disastrous *reinforcement* of business cycles and inflation. Second, banks found that they prefer to borrow from the Fed on the basis of their numerous government securities rather than on their customers' promissory notes. Since 1935, most borrowing is on government securities, and that is why we now speak of the "Discount Rate" rather than of the old-fashioned "rediscount rate." (In England, they speak always of "Bank Rate," which made headlines in September, 1957, by being raised to the high level of 7 per cent in an attempt to hold down inflation and protect the pound's foreign-exchange value.)

the Discount Rate to bring it back into normal alignment with the market.

And when the Fed does raise the Discount Rate, everyone in the market will say: "Aha, the Board still thinks the wind is blowing in the inflationary direction. Money will probably become even tighter." Which shows that the changes in the Discount Rate, as well as being reflections that follow the tightness of credit, can also have important reinforcing *causal* effects upon the credit market.[1]

The above patterns go into reverse when the Fed wants easier credit. The Discount Rate is lowered to reflect the ease already in the market, and the announcement effect of its being lowered usually serves to ease the market further. Thus, after the November, 1957, Thursday when the Discount Rate was cut from 3½ to 3 per cent, stocks and bonds soared in price.

▶ **CHANGING RESERVE REQUIREMENTS**

The Federal Reserve Authorities are given by Congress the power to raise or lower the required legal reserve ratio that the Member Banks must keep against their deposits. If the Fed wants to make credit tight, it could raise the required reserve ratios for the three types of banks by 2 percentage points: up to 22, 20, and 14 per cent. If it wants credit still tighter, it can raise the New York and Chicago requirements up to 26 per cent. If it wants credit still tighter, it would have to ask Congress to give it the right to raise requirements beyond these limits.

If the Fed wants to ease credit conditions, it can do the reverse. It can cut legal reserve ratios—doing this again and again until the three kinds of banks are down to 13, 10, and 7 per cent. To go lower than that would require a new act of Congress.

Changing reserve requirements is a powerful tool. So powerful that it is used sparingly—a change comes only every few years, not every day as in the case of open-market operations.

Exactly how does an increase in required Reserves operate to tighten credit? Suppose the banks had built up deposits in a 5:1 fashion as a result of the required ratio having been 20 per cent. Now suppose the Fed wants to tighten credit and Congress lets it raise the required ratio to 25 per cent. Even if it does nothing by way of open-market operations or discount policy to change bank Reserves, the banks now have to contract greatly their loans and investments—and their deposits. Why?

---

[1] Bank Rate in London has probably been more potent than our Discount Rate. Recently, Canada has tried an interesting experiment: each week it sets its Central Bank Rate automatically 0.25 per cent above whatever rate the free market sets for short-term government bonds.

Raising reserve requirements forces Member Banks to contract:

Before: when 1:5 prevails

Member Bank Assets		Member Bank Liabilities	
Reserves	$20	Demand deposits	$100
Loans and investments	80		
Total	$100	Total	$100

After: when 1:4 prevails

Member Bank Assets		Member Bank Liabilities	
Reserves	$20	Demand deposits	$80
Loans and investments	60		
Total	$80	Total	$80

Table 4. Effect of rise in legal reserve requirements from one-fifth to one-fourth. The same base of Reserves now supports only 4:1, not 5:1, of deposits. What will be happening on Main Street in the transition?

Because now the bank deposits can only be in a 4:1, not a 5:1, ratio. So there will have to be a drop by one-fifth in all deposits!

This painful cut will start to take place at once. For as soon as the Board signs the new fiat raising requirements to 25 per cent, every bank will find itself deficient with respect to Reserves. It will have to sell off some of its bonds and call in many of its loans. The bond buyers will use up their demand deposits, and the borrowers whose loans are called will have to use up their demand deposits to pay back such loans. The process ends only after banks have brought down their deposits to 4 rather than 5 times their Reserves.

Table 4 shows how their combined balance sheets might look after the change. You may be sure that so great a change would result in very high interest rates, in very unavailable credit, in great cuts in I (and possibly in local G), and in great reductions in national income and employment. Hence, this powerful weapon is rarely used.[1]

Probably in the future it will be used primarily to *lower* required reserve ratios, to bring the three kinds of banks into closer uniformity, and to give the banks the growth in Reserves needed to keep our total money supply in line with our growing money national income. (Can you explain why such lowerings of reserve requirements are likely to take place when business is slack rather than brisk? Can you explain how the lowering is likely to expand investment and income?)

---

[1] In 1936–1937 reserve requirements were sharply raised. But at that time banks found loans and bonds so unattractive that they were already holding heavy "excess reserves"— *i.e.*, they were holding more idle cash than the law required. So raising legal requirements did not have great effects on total M: it merely raised interest rates a little and made the Fed feel that by mopping up excess reserves it was getting rid of some of the kindling for a *future* inflationary fire.

▶ MINOR WEAPONS: QUALITATIVE VERSUS QUANTITATIVE CONTROLS

Moral suasion refers to "jawbone control": the Reserve officials express their displeasure if banks are not doing what it is wanted for them to do. Bankers are called in for heart-to-heart talks. An appeal to their community spirit is made. Vague threats concerning future availability of credit may be made, and bank examiners may become especially zealous in going over the books.

Many economists doubt that slaps on the wrist will keep competitive bankers from doing what they want to do. But it is my tentative belief that moral suasion does have some significant effects, especially in the short run. After all, bankers are sensitive to public opinion just like anyone else.

▶ SELECTIVE, QUANTITATIVE CONTROLS

A selective or qualitative credit control is contrasted with an over-all quantitative credit control that operates merely by affecting over-all bank Reserves and over-all credit tightness. Selective credit controls can be very important in countries that have considerable central planning and supervision by the government of the detailed actions of business. To build a house there you may need a permit. Or to float a new stock or bond issue.

The banks, particularly if as in England there are a few great ones, may be called in by the Chancellor of the Exchequer. He may say: "Look here. We want you to favor export industries in making your loans. And favor necessities. And cut back your total loans by 10 per cent before Christmas."

Margin requirements. The above selective credit controls can be very powerful indeed. However, in normal peacetime it is the American custom not to rely on such detailed interferences with the pricing process—with one exception. The Federal Reserve is given power to set "margin requirements" that limit how much people can borrow in order to buy and carry listed common and preferred stocks. Thus, I can in 1958 borrow 50 per cent from my broker but am required to put up the other 50 per cent myself. Back in 1957 I could borrow only 30 per cent.[1]

Control over installment terms. Besides moral suasion and direct controls over margin borrowing, the Fed for many years had the power to set limits on installment contracts. Thus, in the years of the Korean war, the Fed made you put so much down when you bought cars, furniture, and other goods; and

---

[1] Back in the boom market of 1929, there were no rules at all: my father could borrow 70, 80, or even 90 per cent of the value of any stock he bought. Little wonder then once the crash came, brokers began to phone their clients for them to put up more "margin to cover the declining value of their stocks." Since many clients were already operating on a shoestring, they couldn't pony up the extra margin. Result: the broker had to sell their stocks; so just when stocks were already weak, the necessitous selling of low-margin holders added to the downward avalanche. Do you really think you would have liked living in the old days?

this same so-called Regulation W also required you to pay up on your charge accounts before buying more goods on credit. Regulation W seems to have been very effective, and the same has been true of similar regulations in Britain and elsewhere. But it became unpopular, and when the Korean crisis had passed, this power of the Fed was permitted to lapse.

Control over mortgage terms. Congress long empowered the Federal Reserve to set terms for mortgage down payments and number of years' amortization. This so-called Regulation X gave the Board powerful leverage over the pace of house-construction expenditure. By raising down payments and shortening the span of mortgages, the Board could choke off housing. By doing the reverse, the Board could help step up the pace of construction.

This strong weapon was allowed by Congress to lapse in 1953. The Fed, with its philosophy of over-all quantitative controls rather than selective fiats, was perhaps not too sorry to see this power go. But it soon learned that Nature abhors a vacuum. If the Central Bank will not wield these powers, somebody else will. Thus, much housing is subsidized by the government: the Veterans Administration (VA) guarantees mortgage loans and so does the Federal Housing Authority (FHA). Also, there is the "Fannie Mae," the Federal National Mortgage Association, which buys mortgages to make credit for housing more available.

These government agencies, which have no connection with the Federal Reserve, have often done what you would expect them to do. Namely, they have worked at cross-purposes to the Board. In 1956–1957, when the Fed was trying to clamp down on credit, Congress and some executive agencies were doing all they could to funnel new funds into the building market. The same was true of the Small Business Administration, which Congress wanted to make credit easier, rather than tighter.

The moral of all this would seem to be as follows. These days, public policy takes special interest in certain sectors of the credit market. It is not content to let interest rates find their own level in each such market; it seeks to encourage certain activities (housing, small business, etc.) and discourage others (stock speculation, etc.). Whether public policy works itself out under the direction of the Central Bank or outside that organization, the economist has to reckon with these facts of life.

▶ RECAPITULATION OF MONETARY POLICY'S WEAPONS

From discussing the four minor weapons of Federal Reserve policy, we can now return to the three major weapons. The Fed's operations can be summarized thus:

▶ The Central Bank's liabilities form the base of an economy's money supply: its federal reserve notes provide us with currency; its deposit liabilities provide the

Reserves of the Member Banks, on top of which their multiple expansion of demand deposits takes place.

Of the Fed's assets, the gold certificates merely represent its neutral acquiescence with the international flows of gold. But the ebb and flow of its earning assets—its government securities and discounts which together are called Reserve Bank Credit—represents its active control over money in circulation and bank Reserves and demand deposits.

The major weapons it now uses to influence money and credit conditions are, in order of importance, open-market operations, Discount Rate policy, and changing legal reserve requirements.

▶ **THE PYRAMID OF CREDIT**

Figure 1 summarizes the relation between the commercial or Member Banks and the public; between the banks and the Federal Reserve Banks; and between the Reserve Banks and the Treasury. At the bottom of the pyramid is a relatively small amount of gold held by the United States Treasury, about 23 billion dollars' worth in 1957. A little of this is held as nominal "backing" against the relatively minor amount of coins and paper money issued by the Treasury, and a little is held by the Exchange Equalization Fund for use in

The Federal Reserve provides our currency and bank reserves:

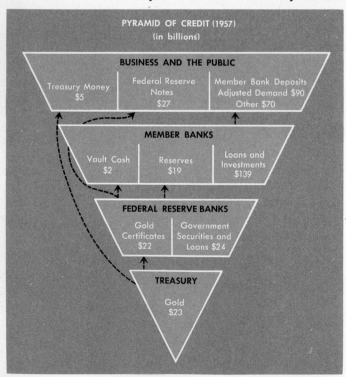

Fig. 1. We have more than enough gold to support outstanding Reserve Bank Credit. It is these latter earning assets—primarily the result of past open-market purchases—that underlie our money supply.

connection with the United States quota in the International Monetary Fund. But by far the largest part is matched by gold certificates in the coffers of the Federal Reserve Banks—some 22 billion dollars in all.

Moving up the pyramid from the Treasury to the Federal Reserve Banks, we find their total liabilities and total assets to be 46 billion dollars, so that Reserve Bank cash reserves are about half their total liabilities.[1]

Besides cash assets, the Reserve Banks hold about 24 billion dollars of loans and investments, almost all in short-term government bills.

Matching their total assets, the Reserve Banks' first principal liability consists of federal reserve note currency. This is held largely by the public, but in degree also by banks as till money or vault cash.

The other principal liability of the Reserve Banks is the legal reserve deposits of the Member Banks. Pyramided upon this 19 billion dollars of Reserves is the volume of bank checking deposit money held by the public.

To test your grasp of these important financial institutions, perform the following review in terms of the different parts of the pyramid: (1) Show what happens eventually to 1 billion dollars of newly mined or newly imported gold. Show how this will give rise to new Member Bank reserves and to new checking deposits, and possibly to a little new paper money in circulation. (2) Show what happens if the Reserve Banks make 1 billion dollars of open-market purchases of government bonds from the public.

▶ FINANCE IN THE WAR AND POSTWAR

The pyramid of credit gives us a still picture. To see the changes that have taken place in recent years, turn to Fig. 2. This pictures the important economic variables published each month in the *Federal Reserve Bulletin*.

At the top is money in circulation. It grew mightily in the war and has

---

[1] The Federal Reserve Banks have the legal requirement of holding at least 25 per cent of their note and deposit liabilities in the form of gold certificates. This 1:4 gold reserve ratio (which should not be confused with the Member Bank 1:5 ratio) is not of much importance today. The Fed stays well above it, as is necessary if the Fed is to be perfectly free to act in *both* an expansionary and a contractionary direction. And should the Fed begin to get close to this legal ratio, Congress would probably do what it did during the war—pass a law lowering the requirement so as to restore to the Fed two-way freedom.

In 1913 the founders of the reserve system thought this gold reserve requirement would be important. They took it so seriously that part of the blame for the 1920 price collapse must be attributed to the fact that no one dreamed that Congress could lower the gold requirement at the time when the Fed was threatening to go below the 35 and 40 per cent ratios that then legally prevailed! The founders of the system would look at today's pyramid of credit and say: Each dollar of gold can give rise to a 20:1 deposit expansion—i.e., 5/1 at the Member Bank level times 4/1 at the Fed level. We know this to be misleading: in that the Fed does not adhere to its 1:4 ratio, each dollar of gold results only in a 5:1 deposit expansion—and not even that if the Fed wants to offset it or if the Treasury wants to "sterilize" it.

How "Reserve Bank Credit" determined our money supply:

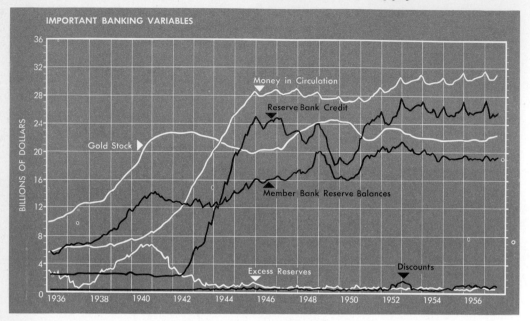

Fig. 2. Money in circulation and Reserves have followed Reserve Bank Credit pretty closely. The Fed has not let gold flows call the tune. Note the tight rein on growth of Reserves that the Fed has kept in recent years. (Late in 1957 it eased credit. Why?)

since shown slow growth. Demand deposits would be too large to show on the same chart; but they too show this same general pattern.

Member Bank reserve balances, what we've been calling Reserves, show a similar but less dramatic pattern. Our major interest is to explain how these Reserves change. Part of the explanation will come from the behavior of the gold stock. But not very much. The Fed will not let undulations in our gold holdings show up in changes in Reserves.

To explain Reserves, we have to turn to Reserve Bank Credit, namely, to the sum of the Fed's government securities and discounts. Can you see how the Fed put on the brakes in 1948–1949, using open-market sales to depress Reserve Bank Credit and sop up bank Reserves? And can you see how it has held the line against what it conceived to be the inflationary peril in the years 1955–1957?

At the bottom of the chart is discounts. Their total is small compared to government securities; but their change in any year is not insignificant in comparison with that year's net open-market purchases or sales. In the short run these discounts operate at cross-purposes to open-market operations. Thus, note how discounts grew late in 1952, just when the Fed was trying to tighten credit. Some economists therefore are critical of discount policy.

But defenders say, "If it weren't for the safety valve of the discount privilege, the Fed wouldn't dare to have so tight a policy of open-market sales. Just as car brakes enable cars to go *faster,* the existence of discounting enables the Fed to pursue a sterner open-market policy."

Excess reserves, as shown at the bottom of the chart, have been pretty small in recent years. When discounts get above excess reserves—so that so-called "net free reserves" are negative—you can be pretty sure money is tight.

But back in the mid-thirties you would have seen a tremendous bulge in excess reserves. Gold flowed here in great amounts: but with banks leery of loans and of further government securities, the result was no multiple expansion—merely a piling up of excess reserves. The Board, nervous always about inflation (even during the slump itself!), couldn't sleep at night for fear that these excess reserves might suddenly become the base of deposit expansion. So, as we've seen, they doubled reserve requirements, to bring excess reserves under control. In ordinary times, when banks can find attractive earning assets, excess reserves never become substantial.

This chapter has now laid the base for next chapter's discussion of the interplay between monetary policy and income determination.

SUMMARY

1. The Federal Reserve is a Central Bank, a bank for bankers. Its duty is to control the community's supply of money.

2. Its five-step mode of action goes thus: it contracts bank Reserves; which causes multiple contractions in total deposits; which makes credit expensive (high interest rates) and hard to get; which depresses private and public investment spending; which puts a damper on money income and prices.

3. The powerful weapons the Fed uses are (*a*) open-market operations, (*b*) Discount Rate policy, and (*c*) changing legal reserve requirements. Minor weapons used at times by Central Banks are moral suasion, and selective controls over margin borrowing, installment sales, and mortgages.

4. Unlike its neutral acquiescence to change in gold supplies, sales by the Fed of government securities to the open market represent a positive act which reduces its assets and liabilities, and which reduces the Reserves of the Member Banks and hence their base for deposits. Powerful day-to-day open-market operations should be understood by every student of monetary policy.

5. The main facts of finance, as shown by the still picture of the credit pyramid or by the chart of changing Reserves and money, are to be understood in terms of this chapter's analysis.

QUESTIONS FOR DISCUSSION

1. In what federal reserve district are you? Where is the nearest branch?

2. Interpret the items on the latest balance sheet of the Reserve Banks.

3. You find gold in a cave. Describe the resulting steps.

4. "Gold movements affected prices only because we use them as a barometer, signaling us to expand or contract the total of money supply. Of course, the gold standard was a stupid system. But it was wiser to tie ourselves to such an imperfect system than to trust corrupt legislatures whose tendency is always to print inflationary paper money." Discuss.

5. Trace through the effects of a 1-billion-dollar open-market purchase.

6. Trace the effects of a doubling of reserve requirements. A halving.

7. List the weapons, of monetary control of the Reserve authorities. How powerful are they (*a*) to control *M*, (*b*) to control interest rates, (*c*) to control prices, (*d*) to control employment and unemployment?

8. Discuss the following 1939 statement of the Reserve Board: "The federal reserve system can see to it that banks have enough reserves to make money available to commerce, industry, and agriculture at low rates; but it cannot make the people borrow, and it cannot make the public spend the deposits that result when the banks do make loans and investments."

9. Discuss monetary policy since mid-1958.

10. Debate qualitative, selective controls versus quantitative controls.

11. Review your understanding of the following concepts:

the five-step sequence	*Discount Rate, discounts*
Reserves and excess reserves	*legal reserve requirements*
availability and cost of credit	*moral suasion, Regulations X*
gold certificates, Reserve Bank Credit	*and W*
federal reserve notes	*margin requirements*
open-market purchases and sales	*selective qualitative controls*
	pyramid of credit

SYNTHESIS OF MONETARY ANALYSIS
AND INCOME ANALYSIS

About this time there was a cry . . . for more paper-money. . . . I was on the side of an addition, being persuaded that the first small sum struck in 1723 had done much good, by increasing the trade, employment, and number of inhabitants in the province, since I now saw all the old houses inhabited, and many new ones building. . . . The utility of this currency became by time and experience so evident, as never afterwards to be much disputed. . . . Tho' . . . there are limits beyond which the quantity may be hurtful.

BENJAMIN FRANKLIN

Chapter 12 showed how saving and investment schedules intersect to determine the level of national income. And the last few chapters have discussed how changes in Federal Reserve policy can affect the community's stock of money.

In this brief chapter, we relate these two analyses. Monetary analysis is seen to fit in well with the modern theory of income determination. And the stage is set for stabilization policy: Central Bank monetary policies and government fiscal policies (public expenditure and taxation, with the implied budget deficit or surplus). These monetary and fiscal policies have to be coordinated to achieve the goal of a progressive economy which enjoys reasonable price stability and lives up to its full-employment production potentialities.

The present chapter shows how stabilization policies work and sketches recent monetary policy. It leaves for the remaining chapter of Part Two the more detailed study of fiscal policy issues.

331

▶ **MONETARY POLICY OPERATES ON THE INVESTMENT SCHEDULE**

Figure 1 uses the tools of income analysis to show how a cheap money policy works. Note the upward shift in the investment schedule induced by the lowering of interest rates and enhanced credit availability that accompanies a multiple increase in total money.

(The same process could have been shown by use of the $C + I + G$ schedules of Chapter 12. An expansionary monetary policy might then operate to wipe out the kind of deflationary gap shown in Fig. 11 of page 240. However, provided we agree to include in our II schedule such local and state public investing as cheaper money does induce, our Fig. 1 pretty much covers the ground.)

Suppose the economy faced an inflationary gap, with II tending to intersect SS to the right of the level of full employment. Can you show how contractionary monetary policy might bring income back to the desired level of full employment without price inflation?[1]

▶ **CHANGING INTEREST RATES AFFECT INVESTMENT PROPENSITIES: A DIGRESSION**

Some economists like to use a graph like Fig. 2 to show exactly how and why Fig. 1's investment schedule does shift upward at each level of income. In Fig. 2, when you raise interest and make credit less available, that moves you northwestward up an "investment-interest demand curve" dd, choking off some investment.[2]

There is one advantage to using the investment-interest demand curve: it warns you that in times of great depression, when businessmen are very pessimistic and when they already have much excess capacity, the dd curve may be almost vertical. (Try penciling in a new vertical $d'd'$ curve.) What does that mean? In this depression case, no matter how much you change interest rates, you may find that you can't coax out much new investment. If a new vertical

---

[1] Some economists used to hope that monetary policy, in addition to affecting investment, would get some help from the saving and consumption side. Higher interest rates, they hoped, would stimulate saving and kill consumption. *I.e.*, they hoped interest increase would shift up the SS schedule in Fig. 1, thereby reinforcing the effect of the downward shift in II.

Experience, and the analysis of Chapter 29, suggest that these effects are probably weak and can't be much counted on. (The interest effects on saving might even be perverse, a rise in interest enabling you to save less in anticipation of your old age.) Except that credit easing might increase the availability of credit to consumers who rely on installment credit, economists today think it unimportant to show such a shift in the SS schedule.

[2] This schedule of investment against interest rates is sometimes called the "marginal efficiency of investment schedule." It and related concepts are discussed in more detail in Chapter 29 dealing with capital theory. Note that each of the indicated investment demand schedules is drawn up with the level of income specified; as interest changes investment, investment will change income via the multiplier and shift the schedule in Fig. 2.

Central Banks ease credit to raise investment schedule:

Fig. 1. By giving banks more Reserves and causing them to bid down interest and make credit more available, the Fed shifts the investment schedule upward and produces a multiplier expansion of income.

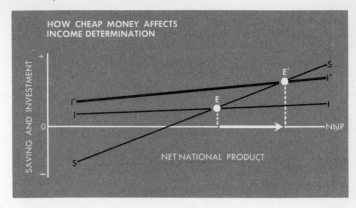

HOW CHEAP MONEY AFFECTS
INCOME DETERMINATION

NET NATIONAL PRODUCT

$d'd'$ holds in Fig. 2, that means the II curve in Fig. 1 just can't be shifted up and income can't be raised by monetary policy alone.

Thus, monetary policy tends not to be very potent in deep depression. This the Fed learned back in the slump of the 1930's. Even when it forced interest rates on short-term government bonds down to one-tenth of $\frac{1}{10}$ of 1 per cent (read that again!), the Fed still couldn't revive plant and equipment or inventory investment spending. When a businessman already has a half-idle plant and excessive inventory, he probably won't invest even if you were to give him credit at zero interest. As the Fed put it, "You can lead a horse to

Higher interest rates choke off investment spending:

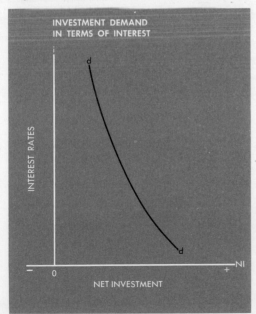

INVESTMENT DEMAND
IN TERMS OF INTEREST

INTEREST RATES

NET INVESTMENT

Fig. 2. Even with the same income level there will be more investment when interest is low with credit easy to get. And tight money will cut investment as you move northwest on dd.

Fiscal policy means government expenditure and tax policy:

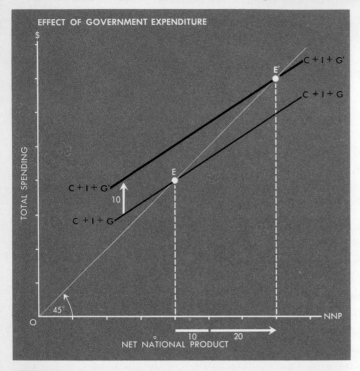

EFFECT OF GOVERNMENT EXPENDITURE

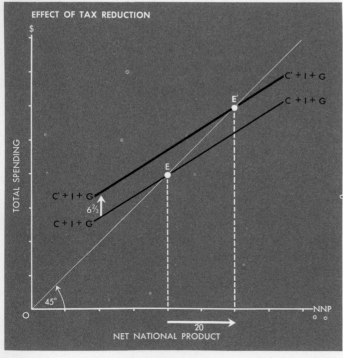

EFFECT OF TAX REDUCTION

Fig. 3. An increase in government expenditures shifts $C + I + G$ up to $C + I + G'$. E' shows the higher income that results.

Lowering taxes has similar effects on income. Lower tax collections give you more Disposable Income out of NNP, and hence shifts upward the consumption schedule. We go from E to E' as a result of the new $C' + I + G$ schedule. (Dollar for dollar, tax reduction is a little weaker than G increase. Why? Because some of tax rebate is saved rather than used to shift up CC. A cut of taxes of 10 shifts CC up only by $\frac{2}{3} \times 10 = 6\frac{2}{3}$ when the MPC is $\frac{2}{3}$.)

water but you can't make him drink." Or as some economists characterize the difference between the Fed's deep-depression and ordinary power: "The Fed can pull on a string, but it can't push on a string."

▶ **FISCAL POLICY AND INCOME DETERMINATION**

Aside from the Central Bank, the government has other ways to affect current spending. As part of its *fiscal policy* it can expand its investment: build useful public roads and schools, hire more civil servants, increase defense expenditure, do a hundred and one useful or foolish things to expand total spending. This could be shown in a saving-investment diagram like Fig. 1.

But better still, you can show it as an upward shift in the G component of the $C + I + G$ schedule that we have used as an alternative way to show income equilibrium. The first chart in Fig. 3 shows how an expansion of public expenditure G will lead to an expansion of income.

The same type of chart[1] can show the other side of fiscal policy—changes in tax collections. To raise NNP the fiscal authorities cut taxes: this gives people higher disposable income, and since they have a propensity to consume out of extra income, this means they will consume more.

How can we show the increased consumption on Fig. 3's second chart? We can show the effect of reduced taxes as an upward shift of the CC schedule that is plotted against NNP and is a major component of the pictured $C + I + G$ schedule. With taxes lower, we subtract less from each level of NNP to get the corresponding level of disposable income. So with higher disposable income corresponding to each NNP, we must show higher consumption—hence the higher CC curve.

So we may summarize the effects of fiscal policy:

▶   Increased G raises income by raising the GG component of $C + I + G$. Reduced taxes raises the CC component of the $C + I + G$ schedule. Both together—which also means deficit financing or a reduction in the budgetary surplus—results in an even greater upward shift of the $C + I + G$ schedule and in equilibrium income. You formulate the reverse case of contractionary fiscal policy.

▶ **WAGE PUSH VERSUS DEMAND PULL ONCE AGAIN**

Now you know how our saving-investment or $C + I + G$ schedules are affected by monetary and fiscal policy. This is a highly useful analysis that business, government, and university economists are employing all the time to understand the movements of our national economy.

---

[1] The present treatment duplicates Chapter 12's page 245 treatment and best handles the effects of personal income taxes. For more complicated analysis of indirect and other taxes, taking account too of tax effects on investment, reference must be made to intermediate texts.

If you think about these tools, you will realize that they are at their best in analyzing the ebb and flow of aggregate demand. In any years when the behavior of prices can best be understood in terms of aggregate demand, these tools will get gold stars for their usefulness.

Here are some examples. The tools worked well to explain the Great Depression of the decade following 1929. MIT's E. Cary Brown has studied the expenditure and taxes history of the federal government during those years, and he finds that events shaped up just about the way the schedules said they ought to. Thus the New Deal, for all the talk at the time, was pushing up taxes along with its increased expenditure; and the states and localities were contracting their public expenditures. So the resulting pattern of NNP was in line with the expectations of income analysis.

Still another example is that of the years right after the war. The tremendous growth in ·the wartime public debt and money supply M was accompanied in the postwar by a very easy money policy. The Fed was then a captive of the Treasury: prior to 1951, when the Treasury signed an "accord" giving the Fed its freedom, it felt obligated to make expansionary open-market purchases of government bonds to "peg" their prices at 100; you know what such purchases do to credit easiness. With so much M, with credit so easy, and with people coming out of the war hungry for consumption and business hungry for plant and equipment, what would you expect to happen? You would expect there to be strong inflationary gaps. You would expect prices to be bid up once employment and capacity were full and output could no longer grow.

Well, that's exactly what happened. There was a tremendous surge in prices. Economic historians, looking back on the years around 1947, now think the commentators were wrong who were then attributing the price rise mainly to union leaders. It is now felt that demand pull rather than wage push predominated in that period: the unions got credit, or blame, for higher wages; but really, with demand so excessive, the wages were chasing soaring prices rather than vice versa.

▶ **A BRIEF HISTORY OF FEDERAL RESERVE POLICY**

The Federal Reserve was set up just in time for World War I. It contributed much to the smooth financing of that war. But, as history shows, it was not able to prevent considerable wartime price inflation.

The twenties. Under the firm hand of Benjamin Strong, who headed the New York Federal Reserve Bank, the Fed became an important influence during the decade of the roaring twenties. People began to speak of a "new era" of perpetual prosperity, with the Federal Reserve being expected to accomplish this miracle. Of course, the subsequent depression ended such talk and led to an equally sweeping dismissal of the virtue and potency of monetary policy.

One perplexing problem the Fed faced in the late twenties was the stock market. How could it tighten credit to speculators without tightening it to "legitimate" business? It never did succeed in resolving this issue: some economists think it was too tough in its 1929 policy; some, that it was too easy. In any case we got *both* the stock-market crash and the Great Depression.

The depressed thirties. As we have seen, neither the Federal Reserve nor the government had the imagination and courage to prevent wholesale collapse of the banking system. Runs on the banks occurred everywhere. And by their actions, desperate depositors brought on themselves the disaster they feared. Only after 1933 did reforms of our banking system take place; and many of these—such as the FDIC—were outside the federal reserve system.

With respect to its open-market operations, many economic historians feel that the Fed did too little during the first years of depression. If in 1930 and 1931 it had absolutely flooded the market with easy credit, through massive open-market operations, these economists believe the worst of the depression could have been prevented. Actually, the Fed did try a little to ease credit, but not as militantly as we should today think so grave an emergency called for. Also, in the fall of 1931, it temporarily tightened credit a little to try to help Britain get back on her feet after being forced off the gold standard.

After 1933, monetary policy became secondary to fiscal policy. Indeed, so great was the flow of gold to our shores, and so great was the increase in its total dollar value after Roosevelt raised gold's price from $21 to $35 an ounce, that the money market began to be flooded with funds even without any active open-market policies.

Short-term interest rates dropped almost to zero. Banks held vast excess reserves, not caring to lend in so depressed times and not caring to buy more short-term bonds yielding less than $37 on each million dollars invested!

Long-term interest rates were slow to fall. Even after 10 years of easy money, loans for business or home construction remained at 4 per cent or higher in most places. Availability of credit was also very poor—despite some government helps by the Reconstruction Finance Corporation (RFC) and occasional direct Federal Reserve industrial loans.

In short, throughout the greatest depression in our history the easiness of money was primarily due to gold inflow and weak loan demand—not to militant easy-money policy by the Federal Reserve.

World War II. The Fed got drafted, so to speak, like everyone else. It helped Secretary of the Treasury Henry J. Morgenthau to peg the structure of government-bond prices.

People generally got high war incomes as production and hours of work soared. They couldn't spend it on consumption goods as direct controls and rationing diverted goods to the war effort. Result: the workers saved mightily.[1]

What did they do with their war savings? They put some in currency, as federal reserve notes expanded. They put some in saving and demand deposits. They put some into Victory bonds. It was up to them.

The Treasury was then running a huge deficit. To whom did it sell the bonds? It sold as many of them to individuals as it could. For the rest, it sold them to the Member Banks and to the Federal Reserve Banks. Where did the Member Banks get the money? The Fed, by its purchase of 1 billion dollars of government bonds, expanded Reserves by that much. This permitted the banks to buy 4 billion dollars' worth of bonds. So the Fed always bought one-fifth of the bonds that the public wouldn't buy, thereby permitting the banks to buy the other four-fifths. Thus we manufactured M out of thin air!

So it went throughout the war. And at low, pegged rates of interest.

The postwar. After the war people generally ended up with vast holdings of government bonds and deposits. They felt rich. And they felt hungry. Hungry for new homes, for new cars, for all the things they had gone without during the war. They wanted to sell their bonds to buy consumption goods and new homes.

Business, which also ended with swollen liquid assets, likewise wanted to invest at a great pace. Why? To make up for capital worn out by three-shift war operation and not then replaced. And to take advantage of the greatly expanded postwar level of business activity and sales. (Remember Chapter 13's acceleration principle?)

What was the result? As the man in the street said: "Too much money chasing too few goods." Or as men said in the chaste downtown clubs: "By continuing to support the Treasury's bond prices, the Fed is being forced to 'monetize' the public debt. When the Fed is forced to buy all government bonds at 100 to please the Secretary of the Treasury, it is forced to make open-market purchases that everyone knows to be inflationary. And during the present great postwar inflation! Instead of leaning against the wind, the Fed in fanning the wind into a hurricane. By gad, I'll write a letter of protest to the *New York Herald Tribune.*"

After the accord. Gradually the Fed began to assert its independence of the Treasury. It lowered its support of government-bond prices a little. But it kept bickering behind the scenes with the Treasury; and the Korean crisis again put it in the uneasy position of buying bonds at a time when inflationary price increases were already raging.

Finally, in March, 1951, the Treasury and the Federal Reserve signed an accord which recognized that the Fed's primary duty is that of stabilizing

---

[1] See Chapter 36 on war finance for more details.

business activity—not stabilizing the government-bond market. Only to prevent crises and disorderly markets would the Fed sacrifice its goal of national-income control by intervening in the government-bond market. Such interventions in the bond market as it makes are, normally, for the purpose of fulfilling its open-market operations designed to keep bank Reserves where prosperity requires them to be and are not to make the Treasury happy.

In 1952 and early 1953 the Fed followed a tight money policy. Why? Because it feared inflation and thought activity too high. When the 1953–1954 recession was set off by inventory trimming and cuts in post-Korean defense spending, the Fed shifted sharply to easy money. This did seem to help construction and some other forms of investment. And coupled with fiscal policy, monetary policy did succeed in keeping that recession a mild one.

▶ A NEW INFLATION?

These are fine examples of our aggregate demand tools. But what about recent years? Some economists have testified before Congress that we may now be in a "new inflation." For years after 1955, prices were rising: wholesale prices, farm prices, cost-of-living prices—in fact, all but a few metal prices.

Everyone was disturbed about the month-after-month announcement of higher prices. But what was it due to? To excessive demand?

Turning to look at each industry, it was hard to perceive excessive demand. Autos just weren't selling well. Farm-equipment salesmen sang the blues. TV producers took out the red ink as sales slumped and as people began to buy the low-profit cheap models. The steel industry operated at 80 per cent of capacity. So it went, in reports about demand for industry after industry.

Yet the price index continued to advance. So some experts began to wonder whether this was not the case of a "wage push" rather than "demand pull."

Money wages were raised each year, and often by more than the growth of productivity. Nor did it seem to take many strikes to accomplish this. The wage push happened outside the unionized industries too. And in the unionized sectors some observers said: "In pushing for higher wages, labor is pushing against an open door. The employers don't fight the increases the way they used to. They act as if they think that the Treasury and the Fed will act so as to keep aggregate demand high enough to buy the higher-cost output; so they grant the wage increases, and this sends up costs of production, which sends up the prices firms charge for their goods. The result is a new kind of inflation. If the Fed and Treasury tried to handle it by their weapons that affect demand, they would create unemployment and a recession. We wonder whether a deliberately created short 1957 recession will be enough to end the whole wage-push psychology of employers and employees."

Economics is not an exact science. Here is another one of those cases where the plot is being acted out in front of us. As in any thriller, we won't know until the third act who is responsible for killing off price stability. And unlike the land of fiction or the laboratory of the experimental scientist, the real world of economics may never reveal to us just what caused our inflation or just what would be the potency of conventional fiscal and monetary policies to affect the rate at which an inflation proceeds.

Part of learning a subject is learning when to reserve judgment. No one yet fully knows how to analyze the issue of wage-push versus demand-pull inflation. We do know that they interact to reinforce each other and that operating on demand may sometimes help to curb an inflation that was triggered off by cost rather than by demand. That's all we are yet sure of.

▶ THE NEOCLASSICAL SYNTHESIS

Critics used to regard the classical principles of economics as out of date. Looking out the window at the long bread lines and the men selling apples on street corners, they said: "Why speak of scarcity? Or efficiency? Or growth? Or fairness? Throw away your tools of supply and demand, your finespun theories of market pricing. Tear up the rule book. We live in a new era in which everything is upside down: attempts to save kill off investment; a hurricane or war is a blessing in that it creates jobs and puts food into the starving bellies of the unemployed."

What is the modern economist's answer to all this? He says: "You are right to question the classical principles. All principles should be subjected to the closest examination with respect to both their logic and their factual relevance. The classical arguments were oversimple, and they admittedly did not allow for the facts of nineteenth- and twentieth-century life. But experience since 1932, and careful logical reasoning, suggests that you had better discard your own false inferences. Everywhere in the free world governments and Central Banks have shown they can win the battle of the slump. They have the weapons of fiscal policy (expenditure and taxes) and of monetary policy (open-market operations, Discount Rate policy, legal reserve ratio policy) to shift the schedules that determine national income and employment. Just as we no longer meekly accept disease, we no longer need accept mass unemployment. That being so, you'll find the classical principles will again apply: but now they apply because our macroeconomics has validated their premise of adequate demand—not because the world is lucky enough to have them apply automatically and at all times."

This is a brave answer. And essentially, most careful economists would today say, an accurate answer. But let us not be too arrogant, too conceited about our modern conquest of instability. Let us quietly add the following qualifications: The worst of the business cycle, which Chapter 13 showed plagued capitalism from its beginning, is probably a thing of the past. But that does not mean that the cycle is gone: we still shall have minor inventory fluctuations, still shall have transitions from war to peace and from one kind of a boom to another. The difference will be this: the age-old tendencies for the system to fluctuate will still be there, but no longer will the world let them snowball into vast depressions or into galloping inflations—no longer will we let our banking system fail and our nation go through the most painful debt deflation and bankruptcy.

And, finally, let's admit that all the political pressures in a democracy do work to make a chronic slump unlikely. But can we be so sure that the same pressures will operate to prevent mild inflation? Even if fiscal and monetary policies could prevent such chronic, mild inflation of a couple of per cent per year, are you sure that they will be used to do so? Do you really think you should put *all* your old-age savings in the form of bonds and money?

SUMMARY

1. Monetary policy fits in with modern income analysis: it can be thought of as shifting the investment schedule so as to lead to a higher or lower level of income spending. Or you can use the $C+I+G$ approach.

2. To show the amount of the shift in the II schedule, economists often plot the demand for investment in terms of interest rates (and availability). This "investment-interest demand schedule" shows how lowering interest will coax out more investment at each income level; and how raising interest will choke off investment. In deep depression, this schedule may be practically vertical, so that II and income will hardly be affected by monetary policy. Monetary policy is then not very potent, as the authorities find themselves "pushing on a string."

3. Fiscal policy too acts on the schedules that determine income. Higher expenditure, by raising G, pushes up the $C+I+G$ schedule and makes for expanded income. Lower taxes, by raising disposable income and consumption corresponding to each level of NNP, shifts up the CC component in $C+I+G$, and thus also serve to raise income. Lowering G and raising taxes does the reverse of all this and lowers income.

4. These tools work well to explain aggregate demand. Many historical events seem well explained by demand-pull analysis. But not all. Some seem to call for a wage-push analysis. Admittedly, these two approaches often interact—with each having a measure of truth. *E.g.*, when demand is strong unions are encouraged to be aggressive in their wage demands; and if demand turned out not to be adequate, some of the wage increases would be rescinded or would serve to raise prices and choke off production as money spending was insufficient to buy all the output at the higher prices. And it is often true that the fiscal and monetary authorities will want to use the weapons of demand to cure the inflation that wage push may be creating.

5. After expecting too much of Federal Reserve monetary policy in the twenties, people became so disillusioned by the thirties as to expect too little from it. During the depression, the gold inflow and weak general investment demand did render conventional monetary expansion programs less effective. However, since the 1951 accord restored to the Fed its freedom to pursue a stabilizing monetary policy, historical events suggest it has an important role to play in helping fiscal policy lean against the wind of excessive or deficient aggregate demand.

6. Modern democracies have the fiscal and monetary tools, and the political will to use them, to end chronic slumps and galloping inflations. This gives us the neoclassical synthesis—the classical principles of pricing of later chapters are validated by successful use of the tools of these chapters. But we must raise the question as to whether democratic pressures are so strong as to prevent mild inflation; and we must not think that curing the worst phases of the old business cycle means that we shall avoid minor fluctuations in the years ahead.

QUESTIONS FOR DISCUSSION

1. Redraw Fig. 1 to show tight monetary policy. Trace your move on Fig. 2.

2. Show that if *dd* is almost horizontal, Fed policy will be very potent.

3. Use Fig. 3 to show that increasing G and taxes at the same time will tend to have canceling effects on income. Difficult question: Can you follow the intricate reasoning back on page 245 which argues that, dollar for dollar, changes in G are a little more potent than changes in taxes—so that a balanced-budget increase in G is likely to be a little expansionary?

4. "Fiscal and monetary authority should be in one agency, or at least be coordinated. Otherwise they may work at cross purposes, one undoing what the other is trying to accomplish." Criticize.

5. Delineate some of the issues involved in the demand-pull versus wage-push debate. Show how these may interact. Discuss therapy.

6. Try to explain what is meant by the neoclassical synthesis. Qualify it.

7. Review your understanding of the following concepts:

II *shifts induced by monetary policy*   *shift of* C + I + G *due to tax and expenditure changes*

the investment demand curve dd in terms of interest   *wage push and demand pull*

neoclassical synthesis

18

FISCAL POLICY AND FULL EMPLOYMENT
WITHOUT INFLATION

I give you this assurance: every legitimate means available to the Federal Government that can be used to sustain prosperity will be used.

PRESIDENT DWIGHT D. EISENHOWER (1954)

We have seen in earlier chapters that the behavior of saving and investment determines the level of national income and employment. We have seen that private investment often fluctuates widely from year to year. History shows how painful and wasteful the business cycle has been in the past; today everyone is in agreement that, unless we succeed in laying the ghost of instability in the future, American free enterprise will be in jeopardy.

What prescription follows from our economic diagnosis? No single answer can be given; there is no single cure-all for the economic ills of society. Business, labor, and agriculture must all attempt to pursue price and wage policies aimed at maintaining a stable, high-employment economy. The federal reserve system can also do much, by way of interest and monetary policy, to prevent an aggravation of the business cycle. But, if all these measures have been tried and they still do not succeed in avoiding the perils of heavy unemployment or extreme inflation, then there is still the public weapon of fiscal policy. This is not to say that fiscal policy, alone, is a cure-all, but it is an important part of any economic program.

You are warned that the subject matter of this chapter is still in a controversial stage. While stress has been placed on limitations as well as on advantages of different fiscal policies, it is idle to believe that, in the present inadequate state of our scientific economic knowledge, economists are in agreement as to the importance of the pros and cons. You should not form your opinions from a hasty reading of some superficially persuasive argument.

A SHORT-RUN AND LONG-RUN FISCAL POLICY

By a positive fiscal policy, we mean the process of shaping public *taxation* and public *expenditure* so as (1) to help dampen down the swings of the business cycle, and (2) to contribute toward the maintenance of a progressive, high-employment economy free from excessive inflation or deflation.

The war years have shown fiscal policy to be a very powerful weapon. Indeed, some would argue that it is like the nuclear bomb, too powerful a weapon to let men and governments play with; that it would be better if fiscal policy were never used. However, it is absolutely certain that, just as no nation will sit idly by and let smallpox decimate the population, so too in every country fiscal policy always comes into play whenever depressions gain headway. There is no choice then but to attempt to lead fiscal policy along economically sound rather than destructive channels. Every government always has a fiscal policy whether it realizes it or not. The real issue is whether this shall be a constructive one or an unconscious, bumbling one.

▶ **THE TASK OF FISCAL POLICY**

Without fiscal and monetary policy, the economic system might in a particular year be threatened with a deflationary gap. Suppose private consumption and investment spending were too weak to provide adequate employment. What action would then be called for?

The Federal Reserve would use expansionary monetary policy to try to stimulate private investment. In the degree that its efforts were not fully successful, the fiscal authorities would still be faced by a deflationary gap. This would be the signal for Congress and the President to introduce tax and public-expenditure policies designed to help the economy again achieve stable full employment.

Likewise in the case where private investment and consumption decisions were threatening the economy with an inflationary gap. With prices rising and employers desperately vying for nonexistent workers, the Fed would initiate contractionary credit programs aimed to reduce the inflationary gap. But if the saving-investment or $C+I+G$ intersections still threatened the economy with an inflationary gap, it would then be the duty of Congress and the President to initiate higher tax rates and/or lower public expenditure programs aimed at restoring a high-employment equilibrium without inflation.

Summary:

▶ Fiscal policies dealing with taxes and public expenditure, in cooperation with stabilizing monetary policies, have for their goal a high-employment economy— but one without price inflation. The fiscal and monetary authorities "lean against the prevailing economic winds," thereby helping provide a favorable economic environment within which the dynamic forces of private initiative can have the widest opportunity for achievement.

▶ OUR IMPORTANT "BUILT-IN STABILIZERS"

You may gain the impression from the above remarks that fiscal policy helps stabilize the economy only so long as government officials are carefully watching trends, are successfully anticipating future developments, and are meeting promptly to take decisive actions. All such "discretionary fiscal policies," which involve the making of explicit decisions, are indeed important. But they are fortunately only part of the story.

The modern fiscal system has great inherent *automatic stabilizing* properties. All through the day and night, whether the President is in the White House or golfing on some distant vacation links, the fiscal system is helping to keep our economy stable. If in 1961 a recession should get under way while Congress was out of session, powerful automatic forces would go instantly into action to counteract it without the need for any committee meetings or for exercise of any human intelligence.

What are these mysterious stabilizers? They are primarily the following.

1. *Automatic changes in tax receipts.* We saw in Chapters 6 and 7 that our federal tax system depends progressively on personal and corporate incomes. What does this mean for stability? It means that as soon as income begins to fall off, and even before Congress makes any changes in tax rates, the tax receipts of the government also fall off. (Today, for each 10-billion-dollar drop in NNP, tax receipts drop by about $3\frac{1}{2}$ billions.)

Now reductions in tax receipts are just what the doctor prescribes in case of a dip in income. So our present tax system is a mighty and rapid built-in stabilizer. (Show that taxes stabilize against upward as well as downward income movements.)

A century ago, writers thought that *stability* of tax revenue was a good thing, and they would have looked with disapproval on the present-day tendency for tax receipts to rise and fall with national income. Today, most believe that the truth is just the reverse. To dampen down a boom, a budgetary surplus is needed. Now there are two ways to produce a surplus: by a reduction in government expenditure, yes; but also by an increase in tax receipts. Indeed, from the standpoint of free private enterprise, tax changes represent the more conservative policy. How lucky we are, therefore, that our present tax system to some degree has "automatic flexibility," with its collections tending to rise in inflationary times and to fall in times of depression. This is a powerful factor stabilizing the whole economy and moderating the business cycle.

2. *Unemployment compensation and other welfare transfers.* In the last 25 years we have built up an elaborate system of unemployment compensation. Soon after men are laid off, they begin to receive payments from the unemployment compensation funds. When they go back to work, the payments cease; the taxes to finance unemployment compensation greatly increase when employment is high. During boom years, therefore, the unemployment reserve funds grow and exert stabilizing pressure against too great spending; conversely, during years of slack employment, the reserve funds are used to pay out income to sustain consumption and moderate the decline.

Other welfare functions—such as relief payments outside the social security system—also show an anticyclical automatic behavior of a stabilizing type.

3. *Farm-aid programs.* The various parity programs to aid agriculture, which we shall discuss later in Part Three, act like built-in stabilizers. When dollar spending drops off and farm prices fall, the federal government pays out dollars to farmers and absorbs surpluses. When inflation brews and prices soar, the government warehouses put forth goods and absorb dollars—thus cushioning any movement.[1]

4. *Corporate savings and family savings.* Not all the credit goes to the government. Our private institutions also have built-in stabilizers. Thus, the custom of corporations' maintaining their dividends, even though their incomes change in the short run, does cause their retained savings to act like a shock absorber or built-in stabilizer.[2] And to the extent that families try to maintain previous living standards and are slow to adjust upward their living standard—to this extent, they too help stabilize. (To the extent they rush out to spend extra income on down payments, or hysterically cut down on consumption when economic clouds arise, they hinder stability.)

Still other stabilizers could be mentioned, but these are the main ones.[3]

▶ **LIMITATIONS OF AUTOMATIC STABILIZERS**

Before leaving the discussion of automatic stabilizers, we should stress two things. First, the built-in stabilizers are our first line of defense but are not by themselves sufficient to maintain full stability. And second, reliance on them in preference to reliance on discretionary programs raises some philosophical and ethical questions.

---

[1] By pushing up the prices of raw materials, parity formulas may also have an "escalating" or destabilizing effect; and to the extent that they simply limit supply at all times, they may merely redistribute rather than stabilize income.

[2] To the extent that corporate investment is itself linked to corporate saving, this stabilizing influence is negated.

[3] Some have advocated increasing the stabilizers by having Congress pass a law making tax *rates* vary automatically with changes in various aggregate price and income indexes. But Congress has not even been willing to vote discretionary power over rates to the President.

The automatic tendency for taxes to take away a fraction of each extra dollar of NNP means that the size of the "multiplier" is cut down. Each dollar swing in investment—whether caused by sunspots, inventions, or anything else—will now have its destabilizing effect on the system reduced but not wiped out completely. Instead of such disturbances' having their effects on NNP multiplied three or more times, there will now because of the automatic stabilizing effect of taxes be a multiplied effect of only 1.5 or 2 times.[1]

> In short, a built-in stabilizer acts to reduce *part* of any fluctuation in the economy, but it does not aim to wipe out 100 per cent of the disturbance. It leaves the rest of the disturbance as a task of fiscal and monetary discretionary action.

Philosophically, some reformers dislike the need to have human beings decide policy. They speak of a "government of laws and not of men." They would advocate setting up automatic rules and mechanisms that would go into action without ever depending on human decisions.

At the present time an automatic gyropilot can keep an airplane pretty stable while the pilot catches a nap. But when something unusual comes up the human pilot must still take over. No one yet has found a gadget with all the flexibility of man. Similarly in the social field: we have not yet arrived at a stage where any nation is likely to create for itself a set of constitutional procedures that will displace the need for discretionary policy formation.

▶ DISCRETIONARY FISCAL POLICY

The principal weapons of discretionary fiscal policy are (1) changing tax rates, and (2) changing public expenditure programs, whether of a "transfer" type or on goods and services.

When governments first began to do something active about depressions, they tended to initiate work on public investment projects for the unemployed. Often these were hastily devised; and in that they aimed primarily to create work for people, they often were rather inefficient. Examples: road building using as little machinery as possible to make the work stretch. Leaf raking during the depression by the WPA relief workers. Trumped-up public projects of little usefulness and lacking careful planning. The extreme case would be the mythical program in which men are hired to dig holes and then fill them up.

Now that governments have long recognized their need to take stabilizing action, the emphasis has shifted from public-works programs over to tax-rate changes. Back in 1932 people did not talk much about using tax reduction to

---

[1] Intermediate texts show that in the simple multiplier formula $1/(1 - MPC)$, we have to cut MPC down to .65 MPC now that .35 of each NNP dollar goes to taxes and only .65 to disposable income. What effect on the multiplier does this attenuation of MPC have? In the multiplier of $3.0 = 1/(1 - \frac{2}{3})$, it cuts the $\frac{2}{3}$ down to .433 and the final multiplier down to only 1.8!

cure unemployment—indeed, they then tried to raise tax rates! But you can be sure that in any future depression one of the first things done will be to legislate reductions in tax rates. Each cut in the personal income tax rate or in business taxes can result in billions of dollars of stimulus to disposable income and to spending.

Why this change in emphasis? In the first place, taxes now loom large in the modern economy in a way that didn't use to be true. With the government taking some 30 per cent of the national income in taxes, it could never find itself with no more taxes to reduce rates on in the struggle against depression.

In the second place, we no longer decide which fiscal weapon to use in an atmosphere of panic and emergency. "How shall we get some money out? What, what can we do in a hurry about this terrible situation?" Such remarks are today replaced by: "Isn't it nice that we didn't let a mild recession snowball into a grave emergency? And given the amount of unemployment that still plagues us, let's sit down and decide rationally whether the American people want to employ the resources still available to them on needed private consumption or on needed collective consumption. If the voters want more shoes, autos, and food, then we should reduce their taxes and let them spend the resulting extra Disposable Income on shoes, autos, and food. But if the voters feel that the available resources could in part be better used in giving us better intercontinental missiles and radar warning systems, better roads and schools, more sponsored basic research and conservation programs, then an expansion in G will be called for."

One thing is clear. Programs to reduce tax rates and programs to spend substantial sums do both take time to get formulated and put into effect. And it takes time for them to have their impact on the economy. Hence, few experts today advocate using such crash programs to wipe out each short-run fluctuation in the economy. By the time such programs are planned and put into effect, you may find yourself faced with an inflationary rather than deflationary situation.

Fortunately, we can rely on the built-in stabilizers and monetary policy to cushion the short-run fluctuations. And we can hope to have ready to go, on a reserve shelf, up-to-date blueprints of useful public programs which can quickly be put into action. (Many years ago when Herbert Hoover was Secretary of Commerce, and later when President, he lobbied successfully to have the government plan its public works—hoping to postpone them in inflationary times and accelerate them during depressed times. In 1931 Congress passed a law to set up such a shelf of public-works projects.)

There is also a new wrinkle in tax planning. Walter Heller, the University of Minnesota's fiscal expert, points out that Congress these days tends to legislate tax reduction for some date ahead. Then when that date arrives, taxes can be speedily cut—even if Congress is not in session. But if, when that date arrives, the situation should turn out to be inflationary and inconsistent with a tax cut, the President can summon Congress to postpone the tax cut. This way the delay in shaping basic tax changes to the condition of the economy seems to have been cut down.

Does this seem too fanciful a mechanism? Actually, things have been working out just that way over the last few years. Thus, in 1953 Congress held on to some taxes scheduled earlier to die. Why? Because brisk business activity called for holding on to such taxes. But in 1954, when we were in a mild recession, the expiring of certain taxes, which Congress had long before provided for, was permitted to take place and proved exactly what the doctor ordered.

All this proves that there is still ample scope for creative social innovation. Now that we have a withholding tax system, the economy responds much more quickly to legislated tax changes than it used to. It should be possible for the American political system to devise various ingenious arrangements for reducing the lag between recognition of the need to act and successful carrying out of the desired program.

▶ THE PROBLEM OF SURPLUS AND DEFICIT FINANCING

When an inflationary gap calls for contractionary fiscal policy, the principle of a balanced budget will almost certainly be violated by the implied expansion of taxes and reduction of expenditure. Similarly, a successful attempt to offset a deflationary gap may put the budget into a deficit.

If the business cycle were perfectly regular, most people would not worry too much as long as the boom-time budgetary surplus were always matched by the depression budgetary deficit. With such regularity, *the budget would be balanced over the business cycle* even though not balanced in every single year or month. There would be no secular trend upward in the public debt or downward.

But how can you be sure that the cycle will be so regular? What if America is in for what Harvard's Alvin Hansen used to call "secular stagnation"— which means a long period in which (1) slowing population increase, (2) passing of the frontier's free land, (3) high corporate saving, and (4) a bias toward capital-saving inventions will mean depressed investment schedules relative to saving schedules. Won't an active fiscal policy designed to wipe out such deflationary gaps then result in your running a deficit most of the time? And won't that mean a secular growth in the public debt?

Contrariwise, suppose population is popping, new inventions are zooming, and investment is generally excessive relative to full-employment saving? If this threatens to go on most of the time, won't active fiscal policy require a budgetary surplus most of the time? Hence, won't such a condition of "secular exhilaration" lead to a secular decline in the public debt?

It must now be apparent that one cannot discuss the important subject of fiscal policy without going into a thorough discussion of the issues raised by the public debt.

B THE PUBLIC DEBT AND MODERN FISCAL POLICY

As a result of World War II the public debt of the federal government is more than one-quarter of a trillion dollars! What are the real problems created by such a debt? Are there any false problems associated with it? What are the important noneconomic factors that must be reckoned with in any discussion of this vital political issue?

▶ THE PUBLIC DEBT AND ITS LIMITATIONS

In appraising the burdens involved in a public debt, we must carefully avoid the unscientific practice of making up our minds in advance that whatever is true of one small merchant's debt is also necessarily true of the government's debt. Prejudging the problem in this way comes perilously close to the logical fallacy of composition; and, instead of permitting us to isolate the true —all too real!—burdens of the public debt, might only confuse the issue.

External versus internal debt. A large *external* public debt, owed to people outside of the United States, would be a real burden and limitation upon the American economy. This is because as a nation we should be forced to ship valuable goods and services abroad to meet the interest charges on the external debt and possibly to amortize some of its principal. If 10 per cent of the national income had to go abroad in this way, the burden would be—if not an intolerable one—nevertheless a weighty one. The American people would have to work harder and longer, and they would have to do without.

There are also burdens involved in an internally held public debt like our present one, *but the burdens of an internal debt are qualitatively and quantitatively different from those of an external debt.*[1]

This is the first and most important lesson to be grasped, without which nobody can go far in understanding the economics of the public debt. The in-

---

[1] The following question is not germane to the present discussion but may call for a few words here. How does an external debt arise? It may have come from our having received goods from abroad during the war, and it is only to be expected that such goods be repaid. Or it may have arisen from the kind of foreign investment to be discussed in Part Five. If foreigners have given us capital goods to develop our resources, the resulting increase in our NNP will probably be more than enough to pay the interest and dividends on the external debt; so we are not the poorer for the whole transaction—but we are poorer than we should otherwise be if somehow the external debt could be conjured away, without at the same time conjuring away the higher productivity made possible by the original foreign investment. All this is later discussed in connection with international trade and development.

terest on an *internal* debt is paid by Americans to Americans; there is no *direct* loss of goods and services. When interest on the debt is paid out of taxation, there is no *direct* loss of disposable income; Paul receives what Peter loses, and sometimes—but only sometimes—Paul and Peter are one and the same person.

Borrowing and shifting economic burdens through time. Still another confusion between an external and internal debt is involved in the often-met statement: "When we borrow rather than tax in order to fight a war, then the true economic burden is really being shifted to the future generations who will have to pay interest and principal on the debt." As applied to an external debt, this shift of burden through time might be true. It is unmistakably false in reference to an internal debt. Why?

To fight a war now,[1] we must hurl present-day munitions at the enemy; not dollar bills, and not future goods and services. If we borrow munitions from some neutral country and pledge our children and grandchildren to repay them in goods and services, then it may truly be said that external borrowing permits a shift of economic burden between present and future generations.

But suppose there is no outside nation to lend us goods. Suppose civilian capital formation has already been cut down to the bone, but still our government needs more resources for the war effort. Suppose Congress is not willing to vote taxes large enough to permit the government to balance its swollen budget or stringent enough to reduce people's spending to where they will release resources for the war effort and stop bidding up prices. The government will then be running a deficit and will build up a huge debt.

Can it then be truthfully said that "internal borrowing shifts the war burden to future generations while taxing places it on the present generation"? A thousand times no! The present generation must still give up resources to produce the munitions hurled at the enemy. In the future, some of our grandchildren will be giving up goods and services to other grandchildren. That is the nub of the matter. The only way in which we can impose a direct burden on the future nation as a whole is by incurring an external debt or by passing along less capital equipment to our posterity.

This explains why the British are a great deal more worried about their small external debt than they are over their vastly greater internal debt; the former directly impoverishes the British Isles. Fortunately, the United States came out of the most costly war in all history with little impairment of capital equipment and external debt.

"We all owe it to ourselves." If an internal debt is simultaneously owed and owned by Americans, why do some people think that the wartime creation of 250 billion dollars of government bonds makes the public more wealthy and more ready to spend? If we draw up a consolidated balance sheet for the na-

---

[1] See Chapter 36 on economics of war for further discussion.

tion as a whole, we see that the (internal) debt represents a kind of fictitious financial wealth, which cancels out as a liability and asset.

Purely financial assets do, however, have important effects. Anybody owning government bonds includes them when drawing up his periodic balance sheet, along with his other assets. But he is a very rare man indeed if he also includes as a present liability the amount of *future* taxes which he may have to pay to finance government interest payments or debt retirement. He does not even have a way of estimating his share of these taxes. The result is that the internal debt, which as a liability should exactly cancel out itself as an asset, tends instead to be counted by people primarily as an asset. Given a nest egg of bonds which they can either sell or cash in, people *feel* richer and more secure and therefore they probably tend to have a higher propensity to consume out of current income.

Debt management and monetary policy. The existence of a large outstanding public debt may also have an influence on the interest rate and on its use to fight the business cycle. Some writers fear that channeling investment funds into the purchase of government bonds will raise the rate of interest to private borrowers. Alexander Hamilton, the spokesman of the conservative Federalist party, had just the opposite opinion. He felt that, rightly managed and in the right amounts, a public debt would be "a national blessing" because it would provide a secure gilt-edge asset that would give businessmen an income and enable them to trade for smaller profits.

As was shown in Chapter 16 on Central Banking, the federal reserve authorities have strong powers to affect rates of interest on government bonds. Therefore, any undue upward or downward pressure of the debt upon interest rates can be offset by open-market purchases and sale of government securities. But—and this is an ironic paradox—the existence of the vast public debt, while it enhances their power, at the same time could serve to inhibit the exercise of effective monetary and interest policy by the Federal Reserve Banks.

It will be recalled that monetary policy is supposed to act so as to raise interest rates and tighten credit conditions when over-all demand threatens to be inflationary. But with large amounts of bonds in the hands of banks and the public, the governmental authorities have a strong incentive toward keeping up the selling price of government bonds—in order to keep interest charges on the debt low and prevent financial embarrassment of financial institutions holding government bonds. If government bonds cannot fall in price, then interest rates cannot be tightened; people and banks are always able to convert their bonds into the cash they need for consumption or investment spending. A large debt, therefore, did in the 1945–1951 period discourage the use of monetary policy to control the business cycle and served to throw an even larger burden on fiscal policy.

Since 1951 this has pretty much ceased to be a problem. As we saw in the last chapter, the accord between the Treasury and Federal Reserve has restored to the latter its freedom to pursue countercyclical monetary policy. Many experts, such as Dr. Robert V. Roosa, vice-president of the New York Federal Reserve Bank, believe that the existence of a broad market in government securities makes possible extensive open-market operations of a stabilizing type and tends to enhance the effectiveness of monetary policy.

The true indirect burden of interest charges. When taxes are used to pay interest charges on the public debt, then money goes from one pocket into another. No direct burden like that of an external debt is involved. But it would be wrong to jump to the hasty conclusion that no burden of any kind is involved. There is an indirect burden that may be very important.

In the first place, although money merely goes out from one pocket and into another, the trousers in question may be worn by different people. The present national debt is very widely held, so that almost every individual has some share, either through outright holdings or through bank deposits and insurance policies. Nevertheless, the statistical evidence suggests that the people who receive bond interest are *on the average* not in the lower income brackets. Thus interest on the public debt constitutes a regressive (Robin Hood in reverse) element in our fiscal system. "Soaking the poor to pay the rich" tends to reduce purchasing power and runs counter to some modern notions of equity. Nevertheless, if it is an evil, it is a necessary evil if past commitments with respect to the public debt are to be scrupulously honored, as they must be.

However, with our present public debt this transfer from one income class to another is probably not its single most important indirect burden. More important, *transferring tax money from Peter to pay bond interest to the same Peter will involve a heavy indirect burden on the economy!* This is because taxation always has some distorting effects on people's economic behavior. Centuries ago houses were taxed on their windows, with the result that people built dark houses, even though the government still collected the same revenue by simply raising rates on the few remaining windows. Similarly, taxing people's income may cause them to work too little, or in many cases too hard in their attempt to maintain the same standard of living. Perhaps of even more importance, high corporation or personal income taxes will often have adverse effects upon people's willingness to venture their capital on risky enterprises. The result: less technological progress and fewer jobs.

At this point, you may protest that this is all nonsense and that there is no net tax burden involved in an internal transfer, since it is being assumed that we all own bonds in proportion to our share of taxes, and in effect are only paying to ourselves. This reasoning is quite mistaken. *Taxes on each individual matched by exactly equal interest payments to him do not cancel out!*

This is so because what is true of all is not true for each individual. Suppose for simplicity that all Americans earn $4,500 a year in wages. Suppose each owns $25,000 in government bonds, which at 2 per cent bring in a yield of $500. To pay this interest the government, let us say, levies 10 per cent (in addition to existing taxes) on total income of $5,000 ($4,500 + $500). Previously it just paid me to work an extra bit of overtime to earn the last dollar of my $4,500. But now the government takes another dime out of the last dollar. I (and every American like me) may now feel it does not pay to work such long hours. By cutting out, say, one-third of my working hours, my income is now only $3,500. The tax has distorted national effort and production.

The unconvinced reader will say at this point: "What if everybody else cuts his hours as you do? Then the extra tax rate will have to be raised from 10 per cent to almost 15 per cent if the total of bond interest is to be covered." True enough. But this only proves the point. The final situation may end up with even a greater distortion of effort and risk taking, and with an even higher tax rate. This all happens because, although the nation cannot avoid raising taxes equal to the interest payment, each individual knows that he can affect his taxes by varying his effort, with his own small interest payments going on anyway, regardless of what he as a single small person does.

The above example is oversimplified and undoubtedly exaggerates the harmful effects of internal transfers. Also, different kinds of taxes differ in their harmful effects; but in any case with our taxes already so high, any further burden due to interest on the public debt is just that much more harmful.

Also we have neglected the beneficial effects of interest payments to banks, universities, widows, and other *rentiers*. If there were no public debt or if interest rates were to fall substantially, then (1) charitable institutions would have to be supported by public and private current contributions more than by interest on endowments, (2) social security and annuities would have to take the place of *rentier* interest, and (3) service charges by banks would have to be increasingly relied upon instead of government bond interest.

▶ EFFECTS ON PRIVATE INVESTMENT

Never forget that there is a tremendous amount of emotion involved in people's attitudes toward the debt, and this we must not dismiss lightly. Like sex or religion, the public debt is a subject we all love to discuss. Many people used to predict the end of the world when the debt reached one-hundredth, one-tenth, and one-fifth of its present level; each year when the dire disaster had not appeared, they renewed their predictions for subsequent years.

Such attitudes may affect private investment. For example, some would argue that government expenditure or deficits may not really add much to purchasing power during depressions. If private investment could be assumed constant, then public expenditures would admittedly have favorable primary effects upon income and employment; more than that, the consumption re-spending of income would give rise to the familiar multiplier chain of favorable secondary effects. But what if private investment is frightened off by government expenditure or by the deficit?

This is certainly a possibility. Businessmen may say, "With that man in the White House spending recklessly, we're going to abandon even the little private investment we had planned." Or a private utility company may curtail investment because it fears the threat of public dam projects. Or when the government spending gives people money to buy in retail stores, the effect in time of deep depression may simply be to permit the merchant to work down his inventory of surplus merchandise; if he does not reorder production goods, the public expenditure has been just neutralized by induced private *disinvestment* (in inventory), and the multiplier chain is stopped dead in its tracks.

On the other hand, there may be favorable effects on private investment that are just the opposite to these unfavorable repercussions of government finance. When current production is at a low ebb and there is excess plant capacity, no prudent businessman feels like undertaking new capital formation. If the government is able to boost retail sales and the production of consumption goods, then businessmen will have the financial ability and at least some motive to renew equipment and build new plants.[1]

Where there are two such opposing tendencies—favorable and unfavorable effects upon private investment—facts rather than arguments must be our guide. Although economics does not permit us to make controlled experiments to settle the point conclusively, the bulk of the statistical data seems to suggest that private investment tends to move on the whole sympathetically with the level of national income. The cash register calls the tune, and in a free-enterprise society, rightly so.

▶ THE QUANTITATIVE PROBLEM OF THE DEBT

We may summarize the above section on the economics of a public debt thus:

1. Our internal debt does not involve the direct burden of an external debt or the same possibility of shifting real burdens between generations.

2. Although we all owe it to ourselves, people tend to treat bonds as a safe liquid asset which increases their willingness to consume out of current income. The huge debt increases leverage but may hamper an anticyclical interest rate policy if the authorities are loath to see bond prices fluctuate.

3. An internal debt involves an important *indirect* burden whenever new taxes must be raised to meet interest payments. This is true even if the typical person was taxed by as much as his own interest payments, but it is further aggravated by the fact that interest receivers are more wealthy than average taxpayers.

To assess the importance of the public debt, we must turn to the facts. Do

[1] An example of this was provided by the discussion in Chapter 13 of the acceleration principle relating induced investment to the upward change in sales.

interest payments on it swallow up most of the national income? How does the total of all interest payments, public and private, compare with past years and with the experience of other countries? What about foreseeable future trends?

To see how the present quarter of a trillion dollar debt compares with the past and some other countries, Table 1 has been drawn up. It shows for selected times and places the size of national debts and their relationship to size of national income and interest payments. Thus, in 1957 our national debt of about 275 billion dollars represented much less than one year of national income, and its interest payments represented only about 2 per cent of net national product. Note that England in 1818, 1923, and 1946 had an internal debt estimated at more than twice national income, and her interest on the debt as a percentage of national income far exceeded anything that we need look forward to. Yet, the century before World War I was England's greatest century —greatest in power and material progress. Nevertheless, as the table shows, her national debt was not substantially reduced; but with the steady growth of her national income, the debt and its interest charges shrank to almost nothing in relative quantitative magnitude.

In view of these statistics and careful qualitative analysis, the reader must form his own judgment as to whether the national debt constitutes as yet a problem of the first magnitude in comparison with the problems of national defense, the nuclear bomb, unemployment, or inflation. Whether productivity will continue to rise in the future, whether labor and management can learn to bargain collectively without strikes and inflation—to many observers these seem more important than the debt itself.

Growth in the economy. In dispassionately analyzing the growth of the debt, one error we must avoid: *we must not forget that the real national product of the United States is an ever-growing thing.*

Our population grows lustily. As to productivity, there is no indication that man-hour efficiency and new techniques have begun to slacken off. Upon this, stagnationists and exhilarationists both agree. What seemed like a big debt in 1790 would be nothing today. What our children will come to regard as a big debt, our great-grandchildren may consider relatively unimportant.[1]

This explains why England and France, in the crucially formative years of the capitalistic system and Industrial Revolution, were able to go on—not only decade after decade but almost century after century—with their budgets in balance less than half the time. This same factor of growth explains why in the United States, where real national production doubles every generation

---

[1] The decade since the war ended provides a dramatic example: in 1945, the public debt was 1.5 times national income; but income grew so much as to halve this ratio in a dozen years. This despite the cold war!

Growing debt holds little peril for a dynamically growing economy:

Table 1. National debt and interest charges relative to national income. The 40-billion-dollar debt that so worried people in the 1930's looks small against the subsequent rise in our income. (Source: *Economic Almanac*, U.S. Department of Commerce; U.S. Treasury; United Nations; *Colwyn Report*; Statistical Abstract of United Kingdom. Data rounded off.)

Year	National debt	Interest charges on national debt	National income	Size of debt in years of national income $(5) =$ $(2) \div (4)$	Interest charges as a per cent of national income $(6) \div 100 =$ $(3) \div (4)$
(1)	(2)	(3)	(4)	(5)	(6)
United States:	(Billions)	(Billions)	(Billions)		
1957	$275	$7.7	$361	0.8	2.1
1939	47.6	1.19	72.5	0.7	1.6
1932	20.8	0.72	41.7	0.5	1.7
1929	16.3	0.73	87.4	0.2	0.8
1920	23.5	1.06	68.4	0.3	1.5
1916	1.2	0.02	38.7	0.0+	0.0+
1868	2.6	0.13	6.8	0.4	2.0
Britain:	(Millions)	(Millions)	(Millions)		
1956	£27,039	£726	£16,331	1.7	4.4
1946	23,774	472	8,411	2.8	5.6
1923	7,700	271	3,800	2.0+	7.1
1913	656	17	2,300	0.3	0.7
1818	840	31	400	2.1	7.7

or so, the public debt might increase by 250 billion dollars in 25 years without its relative percentage burden growing.

This would give the wildest believer in government spending an average deficit of some 10 billion dollars per year before he would have to turn to such even more unorthodox financial expedients as printing money or selling interest-free bonds to the Federal Reserve Banks. Moreover, before turning to such expedients, he would still have open to him the now familiar process of keeping down interest rates on government bonds by a conventional easy-money banking policy. This raises a sobering question.

Could a nation fanatically addicted to deficit spending pursue such a policy for the rest of our lives and beyond? Study of the mechanics of banking and income determination suggests that the barrier to this would not be financial. The barrier would have to be political. And the effects of such a policy depend crucially upon whether it impinges on an economy that is already inflationary or deflationary. And if the electorate and Congress learn the half-truth that expenditure is expansionary while forgetting the fact that unpleasant taxes may be necessary to curb undue expansion, then in the present author's opinion, the long-term outlook may be in the direction of rising prices.

So far this chapter has analyzed and described the principal features of fiscal policy and the public debt. Against this background, the rest of the chapter can stress some important policy implications.

▶ USEFUL VERSUS WASTEFUL FISCAL POLICY

Those who believe in an active fiscal policy set up a perfectionist goal: the maintenance of total effective demand at a level high enough to prevent the wastes of mass unemployment, and low enough so as not to lead to a level of inflationary total spending in excess of total producible goods.

Or, to put the matter in technical terms, they argue that fiscal policy should shape taxes and expenditure, quantitatively and qualitatively, so that the economy's saving and investment schedules will intersect neither to the right nor to the left of the region of high (or full) employment. Many equally competent economists insist that there are other goals of equal or greater importance and that great harm can result from too avid a search for perfection.

It cannot be repeated too often that building pyramids or digging holes and filling them up is indefensible. True, in comparison with a policy of doing nothing about a deep depression, such boondoggling might seem in some ways preferable, because of the favorable respending effects of those who receive government expenditures. But such a policy is surely only the lesser of two evils. Properly planned, useful public works have just as favorable secondary effects, and in addition they fill important human needs.

Nor is it necessary or always desirable to fight a depression with useful public works. If the American people feel that private consumption should have a higher social priority, tax reduction or transfer expenditure should be relied upon. The extra income available from the conquest of unemployment will then be going for privately produced and purchased goods.

Should government expenditure or should tax reduction be pushed if private investment and consumption are lacking? The answer cannot be given simply in terms of financial orthodoxy—the size of the deficit—but rather in terms of what the American people consider to be the pressing national priorities.

If 10 billion dollars of resources were to be released from investment or defense or foreign aid, the American people would wish to use part of this for extra food, extra clothes, extra leisure, etc. This suggests tax reduction (or increase in transfer expenditure). But the American people may also want to spend part of such newly available income on education, on public health, on urban redevelopment projects, on roads, etc. This suggests some use of government expenditure in depressed times.

The one way that the American people should not want to spend their income is upon involuntary unemployment. There should never be any need to indulge in wasteful or inefficient government expenditure; the government should always get something useful for the resources it uses up. If collective consumption projects have a lower social priority than private consumption, then the proper fiscal policy is one of tax reduction and transfer expenditure.

▶ A FUNDAMENTAL DIFFICULTY WITH FULL EMPLOYMENT

One last and important set of qualifications must be made before completing the discussion of fiscal policy and, indeed, of the whole problem of national income determination. In a rough way, we know what is meant by full or high employment; but only in a rough way.

Of course, full employment doesn't mean that every man, woman, and child should be out at work every hour of a 24-hour day. It doesn't mean I can hold out for a job as pitcher with the New York Yankees, or as a $100-a-day carpenter. But it does mean that reasonably efficient workers, willing to work at the currently prevailing ("fair") wage rates, need not find themselves unemployable as a result of too little general demand. Women who want to can work in the home, youths can go to school if they prefer to, and the aged or unwell can retire from the labor force; but none of this because of job shortages.

The real difficulty with full employment lies not in its rough definition but in the fact that *wages and prices may begin to soar while there is still considerable unemployment and excess capacity.* An increase in private investment spending or in government spending may be prevented from effectuating full employment, its favorable dollar effects being wasted by a paper rise in prices.

If businessmen and trade-unions react perversely to an increased demand, fiscal policy cannot be relied upon to achieve and maintain full employment. Some pessimists have argued that there is nothing to do but hope for a large enough "army of the unemployed" to keep laborers from making unreasonable wage demands; thus, a reserve army of 10 million jobless hanging around factory gates might keep wages from rising and labor from becoming obstreperous. Still others might see no escape from the dilemma other than to have some degree of inflation most of the time.

Still other writers would then advocate the use of direct price and wage controls to keep prices from spiraling upward at high employment levels. In the present writer's personal opinion, efficient peacetime, nonemergency, over-all price controls would involve a degree of planning incompatible with past, and probably present, philosophical beliefs of the great majority of the American people. For, as we shall see in Parts Three and Four, the problem of setting appropriate social prices is a tremendously complex one—so complex that the whole nature of our economic system would have to be different, once we had decided not to rely upon market forces.

It is hardly too much to say that this price-wage question is the biggest unsolved economic problem of our time: *Can business, labor, and agriculture learn to act in such a way as to avoid inflation whenever private or public spending brings us anywhere near to full employment?* A wage and price policy for full employment—that is America's greatest problem and challenge.

▶ THE EMPLOYMENT ACT OF 1946

Obviously no one has a crystal ball to read the future, particularly the distant future. The case for and against secular stagnation cannot be definitely assessed. But fortunately—and this requires great emphasis—it is not necessary for Congress or the experts to be able to see a decade or more into the future in order to pursue correct economic policies currently.

In the momentous Employment Act of 1946, both political parties in Congress affirmed the responsibility of the government, and of private enterprise, to fight mass unemployment and inflation. This law provided for a Council of Economic Advisers which each year is to keep Congress and the President informed as to the state of "employment, production, and purchasing power";[1] also a Joint Congressional Committee is set up whose duty it is to study and evaluate the recommendations contained in the President's Annual Economic Report. This chapter's Eisenhower quotation affirms that full-employment policy is bipartisan in American politics.

▶ EPILOGUE: A GRAND NEOCLASSICAL SYNTHESIS

Here at the end of Part Two's analysis of aggregative economics or macroeconomics, it is fitting to formulate an important tenet of modern economics.

▶ *Neoclassical synthesis: by means of appropriately reinforcing monetary and fiscal policies, our mixed-enterprise system can avoid the excesses of boom and slump and can look forward to healthy progressive growth. This fundamental being understood, the paradoxes that robbed the older classical principles dealing with small-scale "microeconomics" of much of their relevance and validity—these paradoxes will now lose their sting. In short, mastery of the modern analysis of income determination genuinely validates the basic classical pricing principles; and— perhaps for the first time—the economist is justified in saying that the broad cleavage between microeconomics and macroeconomics has been closed.[2]*

---

[1] The original Act said nothing of "price stability" and there has been a recent movement to add this in as an explicit goal.

[2] Naturally, one can point out many needed qualifications to this optimistic formulation. But events of recent decades and the most painstaking economic researches in universities, industry, and government justify our concentrating on the doughnut—not on its hole.

SUMMARY

▶ **A. SHORT- AND LONG-RUN FISCAL POLICY**

1. When private investment and consumption spending are producing an inflationary (or deflationary) gap which Federal Reserve monetary policy has not fully offset, the task of fiscal policy is to offset the remaining gap in the attempt to preserve price stability and high employment.

2. The principal fiscal weapons are taxation and expenditure, with emphasis turning more and more these days to stabilizing effects of tax-rate changes. This is in contrast with earlier emphasis on emergency public works.

3. The modern economy is blessed with important "built-in stabilizers." Requiring no discretionary action, tax receipts change automatically when income changes—thereby reducing the size of the multiplier and serving to wipe out part of any disturbance. (The same effect is realized by unemployment compensation and other welfare transfers that automatically grow as income declines; and by farm-aid programs and by the propensity of corporations to pay out in dividends only part of their current earnings.)

Because the automatic stabilizers never fully offset the instabilities of an economy, scope is left for discretionary programs. A "government by laws not by men," in which fiscal and monetary policies work automatically untouched by any human intelligence, is not now anywhere in sight. But social innovations to reduce lags in diagnosis and therapy hold forth promise.

4. When men began to drop the notion that the government's budget had to be balanced in every year or month, they first thought that it would be in balance over the business cycle—with the boom-time surpluses just matching the depression deficits. It is today realized that only by coincidence would the number of years of prosperity just balance in their intensity the number of years of depression.

If, as some believe, we are in for "secular stagnation" with private saving and investment schedules tending much of the time to produce deflationary gaps, fiscal policy will probably succeed in maintaining inflationless high employment only by having a secular increase in the public debt. If, as others believe, we are in for "secular exhilaration" with demand so brisk as to lead much of the time to inflationary gaps, then active fiscal policy will probably mean a bias toward surplus financing and a secular downward trend in the public debt. Perhaps the majority of economists feel there is no need to try to predict what the far future has in store, being prepared to advocate programs that the developing situation shows to be called for.

▶ **B. DEBT AND MODERN FISCAL POLICY**

5. The reader should understand the economic effects of an internal debt: (*a*) the difference between the direct burden of an external and an internal debt, and the ability of a country to shift burdens through time in the two cases; (b) the effect of the public debt on people's financial wealth and consumption habits; (c) the difficulties created by the debt for a countercyclical interest rate policy because of the short-sighted desire of government authorities to stabilize bond prices; (d) the important indirect burden of collecting taxes to pay interest on a debt, even if we all owe it to ourselves.

It is important, also, to know roughly what the size of the postwar federal debt is in relation to national income and interest charges, in order to assess the present, both in terms of the past and in terms of the future. The growth of the debt must be appraised in terms of the growth of the economy as a whole.

6. A full (or high) employment program has as its goal a level of total spending that is neither too little nor too great—so that the saving and investment schedules intersect in the region of full employment. The Employment Act of 1946 represents an important innovation in our republic, affirming responsibility of the government for employment opportunities and setting up executive and congressional machinery for policy action.

7. To the extent that reinforcing monetary and fiscal policies is efficacious in stabilizing the worst excesses of boom and slump, we need no longer fear the clash between private and social virtues or the various paradoxes of a depressed economy. Mastery of the modern tools of income determination at the macroeconomics level will turn out to validate the basic truths in the classical doctrines of pricing and scarcity at the microeconomic level. This is the optimistic "neoclassical synthesis."

QUESTIONS FOR DISCUSSION

1. "No nation can avoid having a fiscal policy. With the government such an important part of the present-day economy, it is almost impossible even to define a 'neutral fiscal policy.' It is even harder to give rational reasons for preferring such a policy to an active fiscal program aimed at preventing inflation and deflation." Examine this statement critically bringing in some noneconomic considerations.

2. List various "built-in stabilizers." Show how they work.

3. What phase of the business cycle are you now in? What expenditure policies would seem appropriate? What taxation policies? Qualitatively, how would you vary the relative importance of different kinds of taxes (such as income-tax rates and exemptions, sales taxes, or property taxes) to compensate for unemployment or inflation?

4. From the early 1870's to the middle 1890's, depressions were deep and prolonged, booms were short-lived and relatively anemic, the price level was

declining. What long-run fiscal policy should have been followed in that quarter of a century? Would your answer be the same for the following 20 years leading up to World War I, a period of rising prices and comparative prosperity?

5. Comment on the 1840 views of the historian Macaulay:

"At every stage in the growth of that debt the nation has set up the same cry of anguish and despair. At every stage in the growth of that debt it has been seriously asserted by wise men that bankruptcy and ruin were at hand. Yet still the debt went on growing; and still bankruptcy and ruin were as remote as ever. . . .

"The prophets of evil were under a double delusion. They erroneously imagined that there was an exact analogy between the case of an individual who is in debt to another individual and the case of a society which is in debt to a part of itself. . . . They made no allowance for the effect produced by the incessant progress of every experimental science, and by the incessant efforts of every man to get on in life. They saw that the debt grew; and they forgot that other things grew as well. . . ."

6. Professor A. P. Lerner has set down the following (abbreviated) principles of "Functional Finance." Criticize:

"There are effective instruments in the hands of the government for maintaining full employment and preventing inflation, but their use is hindered by strong prejudices. The instruments are not available until it is recognized the size of the national debt is relatively unimportant, the interest on the debt is not a burden on the nation, the nation cannot be made "bankrupt" by internally held debt. Every debit has a corresponding credit. Only external debt is like individual debt and impoverishes the nation. The purpose of taxation is never to raise money but to leave less in the hands of the taxpayer. . . . There is no room for the *principle* of balancing the budget. . . ."

7. The Council of Economic Advisers to the President, in its first report under the Employment Act of 1946, questions that "we can always create full employment by pumping enough purchasing power into the system," and the doctrine that we have only to "turn the faucet off and cause a contraction." According to the Council report, ". . . we cannot assume that deficiency of demand in one particular area or of one particular character can be made up just by adding purchasing power in general, for instance through tax relief. . . . If labor is pricing itself out of jobs or manufacturers and farmers are pricing themselves out of a market, or capital is pricing itself out of investment, the basic remedy is the correction of these specific situations, not the injection of some aggregate purchasing power in a dose measured in size to offset an estimated future total of unemployment."

With how much of this would you agree? Why?

8. Formulate, and evaluate, the "neoclassical synthesis."

9. Early in 1958 when America seemed to be going into a recession, President Eisenhower told his news conference that during depressed times running a budgetary deficit is a good thing because then the economy "needs a needle, not a checkrein." What issues does this raise in your mind?

10. Review your understanding of the following concepts:

inflationary and deflationary gap

tax receipts and tax rates

government expenditure on goods and transfers

built-in stabilizers and the reduced multiplier

discretionary policy problems

secular stagnation, exhilaration, and trends in the debt

internal versus external debt

true indirect internal-debt burdens

debt/income ratios here and abroad, today, yesterday, and tomorrow

Employment Act of 1946

neoclassical synthesis

part

THE COMPOSITION
AND PRICING OF
NATIONAL INCOME

3

19 DETERMINATION OF PRICE BY SUPPLY AND DEMAND

> The end is easily foretold,
> When every blessed thing you
>   hold
> Is made of silver, or of gold,
>   You long for simple pewter.
>
> When you have nothing else to
>   wear
> But cloth of gold and satins rare,
> For cloth of gold you cease to
>   care
>   Up goes the price of shoddy.
>
> GILBERT AND SULLIVAN, *The Gondoliers*

Part One of this book gave a description of the modern economic system and described the nature of national income.

Part Two gave the modern theory of income determination: it showed why and how incomes fluctuate; it showed how money and banking fit in with income analysis; and, most significantly, it showed how fiscal and monetary policy can keep the aggregate system working tolerably well.

▶ **PREVIEW**

Now Parts Three and Four will deal with the following important questions: What determines prices of goods? What determines the breakdown of the national income aggregates into various kinds of goods and services? This analysis of Part Three is what used to be called "Value and Price" in the older texts.

It will be followed in Part Four by the closely related analysis of what determines the prices of factors of production. Why are wages growing? Why does the share of land rent in the economy move in this way or that? What determines interest? Why have semiskilled wages been rising relative to white-collar wages? These constitute Part Four's discussion of "Distribution of Income" and we'll see that the tools of supply and demand of this chapter have a vital role to play in its explanation. (As a matter of fact, the supply and demand tools are indispensable if you want to explain the international trade problems of Part Five, or the problems of Automation, Atomic Energy, War, and Development in Part Six.)

▶ MICROECONOMICS VERSUS MACROECONOMICS?

Sometimes this analysis of market pricing is called "microeconomics." That's to distinguish it from "macroeconomics," which deals with the big picture—with the macro aggregates of income, employment, and price levels. But don't think that microeconomics is dealing with unimportant details. After all, the big picture is made up of its parts. Mere billions of dollars would be meaningless if they didn't correspond to the thousand-and-one useful goods and services that people really need and want. And who would be impressed by a vast national income if its distribution among human beings was a matter of caprice and pointless inequality?

No, there is not really any opposition between micro- and macroeconomics. Both are absolutely vital. And you are only half-educated if you understand the one while being ignorant of the other. We can't even say which comes first: some books begin with the one; some begin with the other. And even those which begin with macroeconomics—like this one—surveys show are used by about 40 per cent of the teachers to teach market pricing prior to teaching national income determination.

Twenty-five years ago our society had such poor mastery over its macroeconomics as to make people naturally give less emphasis to microeconomics. With millions starving because of a slump, who could get excited about whether mutton or pork were in a proper relative-price configuration. Or who thought much about white-collar wage trends relative to semiskilled wages, when the unemployed tramped the street in shirts so faded you couldn't even tell their color.

Today we hope all that is changed. Man has gained considerable mastery over his macroeconomic problems, and hence it is natural for the classical problems of microeconomics to move back to the forefront of his interest and attention.

▶ WHAT, HOW, AND FOR WHOM

Recall our discussions in Chapters 2 and 3 of the three basic problems every economy must face. (1) *What* shall be produced of the great variety of possible goods and services, and in precisely what quantities? (2) *How* shall society combine its different productive factors—land, labor, etc.—to produce each good: shall we use this technique or that, growing wheat in a labor-intensive way or using much land per unit of labor? (3) *For Whom* shall goods be produced, which is the problem of how the national product is to be distributed among the different members of the populace with their different skills and ownerships of land and capital goods?

Chapter 2 showed that a variety of systems could be thought of to solve these three problems. What, How, and For Whom might be determined by custom or by instinct. Or by centralized, collective fiats. But Chapter 3 indicated that the modern mixed economy relies primarily on none of these to solve its basic problems. Instead it relies on a system of markets and prices.

So you remember how we spoke of the consumer as being king. Or rather, with every man a king, of each man as a voter who uses his money like votes to get the things done that he wants done. Now our task is to see just how this spending of money votes takes place.

► THE MARKET MECHANISM

Let's take an example. You wake up this morning with an urge for a new pair of shoes. You wouldn't think of saying: "I'll go down to the city hall and vote for the mayor who will give me a new pair of shoes. Of course, I mean a new pair of size 9, soft-leather, dark-brown shoes."

Or, to take an actual case from history, suppose men begin to get prosperous enough to afford meat every day rather than having to fill up on potatoes. How does their desire to substitute meat for potatoes get translated into action? What politician do they tell? What orders does he give to farmers to move from Maine to Montana? How much extra pay does he decide will be needed to bribe landlords to take land from potato production to cattle grazing? And how does he make sure that people get what they want of pork and lamb as well as of beef? And who is to get the choice cuts of the beef?

But, why belabor the obvious. You know very well it never worked itself out that way at all. What happened was this. Consumers began to stop buying potatoes. They began to buy meat. That raised the price of meat and cut the price of potatoes. That gave losses to the potato growers and gains to the ranchers. Ranch labor too found it could hold out for higher wages, and many a potato digger quit his job for a better paying job elsewhere. In time, the higher meat prices brought out larger productions of beef, pork, and lamb. And the different parts of the cow—its horn, hide, liver, kidneys, choice tenderloin, and tough ribs—got auctioned off among the populace for what each part would bring.

You don't believe the last sentence? You perhaps think that some important businessman or government official sets the relative prices of the different cuts of meat? Well, look then at what happened when science discovered that liver was good for anemia. Kidneys, for reasons that happen to be obscure to me, previously used to sell for much more than liver. In fact, according to the records you could then hardly give liver away. Now go to any butcher shop. Price liver and, if you can find any, price kidneys. A veritable revolution has taken place!

Well, similar revolutions are taking place in the economic market place all the time. As people's desires and needs change, as engineering methods change, as supplies of natural resources and other productive factors change, there is registered in the market place changes in the prices and the quantities sold of goods and of productive factors.

The purpose of this chapter is to show how supply and demand work themselves out in the competitive market for one such good. We will define a demand curve. And we'll define a supply curve. And we'll see how the market price reaches its competitive equilibrium where these two curves intersect— where the forces of demand and supply are just in balance.

To be sure, not all markets are today competitive. We'll see in later chapters that elements of monopoly power or of market imperfection may enter in. And these imperfections will require us to modify the competitive model. After we've learned how to handle such cases, we'll recognize that the world is a blend of competition and imperfections—which means that the competitive analysis, properly qualified, is still an indispensable tool for the understanding of modern reality.

▶ **THE DEMAND SCHEDULE**

Let's start with demand. Everyone has observed: the higher the price charged for an article, the less will be the quantity of it bought. And other things being equal, the lower is its market price the more units will people buy.

▶ Thus there exists at any one time a definite relation between the market price of a good (such as wheat) and the quantity demanded of that good. This relationship between price and quantity bought is called the "demand schedule" or "demand curve."

A demand schedule relates quantity demanded and price:

	Price per bu. P (1)	Quantity demanded, million bu. per month Q (2)	Total revenue, millions per month $R = P \times Q$ (3) = (1) × (2)
A	$5	9	$45
B	4	10	—
C	3	12	—
D	2	15	—
E	1	20	$20

Table 1. Demand schedule for wheat. At each market price, there will at any time be a definite quantity of wheat demanded. At lower prices, quantity demanded will go up as people substitute this food for other goods and feel they can afford to gratify their less important wants for this good.

A downward-sloping curve portrays demand:

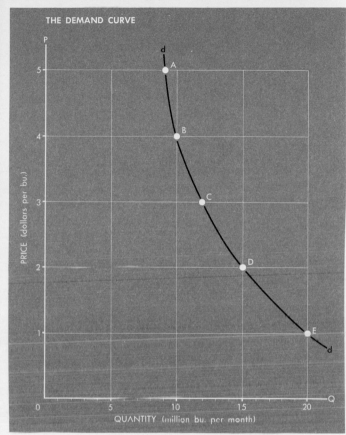

THE DEMAND CURVE

PRICE (dollars per bu.)

QUANTITY (million bu. per month)

Fig. 1. Prices are measured on the vertical axis and quantities demanded on the horizontal axis. Each pair of Q,P numbers from Table 1 is plotted here as a point, and a smooth curve passed through the points gives us the demand curve. The fact that dd goes downward and to the right portrays the very important "law of downward-sloping demand."

The preceding hypothetical table gives an example of a demand schedule. At any price, such as $5 per bushel, there is a definite quantity of wheat that will be bought by all the consumers in the market—in this case 9 (million) bushels per month. At a lower price, such as $4, the quantity bought is even greater, being 10 (million) units. From Table 1 we can determine the *quantity bought at any price,* by comparing Column (2) with Column (1).

The total number of dollars of revenue received for the sale of wheat is equal to the number of bushels sold times the price per bushel. Thus if the price is $5 and the quantity sold 9 (million) bushels, then the total revenue received from the sale of wheat is 45 million dollars. You can easily fill in the missing blanks in the total revenue column (3) of Table 1.

▶ **THE DEMAND CURVE**

The same numerical data of Table 1 can be given a more graphic interpretation. On the vertical scale in Fig. 1 we represent the various prices of wheat, measured in dollars per bushel. On the horizontal scale, we measure the quantity of wheat (in terms of bushels) that will be bought per month.

Just as a city corner is located as soon as you know its street and avenue, so is a ship's position located as soon as you know its latitude and longitude. Similarly, to plot a point on this diagram, we must have two coordinate numbers: a price and a quantity. For our first point *A*, corresponding to $5 and 9 million bushels, we move upward 5 units and then over to the right 9 units. A circle marks the spot *A*. To get the next circle, at *B*, we go up only 4 units and over to the right 10 units. The last circle is shown by *E*. Through the circles we draw a smooth curve, marked *dd*.

This picturization of the demand schedule is called the "demand curve." Note how quantity and price are inversely related. The curve slopes downward, going from northwest to southeast. This may be given a name: the *law of downward-sloping demand*. This law is true of almost all commodities: wheat, electric razors, cotton, ethyl gasoline, and corn flakes.

▶ *The law of downward-sloping demand: when the price of a good is raised, less of it will be demanded.* What is the same thing: *If a greater quantity of a good is thrown on the market, it can be sold only at a lower price.*

Why does my quantity demanded tend to fall as price rises? For two main reasons. When the price of a good rises, I naturally try to *substitute* other goods for it. (Tea for coffee, for example.) Also when a price goes up, I find myself really poorer than I was: and I will naturally cut down on my consumption of most normal goods when I feel poorer.

Here are examples illustrating cases where I buy more of a good as it becomes more plentiful and its price drops. When water is very dear, I demand only enough of it to drink. Then when its price drops, I buy some to wash with. At still lower prices, I bring in still other uses; finally when it is really very cheap, I water flowers and use it lavishly for any possible purpose. (Note, too, that someone poorer than I will probably begin to use water to wash his car only at a lower price than that at which I buy water for that purpose. Since market demand is the sum of all different people's demands, what does this mean? It means that even after my demand stops expanding much with price decreases, the total bought in the market may still be expanding as new uses for new people come into effect.)

▶ ELASTIC AND INELASTIC DEMANDS

Different goods vary in the *degree* to which their use expands in response to a reduction in price. In fact, wheat was not a strong example to illustrate our law of downward-sloping demand, because its demand is rather "inelastic." I.e., when you cut wheat's price by 10 per cent, you expand its consumption by a lot less than 10 per cent.

Henry Ford believed the auto demand schedule was elastic:

	Price per unit P (1)	Quantity demanded, thousands per year Q (2)	Total revenue, millions per year $R = P \times Q$ (3) = (1) × (2)
A	$2,500	10	$ 25,000
B	2,000	60	120,000
C	1,500	120	180,000
D	1,000	200	200,000
E	500	300	150,000

Table 2. Demand schedule for autos. Autos, like wheat or anything else, have a demand schedule. But this hypothetical table illustrates that quantity of autos demanded will respond more "elastically" to price changes than will wheat quantity. (Thus, a 1% cut in P results in more than a 1% rise in Q, thereby raising total revenue, $R = P \times Q$, and portraying "elastic" demand.)

The demand for automobiles, at least in the good old days of the Model T Ford, might have been a better example because it represents an "elastic" demand. When Henry Ford cut his price by 10 per cent, the number of Fords demanded went up by much more than 10 per cent. This can be illustrated by the hypothetical Table 2.

Now let's plot the demand curves for automobiles and for wheat upon the same chart, by a careful juxtaposition of scales (Fig. 2). Immediately we see their difference. The two curves are made to have the point C in common, and at this point the automobile curve is much flatter. On it, the quantity demanded is very *elastic* with respect to price changes. Contrariwise, the wheat curve is relatively steep because its demand is rather *inelastic* at C.

Demand elasticity measures percentage responsiveness of Q to P:

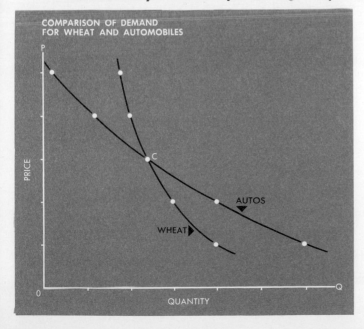

COMPARISON OF DEMAND FOR WHEAT AND AUTOMOBILES

P

PRICE

C

AUTOS

WHEAT

0   QUANTITY   Q

Fig. 2. A percentage change in P at point C is seen to lead to a greater percentage change in auto Q than in wheat Q. So auto demand is more elastic there than wheat demand.

▶ ELASTICITY OF DEMAND AND TOTAL REVENUE

Now how shall we decide whether the demand curve is (1) *elastic* at a given point on it, (2) *inelastic* at that point, or (3) a *borderline* case between being elastic and being inelastic? Here are our definitions concerning elasticity.

▶ A demand curve is *inelastic* at a given point if a one per cent cut in its price will expand its quantity by *less* than one per cent.

Demand is *elastic* at any point where a one per cent cut in P leads to *more* than a one per cent increase in Q. (I.e., Q responds relatively "elastically").

Demand is at the borderline called "unitary elasticity" if a halving of P is just matched by a doubling of Q and a one per cent cut in P is just matched by a one per cent rise in Q—so that total revenue, $P \times Q$, remains unchanged.

The way total revenue changes gives us a quick way to test whether we are at an elastic or inelastic point. If cutting P also cuts total revenue, demand must be *in*elastic. If cutting P raises total revenue, which must be because Q has responded so "elastically," then demand is elastic. If total revenue remains the same whether you raise or lower P, then demand is of unitary elasticity.

▶ MEASURING ELASTICITY

Economists often use a numerical coefficient called E to measure elasticity. Elastic demand means E is greater than 1.0 and inelastic demand means E is less than 1.0. Unitary elasticity gets its name from the fact that it has E just equal to 1.0.

How do we measure E? We do so by the following numerical ratio:[1]

$$\text{Elasticity coefficient } E = \frac{\text{per cent that } Q \text{ has risen}}{\text{per cent cut in } P}$$

▶ EXAMPLES CONCERNING ELASTICITY

The important thing is not numerical formulas of elasticity but the general idea. How total revenue changes when price drops or rises, or what's the same thing when quantity increases or falls—that is what businessmen and farmers are interested in. So here are a few examples based on our previous tables.

---

[1] Example: to calculate the elasticity coefficient between points A and B in Table 1 or Fig. 1. Let P drop from 5 to 4. Is this a 20 per cent or a 25 per cent drop? To save argument, let's always relate the cut to the original bigger P; so this is a 20 per cent cut in P. Q increases from 9 to 10, and to save argument we'll relate the change to the bigger Q, saying "Per cent Q has risen is 1/10 or 10 per cent." Hence, here $E = \frac{10}{20} = .5$, representing an inelastic demand. You can check this inelasticity by showing how the price cut has reduced total revenue. (Note: some advanced texts relate the changes in P or Q not to the biggest P or Q but to the *average* of the two Ps or two Qs. Our simple rule gives similar results.)

Turn back to Table 1 and look at Column (3). Notice that, every time we cut the price of wheat, the total revenue received from its sale goes down. Hence, the wheat demand curve is inelastic at all the points shown.

Contrast this with the automobile data of Table 2. As we cut the price of an automobile from $2,500 to $2,000, what happens to total revenue? Dollar revenue actually rises. Why? Because the quantity sold increases by a much larger percentage than the price falls. Therefore, between *A* and *B,* the automobile demand curve is certainly elastic. The same is true between *B* and *C* and between *C* and *D*.

But note what happens when the price of automobiles falls below *D*. Total revenue ceases to rise. The automobile demand curve has become inelastic between *D* and *E*. Clearly, somewhere near *D*, it went from being elastic to inelastic. Somewhere around *D* we can expect to find the borderline case of unitary elasticity, with total revenue remaining unchanged as price is cut.

An artificial demand schedule for movies is shown in Table 3. It is drawn up on the assumption that total revenue is the same at every price; hence it is a case of unitary elasticity. You should be able to fill in the missing *P* and *Q* in the table. Figure 3 plots this important borderline case of unitary elasticity. Though elasticity is everywhere exactly 1.0 the curve has a much flatter slope at low *P* than at high. Why? Because as *P* falls *Q* must expand always enough to keep total revenue, $R = P \times Q$, constant. The constant total revenue is shown in Fig. 3 by the equal areas of the rectangles whose altitude in every case depicts *P* and whose base depicts *Q*, with area as their revenue product.

Two warnings should be given. Beginning students of economics often associate elasticity with geometrical flatness of the demand curve, and they associate inelasticity with geometrical steepness. This involves a slight oversimplification. True enough, a perfectly vertical curve does have zero elasticity, and a perfectly horizontal curve does have infinite elasticity. Nonetheless, our movie case of Fig. 3 warns us that even though elasticity remains the same along a curve its steepness will change.

Or consider the example of a demand curve which is a straight line. Its slope or steepness is everywhere the same. Is its elasticity everywhere the same? Definitely not, as calculation of its total revenue will show. As we go from its highest price downward, its revenue rises, which means elasticity is greater than 1. At the halfway point its elasticity is exactly 1 because there total revenue turns out to be at its maximum. At still lower prices, its demand becomes inelastic.[1]

Where has the beginning student gone wrong? He has forgotten that elastic-

---

[1] These properties of a straight-line demand curve are proved in more advanced texts. Or the reader may verify them by referring to Table 2 and Fig. 2 of Chapter 24, p. 458, which illustrate just such a demand situation.

If doubling movie prices will just halve attendance, total revenue is constant:

	Price per ticket P (1)	Quantity demanded, per day Q = R ÷ P (2) = (3) ÷ (1)	Total revenue R (3)
A	$5.00	240	$1,200
B	4.00	300	1,200
C	3.00	___	1,200
D	___	600	1,200
E	1.00	1,200	1,200

Table 3. Schedule to illustrate unitary elasticity of demand. Column (3)'s total revenue, R = P × Q, is everywhere constant—so given either P or Q, you can get the other by dividing into R.

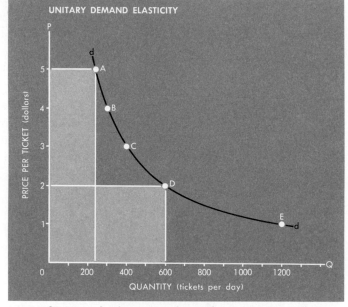

UNITARY DEMAND ELASTICITY

Fig. 3. Total revenue, R, is measured at any point by the shaded rectangular area the point forms with the axes. Why? Because R = P × Q and multiplying the P altitude by the Q base does give the rectangle's area P × Q. Note that the slope varies along this curve, but E = 1.0 everywhere and the rectangle's revenue area is everywhere the same.

ity depends on *percentage* changes; it does not depend on *absolute* changes alone as does geometrical steepness of the curve.

This same example teaches us a second truth: *Elasticity is usually different at each different part of a good's demand curve.* Earlier, I spoke loosely of the demand for wheat being inelastic and that for autos being elastic. But actually, we saw that, at low enough prices, the demand for automobiles turned inelastic. Similarly, had the wheat curve been extended to much higher prices, it would have finally become elastic as it approached the vertical axis.

What then do we mean when we say that a commodity has inelastic demand? What we really mean is the following: At the price levels for the commodity *that have generally been prevailing in the market,* its demand is inelastic. That is all such a statement can mean.

► ELASTICITY IN PERFECT AND IMPERFECT COMPETITION

A few illustrations show the importance of the concept of elasticity. If a monopolist should gain control of a very necessary commodity much desired by people, like penicillin, he can take advantage of its inelasticity of demand and make great profits by jacking up his price until he ceases to face inelastic demand.

On the other hand, in a highly competitive trade, where patents and customer good will are not important, demand for any *one* firm's output will be very elastic. Why? Because at the slightest raising of its price, buyers will go elsewhere and substitute the output of other firms. Thus one small wheat farmer has such a negligible effect upon the price at the Chicago Board of Trade that the demand for his wheat is infinitely elastic. He can sell 100, 200, or 1,000 bushels of wheat without affecting the price. But at the very slightest price rise over that of the market, he loses *all* his sales. His demand curve is therefore very flat as in Fig. 4.

► Though industry demand slopes downward, each perfect competitor—being too small to affect price—faces a horizontal (or infinitely elastic) demand.

In the first chapter we learned that it is a fallacy to think that what is true for each is also true for all together. Here we have an instance as applied to farmers. Although the demand for each competitive farmer's wheat is very elastic, we already know that the demand for all wheat is very inelastic. The difference results from the great disparity of the horizontal scale of Fig. 4 and the scale of Fig. 1. Farmer Brown's piddling few carloads will not move us

A perfect competitor can sell all he wants to at the market price:

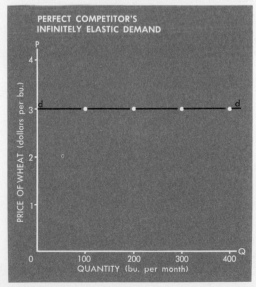

Fig. 4. The perfectly competitive individual seller is such a small part of the total market that he can sell all he wishes without depressing the prevailing price. Under imperfect competition, a firm's demand curve slopes downward.

1/1,000 inch along the industry's demand curve. Price on the diagram, Fig. 1, will be imperceptibly changed. No wonder Brown finds *his* demand is elastic. What if all the millions of Browns, Smiths, and O'Malleys bring a few carloads to market? Then we move a substantial distance along the whole industry's inelastic wheat-demand curve.

In fact, when all farmers are lucky enough to have a large crop, their total revenue actually goes down. Does this mean that farmers pray for drought and bugs? Not necessarily. The more calculating ones pray for bugs on everyone else's field, but none on their own. But since that cannot be expected to happen often, the next best thing is for everyone to have some bugs.

Now we begin to understand what we shall study in detail in later chapters: (1) why farmers wish to restrict crop production to raise their incomes and (2) why they cannot rely on each individual farmer to do his part in restricting, unless government force or bribery is employed.

▶ THE SUPPLY SCHEDULE

Enough has now been said of demand. Let's now turn briefly to the sellers' side, or to the supply schedule. The demand schedule related prices and the amounts consumers wish to buy. How is the supply schedule defined?

▶ By the *supply schedule or curve* we naturally mean the relation between market prices and the amounts that producers are willing to produce and sell.

Table 4 illustrates the supply schedule for wheat, and Fig. 5 plots it as a supply curve. Unlike the demand curve, the supply curve for wheat normally rises upward and to the right, from southwest to northeast. At a higher price of wheat, farmers will take acreage out of corn cultivation and put it into wheat. Also they can afford the cost of more fertilizer, more machinery, and poorer land. All these factors increase output with higher prices.[1]

▶ EQUILIBRIUM OF SUPPLY AND DEMAND

For the moment let us say no more about the costs and other things that determine the supply curve. We take it as given. Let us now combine our analysis of demand and supply to see how competitive market price is determined. This is done in Table 5.

So far we have been considering all prices as possible. We have said, "If price is such and such, sales will be such and such; if price is so and so, sales will be so and so; etc." But to just which level will price *actually* go? And how much will then be produced and consumed? The supply schedule

---

[1] The advanced student can define elasticity of a rising supply curve as (per cent rise in Q) ÷ (per cent rise in P). We need not do so here. Also he'll note that some supply curves do bend back toward the northwest.

The supply schedule relates price and quantity supplied:

Table 4. Supply schedule for wheat. At each P, there is listed the Q that producers will want to supply.

	Possible prices per bu.	Quantity sellers will supply, million bu. per month
A	$5	18
B	4	16
C	3	12
D	2	7
E	1	0

The supply schedule can be plotted as a curve:

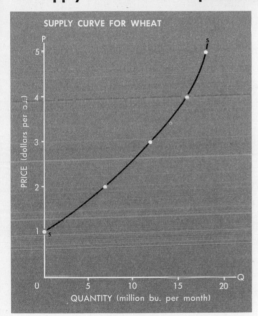

Fig. 5. Each Q,P pair of Table 5 is here plotted as a point. A smooth curve passed through them gives the supply curve, ss.

alone cannot tell us. Neither can the demand schedule alone. But both to-gether can.

Let us do what an auctioneer would do, *i.e.,* proceed by trial and error. Can situation *A* in Table 5, with wheat selling for $5 per bushel, prevail for any period of time? The answer is a loud and clear, No. At $5, the producers will be bringing 18 (million) bushels to the market every month [Column (3)]. But the amount demanded by consumers will be only 9 (million) bush-els per month [see Table 5, Column (2)]. As stocks of wheat pile up, com-petitive sellers will cut the price a little. Thus as Column (4) shows, price will tend to fall. But it will not fall indefinitely down to zero.

To see this, let's try the point *E* with price equal to only $1 per bushel.

Can that price persist? Again, obviously not. For a comparison of Columns (2) and (3) shows that consumption will exceed production *at that price*. Storehouses will begin to be emptied; disappointed demanders who cannot get wheat will tend to bid the price up. This upward pressure on price is indicated in Column (4) by the rising arrow. We could go on to try out other prices, but by now the answer is obvious.

▶ The only equilibrium price, *i.e.*, the only price that can last—is that at which the amounts supplied and demanded are equal. Competitive equilibrium is always at the intersection point where the supply and demand curves meet.

Only at *C*, with a price of $3, will the amount demanded, 12 (million) bushels per month, exactly equal the amount supplied, 12 (million). Price is at equilibrium, just as an olive at the bottom of a cocktail glass is at equilibrium, because there is no tendency for it to rise or fall. Of course, this stationary price may not be reached at once. There may have to be an initial period of trial and error, of oscillation around the right level before price finally settles down and supply balances demand.

Figure 6 shows the same result in pictorial form. The supply and demand curves are superimposed on the same diagram. They cross at one intersection point. This point *C* represents the equilibrium price and quantity.

At a higher price, the white bar shows the *excess* of supply over demand. The arrows point downward to show the direction in which price will move because of the competition of *sellers*. At a price lower than equilibrium price, $3, the white bar shows that demand overmatches supply. Consequently the eager bidding of *buyers* requires us to point the arrow indicators upward to show the pressure that they are exerting on price. Only at the point *C* will there be a balancing of forces and a stationary maintainable price.

This gives the essence of the doctrine of supply and demand.

Equilibrium market price is at the point where supply and demand match:

	Possible prices per bu. (1)	Quantity demanded, million bu. per month (2)	Quantity supplied, million bu. per month (3)	Pressure on price (4)
A	$5	9	18	Falling
B	4	10	16	Falling
C	3	12	12	Neutral
D	2	15	7	Rising
E	1	20	0	Rising

Table 5. Supply and demand schedules for wheat. Only at $3 will quantity demanded by consumers equal quantity supplied by producers. At any lower price, demand would exceed supply; at any higher price, supply would exceed demand.

The equilibrium market price is where demand and supply curves intersect:

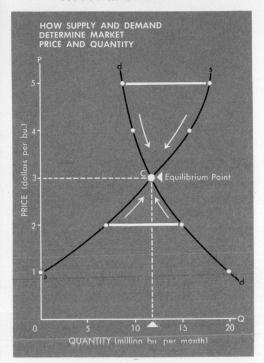

HOW SUPPLY AND DEMAND DETERMINE MARKET PRICE AND QUANTITY

PRICE (dollars per bu.)

C ◀ Equilibrium Point

QUANTITY (million bu. per month)

Fig. 6. At the C intersection, the amount supplied just matches the amount demanded. At any lower *P*, the excess of demand will force *P* back up; and at any *P* higher than the equilibrium, the amount supplied will be excessive and *P* will be forced back down to the equilibrium level.

▶ EFFECT OF A SHIFT IN SUPPLY OR DEMAND

Now we can put the supply and demand apparatus to work. Gregory King, an English writer of the seventeenth century, noticed that when the harvest was bad, food rose in price and farmers got more money than when the harvest was good. This puzzled him. Let's try to explain what happens by our diagrams.

Figure 7 shows how a spell of bad weather will reduce the amount that farmers will supply at each and every market price, and thereby displace the equilibrium point, *E*. The *ss* curve has shifted to the left and has become *s's'*. The demand curve hasn't changed. Where does the new supply curve *s's'* intersect *dd*? Plainly at *E'*, the new equilibrium price where demand and the new reduced supply have again come into balance. Naturally *P* has risen. And because of the law of downward-sloping demand, what has happened to *Q*? It has gone down. And one more striking fact. Because wheat has an inelastic demand, total revenue ($= P \times Q$) has gone up. The drop in the harvest has generated a price rise much greater in percentage terms than itself.

Suppose the supply curve shifted far rightward because of good weather and new fertilizers. Show the new equilibrium for *P*, *Q*, and total revenue.

Diagrams show effects on price of demand and supply shifts:

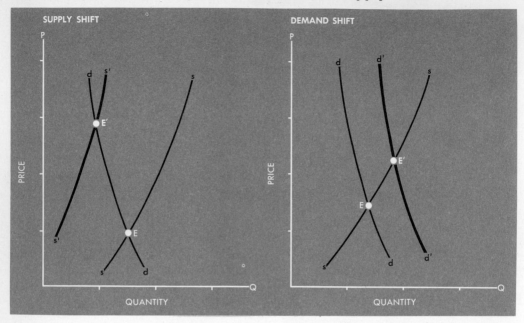

SUPPLY SHIFT

DEMAND SHIFT

Fig. 7. If supply shifts leftward for any reason, the equilibrium price intersection will travel up the demand curve, giving higher P and lower Q.

If demand shifts rightward, the equilibrium will travel up the supply curve.

Our apparatus will also help us analyze the effect of an increase in demand. Suppose that rising family incomes make everyone want more wheat. Then at each unchanged P, greater Q will now be demanded. The demand curve will shift rightward to d'd'. The right-hand Fig. 7 shows the resulting travel up the supply curve as enhanced demand raises competitive price.

▶ MOMENTARY, SHORT-RUN, AND LONG-RUN EQUILIBRIUM

Alfred Marshall, Cambridge's great economist at the turn of the century, helped forge these tools of supply and demand. We can review our understanding of equilibrium and at the same time advance our knowledge if we survey Marshall's important emphasis on the *time element* of the problem.

He distinguishes at least three time periods: (1) *momentary* equilibrium when the supply is fixed; (2) *short-run* equilibrium when firms can produce more within given plants; and finally (3) *long-run* equilibrium (or "normal price") when firms can abandon old plants or build new ones and when new firms can enter the industry or old ones leave it.

Let's imagine that the demand for a perishable good such as fish that can't be preserved increases from dd to d'd'. With the supply of fish unchanged, the stronger demand will bid up sharply the momentary price of fish. This is shown in Fig. 8a where the fixed supply curve $s_m s_m$ runs up to the new demand curve $d'd'$ to determine the new sharply higher, momentary equilibrium price shown at E'. The price has had to rise so much in order to ration out the limited supply of fish among the now eager demanders.

But with so high a price prevailing in the market, skippers of the fishing boats will be motivated to hire more men and to use more nets. Even if they haven't the time to get new boats built, they will in the short run begin to bring to the market a higher supply of fish than prevailed in the old momentary equilibrium. Fig. 8b shows the new $s_s s_s$ short-run supply schedule, and shows that it intersects the new demand curve at E'', the point of short-run equilibrium. Note that this equilibrium price is a little lower than the momentary E' price. Why? Because of the extra supply of fish induced in the short run by more intensive use of the same number of boats.

Figure 8c shows the final long-run equilibrium or normal price. The higher prices that long prevailed have coaxed out more shipbuilding and attracted more trained sailors into the industry. Where the long-run supply

Effect of demand increase on price varies in the three time periods:

1st, the new momentary equilibrium raises P to ration out the unchanged supply:	2d, short-run equilibrium coaxes out increased supply from existing plants:	3d, normal long-run equilibrium comes when new plant and all resources vary, with price finally adjusting to all costs:

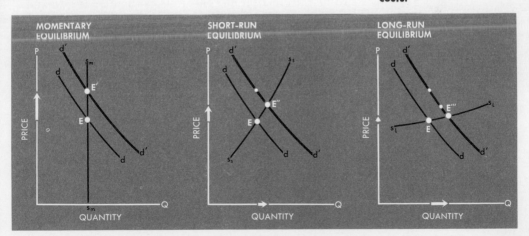

Fig. 8. Marshall distinguishes three different time periods depending upon whether supply elements have time to make (a) no adjustments, (b) some adjustments of labor and variable factors, (c) full adjustment of all factors and all costs to price. (The upward slope of $s_L s_L$ puts this case in the "increasing cost" category discussed on the next page. What would $s_L s_L$ be like in the "constant cost" case? Why might a very small industry have constant costs?)

curve $s_L s_L$ intersects the demand curve $d'd'$ at E''' is the final equilibrium reached after all economic conditions have adjusted themselves to the new level of demand.

Note that the long-run equilibrium price is not so high as the short-run equilibrium price and not nearly so high as the momentary equilibrium price. Yet it is a little bit higher than previously prevailed when demand was lower. Had the fish industry used no factors of production peculiar to itself and had it been so small as to be able to attract from the rest of the economy without raising their prices all the factors it needed to duplicate and reduplicate its previous outputs, it might have been able to supply all the new demand for fish with no increase in its long-run costs or price. In that case the long-run supply schedule would have been horizontal, and Marshall would have referred to it as a "constant-cost" case. But if its ships, nets, and men have to be coaxed away from other employments by a rise in their factor prices, the $s_L s_L$ long-run supply curve will be gently upward sloping as in Fig. 8c. Marshall would call this a case of "increasing cost" and would regard it as the normal one to be met in most sizable industries.

The reader can test his knowledge by now assuming a downward shift in the demand curve back to dd. Show what happens in the new momentary run. In the short run. In the long run.

▶ WHAT SUPPLY AND DEMAND ACCOMPLISHED

Having seen how supply and demand work, let's take stock of what has been accomplished. The scarce goods of society have been rationed out among the possible users of them. Who did the rationing? A board? A committee? No, the auctioneering mechanism of competitive price did the rationing. It was a case of "rationing by the purse."

For Whom goods are destined was *partially* determined by who was willing to pay for them. If you had the money votes, you got the fish. If you didn't, you went without. Or if you had the money votes, but preferred not to spend them on fish, you did without. The most important needs for goods—if backed by cash!—got fulfilled.

At the same time, the What question was partially being answered. The rise in market price was the signal to coax out a higher supply of fish. It was the signal for men to move from farms to the sea. For wood to become unavailable for homes and available for ships.

Even the How question was partially being decided in the background. For with fish now dear, men could afford expensive nets and could go to more distant seas, and so forth.

Why the word "partially" in my description of how the competitive market helped solve the three problems? Because this fish market is but one market of many. What is happening in the meat market also counts. And what is happening in the market for wood, rope, and men obviously matters much. As we'll see, the pricing problem is one that involves *interdependent markets* and not just what Alfred Marshall would have called the "partial equilibrium" of a single market.[1]

SUMMARY

1. A basic problem of microeconomics is how the mechanism of market pricing grapples with the economy's triad of problems: What, How, and For Whom.

2. By the demand schedule we mean a table showing the different quantities of a good that people will at any time buy at each different price. The same relationship plotted on a diagram is the demand curve.

3. With few exceptions, the higher the price, the lower will be the quantity sold, and vice versa. Almost all commodities are subject to this "law of downward-sloping demand," but in different degrees.

4. Elasticity of demand depends on what happens to total revenue as price is cut. Demand is elastic, inelastic, or unitary, depending upon whether a reduction in price increases, decreases, or does not change total revenue. The numerical coefficient of elasticity of demand is defined as the percentage increase in quantity divided by the percentage cut in price.

5. A perfect competitor is defined as a seller too small to have an appreciable effect on the price of the good he sells. His demand curve is, by definition, horizontal and of infinite elasticity. An imperfect competitor is one who has some degree of monopolistic control over the price of his goods. His demand curve is of less than infinite elasticity of demand and slopes downward.

6. The supply curve or schedule represents the relationship between the prices and the quantities of a good that producers will be willing to sell. Usually, but not always, the supply curve rises upward and to the right, the higher prices calling forth larger supplies.

7. Market equilibrium can take place only at a price where the quantities

---

[1] The alert reader will not have to be reminded that the competitive market gives goods to those with money votes and does so efficiently. But the distribution of the money votes depends on how much you can sell your labor and property for in competitive and imperfectly competitive factor markets, and it is affected in an important way by (1) how lucky you are, (2) how lucky your parents and in-laws were, (3) the advantages and disadvantages of your genetic and acquired skills and aptitudes. If a student writes on a final exam, "For Whom is decided (in part) by how people decide to use their money votes," he is not wrong. Indeed he gets maybe 30 per cent credit. But he won't get the other 70 per cent unless he adds, "The basic problem in For Whom is the process by which the money votes themselves get determined, which is primarily not by supply and demand in a single good's market but by supply and demand in the labor, land, and other interdependent factor markets of Part Four."

supplied and demanded are equal. At any price higher than the equilibrium intersection of the supply and demand curves, the quantity supplied will exceed the quantity demanded; downward pressure on price will result as some sellers undermine the going price. Similarly, the reader can show why a price lower than the equilibrium price will meet irresistible upward pressure.

8. Marshall stressed the time element: (a) *momentary* equilibrium of fixed supply, (b) *short-run* equilibrium with output varying within fixed plants and firms, and (c) *long-run* equilibrium of normal price, when numbers of firms and plants, and all other economic conditions, have adjusted themselves to the new level of demand.

9. Competitive pricing rations out the limited supply of goods to those with desire or need backed by money votes. Along with helping decide For Whom, it signals changes in What shall be produced, and in How goods shall be produced. But any one market only "partially" helps solve the What, How, and For Whom because of our need to consider its interdependence with other commodity and factor markets.

QUESTIONS FOR DISCUSSION

1. What factors might increase the demand for wheat? The supply?

2. Which of the following do you think has the most inelastic demand: perfume, salt, penicillin, cigarettes, ice cream, chocolate ice cream, Sealtest chocolate ice cream? Why?

3. Comment on the following: "How can price be determined by the equality of supply and demand? After all, the 'amount bought' must be the same in every transaction as the 'amount sold.' How then could they be different at every price but the unique equilibrium price?"

4. What would cheap mechanical pickers do to cotton price? To farm wages?

5. Spell out the arguments which show that price must settle down at the equilibrium intersection of supply and demand. Imagine that price is at first too high. Then too low.

6. Explain Marshall's three different kinds of equilibrium.

7. Here are two teasers that beginners will find puzzling and may skip. "I raise my price by 1 per cent—*i.e.*, from 100 to 101. My quantity sold drops from 100 to 99. I thought this meant an elasticity of unity. But . . . when I calculate my new total revenue it is 9,999, whereas my old revenue was 10,000. Why?"

(Hint: Elasticity is very near to unity but really is a bit above 1.0. The trouble comes from the fact that a change of 1 in P and of 1 in Q look of equal percentage importance if we relate them both to the *original* 100; but if we relate the change of 1 in P to the *new* 101 we see that it is a smaller percentage change than is the change of 1 in Q. Thus, the percentage change in quantity is really a little bigger than the percentage change in price—and hence demand is slightly elastic. Note that this discrepancy becomes smaller and smaller as we make the percentage changes smaller and smaller, becoming negligible in the limit. Note too that the arithmetic of page 374's footnote does properly handle this paradoxical case.)

"RCA slashes the price of its records in half. As a result the quantity it sells exactly doubles. Show that demand elasticity *is* exactly unitary—even though P has dropped 50 points from 100 to 50 while Q has gone up 100 points from 100 to 200."

(Hint: Calculate total revenue; or use the footnote's largest P and largest Q when computing the base for percentages. Again, the paradox comes from the fact that percentages are ambiguous when finite moves are made. The advanced student knows one way out of the difficulty: plot the demand curve on *double-log* paper and join the two points by a straight line. The reciprocal of the line's slope is the numerical elasticity.)

8. Review your understanding of the following concepts:

microeconomics, macroeconomics   *supply schedule or curve*
What, How, For Whom   *equilibrium intersection*
demand schedule or curve   *Marshall's three time periods*
total revenue, $P \times Q$ *how supply and demand in one*
elasticity, inelasticity, unitary   *market "partially" solves*
  elasticity   *What, How, and For Whom*

SUPPLY AND DEMAND (CONTINUED): SOME APPLICATIONS

Other things being equal, as economists are fond of saying, there is a unique schedule of supply or demand at any instant of time. But other things will not remain equal. The demand for cotton is declining over the years because of reductions in the price of rayon. The supply schedule of gasoline is increasing because technological progress permits more to be produced at the same cost. As costs and tastes change, as incomes vary, as the prices of rival products (coffee in relation to tea) or cooperating products (sugar in relation to tea) change, our schedules will shift. What will be the effects on consumption, production, and price? That we must now study.

All beginners in the field of economics must beware of a common error. They must take care not to confuse an increase in *demand*—by which is meant a shift of the whole curve to the right and upward, as more is bought at each and every price—with an increase in the *quantity demanded* as a result of moving to a lower price *on the same demand curve*. By "demand" is meant the whole demand curve; by "supply" is meant the whole supply curve; by an "increase" in demand or supply is meant a shift of the whole curve in question to the right. To indicate a single point on a demand curve, we speak of the "quantity bought" or the "quantity demanded" *at a particular price*. A movement *along* the same curve is "a change in the quantity demanded as a result of a price change." It does not represent any change in the demand schedule. The need for this warning will appear in a moment.

▶ **INCIDENCE OF A TAX**

We can illustrate the case of a shift in the entire curve by referring back to Table 5 and Fig. 6 of last chapter's p. 380, which portrayed hypothetical supply and demand schedules for wheat. These resulted in an equilibrium price of $3 per bushel.

Let us now introduce a new factor which will disturb this equilibrium. In particular, let us assume that the government imposes a sales tax on wheat. On each and every sale, the producer is required to pay a tax of $1 per bushel of wheat. What is the final effect or "incidence" of the tax? Does its burden fall back completely on the producer who must in the first instance pay it? Or may it be shifted forward in part on to consumers? The answer can be derived only by the use of our supply and demand curves.

There is no reason for the demand curve of the consumers to have changed at all. At $3 consumers will still be willing to buy only 12 (million) bushels; they neither know nor care that the producers must pay a tax.

But the whole supply curve is shifted upward and leftward: leftward because at each market price the producers will now supply less as a result of the tax, upward because to get the producers to bring any given quantity to market, say 12 (million) units, we must give them a higher market price than before—$4 rather than $3, which is higher by the exact amount of the $1 tax.

The student should be able to fill in a new supply column, resembling the Column (3) in Chapter 19's Table 5, but with each price raised by $1. In Fig. 1, on the next page, the demand curve dd is unchanged, but the supply curve ss has been shifted everywhere up by $1 to a new parallel supply curve $s's'$.

Where will the new equilibrium price be? The answer is found at the intersection of the new demand and supply curves, or at C' where $s's'$ and dd meet. Because supply has decreased, the price is higher. Also the amount bought and the amount sold are less. If we read the graph carefully, we find that the new equilibrium price has risen from $3 to about $3⅔. The new equilibrium output, at which purchases and sales are in equilibrium, has fallen from 12 (million) per month to about 10.6 (million) bushels.

Who pays the tax? Well, the wheat farmers do in part because now they receive only $2⅔, ($3⅔ − $1), rather than $3. But the consumer also shares in the burden, because the price received by the producer has not fallen by as much as the tax. To the consumer, the wheat now costs $2⅔ plus the $1 tax, or $3⅔ all told. Because the consumers need wheat so badly, they pay ⅔ of the tax, and the producers pay ⅓ of the tax. As a final burden, the community is poorer because it is consuming less wheat.[1]

To check his understanding of the above reasoning, the student should consider the case of an opposite shift in supply. Let the government pay producers a subsidy of $1 per bushel of wheat instead of taxing them this

---

[1] Don't think there is only one way to handle this tax problem. If the consumer were thought of as paying the tax in the first instance, you could subtract $1 everywhere from his dd curve. The new $d'd'$ will intersect ss at the same new Q, and the same $2⅔ and $3⅔ prices will prevail. It goes without saying that all these figures are hypothetical.

A tax on wheat falls both on consumer and producer:

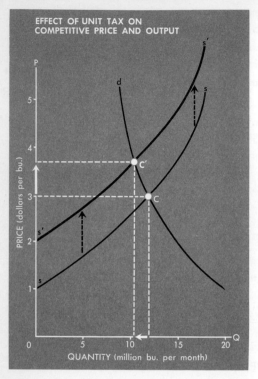

EFFECT OF UNIT TAX ON
COMPETITIVE PRICE AND OUTPUT

Fig. 1. A $1 tax shifts *ss* up $1 everywhere to give *s's'*. This intersects *dd* in new equilibrium at *C'* where price to consumer has risen $⅔ above old *C* equilibrium and where price to producer has fallen by $⅓. The thick white arrows show change in *P* and *Q*. (Had *dd* been very elastic and flat relative to *ss*, most of the $1 tax would have fallen on the producer.)

amount. Shift *ss* down to the new curve *s"s"*. Where is *C"*, its intersection with *dd*? What is the new price? The new quantity? How much of the benefit goes to the producer? How much to the consumer?

▶ A COMMON FALLACY

By now the student has mastered supply and demand. Or has he? He knows that a tax will have the effect of raising the price that the consumer will have to pay. Or does he know this? What about the following argument of a kind often seen in the press and heard from the platform:

> The effect of a tax on a commodity might seem at first sight to be an advance in price to the consumer. But an advance in price will diminish the demand. And a reduced demand will send the price down again. It is not certain, therefore, after all, that the tax will really raise the price.[1]

---

[1] H. D. Henderson, *Supply and Demand* (Cambridge, London, 1922), p. 27 analyzed this fallacy. The quotation could have been made even more fantastic as follows: "Price goes up and demand falls. This sends price down which makes demand rise. This makes price go up. But the higher price makes demand fall. . . ." And so we have a perpetual oscillation in price, up and down, down and up. The student should spot the error.

Well, what about it? Will the tax raise the price or not? According to the editor's written word and the senator's oratory, the answer is "no." Evidently, we have here an example of the treachery of words. One of the four sentences in the quotation is false because the word "demand" is being used in the wrong sense. The student has already been warned against confusing a movement *along* an unchanged curve with a shift in the curve.

Actually, the correct answer would be more or less as follows:

A tax will raise the price to the consumer and will lower the price received by the producer, the difference going to the government. At the higher price a smaller quantity will be bought by consumers. This is as it should be because producers are also supplying a smaller quantity at the lower price which they receive. Thus the amounts bought and sold are in balance where the new supply and demand schedules intersect, and there will be no further change in price.

► IS THE LAW OF SUPPLY AND DEMAND IMMUTABLE?

Competitive price and quantity are determined by supply and demand. But don't prices depend on other factors such as the amount of gold production or whether there is a war going on? Actually, price does depend on many such factors. However, they are not *in addition* to supply and demand but are included in the numerous forces which determine or *act through* supply and demand. Thus if new gold production gives everyone higher incomes, it will shift demand curves and raise prices. But it is still true that competitive price is determined by supply and demand.

At this point a thoughtful reader should be moved to voice protest. Nothing much has been said about price as being determined by cost of production. Shouldn't this be listed as a third factor in addition to supply and demand? Again our answer is the same. *Competitive price is affected by cost of production only to the extent that the latter affects supply.* If God sends manna from heaven without cost but in limited supply, then its price will not be zero but will be given by the intersection of the demand and supply curves. On the other hand, if it would cost $50,000 to print the national anthem on the head of a pin, but there is no demand for such a commodity, it simply will not be produced and would not command $50,000 if it were produced. (What the market price of something nonexistent should be called I leave to the pleasure and imagination of the reader.)

This doesn't mean that cost of production is unimportant for price determination. Under competition it is especially important. But its importance shows itself *through its effects upon supply*. Businessmen do not produce for their health. If they cannot get a price high enough to cover their past costs, then they will not like it. Nevertheless, under competition once the crop is in, so to speak, there is not much they can do about it. But they will not continue *in the future* to supply goods at prices that fail to cover the *extra* costs incurred to produce these goods. Thus supply depends intimately on cost, especially on "extra costs," and so too must price. (Later we'll give details.)

Moreover, to say that price equals cost does not in itself tell us which is the cause of which. In many cases where an industry uses a productive factor highly specialized to itself (*e.g.*, baseball players, opera singers, vineyard land), *price determines cost rather than vice versa*. Grain land is dear because the price of grain is high. Apartment buildings sell for little because rents are low. This type of relationship was overlooked by the Massachusetts dairy farmers who petitioned during World War II for a higher milk price "because the price of cows is high." If their request had been granted, they would soon have observed the price of cows chasing the milk price upward.[1]

These examples show us that supply and demand are not ultimate explanations of price. They are simply useful catchall categories for analyzing and describing the multitude of forces, causes, and factors impinging on price. Rather than being final answers, supply and demand simply represent initial questions. Our work is not over but just begun.

This should help to debunk the tendency of neophytes who have just mastered the elements of market price determination to utter sagely, "You can't repeal the law of supply and demand. King Canute could not command the ocean tide to retreat from his throne on the seashore. No more can government get around or interfere with the workings of supply and demand."

It would be better never to have learned any economics than to be left with this misleading half-baked untruth. Of course the government can affect price. It can do so by affecting supply or demand, or both. In much of the next chapter we shall examine how government programs for restricting farm production can raise price and income by cutting down on supply. Similar programs by government cartels have been pursued all over the world: Brazil has burned coffee to raise its price; Britain during the 1920's pursued the "Stevenson policy" of artificially controlling the price of rubber; sugar is still under international control.

These governments have not violated the law of supply and demand. They have worked through the law of supply and demand. The state has no secret economic weapons or tricks. What is true for the state is also true for individuals. Anyone can affect the price of wheat so long as he has money to throw on the market or wheat to hold off it.

Every trade-union influences wages, or tries to, by directly or indirectly affecting the supply of labor. Anyone with a somewhat distinctive commodity

[1] Where a factor of production is inelastic in supply, as in all these cases, its cost is "price-determined" rather than "price-determining" and its return is called an "economic rent." See Case 3 in the Appendix to this chapter and also Part Four's Chapter 27.

may try by advertising to increase the demand for his product, and by restricting supply to raise price above his extra costs of production. It should be remembered, however, that as soon as individual producers become important enough to affect the price of the things they sell, then they cease to be perfect competitors in the strict sense, and their behavior must be analyzed in terms of a blend of monopoly and competition, *i.e.*, in terms of imperfect competition as described in Chapter 25.

▶ PRICES FIXED BY LAW

There is one important interference with supply and demand whose effects we must analyze. The government sometimes sets a maximum price by law, or a minimum wage. During the war ceilings were placed on items in the cost of living. A floor of $1.00 is placed on hourly wages of most factory workers. These interferences by law are quite different from government actions, previously described, which work through supply and demand.

Consider, say, the market for sugar, which has ordinary curves of supply and demand such as we have repeatedly met in this chapter. Suppose that the government through an Office of Price Stabilization (OPS) establishes an order prohibiting sugar from rising above 7 cents a pound (retail). Now because of prosperity or bad crops, let demand be so high and supply so small

A legal maximum price, without rationing, leaves a gap between demand and supply:

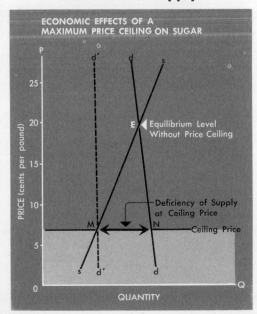

Fig. 2. Without a legal price ceiling, price would rise to E. At the artificial ceiling price, supply and demand do not balance and some method of rationing, formal or informal, is needed to allocate the short supply and bring the effective demand down to d'd'.

that the equilibrium price would have been 20 cents a pound if the government had not intervened. This high price would have contributed to profiteering in that industry, it would have represented a rather heavy "tax" on the poor who could least afford it, and it would only have added fuel to an inflationary spiral in the cost of living, with all sorts of inflationary reactions on workers' wage demands, and so forth.

Therefore, the government through Congress and the OPS decides to hold the line on prices. It passes a law putting a maximum price on sugar at the old level of 7 cents a pound. The line MN represents the legal price ceiling. Now what will happen?

At the legal ceiling price, supply and demand do not match. Consumers want thousands of pounds of sugar in excess of what producers are willing to supply. This is shown by the gap between M and N. This gap is so large that there will not long be enough sugar on grocers' shelves or in the warehouse to make up the difference. Somebody will have to be drinking bitter coffee. If it were not for the maximum price law, that somebody would gladly bid the price up to 8 or 9 cents or more, rather than do without sugar. As in our earlier discussion (Chapter 19, Fig. 6), we could show this by putting an upward pointing arrow perpendicular to MN. The arrow would not stop pointing upward until price had been bid up to the equilibrium level of 20 cents.

It is against the law for the consumer to bid a higher price. Even if the consumer should be so unpatriotic, the seller could not legally take the higher price. There follows a period of frustration and shortage—a game of musical chairs in which somebody is left without a seat when the orchestra stops playing. The inadequate supply of sugar must somehow be rationed. At first, this may be done by "first come, first served" with or without limited sales to each customer. Lines form and women have to spend much of their time foraging for food. But this is no solution since somebody must be left at the end of the line when the sugar is gone.

The price mechanism is stymied and blocked. Nonmonetary considerations must determine who is the lucky buyer and who the unlucky one: the accident of being in the store when the sugar is unveiled, the warmth of the smile that the customer flashes on the grocer, her previous standing at the store in question, and the amount of other things the customer is willing to buy.

Nobody is very happy, least of all the harassed grocer. Were it not for the community's elementary sense of fair play, the situation would soon become intolerable. Patriotism is more effective in motivating people to brief acts of intense heroism than to putting up day after day with an uncomfortable situation. So it is no wonder that black markets occasionally develop. The really surprising thing is how infrequently they do occur.

If for political or social reasons market price is not to be permitted to rise high enough to bring demand down to the level of supply, the only solution under these circumstances lies in outright coupon or point rationing.

Once this is adopted most people heave a sigh of relief, because now sellers need not turn people away and buyers can count upon getting their fair quota of the limited supplies. Of course there are always a few women and soapbox orators, who are longer on intuition than brains and who blame their troubles on the mechanism of rationing itself rather than on the shortage. "If only the government could print more coupon points," they sigh. As if that would help rather than hurt the situation! Such people are like the ignorant ancient kings who used to slay the messengers bringing them bad news. They add spice to the human comedy but need not be taken seriously.

Just how do ration coupons work out in terms of supply and demand? Clearly the OPS tries to issue just enough of them to lower the demand curve *to d'd' where supply and the new demand balance at the ceiling price.* If too many coupons are issued, demand is still too far to the right and we encounter the old difficulties, but in lesser degree. If too few coupons are issued, stocks of sugar will pile up. This is the signal for liberalizing the sugar ration.

One goes to an insane asylum to learn to appreciate normal human behavior. So too, the breakdown of the price mechanism during war gives us a new understanding of its remarkable efficiency in normal times. Goods are always scarce, in the sense that there is never enough to give everyone all he wishes. Price itself is always rationing scarce supplies: rising to choke off excessive consumption and in order to expand production; falling to encourage consumption, discourage production, and work off excessive inventories.

▶ MONOPOLY INTERFERENCES WITH SUPPLY AND DEMAND

Competitive supply and demand is one way of organizing an economy. It's one way of getting the job done but of course it's not the only way. Certainly if one or a few producers could get monopoly control of an industry, they could move the final outcome away from the competitive equilibrium point. As we'll later see, a monopolist could reduce output and make the consumers travel up their demand curves to higher prices.

Is such an interference with supply and demand a "good thing?" If the monopolist were a more worthy soul than the rest of us, or if he were much poorer than the rest of us with greater need for money, some might rise to defend his act of raising price. Or if he were a Robin Hood, who took our money and devoted it to better causes (charity, scientific research) than we would do, some might still defend him.

Chances are though that anyone in a position to contrive a monopoly will be at least as well off as his customers, and there isn't much reason to think he'd be of finer clay than anyone else. And though Robin Hood may have been all right in his day, in our day we tend to think it's the government that ought to do any subsidizing of worthy causes, not self-appointed do-gooders, and we hope that it can be more efficient in financing its good causes out of tax revenues than any Robin Hood could ever be.

So what probably needs emphasis is this: *Any haphazard interference with competitive supply and demand is likely—save in some exceptional circumstances—to be a bad rather than a good thing.*

Thus, a monopolistic interference reduces output needlessly. The fact that it produces such scarcity is reflected in the higher price it creates. The monopoly may also lead to a bad distribution of income in that it may give extra income to one who already has as much income as he deserves.

At this point monopoly's reduction in output perhaps needs more stressing than its distortion of the income distribution. For what if we taxed away the monopolist' ill-gotten gains?[1] We would then have rectified the income-distribution distortion of monopoly. But the community would still be left enjoying less of the consumption goods that it really wants and that it is really capable of producing.

Like sin, monopoly is one of those things most people are against. So I don't have to labor the point that monopoly interferences with supply and demand are probably a bad thing.

▶ GOVERNMENT AND OTHER INTERFERENCES WITH SUPPLY AND DEMAND

But what about government interferences? Surely the government means well and its interferences are not to be so harshly judged?

Well, that all depends. If the government happens to know better than people what is really good and evil, its interferences may improve matters. An example might be opium. We don't treat the consumer as a sovereign who can decide how much opium he'll spend his money votes on. Where opium is concerned we adopt a paternalistic attitude, treating the consumer a little the way we treat lunatics, minors, and other "incompetents."

But where eight-cylinder cars or cigarettes are concerned, we usually are content to let the consumer spend or squander his own dollars in his own way. We recognize that advertising has given us one set of tastes, which may or may not be intrinsically better than some other set of tastes, but in the interests of freedom we do treat the consumer as sovereign.

---

[1] Or what if so many monopolists entered the industry, with all keeping their price too high, but with total business so divided up among them that none ends up making any exorbitant monopoly profit? Then the evil effect on the income distribution would not exist, but the resulting wasteful pattern of over-capacity in the industry and too-high price could persist until doomsday. More on this when Chapter 25 treats imperfect competition.

The matter becomes more complicated if the sellers or the buyers in a market happen to be especially rich, or especially poor, or especially "deserving," or especially "undeserving."

For example, imagine an artificial case where a million very rich producers sell milk in competitive markets to 50 million very poor people. Some people would then be tempted to approve of any interference that lowered milk price. "That leads to what we regard as a fairer income distribution," they'd probably say.

It's not the economist's business to force his own ethical preferences on the whole community. I might happen to like rich people and dislike poor people. I might like to see the rich get more and the poor get less. The fact that I am a Ph.D. in economics wouldn't give me the right to foist such views on others, any more than that degree would give Professor Blank in my department the right to foist on the world his view about how worthy the poor are. As a citizen, an economist gets only one vote in these ethical matters.

But this is what we both might say:

▶   Interfering with the competitive supply and demand mechanism is an inefficient[1] way of correcting the income distribution. Whatever distribution you want to end up with can often be more efficiently reached by using the tax system to redistribute income rather than using *ad hoc* Robin Hood interferences in a single market. If taxation always could be counted on to keep society's For Whom problem optimally solved, then perfect competition (were it to prevail!) could be counted on to solve most What and How problems efficiently.

Naturally, all this is a controversial area. There is no one answer. And any

[1] The fact that buyers and sellers are different people who may be of different incomes or worth hides the truth that the competitive equilibrium point has certain allocative efficiency properties in solving the What and How economic problems. So consider a simplified case where I trade only with myself. I have 10 hours of leisure worth exactly $2.50 per hour to me. I can produce 1 Q unit with each hour of work or sacrificed leisure. Suppose the first Q unit is worth exactly $4 to me, and successive further Q units are worth $3, $2, $1, and $0, to me. Figure 3 shows *my* supply and demand for Q. Equilibrium is at E where I consume exactly $2Q$. I get $4 + $3 of "satisfaction" from them (as shown by the light shading) and 8 times $2.50 from my 8 hours left of leisure (as shown by the heavy shading): or $27 of satisfaction in all—as shown by the sum of the areas. You can show that any disturbance which makes me work 1 hour too much or too little kills off $.50 of my satisfaction. Distortion of a second hour kills off $1.50 of satisfaction; and so it goes, with each further distortion taking a heavier and heavier toll—as shown by the growing discrepancy between dd' and ss'.

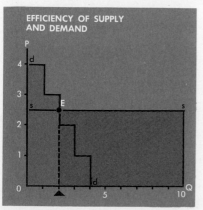

EFFICIENCY OF SUPPLY AND DEMAND

Fig. 3.

observer of the modern world can see that nations everywhere do interfere with the price system at many points. Examples: House rents are often controlled. Blood for transfusions is not primarily obtained by commercial bidding, but rather involves much voluntary effort. (Why?) Doctors often charge more to rich than poor patients, in part subsidizing the latter from revenues of the former. (Why this private system of taxation?) Milk and other foods are often subsidized by governments. Indeed, the next chapter will deal with the extensive agricultural aid programs which the federal government has been following.

SUMMARY

1. The apparatus of supply and demand enables us to analyze the effects of shifts in either curve or in both simultaneously. Beginners must avoid the pitfall of confusing the expression "an increase in demand" (*i.e.,* an outward shift of the whole demand curve) with "an increase in quantity demanded" as a result of a reduction in price) *i.e.,* a movement down an unchanged curve).

2. A tax of so many dollars per unit of a good will lead to a new equilibrium intersection and will be borne more largely by consumers to the degree that the demand is inelastic relative to the supply.

3. A thousand forces affect price. But in a free competitive market they do so only by acting through supply and demand. For example, cost of production affects competitive price only through affecting supply; not otherwise.

4. Although the government usually affects price by operating on either supply or demand, occasionally it passes laws that interfere with the workings of competitive markets. Under such circumstances, supply and demand need not be equal; some producer or consumer may *wish* to sell or buy more than he is able to do at the legal price. Unless the discrepancies are parceled out by legislation (rationing, etc.), disorder and black markets may result.

5. Haphazard, arbitrary interferences with supply and demand will often be harmful. Monopoly interference provides an obvious case, and here the evil is not so much that the distribution of income is distorted as that society unnecessarily has to put up with reduced output of a good that it really wants and it really can afford. Even in cases where government is interfering with supply and demand for the purpose of achieving some desired distribution of income or some other social goal, there may be hidden costs in the use of so inefficient a device—and it may often be the case that the same goal could better be accomplished by use of the tax system and preservation of the efficiency of market pricing.

QUESTIONS FOR DISCUSSION

1. Examine the diagram below, which shows demand and supply curves for wheat for different years, and then fill in the table alongside showing the price of wheat for each of the four years.

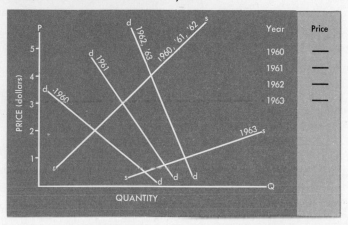

Year	Price
1960	___
1961	___
1962	___
1963	___

2. Show that, when demand is very inelastic, a sales tax will fall mostly on consumers. If demand is elastic, show the reverse. What if supply were very elastic, as in the case of a completely horizontal *ss* curve? What if supply were completely inelastic?

3. A ship arrives in port with an exceptionally large cargo of fish that will not keep. Use the market demand curve to show what determines the momentary equilibrium price. What if the fish could be stored? What common-sense modifications would you have to make in your conclusions?

4. Suppose that over the long run it costs $10,000 a trip to pay for a fishing ship's expenses. Suppose that each trip averages 50,000 pounds of fish. What will the long-run equilibrium price of fish be? Explain in terms of supply and demand. (Hint: Draw in a long-run horizontal supply curve at the proper level.)

5. Review your understanding of the following concepts:

demand versus amount de-
  manded

shift versus movement along a
  curve

incidence of a tax

cost of production, supply, and
  price

government actions to influence
  supply and demand curves

rationing and price fixing

monopoly reduction of output
  versus monopoly distortion of
  income distribution

possible efficiencies sacrificed
  when government interferes
  with supply and demand to
  achieve what it deems a worthy
  goal

APPENDIX: CASES ON SUPPLY AND DEMAND

Proposition 1

(a) As a general rule an increase in demand, supply being constant, will raise price. (b) Probably also, but less certainly, it will increase the quantity bought and sold. A decrease in demand has opposite effects.

Proposition 2

An increase in supply, demand being constant, will almost certainly lower price and increase the quantity bought and sold. The effects of a decrease in supply are just the opposite.

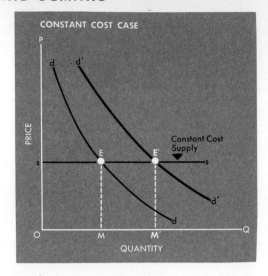

Fig. 4.

These two important propositions summarize the qualitative effects of shifts in supply and demand. But the exact quantitative degree of change in price and quantity depends upon the specific shapes of the curves in each instance.

As we'll see in detail later, behind every competitive supply curve there are cost considerations on the part of producers. If producing more of a good sends up the competitive producer's costs, the market will have to offer a higher price when it wants to coax out an increase in amount supplied. On the other hand if the industry finds it easy to buy more of every factor at unchanged factor prices, so that it can merely duplicate on ever larger scale its mode of production, then there will be an indefinitely large supply of output forthcoming even at the same market price.

Here then are a number of possible cost and supply situations.

Case 1. Constant cost. Imagine a manufactured item, like razor blades, whose production can be easily expanded by merely duplicating machinery, plant space, factories, and labor. To produce 100,000 blades per day simply requires us to do the same thing as when we were manufacturing 1,000 per day, except on a hundredfold scale. In this case the supply curve, *ss,* in Fig. 4, is a horizontal line at the constant level of unit costs.

A rise in demand will shift the new intersection point *E'* to the right, raising quantity but leaving price the same.

What will be the effects of a sales tax of, say, 5 cents per blade, on output and price paid by the consumer? Fill in the diagram.

Case 2. Increasing costs and diminishing returns. Suppose an industry like wine-grape growing requires a certain kind of soil and location (sunny hillsides, etc.). Such sites are limited in number. The annual output of wine can be increased to some extent by adding more labor and fertilizer to each acre of land and by bidding away more hill sites from other uses. But as we saw in Chapter 2, the law of diminishing returns will begin to operate if variable factors of production, like labor and fertilizer, are added to fixed amounts of a factor like land. Why is that? Because each new variable addition of labor and fertilizer has a *smaller proportion* of land to work with. By the same token, each fixed unit of land has more labor and fertilizer cooperating with it. Therefore land's productivity and earnings are higher. The result: getting extra amounts of wine sends total costs up more than proportionately.

Therefore, the cost per unit of wine is rising. The supply curve travels upward from southwest to northeast because at *lower* market prices, *less* will be supplied. At higher prices, *more* will be supplied.

Figure 5 shows the supply curve *ss*. What will be the effect on price of an increase in demand? Effect on quantity?

Show by a diagram that a tax of 5 cents per ounce of wine will raise price to the consumer by less than a similar tax on razors did. Why? What will be the effect on the price received by the producer? If the original demand curves for wine and razors are similar, show the fall in output will be *greater* for razors than for wine. Why?

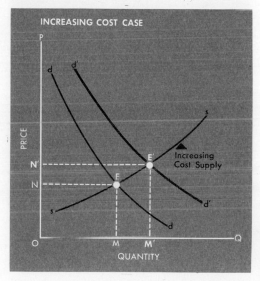

Fig. 5.

Case 3. Completely fixed or inelastic supply and economic rent. Some goods or productive factors are completely fixed in amount, regardless of price.

Thus, there is only one Mona Lisa painting. Nature's original endowment of the "natural and indestructible" qualities of land can also often be taken as fixed in amount. Raising the price offered for land cannot create more than four corners at State and Madison in Chicago. High-paid

artists and businessmen who love their work would continue to work at their jobs even at low pay. Once a bridge is built, it must earn "what the traffic will bear" regardless of past sunk costs. (Find other examples.)

In all such cases the supply curve goes straight up and down, at least in the relevant region. Look at Fig. 6. A higher price cannot elicit an increase in supply; nor is the higher price necessary to bring out the existing supply, for even at lower prices the same amount will still be forthcoming. Because it is price-determined rather than price-determining, the return to the factor of production is called a "pure economic rent or surplus," which need not be paid to call out the required supply.

If now demand shifts upward, the whole effect is to raise price. Quantity is unchanged. And the rise in price exactly equals the upward shift in demand.

Likewise if a tax is placed upon the commodity, its whole effect is to reduce the price received by the supplier by exactly the amount of the tax. The tax is shifted back completely to the supplier, who absorbs it all out of his economic rent or surplus. The consumer buys exactly as much of the good or service as before and at no extra cost.

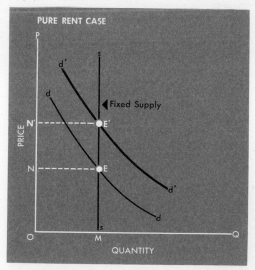

Fig. 6.

Case 4. A backward rising supply curve. Early explorers into new lands often noted that, when you raised the wages of natives, you received less labor rather than more. If wages were doubled, instead of working 6 days a week for their minimum of subsistence, the natives might go fishing for 3 days. The same has been observed among so-called "modern civilized people." As improved technology raises real wages, people feel that they ought to take part of their higher earnings in the form of more leisure and less work. This partly explains why over the decades the average factory working week has dropped from 84 to 40 hours, and why wives, children, and aged parents of workers do not have to find jobs in such great numbers to help make ends meet.

Figure 7 indicates the supply curve of labor in this case. At first it rises as higher wages coax out more labor, but beyond the point *T* higher wages induce more leisure and less work. An increase in demand does increase the price of labor in agreement with Proposition 1 (*a*). But note how lucky we were to have added the words "but less certainly" in 1 (*b*)! For the increase in demand has *decreased* rather than increased the quantity of labor.

A partial verification of such a possibility is found in the fact that a decrease in demand for farm products during a depression often causes farmers to work harder in order to restore their incomes. The result: More rather than less is produced in response to a decrease in demand.

Case 5. A possible exception: decreasing cost. Heretofore our examples have agreed with Proposition 1 (*a*), that an increase in demand raises price. But what about the often observed case where an increase in demand is followed by economies of mass production and decreasing costs?

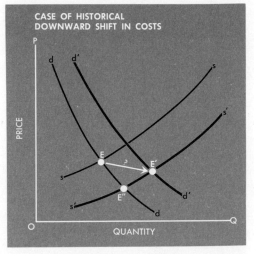

CASE OF HISTORICAL DOWNWARD SHIFT IN COSTS

Fig. 8.

A good theory must make room for all the facts. So we must frankly admit our first proposition may break down and have exceptions. Of course, we can try to save face by pointing out that many of the important reductions in cost following an increase in demand really represent *permanent downward shifts* in the supply curve rather than movements down a falling supply curve.

Let's illustrate this by the case where the government increases its demand for radar sets. The first few sets built must be constructed in the laboratory by experimental methods. They are tailor-made, and very expensive per unit. But the know-how gained in the process makes possible the further

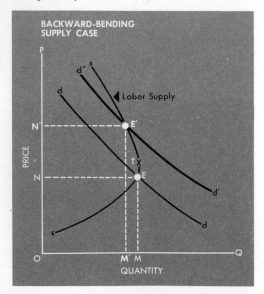

Fig. 7.

production of sets for much less per unit. Even if demand went back again to its previous level, price wouldn't return to its previous higher level. In traveling along Fig. 8's arrow *EE'* marked with a question mark, we are not moving reversibly along the supply curve. Instead, the supply curve has shifted irreversibly downward from *ss* to *s's'*, so that, even when demand is back again at *dd,* the price is now lower at *E"* than it was originally.

The case discussed really does not come under the heading of Proposition 1, but under Proposition 2 dealing with shifts in supply. The final result agrees with the latter's conclusion that an increase in supply will lower price and increase quantity. (Compare *E* and *E".*) But the present case is still an unusual one because the shift of supply has been *induced* by a shift in demand.

From the standpoint of economic history, there is tremendous importance in such cases of reduced cost over time as a result of technological progress partly induced by the expansion of a mass market. Goods are constantly being improved in quality and cheapened in price.

What about the case of genuine *reversible* economies of large-scale production—cases where going back to small-scale production does again send costs up? The alert modern economist will not deny its importance. But he will point out that in a competitive industry each firm will have *already* expanded its output to where the *extra* cost of producing a unit of output has begun to turn up. This is so because each competitive producer will have no fear of spoiling his own market and will have had every incentive to expand his production through and beyond the decreasing cost stage.[1] (Later chapters analyze the imperfect competition that results when

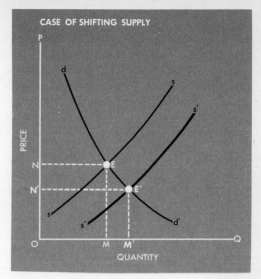

CASE OF SHIFTING SUPPLY

Fig. 9.

a few firms have decreasing cost and hence expand to capture much of the market.)

Case 6. Shifts in supply. All the above discussion, with the exception of part of Case 5, dealt with a shift in demand and no shift in supply. To analyze Proposition 2, we must now shift supply, keeping demand constant. This is done in Fig. 9.

If the law of downward-sloping demand is valid, then increased supply must send us *down* the demand curve, decreasing price and increasing quantity. The student may verify, by drawing diagrams or by comparing automobiles and wheat, the following quantitative corollaries of Proposition 2:

a. An increase in supply will decrease price most when demand is inelastic, and decrease price least when demand is relatively elastic.

b. An increase in supply will increase quantity least when demand is inelastic, most when demand is elastic.

---

[1] There remains one possibility discussed in advanced economic textbooks. If an increased demand for an industry's product causes each firm's cost curve to *shift downward* (a) because cheaper and better trained labor becomes available, (b) because better information centers and markets are created, (c) because productivity of factors in one firm is enhanced by expanded pro- duction elsewhere, or (d) because raw materials produced at decreasing costs by other quasi- monopolized industries become cheaper, then this industry may have a truly reversible, com- petitive supply curve which is downward slop- ing. Marshall called this a case of "*external econ- omies*" of production, *i.e.,* external to each firm.

What are common-sense reasons for these? Illustrate with autos or wheat.

Three Exceptions

In concluding, three rather unimportant exceptions to the universal law of downward-sloping demand will be briefly mentioned.

First, items such as diamonds or women's hats that are valued not for their intrinsic qualities so much as for their "snob appeal" and expensiveness may fall off in demand if their price is cut. Chic shops sometimes find they do better in moving a slow-selling item if they raise its price.[1] Customers think, "It really must be good if it costs so much," as if it were universally true that "You only get what you pay for." Thorstein Veblen[2] coined the phrase "conspicuous consumption" for cases where things are valued because their price tag shows all over them.

A second exception to the law of downward-sloping consumption may be important. When the price of steel or a share of common stock is first lowered, buyers may not think to themselves, "Ah, this is now cheap. I will buy." Instead they may think, "Aha! Price is falling and will probably fall still more. I'll cut down on my orders and wait until the price falls farther." The same effect (in reverse) is often observed when prices begin to rise: buyers rush to buy in anticipation of still higher prices. Result: in the short run amount demanded may rise rather than fall with increases in price.[3]

The third exception is trifling, but interesting as a curiosity. Certain items, like potatoes, are bought in great quantity by poor people just because they are cheap and filling. In nineteenth-century Ireland, the peasants were so poor that a good deal of their income was spent in this way. Only in good times did they have a little money to spend on meat, bread, and perhaps a few lace curtains. Now what would happen if the price of potatoes should rise? To the despairing housewife this would be just like a cut in her man's income. The family now becomes so poor that, paradoxically, it has to give up all meat and luxuries and fill up even more than before on potatoes. So, the higher the price, the more may potatoes be demanded!

The student may try his hand at finding still other exceptions. But he must not commit the cardinal error of confusing a shift in demand with a movement along the curve. He will receive harsh treatment at the bar of justice if he offers, as a fourth exception, the fact that in prosperity price goes up and so does the quantity demanded. Why?

---

[1] A Boston night club claims to be the "most expensive place in town."

[2] T. VEBLEN, *The Theory of the Leisure Class* (Macmillan, New York, 1899).

[3] This is a dynamic effect hinging not on high or low levels of price but on "the rate of change of price." The destabilizing effects of this are shown in connection with Chapter 22's discussion of stock-market speculation.

21

SUPPLY AND DEMAND AS APPLIED TO AGRICULTURE

American farm leaders are correct in arguing that our agriculture still must look forward to a definite "surplus" problem. What they tend to overlook, however, is of what our "surplus" consists. Fundamentally America's long-term agricultural problem is not one of "surplus" cotton, wheat or grapefruit. Rather it is one of "surplus" farmers.

WILLIAM H. NICHOLLS

The economist's model of perfect competition, in which a homogeneous product is produced by many different people and auctioned off in a well-organized market, does not fit most of American life at all closely. Therefore, in Chapters 24 and 25 we shall have to supplement it by the new tools of imperfect or monopolistic competition.

There is, however, one great area that does provide a valuable application of the basic tools of supply and demand. Agriculture is an important problem area. It makes the news. It shifts votes. No one can possibly understand the vital policy issues in this field without first understanding the basic economic concepts of supply and demand. This chapter describes the general agricultural problem and applies those tools to it.

▶ **RELATIVE DECLINE OF AGRICULTURE**

Farming is still America's largest single industry. But the percentage of people engaged in farming has been declining steadily for the last two centuries. We used to be a nation of farmers. That's no longer true. Though farmers still swing much political weight, today only 1 out of any 10 American workers works in agriculture!

Why this relative shift away from farming? The answer is simple: Country people prefer to move to town and city. Young people seek higher incomes in the city; they seek shorter hours; they seek what they seem to regard as the better social life in town.

Many social observers deplore the exodus away from the country, cities having a bad reputation among moralists. But this is a free country, and if people want to leave the farms, they simply pick up and go. This pattern is nothing new. It has been going on throughout our history. In each depression the cityward flow has slowed down, only to resume again in prosperity.

Differential birth rates. In a way, it is lucky this is so. For, as we saw in Chapter 2, birth rates are much higher in rural areas than in cities. If it were not for this migration, cities would grow smaller and smaller; the rural share of total population would grow larger and larger. What does the law of diminishing returns tell us this would mean? It would mean a great reduction in the productivity of each man-hour spent on the farm. And what does our common sense tell us must then be the law of the market place if an increasing part of the nation's production were to take the form of food and fiber rather than other products? Obviously, the dollar prices of foods would go way down in comparison with the dollar prices of other things. The land would become crowded with many people, each producing little and each unable to buy many of the comforts of life with his produce.

Does this sound far-fetched? It is a true picture of about two-thirds of the globe. In Asia especially, standards of living are pitifully poor. With three out of every four persons engaged in producing the food necessary for life, only one out of four can be producing the bare comforts of life. Contrast this to the United States, where each worker is today efficient enough to feed 16 other people well!

Technological change and patterns of taste. Besides the differential in birth rates, there are two other reasons why agriculture is declining in relative importance: Technological progress has been greatly reducing the number of people needed to produce any given total of food and fiber. Use of the tractor, the combine, the cotton picker, irrigation, fertilizer, selective breeding of hybrid corn and livestock, and numerous other examples come to mind.

Coupled with the improvement in laborsaving technique is the unshakable fact that, *as we get richer, we do not want to expand our food consumption by as much as we want to expand our consumption of city products.* This has been shown by almost every statistical investigation here and abroad.

So birth rates, tastes, and technology dictate that agriculture must export people to industry.

▶ POVERTY IN AGRICULTURE

An enduring American vision is that of the "family farm." This is run by father, mother, and children, with possibly a little outside help; it is a reasonably efficient unit and it produces at least a minimum income level, comparable to that of city living after taking account of the extra pleasures and duties that go with self-reliant country living.

Let us turn from vision to fact. Professor Theodore Schultz of the University of Chicago has pointed out that this definition automatically excludes numerous sharecroppers; and from the 5½ million remaining farms of 1940, Schultz eliminates country residences, large nonfamily farms, and about 1 million subsistence farmers who did not earn a cash income of even $600 in 1940. This leaves about 3 million farms that *might* be classed as family farms. But in Schultz's judgment about half of these, which had prewar farm incomes of less than $1,200 or $1,500, could not be regarded as representing a reasonably efficient use of resources. So in the end, he finds that only a fraction of all American farms were before the war at all like the American dream.

Even today most family farms are not fully sharing in the nation's economic progress. The sad fact is that 100,000 farmers with the largest farms produce more than do the 2,500,000 poorest farm families (who don't even earn $2500 a year). These 2 per cent largest farmers get no less than 26 per cent of total farm receipts. This means that most farm land is very low producing. A hidden surplus of population exists in the form of low-productivity marginal farm residents. Family farms will have to grow in size and shrink in number.

The *paid farm laborer* was, before the war, one of the lowest paid of all workers. It is estimated that two-fifths of the 2½ million farm laborers received less than $250 per year over and above their keep! And only one-fifth received more than $500. During the war, the drafting of farm hands and the upswing in farm earnings sent farm wages up. By 1958 farm wages had increased sixfold in comparison with the average before World War I, but still averaged little more than $45 a week (plus house, but without board). Even if the increase persists, this is still a low wage, considering the length of the working day and the exertion involved.

The Southern white or Negro *sharecropper,* who owns neither land nor tools and who lives during the year on credit and goods advanced from the company store, is a more complex case. In ordinary years, he is lucky if the cotton crop brings him enough cash to pay off the I.O.U.'s that he has incurred. Often he is chained to risking everything on a single crop—cotton —because it cannot be eaten or easily stolen. A week after the harvest he is again in debt, again on the interminable annual treadmill. In exceptional years when the crop sells for a high value, he may make a profit high enough to pay back past debts and still have something left over. He is therefore a capitalist in a certain sense, but usually he would gladly change this status for decent wages. This explains the influx of Southern Negroes and poor whites into the Northern cities during the two wars and since.

The *tenant farmer* represents another intermediate case typical of all parts of the United States. Ordinarily, he rents land for a fixed price or on some sort of sharing basis. He may live on the farm, provide all the labor, occasionally own half the equipment and half the livestock, and quite commonly share 50–50 in the annual return. Under the most favorable circumstances, tenant farming represents the stepladder by which a young farmer is able to climb to ownership of his own establishment. But when agriculture is depressed for many years, as in the period between the two world wars, even independent farmers lose their holdings through widespread mortgage foreclosure, and the traffic on the ladder may be predominantly downward.

▶ INSTABILITY IN AGRICULTURE

Farming is an up-and-down industry. Corn, wheat, beef, pork, and other farm products are sold in highly competitive markets whose prices change yearly, daily, hourly, and by the minute. The farmer swings at the very end of our seesawing economy. Good times bring him great percentage increases in income. Depressions cause his cash income to drop away to very little. The farmer particularly benefits from wartime demand conditions; and unlike most of the community, the farmer can ride out an inflationary period of skyrocketing prices. But since 1947 farm income has been sliding downward relative to other incomes.

If we look closely at farm statistics, we note a surprising fact. Farm *incomes* fluctuate between boom and bust to a greater degree than do nonfarm incomes, but farm *production* is remarkably more stable than is industrial production. Even the weather, which is a great threat to stability of income in any one farm region, does not cause sizable fluctuations in total farm crops over the whole nation. During the last quarter century, industrial production had an average year-to-year variation of about 14 per cent, while agricultural production had less than a 4 per cent average variation.

No wonder the farmer feels he is at the mercy of a fluctuating market. His supply curves are relatively inelastic for many reasons: (1) His own effort may increase when P is low as he desperately tries to maintain his family's income; (2) many of his costs go on anyway, whether he produces much or little, and if he can't save much extra cost by cutting his Q, why do so?

Amount demanded of farm products, in addition to growing little when income rises, is also quite inelastic to price changes. What then is the result of the condition (a) relatively inelastic demand coupled with (b) relatively inelastic supply?

To answer this, take a clean sheet of paper. Draw on it a quite-vertical supply curve intersecting a quite-vertical demand curve. Now shift either curve the least little bit. Do you see how great are the resulting shifts in P! How would you like it if your baby's operation or your daughter's college education depended upon a tiny shift of supply and demand with a resulting whopping change in your family's income?

Figure 1 will show that fluctuations in the prices received by farmers are greater than the fluctuations in the prices of the things they must buy. In the Great Depression days of the early 1930's prices received by farmers dropped about twice as far as did prices elsewhere. Even in the prosperous 1920's the farmer did badly; and remember, to make things worse, he then carried a heavy burden of mortgage debt incurred during the tremendous land boom at the end of World War I. Farmers are today asking: "Is the 1960 era another era like the 1920's when everyone prospered but us?"

▶ GOVERNMENT AID TO AGRICULTURE

Agriculture may be the unlucky stepchild of nature, but it is certainly the favored foster child of government. From the beginning of time, the public seems always to have hated a landlord and loved a farmer. So there is fairly widespread support among the electorate at large for aid to the farmer.

Prior to 1929, the principal government aid to agriculture came through our public land policy aimed at getting acreage into the hands of settlers and through the elaborate practical and scientific aids to improved agricultural methods and conservation. The work done in agricultural experiment stations at the so-called state land-grant colleges is well known; and in every farm district, the government-paid county agent is an important source of help toward efficient farming.

But in 1929 under the Hoover administration, the Federal Farm Board was set up. A new era of direct aid to farmers began. Subsequently under various alphabet agencies (the AAA, the CCC, etc.) the government has stepped in to "interfere with the natural laws of supply and demand" so as to increase the stability and level of farm incomes.[1] Both political parties have pledged themselves to a continuation and extension of such activities; the powerful Farm Bureau Federation, Grange, and Farmers' Union maintain close contact with Washington to make sure Congress knows farmers' wishes.

▶ THE PARITY CONCEPT

The years 1910 to 1914 are often looked back upon as the golden age of agriculture. So over the years there grew up political pressure to have the government somehow guarantee to the farmer prices as favorable as then prevailed. This is the root notion of "parity."

---

[1] Also, the Farm Credit Administration (FCA) and the Rural Electrification Administration (REA) are government agencies set up to help the farmer borrow at low interest rates and to bring him electric power.

Parity is the ratio of prices the farmer gets to prices that he pays:

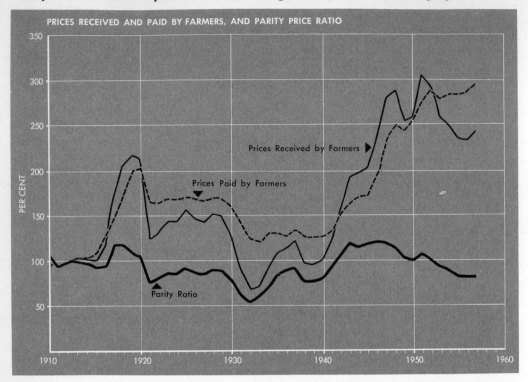

Fig. 1. If the change since 1910–1914 in prices farmers receive for their products just matched the change in the prices they pay for goods, the parity price ratio curve would be at 100. Its being recently around 80 shows that prices received by farmers have not risen as much as have prices they must pay.

In practice, several complexities enter into any parity formula. As Fig. 1 shows, the prices of the things the farmer buys have risen. So to arrive at the parity figure, we must take (1) today's actual price in relation to the 1910–1914 price, and then correct this ratio by dividing it through by (2) today's prices of the things farmers buy in relation to what they were in the base period. If the resulting ratio is below 100, what does that mean? It means farmer's prices have fallen behind other prices.

Parity sounds simple, doesn't it? And rather fair, especially since we all like farmers and their votes? Why then the fight to have the government drop its support of prices at 90 per cent of parity in favor of "flexible price supports" at 70 to 90 per cent of parity—or even the abandonment of all government price supports?

Deeper analysis shows that, as demand and supply change over a long period of time, the attempt to peg price at any arbitrary level will result in a literal avalanche of surplus farm goods. The dollar costs of aid will become astronomical. The distortions of production will become cumulatively greater and greater. Thus, the government storage bins are bursting, and even the moth-ball fleet of abandoned warships has had to be used for storage; grain has had to be stored on the ground itself. And the end is not in sight.

The reason for all this we shall see in detail in a moment. It is enough here to point out that technology on the farm has changed greatly since 1914. Then we used horses and mules; now, tractors. Then we used conventional seed; now, hybrid varieties. In short, the real costs of production have gone down immensely since then; so to peg prices at the old levels calls forth a supply much larger than will ever be bought in the market at the parity prices.[1] For the efficient farmers, it means incomes running into six figures! And it keeps inefficient farmers from going to higher-productivity occupations.

Farmers boast of their independence; and when they come to the government for help—as they most certainly do—they claim they don't want a handout, but rather that they want to "earn" their subsidies. But actually, in many postwar years, more than half of what the farmers collected in the market place for certain crops—such as peanuts, sorghum grain, and others—has in fact come from government aid programs!

▶ FORMS OF GOVERNMENT AID

What are the economic mechanisms by which government can help, or seem to help, the farmer? They are principally five in number:

1. Outright gift or relief payments, given to needy farmers who have established their need and misery.

2. Programs by the government that aim to increase the demand for farm products or cut their real cost of production.

3. Crop-limitation programs (such as the "Soil Bank") that aim to cut supply and raise price.

4. Purchase-loan storage programs to guarantee or support prices.

5. Finally, purchase-and-resale differential subsidy plans connected with the names of Eisenhower's Secretary of Agriculture Benson and Truman's Brannan.

Gifts and relief. There is nothing complicated about outright gifts or transfer payments, and we need say little about them here. The farm pressure groups don't particularly want them, even though in strictest economic logic they are the most defensible of all: If our republic wants to favor farmers and provide minimum standards for all, outright gifts will clarify exactly what is involved and what it costs, thereby enabling the electorate to rationally decide on what it wants to do.

---

[1] This is so obvious that the 1910–1914 parity is recomputed today for particular crops, taking into account price changes and cost changes in comparison with data over the 10 years just past. This permits parity to adjust slowly to changing real costs.

Demand promotion and research. Little too need be said about attempts by the Department of Agriculture to find new chemical uses of farm products, or to send out circulars telling people to eat better diets. (It may also get Congress to provide funds to provide cheap school lunches and other demand-raising programs.) Such activity goes a long way back in our history, as does government aid to land-grant colleges' experimental work to increase farm productivity. Not only will the Department of Agriculture send a farmer a pamphlet on baking an angel-food cake or running a Halloween party; it will also send a county agent to teach him good conservation methods, how to keep records, and how best to till his soil. Some observers think it odd that while one branch of the government is trying to get the farmer to produce less, another branch is trying to improve his productivity!

► **ECONOMICS OF THREE MAIN AID PROGRAMS**

For the remaining three programs, the tools of supply and demand are absolutely necessary. Let's see how each of the three cases works.

1. *Crop-restriction and Soil Bank.* The Secretary of Agriculture has the legal right to propose acreage controls limiting total acres that can be planted of a given crop and assigning acreage quotas for each farmer. All the wheat farmers, for example, vote on whether they want these acreage controls. They always tend to vote Yes by whopping majorities. Why? Because they like to cut down on acreage and get low quotas? No. Rather because they know that failing to limit crops will send prices way downward.

Since 1956 the Madison Avenue name of "Soil Bank" has been introduced to cover the program in which farmers agree to withdraw some acres of land from production, putting them into the Soil Bank in return for a payment equal to the profit that could have been earned on them. This cut in acreage is designed to reduce output of surplus wheat, cotton, corn, tobacco, and rice. (Some of the withdrawn acres aim to promote long-run conservation by going into grass, trees, and water-conserving uses.)

Of course, when a wheat farmer puts 10 of his 100 acres in the Soil Bank, he picks the worst ones. And he cultivates his other 90 so much harder as to produce from them almost as much wheat as he used to be able to produce from the whole 100. (He might also be able to put the 10 Bank acres into alfalfa or sorghum, thereby adding to the surplus of feed crops which compete with wheat.) For these and other reasons, don't think that the Soil Bank is a *permanent* way of reducing the supply curve by much.

Figure 2 shows how crop restrictions actually work. Before the government steps in, the supply and demand curves are given by *ss'* and *dd'*. The equilibrium price would be at *E*. The farmers now limit their acreage; and let's suppose, even though many of the facts suggest that this is not a true

A cut in farm supply raises price and total revenue:

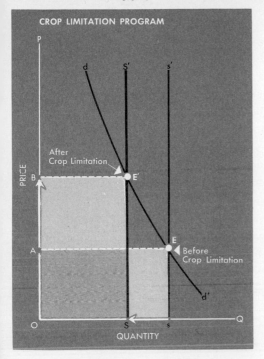

Fig. 2. Suppose the Soil Bank or allotment program succeeds in cutting supply from *ss'* to *SS'*, thereby raising price to *E'*. Provided demand is Inelastic, total farm Income (measured by the *E* and *E'* rectangular areas) is thereby increased.

supposition, that the program does succeed in limiting the supply produced of the farm crop. What has the result been?

The new supply curve is shown by *SS'*. It intersects the demand curve at the new higher equilibrium price shown by *E'*. The consumer is paying a higher price and consuming a smaller quantity. The farmer is receiving a higher price. But he is selling a smaller output. Is he better or worse off?

The answer depends primarily upon the elasticity of demand. If the demand curve for agriculture is inelastic, as many authorities believe, then a cut in output will raise price so much that the total revenue collected will actually increase.

▶   If the demand for farm products is inelastic rather than elastic, then a program of crop reduction will result in higher total receipts to the farmer. And since he also saves a little costs when he produces less, his net revenue goes up by even more than his total receipts do.

Before leaving this first and simplest case, let's recall that we can read off total revenue from a demand-curve diagram: Total revenue at a point like *E* can be shown by the area of the rectangle that *E* forms with the two axes. Remembering that the area of any rectangle is always equal to its altitude times its base, look at the rectangle *OAEs*. Note that its altitude *OA* is price. Note that its base *Os* is quantity. Its area, therefore, represents price times quantity, or total dollar revenue.

We can now picture our above result. Because the demand curve is inelastic, the area of the rectangle formed by means of the new equilibrium point *E'* is necessarily *greater* than the area formed by the old equilibrium point *E*. Does your eye confirm the fact that the new rectangle more than makes up in height what it loses in width? (The reader can show how this whole argument goes into reverse if the demand curve is elastic.)

2. *Parity price through government purchase or loan support.* This case is a little harder. Now government guarantees the farmer a price higher than would have prevailed in the market. This "price floor" is shown by the white line *BB'* in Fig. 3. At so high a price, consumers will not buy all the crop supplied. Consumers will be on the demand curve at the point *C*. But farmers are supplying the full amount shown by the point *F*. If government does nothing, price must fall to *E*, which is below the parity price.

So what does the government have to do? By outright purchase or through some kind of loan red tape, it must acquire the unsold portion between *C* and *F*, marked with an arrow. This either will go into storage or will have to be left to rot. What then has the final result been?

Government loans or purchases support price
by acquiring unsold surplus:

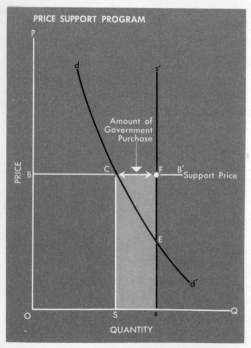

Fig. 3. The government keeps price at indicated floor or support price *BB'* (near or at parity) by acquiring for storage unsellable surplus shown by *CF*. The shaded area shows the total cost to the government of raising market price from *E* to *F*. Note that consumers pay the higher price and get no current benefit from the *CF* part of the crop.

The government has incréased the price received by the farmer from E to F. But unlike the previous case, the farmers can now sell as much as they want to; so the increased price is clear gravy to them, representing a clear increase in their incomes. The consumers are now paying a higher price and buying less; to them Case 2 is just as bad as Case 1. Who then is footing the bill for the extra income now received by the farmers in comparison with the previous case? Obviously, the government: The Treasury is having to shell out an amount of dollars equal to the part of the crop they must buy times the full market price. (In terms of area, the Treasury's expense is shown by the shaded area $CFsS$. Can you explain why?)

Of course if the demand curve dd' were in later years to shift upward so that it intersected the supply curve at F or above, then the Treasury would not have to do anything to ensure parity. Indeed, it might in such a prosperous year exactly reverse the above procedure; instead of buying part of the crop to add to storage, it might take food out of storage and sell it. The interested reader can draw a new curve DD', showing how this reverse process works. (Hint: Now the Treasury collects revenue instead of incurring costs, as actually did happen during World War II.)

3. *Subsidized producer-consumer price differential.* This is the hardest case of all. Although originally proposed by Truman's Secretary of Agriculture Brannan for perishable goods, this resale proposal has also been advocated by Eisenhower's Benson with respect to butter and was passed by the Republican Congress with respect to wool.

Here, the farmer is again guaranteed the BB' parity price just as in the previous case. But Fig. 4 must now show the new fact that food, instead of being left to rot in storage, is to be sold to the public for current consumption at whatever market price it will bring.

How is the farmer to receive the parity price if market price proves to be below that figure? The Department of Agriculture simply writes him a check for the difference. In effect, then, it is much as though the government had bought the crop at the parity price—as in Case 2's loan support—but had then sold it on the open market for whatever price it would bring. Next page's Fig. 4 illustrates the essence of the result.

Every bit produced, as shown by the ss' supply curve, will now go to the consumer. Consumption will end up at the original point E. Why? Because the "law of supply and demand" tells us that, for consumers to buy the full crop, price must fall to the point where the demand curve intersects the market supply. But producers are promised the parity price for their entire crop. So the price they are to receive is indicated by F (just as in Case 2). Who pays the difference? The government—by sending each primary producer a check, whose amount per bushel is shown in Fig. 4 by the vertical arrow EF.

How much does this cost the government? The answer is clear, once we

Benson-Brannan plan pays farmers gap between actual consumer's price and producer's supported price:

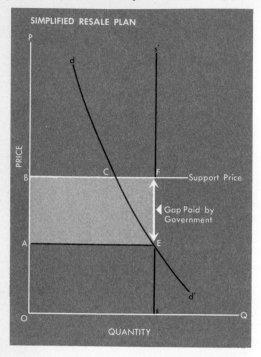

SIMPLIFIED RESALE PLAN

Fig. 4. The government lets price to consumer fall to *E*. It then makes up, by direct payments to farmers of *FE* per bushel, the difference between the low market price and the desired support price. The shaded area shows the cost to government of the direct payments involved in such a two-price system.

realize the government must pay the difference between the producers' and consumers' price *on each and every unit produced!* (In terms of area, the expense to the government is the shaded rectangular area *ABFE*. Here the shaded rectangle goes all the way leftward to the price axis, whereas back in Case 2 the shaded rectangle of government expense went all the way downward to the quantity axis.)

An important but tricky question is the following: Will the Benson-Brannan plan of Case 3 cost the Treasury more or less than would Case 2's plan of having the government withhold from the consumers part of the crop? The answer to this complicated question turns out to depend upon our old friend elasticity of demand and upon nothing else.

Look at the problem this way: Under either plan the *producers* are equally well off, being at *F* in both cases and receiving the same total income. Remember, too, that under either plan the producers' revenue can come from only two sources: the total revenue paid by the consumers plus the government's contribution. Hence, to answer the question, "Which plan costs the government more dollars?" we need only answer the much simpler question, "Which plan collects the greater total revenue from consumers: the plan where the consumers pay a high price and buy little; or the plan where consumers pay a low price and buy much?"

But note: this is nothing but the question we have met again and again in connection with the definition of elasticity. A point high up on the demand curve like *C* will collect more total revenue than a point low down like *E* provided the demand is *inelastic* in that interval. If demand were *elastic*, then the reverse would be true.

So now we can answer the question of relative cost as follows: The Benson-Brannan plan of making more food available to consumers will currently cost the Treasury more money than will a purchase-for-storage-or-destruction program provided the demand curve is *inelastic*. If it is *elastic*, the reverse will be true. (Needless to say, a plan that makes more food available to consumers may be considered by some citizens the preferable program, even if it costs the Treasury more money. And to the degree that, the government really wants a larger stockpile of food against a future war emergency or shortage period, the value of the inventory it is acquiring will have to be taken into account.[1])

► ISSUES IN FARM AID

When a Senator speaks of an excess of farm supply over demand and of a crop surplus, what does he mean exactly? He must mean that the amount supplied would exceed the amount demanded *at the existing or desired market price.* He can't sensibly mean that supply would be above demand *at every price,* however low.

In the early New Deal years the emphasis was on crop reduction, and there was much editorial weeping for the little pigs being killed and crops aborted. Then, after the Supreme Court declared the Agricultural Adjustment Act unconstitutional, the emphasis shifted to price supports through government purchase and loan. Huge government surpluses naturally resulted, but the war happened to come along and made those surpluses worthwhile. Again in the postwar the old problem of excess production returned.

To continue to support prices at parity or even 90 per cent of parity would have been collossally expensive in view of the great improvements in farm productivity. And such a support program would have resulted in more government inventory than warehouses could hold. So the palmy 1945–1947 days of farm prosperity have been steadily ebbing away and Congress has been forced into abandoning 90 per cent of parity.

Even a flexible-price support program at 70 per cent of parity has resulted in such tremendous production outpouring as to bring the emphasis back again to crop restriction, now in the guise of the Soil Bank as well as in a continuation and a stiffening of allotment programs. But with each cut in

[1] All this will remain for a long time a political issue. No one will begrudge the farmer his desire to be free from wildly fluctuating prices. In the next chapter we shall see how private speculators on an organized exchange are supposed in traditional economic theory to be able to iron out any *foreseeable* fluctuations. The question remains whether, gifts aside, we can expect the government to make better forecasts of the uncertain future than can private speculative markets, and through its storage program more successfully stabilize prices.

acres, the ingenuity of farmers in growing more per acre has shown that this too can only be a stop gap.

Only a stop gap too has been the practice of dumping our surpluses abroad. What does this mean? It means that we sell cotton and wheat for less abroad than at home, figuring that anything we can get for these white elephants is all to the good. And it means we give to our allies or friends in the form of foreign aid some of our surplus crops. Naturally our dumping wheat abroad infuriates our Canadian friends, whose export markets are undercut. And it infuriates our domestic textile producers to have their foreign rivals producing textiles at a competitive advantage out of American cotton that has been sold abroad for less than we charge at home.

► **WHAT ECONOMIC ANALYSIS CAN SUGGEST**

At the end of the last chapter we saw that there is often a strong case for sticking to the competitive market's outcome. The main exception was (1) when the people helped by government interference are somehow strongly preferable to those who are hurt and (2) in case it can be shown that there is no better way of helping them out of general taxes. How does this apply to the farm problem?

Many tough-minded economists would argue that much of our government aid now goes to very prosperous commercial farmers. They would argue that if the public realized how much of the artificial dollar aid is going to farmers who earn $20,000 a year or at least incomes way above the median income level, voters would not approve such expensive aid. And if the public realized how the really poor farmers, those whose poverty makes them most deserving from the need standpoint, have so little of the aid filtering down to them, again there might be a political turnaround.

What kind of a political turnaround? One that involves giving whatever aid you decide to give to farmers in a more efficient way—so as to leave the rest of us with more than under present inefficient arrangements. And one that involves more pinpointing of the aid given to those who actually merit it by need.

Such a turnaround would involve more reliance on market forces in determining food and fiber prices. As prices fell, consumers generally would be able to afford more food and especially more of the expensive protein foods like milk and meat. Commercial farmers would have pressure on them to become more efficient, and many of the remaining family farmers would find their incomes so low in agriculture as to be driven into industry. The really poor farmers would, under such a program, receive welfare aids—not so much because they are farmers but for the same reason that government welfare aid is given to any families who are in poverty and who need rehabilitation. The tough-minded economists who argue like this say:

► In terms of resource allocation the American people so little value an extra unit of food relative to other things, and our technology so easily permits us to produce an extra unit of food, as to make it most worthwhile for us to equate supply and demand for food at low prices—at prices so low as to coax resources out of agriculture and into industry where they will produce things for which there is a demand in the form of consumers' money votes unbuttressed by artificial government aids.[1]

► **THE LONG-RUN SOLUTION?**

Does all this sound cruel and heartless—too tough-minded? Speaking as but one citizen, I must confess that I do find it a little extreme in that it gives too little weight to the argument that a civilization is happier which seeks to protect any group in it from sudden and drastic changes in its status. But in any case there is little danger that it will soon be put into action. The politics of agricultural aid is too intense to make any major changes in present practices likely.

None the less this economic analysis does point out the only ultimate solution. That solution, as portrayed in the quotation from Vanderbilt's expert agricultural economist, W. H. Nicholls, is to reduce our surplus of farmers. No doubt this has to be done gradually. And it is actually happening every year. Each year there are fewer and fewer people in agriculture.

If you feel like mourning over this century-old trend, consider the following parable.

Back in Andrew Jackson's day, the American people discovered that cheap western land was depressing farm prices. So they then introduced an AAA program. Later the Whigs stepped up this program, and in the post-Civil-War Grant Administration, the program was stepped up still further.

To restore the golden age of 1820, the government bought and burned crops. This became so expensive that it also had to give each farmer an acreage quota. By 1860 each farmer had to leave one acre fallow for each acre he cultivated. By 1900 he could cultivate only 1 acre in 10. By 1970, so rapid was technological innovation that he could cultivate only 1 acre in 30. And even then, the government found itself taxing one-third the Net National Product for purchases of crops to burn. Yet America's 50 million people—her population couldn't grow much under such a regime!—were so dedicated to helping agriculture that they cheerfully carried the burden. And why not?

[1] Footnote readers can refer to p. 397's note for a graph of this argument that uninterfered-with equilibrium pricing is most efficient. This type of argument would take explicit notice of the fact that in a future war food might be important, but would argue that present subsidies are both inefficient and exorbitant from this viewpoint.

More than half of the working force had to labor on the 1 acre in 30 in order to support the other half. The average income per head was in 1970 about that which prevailed in Japan, a country unlucky enough not to have a wonderful agricultural aid program.

Everybody was happy. Except for one thing. Americans feared that with so low an income they would be unable to equip a strong army against the Russians, who each year foolishly encouraged their farm and city productivity and who looked with longing eyes on all 30 out of each 30 lush North American acres.

Of course, this is a rather silly parable. It overstates the case and that's not fair. And yet . . . And yet . . . for all its foolishness might there not be a trace of a moral in it?

SUMMARY

1. Although the rural birth rate is higher than the urban, a persistent cityward migration means that the percentage of the population engaged in agriculture is declining. Improvements in agricultural techniques mean that the same total of food can be produced with fewer workers; and as incomes increase, the increase in demand for food is less than proportionate. Farm income is low and unstable; as a result, government adopted a variety of programs to support farm-product prices and maintain farm incomes.

2. Pegging prices at any ancient parity formula, despite its superficial plausibility and fairness, utterly disregards basic changes in demand and real costs of production. As time passes, such a parity will produce prices differing sharply from "natural competitive" levels here and abroad. The result: huge surpluses and growing distortions of efficiency.

3. Aid programs involving direct gifts or promotion of demand and of cost research require no deep economic analysis. But the tools of supply and demand are needed to understand the three aid programs: (1) crop limitation and Soil Bank, (2) government price support by purchase-loan storage programs, (3) resale to consumers at competitive market prices of food bought at a pegged price, with the government footing the bill for the differential.

4. Because high and inflexible parity support causes storage to grow astronomically and sends the government's aid costs skyward, Case 2 in practice leads to more and more of Case 1. (Farmers like 2 and accept 1 only as a necessary evil; consumers dislike 1 and 2, but like 3.)

5. The long-run solution must involve maintenance of prosperity outside agriculture, so that people can continue to move to the lines of highest productivity and so that demand for agriculture will be optimally high. But mere prosperity in industry is not enough. The 1920's and 1950's show that the city and town can prosper while the country's economic position deterio-rates. In the long run, resources have to be helped to move out of low-efficient rural uses and into more productive other uses. That means a continuation of the trend toward fewer farmers.

QUESTIONS FOR DISCUSSION

1. Give reasons for past and future migration from country to town. Do noneconomic factors reinforce or work against the basic economic fact of relatively low farm income?

2. Contrast cyclical patterns of agriculture and industry. Use curves.

3. Describe government indirect and direct farm aids. Explain "parity."

4. Why might limiting a farm's acreage in one crop not reduce the total of it much? How would it affect noncontrolled crops? Fertilizer demand?

5. In Fig. 2, label the intersection of AE and SE' with the letter R. Then show that $REsS$ is greater in area than $RABE'$ if demand is elastic. Give a detailed interpretation in terms of total revenue to justify your answer. What if demand were inelastic between E' and E?

6. Write a parable of the next 20 years under all-out aid to agriculture.

7. Debate the merit of taking a dollar from the 9 in 10 outside of farming and giving it to the 1 in farming. Distinguish ways of giving him the dollar.

8. What is your short- and long-run solution for agriculture?

9. Review your understanding of the following concepts:

inelastic farm demand and supply
farm technology and declining per cent of income spent on food
rural birth rates
pre-New Deal farm aids

Q limitation, P support, direct payments with consumer and producer P's different
pros and cons of free farm prices
dumping
long-run solutions

THE 22 DYNAMICS OF SPECULATION AND RISK

De Camptown race track five miles long,
Oh doodah day!
Gwine to run all night!
Gwine to run all day!
I'll bet my money on de bobtail nag,
Somebody bet on de bay.

STEPHEN C. FOSTER

The present chapter applies the tools of supply and demand to analyze price relations across space and time. It introduces the important problems involved in risk, insurance, speculation, and gambling. It deals not alone with the purchase and sale of actual commodities like corn or cotton, but also with the purchase and sale of something more mysterious—the purchase and sale of bits of paper.

These bits of paper may be shares of common stock, which represent ownership of various corporations. Or they may be bits of paper called "commodity futures": these are contracts that brokers deal with on organized commodity exchanges like the Chicago Board of Trade or the New Orleans Cotton Exchange. You and I may buy or sell such commodity futures even though we have never seen any *real* cotton or corn. As speculators in such futures the last thing in the world we would want to happen would be for a truck to roll up to our door seeking delivery of real honest-to-goodness corn or cotton. Yet, as we'll see, even though speculators never touch the real thing, they may under certain conditions be helping to even out the consumption of the crop between harvest times and be helping to carry over between seasons the proper amount of grain and fiber.

In his autobiography, the elder statesman, Bernard Baruch, said that 10 years after he heard Professor George B. Newcomb lecture on supply and demand at C.C.N.Y., he had made more than a million dollars from speculation—implying that those lectures may have had something to do with it. Well, this chapter isn't going to make you rich and if you skip it your knowledge of the rest of the book won't much suffer. But the subject of speculation is a fascinating one and can serve as an example of important applications of supply and demand. Inevitably though it is a complicated subject which no elementary book can pretend to treat completely.

► GEOGRAPHICAL PRICE PATTERNS

In a well-organized competitive market, there tends to be at any one time and place a single prevailing price. This is because of the action of professional speculators or *arbitragers* who keep their ear to the market and, as soon as they learn of any price differences, buy at the cheaper price and sell at the dearer price, thereby making a profit for themselves—at the same time tending to equalize the price.[1]

Two markets at a considerable distance from each other may tend to have different prices. Wheat in Chicago may sell for a few cents more per hundred than in Kansas City, because of the shipping, insurance, and interest charges involved in transportation. But if ever the price in Chicago should rise by more than the few cents of shipping costs, speculators will buy in Kansas City and ship to Chicago, thereby bringing the price up in Kansas City and down in Chicago to the normal differential charge.

Nobody legislates these patterns. They follow from supply and demand.

► SPECULATION AND PRICE BEHAVIOR OVER TIME

In an ideal competitive market there tends to be a definite pattern of prices *over time* just as there is over space. But the difficulties of predicting the future make this pattern a less perfect one, so that we have an equilibrium that is constantly being disturbed but is always in the process of reforming itself—not unlike the surface of the ocean.

Stabilizing seasonal patterns. Let us consider the simplest case of a grain that is harvested at one period of the year. This crop must be made to last all the year if privation is to be avoided. Since no one passes a law regulating the storage of grain, how is this desirable state of affairs brought about? The answer is, Through the attempts of speculators to make a profit. A well-informed speculator who is a specialist in this grain realizes that, if all the grain

---

[1] On the floor of the Chicago Board of Trade, the important market for grain, some hundred important "pit scalpers," or dealers, are said to make all their profits on price changes within each day, closing out all their transactions every night and sleeping peacefully until the next day.

is thrown on the market in the autumn, it will fetch a very low price because of the glutting of the market. On the other hand, months later with almost no grain coming on the market, price will tend to skyrocket up.

This is what would tend to happen were it not for the action of speculators. They realize that by (1) purchasing some of the autumn crop while it is cheap, (2) withholding it in storage, and (3) selling it later when the price has risen, they can make a profit. This they do. But in doing so, they increase the autumn demand for grain and raise its autumn price; and they increase the spring supply of grain and lower its price at that time. At the same time that they are equalizing the price over the year, they are also equalizing the supply coming on the market in each month—which is as it should be.

Moreover, if there is brisk competition among speculators, none will make an excessive profit over the costs that he incurs (including of course the wages necessary to keep him in this line of activity). Actually the speculator himself may never touch a grain of wheat or a bale of cotton, nor need he know anything about storage, warehouses, or delivery. He merely buys and sells bits of paper, but the effect is exactly as described above.

Now there is one and only one monthly price pattern which will result in neither profits nor losses. A little thought will show that it will not be a pattern of constant prices. Rather will the ideal price pattern involve lowest prices in the autumn and then gradually rising prices until the peak is reached just before the new wheat comes in. The price must rise from month to month to compensate for the storage and interest costs of carrying the crop in storage—in exactly the same way that the price must rise over space from one mile to the next to compensate for the cost of transportation. Figure 1 shows the behavior of prices over an ideal yearly cycle. The increase in price from month to month is not constant, because of the accelerated growth of compound interest on the money tied up in the stored crop.[1]

Stabilizing foreseeable fluctuations. Not all fluctuations in activity can be so accurately forecast as the seasonal harvesting of a crop. No one can predict with confidence next year's weather or whether a depression will develop in the near future. But to the extent that speculators can form any accurate guesses today about the future *scarcity* of a commodity, they will tend to buy it now for *future* delivery, thereby causing (1) a withdrawal of present supply, (2) an increase of present price, (3) an increase in amount stored, (4) an increase in future supply, (5) a reduction in future price—or in all a relative stabilization of price and consumption over time. The reader should trace through the opposite process by which speculators stabilize prices when

---

[1] Do I need a crystal ball to tell me price will rise enough for it to pay me to store wheat today? No. The market today will quote me a future price—for delivery of wheat some months from now—and when this future price sufficiently exceeds the current spot price, I get the signal to store wheat.

For a good to be stored, expected price rise must match storing cost:

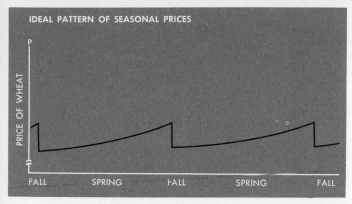

IDEAL PATTERN OF SEASONAL PRICES

PRICE OF WHEAT

FALL   SPRING   FALL   SPRING   FALL

Fig. 1. Ideally, P is lowest at harvest time, rising gently with accumulated storage costs until the next harvest. This pattern evens out consumption as compared to harvest glut with very low autumn price and summer scarcity with sky-high price.

they correctly foresee an exceptionally large future crop and a low future price: how they then begin to "sell short"[1] for future delivery, tending to depress current prices, increase present consumption, decrease carry-over of stocks, and so forth.

Spreading of risks. Aside from their possible influence toward stabilizing prices, speculators have another important function. By being willing to take risks on their own shoulders, they enable others to avoid risk.

For example, a miller must carry large inventories of grain in the course of his business. If the price of grain goes up, he makes a windfall capital gain; if down, he makes a windfall loss. But let us suppose that he is content to earn his living by milling flour and wishes to forego all risk taking. This he can do by a process called "hedging." This complicated procedure is rather like a man who bets on Army to win the Army-Navy game, and then washes out this transaction, or covers it, by placing an equal bet on the Navy. Whichever side wins, he comes out the same, his left hand winning what his right hand loses.[2]

[1] There is really nothing mysterious about selling short. I simply put in an order to my broker in which I agree, in return for a certain price *now,* to deliver *at some later date* (usually but not always exactly specified) an amount of grain. Usually at the time of putting in the order, I do not have on hand the grain. But I legally fulfill my contract by later "covering"; *i.e.,* buying the grain and making delivery. If I later have to pay a higher price in covering than I now receive when selling short, then I take a loss. But if I have guessed right and prices do fall in the intervening period, then I "buy in" for less than I have received and make a profit. Selling short in the stock market works out similarly, except that I am free to cover and make future delivery of the stock at any time I please. In the meantime, the man who has bought the stock receives his stock shares. How? As a result of the fact that my broker, obligingly, lends me the stock certificates to make delivery. Later when I cover, I buy in some stock and turn over the certificates to my obliging broker.

[2] Likewise the miller, in quoting his present price for flour, will do so only after having bought a "future contract" for delivery of wheat to replace his used-up inventory of grain. If the price of wheat should go up a month from now, then the miller will have made a loss by selling his flour too cheap. But the gain he makes on his future purchase just cancels out his loss, and so he is "hedged" against risk.

To the extent that speculators forecast accurately, they provide a definite social service.[1] To the extent that they forecast badly, they tend to aggravate the variability of prices. Were it not for the detailed statistical information provided by the Department of Agriculture and private agencies, the traders of the Chicago Board of Trade would find themselves at the mercy of every idle rumor, hope, and fear. For speculation is essentially a mass contagion, like the inexplicable dancing crazes that swept medieval villages, the Dutch tulip mania that sent the price of a single bulb higher than that of a house, the South Sea Bubble in which companies sold stock at fabulous prices for enterprises which would "later be revealed."

▶ **THE GREAT STOCK-MARKET CRASH**

This was illustrated more recently in the United States during the fabulous stock-market boom of the "roaring twenties." Housewives, Pullman porters, college students between classes—all bought and sold stocks. Most purchases in this wild "bull" market were "on margin"; *i.e.,* the buyer of $10,000 worth of stocks had to put up only $2,500 or less in cash, borrowing the difference by pledging his newly bought stocks. What matter that he had to pay his broker 5, 6, or 10 per cent per year on his borrowing when in one day Auburn Motors or Bethlehem Steel might jump 10 per cent in value!

The most wonderful thing about a bull market is that it creates its own hopes. If people buy because they think stocks will rise, their act of buying sends up the price of stocks. This causes them to buy still further, and sends the dizzy dance off on another round. And unlike a game of cards or dice, no one loses what the winners gain. Everybody gets a prize! Of course, the prizes are all on paper and would disappear if everyone tried to cash them in. But why should anyone wish to sell such lucrative securities?

When the whole world is mad, 'tis folly to be sane. Suppose one were so wise or so naïve as to believe that the public-utilities holding companies were paper pyramids on cardboard foundations; or that Florida dream real-estate developments were midway between pine thicket and swamp; or that private foreign loans to South America and Europe were being frittered away in roads to nowhere or on public swimming pools? What could such a social misfit do? He would soon learn the first rule of property values: "A thing is worth what people *think* it is worth." Unfortunately, to be successful this has to be applied in connection with the second rule, which is as hard to follow in practice as belling the cat or catching birds by putting salt on their tails: "Don't be the sucker left holding the bag."

When the black October crash of 1929 came, everyone was caught, the big-

---

[1] We'll see why on page 432.

Only thing sure about stock prices is that they will fluctuate:

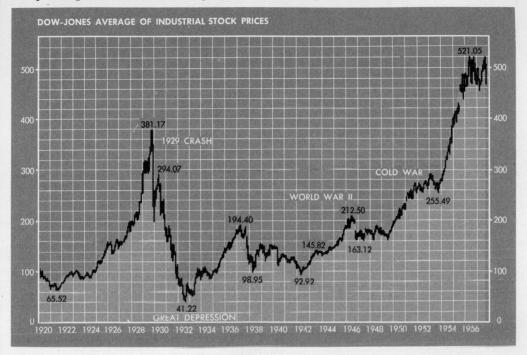

DOW-JONES AVERAGE OF INDUSTRIAL STOCK PRICES

521.05

381.17

1929 CRASH

294.07

COLD WAR

WORLD WAR II

212.50

255.49

194.40

145.82

163.12

98.95   92.92

65.52

41.22

GREAT DEPRESSION

1920 1922 1924 1926 1928 1930 1932 1934 1936 1938 1940 1942 1944 1946 1948 1950 1952 1954 1956

Fig. 2. As money national income rises, from real growth and price-level increases, the trend in common stock prices is upward. But note the severe oscillations. (Source: Barron's Publishing Co.)

league professionals and the piddling amateurs—Andrew Mellon, John D. Rockefeller, the engineer in the White House, and the economics professor from Yale. The bottom fell out of the market. Brokers had to sell out the "margin" accounts of investors who could no longer pony up extra funds to cover the depleted value of their collateral,[1] sending the market down still further. Even those who did not buy on margin lost one-third of their capital by the end of the year, and five-sixths by 1932!

The bull market was over. The bear market had taken its place. And, as the former had lived on its dreams, so the latter was consumed by its own nightmares. Billions of dollars of security values were wiped out every month, taking with them not only the capital of gamblers out for speculative gains, but also the widow's mite supposedly invested for steady income. A "blue chip" stock like United States Steel fell from a 1929 high of 261 to a 1932 low of 21, while less respectable securities dropped off the Board completely. Even though President Hoover and his administration were friendly toward busi-

[1] Frederick Lewis Allen's amusing and interesting chronicle of the 1920's, *Only Yesterday*, gives a detailed account of the role of the stock-market boom in American life.

ness, in vain did they try to restore confidence by predicting "prosperity is just around the corner" and "stocks are excellent buys at their present levels."

Finally, after the great banking crisis of 1933 and the NRA, the stock market began to follow general business recovery. Figure 2 shows the movements of stock-market values over the whole period. Although stocks were bullish in 1936–1937 and again during World War II, it was not until the mid-fifties that they returned to anything like the peak levels of 1929. The 1957 drop of stock prices by more than 20 per cent reminded people that the market is never a one-way street.

▶ OUTGUESSING THE MARKET?

To the age-old question, does the market follow business activity or business activity the market, no simple answer can be given. It is reasonably clear that business activity, national income, and corporate earnings determine stock prices and not vice versa; and also that the psychological effects of market movements no longer have primary importance, but are in the nature of a grim national side show. But still the market can occasionally *anticipate* changes in national income and total purchasing power. It then appears to be leading them when really it is following what it thinks they will be later.

How to invest. There are no simply stated foolproof rules for making money out of the stock market. Anyone who can accurately predict the future course of business activity will prosper, but there is no such person. At least four main classes of investors and speculators can be distinguished:

1. The group who simply buy and hold. Because the national economy has a long-time upward trend, they fare reasonably well over the long run. They might do even better if they would follow the statistical advice of investment services as to how to switch to companies of more favorable growth prospects.

The effect of this group is neither to stabilize or destabilize prices; to the extent that they freeze shares off the market and limit the number of tradings, they tend to make the market more "thin." In a thin market there are so few transactions that the attempt to buy a few hundred shares may send its price up a few points because of the absence of ready sellers around the ruling market price. An attempt to sell may depress the price a few points.

2. At the other extreme are the hour-to-hour, day-to-day ticker watchers, to be seen in every brokerage office. Generally speaking, they buy and sell, sell and buy. By and large, they make money only for their brokers.

This group has the effect of making the market less thin. Because of them, any investor can expect to be able to liquidate his market holdings at any time at some price, although not at a price predictable in advance nor that he would like. Still even this restricted "liquidity" enhances the attractiveness of securities traded on organized exchanges over and above the unlisted issues of smaller companies bought and sold by brokers over the counter.

3. In between are those speculators who play intermediate swings of many months or years. The least successful of these are the amateurs whose entrance into the market at the top when it is too late is the signal for the "smart money" to leave. The most successful speculators are those who are able to avoid the extremes of enthusiasm of the mob and to discern underlying business conditions. This does not mean that they simply buy because a stock looks low and sell when it looks high. On the contrary, they buy when stocks look as if they will continue to rise. When a drop seems imminent, they sell short or, more conservatively, they simply go into cash or high-grade bonds. It takes cool nerves to sell short because on the whole the market is overoptimistic. But if a single individual does it cleverly, he may achieve success in avoiding the losses of a bear market.

The behavior of such speculators is often destabilizing to prices. They "pile on" to a price rise and send it farther; they similarly *accentuate* a decline.

4. Finally, there are individuals who study special situations. From public or inside sources, they learn in advance of changes in the fortunes of particular companies: of rumored bankruptcies, of special stock dividends, split-ups, or mergers, of likely earnings and dividend announcements, etc. When combined with the successful characteristics of the third group, members of this group—such as the elder statesman of two wars, Bernard Baruch—make the largest profit from the market. Since World War II some alert operators have been able to run $1,000 up to $1,000,000 or more—at the same time keeping profits in the form of less heavily taxed capital gains.

But the investor must take to heart Baruch's caution:

> If you are ready to give up everything else—to study the whole history and background of the market and all the principal companies whose stocks are on the board as carefully as a medical student studies anatomy—If you can do all that, and, in addition, you have the cool nerves of a great gambler, the sixth sense of a kind of clairvoyant, and the courage of a lion, you have a ghost of a chance.

▶ GAMBLING AND DIMINISHING UTILITY

The defenders of speculation resent the charge that it represents simply another form of gambling, like betting on the horse races or buying a lottery ticket. They emphasize that an uncertain world necessarily involves risk and that someone must bear risks. They claim that the knowledge and the venturesomeness of the speculator are chained to a socially useful purpose, thereby reducing fluctuations and risks to others. We have seen that this is not always the case and that speculation may be destabilizing; but certainly no one can deny all validity to the above claims.

Why is gambling considered such a bad thing? Part of the reason, perhaps the most important part, lies in the field of morals, ethics, and religion; upon these the economist is not qualified to pass exact judgment. There is, however, a substantial economic case to be made against gambling.

First, it involves simply *sterile transfers of money* between individuals, creating no new value.[1] While creating no value, gambling does nevertheless absorb time and resources. When pursued beyond the limits of recreation, where the main purpose after all is to "kill" time, gambling subtracts from the national income.

The second economic disadvantage of gambling is the fact that it tends to promote *inequality* and *instability of incomes*. People who sit down to the gaming table with the same amount of money go away with widely different amounts. A gambler (and his family) must expect to be on the top of the world one day, and when luck changes—which is the only predictable thing about it—he may almost starve.

Law of diminishing marginal utility. But why is inequality of income over time and between persons considered such a bad thing? One answer is to be found in the widely held belief that the gain in well-being achieved by an *extra* $1,000 of income is not so great as the loss in well-being of foregoing $1,000 of income. Therefore, a bet at fair odds involves an economic loss: the money you stand to win balances the money you may lose, but the satisfaction you stand to win is less than the satisfaction you stand to lose.

Similarly, if it can be assumed that individuals are all "roughly the same" and are ethically comparable, then the dollars gained by the rich do not create so much "welfare" as the dollars lost by the poor. This has been used not only as a criticism of gambling, but as a positive argument in favor of "progressive" taxation aimed at lowering the inequality of the distribution of income.[2]

Just as the law of diminishing returns was seen to underlie the Malthusian theory of population, so is the "law of diminishing (marginal or extra) utility" used by many economists to condemn professional gambling. According to this theory, as money income increases, each new dollar adds something to well-being, but less and less. In the same way, each extra unit of any

---

[1] Actually in all professional gambling arrangements, the participants lose out on balance. The leakage comes from the fact that the odds are always rigged in favor of the "house" so that even an "honest" house will win in the long run. Moderate gambling among friends may be considered as a form of consumption or recreation activity whose cost to the group as a whole is zero.

[2] Economists used to think that they could scientifically prove the desirability of income redistribution by this type of argument. Today it is widely realized that such an argument is based on implicit ethical judgments concerning the deserts of different people and that an issue like this one must be decided on a-scientific ethical grounds. The issue of incentives must also enter in forming any decision on policy, since redistributing the pie may lessen its total.

Each new sugar unit adds to total utility, but extra utility diminishes:

Sugar consumed	Total utility	Extra utility of last unit
0	0	
1	4	4
2	7	3
3	9	2
4	10	1
5	10	0

Table 1. Total and marginal utility schedule of sugar. The extra utility which comes from each extra unit of sugar is called by economists "marginal utility." See how the marginal utility steadily falls.

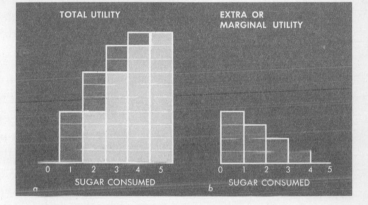

Fig. 3. The dark blocks show the extra utility added by each new unit. The fact that total utility increases at a decreasing rate is shown on the right by the declining steps of marginal utility.

good that can be bought with money contributes less and less satisfaction or utility. When we get as much of a good as we wish (*e.g.*, water), it becomes a "free good" because still further units add nothing new to our utility.

As an example of this law, consider the utility or satisfaction to be derived from consuming more or less sugar per year. The accompanying hypothetical table shows how many units of utility are associated with an individual's consumption of different amounts of sugar per year.

The first part of Fig. 3 shows how *total utility* grows with the amount of sugar consumed; the second, how much *extra* or *marginal utility* is added with each new pound of sugar consumption. The first set of blocks is increasing, but the law of diminishing utility causes the second set to be decreasing; *i.e.*, the steps go downhill. Note that the sum of all the blocks in the second diagram is equal to the last pillar of blocks in the first. This portrays the fact that total utility is the sum of the extra utility added by each of the units.[1]

---

[1] Many economists don't believe utility is numerically measurable, and next chapter's discussion of demand does not depend upon its measurability. By observing people's bets, we might reverse the arguments of this chapter and make numerical guesses as to people's probable utility schedules. None of our results depends crucially on measurability of utility.

▶ **WHY IDEAL STABILIZATION BY SPECULATORS IS OPTIMAL**

We can now use the tools of marginal utility to show how ideal speculation would maximize total utility over time. Suppose every consumer has the utility schedule for sugar of Table 1 and Fig. 3, which holds in each year independently of any other year. Now suppose that in the first of two years there was a big sugar crop—say 3 units per person—and in the second a small crop of only 1 unit per person. If this crop deficiency could be foreseen, how should the consumption of the two year's 4 unit total be spread over the two years?

If we agree for simplicity to neglect all storage, interest, and insurance charges, you can prove that *total utility for the two years together will be maximized only if consumption is equal in each of the years.*

Why is uniform consumption better than any other division of the available total? Because of the law of diminishing utility. Here's the reasoning.

Suppose I consume more in the first year than in the second. My last unit's marginal utility will then be low in the first year and high in the second. So if I carry over sugar from the first to the second year, I'll be switching from low to high marginal utilities— and that will maximize my total utility.

But isn't that exactly what the ideal speculation pattern would accomplish?

If speculators can neglect interest, storage, and insurance charges, and happen to accurately forecast next year's low crop, what will they do? They'll figure it pays to carry sugar over from this year's low price resulting from the high crop, instead hoping to sell at next year's scarcity price. But as each speculator subtracts from this year's supply and adds to next year's, what must finally happen? Equilibrium can take place only when the two prices have been equalized! Then there will be no further incentive to carry over more crop.[1] (Of course, a small payment for the speculator's effort might

[1] A graph could illuminate this argument. If Table 1's satisfactions could be measured in dollars, with each dollar always denoting the same marginal utility, the demand curves for

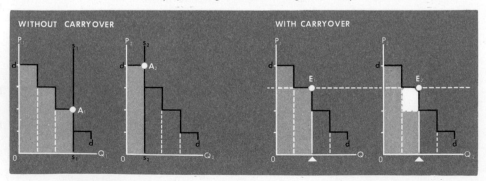

Fig. 4. The light slabs measure total utility. Carrying one unit to second year equalizes Q and P and increases total utility by the amount of the white block.

have to be included—but we've agreed to waive all costs just to keep the example simple.)

Don't for a moment get the impression that real flesh-and-blood speculators can guess the future correctly. They often make mistakes and often are prey to rumors and mass enthusiasms. So the process isn't as ideal as here pictured. Still to the degree that speculators can intelligently foresee the future—and those who have a terrible batting-average may get eliminated fast as their capital is lost—they (and for that matter, *farsighted* government agencies too) may help to provide a useful stabilizing function.

▶ **ECONOMICS OF INSURANCE**

We are now in a position to see why insurance, which appears to be just another form of gambling, actually has exactly opposite effects. For the same reasons that gambling is bad, insurance is economically advantageous. Whereas gambling creates risks, insurance helps to lessen risks.

In buying fire insurance on his house, the owner seems to be betting with the insurance company that his house will burn down. If it does not, and the odds are heavily in favor of its not burning, the owner forfeits the small premium charge. If it does burn down, the company loses the bet and must reimburse the owner to the tune of the agreed upon loss. (For the obvious reason of removing temptation from hard-up home owners who like fire engines and excitement, the face value of the policy tends to be something less than the money value of the property insured.)

What is true of fire insurance is equally true of life, accident, automobile, or any other kind of insurance. Actually at the famous Lloyd's of London, which is a place for insurance brokers to come together, you can arrange to insure a ball team or vacationer against rain, dancers against infantile paralysis, a hotel keeper against a damage suit from the widow of a man killed in a fight with another man who bought a drink in the hotel's cocktail lounge, and you can get numerous other bizarre policies. But by the common law, Lloyd's cannot bet $10,000 with me that it will not snow on Christmas, since I do not have an "insurable interest" of that amount and the bet would be unenforcible in the courts. But a ski resort owner, who stands to lose that much if it does not snow, would have such an insurable interest and could buy such a policy. Economic theory shows what the difference is between these two cases.

---

the two years would look just like Fig. 3b's marginal utility schedule. Figure 4's two curves show what would happen if there were no carryover—with price first determined at A_1 where $s_1 s_1$ intersects dd and second at A_2 where the lower supply $s_2 s_2$ intersects dd. Total utility of the shaded areas would add up only to $(4+3+2)+4$ or $13 per head. But with optimal carryover to the second year of one unit by speculators, P's and Q's will be equalized at E_1 and E_2, and now the total utility of the light areas will add up to $(4+3)+(4+3)$ or $14 per head. (Show that the gain in utility of $1 is measured by the white block, which represents the excess of the second unit's marginal utility over the third unit's marginal utility.)

The insurance company is not gambling because what is unpredictable and subject to chance *for the individual* is highly predictable and uniform *in the mass.* Whether John C. Smith, age twenty and in good health, will live for 30 more years is a matter of chance, but the famous *law of large numbers* guarantees that out of 100,000-odd twenty-year-olds in good health only a definite proportion will still be alive at the end of such a period of time. The life-insurance company can easily set a premium at which it won't lose money. Certainly therefore, the company is not gambling. What about the buyer of insurance, is he gambling? Actually it is not too hard to show the reverse to be true: the man who does not insure his house is doing the gambling. He is risking the whole value of his house against the small premium saved. If his house does not burn down in any year, he has won his bet; if it does, as occasionally must happen, he loses his bet and incurs a tremendous penalty.

At this point, a sporting man will say, "So what? Of course, a man gambles when he doesn't buy insurance. But the odds on such a bet are not unfavorable. In fact, they are favorable, because we know that the insurance company is not in business for its health. It must keep records, it must support insurance salesmen, and so forth. All this costs money and must be 'loaded' on to the insurance premium, detracting from the perfect mathematical odds of the buyer and making the odds for the nonbuyer a little better."

To which a rational man will reply. "When I am among friends, I don't mind a small game of chance for relaxation even at slightly unfavorable odds. But when a big bet is involved, even if the odds are favorable, then I pass. I insure my house because I hardly miss the premium each year, and if it should burn down without being covered, I would feel the loss an awful lot. When I insure, my living standards over time and my income remain the same, come what may. When I don't insure, I may be up for a while, but I risk going way down."

Obviously, the law of diminishing utility—which makes the satisfaction from wins less important than the privation from losses—is one way of justifying the above reasoning. *This law of diminishing utility tells us that a steady income, equitably divided among individuals instead of arbitrarily apportioned between the lucky or unlucky people whose house did or did not burn down, is economically advantageous.* Also, when a family chooses to buy hospital and medical insurance, there is also the belief that this will be a relatively painless way of making itself "save against a rainy day." This self-imposed "compulsory saving" feature is another benefit of insurance.

▶ WHAT CAN BE INSURED

Undoubtedly then, insurance is a highly important way of spreading risks. Why then can we not insure ourselves against all the risks of life? The answer lies in the indisputable fact that certain definite mathematical conditions are necessary before sufficiently exact actuarial probabilities can be determined. What are these?

First, we must have a *large number of events*. Only then will there be possible a pooling of risks and a "cancellation of averages." The bank at Monte Carlo knows there is safety in numbers. The lucky streak of an Arabian prince will be canceled by the losings of a fake Balkan countess or by her next night's losings. Once in a blue moon someone may "break the bank" but in a few more lunar cycles the "house" will more than break even.

But large numbers are not enough. No prudent fire-insurance company would confine itself to the island of Manhattan even though there are thousands of buildings there. *The uncertain events must be relatively independent*. Each throw of the dice, each chance of loss by fire, should stand relatively by itself. Obviously a great fire, like that of Chicago in 1871 or in San Francisco after the earthquake, would subject all the buildings in the same locality to the same risk. The company would be making a bet on one event, not on thousands of independent events. Instead, it must diversify its risks. Private companies cannot, without government aid, bear the risks of nuclear-bomb insurance. And it is not possible to buy unemployment insurance from a private company. Depressions are great plagues which hit all sections and all classes at one and the same time, with a probability that cannot be computed in advance with any precision. Therefore only the government, whose business it is to take losses, can take the responsibility of providing unemployment compensation.

But there still remain, and probably always will, numerous risks of personal and business life. No one can insure the success of a new beauty shop, a new mousetrap, or a hopeful opera singer. Without error there cannot be trial; and without trial, there cannot be progress.

SUMMARY

1. The intelligent profit-seeking action of speculators and *arbitragers* tends to create certain definite equilibrium patterns of price over space and time. To the extent that speculators moderate price and consumption instability, they are performing a socially useful purpose. To the extent that they provide a market and permit others to hedge against risk, they are performing a further socially useful function.

2. But to the extent that speculators pile on to price changes and cause great fluctuations in stock prices, commodities, and foreign exchange rates, their function is a harmful one.

3. The economic principle of diminishing (marginal) utility is one way of showing why consumption and price stability is good, and why gambling is economically unsound and insurance is sound. There are necessarily, of course, fundamental and important differences between private and social insurance or social security.

QUESTIONS FOR DISCUSSION

1. Pretend that you are engaging in some stock or commodity transactions. Start out with $10,000 and follow the newspapers to see how you make out.

2. How does ideal speculation work to stabilize seasonal prices?

3. "I can't afford to sell my United States Steel stock today (1930) because if I do I'll take such a great loss over what I paid for it in 1929." Appraise.

4. "I love the thrill of gambling, of risking all on the turn of a card. What do I care for odds or economic principles?" Can economic science pass judgment on whether such a person should gamble or not?

5. Can you reverse the reasoning concerning the desirability of gambling and insurance so that it will apply to two individuals with increasing rather than decreasing marginal utility of income?

6. List some important differences between private and social insurance.

7. For a year after late summer, 1953, American business was in a recession. Yet Fig. 2 shows the stock market was rapidly rising—and by 1956 the Dow-Jones Industrial Averages reached 420, going well beyond the 1929 peak. In 1957 it fell. Use hindsight (which is the clearest "sight" of all in the market) to give the causes of this rise and subsequent dip.

8. Review your understanding of the following concepts:

spatial P equality but for transport costs	total versus extra or marginal utility
ideal seasonal price pattern	law of diminishing marginal utility
hedging, speculation, and short-sale	
mania and mob psychology	stability versus instability of consumption
1929 market crash	gambling versus insurance
types of equity investors	social versus private insurance

23 THE THEORY OF CONSUMPTION AND DEMAND

What is a cynic? A man who knows the price of everything, and the value of nothing.

OSCAR WILDE

In a competitive market, price is determined by the schedules of supply and demand. In this chapter, we may briefly digress in order to analyze what is going on behind the market demand curve for consumer goods.

▶ SUMMING INDIVIDUAL DEMANDS TO GET MARKET DEMAND

The market demand curve for a good like beef is arrived at by summing up the amounts of beef that will be demanded by each consumer. Each consumer has a demand curve that can be plotted against the price of beef. It generally slopes downward and to the right, dropping from northwest to southeast. If all consumers were exactly alike in their demands and there were 1 million consumers, then we could think of the market demand curve as a millionfold enlargement of each consumer's demand curve.

But people are not all exactly alike. Some have high incomes; some have low. Some greatly desire beef, while others prefer pork or vegetables. What must we do to the demand schedules or curves of each consumer to arrive at the total market demand curve? All we have to do is calculate the sum total of what each and every consumer will consume at any given price; we then plot that total amount as a point on the market demand curve; or if we like, we may set the total down in a table like those first seen in Chapter 19.

▶ Summary: We always sum individual demands at each price to end up finally with the market demand curve. (Figure 1 on the next page shows how demand curves are "horizontally added.")

437

To get market demand, we add all consumers' demand curves:

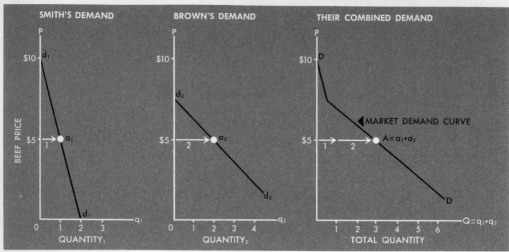

Fig. 1. At each price, such as $5, we add quantities demanded by each man to get market quantity demanded. (Do you see that same addition process could get you market supply from individual producers' supply curves?)

▶ THEORY OF CONSUMER'S CHOICE

But suppose we want to go behind the individual's demand curve. Why do you buy 100 pounds of beef a year when the price is $1 per pound and only 25 pounds when the price rises to $2 a pound? Why does a fall in the price of pork cause you to cut down on your beef purchases? Why might an increase in the price of sauce to put on your beef cause you to cut down a little bit on your beef purchases? Why does an increase in your income cause you to increase your purchase of beef and reduce your purchase of potatoes?

A theory of utility was developed in the nineteenth century to explain the way a consumer arrives at decisions on what to buy. Here's how it goes.

To begin with, the consumer starts out with a certain amount of income that he—or perhaps we should say "she"—can spend. In addition, he is confronted with a whole array of market prices for all the things he can buy. The prices are quoted to him, and ordinarily are beyond his power to alter.

Immediately the problem of choice becomes apparent. If goods were free, or if his income were great enough so that he could buy every last thing that suits his fancy, this would not be so. But as things are, the more he buys of one good, the less he can buy of others. Therefore, the advantages of any good must be balanced against the advantages of all the rest. In performing this calculation of comparing goods, it is not enough for him simply to balance the advantage of different goods on an equal basis. A steak may be preferred to a can of Spam, but if the steak costs ten times as much, he may decide to buy the Spam. That is, it is extra satisfaction or marginal utility secured *per unit of money expended* that matters to him. The satisfaction to be derived from different goods is not to be equal if their prices differ; but their extra satisfactions must end up *proportional* to the respective prices of the goods.

The theory being described assumes that the consumer has rather definite opinions about his own (family's) preferences as between different amounts of goods. If a psychologist quizzed him about them, he could probably answer many of the questions. But not necessarily all. Many of these opinions are on the subconscious level because he has come, through repeated experience, to make decisions almost automatically. As a matter of fact, most people like to keep deliberate decision making down to as low a level as possible.[1]

In any case, the consumer, possessed of a given income and set of prices of goods, is thereby confronted with a wide range of final batches of goods. Automatically or unconsciously, he can compare them and finally pick out the best combination, or what is called the "optimal equilibrium combination."

Equal extra (or "marginal") utility per dollar. How shall we characterize this equilibrium position? Clearly, it is one from which the consumer will not care to depart. He will be unwilling to give up buying something of one item in order to substitute something of another. Why? Because he has already made his choice of the best combination, and any other combination is inferior.

Or to put the matter another way. He buys more and more units of all commodities until the last little units of each of them yield him satisfactions that are proportional to their respective prices. When the last 10-cent pound of beans yields twice as much satisfaction as does the last 5-cent pound of sugar, then he stops, knowing that he has arrived at the equilibrium point. Notice that the critical satisfactions to be compared concern not the total quantity of each commodity consumed but only the *last* or "marginal" increments. *At this best point the marginal utility per last cent or nickel is the same in all uses;* this is a necessary condition for equilibrium.

Why? Because if it were not—if the last penny spent on sugar yielded *less* satisfaction than that spent on beans—it would pay him to switch a penny from sugar buying to the purchase of some more beans. When it no longer pays to switch purchases, because the satisfaction per penny from beans has

---

[1] Some daring economists assume that the consumer experiences a definite quantitative amount of satisfaction or anticipated pleasure when confronted with a given batch of goods. This definite psychological quantity or sensation is given the name "utility." If a first batch of goods and services, *A*, registers a higher utility score than a second batch, *B*, and they cost the same, then he will buy *A* and not *B*.

More cautious writers prefer to be agnostic on the question of utility as a magnitude. All they assume is that the consumer can compare *A* and *B* and know which he prefers. Whether this is done by giving each some numerical score, these writers do not claim to know; nor do they care since the "facts" of consumer's behavior are the same in either case. (As the last chapter showed, a certain kind of measurability of utility may be possible and relevant in *probability* statistics: but it is not needed here.)

finally fallen to the level of that from sugar, then he has reached the equilibrium position and will stop. This shows us, by the way, that the equilibrium position in this field, as in other parts of economic life, is usually approached only after a period of trial and error.

▶ HEART OF THE THEORY RESTATED

The few pages above summarize all that there is to the theory of consumer's behavior. The discussion could be amplified by numerous diagrams and tables, but that is not really necessary. The beginning student of economics need keep firmly in mind only the following three sets of propositions:

1. A consumer with only a finite income, confronted with (nonzero) prices, cannot buy as much as he wants of everything. He must choose and balance, and in doing so must take relative prices into consideration.

2. The consumer is supposed to have a fairly definite set of preferences so that he knows whether a given situation is better, worse, or indifferent as compared to another situation.

3. The consumer is able, therefore, to select out of all possible situations available to him because of (1) the one which is "best" as determined by (2) . This is the *equilibrium situation*, characterized by the condition that no further substitution between goods is desirable, because already expenditure has been allocated among goods until *the last penny spent on each commodity gives the same marginal utility or satisfaction as does the last penny spent on every other commodity.*

▶ PRICE AND INCOME CHANGES IN DEMAND

This theory explains how the amount demanded of each good is determined, once the consumer is given a set of prices and income. So it will also explain why the amount demanded of a good will change when (1) its price changes, or for that matter when (2) income or (3) the price of some *other* good changes.

The first of these three changes, involving the variation in quantity demanded of a good as its own price is raised or lowered, is nothing other than our old friend the demand curve. The second, which relates variations in demand to income changes, is of the greatest importance both in comparing the behavior of rich and poor and in connection with the effects of ups and downs in national income and employment. The wealth of facts on this subject has earlier been discussed in terms of family budgets and the propensity to save or consume.

▶ CROSS RELATIONS OF DEMAND

Let us look at the third case in which the amount demanded of one good changes when the price of another good changes. This rather interesting case of cross interrelationship can be disposed of briefly because its results are in line with general experience.

Thus everyone knows that raising the price of tea will decrease the amount demanded of tea. It will also affect the amounts demanded of other commodities. For example, a higher price for tea will lower the demand for a commodity like lemon; *i.e.,* it will shift the whole demand schedule of lemon downward. But it will also increase the amount demanded of coffee. Probably it will have little or no effect on the demand curve for salt.

We say, therefore, that tea and coffee are *rival,* or *competing,* products, or *substitutes.* Tea and lemon on the other hand, are *cooperating,* or *complementary* commodities, or *complements.* The in-between pair of tea and salt are said to represent *independent* commodities. The reader will of course be able to classify such pairs as beef and pork, turkey and cranberry sauce, automobiles and gasoline, truck and railroad freight, oil and coal.

▶ DEMAND SHIFTS FROM INCOME OR OTHER-PRICE CHANGES

Just as changing other prices will shift the demand for tea, so, too, will increasing consumers' incomes cause them to demand more tea and more of almost all goods. And decreasing their incomes will decrease their tea consumption.

Let's now show what all this means in terms of our old friend the demand curve. This curve is, of course, simply the graphical picture of the response of quantity bought of a good to the change in its *own* price. But quantity bought may change also as a result of changes in the *prices of other goods* or as a result of a change in the consumer's *income.* The demand curve is drawn on the assumption that these other things *do not* change. But what if they do? Then the whole demand curve will *shift* to the right or to the left.

Figure 2 illustrates such changes. Given a certain income and established

Change in income or other-good's price shifts demand curve:

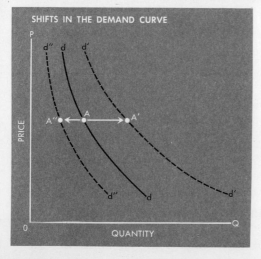

SHIFTS IN THE DEMAND CURVE

PRICE

QUANTITY

Fig. 2. Higher income will shift *dd* to *d'd'*. (Explain why. And why lowering income will shift *dd* to *d"d".*) Similarly a rise in coffee price might shift tea's *dd* out to *d'd'*. (What would a cut in coffee price do? Or a great rise in lemon price?)

prices for all other goods, then we can draw the consumer's demand for tea. First, assume price and quantity are at the point A. Suppose now that his income rises. Even though the price of tea is unchanged, he will in all probability buy more tea than before; hence the demand curve will have shifted to the right—say to $d'd'$, with A' indicating his new total purchase of tea. If his income should fall, then we may expect a reduction in quantity bought—there *must* be a reduction if income falls far enough. This we illustrate by $d''d''$ and by A''.

We can also use Fig. 2 to illustrate the effect of changed prices of other goods. A fall in the price of coffee may well cause our consumer to buy less tea; the demand curve shifts to, say, $d''d''$. But what if the price of lemon were to fall? The change may be small or nonexistent. But if there is any change, it will be in the direction of *increased* tea purchases—a rightward shift of dd. Why this difference in response? Because coffee is a rival, a substitute product for tea; lemon is a cooperating, a complementary commodity with respect to tea.

▶ **RESPONSE OF QUANTITY DEMANDED TO OWN PRICE**

So much for income and crisscross relationships between goods. Returning now to the relationships between a commodity and its own price, we are in a position to understand why the *law of downward-sloping demand* probably holds true; *i.e.,* why more will be bought at a lower price.

Substitution-effect. The first factor explaining diminishing consumption when price rises is an obvious one. If the price of tea goes down while other prices do not, then tea has become relatively cheaper. It pays therefore to *substitute* some tea for other goods in order to maintain one's standard of living most cheaply. Thus tea becomes a relatively cheaper source of stimulation than before, and more of it will be bought and less of coffee or cocoa. Similarly, a cheapening of movies relative to stage plays may cause the consumer to seek more of his amusement in the cheaper direction. The consumer is doing here only what every businessman does when cheapening the price of one productive factor causes him to adjust his production methods so as to substitute the cheap input for other kinds of inputs; by this process of substitution, he is able to produce the same output at lower total cost.

Income-effect. In the second place, being able to buy a good at a lower price is just like having an increase in your (real) income, particularly if you have been buying a great deal of the commodity. With a higher real income you can afford to buy more of tea, and of every good. And unless the good is of the so-called "inferior" variety like bologna or potatoes, you will ordinarily choose to buy something more of it once your real income has risen.

Of course, the quantitative importance of each of these effects varies with the good in question and with the consumer. Under some circumstances the resulting demand curve is very *elastic:* as where the consumer has been spending a good deal on the commodity and where ready substitutes are available—for example, a drunkard's demand for Scotch whisky. But if the commodity is like salt, which involves only a small fraction of the consumer's budget, is not easily replaceable by other items, and is necessary in small amounts to complement more important items, then demand will be *inelastic.*

▶ THE PARADOX OF VALUE

The preceding theories help to explain a famous question that troubled Adam Smith whose book, *The Wealth of Nations* (1776), marks the beginning of modern economics. He asked, "How is it that water, which is so very useful that life is impossible without it, has such a low price—while diamonds, which are quite unnecessary, have such a high price?"

Today even a beginning student can give a correct answer to this problem. "That's simply explained," he will write on an examination. "The supply and demand curves for water are such that they intersect at a very low price, while the supply and demand curves for diamonds are such that they intersect at a high price."

This is not an incorrect answer. Adam Smith could not have given it because supply and demand curves as descriptive tools had not yet been invented and were not to be for 75 years or more. But after he had mastered the lingo, old Adam Smith would naturally ask the question, "But *why* do supply and demand for water intersect at such a low price?"

The answer is by now easy to phrase. It consists of two parts. (1) Diamonds are very scarce, the cost of getting extra ones is high, and water is relatively abundant, with its cost low in most parts of the world.

This first part would have seemed reasonable to even the classical economists of more than a century ago, who would probably have let it go at that, and would not have known how to reconcile these facts about cost with the equally valid fact that the world's water is more *useful* than the world's supply of diamonds. (In fact, Adam Smith never did quite resolve the paradox. He was content simply to point out that the "value in use" of a good—its total contribution to economic welfare—is not the same thing as its "value in exchange"—the total money value or revenue for which it will sell.)

But today, we should add to the cost considerations of (1) the following: (2) the *total* usefulness of water does not determine its price or demand.

Only the relative usefulness and cost of the *last* little bit of water determine its price. Why? Because people are free to buy or not buy that last little bit. If water is priced higher than its last extra usefulness, then that last unit cannot be sold. Therefore, the price must fall until it reaches exactly the level of usefulness of the last little bit, no more and no less. Moreover, because every unit of water is exactly like any other unit and because there is only one price in a competitive market, *every unit must sell for what the last least use-ful unit sells for.* (As one student put the matter: The theory of economic value is easy to understand if you just remember that the tail wags the dog.)

Now we know that the more there is of a commodity, the less becomes the relative desirability of its last little unit—even though its total usefulness always grows as we get more of the commodity. So, it is obvious why a large amount of water has a low price. Or why air is actually a free good despite its vast usefulness. The later units pull down the market value of all units.

This completes the brief excursion behind the supply and demand curves which uses the marginal utility concept to explain Smith's paradox of value.

▶ CONSUMER'S SURPLUS: A DIFFICULT CONCEPT

This discussion emphasizes that the accounting system which records the "total economic value" or revenue of a good (price × quantity) differs from the measurement necessary to record "total welfare." The total economic value of air is zero; its contribution to welfare, very great.[1] Similarly, if we increase the quantity produced of a commodity, we obviously increase the community's welfare; but if it is a good like wheat whose demand is inelastic, we do at the same time destroy some economic value.

Thus, there is always kind of a gap between total welfare and total economic value. This gap is in the nature of a *surplus,* which the consumer gets because he always "receives more than he pays for."

Nor does he benefit at the expense of the seller. In a swap, one party does not lose what the other gains. Unlike energy which cannot be created or destroyed, the well-being of all participants is increased by trade.

It is not hard to see how this surplus arises. Each unit of a good that the consumer buys costs him only as much as the last unit is worth. But by our fundamental law, the *earlier* units are worth *more* to him than the last. Therefore, he enjoys a surplus on each of these earlier units. When trade stops benefiting him and giving him a surplus, he stops buying.

As final clinching evidence that the consumer always receives a surplus, we may cite the fact that a ruthless seller could present the consumer with an ultimatum: "Either you pay me an extra amount of money for the whole block of the good that you are consuming, or you must go without all the units, from first to last. Take it or leave it!" The consumer would certainly be willing to pay an extra amount rather than do without the good altogether.

Many ingenious ways have been suggested for measuring this consumer's surplus, but they are of no particular significance.[2] The important thing is to

---

[1] Or, as Smith would say, its value in use is very great; its value in exchange, negligible.

[2] In p. 397's footnote, consumer surplus could be measured by the area *dEs:* this is the triangular area under the demand curve but above the revenue rectangle actually paid. (Thus, you pay only $2.50 each for the units worth $4 and $3 to you, so your consumers surplus is $ $(4 - 2\frac{1}{2}) + $ $(3 - 2\frac{1}{2}) = $1\frac{1}{2} + $1\frac{1}{2}$, or $2 in all.

see how lucky the citizens of modern efficient communities really are. The *privilege of being able to buy a vast array of goods at low prices cannot be overestimated.*

This is a humbling thought. If ever a person becomes arrogantly proud of *his* economic productivity and *his* level of real earnings, let him pause and reflect. If he were transported with all his skills and energies intact to a primitive desert island, how much would his money earnings buy? Indeed, without capital machinery, without rich resources, without other labor, and above all without the technological knowledge which each generation inherits from society's past, how much could *he* produce? It is only too clear that all of us are reaping the benefits of an economic world we never made.

The organizer of industry who thinks that he has "made" himself and his business has found a whole social system ready to his hand in skilled workers, machinery, a market, peace and order—a vast apparatus and a pervasive atmosphere, the joint creation of millions of men and scores of generations. Take away the whole social factor and we have not Robinson Crusoe, with his salvage from the wreck and his acquired knowledge, but the naked savage living on roots, berries, and vermin.[1]

SUMMARY

1. A consumer with a given money income, confronted by finite prices, is limited in what he can buy and so must choose and substitute. To the extent that he is acting rationally, he will consciously or unconsciously substitute one good for another until he has reached the highest level of satisfaction. At this equilibrium point, the last penny spent on each kind of good will yield exactly the same extra satisfaction or marginal utility.

2. The equilibrium amount demanded of any good will change when either income, its own price, or the price of some other good changes. The last change introduces the notion of competing, independent, or complementary goods.

3. The drop in purchases of a good when its price rises[2]—or the relation between scarcity of a good and its price—is the basic economic *law of downward-sloping demand.* Together with the important recognition that it is the cost and desirability of the last unit of an article which is all important, this law and the marginal utility reasoning associated with it help to explain Adam Smith's famous paradox of value concerning water and diamonds.

4. Consumer's surplus is a reflection of the fact that the total economic welfare of any good is greater than its total monetary value. This is because all units of a good, being interchangeable, sell for as little as the last is worth. Consequently, the consumer is receiving a surplus on all previous units.

[1] L. T. Hobhouse, *The Elements of Social Justice* (Holt, New York, 1922), pp. 162–163.
[2] This is explicable in terms of "substitution-effect" and "income-effect."

QUESTIONS FOR DISCUSSION

1. "I don't know much about art, but I do know what I like." Is this a correct statement? Do people know what they like in the way of consumption goods? Do they usually like "what is good for them"?

2. Why is it nonsensical to say: "In equilibrium, the last little bits of satisfaction derived from all goods must be equal"? Write out a correct statement.

3. How much would you be willing to pay rather than give up all movies completely? How much do you spend per year on movies?

4. "You only get what you pay for." Is this true?

5. How would you go about measuring your own utility? With an X-ray machine, a yardstick, a Geiger counter, a smile recorder, a blood-pressure instrument, a cash register, a record of your gambling on the races, or records of your budget behavior in buying food and clothing? Or do you think it impossible?

6. Review your understanding of the following concepts:

market versus individual demand curve

maximizing utility from income

proportionality of prices and marginal utilities

equating marginal utility of last penny spent on each good

cross-elasticity, complements, substitutes

demand shifts

"substitution effect" and "income-effect"

paradox of value, total and marginal utility, scarcity, cost

consumer's surplus from buying worthwhile early units at last unit's worth

take-it-or-leave-it offer

APPENDIX: GEOMETRICAL ANALYSIS OF CONSUMER EQUILIBRIUM

It is instructive to show graphically, and without using the language of numerical utility, exactly what the consumer's equilibrium position looks like.

The Indifference Curve

We start out by considering a consumer with a given money income,[1] all of which he spends on consumption. He buys only two commodities, say food and clothing, at definite quoted prices. We suppose the consumer can tell us whether (1) he prefers a given combination or batch of the two goods, say 3 units of food and 2 of clothing, to some second combination or batch, say 2 units of food and 3 of clothing or (2) he is "indifferent" as between the two combinations or (3) he actually prefers the second batch of goods to the first.

Let us suppose that actually these two batches are equally good in the eyes of our consumer—that he is indifferent as to which of the two he receives. Let us go on to list in Table 1 some of the other combinations of

---

[1] By income and consumption, we always mean income and consumption per year or per day. For brevity, the fact that these are rates over time is taken for granted.

Food-clothing batches which give equal utility are "indifferent":

	Food	Clothing
A	1	6
B	2	3
C	3	2
D	4	1½

Table 1. Indifference combinations. Getting more of one good compensates for giving up something of the other. The consumer likes situation A exactly as well as B, or C, or D.

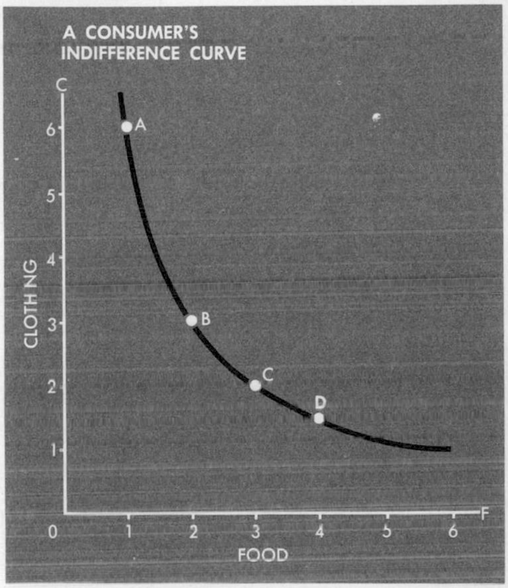

Fig. 3. The food-clothing combinations that yield equal satisfaction can be plotted as a smooth "indifference curve" (or so-called "equal-utility contour"). This is concave from above in accord with the Law of Substitution which says: As you get more of a good, its "substitution ratio" or "indifference slope" diminishes.

A CONSUMER'S INDIFFERENCE CURVE

goods between which the individual in question is likewise just indifferent.

Figure 3 shows these combinations diagrammatically. We measure units of clothing upon one axis and units of food upon the other. Each of our four combinations or batches, A, B, C, D, is represented by a single point. But these four are by no means the only combinations that would leave our consumer just indifferent as between them. Another batch, such as 1½ units of food and 4 of clothing, might be ranked as just equal to any of A, B, C, or D above, and there are many others. The curved line of Fig. 3, linking up the four points, is an "indifference curve." *Every* point thereon represents a different combination of the two goods; and the indifference curve is so drawn that, if our consumer were given his choice of any

point on it, he would not know which one to choose. All would be equally desirable to him, and he would be indifferent as to which batch he received.

It should be noted that this indifference curve is of concave curvature viewed from above. As we move downward and to the right along the curve—a movement which implies increasing the quantity of food and reducing that of clothing—the slope of the curve becomes flatter. The curve is drawn so because this illustrates a property which seems most often to hold true in real life and which we may call the Law of Substitution:

The scarcer a good, the greater its relative substitution value; the marginal utility of the good that has become scarce rises relative to the marginal utility of the good that has become plentiful.

For example, the consumer who is at position *A* in Table 1 is willing to give up 3 units of clothing in order to get a second unit of food; thus at *A*, he would swap 3 of his 6 clothing units in exchange for 1 extra food unit. But when he has moved to *B*, he would sacrifice only *one* of his remaining clothing supply in order to obtain a third food unit—a one-for-one swap. And for a fourth unit of food, he would sacrifice only ½ unit from his dwindling supply of clothing.

If we join the points *A* and *B* of Fig. 3, we find that the slope of the resulting line (neglecting its sign) has a value of 3. Join *B* and *C*, and the slope is 1; join *C* and *D*, and the slope is ½. These figures—3, 1, ½—are simply the "swapping terms" that we noted just above.

But to move from *A* to *B* is to move a considerable distance along the curve. What about the swapping terms for smaller movements? If the consumer is at *A* and we consider a movement to the intermediate position (not shown in Table 1) of 1½ food and 4 clothing, the swapping ratio would be 4. And it is clear that, as the movement along the curve grows smaller, the closer the swapping terms come to the actual slope of the indifference curve.[1]

So the slope of the indifference curve is the measure of the terms on which—for very small changes—the consumer would be willing to exchange a little of his supply of one good in return for a little more of the other. And an indifference curve which is concave

---

[1] By the arithmetic slope of the indifference curve, we mean this: To find the slope of the curve at, say, the point *B*, take a ruler and place it so that it is just tangent to the curve at *B*— it touches the curve, but does not cross it either above or below *B*. Mark the points at which the ruler's edge crosses the two axes. The slope is the ratio of the distance cut off on the vertical axis to the distance cut off on the horizontal axis; *e.g.*, at *B*, the slope is 6/4, or 1½. Intermediate texts refer to the slope of the indifference curve at any point as the "substitution ratio," or "the marginal rate of substitution," or the "relative marginal utility ratio" at that point.

in the manner of Fig. 3 conforms to the law of substitution earlier noted. As the consumer's supply of food increases—and his clothing dwindles—less and less favorable will be the terms on which he could be persuaded to take a little extra food in exchange for a little sacrifice of clothing. The precise shape and slope of an indifference curve will, of course, vary from one consumer to the next; but for this introductory discussion, it seems reasonable to assume that the general concave shape of the curve in Fig. 3 is typical.

The Indifference Map

Table 1 is but one of an infinite number of possible tables. We could have started out with a still higher level of satisfaction or indifference and listed some of the different combinations that belonged to it in the mind of our consumer. One such table might have begun with 2 food and 7 clothing; another with 3 food and 7 clothing. Each table could

Every point lies on one of the many indifference curves:

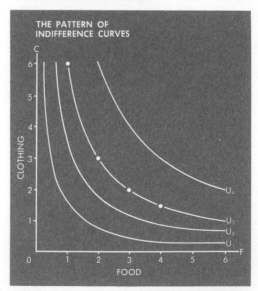

Fig. 4. The curves labeled U_1, U_2, U_3, U_4 represent indifference curves, or equal-utility contours. (Why is it better to be on a farther-out indifference curve?) U_3 is the curve of Fig. 3.

be portrayed graphically; each has its corresponding curve. Figure 4 shows four such curves; the old curve of Fig. 3 is now labeled U_3. This figure is analogous to a geographical contour map. A person who walks along the path indicated by a particular height contour on such a map will find that he is neither climbing nor descending; similarly the consumer who moves from one position to another along a single indifference curve enjoys neither increasing nor decreasing satisfaction from the change in the flow of goods he is getting. Of course, only a few of the possible indifference curves or equal-utility lines are shown in Fig. 4.

Note that, as we increase both goods and hence move in a northeasterly direction across this "map," we are crossing successive indifference curves; we are reaching higher and higher levels of satisfaction. Unless the consumer is satiated, he would be enjoying increasing satisfaction from receiving increased quantities of *both* goods. Hence curve U_3 stands for a higher level of satisfaction than U_2; U_4, for a higher level of satisfaction than U_3 and so forth.

The Consumption-Possibility Line

Now let us set the consumer's indifference map aside for a moment and consider his fixed income. He has, say, $6 per day to spend, and he is confronted with fixed prices for food and clothing—say $1.50 for food, $1 for clothing. It is clear that he could spend his money on any one of a variety of alternative combinations of food and clothing. At one extreme, he could buy 4 food units and no clothing; at the other, 6 clothing units and no food. Table 2 illustrates some of the possible ways in which his $6 could be allocated.

Figure 5 shows these five possible positions on a diagram with axes similar to those of Figs. 3 and 4. Each position is indicated by a small circle, and it will be noted that they all lie on a straight line, which is labeled *NM*. Moreover, any other attainable point, such as 3⅓ food units and 1 clothing unit, would lie upon *NM*.[1] *NM* sums up all the possible

Fixed income and market *P*'s imply limited consumption possibilities:

Food	Clothing
4	0
3	1½
2	3
1	4½
0	6

Table 2. Alternative consumption possibilities. The costs of these budgets (reckoned as $1.50 F + $1 C) all add up to $6 income.

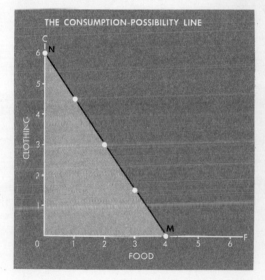

Fig. 5. *NM* is the consumer's consumption-possibility line. When he spends just $6 daily, with food and clothing prices $1.50 and $1, he can choose any point on this line. (Why is its slope $1.50/$1 = ³⁄₂ or 1.5?)

---

[1] This is so because if we designate quantities of food and clothing bought as F and C, respectively, total expenditure on food must be $1½$F$ and total expenditure on clothing, 1C$. If daily expenditure is $6, the following equation must hold: $6 = $1½$F$ + 1C$. This is a simple linear equation—the equation of the line *NM*. Note:

$$NM\text{'s arithmetic slope} = \$1\tfrac{1}{2} \div \$1 = \text{price of food} \div \text{price of clothing}$$

Equilibrium is where consumer has reached highest satisfaction level:

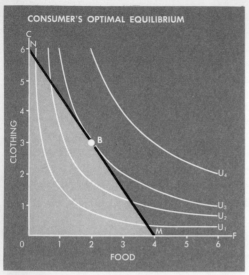

CONSUMER'S OPTIMAL EQUILIBRIUM

Fig. 6. At B the consumer reaches highest indifference curve attainable with his fixed income. B represents tangency of consumption-possibility line with highest indifference curve. (Why? If slopes were unequal, NM would intersect U contour and you could cross over into higher satisfaction levels.) At tangency point B, "substitution ratio" equals price ratio P_F/P_C. This means all goods' marginal utilities are proportional to their prices, with marginal utility of the last dollar spent on every good being equalized.

positions that our consumer could occupy in spending his $6 income.

The slope of *NM* (neglecting its sign) is 3/2, which is necessarily the ratio of food price to clothing price; and the common sense of this line is clear enough. Given these prices, every time our consumer gives up 1½ clothing units (thereby dropping down 1½ vertical units on the diagram), he can gain 1 unit of food (*i.e.*, move east 1 horizontal unit). Or what is the same thing, he can exchange 3 clothing units for 2 food units. We can call *NM* the consumer's "consumption-possibility" (or "budget") line.

The Equilibrium Position

Now we are ready to put our two parts together. The axes of Fig. 5 were the same as those of Figs. 3 and 4. We can superimpose the consumption-possibility line *NM* upon the consumer's indifference map, as in Fig. 6. He is free to move anywhere along *NM*. Positions to the right and upward of *NM* are barred to him unless he spends more than $6 daily, and positions to the left and below *NM* are unimportant, since we assume that he will want to spend the full $6. Where will the consumer move? Obviously to that point which yields the greatest satisfaction;

or, in other words, to the highest available indifference curve, which in this case must be at point *B*. At *B*, the consumption-possibility line just touches—but does not cross[1] —the indifference curve U_3; this is the highest curve he can reach.

Geometrically, the consumer is at equilibrium where the slope of his consumption-possibility line is exactly equal to the slope of his indifference curve. And as we have already noted, the slope of the consumption-possibility line is the ratio of food price to clothing price. We may say, then, that equilibrium is attained when the consumer's *substitution* ratio is just equal to the ratio of food price to clothing price.[2]

---

[1] At any point other than *B* on *NM*, *NM* is crossing indifference curves. And as long as the consumer can keep crossing indifference curves, he can keep moving to higher ones.

[2] The substitution ratio, or slope of the indifference curve, can be shown to be nothing but the ratio of the marginal utility of food to the marginal utility of clothing. So our tangency condition is just another way of stating that a good's price and its marginal utility must be proportional, in equilibrium—with the consumer there getting the same marginal utility from his last penny spent on food as from his last penny spent on clothing.

Changes in Income and Price

Our understanding of the process will be furthered by considering the effects of (1) a change in money income and (2) a change in the price of one of the two goods.

1. Assume first that the consumer's daily income is halved, the two prices remaining unchanged. We could prepare another table, similar to Table 2, showing the consumption possibilities that are now open to him. Plotting these points on a diagram such as Fig. 7, we should find that the new consumption-possibility line occupies the position N'M' in Fig. 7. The line has made a *parallel*

2. Now let us return our consumer to his previous daily income of $6, but now assume that the price of food rises from $1.50 to $3. Again we must examine the change in the consumption-possibility line. This time, we shall find that it has pivoted on the point N and is now NM",[3] as in Fig. 8. The common sense of such a shift is clear. Since the price of clothing is unchanged, the point N is just as available as it was before. But since the price of food has risen, point M, which meant 4 food units had been purchasable, is no longer attainable. With food costing $3 per unit, only 2 units can now be

When income or a *P* changes, we find new equilibrium:

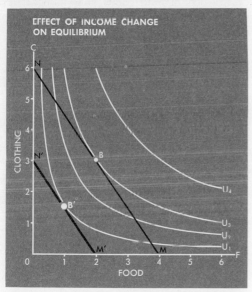

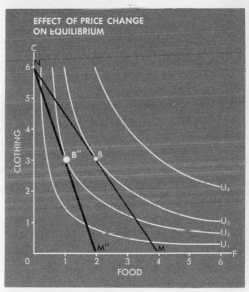

Fig. 7. An income change shifts the consumption-possibility line in a parallel way. Thus, halving income to $3 shifts NM to N'M' and moves equilibrium to B'. (Show what raising income will do to the equilibrium.)

Fig. 8. A rise in the price of food makes the consumption-possibility line rotate from NM to NM". New tangency equilibrium is at B". (Can you handle a clothing price change?)

shift, in the southwesterly direction.[1] The consumer is now free to move only along this line. Again he will move to the highest attainable indifference curve, or to the point B'. A similar tangency condition for equilibrium again applies.[2]

[1] The equation of the consumption-possibility line is now $3 = $1½F + $1C.

bought with a daily income of $6. So the new consumption-possibility line must still pass through N, but it must pivot around N

[2] Join B' and B by a smooth curve to generate the important budgetary income expenditure patterns of Chapter 9, Fig. 1, p. 164.

[3] The equation of the consumption-possibility line is now $6 = $3F + $1C.

and pass through M'', which is nearer to the origin than the old point M. (The new line has a slope of 3/1. Why?) Equilibrium is now at B''; we have a new tangency situation in that equilibrium.

To clinch his understanding, the reader should work out the cases of (1) an increase in income and (2) a fall in the price of clothing or food.

SUMMARY TO APPENDIX

1. If a consumer has a fixed money income, all of which he spends, and is confronted with market prices of two goods, the consumption-possibility line upon which he is free to move is a straight line. The steepness of the line's slope depends on the ratio of the two market prices; how far out from the origin it lies depends on the size of his income.

2. The consumer will move along this consumption-possibility line until he reaches the highest indifference curve attainable. At this point, the consumption-possibility line will touch, but not cross, an indifference curve. Hence equilibrium is at the point of *tangency,* where the *slope of the consump-*

tion-possibility line (the ratio of the prices) exactly equals the *slope of the indifference curve* (the substitution ratio or relative-marginal-utility ratio of the two goods).

3. A fall in income will move the consumption-possibility line inward, usually causing less of both goods to be bought. A change in the price of one good alone will, other things being equal, cause the consumption-possibility line to pivot so as to change its slope. In any case, whatever change has occurred, a new equilibrium point of highest satisfaction will be reached. It will be identified by a new point of tangency, where marginal utilities are again proportional to market prices.

QUESTIONS FOR DISCUSSION

1. Explain why an indifference curve can be drawn through every point on an indifference map. Can you explain why two indifference curves could never cross?

2. If the consumer is at a point on his consumption-possibility line where it crosses an indifference curve, explain why he cannot have reached equilibrium. Which way would he move?

3. Can you generate the ordinary *dd* food

demand curve from Fig. 8?

4. Review your understanding of the following concepts:

    indifference curves
    slope or substitution ratio
    consumption-possibility line
    optimal tangency equilibrium
    $P_F/P_C = substitution\ ratio$
    parallel and pivoted shifts

24 EQUILIBRIUM OF THE FIRM: COST AND REVENUE

Both monopolistic and competitive forces combine in the determination of most prices.

EDWARD H. CHAMBERLIN

In the last several chapters we have studied the workings of competitive supply and demand in considerable detail. For the most part, we have been studying what the economist calls the case of "perfect competition."

Perfect competition means something very definite to the economist. As we'll see, the economist means by it something *much stronger* than does the man in the street or the businessman when he talks of "strong rivalry and keen competition among different business firms and industries."

The special case of perfect competition is a very important special case. But it is only one case. It cannot faithfully represent many of the facts about modern industries. The real world—as we know it in America, Europe, or Asia—contains significant mixtures of monopoly imperfections along with elements of competition. The real world, then, is for the most part to be classified in the realm of "imperfect competition": it is neither perfectly competitive nor perfectly "monopolistic."

The remaining chapters of Part Three, therefore, will give us the tools to analyze imperfect as well as perfect competition. They will show what modifications have to be made in any conclusions that were based on an analysis of perfect competition. We shall see that the way a pricing system succeeds in solving the basic problems of What, How, and For Whom is affected in important degree by any elements of monopolistic imperfection that may be involved in numerous modern industries.

▶ PERFECT COMPETITION STRICTLY DEFINED

Exactly how does the economist define "perfect competition?" His requirements are very stringent indeed. He says that competition isn't really perfect unless numerous producers sell an exactly *identical* product, as like as two peas in a pod or two grains of Winter Wheat No. 2. With each firm's product so much like every other firm's product, it has no way of raising its price above that which prevails in the market. And with so many other firms producing the good, if one firm doubles or redoubles its output, it will still be too small to depress market price appreciably.

By definition, then,

▶ A "perfect competitor" is one who can sell all he wishes at the going market price, but is unable in any appreciable degree to raise or depress that market price. And by definition, a "perfectly competitive industry" is one made up exclusively of numerous perfect competitors. In all likelihood it has some kind of organized, auction mechanism or exchange where market price is quoted (and where may even be quoted market prices for "future delivery at stipulated date" of the good).

Notice how strict this definition is. Think of any commodity that comes to mind: razor blades, tooth paste, steel, aluminum, potatoes, wheat, cigarettes, tobacco, nylon, cotton. Which fit in with the strict definition of perfect competition? Certainly not razor blades or tooth paste or cigarettes. Did you ever hear of an auction market for blades, or tooth paste, or cigarettes?

Neither aluminum nor steel meet the definition of perfect competition. For a long time there was only one aluminum company, Alcoa (Aluminum Company of America); and even today there are only Alcoa, Reynolds, Kaiser, and one or two others. Contrast this with the case of thousands, if not millions, of cotton and wheat farmers.

What about steel? U.S. Steel Co. and Bethlehem are the giants. Together with Republic Steel, Jones & Laughlin, and a few other firms that constitute Little Steel, they produce a large fraction of the total market. It is true that one plant's steel output may be much like another's, but it is not true that Bethlehem or Republic are so weak that each could not depress the price of steel by throwing on the market as much as it wanted to.

When you go down the list, you'll find that only potatoes, tobacco, wheat, and cotton come within our strict definition of perfect competition. Nylon must compete with cotton: that is very true. But in the economist's strict sense, nylon is not a product produced under "perfect competition" nor is its producer a "perfect competitor" in the economist's sense of the term.[1]

---

[1] Sometimes economists use various synonyms for perfect competition: they often call it "pure competition," in contrast to "impure, or imperfect, or monopolistic competition"; or they occasionally call it "atomistic competition," to convey the notion of numerous small firms which combine like a multitude of tiny atoms to make up the industry. Occasionally, too, an economist will say: "By perfect, I mean really perfect. The wheat market isn't 'perfect competition' unless everyone in it is perfectly informed about all the future, with there being nowhere any uncertainty." However, that's not the sense used here for perfect competition. The price of wheat will fluctuate in a way that no one can now foresee, but so long as no seller can appreciably influence wheat price, we'll agree to call the wheat market perfect. (Naturally, once you bring government control programs into the wheat picture, as in Chapter 21, you're bringing monopolistic imperfections into this perfect competition setup.)

Acid test for imperfect competition is slope of firm's demand:

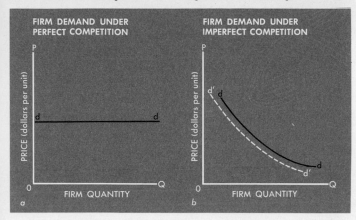

FIRM DEMAND UNDER PERFECT COMPETITION

FIRM DEMAND UNDER IMPERFECT COMPETITION

PRICE (dollars per unit)

FIRM QUANTITY

Fig. 1. The perfect competitor can sell all he wants along his horizontal *dd* curve, never depressing market price.

But the imperfect competitor will find his demand curve sloped downward, as his increased Q forces down the P he can get. Unless he is a sheltered monopolist, a cut in his rival's P will appreciably shift his own *dd* leftward to *d'd'*.

Figure 1 shows the acid test to determine whether a given producer is a "perfect competitor" or an "imperfect competitor." Plot the price he can get for each amount he sells: if his demand curve is horizontal as in Fig. 1*a*, showing that he has no control over price at all and can sell all he wants to at the going price, then he is indeed a perfect competitor.

▶ **IMPERFECT COMPETITION DEFINED**

But suppose the single firm finds itself facing a demand curve which slopes appreciably downward as in Fig. 1*b*—which means that when it insists on throwing more on the market, it definitely does depress price along its *dd* curve—then the firm is classified by the economist as an "imperfect competitor."

Mind you that doesn't mean that its owner is of poor character, that he beats his wife or fails to pay his bills. Nor does the fact that a firm is an imperfect competitor mean that it is not keenly seeking to outsell and outadvertise its rivals. Intense commercial rivalry and "perfect competition" are not at all the same thing: indeed Farmer Jones, perfect competitor, will do no advertising at all. Why should he? He can sell all the wheat he can produce without depressing market price. But American Tobacco Company, producer of Lucky Strike cigarettes and an imperfect competitor, will spend much of its energies in trying to outsell Chesterfields, the snuff industry, and maybe the candy industry too.

The final test then is always in the horizontality of the demand curve. It doesn't matter whether the firm is profitable or unprofitable; or whether it has patents, secret know-how, trade-marks, or other advantages which give it control over market price.

▶ So long as a firm's demand curve tilts downward—looking like the industry demand curves of earlier chapters rather than like the horizontal demand curve of each small perfect competitor in a perfectly-competitive industry—it is classified as an "imperfect competitor." (This doesn't mean it has absolute monopoly power over the price it can charge: as we'll see there are varying degrees of monopolistic imperfection in different imperfectly competitive markets.) [1]

▶ **IMPERFECT COMPETITION: MONOPOLY, OLIGOPOLY, AND DIFFERENTIATED PRODUCTS**

Monopoly. How imperfect can imperfect competition get? The extreme case would be that of a *single* seller with practically complete monopoly power. (He's called a *monopolist* from the Greek word "mono" for "one" and "polist" for "seller.") He is the only one producing in his industry, and there is no industry that produces a close substitute for his good. (In Fig. 1*b*, a change in another firm's price would shift the monopolist's *dd* curve negligibly.)

Exclusive monopolies, like public utilities or telephones, are usually regulated by the government; and even they must usually take account of the potential competition of alternative products—oil for gas, or cables for telephones. This shows how relatively unimportant complete monopolies are.

Oligopoly. This horrible-sounding word means "few sellers" (and like monopoly comes from the Greek stem "oli" for "few"). An oligopolist is one of a *few* sellers who produce an *identical* (or almost identical) product. Thus, if A's steel is much the same as B's steel, then the smallest price difference will drive the consumer from A to B. Neither A nor B could be called a monopolist. Yet, if the number of sellers is few, each has a very appreciable effect on market price.

Oligopoly is thought to be common in a number of our basic industries where product is fairly homogeneous and size of enterprise large. Another example would be that of moving freight between New York and Chicago by any of the three or four alternative rail routes. In the old days when rail rates were unregulated, there would be periodic price wars in which each railroad undercut the other in the attempt to gain more of the business: sometimes it would become cheaper to move freight from New York to Chicago than to move it from New York to Buffalo; and occasionally it might be cheaper to move freight from New York to Buffalo via Chicago, with all the implied wasteful cross-haulage.

Differentiated products. This is the last in our list of imperfect competitors. Here there may be many or few sellers, but now they do not produce identical products. Instead they produce "differentiated products": *i.e.*, products which differ somewhat in real qualities or which the buyer thinks differ in real qualities. My toothpaste is a little different from yours; and if I raise my price above yours, I may still hope to sell a good deal to those consumers who have been persuaded by my advertising or by past use of my product.

---

[1] The standard book on all this is E. H. Chamberlin, *Theory of Monopolistic Competition* (Harvard University Press, Cambridge, Mass., 1957, 8th edition) especially Chapters 1 and 4. Chamberlin prefers the word "monopolistic competition" for what is here called "imperfect competition," but that may give the impression to the layman that there is something especially nasty, or illegal, in not being a perfect competitor—which is not Chamberlin's view.

Advertising, brand names, trade-marks, patents, and custom may explain why there is product differentiation. Or it may merely be that a given barber shop or grocery store is in a locality near to certain consumers: the fact of this nearness may give it a measure of monopoly power; and yet if its price gets too high, it will find itself losing trade to more-distant competitiors. (In Fig. 1*b*, when your rivals cut their *P*, your *dd* curve shifts appreciably.)

All these categories overlap. Take the auto industry. Is it oligopoly or differentiated product? Sellers are indeed few: the "Big Three" (GM, Ford, Chrysler) sell all but a few per cent. Still a Ford has different chrome from a Chevy, so there is product differentiation. Yet if Ford shaded its price, could Plymouth and Chevy afford not to?

▶ BRIEF SUMMARY OF KINDS OF COMPETITION

Table 1 presents a brief picture of the various possible categories of imperfect and perfect competition.

Most industries are imperfectly competitive—a blend of monopoly and competition:

Table 1. Types of competition.

Kind of competition	Number of producers and degree of product differentiation	Part of economy applicable to	Degree of control over price	Methods of marketing
Perfect competition	many producers; identical products	a few agricultural industries	none	market exchange or auction
Imperfect competition				
Oligopoly	few producers; little or no difference in product	most firms and industries	some	advertising rivalry, administered prices
Differentiated products	many or few producers; many real or fancied differences in product			
Complete monopoly	single producer; single product without close substitutes	a few utilities	considerable	promotional and "institutional" public-relations advertising

▶ **PRICE, QUANTITY, AND TOTAL REVENUE**

For the rest of this chapter, we want to analyze how a business firm will rationally decide to determine its best output and price. Since imperfect competition includes perfect competition as a limiting case where the slope of the demand curve becomes inappreciable, we can concentrate on the general case of an imperfect competitor. Call him John Doe, Inc. or anything else. For simplicity, suppose he produces a single good, Q.

From its demand schedule, firm derives its total revenue schedule:

Quantity Q (1)	Price P (2)	Total Revenue $R = P \times Q$ (3)
0	$144 or more	$ 0
1	134	—
2	124	248
3	114	—
4	104	—
5	94	—
6	84	504
7	74	518
8	64	512
9	54	—
10	44	—

Table 2. Demand and revenue schedules for imperfect competitor. Always $R = P \times Q$. When you have filled in all the missing data, can you verify that the firm will not "charge all the traffic will bear." It maximizes its total revenue not at highest possible P, but at P of $74. (Why would this be its equilibrium point of maximum profit in the case where its production costs were negligible?)

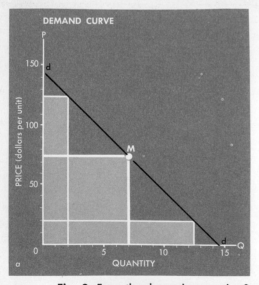

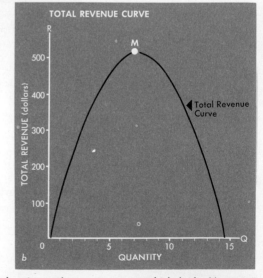

Fig. 2. From the demand curve, the firm plots its total revenue curve—which looks like a hill whose slope is rising as long as demand is elastic and falling after demand becomes inelastic. (Can you see that the revenue rectangle of the demand curve reaches its maximum at point M, where $Q = 7$?)

Table 2 represents the original demand schedule for the firm. The reader should fill in the missing figures in the total revenue column of Table 2.

How much will the firm produce, and at what price? This question cannot be answered until we know something about its costs of production. For the moment, though, let's neglect all costs. The firm, even if it has no costs, will not charge the highest possible price of $134. Why not? Because then it does not maximize its revenue and profits. It is then collecting the highest possible (average) revenue per unit, but it is selling only one unit, and collecting only $134 of total revenue.

Actually, with zero costs the best quantity for the firm is 7 units, and the best price is $74. This answer is derived from an examination of the total revenue column, $R = P \times Q$, where the point of highest total revenue is stressed. Price is not there at a maximum; neither is quantity. But *total* revenue is being maximized. Figure 2, accompanying Table 2, shows the relation between the demand curve and the total revenue curve.

▶ **TOTAL AND MARGINAL COSTS**

It is now simple to introduce costs into the picture. The firm had to make a guess at its demand curve. Similarly, it must try to estimate the approximate dollar expense that will be incurred in producing different outputs. Although the accounting difficulties in arriving at such a total cost curve are very great and may involve considerable guesswork, the firm's accounting and production departments must try to determine which costs are *fixed,* independently of changes in output, and which are *variable costs* changing with output. Table 3 and Fig. 3 on the following two pages give an example of such a cost estimate for a certain firm.

Fixed costs. Column (1) indicates the different levels of production per unit time, going from 0 up to 10 units. Column (2) indicates that the firm's fixed costs per time period are $256 even if it produces nothing. By definition, fixed costs are fixed; they remain at $256 at all levels of output. They result from past commitments, from costs already "sunk," overhead expense, etc.

Variable cost. Column (3) lists the estimated amounts of total variable costs per unit time at different levels of production. By definition, variable costs are zero when no output is being produced. But they change with quantity, Q. At first as output increases, variable costs grow quite rapidly. But as output increases further, *economies of mass production* come into play and variable costs do not seem to be increasing proportionately with output. Later on, though, as diminishing returns set in, short-run variable costs begin to shoot up more rapidly than output.

Total cost. This is given in Column (4). It is nothing but the sum of fixed and variable costs. It must begin, therefore, even with zero production, at $256

Total cost curve comes from adding fixed and variable cost curves:

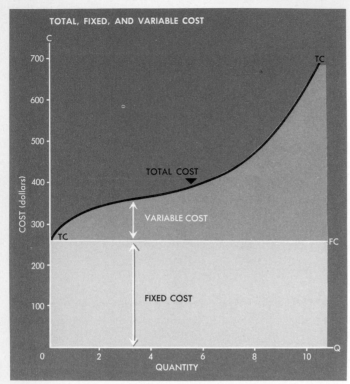

Fig. 3. The *FC* curve is horizontal by definition. The Variable Cost curve is measured as the distance above the *FC* curve. Total Cost always equals their sum: $TC = FC + VC$.

and increase from there on like variable costs. Figure 3 illustrates the three different cost categories pictorially.

Average cost. Of the three cost schedules discussed, clearly the basic one is total cost. The other two are refinements that can easily be calculated from it. Still, accountants find it sometimes convenient to make still other cost calculations. Thus, in Column (6) of Table 3 is listed *average* or *unit cost* of production. This is easily derived by dividing total cost by the number of units of output in order to get the average cost per unit.

Average costs are very high at first because the large fixed costs are saddled on to so few units. In fact, when output is zero, costs per unit have to be infinite. If only one unit were produced, average costs would be $320. But as more is produced, the $256 of fixed cost is spread over more and more units. This explains the early rapid decline of average costs in Fig. 4.

After the overhead has been spread thin over many units, fixed costs can no longer have much influence on average costs. Variable costs become important, and as average variable costs begin to rise because of limitations of plant space and management difficulties, average costs finally begin to turn up. Thus, in Table 3, Column (6), and in Fig. 4, average costs are at their lowest at

8 units, where they are only $60 per unit. Expanding output beyond this point causes average costs to rise. Thus, the average curve is U-shaped: falling at first because of spreading the overhead and economies of mass production, but ultimately rising because of some kind of diminishing returns.

Marginal cost. The businessman must decide how much to produce so as to make the greatest profits. He will be more interested, therefore, in the *extra* costs of changing output rather than in over-all average costs.

Column (5) of Table 3 lists the difference in total costs for each extra unit

From schedule of total cost, all other costs can be computed:

Table 3. Total, fixed, and variable cost; average and marginal cost per unit. Fixed cost always equals your total cost at Q = 0. FC never changes. Variable cost is what has to be added to fixed cost to get total cost. (Check this for each and every Q.)

Quantity Q (1)	Fixed cost FC (2)	Variable cost VC (3)	Total cost TC = FC + VC (4)	Marginal cost per unit MC (5)	Average cost per unit AC = TC ÷ Q (6)
0	$256	$ 0	$256		Infinity
				$ 64	
1	256	64	320		$320
				20	
2	256	84	340		170
				15	
3	256	99	355		118.33
				13	
4	256	112	368		92
				13	
5	256	125	381		76.20
				19	
6	256	144	400		66.67
				31	
7	256	175	431		61.57
				49	
8	256	224	480		60
				73	
9	256	297	553		61.44
				103	
10	256	400	656		65.60

Average cost per unit comes from dividing total cost by number of units produced (i.e., AC = TC ÷ Q).

Marginal cost per unit is very important. MC is the "extra cost" that comes from producing an "extra unit of Q." You get it by subtracting from new larger TC the previous TC you had when you were producing one less unit. [Important: check column (5) to verify your understanding of this.]

The average cost curve is generally U-shaped:

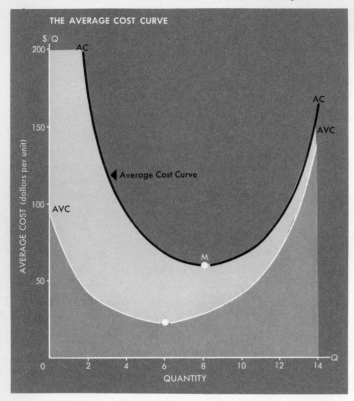

THE AVERAGE COST CURVE

Average Cost Curve

Fig. 4. Average cost comes from dividing total cost by number of Q. It begins high because FC is then spread over so few units. As Q grows, the FC/Q part of average cost steadily declines. (This so-called "spreading of the overhead over more units" is shown by the narrowing light-shaded area between the AC curve and the curve that measures "average variable cost per unit.") AC reaches its minimum at the bottom-of-the-U point M. Average cost eventually rises when the rise in average variable costs finally outweighs the fall in average fixed cost.

of output. Such extra costs are important enough in economic theory to rate a distinctive name: *marginal cost*. Thus, the marginal cost in going from the fifth unit to the sixth unit is got from Column (4) by subtracting the total cost of 5 units from the total cost of 6 units. This gives $400 − $381, or $19. (What is marginal cost or *MC* in going from the eighth to the ninth unit? Why?)

Figure 5 shows the behavior of marginal cost. The *MC* curve of extra cost is quite independent of fixed costs. Why? Because fixed costs go on anyway, whether or not you produce an extra unit. At first marginal cost is falling. It is far below average cost; and with each extra unit costing less than the average unit cost, what must be happening to average cost? It must be in the process of being pulled down, and must be a gently falling curve. Similarly, when extra costs finally rise above average cost, they pull up the average: so *MC* cuts *AC* at its bottom.[1]

---

[1] Parable of the reformed loafer: J. got worse and worse grades his first few terms in college. Each term's marginal grade average was then pulling down his cumulative average grade. Then he met K. and she reformed him. His term grades slowly improved. But not until his marginal grade got above his average, did his average turn from dropping to rising. Some time *after* his reform, his cumulative average reached its minimum—where his *MC* cut his *AC* curve at its bottom. To be sure you understand why, make up a parable about the slow-starting baseball batter.

Marginal or "extra cost" is a vital economic concept:

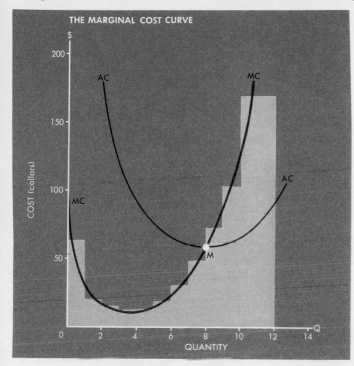

THE MARGINAL COST CURVE

Fig. 5. Marginal cost is always the "extra cost" of "extra output." It comes from Table 2's *TC* by carefully subtracting before and after costs. When the steps are smoothed to a smooth curve, we get the MC curve. (It is no accident that MC cuts the AC curve at its bottom. When the last unit costs you more than the average, it must pull up the average—so the AC curve must begin to rise at point M.)

▶ **MARGINAL REVENUE AND PRICE**

Go back now to the revenue or demand part of the picture. Just as we define marginal cost as extra cost, we define *marginal revenue* as the *extra* revenue resulting from selling an *extra* unit of goods. Marginal revenue would be derived from the total revenue column of Table 2. This is indicated in Table 4, which repeats Table 2 but has one new column for marginal revenue.

At first, the reader may wonder why there is any difference between price, Column (2), and marginal revenue, Column (4). In going from 2 to 3 units of output, why isn't marginal revenue equal to the price at which the third unit is sold? Why isn't it, therefore, $114 instead of the indicated figure of $94?

True, the third unit is sold for $114. But to get it sold, we had to cut the price on the previous 2 units by $10 each (from $124 to $114). This loss on the previous units must be charged up against the third unit in reckoning marginal revenue; thus, the marginal revenue is $114 − (2 × $10), or $94. Generally speaking, marginal revenue is less than the price, as indicated by the fundamental formula:

Marginal revenue of nth unit = difference in total revenue
  in going from (n − l) to n units
  = price of nth unit minus
    loss in revenue on previous units resulting from price
    reduction

Marginal (or "extra") revenue is a vital economic concept:

Table 4. Marginal revenue and price. MR is defined as the change in total revenue when you sell one extra unit of output. [Each row of Col. (4) comes from subtracting Col. (3)'s row above it from the row below it.] Note that for every imperfect competitor like the present firm MR always falls below price.

Quantity Q (1)	Price P (2)	Total revenue $R = P \times Q$ (3)	Marginal revenue MR (4)
0	\$144 $+$	\$ 0	
			\$134
1	134	134	
			114
2	124	248	
			94
3	114	342	
			74
4	104	416	
			54
5	94	470	
			34
6	84	504	
			14
7	**74**	**518**	
			−6
8	64	512	
			−26
9	54	486	
			−46
10	44	440	

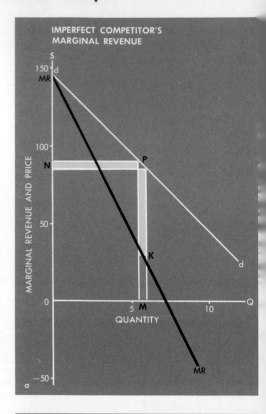

Fig. 6a (Above). Marginal revenue is less than price under imperfect competition. When *dd* slopes downward, marginal revenue falls even more rapidly. Marginal revenue becomes negative when demand becomes inelastic and more Q reduces total revenue. The shaded area *NP* shows the loss on previous units when the imperfect competitor sells one more small unit of Q. *PK* shows the same loss area subtracted from market price *PM* to give marginal revenue *KM*.

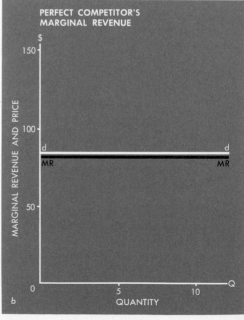

Fig. 6b. With a horizontal *dd*, the perfect competitor has no loss on previous units. So the MR and *dd* curves are identical.

The intelligent firm seeks its Best-Profit point:

Table 5. Summary of firm's Revenue, Cost, and Profit.

Quantity Q (1)	Price P (2)	Total revenue $R = P \times Q$ (3)	Total cost $TC = FC + VC$ (4)	Profit Pro (5) = (3) −(4)	Marginal revenue MR (6)	Marginal cost MC (7)
0	$144 +	$ 0	$256	−$256		
1	134	134	320	−186	$134	$ 64
2	124	248	340	−92	114	20
3	114	342	355	−13	94	15
4	104	416	368	+48	74	13
5	94	470	381	+89	54	13
6	84	504	400	+104	34	19
7	74	518	431	+87	14	31
8	64	512	480	+32	−6	49
9	54	486	553	−67	−26	73
10	44	440	656	−216	−46	103

This brings together all demand and cost data. See that the firm will find its Best-Profit point at unshaded row where Q = 6, P = $84, and Profit = $104, the maximum. For Q<6, MR>MC and firm expands; for Q>6, MR<MC and firm will contract output. (If you accurately interpolate MR and MC to get them at exactly Q = 6.0 and not between 5 and 6 or 6 and 7, you'll find MR = $24 = MC there exactly.) MR = MC is the condition for maximum profit.

Figure 6a illustrates the loss on previous units by its horizontal shaded area. Only under perfect competition, where the sale of extra units will never depress price at all, is the loss-in-revenue term zero. Only then will price and marginal revenue be identical.[1] (See Fig. 6b.)

If elasticity of demand as defined in Chapter 19 falls to less than unity, so that the percentage decrease in price always exceeds the percentage rise in quantity sold, any increase in output will actually *lower* total revenue. In other words, marginal revenue will become negative. Why? Because the second term in our formula—the loss on previous units—will outbalance the first term—the price received on the last unit. The firm would profit more under such conditions to burn up extra output rather than let it "spoil the market" so badly.

▶ MAXIMIZING PROFITS: THE BEST-PROFIT POINT

We may now bring all our relevant facts together in a supertable, Table 5. Total profit is, of course, the column of greatest interest in this table.

[1] The interested reader might check the relationship between price and marginal revenue in Table 4 at some one or more points, by calculating the loss in revenue resulting from the price reduction necessary to get the last unit sold.

What quantity will maximize total profits, and what price? The simplest way to solve this problem is to compute Column (5), total profit, which is simply the difference between total revenue and total cost. Running our eyes down this column tells us:

The optimal quantity is 6 units, with a price of $84 per unit. No other situation will give us as much profit as the $104 which that situation brings in.

Another way of arriving at the same result is to compare marginal revenue, Column (6), and marginal cost, Column (7). As long as a step toward extra output gives us more marginal revenue than marginal costs, our profit is increasing and we continue to produce more output. But whenever marginal cost exceeds marginal revenue, we contract output. Where is equilibrium?

▶ Best-Profit equilibrium is *where marginal cost and marginal revenue are in balance*. Here alone is the optimal situation of maximum profits.

This second way of finding the optimum point by comparing marginal cost

Best-Profit point is shown by total or marginal curves:

1st, by curves of total revenue, total cost, and profit

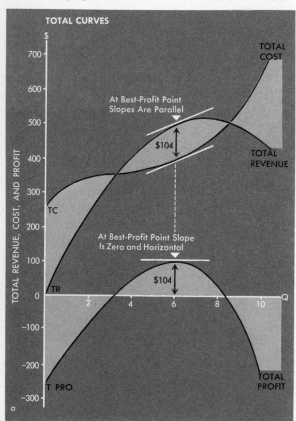

Fig. 7a. The vertical distances between the *TR* and *TC* curves define Total Profit, which is plotted below. Where *TR* and *TC* have equal slopes, and *TPro* has horizontal slope, you find Best-Profit point.

and revenue is neither better nor worse than the first method of simply examining total profits. They are really exactly the same thing.

▶ GRAPHICAL DEPICTION OF FIRM'S OPTIMUM POSITION: TOTAL CURVES

The three curves of Fig. 7a illustrate these procedures. *Total revenue* is a hill
whose slope is rising as long as demand is elastic, and falling after the demand
has become inelastic. *Total costs* are rising, because you usually can't get extra
output for nothing. *Total profit* is the difference between total revenue and
cost. It is shown in two places on the diagram by light shading: directly by
the lowest curve, and also as the vertical distance between the two upper
curves of revenue and cost.

At small outputs, total cost exceeds total revenue and the firm cannot break
even; again at very large outputs, price is so low and costs so high that it is
again "in the red." In between is the optimum point of maximum profit.

2d, by curves of marginal revenue and marginal cost

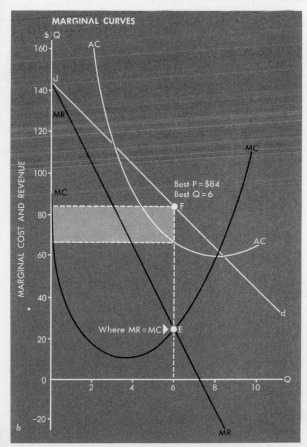

Fig. 7b. The same Best-Profit point is
shown where the marginal cost curve intersects the marginal revenue curve at E. This
Q = 6 sells on the demand curve for
P = $84 as shown at F. (Can you explain
why the shaded rectangle measures total
profit of $104, and why any other such
rectangle would have smaller area?)

This optimum quantity is clearly 6 units. Here total profit is at a maximum. Here the vertical difference between the two upper curves is greatest.[1]

▶ The Best-Profit point is the quantity at which the slopes of the total revenue curve and the total cost curve are exactly parallel; and where the slope of the total profit curve is zero and horizontal.

At any smaller outputs, such as 4 units, the two slopes are widening out; therefore, the vertical distance between the two curves is increasing and the firm will expand its output. At any output larger than the optimum, the two slopes are narrowing; by moving backward, we can increase the vertical distance between revenue and cost. Only at the optimum point, where the slopes are exactly parallel, will it pay to move neither to the right nor to the left. This is the firm's equilibrium of maximum profits—its Best-Profit point.

▶ USING MARGINAL CURVES

These respective slopes of the total cost and total revenue curves are nothing but our recent acquaintances, marginal cost and marginal revenue. In Fig. 7b, the same determination of best output is shown in a new way. The MC and MR curves are plotted for each output (either from smoothing Table 5 data or reading off the numerical slopes from Fig. 7a). Where the MC curve exactly intersects the MR curve, at 6 units, is our most profitable output.

Now that we know the best quantity is 6 units, we can run up to the demand curve and find our best price (or average revenue) of $84.

We are once again led back by the geometry to our fundamental rule.

Profits are at a maximum when
Marginal cost = marginal revenue

This completes our survey of how a rational firm will find its Best-Profit equilibrium.

▶ BYGONES, MARGINS, AND ALTERNATIVE OPPORTUNITIES

While economic theory doesn't try to make you a successful businessman, it does tip you off to a few important principles or ways of thinking. What are they?

First, the economist always stresses the "extra" or "marginal" costs and advantages of any decision. He says:

Let bygones be bygones. Don't look backward. Don't moan about your sunk costs. Look forward. Make a hard-headed calculation of the *extra* costs you'll incur by some decision and weigh these against the *extra* advantages. Cancel out all the good things and bad things *that will go on anyway* whether you make an affirmative or negative decision on the point under consideration.

---

[1] The optimum price cannot be immediately indicated on this diagram. However, knowing the quantity to be 6, we can easily determine the price, $84, by consulting the table; or we can read off price by running up to the demand curve of Figs. 2 or 7b at a Q of 6 units.

This disregarding of bygones is extremely important and most successful decision-makers practice it instinctively even if they have not had a formal course in economics. Here is an application of this principle:

The King taxes a monopolist a flat-sum for his match monopoly franchise. How will this affect the new Best-Profit P and Q? If you've grasped the tools of this chapter, you'll discover that a flat-sum tax won't shift either the MR or MC curve. If the monopolist successfully maximizes his profits before and after the tax and if nothing else changes and if he stays in business, *the flat-sum tax will have absolutely no effect on price or output,* being borne completely by the monopolist! (Can you verify this?)

A second principle that economics alerts you to is very similar. Most cost calculations are really *calculations of alternative opportunities.*

Example: if I put $100 into a new printing press, I don't have that money to spend on bubble gum or on a new Linotype machine or on a saving bond.

Seems obvious, doesn't it? Yet how many low-income farmers would stay in that business if they rationally figured how much their labor might be worth if they somehow moved to the city or to town? And how often in time of inflation do small merchants sell off their inventory of goods at some markup over their original cost, forgetting that they can't replace those goods at anything near the same cost—and *what is here the important point,* not stopping to realize that during a steady inflation, they'll be able to do better in the future if they hold the goods back until prices have risen?

One final example will illustrate both the principle of looking forward to calculate marginal consequences and the principle of scrutinizing alternative opportunities.

During World War II aluminum was scarce. So was the electric power needed to refine aluminum. The TVA and Northwest power dams sold power at lowest money costs; but they were jammed to capacity. Brooklyn, N.Y. had about the highest power rates in the country but it did have some excess capacity. The War Production Board rightly said: "Even though power nominally costs a lot more dollars in Brooklyn than in Tennessee or Washington, let's refine some aluminum there."

That was a good decision, just as it was a bad decision (or maybe lack of decision) for TVA salesmen to keep on during the war trying to sign up homeowners to heat their homes with electricity, which was then a very expensive way of keeping warm from the social and technical if not from the dollar viewpoint. (To understand how dollar P and socially relevant costs and utilities got so far out of line might require studying many semesters of economics.)

▶ **HOW IMPERFECTION OF COMPETITION AFFECTS RESOURCE ALLOCATION**

In the next chapter we'll study some of the important cases of imperfect competition. This will involve us in important public questions that lie in the field of "antitrust policy."

As preparation, let's briefly see how imperfections of competition affect the efficiency with which a free-price system solves the important problems of What, How, and For Whom. Suppose that under free pricing, firms do definitely face a sloping demand curve so that their marginal revenue is below their price.

Then to the degree that such imperfect competitors intelligently pursue their self-interest, will they still be led by Adam Smith's Invisible Hand to do the acts needed to promote the general interest?

No, they will not. There is now a flaw in the picture. When I as a businessman take account of marginal revenue, I am making sure that I won't "spoil my market." I am contriving, in my small way, to keep my good scarce lest I depress my own receipts. Naturally I'm not keeping the good completely scarce: that would yield me zero revenue. But I am desisting from cutting my price down to my marginal cost. Unlike the perfect competitor on the farm, who throws all his Q on the market up to the point where his MC equals the P he gets, I hold back enough Q to keep my MC at MR, which is below P.

How does this divergence between price and marginal cost affect the goodness or badness of the way the economy is organizing its production and distribution? This is a complex question, about which we'll learn more in later chapters. Here we can only highlight a few of the issues.

First, as an imperfect competitor I may be earning more than if the government somehow made me compete like a perfect competitor. If so, is that a good or bad thing? Am I more worthy? Am I more poor and more in need? (And will I use my gains to subsidize the arts or in vulgar display? Will I use my profits to sponsor new industrial research or to sponsor research in ways to convince consumers that my Q is better than other firms' Q?)

When the man-in-the-street thinks of the monopoly problem, he gives most weight to the above type of questions—to the way it affects the For Whom problem of distribution.[1] *Even if it has no harmful effect on income distribution, imperfection of competition could still represent an important economic evil.* To see this, imagine that all money votes are distributed properly and that I am the only imperfect competitor in the system. Everyone else is a perfect competitor, who keeps his MC equal to his P.

Price is the signal that consumers use to indicate how much they value various goods. Costs, and particularly marginal costs, are the indicators of how much each good's production uses up of society's valuable resources: our scarce

---

[1] As the next chapter shows, imperfect competition might not result in anyone's making a profit if there is "free entry" into the industry in question. Yet P might still stay above MC, and so the result might be tremendous wastage of resources as we have too many corners with too many gasoline stations, each with too many idle attendants (who don't even end up being well rewarded for being imperfect competitors). To be sure, more gas stations could mean shorter walks for people out of gas and more consumer convenience generally; but who is to say that the optimal amount of such differentiation-of-product convenience is being provided under any particular regime of imperfect competition?

land, our sweaty labor, and other resources that could produce other goods. Everywhere else, competitive firms are giving people what they most want and are producing right up to the point of $P = MC$ where goods are shown to be worth what they cost.

But take me, the imperfect competitor—the one rotten apple in the barrel. What am I doing? I'm not forcing people to buy from me. But the fact that I face a sloping demand curve shows that I do have some control over price. How am I using my power? Do I produce goods up to the point where their social cost—as measured by my MC—is equal to what the last unit of the good is worth to society—as measured by market P resulting from consumer money votes?

No. Instead, what am I doing? Instead I am contriving to keep things a little scarce. I am contriving to keep P above MC because that way I set $MR = MC$ and thereby maximize my profit. So society doesn't get quite as much of my good as it really wants in terms of what that good really costs society to produce!

Don't think I'm a villain. If I didn't intelligently try to maximize my firm's profits, I'd probably be displaced by the stockholders or be sued. Even if I owned the company and chose to equate P to MC, I'd be shunting money from my wife and children to the public at large. While there's no law against my being such an altruist, a Santa Claus, yet the betting odds may be against this. And in any case such an optimal solution to the problem *by chivalry* has nothing to do with Adam Smith's Invisible Hand—which insisted that *self-* interest (not altruism) would perform the miracle of providing for the general interest.

The clue to the Invisible Hand paradox is this: Adam Smith would have to rely on strictly defined "perfect competition" to get his result. As soon as we have imperfect competition in the real world, we have left the Garden of Eden and there arises next chapter's problems of how to minimize the evil and wastes involved in such imperfections of competition.

SUMMARY

1. Most market situations in the real world can be thought of as falling on a line somewhere between the limiting extremes of perfect competition and complete monopoly. Imperfect competition involves some control by the firm over its price, by virtue of the fact that there are not *a very large number of rivals* who sell *exactly the same product* as it does. (Note the italicized words.) Oligopoly (few sellers of similar products) and sellers of differentiated products are important cases for analysis.

2. From the firm's demand curve, we can easily derive its total revenue curve. From the schedule or curve of total revenue we can easily derive its marginal revenue—the extra revenue resulting from the sale of an extra unit of output. Ordinarily, marginal revenue will fall short of price because of the *loss on all previous units* of output that will result when we are forced to drop our price in order to sell an extra unit of output.

3. Total cost can be split up into fixed and variable costs. Marginal cost represents the *change* in total cost when we produce an extra unit of output. It is not the same thing as average cost per unit, which is the ratio of total cost to total output. Because of "spreading the overhead" and any economies of scale, the average cost curve at first falls, later rising in a U-shaped fashion as the firm's production begins to near "capacity."

4. A firm will find its maximum profit position where the last little unit it sells brings in extra revenue just equal to its extra cost. This same result can be shown graphically by the equality of the slopes of the total revenue and total cost curves. In any case, *marginal revenue = marginal cost* must hold at the equilibrium position of maximum profit.

5. Economic reasoning leads to an emphasis upon marginal advantages and disadvantages—to a cancellation of bygones and factors that go on no matter how you make a decision. It also emphasizes careful preoccupation with *alternative opportunities*.

6. Imperfection of competition, by divorcing P and MC of some goods, acts as one extra deterrent to Adam Smith's Invisible Hand, which tries to convert mankind's selfish interest to a best solution of society's What, How, and For Whom problems.

QUESTIONS FOR DISCUSSION

1. List distinguishing features of perfect and imperfect competition.

2. What does it mean to say that a corporation charges "what the traffic will bear"?

3. How would you divide these various elements of cost as between fixed and variable costs: payrolls, power and light, taxes, depreciation, executives' salaries, raw materials?

4. Carefully define: marginal cost, marginal revenue. Relate latter to price.

5. What is the numerical value of marginal revenue when the demand curve is of unitary elasticity, as in Table 3 of Chapter 19? Why?

6. What would average and marginal cost look like if fixed costs were $100, average variable costs were constant at $10 per unit (total variable costs increasing proportionally with output)? Plot marginal cost, average (total) cost, average variable cost, and average fixed cost on the same diagram.

7. "A lump-sum tax on a firm will have no effect on its best output and price as long as the firm stays in business. Similarly, a 10 per cent tax on a firm's profits will not change its best price or output." Why are these statements true, at least in the short run? Could the same be said of a tax on sales or on each unit produced? Why not?

8. Figures 7a and 7b each describe the Best-Profit equilibrium position. Explain in detail that they are really two different ways of describing exactly the same fact—namely, that a firm will stop when the extra cost of a further move just balances its extra revenue.

9. "We reckon bread's cost in dollars and cents. But underneath, its cost is really in terms of the coffee and wool you could produce with its capital, labor, and land—and in terms of the sweat, disutility, and foregone leisure of its productive factors." If competition were perfect, would P always properly reflect these various real factors?

10. Review your understanding of the following concepts:

perfect versus imperfect competition

monopoly, oligopoly, product differentiation

rivalry versus perfect competition

total and marginal revenue, in relation to P

total, fixed, and variable cost

average cost, marginal cost, and average variable cost

$MR = MC$ condition for Best-Profit

bygones versus relevant alternative opportunities

imperfection of competition and Adam Smith's Invisible Hand

APPENDIX: COST IN RELATION TO COMPETITIVE SUPPLY

There is nothing mysterious about the above relations of profit maximization. They simply represent common sense and elementary arithmetic. There is no reason why they should not apply to the perfectly competitive wheat farmer as well as to a firm employed in an imperfectly competitive field. So this Appendix will apply our MC tools to show what lies behind the competitive industry's supply curve—just as Chapter 23 showed what was underlying the industry demand curve.

Equality of Price and Competitive Marginal Cost

One special feature is present in the case of the perfect competitor. At his optimum posi-

tion, marginal revenue must, of course, equal marginal cost. But as we earlier learned, the perfect competitor can sell all he wishes at a given price. Let us repeat this important characteristic of perfect competition. The market price is given to each small, competitive seller. Marginal revenue and price then turn out to be identical, there being no loss on previous units to be subtracted from the price received from the extra unit sold.

We may combine the above statements, therefore, and say:

► A perfect competitor, who has no fear of spoiling the market, will always produce to the point where marginal costs begin to exceed price; or at his equilibrium

Marginal cost = price

Rising Marginal Cost As the Short-run Supply Curve

Now we can predict how much the firm will supply at different prices. If we retain our previous costs, we shall be able to read from Fig. 8 the supply schedule for the firm in terms of price. Its smooth curve shows marginal costs when our units are made indefinitely divisible.[1]

Thus, when the market price at which the firm can sell is $100 per unit, production is pushed to the point marked A, or to about 9.4 units. Only at that quantity does marginal cost equal price. Only there are profits maximized. (To test your understanding of this point, show what the amount supplied would be at higher prices than $100. E.g., place your ruler at $P = \$110$ and read off the amount supplied from the MC curve.)

Suppose price were only $80. What would the firm supply? The $80 price line is seen to intersect the MC curve twice: once at around 8.9 units and again at around 0.1 unit. Our formula, price $= MC$, is ambiguous. It gives too many answers. Which is the right one?

There is only one final test. We must compute total profit and see where it is larger. The answer is quite obvious. The larger output is the correct one. For if the firm produces only around 1 unit, its revenue is

[1] This assumes *fractions* of a unit can be produced and sold. Why rule out fractions? Of course, a farmer cannot sell one-third of an egg, but he certainly *can* sell one-third of a carload

80×1, its cost in Table $3 = \$320$, and its profits are around $-\$240$. But if it produces about 9 units, its profits are about $(\$80 \times 9) - \$553$ or about $\$167$. The best output, therefore, is at B, not at B'.

It is not difficult to patch up our price $= MC$ rule so that it will not let us down again and make us recompute profit. When price or marginal revenue equals marginal cost, we can only be sure that profit is standing still. But whether it is leveling off "at the top of the hill of profits," or "at the bottom of the valley," our formula does not tell us. We must, therefore, add to the $MR = MC$ requirement the condition that *marginal cost must be shooting up more rapidly than marginal revenue*. At B this condition was met; at B' the opposite condition held. A little calculation shows that this fact makes B' the worst rather than the best place to be. It pays to move to either the right or the left of that point, because profits are there at a minimum.

Decreasing Costs and the Breakdown of Perfect Competition

It follows that from now on our rule under perfect competition must take the form

Price = marginal cost, and marginal cost must be rising

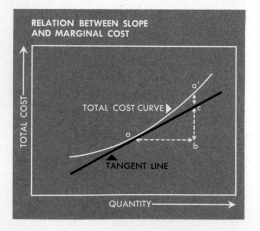

RELATION BETWEEN SLOPE AND MARGINAL COST

TOTAL COST CURVE ▶

TANGENT LINE

TOTAL COST

QUANTITY

of eggs. Even if single eggs represent our units of measurement, he can sell eggs at the rate of 1 every 3 hours, which is one-third of an egg per hour. The careful reader will already have noted that we used continuously divisible units whenever we identified marginal cost with the geometrical slope of the total cost curve. Actually, we have been using two slightly different concepts of marginal cost, as the accompanying diagram makes clear.

The distance from a to b represents one extra unit of output. The distance from b to a' represents the resulting increase in total cost, which is the first and simplest definition of marginal cost. The second definition is given by the slope of the total cost curve at the point a, or what is the same thing numerically, by the distance from b to c. In the limit as the size of the extra units becomes small, the discrepancy between the two definitions—or ca'—becomes negligible.

Firm's rising MC curve gives its short-run supply curve:

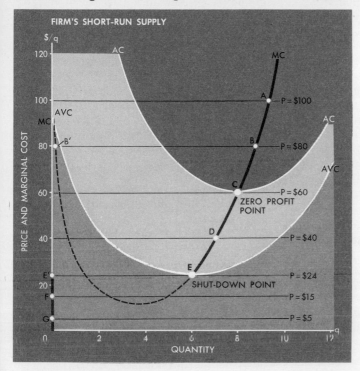

FIRM'S SHORT-RUN SUPPLY

Fig. 8. The profit-seeking competitor will respond to each horizontal demand curve's P by moving to where it intersects MC, with P = MC. Always, though, MC curve must be rising at a Best-Profit supply point.

In short run, supply curve can fall below full costs as firm disregards fixed costs and minimizes its losses. But if P falls below bottom of AVC, firm will shut down.

In long run, supply curve can't fall below bottom point of AC, since firm will not permanently produce at a loss.

Alternatively, we can say: The supply curve of the firm consists of no part of the U-shaped marginal cost curve (in Fig. 8) which is falling. For, if marginal cost is falling, the firm has every reason to expand its output further, each new step bringing it the same extra revenue but lower extra cost.

This second part of our rule is not just a theoretical refinement. It shows us how and why competition tends to break down! Technology of a given industry often becomes more and more complicated so that efficient production is possible only on a gigantic scale. Until this scale is reached, average and marginal costs tend to fall. Competitive firms tend, therefore, to expand their output. A period of cutthroat or ruinous competition may follow in which all firms have heavy losses. Finally, those few firms which have the most resources or which enjoyed the earliest start will drive the others out of the field, leaving us no longer with perfect competition but with imperfect competition.

Although other factors than cost are involved, this seems to be what happened in the auto industry. Out of a 100-odd American car manufacturers, only five are left. And of these, only three count for much.

The same thing may happen to the appliances industry in the next few decades. Why doesn't it happen to wheat farming? Because each farmer's marginal cost curve turns up long before he is sufficiently important to affect the market price. Were an invention discovered that made a million-acre farm the most efficient size, you can be sure farming would cease to be as perfectly competitive as it is.

Minimizing Losses and Deciding When to Shut Down

Let's return to the supply curve of our hypothetical firm. If price drops to $60, the firm will produce 8 units and will just break even.

(This includes wages of managers, and a normal return on invested capital.)[1]

What if price drops down to below $60, the level of lowest average cost? Suppose times are so hard that the market price is only $40. If the firm produces about 7.1 units, as indicated by the point D where $P = MC$, its total revenue will be around $280, $40 × 7, while its total costs will be about $431 (see Table 3). The firm is "in the red," producing at a loss of some $140 to $150. Our formula of marginal cost and price seems to have led us to ruin.

But has it? If the firm chooses to shut down completely rather than run at a loss, its revenue will be zero and its fixed costs will still be $256. Obviously, its loss would then be $256, an even greater sum than when it is producing 7.1 units. In other words, equating marginal costs to marginal revenue is optimal even when profits are negative, because in that way losses are kept to a minimum. A rational businessman will disregard his fixed costs entirely in deciding whether to accept some extra business, for he knows fixed costs will go on anyway and, therefore, must "cancel out of any decision." As long as he receives total revenue in excess of his variable costs, so that he has something above his out-of-pocket costs, he is better off to accept the extra business.

What happens if price continues to decrease, down below even $24? At that figure, if the firm produces 6 units, its total revenue will be $144 and its variable cost will also be $144. It will be just indifferent between producing or shutting down completely, because in either case it will lose $256.

At any price below $24, say at $15, the firm will not even recover its variable costs. Obviously, therefore, it will choose to shut down. Our marginal comparison formulas are no longer relevant.[2]

We may summarize by saying that any costs that are strictly fixed should be treated as bygones if necessary. "There is no use crying about spilt milk." To make the best of the situation, we minimize our losses by equating marginal cost to price—and marginal cost is unaffected by fixed costs.[3] It is better to earn something above our variable costs which can be applied toward our fixed cost commitments, than to have to pay out fixed costs while receiving nothing.

▶ In summary, the firm's short-run supply curve will be the rising part of its marginal cost curve, where that curve is above the AVC curve of average variable cost (so that the firm is getting more revenue than the variable costs it would save by shutting down).

Long-run No-Profit Lowest-Cost Equilibrium
This analysis referred to the short run. In the long run our fixed commitments finally expire. Contracts terminate. Buildings wear out, and the decision arises as to whether they should be replaced or contracts renewed. In deciding this question, no costs are (as yet) fixed. In the long run, therefore, the firm is not forced to produce at a loss. It will still produce that output at which marginal cost equals price.

▶ Always, therefore, in the long run a competitive firm will produce where its $MC = P$, but where P must be at least as great as its AC. Why must price be greater than or equal to average cost

---

[1] Recall our discussion of "alternative opportunities." We'll see later in Chapter 30's treatment of "profit" how important are the returns that owners receive on the labor, land, and capital they themselves provide for their firm. Of course, all this applies as much to imperfect competitors as to this Appendix's perfect competitors.

[2] They tell us producing 5 is better than 4 or 6. But all are worse than producing 0 units. To take any business that more than covers its variable costs is a good rule for an imperfect competitor too—provided he can't wangle a better bargain and provided this won't spoil his market elsewhere or at a later time.

[3] In Column (4) of Table 3, the same fixed costs are in the total cost figures for both the tenth and the ninth unit. So they cancel out of all marginal cost computations. Why?

in the long run? Because a firm won't willingly stay in the industry in the long run if it isn't covering all its recurring costs (including as costs the returns it could earn elsewhere on any factors being supplied by its owners).

We can state a stronger long-run equilibrium condition in an important special case. This is the case of "absolutely free entry" where (1) as many firms as want to can enter or leave the industry, (2) with each firm having the ability to produce just like the old firms—being able to use the same engineering knowledge and to buy the same productive factors at the same prices.

In this special case, could any of the firms go on making a profit in the long run over and above the normal return on their capital? Obviously not. Such a profit would attract new entrants, and they would keep coming in until they had depressed price down to every firm's minimum average cost, with no "profit" left over. Similarly, P could not in the long run permanently stay less than AC—else firms would be leaving.

▶   At long-run competitive equilibrium under "absolutely free entry," each firm would be producing where both its marginal cost and its average cost equalled market price. (The firm itself selfishly makes $MC = P$. But it is the actions of its selfish competitors which forces P down to equality with the firm's AC.) The combined condition of equilibrium can then be written

Marginal   cost = price = average   cost = "bottom-of-the-U" lowest AC

Figure 8 reminds us that marginal and average costs are equal only where the marginal cost pierces the average cost at its bottom. At higher or lower Q, MC is raising or lowering AC.

Perfect Competition and Darwinian Efficiency
Society would be lucky if the condition for absolutely free entry of thousands of competitors held in every industry. Why lucky?

Because then the Invisible Hand would very clearly be determining the best solution to the how-goods-shall-be-produced problem. Perfect competition would then operate just like the ruthless Darwinian struggle-for-existence to ensure that each viable firm produced at minimum average cost, with the industry getting its goods produced at the rock-bottom total cost possible.

But unlike Darwin's jungle which is "red in tooth and claw," the competitive solution would have nice checks and balances—so that when each firm, each laborer, each landowner was avidly doing what he was forced to do, he would get the market-determined wage, interest, and rent. For a productive society these could be handsome factor returns, quite unlike conditions of the jungle where life is short, hard, and brutish.

Alas, what makes all this so often inapplicable in real life is the fact that the cost curves may be decreasing to such a degree that if each firm were somehow made to produce down to the bottom of its U, we'd find only a *handful of firms* in the industry and not the great number needed to keep perfect competition perfect.[1]

Firm and Industry
This completes our brief look at each competitive firm's equilibrium. Let's end this Appendix by showing how all firms' supply curves combine to give the competitive industry its supply curves.

With Marshall, we distinguish different time periods: momentary, short-run, and long-run. In every case we add all the firm supply curves together horizontally at each P as we did for different consumer's demand curves at the beginning of Chapter 23.

----

[1] Uncertainty conditions would make decreasing costs even more likely. Also, product differentiation and transport costs, by reducing the size of the market for each homogeneous product, make it all the more likely that "bottom-of-the-U" output will be an appreciable fraction of the total market. In all such cases, *laissez faire* or Darwinian warfare tends toward the *breakdown* of perfect competition and to various forms of oligopoly and imperfect competition.

We add all firms' supply curves to get competitive industry's supply curve:

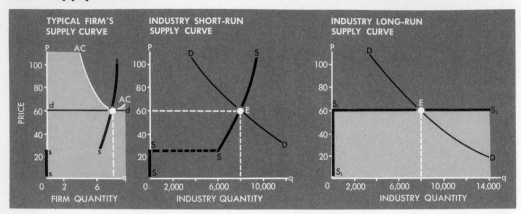

Fig. 9. Adding together all the firms' short-run *ss* curves of 9a gives the much flatter industry short-run supply curve *SS* of 9b. (If all of a thousand firms were exactly alike, the industry's curve would be a thousandfold scale increase that would look very flat indeed if the draftsman didn't change the scaling.)

In the long-run, the number of firms can gradually grow or diminish, gradually shifting the short-run supply *SS* rightward or leftward. The resulting long-run equilibrium with $P = AC$ and no profit will be at the bottom-of-each-firm's-U. As we sum as many or as few firms as the demand will support, we trace out in 9c the industry's horizontal long-run $S_L S_L$ curve, which is at the bottom-of-the-U level. (In this extreme constant cost case, shifts in demand do change long-run Q but not P. In more usual case, $S_L S_L$ slopes gently upward, as expansion of this industry makes the factors it uses rise in price to all its firms.)

Momentary equilibrium. If each firm is frozen with a fixed momentary supply curve that is vertical, we easily get the industry's momentary supply curve as the sum of their fixed supplies—and this too must be vertical. This is so simple a case that no more need be said beyond p. 382's discussion.[1]

Short-run equilibrium. By definition, the number of firms is fixed in the short run, but each can produce more or less Q along its *MC* curve. Each firm's fixed cost, *FC,* is unchangeable in this short run and will be disregarded by the rational profit maximizer. We have seen that he will have an *ss* supply curve which is the part of his *MC* curve that is rising and is above his average variable cost curve.

---

[1] If the good were nonperishable, the picture would be more complicated and we'd need Chapter 22's analysis of storage and speculation.

To get the industry short-run *SS* curve, we simply at each P add such *ss* curves for every firm. The result will look much flatter than any firm's curve. Why? Because each change in P will now bring out a thousand-fold greater industry response than for each of the thousand small competitors. (With 1,500 firms the industry *SS* curve would look flatter still.)

See Figs. 9a and 9b for the relationship between the typical firm's cost and supply and the industry's short-run supply curve.

Long-run equilibrium. In the long run all fixed cost commitments finally expire and a conscious decision must be made about their renewal. In this sense, short-run fixed costs are converted into long-run variable costs.

In the long run the number of firms will vary. If entry is absolutely free, new firms will keep coming into the industry so long as

P remains above the bottom of each firm's average cost curve and an excess profit is to be made. Provided the industry is a small one compared to all the other industries which use the same land, labor, and other productive factors, the enlarged number of firms will always be able to produce with the same old U curves. What then is the final equilibrium in this extreme constant-cost case?

Figure 9c shows that the industry's long-run supply curve—marked S_LS_L—will be a horizontal curve at the level of bottom-of-the-U average cost. In this constant-cost case an increase or decrease in demand will in the long run simply change quantity by changing the number of firms. It will have no affect on price in the long run nor on the scale and costs of each firm that stays in the industry, since each such firm will always be forced to the bottom of its U.[1]

---

[1] If the industry is of appreciable size and uses factors in different intensities from the bulk of other industries, its own expansion will raise the wages and prices of its factors, thus shifting each firm's U up a little. So when you add their shifting bottoms, you will get a gently upward-sloping long-run industry supply curve. This case of slight increasing costs would probably be most typical of a competitive world. It corresponds exactly to the bowed-out production-possibility curves for guns and butter of Chapter 2. As we'll see, it is quite efficient for the costs of things to rise when people want more of them and for their factors to be then awarded higher P's so as to ration them out in their most valuable uses. (Intermediate texts sometimes draw a "long-run envelope curve" to our U's, to show

Uncertainty Qualifications

A concluding reminder is needed. Equilibrium positions are always being disturbed in real life. And as the economy races toward a new equilibrium, along comes a new disturbance sending it off in still another direction. Moreover, the actors in life's scenario have no crystal balls to tell them how the story is going to end.

What is the moral? Just this. Temporary profits or losses in an industry may be very great. Prices may fluctuate considerably. Even in the longer run, equilibrium may turn out to be kind of a statistical equilibrium with the losses of some going to cancel the gains of others.[2] And if for some reason people are chronically overoptimistic about an industry, then it may long continue to show negative profits. As fast as one firm commits suicide, a new optimist is born.

Important as is this qualification, don't lose sight of the vital fact that a perfectly competitive system is always moving to restore a disturbed equilibrium. The way it travels is the important thing, not whether it reaches a quiescent destination.

---

that each firm might replicate plants. This changes none of our conclusions.)

[2] Don't forget that one farmer's acres are unlike another's. One man's energies and effectiveness are unlike another's. So taking account of these differences in effectiveness, you will expect great differences in the actual long-run take-home returns of different competitive firms. Later discussions of rent and profit will return to these issues, which show "free entry" to be a complicated concept.

SUMMARY TO APPENDIX

1. For a perfect competitor, marginal revenue and price are exactly the same thing, there being no loss on previous units for him to worry about. The maximum condition, *marginal revenue equals marginal cost,* can for the perfect competitor be rewritten: *Price equals marginal cost.* It always pays him to expand his output up to the point where the cost of the last unit begins to exceed the market price of the good.

2. It must follow then that the supply curve of the firm is its marginal cost curve, provided that the curve is rising and provided that the price has not fallen so low that he finds it better to shut down completely rather than fail to recover even his variable costs.

3. If price and marginal cost are in excess of the firm's average cost, it will be making a positive profit. If price and marginal cost are below the firm's average cost, it will be making a loss; if this continues for a long time, it will prefer eventually to go out of business rather than reinvest its money in replacing its worn-out plant. If new competitive firms can come into the industry and produce at the same cost as the given firm, any positive profits (in excess of a "normal return" on capital and labor invested) will in the long-run equilibrium be competed away. In this final equilibrium, *price and marginal cost will both be equal to minimum average cost.*

4. The sum of all the competitive firms' short-run supply curves gives the industry's supply curve. In the long run, when the number of firms in the industry can change, the industry's supply curve will become flatter and more elastic.

5. If production of a given commodity is subject throughout an extended range to decreasing marginal costs, then a few firms will expand to dominate the market and perfect competition will be impossible. And uncertainty conditions in all cases imply continual disturbance of any equilibrium.

QUESTIONS FOR DISCUSSION

1. Explain in common-sense terms why a perfect competitor sets $MC = P$.

2. How does total revenue look to a perfect competitor? Redraw Fig. 7a.

3. When would you decide to shut down a plant? To take on new business?

4. How is the supply curve of the industry related to firm's cost: in the short run and in the long run?

5. Why is a falling MC curve never a supply curve? (Hint: Show competition would then become "cutthroat" or "ruinous.")

6. "If there is free competitive entry of new firms, price must fall to the level of minimum average costs." Show why P cannot in the long run be lower or higher than this equilibrium level.

7. Review your understanding of the following concepts:

$P = MC,$ *long-run* $P = MC = AC = minimum$ AC

exclusion from the supply curve of points where MC is falling or below AVC

absolutely free entry

firm and industry supply curves in different time periods

Darwinian struggle and perfect competition

uncertainty effects

decreasing cost and breakdown of competition

25 PATTERNS OF IMPERFECT COMPETITION

The whole logic of private enterprise rests on the fundamental assumption of active competition in free markets. If such a system is to be preserved, it is essential that competition be kept active and markets free.

COMMITTEE ON CARTELS AND MONOPOLY OF TWENTIETH CENTURY FUND

The last chapter has now paved the way for a bird's-eye view of the actual market structure of modern-day industry. How do firms go about setting their prices? What is the role of the theoretical tools used in the last chapter to analyze profit maximization?

What are some of the important patterns of imperfect competition? Finally, what issues for public antitrust policy do they raise?

► DO FIRMS MAXIMIZE PROFITS?

To what degree do businessmen actually try to maximize their profits? To what extent do they succeed if they do try to? These are not easy questions to give precise answers to. Certainly this much is true: If a firm is absolutely reckless in calculating costs and revenues, then the Darwinian law of the survival of the fittest will probably eliminate it from the economic scene.

Therefore, those firms which actually do manage to survive cannot be completely oblivious to the maximization of profits. But that does not necessarily mean that every firm is seeking desperately to squeeze out the last little ounce of profit from every transaction. As soon as it becomes of any considerable size, it can afford to relax a little in its maximizing activities. Moreover, it is probably good business to take the long view and not concentrate on purely immediate gains. Many acts of altruism and apparent generosity can be amply defended in terms of public relations and the maximization of long-run profits.

Consider a firm that is maximizing its profits in a fairly sensible manner. Does that mean it is calculating elaborate geometrical curves of cost and revenue and from them deriving elaborate measures of marginal cost and revenue? Obviously not, as you will soon learn if you inquire about current business practices. But even if the firm is not itself tackling the problem with conscious awareness of the particular marginal tools of the theoretical economists, *to the extent that it is truly making a pretty fair guess as to where its highest profits are realized,* it will be succeeding in making extra revenue and extra cost approximately equal. It does this without curves, just by feeling its way to the optimum by trial and error.

▶ **MARKUP PRICING**

One of the reasons why business is a fascinating activity is the fact that inexact guesses must be made on the basis of incomplete information. It is no small task for a large or small business to make an estimate of the shape of the demand curve for its products. A railroad can only guess whether a 20 per cent cut in fares will bring it many more customers. A company has no exact way of judging the elasticity of demand for its many products.

Realistically speaking, we must recognize that modern business firms—even the largest—cannot accurately determine marginal revenue and marginal cost. They cannot determine their optimum price and output with nice exactitude. Yet the day's work must somehow get done. Prices must be set on their products. Here is where average or unit cost often plays an important role.

Put yourself in the position of the president of a company producing many products. Prices are partly at your disposal. Your last year's sales are known to you, but your next period's sales can only be guessed even if you leave prices unchanged. Not knowing the extent or elasticity of demand for your products, you will be unable to determine marginal revenue. What will you do?

Probably, you will call in your accountants and sales managers. "Boys," you will say, "what is our likely volume if we stay on our toes and keep our share of the market?" In answering, the sales force will have to guess at the probable level of business activity, consumers' needs, etc.

After they have made their estimates, you will turn to the cost experts and probably ask for the unit (or average) cost of producing each product in question at those levels of output. There will be plenty of headaches in aiming at any sort of figure. For example, how shall the administrative and plant overhead costs be allocated between different products? Or if a given process simultaneously creates joint products like meat and hides, how shall the costs be allocated between them? Or if a building will last for many years, how much should be charged against current operations?

Headache or no headache, it is the practice of accountants to come out with some sort of answer as to unit costs. Management must now decide by how much to mark up price over the cost figure. Depending upon its estimate of the consumers' reaction and the pricing policy of its competitors, the firm may perhaps decide on a 5, 10, or 30 per cent markup.[1] Whether aware of it or not, the businessman is making some kind of an implicit guess about his demand elasticity in setting his markup.

In bad times when price competition is particularly keen, businessmen may even set prices at less than "full costs" because of the realization that fixed expenses will go on whether or not production is at a low level. But price will never be set below unit *variable* costs unless the item in question is being used as a "loss leader" to attract other business now and in the future, or unless the firm is willing to incur temporary losses in order to crush a rival and drive him out of business completely.

▶ BREAK-EVEN CHARTS AND "ADMINISTERED PRICES"

Businessmen often speak of their break-even points. You will hear them complain that postwar union wage demands have raised the level of their break-even points to a dangerous degree, so that, if there is any slackening of the peak full-employment levels of sales, then profits may soon turn into losses. What is meant by the concept of a "break-even point"?

Usually it means the following: In many industries, it turns out that variable costs increase pretty much in direct proportion to output. Double output and you double total variable costs; triple output and you triple total variable costs; no matter how you change output, as long as you stay within the limits of your plant's capacity, unit variable costs seem to be just about a constant. If this is a tolerable approximation to the truth, then your total cost curve has been simplified down to being a straight line.

Let's further suppose that you have already fixed upon the price you are going to charge. Probably you used some sort of markup rule to do so, but however you made your decision does not much matter.

If you are like most firms, you won't be changing your P every day and every hour. Probably you name a so-called "administered price"—and subject to varying discounts and other reflections of demand elasticity—you stick to it until further notice.

If your unit variable costs are constant for each extra bit of output and your revenue from that bit of output constant, it is clear that your profits will grow with your sales. As a matter of fact, at small outputs you will not even be earning enough to cover your fixed costs; but as your sales increase, this loss

[1] General Motors, one of the world's most successful enterprises, has used such markup methods for 30 years! Note that the average costs used prior to markup for most firms will *not already* include a return on the firm's own capital.

With fixed price, falling sales lead finally to losses:

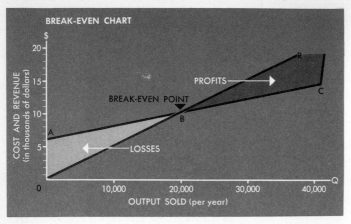

Fig. 1. With P fixed, increased demand for Q expands total revenue along OR. With average variable and marginal costs fairly constant up to the capacity point C, total cost follows ABC. So profits are shown as the vertical difference between the curves —with B the break-even point where losses change to profits.

will dwindle and you will reach a point where you just cover your fixed and variable costs. Your sales have now reached the break-even point.[1]

Beyond this break-even point, your profits will begin to materialize. Anything you can do to increase your sales will be all to the good. Figure 1 gives a geometrical picture of a break-even point chart. OR shows how your revenue grows as you succeed in selling more goods at the same price. ABC shows how your costs grow from the initial fixed-cost point A to the level of plant capacity C, where costs begin to shoot up rapidly. The break-even point is at B. If your sales fall below this level, you are incurring losses, whose magnitude is shown by the light area between the two schedules. If your sales increase beyond the break-even point, your profits increase more and more, as measured by the dark area between the two schedules. By locating his position on a chart such as this one, the businessman is constantly stimulated to reconsider his price policy, his production methods, and his sales-promotion techniques. (Figure 2 shows the shifts in demand that generate the break-even chart.)

Many investigators of actual business pricing policies have testified that corporations often do follow the above-described practice of quoting prices on a "cost and markup" basis, hoping thereby not only to recover their "full cost outlays," but also to make a return on their investments. This theory therefore seems realistic, but it is not very informative. It stops tantalizingly short of telling us *why* the average markup is 40 per cent in one industry and 5 per cent in another; or why, before the war, General Motors in the automobile industry was able to earn 30 per cent on the book value of its invested capital while Ford, almost as large, could earn only about ½ of 1 per cent on its capital.

---

[1] Don't confuse this with the break-even point of consumption and income met in Part Two's discussion of saving. There is only a geometrical resemblance between the two concepts.

How shifts of the demand curve generate the break-even chart:

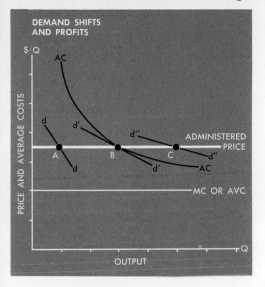

DEMAND SHIFTS
AND PROFITS

$/Q

AC

PRICE AND AVERAGE COSTS

d

d'

d''

ADMINISTERED
PRICE

A   B   C

d'''

d

d'

AC

MC OR AVC

OUTPUT

Q

Fig. 2. At *B* on *d'd'*, the firm breaks even. At *A* on *dd*, it shows losses. At *C* on *d"d"*, it makes profits.

▶ ILLUSTRATIVE PATTERNS OF PRICING UNDER IMPERFECT COMPETITION: "SICK" INDUSTRIES

We can now put our tools to work to see how pricing works itself out in various real life situations. What appears at first to be a terribly complicated and confusing industrial situation, almost without rhyme or reason, is gradually seen to make sense once you cease trying to force it into the mold of perfect competition and instead use the concepts of imperfect competition analysis.

Many fields are characterized by an excessive number of firms. Most of these do a small volume of business and remain in the industry only until they have lost their capital. Grocery stores, taverns, restaurants, night clubs, and gasoline stations are typical examples taken from retail trade. But much the same thing is true of the textile trade, the dress trade, and many others that require little initial capital.

Why don't such unprofitable concerns leave the industry? The answer is, They do. But as fast as they leave, new firms enter the industry, leaving the total number unchanged or even growing.

Why do new firms enter the industry in the face of the fact that most existing firms are making losses? Apparently, partly out of ignorance and partly because "hope springs eternal." An old couple putting their lifetime savings of a few thousand dollars into a little retail grocery store do so in the belief that *their* venture will be different, theirs will succeed—and anyway, in the grocery business no one need starve. But alas, with no special business aptitude and with less than the minimum amount of capital necessary for efficient operation, they last in business only until their original capital has gone.

Or in the dress trade, a worker will often save his money in order to become his own boss. He knows that most concerns are not covering their costs, but he also has heard of a few lucky firms whose special "novelty styles" have become a smash hit and have yielded large monetary profits. Even though the odds are heavily weighted against the new entrant, he is willing to buy a ticket in the sweepstake of success.

The only thing that can be said for such small businesses is that they make jobs. But the jobs they make are largely an illusion as far as pay is concerned, and represent boondoggling of as reprehensible and unnecessary a kind as would be public-works projects aimed at simply digging holes and filling them in again.

▶ WASTES OF IMPERFECT COMPETITION

These chronically overcrowded industries need not be what the economist has called "perfectly competitive"—although in the case of agriculture or "cotton gray goods," they may happen to be approximately so. Too many firms in such a competitive industry is a bad thing, involving as it does wastes of resources and losses. But at least in such a competitive industry the consumer partly gains, through lower prices, what the producers are losing.

Unfortunately, in most chronically overcrowded sick industries market competition is quite imperfect. Being inefficient producers, the small concerns do not sell very cheaply. Instead of competing on a price basis, they tend to charge fairly high prices and simply to divide the business.

▶ The resulting economic situation under this form of imperfect competition may be worse even than under complete monopoly: not only is price excessive, but in addition valuable resources are wasted because each firm has too much idle plant and manpower. The situation is triply bad: producers make losses, resources are wasted, and the prices charged the consumer are too high.

A diagram will show how imperfect competition may result in wastage of resources, too high price, and yet no profits for the imperfect competitors. It will also show how the spirit of Marshall's long-run time analysis can be applied to the sector of imperfect competition characterized by free entry.

Figure 3 shows a typical imperfect competitor—say a local barbershop that can count on some of its customers' being unwilling to walk a long way to get a haircut. Its original demand curve dd slopes downward; and guesses at marginal revenue and cost—not shown—cause it to produce at the original point E. It is maximizing positive profit and charging more than full unit costs.

But now other barbers see this profit opportunity. They move in. There is now one barbershop for every three blocks rather than every four. What happens to the demand curve for our typical barber? Clearly, entry of new competitors divides up the existing business and causes demand to shift down-

Entry of rival firms cuts demand of each and wipes out profit:

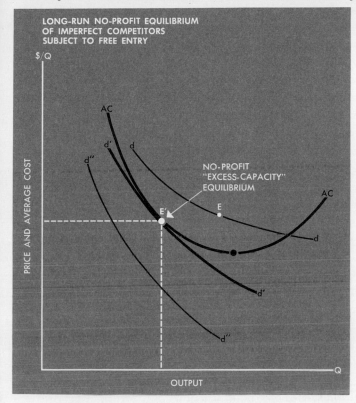

LONG-RUN NO-PROFIT EQUILIBRIUM
OF IMPERFECT COMPETITORS
SUBJECT TO FREE ENTRY

$/Q

PRICE AND AVERAGE COST

AC

d' d

d''

NO-PROFIT
"EXCESS-CAPACITY"
EQUILIBRIUM

AC

E'   E

d

d'

d''

OUTPUT

Q

Fig. 3. Free entry of numerous imperfect competitors shifts the firm's sloping demand curve leftward until long-run no-profit equilibrium is reached at tangency point E'. Here profits are maximized but are still zero. Here P is above $MR = MC$ and above the minimum-unit-cost point. (Starting from d''d'' and losses, show how *exit* of firms brings you back to d'd' and E'.)

ward and leftward to $d'd'$. Now at the new Best-Profit point, the barber makes no profit, as can be seen from the fact that the new demand curve just touches tangentially the average cost curve. In the background, marginal cost is equated to new marginal revenue—but that serves only to avoid losses, not to produce a positive profit. (Why couldn't $d''d''$ represent equilibrium?)

The long-run equilibrium at E', which Marshall might shudder to call "normal," very clearly shows that price is higher than the most efficient cost level which prevails at the bottom of the U-shaped average-cost curve. The barbershop has excess capacity, with empty chairs much of the time. (Of course, customers have to walk only three blocks now, not four. And that's worth something. But note they've never really been given the choice of a slightly longer walk and haircuts at the lower prices that efficient capacity utilization would make possible.[1])

[1] Again and again in our discussion of pricing "efficiency" we've seen what is proved rigorously in advanced texts: price in excess of marginal cost leads to a state from which it would be possible theoretically to make everybody better off—barbers, bald people, long-haired people who hate long walks and waits, and everybody else. But don't leap from this to the invalid inference that variety doesn't matter or that enforcing $P = MC$ everywhere would (in decreasing cost situations with differentiated products) lead to the "ideal" amount of variety. Here is a case where defining an optimum is, even conceptually, a difficult social task.

▶ **EVILS OF OLIGOPOLY**

At the other extreme are industries in which there are only two, three, or a few sellers, all producing almost exactly the same products. Recall that such a case of few sellers, each with similar products, is called "oligopoly." In such cases, there is the temptation for each firm to try to undersell the others by the least little bit in the hope of getting a larger share of the total business.

Recall from Chapter 24 the railroad price wars of the past century. Customers shipping goods from Chicago to New York always pick the route that offers even a few pennies of extra cheapness. Thus, each of the three or four trunk lines would intermittently undercut the existing rate schedules, until finally a disastrously low level of rates was reached. At the same time, for short hauls where shippers had no alternative, the railroads would jack up the rates—thus creating an anomalous, discriminatory pattern of charges. The Interstate Commerce Commission was established in 1887 to regulate railroad rates and earnings and prevent such unstable price conditions.

Even without government regulations, in industries characterized by heavy overhead costs and identical products, there usually grows up the realization that competition is ruinous. Formal or informal meetings are held, whose theme song is "We're all in it together." Each firm is taught the lesson that others firms will not stand idly by while it cuts its prices; rather they too will cut their prices, so that everyone will end up worse off.

Therefore, tacitly or explicitly, the firms try to agree on a price that maximizes the profits of all. Trade associations, keeping one eye on the Justice Department lawyers who enforce the Sherman Antitrust Act, may impose penalties on any chiseler in the industry who makes secret price concessions. Occasionally, as new conditions or firms upset the *status quo* in the industry, another price war may break out—to last until everyone has again learned his lesson and the morale of the industry is restored.

In appraising oligopoly we must note that the desire of corporations to earn a fair return on their past investments can at times be at variance with the well-being of the consumer. Too much plant capacity may have been built in the industry in the past; but that isn't justification for continuing high prices and scarce output. Competition, which the businessman regards as destructive, cutthroat, and ruinous may actually be the only way to get the redundant plant capacity into operation or to discourage its maintenance. (Having made the mistake of building the plants, society ought not to add the further error of failing to use them to best advantage.) Losses or subnormal profits is the free-enterprise way of discouraging excess capacity.

The steel and other metal industries are examples of this pattern of imperfect competition. They illustrate how difficult it is to know what to do about oligopoly. Oligopolists soon realize that they have to charge about the same price for their products. No one can hope to cut his price without others retaliating. But if they must have a common price, it is obviously to their advantage that it be a high one.

Figure 4 shows the high-price, excess-capacity equilibrium for oligopolists who need not fear competitive entry and who are resigned to a uniform *P* for all sellers. The *dd* curve assumes each shares the common market, and each will want the common price to be high enough to yield maximum profits.

That's why in the old days cartels used to be formed to keep price high. Those who cut prices were heavily fined, and elaborate meetings were held to divide up the business. (This still goes on in many parts of Europe.)

But today we don't let this happen. Judge Gary of U.S. Steel, if he were alive today, wouldn't be allowed to hold his little "dinners" at which the industry got together to divide up markets and protect price margins.

Yet, what many people don't realize, is the fact that once a few oligopolists

When sellers are few, their most profitable common price is high:

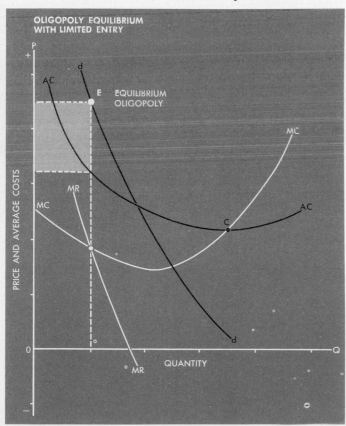

Fig. 4. Oligopolists who need fear little potential competition from new competitors may, tacitly or collusively, get used to charging that common price for their identical products which maximizes their profit—as at *E*. Then price is above *C*, the bottom of the U-shaped cost curve. (Actually, more advanced texts show that if three oligopolists like this one were to merge, they'd make even more profit by shutting down one plant and charging *less* to the consumer!)

realize they are all in the same boat together, they may be able to adopt habits and customs in pricing which do keep prices from being cut to the bone whenever industry capacity is excessive. They don't have to meet for dinner. They don't have to write letters. They don't even have to wink when passing on the street. All they have to do is use a "rule of reason," of "live and let live"—and to follow the "golden rule" (not in terms of doing to the customer what is best for him but doing to your fellow oligopolist what you would have him do unto you).[1]

How does all this work out these days in practice? Well, in 1954 we went into a little recession. Steel production went down to two-thirds of capacity. Some stock-market speculators feared this would initiate a wave of price cuts, which would reduce steel companies' earnings and bring down their stock prices. Did it work out that way? Not at all. The industry discovered it could still make money at those levels as it did again in 1957 when it worked at only 75 per cent of capacity. (Firms were still above their "break-even point" so long as price morale stayed high in the industry.)

In a perfectly competitive industry, when demand shifts leftward, P will fall. Profits will decline greatly. Yet competitive Q may not fall much at all, being sold for whatever it will fetch. The consumer does benefit from what the producer loses, and in time output will adjust to the new state of demand.

By contrast, under oligopoly price tends to stay firm with output taking up the great variation. Plants stand idle, and the product is not cheapened in the hope of coaxing out new quantity demanded.

▶ WHAT TO DO ABOUT MONOPOLY IMPERFECTIONS

Is there no hope for oligopoly? Yes, there is.

For one thing, if we make sure that barriers to entry are kept to a minimum, the fear of potential competition and the actuality of it may help to keep the oligopoly price down.

For a second thing, if government antitrust policy bears down hard on the slightest sign of collusion to keep prices firm and control supply, the oligopolists may find it harder to equate their marginal revenue and cost at a level high above society's true marginal cost.

For a third thing, some economists—such as Columbia's George J. Stigler—would argue that large firms should be broken up into many small pieces. He thinks the bottom of U-shaped cost curves comes early enough to make this a practical possibility that will not sacrifice any appreciable economies of large-scale production. With sellers now numerous, he hopes that competition can become much more like perfect competition than like oligopoly. (Needless

[1] In 1946 the Supreme Court held that cigarette oligopolists could be guilty of price fixing even when there was no overt collusion!

to say, Stigler is against any mergers that might reduce numbers still further; and he believes that many of today's giants grew from mergers which had as their goal not productive efficiency but rather monopoly control over market price.)

This is plainly a controversial area. Even the Supreme Court changes its mind on the legalities of the issues. As we'll see, it did break up Standard Oil of New Jersey back in the days of John D. Rockefeller, and also the old American Tobacco Company. But after World War I it held that applying a "rule of reason" to U.S. Steel did not require that giant to be broken up.

In 1946 and 1950 the Court plainly welcomed the demise of Alcoa's monopoly position in aluminum as Reynolds and Kaiser became important producers. (True, aluminum had to compete all along with copper and steel; and in the du Pont Cellophane case, the Court held that since cellophane had to compete with other wrapping products, its producer did not have a monopoly.) Also the Court made the big motion-picture producers get out of the theater business.

We'll see in later sections that it's the Antitrust Laws which help fight monopoly imperfections, and later we'll review their history.

▶ BIGNESS MAINTAINED BY RESEARCH AND ADVERTISING

Still another common industrial pattern to note is that of a firm that has considerable control over price by virtue of its technological efficiency, its patents, its trademarks, and its slogans. Its "monopoly profits" are plowed back into further research and advertising, so it is always able to keep abreast or ahead of its rivals. General Electric, RCA, and du Pont are perhaps typical of such companies. In setting prices, a "reasonable" markup over computed unit costs is introduced. Long-run considerations such as the possibility of developing new mass markets keep the firm from "charging all that the traffic will bear" in the immediate future. Moreover, fears of new rivals and aroused public opinion often keep the corporation from being "hoggish" in setting prices.

Because research and advertising are expensive and their results cumulative, success tends to breed success, and profits tend to breed more profits. Therefore, small business claims it cannot always effectively compete with such firms. In other words, industrial research may be subject to economies of large scale which cannot be enjoyed by small businesses.[1]

The instances of beer, cigarettes, and soap remind us that advertising and research are quite different things. Budweiser beer may stay large because a national audience has been persuaded of its merits. And much soap advertising

---

[1] Also, large firms are great "poolers of risks," being favored by the statistical fact that when you aggregate independent risks you cancel out much of the variation. (In fact, quadruple the size of the firm and you will halve the average risk or variation per dollar—as probability books will show.)

is more aimed to solidify the sales of one brand than to expand total soap use and cleanliness. Yet in many cases, it will not be easy to decide whether a certain bit of applied industrial research is for the purpose of technical improvement or for market improvement.

While admitting the efficiency and progress of some of the firms described, critics go on to argue that society would be *still* better off if the full advantages of efficiency were passed on to consumers or plowed back into research aimed at technological improvements and not simply at profits; and if fewer advertising dollars were spent on "soap operas" and jingles and more research dollars went into fundamental science rather than into patentable gadgets. Obviously, this is a controversial subject, upon which each citizen must form his own judgment.

▶ PUBLICLY REGULATED MONOPOLIES

As a last case, let's consider a complete monopoly licensed by the state and under government regulation. Such public utilities include gas and light companies, telephone and communication services, railroads and public carriers, etc. Since it is obviously uneconomical to have two local sets of telephone wires, an exclusive franchise is given to a single company. (Why is not the same thing true of milk delivery?)

But having given the utility company a complete monopoly, the state steps in to protect the consumer by setting maximum rates. Usually this is done by public regulating commissions, which specify the maximum prices that can be charged for each kind of service.

In setting such prices it has long been customary to pick prices that will try to give the company a fair return on its capital. Rates such as 5, 6, or 7 per cent are often selected as representing a fair return. (Of course any "guarantee" of a rate of return raises the problem of motivating the utility to keep efficient and cost conscious.)

Complex is the question of determining the *capital value* base of the company to which this "fair rate" is to be applied. Three measures of fair capital value have been suggested at times: (1) *original cost* (minus depreciation) — or the sum of all past prudent investments; (2) *current reproduction cost* (minus depreciation) —or the cost of replacing the company's equipment at present prices, corrected for age and condition of the property; and (3) *capitalized market value* of the public utility's securities or assets.

Of these methods, the third is universally recognized to be nonsensical. As was shown in the earlier discussion of good will (Chapter 5), the market value of any income-earning property is given by capitalizing its annual return by the interest rate.[1] For a regulating authority to use capitalized

---

[1] The capitalization process is more fully discussed in Chapter 29's Appendix.

market value as a base for measuring capital would be tantamount to recognizing *any level of earnings,* high or low, as fair. Once having been capitalized into a new base, excessively high earnings will appear as only moderate interest returns, and the same is true of excessively low earnings. The method of capitalized earnings begs the question that the authorities must answer!

The American courts have, therefore, vacillated between *original* cost and *reproduction* cost. So long as the general price level does not change, the two are not very different. But over a period of decades, when prices may greatly increase, reproduction cost will involve higher earnings and rates than original costs. In periods of declining prices, the reverse discrepancy is to be observed: the use of original cost leads to greater leniency to the nonspeculative investors in public-utility securities. But reproduction cost leads to a more flexible price structure and gives less weight to the dead hand of past costs.[1]

▶ BRIEF HISTORY OF ANTITRUST POLICY

Around the turn of the century, America went through a period of widespread trust formation. Small companies were merged into large; big and small companies combined collusively to limit supply and raise price. Huge stock-market promotion schemes flourished.

The public was naturally growing concerned over the growth of monopoly. In 1890, the Sherman Antitrust Act was passed, making it illegal to monopolize trade or to conspire in restraint of trade. On paper, this Act represented a major advance over the previous common-law restrictions on monopolistic conspiracies. But it was adopted with little discussion, indeed without attracting much attention of a favorable or unfavorable nature; and beyond an antipathy toward "monopoly," there is no evidence that anyone had clear notions concerning which actions were to be regarded as legal or illegal.

In the early 1900's, the Republican administrations of Theodore Roosevelt

---

[1] From the standpoint of the advanced discussions of "welfare economics," neither method is ideal. Some writers in this field have set up a perfectionist formula that would involve pricing of public-utility services at not more than the extra or marginal costs of services. (We've seen why $P = MC$ is "efficient.") However, marginal cost pricing is a doctrine which, as a practical matter, few economists would endorse all the way. It could lead to excessive returns to the owners if demand was large in comparison with capacity. But with decreasing cost situations so likely in the public utility area, it would probably lead to inadequate returns to original investors. Although the state could then, if it wished to, secure by a subsidy justice for investors without interfering with the desirable output or price, this would represent a considerable departure from present practice.

The great regional power projects such as the TVA and Bonneville Dam are from one viewpoint partial approaches toward such a system of pricing. However, the fact that the government can raise capital in larger sums and at lower costs than private industry, and the fact that the same set of dams can simultaneously achieve the ends of national defense, navigation, flood control, and irrigation make any simple yardstick comparison between private and public operations impossible.

and William Howard Taft witnessed the first surge of activity under the Sherman Act. Thus, the Supreme Court prevented Morgan and Harriman from using a holding company to bring about a merger of their Northern Pacific Railroad with Hill's Great Northern. Later, the Supreme Court ordered the American Tobacco Company and Standard Oil each to be broken up into a number of separate companies.

By the end of this first period, the Supreme Court had enunciated the "rule of reason": Only *unreasonable* restraints of trade (agreements, mergers, predation, and the like) were to come within the scope of the Sherman Act and to be considered illegal. The Clayton Antitrust Act (1914), in addition to seeking to exclude labor from antitrust action, tried to define illegal behavior more specifically, so that all matters would not have to be left to the subjective opinion of federal judges; but the problem of defining proper norms was left as vague as ever. The Federal Trade Commission Act (1914) also extended the government's powers to police competition.

The U.S. Steel case, mentioned above, affords a good example of the state of affairs in the period which followed the burst of antitrust activity under Roosevelt and Taft. This case began before World War I, but the arguments persisted until it was finally settled in 1920, when the Court held that U.S. Steel was not a monopoly. Mere bigness was not of itself a crime if the corporation in question behaved with proper discretion.

During the 1920's, antitrust action languished somewhat. And with the coming of the depression in the early 1930's, people ceased to worry about price increases; pressure came from business—especially small business—for legislation to keep prices *up* rather than down.

▶ **THE FEW ANTITRUST LAWS WHICH WEAKEN COMPETITION**

The Sherman Act, the Clayton Act, the Celler Merger Act (1950), and most of the antitrust laws have contributed enormously toward improving the degree of competition in our system. All who value the capitalistic way of life should applaud this kind of public intervention which contributes toward lessening the imperfections of competition.

Unfortunately, during the Great Depression there grew up a move to pass laws that were called "antitrust laws" but which actually tended to make competition more imperfect. Thus, the NRA (National Recovery Act of 1933), under the guise of recovery from depression, blatantly promoted industry-wide codes and cartels with collusive price maintenance. (This act was later declared unconstitutional.)

Another example is the Robinson-Patman Act (1936). This tries to keep one businessman from vigorously cutting his prices by selling the same product under a different brand name, and in various other ways serves to limit competition. Instead of concentrating on bringing *P* down for the consumer, it concentrates on keeping many firms in business, even though some may be inefficient.

Still other examples are provided by *resale price maintenance* laws of the Miller-Tydings and McGuire type. These try to make it hard or impossible for one merchant to undersell another on given brand-name products. In the late 1950's these price-maintenance laws have more and more been under heavy attack by courts and the public.

Often legislators, lawyers, and judges have been against bigness even when it promoted efficiency and lower consumer prices. Thus in the A & P case, this grocery chain's biggest crime in the eyes of many was that its size gave it the ability to sell groceries at a much smaller markup than could its myriad of competitors. Terrified by the quite unrealistic possibility that its price cutting would drive out all competitors and *then* permit it to raise its prices high, critics of the A & P tried to use the antitrust laws against it.

From these perversions of the antitrust philosophy, you can see that the economists' preoccupation with how well the pricing system serves to determine What, How, and For Whom is not quite the same thing as the judge's preoccupation with who is a nasty man who has been doing nasty things and with whom.

▶ ANTITRUST SINCE THE WAR

Fortunately, by the late 1930's the government took up antitrust with renewed vigor. Thurman Arnold, head of the Antitrust Division, even tried to tackle the building industries with its notoriously backward technology. Industries such as glass, cigarettes, cement, and many others all came under vigorous attack.

All this means costly litigation. The Antitrust Division now has hundreds of times as many lawyers as it did in the days of Teddy Roosevelt. Prosecutions and court cases have increased greatly in number.

Examples are the 1946 Cigarette case, and the 1948 Cement case (which abolished the "basing point" system of quoting prices at every point in a region at so much more than the price at a given point—like the old "Pittsburgh-plus" pricing of the steel industry). In 1957 the Supreme Court ruled that du Pont unduly dominated General Motors and ordered it to make arrangements to get rid of its GM stock—which illustrates how tough the attitude toward old or new mergers has become. (Shall Bethlehem and Youngstown Steel be permitted to merge? Bethlehem thinks so, but the Attorney General thinks otherwise.) [1]

[1] Lest you think the government wins all its cases, there was its attempt to prosecute the leading investment bankers for monopoly practices, which was dismissed decisively by the District Court.

▶ **FUTURE OF ANTITRUST POLICY: WORKABLE COMPETITION**

In summary, both Republicans and Democrats are spending more and more money on lawyers and investigators to enforce the antitrust laws with ever-increasing vigor. Firms no longer dare to use group practices which used to be standard in American industry.

Judges are tougher and tougher in their judgments. More and more do they weaken the powers that a business firm has to exploit its patents and its market advantages. Even after a case has been decided against a company, it is not off the hook. It must enter into "consent decrees" which bind it to follow certain policies, and the judge may for years afterward keep his careful eye on the firm's performance. (The *United Shoe* case is a good example, where the company had to agree to sell its machines instead of renting them.)

As we've seen, the economist and the lawyer do not always see eye to eye. The economist often feels that lawyers and the courts have concentrated on the letter of the law, without defining its spirit with any precision. If a businessman should be caught with an indiscreet set of letters in his files, the Court throws the book at him. But if another company has consistently done the same thing in less overt fashion, it is immune from prosecution. The legal mind is not so much concerned with the height of prices, which it has no means of measuring, as it is with the methods by which prices are set. Yet the economic and legal minds do seem today to be coming closer together.

Again and again in Part Three we have stressed the basic problem of how a pricing system solves society's questions What, How, For Whom. This frames the rational goal of antitrust policy.

We can't expect competition to become everywhere perfectly perfect in the strict sense of the economist. But what we can strive for is what Columbia's venerable economist, J. M. Clark, years ago called "workable competition." By public and private policies we can hope to improve the efficiency with which market prices reflect underlying individual needs, desires, and wants against the background of true costs of goods—costs in terms of alternative goods that could be produced and in terms of used-up scarce productive factors which involve sweat and disutility.

Part Four will be concerned with the exactly similar problems that arise in connection with the pricing of land, labor, and capital. Again, the function of such pricing in solving society's problems must be the focal point of interest.

SUMMARY

1. Few business firms are able to develop exact curves of cost and revenue. This does not mean that they are oblivious to profit maximization. In terms of trial and error, they may be doing a tolerably good job of keeping alive as a business entity and of achieving long-run optimum profits.

2. Under imperfect competition, a firm may have to make rough guesses in setting its price. Often it will use some kind of a *markup* over an estimate of unit cost. Break-even point charts may play an active role in the businessman's thinking about the pricing problem.

3. Nonetheless, it is market conditions that usually determine how much of a markup any firm can safely count on getting; so in a sense the problem is merely reposed. Only factual investigations of each situation can tell what the result is likely to be.

4. Chronically sick industries characterized by overentry; wasteful no-profit equilibrium with too many, too small, too dear imperfect competitors; oligopoly, with or without "administered prices"; big quasi-monopolies maintained by diligent research and new product development or by forceful advertising; and regulated public utilities—these are a few important patterns of imperfect competition.

5. Public policy with respect to the antitrust problem has contributed much toward lessening the degree of imperfections of competition. Britain and other nations are beginning to imitate our legislation on this subject.

Once economists realize that perfect competition is not a universally attainable norm, the problem of defining and attaining "workable competition" becomes paramount.

QUESTIONS FOR DISCUSSION

1. Give examples of behavior by business firms suggesting that they do seek to maximize their profits. Give some apparent exceptions.

2. Suppose you ran an electric company. How would you go about maximizing profits? How would you estimate elasticity of demand? Would an economic textbook be the place to learn how to be successful in this respect?

3. What is meant by markup pricing? Show how this might work.

4. Explain the assumptions underlying a break-even chart. Is it just a special case of the last chapter's Fig. 4? Where would your profits be greatest on such a chart? Are you free to move there of your own volition?

5. Describe the pattern of imperfect competition in the auto industry, cigarette industry, aluminum industry, mousetrap industry, women's-dress trade, retail grocery trade, barbershop trade.

6. (a) A perfectly rational entrepreneur will disregard his fixed costs in setting price. (b) Heavy fixed or overhead costs often make for cutthroat or ruinous competition which leads to monopoly and the death of competition. Are (a) and (b) inconsistent? Why not?

7. "The tragedy of monopolistic competition often has nothing to do with excessive profits. Rather there may be no profits at all, the high price being frittered away in small volume and inefficient production." Discuss.

8. "It is utopian to try to break monopolies up into even a few effectively competing units, because the basic cause of monopoly is the law of decreasing cost with mass production and, in any case, a few competitors are not enough to duplicate the pricing patterns of perfect competition." Discuss both parts of this statement.

9. "The A & P Company is not bad just because it is big." Discuss.

10. Show that companies may be tempted to merge in order to gain tax advantages. (Hint: Suppose Kaiser has sizable losses in producing autos and Willys has profits. The Kaiser losses can be "carried forward" to offset later Willys' profits.)

11. Eisenhower's Justice Department permitted Hudson and Nash to merge, permitted Studebaker and Packard to merge, but forbade Bethlehem and Youngstown to merge. All these decisions were made in the interest of promoting competition. Do you think they are necessarily inconsistent? Give arguments pro and con.

12. "The modern corporation is a good pooler of risks. Other things being equal, the larger the firm, the more it can cancel off one risk against another, the more it can economize on inventory and excess peak capacity, and the more it can spread the indivisible costs of the best-grade research among its many units. Larger size tends to help, and if it emulates the example of General Motors and other efficient decentralizers of decision making, there are almost no penalties from larger size. I conclude that trying to prevent monopolies is a fight against nature." Comment critically.

13. Review your understanding of the following concepts:

markup pricing	*utility rate regulation*
break-even chart	*fair return on original or re-*
free entry	*production cost or on market*
no-profit equilibrium of pro-	*valuation*
ducers of differentiated prod-	*Sherman and later major anti-*
ucts	*trust acts*
oligopoly, with or without tacit	*NRA, resale price maintenance*
collusion	*challenge of "workable compe-*
bigness, research, and advertis-	*tition"*
ing	

part

DISTRIBUTION OF INCOME:

THE PRICING OF THE

PRODUCTIVE FACTORS

26 THEORY OF PRODUCTION AND MARGINAL-PRODUCTS

Knowledge is the only instrument of production that is not subject to diminishing returns.
                                                                    J. M. CLARK

In the next few chapters of Part Four we shall be primarily concerned with how factors of production get priced in the market place—with the determination of (1) *rents* of land and other resources, (2) *wages* of various kinds of labor, (3) *interest* rates on capital assets, and (4) *profit*.

Economists call this the problem of "distribution." They don't mean by this word what the man on the street means when he refers to distribution as the marketing of goods and the carrying of goods to the final consumer. Part Four's distribution deals with the problem of For Whom goods are to be produced. The same pricing of factors by supply and demand that is determining For Whom will be shown to also be solving the How-society-is-to-produce problem.

The key to such factor pricing will turn out to be provided by the economic theory of production. So, as a prelude to our general discussion of distribution of income, this chapter investigates the theory of production. It defines the important economic concept of "marginal-product." Then it relates this concept to our old friend the law of diminishing returns. And finally the chapter shows that the demand curves for the various factors of production—the demands for labor, land, etc.—are to be expressed in terms of marginal-products.

▶ **TECHNICAL LAW RELATING OUTPUT TO INPUT: THE "PRODUCTION FUNCTION"**

The theory of production begins with specific engineering or technological information. If you have a certain amount of labor, a certain amount of land, and certain prescribed amounts of other inputs such as machines or raw materials, how much output of a particular good can you get? The answer depends upon the state of technology: if someone makes a new invention or discovers a new industrial process, the obtainable output that you can get from given factor inputs will go up. *But at any one time, there will always be a maximum obtainable amount of product for any given amounts of factor inputs.*

This technical law relating inputs to outputs is so important that economists have given it a name. They call it the "production function." (Example: An agricultural engineer lists in a thick book the various combinations of land and labor that will produce various bushels of corn. On one page of the book he lists the alternative combinations of land and labor needed to produce 100 bushels of corn; on another page, the input combinations that will produce 200 bushels of corn; etc. The totality of the technical information on all the pages of the book is what the economist calls the production function. Example: The chemical engineer's listing of the various ways of producing a given octane gasoline.)

▶ **ALTERNATIVE SUBSTITUTION POSSIBILITIES FOR FACTORS**

That's all there is to the concept of the production function: the technical relation between various inputs and output. But an important property of the production function should be stressed. A schoolboy with little knowledge of economics or engineering will jump to the conclusion that there is only *one* way to produce a given output. He thinks that no matter how high the wages of labor rise relative to the rent of land, farmers will still produce their corn with exactly the same land and labor input proportions.

Engineers and economists know better. They know that when labor is scarce and land plentiful—as in colonial America, which contrasted strongly with densely populated Europe—farmers found it cheapest to produce corn by extensive agriculture. High wages and low land rent made them substitute land for labor in production.

So don't forget that normally the production function tells us there are *numerous alternative factor input combinations to produce the same output.* And note that this has an important bearing on how businessmen minimize their costs of production, as we'll now see.

▶ **BEHIND THE COST CURVE: LEAST COST THROUGH FACTOR SUBSTITUTION**

In earlier chapters we've repeatedly dealt with cost curves of a business firm. We took these curves for granted, supposing that accountants had somehow given costs to us. Now we realize that the theory of production must explain how these cost curves of minimum total expense were actually arrived at.

How were they arrived at? Evidently, the firm succeeded in achieving Least-Cost production only after it had successfully *substituted* cheap inputs for dear inputs. The resulting cost curve came from then jotting down at each and every output the total wage and other factor costs that resulted *after* the right factor substitutions had been made to achieve Least Cost.

Can we give a common-sense explanation of the equilibrium condition of substitution for the firm at such a Least-Cost factor combination? Yes, we can, in terms of comparing (1) each factor's market price with (2) the *extra product* it gives us. Here's our reasoning.

Suppose an acre of land happens to rent for exactly as much as the wage of a unit of labor. For example, suppose each has a factor price of $2 per unit in the market: a $2 wage and a $2 land rent. What will then have to be true about the extra product of labor as compared to the extra product of land at the Least-Cost point? Necessarily, you will find yourself substituting labor for land so long as labor's extra product is greater than land's extra product. That way you'll be getting more from an extra dollar spent on labor than from the dollar spent on land.

Where will you stop substituting? You will find yourself at the Least-Cost stopping point only when the *extra products* of the equally priced land and labor are themselves *exactly equal*. For, only then will you be getting the most from each last dollar spent on labor and capital: the most product for your money; the Least Cost for the given output.

This substitution rule of making different factors' extra products equal is valid only when land and labor happen to have the same factor price. But equal factor prices is too special a case.

If a unit of land costs 10 times a unit of labor, it would be absurd to stop at the point of equal extra products. Where then should be your stopping point? Evidently you ought to go on substituting the cheap labor for the dear land until you get to the point where the extra product of a land unit is exactly ten times the extra product of a labor unit. There and only there you'd be getting the most for your money, producing at Least Cost. Here then is the common-sense general rule:

▶ Achieve Least Cost by substituting factors until their *extra products are exactly proportional to their respective factor prices*. For, only then will it be true that the *extra product per last dollar* spent on labor is exactly the same as your *extra product per last dollar* spent on land. This universal *equality of extra product per last dollar* has to be satisfied if no further cost-saving substitutions are to be possible.

A little further on, we shall reformulate this common-sense rule in terms of the fancier name for extra product that economists call "marginal-product."

▶ MARGINAL-PRODUCTS DEFINED

Remember, back in Chapter 2, the law of diminishing returns? Figure 1 reproduces page 24's Table of diminishing extra corn product for varying labor units added to fixed land. Back there, we were using the production function concept without yet knowing the name.

Now we can introduce the economist's fancier name for extra product. In economic theory the word "extra" is typically replaced by the word "marginal." (Examples: The extra utility of a good is its marginal utility. The extra cost of a good is its marginal cost. The extra amount spent on consumption out of an extra dollar of income is the marginal propensity to consume. So it goes.) It is natural, then, to give the following definition:

▶ The marginal-product of a productive factor is the extra product or output added by one extra unit of that factor, while other factors are being held constant. Labor's marginal-product is the extra output you get when you add one unit of labor, holding all other inputs constant. Similarly, land's marginal-product is the change in total product resulting from one additional unit of land, with all other inputs held constant. Etcetera for any factor.

Note that the marginal-product of a factor is expressed in *physical* units of corn per unit of extra input. So careful economists often speak of "marginal-physical-product" rather than plain marginal-product—particularly when they want to avoid any possible confusion with a later dollar concept called "marginal-revenue-product."

▶ MARGINAL-PHYSICAL-PRODUCTS AND DIMINISHING RETURNS

Column 3 of Fig. 1's table can now be identified with the name "marginal-physical-product." The lower chart shows the steady drop of labor's marginal-physical-product. This reflects the fact that the upper chart shows total product rising in ever-smaller steps as we hold land constant and add equal extra units of labor. The law of diminishing returns could be renamed "the law of diminishing marginal-physical-product."

What's true for one input is also true for another. We can interchange land and labor, now holding labor constant and varying land. We could make up a new table, showing land's marginal-physical-product in its column. And this too would presumably obey the law of diminishing returns. Why? Because now each of the extra land units would have less and less of the fixed labor factor to work with.

▶ RESTATEMENT OF THE LEAST-COST RULE OF BEST SUBSTITUTION

We saw that you reached Least Cost by substituting until there is equality of the extra product got per last dollar spent on each and every factor. We can now restate this rule in terms of marginal-physical-products, in any of the three following equivalent forms.

Least-Cost rule of best substitution:

Diminishing returns restated as law of diminishing marginal-physical-product:

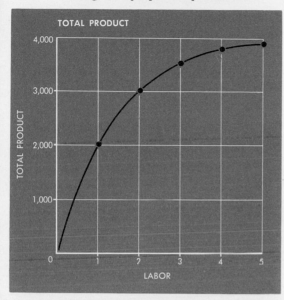

Units of labor	Total product	Marginal-physical-product
0	0	
		2,000
1	2,000	
		1,000
2	3,000	
		500
3	3,500	
		300
4	3,800	
		100
5	3,900	

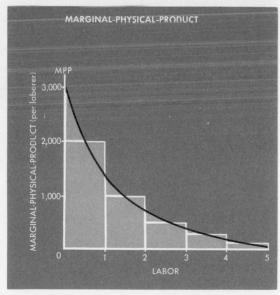

Fig. 1. In the lower diagram the slabs of marginal-physical-product have been smoothed by a curve. The area under the marginal-physical-product curve (or of the slabs) adds up to the total product shown above. (E.g., 2,000 + 1,000 + 500 = total product of 3,500 for three men. What gives total product of four men?)

1. Substitute until all factor marginal-physical-products are *exactly proportional* to their respective market factor prices.
2. What is precisely the same thing, substitute until the *marginal-physical-product per last dollar* spent on any factor is *exactly the same* for each and every factor.

3. What is still another way of describing the same thing, Least-Cost equilibrium requires the following condition:

$$\frac{\text{Marginal-physical-product of } A}{\text{Price of } A} = \frac{\text{marginal-physical-product of } B}{\text{Price of } B} \cdots$$

This condition holds for a third or any number of factors.

These three formulations all say the same common-sense thing. When you understand the last, you understand them all. You should realize that if

$$\frac{\text{marginal-physical-product of } A}{\text{Price of } A} \text{ were greater than}$$

$$\frac{\text{marginal-physical-product of } B}{\text{Price of } B},$$

you'd be getting more for an extra last dollar spent on A than on B. Then you could lower costs by substituting A for B; and as you so substitute, the law of diminishing returns tells you that marginal-physical-product of A will fall and marginal-physical-product of B will rise—until the desired Least-Cost equilibrium equality is reached and further substitution ceases.

The common sense of all this is fairly simple. A consumer maximizes his total satisfaction only when he spends his money on different goods until the marginal utility per dollar has become exactly equal in every use. An eager student will try to reallocate his study of different courses until the last hour spent on each can be estimated to yield the same contribution to his grade average or scholarly fame. A similar equalization rule holds for the substitutions that will minimize cost.

► **HOW CHANGING FACTOR PRICES INDUCE SUBSTITUTION**

Production theory has now told us what was going on behind the cost curves of Part Three. The first part of this chapter is therefore complete. To test your understanding, work out the following example.

What happens to the cost curve and to the way factors are combined when price of A rises and price of B stays the same? Costs will naturally now rise, because the A input you buy costs more. The cost curve therefore shifts upward. But note that there will also be induced a substitution of the now cheaper B for input A. (With labor dear, you'll now use less men per acre and produce your corn by more extensive agriculture.) The induced factor substitution ceases when we've restored the proportionality of marginal-physical-products to the new factor prices.

► **FINAL FACTOR DEMAND AT BEST-PROFIT OUTPUT**

We now know what the demand for each factor—labor or land—would be for each of the various possible levels of output. But the factor markets are interested in actualities, not possibilities—in what your final output will be. The labor and land auctioneers ask: Exactly what will be your final demand for labor, for land, for machines at each given wage, rent, and machine rental?

To get these unique demands we merely have to add to our Least-Cost rule an important result of Part Three: we recall that your maximum-profit output always comes when you have produced until marginal cost just matches marginal revenue; that $MR = MC$ gives Best-Profit output.

Table 1 shows how we find the demand for factors. The first two columns give our cost data, the cost curve. At every point, we now know what's behind these cost data: namely, our substitution rule about marginal-physical-products being proportional to factor prices.

But Column (3) gives the firm's demand curve, and from it we calculate Column (4)'s Total Revenue. Comparing costs and revenue, we recognize that the Best-Profit output is at 400 units. Why? Because that is where $MR = MC$. So it is the factor demand appropriate to this unique Best-Profit output that gives us our desired amount demanded of factors by the firm.

▶ **FROM PHYSICAL PRODUCT TO DOLLARS: "MARGINAL-REVENUE-PRODUCT"**

How can you arrive in one step at this amount that you will demand of factors? You will find yourself wanting to go beyond marginal-physical-product to a new concept of "marginal-revenue-product." You're not in business for your health; it's dollars you're interested in. To you the important thing about hiring an extra land unit is not the extra *physical* corn it brings you, but rather the extra *dollars* it brings you. You say:

"An extra man costs me $2 wages. What does he bring me? He brings me his marginal-physical-product of, say, 4 bushels. Now what extra dollars do I get from this? Let's see: my marketing experts tell me that my marginal revenue is now $1.50 per bushel. (They calculated this from the demand-curve

From all Least-Cost outputs, we pick the Best-Profit output:

Table 1. At all three outputs, Least-Cost proportionality of marginal-physical-products to factor-prices is satisfied in the background. But only at 400 output is Best-Profit of $100 being made, with $MR = MC$. Final derived demand for factors comes from this point of Best-Profit output.

Output q	Least-Cost TC	Demand curve price p	Total revenue $p \times q$ TR	Comparison of MR and MC	Total Profit
200	$300	$1.75	$350	$MR > MC$	$ 50
400	500	1.50	600	$MR = MC$	100
600	700	1.25	750	$M < MC$	50

data of Table 1.) So it appears to me that the labor unit has really brought me extra revenue product of 4 × $1.50 = $6.

"Will I hire a man who costs $2 extra and brings me $6 of extra dollar revenue product? I sure will. And I'll keep hiring labor until diminishing returns and falling corn price bring extra revenue product down to the $2 factor price. Then I'll quit hiring further men."

Notice that you've been groping in a common-sense way for a new concept: for marginal-physical-product multiplied by marginal (dollar!) revenue—which means the extra revenue product that the factor brings you. Economists give a definite name to this concept: namely, "marginal-revenue-product." Here is its exact definition.

▶ Marginal-revenue-product is defined as the extra *dollars* of revenue that the marginal-physical-product of a factor actually brings you when you sell the extra physical product. Marginal-revenue-product for each factor must therefore always be marginal revenue times marginal-physical-product. Thus

Marginal-revenue-product of A = MR × marginal-physical-product of A
Marginal-revenue-product of B = MR × marginal-physical-product of B
Etc.

It is this marginal-revenue-product that gives us the factor demand curves of Part Four's distribution theory, as we'll see after a digression on the evil of monopoly.

▶ MONOPOLY EVIL OF RESTRICTED FACTOR DEMAND: A DIGRESSION

If you are a perfect competitor, no matter how much physical product you send to market you'll be too unimportant to affect market price. In that special case, marginal-revenue-product will be simply marginal-physical-product times the market price you actually get for the extra corn units sent to market.

But in the frequent case where you are big enough to affect market price, you won't include in marginal-physical-product *all* that the extra physical product itself actually sells for. Why not? Because you know that selling this extra product has moved you down your *tilting* demand curve; this extra product has forced *all the earlier product* to sell for less; and this loss on all the earlier product has to be subtracted from the receipts of the extra product before you've arrived at the hard-boiled correct figure of what it's worth to you. Fortunately, our original definition in Chapter 24 of marginal revenue was designed explicitly to take into account all such losses on previous units. So we have taken care of this fact in insisting that marginal-revenue-product be calculated by multiplying marginal-physical-product by MR. Only in perfect competition, where P and MR are exactly the same (there being no loss on previous units), can we calculate marginal-revenue-product by P × marginal-physical-product.

This technicality reminds us once again of the evil involved in monopolistic imperfection. A monopolist tends to produce too little because of his fear of "spoiling the market." He connives and contrives to produce scarcity. How does this show up in production theory? *It shows up by his hiring less factors than would a competitor.* Why? Because the monopolist's calculation of his marginal-revenue-product always multiplies the factors' marginal-physical-products by a *MR* term which falls far short of *P*—falls short because of the canny monopolist's calculation of loss on previous units that comes with spoiling the market by extra product.

Thus, the restrictionist philosophy of cartels, oligopolists, and all kinds of imperfect competitors shows up as too small factor demand. The evil burden of monopoly, like a tax, may be shifted backward onto productive factors as well as forward onto consumers.[1] This ends our digression.

▶ FACTOR DEMAND CURVES FROM MARGINAL-REVENUE-PRODUCTS

We have now seen exactly what determines any firm's demand curve for productive factors. Seeking maximum profit, each firm will hire a factor up to the point where its marginal-revenue-product exactly equals its factor price in the market. That point maximizes profits. We can summarize thus.

Best-Profit Marginal Equivalence in Factor Hiring:

1. Each input will be hired up to the point where its marginal-revenue-product is finally equal to its ruling market price; thus in the final Best-Profit equilibrium position

Marginal-revenue-product of A = price of A
Marginal-revenue-product of B = price of B
Marginal-revenue-product of C = price of C

. . .

. . .

Marginal-revenue-product of Z = price of Z

2. When a factor's price goes up, less of that factor will be used—as other factors are substituted for it and as rising cost reduces output—until the equilibrium relation is again restored. Both effects are important: factor substitution and output reduction.

Figure 2 gives this chapter's results in a nutshell. It illustrates how the factor demand curve is derived from the commodity demand curve and from

[1] A footnote in Chapter 28's discussion of wages discusses a quite different evil of imperfect competition. If a firm dominates its factor markets, it may have monopoly power in the *buying* of factors. (Economists call it a "monopsonist" from the Greek words for "single buyer.") Then it refuses to hire men up to the point where their marginal-revenue-product equals their market wage? Why? Because it knows that it is big enough to *push up the market wage on all its men* when it tries to hire one extra man. That man costs it his $2 wage plus maybe $.01 on each of the previous 100 men; so unless he adds $3 of marginal-revenue-product he won't be hired! Such monopsony also restricts output and invites labor unionization.

Derived factor demand . . .

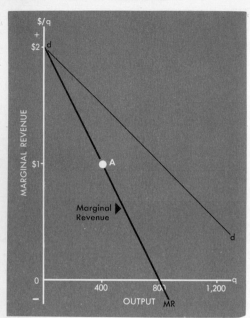

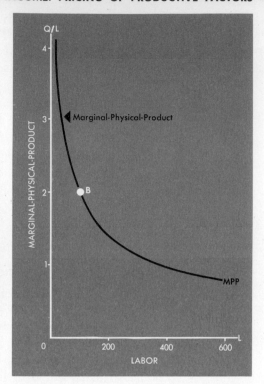

the curve of marginal-physical-product. It illustrates why the factor demand curve is sloping: because of diminishing returns, reinforced by falling marginal revenue.

▶ A REALISTIC QUALIFICATION

An important qualification must sometimes be made. We have calculated the marginal-physical-product of any one input by (1) holding all the other inputs constant and then (2) increasing the input in question by 1 unit. The resulting increase in physical product was then measured, and that was identified as the factor's marginal-physical-product. Now in some technological processes the factor inputs work very intimately together, so that, when you increase only one of them, holding the others constant, you get *zero extra product;* and, when you decrease one factor alone, you lose *the whole product* produced by both together; only when you change them both *in combination* do you seem to get a nice smooth curve of marginal-physical-product.

Certainly such discontinuities can sometimes happen, but perhaps they do not occur quite so often as some critics have claimed. Thus, critics often point out examples where one man is always using one shovel or where it seems to take a certain amount of gold to produce a watch band and no amount of labor can substitute for this gold. But actually in any digging operation, extra shovels must usually be kept on hand; and if shovel prices were very high and

. . . comes from marginal-revenue-product:

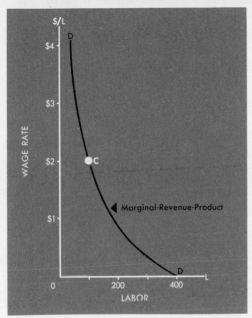

Fig. 2. To get labor's demand at C, we multiply A's marginal-revenue by B's marginal-physical-product. This gives us at C labor's marginal-revenue-product. All other points on DD we get in a similar way. The whole point of production theory is to develop this important factor demand curve.

wages were low, workers on different shifts might use the same implements so that the shovel requirements could be kept down to a minimum; also, we might in time change the size of the shovels or introduce bulldozers, thereby changing the proportions of the factors. Or in the above case of the gold watch band, there will almost certainly be some waste of metal in the form of shavings and dust; and if wages were low enough relative to the price of gold, it would pay us to hire more men to produce the same number of watch bands out of less gold—the labor being, in effect, a substitute for the use of more gold.

Numerous other arguments and examples could be given in reply to those who stress fixity of factor-proportions and discontinuities in substitutability and marginal-products. Nonetheless in some technical processes, there may not be continuous substitutability between the various inputs, and so the calculated marginal-physical-products may become very erratic and lumpy. It was once thought that this would spoil the economic theory of production. But that is fortunately not so.

If you own a business with this type of technology, you can still apply all the Least-Cost and Best-Profit principles outlined above—in fact, it will be easier for you to do so, inasmuch as your engineers can then rule out many factor combinations from the very beginning. If adding a man without adding other inputs will result in no extra product, then nobody but a fool would ever be tempted to do this. And if adding a combined dose of labor and machines gives rise to a big increase in revenue product—bigger even than the combined factor-costs of the labor *and* machines—you will, of course, add such a combination. You will continue to add such combinations until finally the law of diminishing physical returns or the law of diminishing marginal revenue acts to bring the *combined* marginal-revenue-product down to the combined factor-cost.[1]

The difference that technical discontinuities and lumpinesses make in our results is the following: In such cases, when the factor-price first changes, it may not pay the firm to change the way it combines that factor with other factors. Then after the factor-price has changed a lot, it may suddenly pay the firm to make a drastic rearrangement over to an entirely new and different combination of factors. Thus, such discontinuities have no other effect on our theory of production than to make it likely that the derived demand for a factor will show patches of inelastic demand (with little change in amount bought) coupled with occasional *huge discontinuities* of demand. Nonetheless the firm's demand curve for each factor is still well determined, just as it is in the nicely continuous case. Our same logic still applies.

▶ DEMAND FOR FACTORS A DERIVED DEMAND

We conclude this chapter with some elementary observations about factor demand.

Why do people demand a finished good like a magazine or an overcoat? They do so because of the satisfaction which they hope to enjoy from its use. But when a businessman demands a factor input, why is that? Surely not for the direct satisfaction that he hopes to get from those inputs. He wants the productive factors because of the production and revenue that he hopes to secure from them.

Satisfactions are in the picture, but at one stage removed. The satisfactions that we consumers get from an overcoat help to determine how much a textile company can sell the coat for and how many coats it can sell. Therefore you would be right in insisting that consumer satisfactions do *ultimately* determine the firm's demand for inputs.

Still, the firm's demand for labor is *derived indirectly* from the consumer demand for its final product. That is why economists speak of the demand for productive factors as a "derived demand." Effort involved in making coats is of no interest to society for its own sake; we pay men to sew because of the satisfaction to be gained from the finished product. Sometimes the derived demands go through many stages: Wool is wanted to spin yarn; yarn is wanted to weave cloth; cloth is wanted to make coats. All the previous demands are

---

[1] Occasionally in advanced economic works, the words "marginal-*net*-product" are used instead of "marginal-product" to describe cases like the above. In Chapter 27's Appendix there is some discussion of how intercommodity substitution helps determine factor prices even where intracommodity factor substitution is technically impossible.

derived from the ultimate consumer demand for the satisfactions to be secured from the finished product.

▶ **DEMAND FOR FACTORS A JOINTLY INTERDEPENDENT DEMAND**

Another peculiarity about the demand for inputs stems from this technological fact: Factors usually do not work alone. A shovel by itself is worthless to me if I wish a cellar; a man with his bare hands is equally worthless. Together the man and shovel can dig my cellar. In other words, the quantity of a good produced depends *jointly* upon all the available inputs.

We cannot say which is more important in producing a baby—a mother or a father. So, too, we cannot in most cases hope to demonstrate how much of the physical product has been *caused* by any one of the different factors *taken by itself*. The different factors *interact* with each other. Usually they reinforce each other's effectiveness, but sometimes they get in each other's way and compete rather than complement each other.

What are some of the consequences of this jointness or interdependence between the productivities of the different factor inputs? One obvious consequence is this: The amount of labor demanded will depend on its wage rate, but the labor demanded will also depend upon the price of machines. The same is true of the demand for machines. By raising miners' wages, John L. Lewis creates good business for power tools. *Thus, the demand for each input will depend upon the prices of all inputs, not on its own price alone.* Cross elasticities between different factors are as important as regular elasticities.

SUMMARY

1. Distribution is concerned with the determination of different people's income or with the basic question For Whom economic goods are to be produced. It studies the problem of how the different factors of production—land, labor, capital, entrepreneurship, and risk taking—are priced in the market place, or how supply and demand interact to determine all kinds of wages, rents, interest yields, profits, etc. (Needless to say this primary distribution of market-determined income is then modified by government taxes and expenditure programs to create ultimately the final actual pattern of individual and family income.)

2. To understand why the demand curves for the factors of production are what they are, we must investigate the theory of production and cost within a firm. This is because the demand for inputs is a *derived demand*—derived indirectly from the final demand by the consumer. The problem is complicated by the fact that the demand for factors is a *joint demand*—joint because the factors interact with each other in producing final product.

3. If he is given ruling market prices of all factors and is given engineering, technical information about the effects of factor changes on final product, the businessman can solve the two problems: (a) of substituting the different factors for each other so as to realize the Least-Cost combination—at which he has *equalized the marginal-physical-product per dollar spent on every factor used*—and (b) of finally determining which of all possible outputs is his Best-Profit position where $MR = MC$.

4. An exactly equivalent condition of factor equilibrium is the following: *equality* of marignal-*revenue*-products with factor-prices. Why must this hold in the Best-Profit equilibrium? Because any businessman with common sense will stop hiring any factor at the point where its market price has begun to exceed what its marginal-physical-product will bring in to his firm in actual dollars of marginal revenue.

5. Our analysis has shown why, when a factor's price rises, the quantity of it that is demanded will tend to fall. Higher labor price will cause other factors to be substituted for it in producing each output; and higher labor cost probably means that the Best-Profit output will be at the lower level where MR equals a now higher MC. What is the same, the marginal-revenue-product demand curve for the factor tilts downward because of technical diminishing returns, reinforced by spoiling of the monopolist's market. (This last fact reminds us that monopolists produce too little and hire too few factors.)

6. We must slightly qualify our theory if there are technical discontinuities in the substitutability of different factors in production; but these cases of fixed-proportions will not spoil our theory of production. The firm will then work with various combinations of more than one factor and will find it easier rather than harder to make all its decisions. Its derived demands for the separate factors will still be perfectly well determined—although possibly inelastic and discontinuous in patches.

In the next few chapters we shall apply these principles of derived demand to show how supply and demand operate in the factor markets to determine rents, wages, and other factor-prices. An Appendix to this chapter gives a review of the theory of production for those interested in a more geometrical approach.

QUESTIONS FOR DISCUSSION

1. What are the two major production problems a firm must solve? How would the responsibility be divided up among engineers, cost accountants, personnel people, etc.?

2. Convince a skeptic of the truth of the rule that to reach a Least-Cost

point you must equalize the marginal-productivity-per-dollar spent on every factor. Show this to be true even when we have not yet decided on the Best-Profit output.

3. Define marginal-revenue-product, distinguishing it from marginal-physical-product. Give common-sense explanation to show that profit isn't at a maximum unless each factor-price exactly equals its marginal-revenue-product.

4. Wheat can be grown with various combinations of land, machinery, labor and fertilizer. What information is necessary in order to decide what combination should be chosen? Give the steps of your decisions.

5. A firm finds that the demand for its product has increased (the demand curve has shifted to the right). Explain the process that it should follow in order to reach a new equilibrium with respect to price, output, and quantities of factors hired.

6. Show that when a factor-price falls there is (a) a substitution-effect and (b) an output-effect that tends further to increase the demand for the factor. Show that the factor demand curve slopes down because of (c) diminishing physical returns, and (d) diminishing dollar returns. (Use Fig. 2.)

7. Give examples of derived demand and joint demand.

8. Give examples of discontinuities and lack of substitutability. Does this make the Least-Cost and Best-Profit questions more or less difficult?

9. Review your understanding of the following concepts:

For Whom, How, factor pricing, distribution theory
production function
marginal-product, marginal-physical-product, marginal-revenue-product, marginal-physical-product per last dollar spent on each factor
diminishing returns

substitution rule of Least Cost
$MR = MC$ *and Best-Profit Q*
monopoly output and factor restrictions
technical lack of substitutability
derived demand
joint demand

APPENDIX: GRAPHICAL DEPICTION OF PRODUCTION THEORY

This chapter's production theory can be graphically presented. Table 2 is a numerical example of a simple production function relating output to two inputs: labor and capital. It is in the form of a two-way table, looking like a baseball schedule or a mileage chart of distances between cities.

Along the left-hand side are listed the varying amounts of capital, going from 1 unit up through 6. Along the bottom are listed amounts of labor, going from 1 through 6. Output corresponding to the specified capital row and labor column is listed inside the table.

If we are interested in knowing exactly what output there will be when 5 units of capital and 2 units of labor are available, we count up 5 units of capital and then go over 2 units of labor. The answer is seen to be 448 units of product. Similarly, we find that 3 units of capital and 6 of labor will produce 600 units of output. Thus, for any combination of labor and capital, the production function tells us how much product we shall have (using, of course, best methods as decided by the technical engineer).

The Law of Diminishing Marginal-Physical-Product

The law of diminishing returns can be nicely illustrated by Table 2.

First recall that we have given the name "marginal-physical-product of labor" to the extra production resulting from *one* additional unit of labor. At any point in Table 2 the marginal-physical-product of labor can be derived by subtracting the given number (representing product at that point) from the number on its right lying in the same row. Thus, when there are 2 units of capital and 4 units of labor, the marginal-physical-product of an additional laborer would be

48, or the number 448 minus the number 400.

By the "marginal-physical-product of capital" we mean, of course, the extra product resulting from one additional unit of capital, labor being held constant. It involves a comparison of adjacent items in a given column. Thus, when there are 2 units of capital and 4 units of labor, the marginal-physical-product of capital is 90, or 490 − 400. The reader should be able to compute the marginal-physical-product of labor or capital at any point inside the table.

Having defined what we mean by the marginal-physical-product of an input, we are now in a position to restate the law of diminishing returns:

As we hold a fixed input constant and increase a variable input, the marginal-physical-product of the variable input will decline—at least after a point.

To illustrate this, hold capital constant in Table 2 by sticking to a given row—say that corresponding to capital equal to 2 units. Now let labor increase from 1 to 2 units,

The production function summarizes technology:

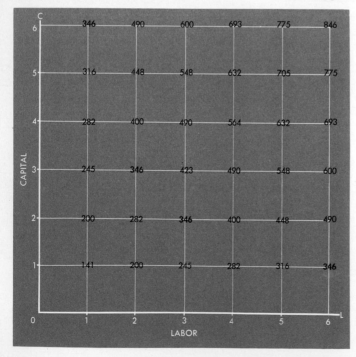

Table 2. Production function relating amount of output to varying combinations of labor and capital input. When you have 3 capital units and 2 labor units available, the engineer tells you your maximum obtainable output is 346 units. Note the different ways to produce 346; and to produce 490.

How we graphically find Least-Cost point:

1st, factors can be substituted to produce the same output

	Labor L	Capital C	Total cost when $P_L = \$2$ $P_C = \$3$	Total cost when $P_L = \$2$ $P_C = \$1$
A	1	6	$20	—
B	2	3	13	$7
C	3	2	12	—
D	6	1	15	—

Table 3. Equal-output factor combinations. More labor can be substituted for less capital to produce 346 units. When $P_L = \$2$ and $P_c = \$3$, calculate total of wage cost plus capital cost to show that their combination gives lowest cost $12 at C. Show that lowering P_c to $1 causes capital to be substituted for labor as you move from C to B.

from 2 to 3 units, and so forth. What happens to product at each step?

As labor goes from 1 to 2 units, product increases from 200 to 282 units, or by 82 units. But the next dose of labor adds only 64 units, or 346 − 282. Diminishing returns has set in! Still further additions of a single unit of labor give us, respectively, only 54 extra units of output, 48 units, and finally only 42 units. The reader should check some other row to verify that the law of diminishing returns holds there too. He should also verify that the same law holds true when labor is held constant and capital is added in a number of steps. (Hint: Examine the changes in product in any *column*.)

At this point, it is well to recall the explanation given for diminishing returns. In Chapter 2, this was attributed to the fact that the fixed factor decreases *relative* to the variable factor. Each unit of the variable factor has less and less of the fixed factor to work with, and it is only natural that extra product should begin to fall off.

If this explanation is to hold water, there should be no diminishing returns when both factors are increased in proportion. When labor increases from 1 to 2 and capital *simultaneously* increases from 1 to 2, we should get the same increase in product as when both increase simultaneously from 2 to 3. This can be verified from Table 2.[1] In the first move we go from 141 to 282, and in the second move the product increases

from 282 to 423, an equal jump of 141 units.

Also, this explanation of diminishing returns in terms of the proportions of the inputs would lead us to expect that increasing capital will improve the marginal-physical-product of labor. Again this can be verified from our table: The fifth unit of labor adds 48 units of product when there are only 2 units of capital; but at 3 units of capital, a fifth unit of labor adds 58 units of product.

Least-Cost Factor Combination for a Given Output

The numerical production function shows that the engineer is not able to tell us definitely how any given output is to be produced. There is more than one way to kill a cat. And there is more than one way to produce any given output. Thus, the bold-face numbers in Table 2 show that the output $q = 346$ can be produced in any one of the ways shown in Table 3.[2]

As far as the engineer is concerned, each of these combinations is equally good at producing an output of 346 units. But the accountant, interested in keeping profits of the firm at a maximum and costs at a minimum,

---

[1] Not all production functions met with in real economic life would have these special properties of so-called "constant returns to scale." Recall Chapter 2's discussion of increasing returns to scale or economies of mass production.

[2] You can and should make up a similar table for output equal to 490 or some other number.

2d, equal-output factor combinations can also be graphed

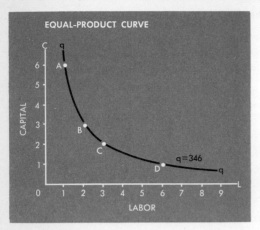

Fig. 3. All the points on the curve represent the different combinations of capital and labor that can be used to produce the same 346 units of output.

knows that only one of these four combinations will give Least Cost. Just which one will depend, of course, on the respective prices of the two factors of production.

Let's suppose that the price of labor is $2 and the price of capital $3. Then the sum of the labor and capital costs in situation A will be $20 $(=1 \times \$2 + 6 \times \$3)$. And costs of B, C, and D will be respectively, $13, $12, $15. At these stated input prices, there is no question but that C is the best way of producing the given out-put.

If either of the prices of the inputs changes, the equilibrium proportion of the inputs will always change so as to use *less* of the input that has gone up relatively most in price. Thus, if labor stays at $2 per unit but capital falls to $1 per unit, the new optimal combination will be B, where more capital is used and less labor and where total cost is only $7. The reader should verify this by computing the new total expense of all other combinations and seeing that they are higher. (Pencil in missing costs in Table 3).

Exactly the same sort of thing can be done for any other output; as soon as all input prices are known, we can experiment until we have found the Least-Cost input combination. (To clinch your understanding of the principles involved, work out the optimum production decision and cost for out-

put equal to 490 units when price of labor is $2 and price of capital is $3.)

Equal-Product and Equal-Cost Contours: Graph of Least-Cost Position

The common-sense numerical analysis of the way in which a firm will combine inputs to minimize costs can be made more vivid by the use of diagrams. From the production schedule we can draw a picture of the different input combinations that will produce a given output. Figure 3 is the exact counterpart of Table 3. In it the smooth curve indicates the different combinations of labor and capital that yield an output of 346 units. This could be called a "production-indifference curve" by analogy with the consumer's indifference curve of the Appendix to Chapter 23. But a more expressive name would be to call it an "equal-product" curve. (You should be able to draw in on Fig. 3, as a dotted curve, the corresponding equal-product curve for output equal to 490. You should realize that an infinite number of such equal-product contour lines could be drawn in, just as a topographical or weather map could be covered with an indefinitely large number of equal-altitude or equal-barometric-pressure contour lines.)

Given the price of labor and capital, the firm can evaluate the total cost for points A, B, C, and D or for any other point on the

3d, equal-cost lines are parallel contours

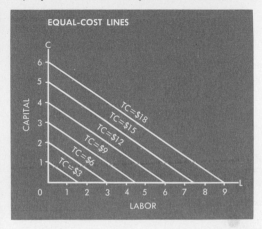

Fig. 4. Every point on a given line represents the same total cost. The lines are straight because of constant factor-prices, and they all have a numerical slope equal to the ratio of labor price to capital price, $2/$3 and hence are parallel.

equal-product curve. Obviously, it will be maximizing its profits only when it has found that optimum point on the equal-product curve at which it reaches Least Cost. Purely as a graphical trick, the firm might try to save itself much tedious arithmetical computation by evaluating once and for all the total cost of every possible factor combination of capital and labor. This is done in Fig. 4, where the family of parallel straight lines represents all possible equal-cost curves when the price of labor is $2 and the price of capital $3.

To find the total cost for any point we have simply to read off the number appended to the equal-cost line going through that point. The lines are all straight and parallel because the firm is assumed to be able to buy all it wishes of either input at constant prices. The lines are somewhat flatter than 45° because the price of labor P_L is somewhat less than the price of capital P_C. More precisely, we can always say that the arithmetic value of the slope of each equal-cost line must equal the ratio of the price of labor to that of capital—in this case $2/3$.[1]

It is now easy to recognize the optimum equilibrium input position of the firm at which total costs are minimized for the given output. The single equal-product curve has superimposed upon it the family of equal-cost lines. This is shown in Fig. 5. The firm will always keep moving along the heavy concave curve of Fig. 5 as long as it is able to cross over to lower cost lines. Its equilibrium will, therefore, not be at A, B, or D. It will be at C, *where the equal-product curve touches (but does not cross) the lowest equal-cost line.* This is, of course, a point of tangency, where the slope of the equal-product curve just matches the slope of an equal-cost line and the curves are just kissing.

We already know that the slope of the equal-cost curves is P_L/P_C. But what is the

_____
[1] The careful reader will notice the parallel between the geometry of this section and that of the analysis of consumer equilibrium in the Appendix to Chapter 23. Each equal-cost line indicates all of the possible different quantities of labor and of capital that the firm might buy

for any given cost outlay. Each line is straight since its equation is $TC = \$2L + \$3C$. In Chapter 23's Appendix, the consumer is buying goods, not factor services; otherwise his "consumption-possibility line" exactly parallels the equal-cost lines we are now discussing. We can explain similarly why the slope of an equal-cost line equals the ratio of the two prices involved.

But note this difference: The consumer was assumed to have a fixed budget; hence, he had but one consumption-possibility line. The firm is not limited to any particular level of costs; so it must consider many equal-cost lines before discovering its equilibrium.

4th, we move on equal-product curve to Least-Cost line

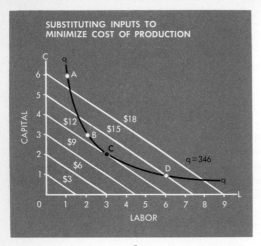

Fig. 5. Where the equal-product curve touches (but does not cross) the lowest total cost contour is the Least-Cost optimum position. This tangency means that factor-prices and marginal-physical-products (or "substitution ratios") are proportional.

slope of the equal-product curve? This slope is a kind of "substitution ratio" between the two factors, and it depends upon the *relative* marginal-physical-products of the two factors of production—just as the rate of substitution between two goods along a consumer's indifference curve was earlier shown to equal the ratio of the marginal or extra utilities of the two goods (Appendix to Chapter 23).

Least-Cost Conditions

Thus, our Least-Cost equilibrium can be defined by any of the following equivalent relations:

1. *The ratio of the marginal-physical-products of any two inputs must equal the ratio of their factor-prices.*
That is,

Substitution ratio or
$$\frac{\text{marginal-physical-product of labor}}{\text{marginal-physical-product of capital}}$$
$$= \frac{\text{price of labor}}{\text{price of capital}}$$

2. *The marginal-physical-product-per-dollar received from the (last) dollar of expenditure must be the same for every productive factor.*
That is,

$$\frac{\text{Marginal-physical-product of } L}{\text{Price of } L}$$
$$= \frac{\text{marginal-physical-product of } C}{\text{price of } C} = \cdots$$

This condition holds for any number of inputs. Relation 2 is discussed in detail in the main body of the chapter. (It could also be derived from relation 1 by transposing terms from one numerator to the other denominator, *i.e.,* by "interchanging means," as is always algebraically permissible.)

But the student should not be satisfied with any such abstract explanation. He should always remember the common-sense economic explanation which shows how a firm will redistribute its expenditure among inputs if any one factor offers a greater return for each last dollar spent on it. Finally, we may state the above Least-Cost relations in the form:

3. *Input prices and their marginal-physical-products must be proportional, the factor of proportionality being marginal cost.*[1]
That is,

---

[1] Why are these marginal-physical-products-per-dollar each equal to the reciprocal of marginal cost, or to $1/MC$? Because extra output per dollar is nothing but the upside down of extra dollars per unit of product, which is what we always have meant by MC.

MC of output $\times$ marginal-physical-product of
labor $=$ price of labor

MC of output $\times$ marginal-physical-product of
capital $=$ price of capital

and so on for any number of inputs.

Marginal-Revenue-Product Condition of Best-Profit

The Least-Cost relationships 1, 2, and 3 are all equivalent. Each holds at every point along the total cost curve, *whatever be the output*. They do *not* tell the firm where it should finally produce.

But now we add the Best-Profit condition that $MR = MC$, and we recall the definition of marginal-revenue-product as equal to marginal-physical-product times marginal revenue. Then we can now combine the Least-Cost relations of 3 and the Best-Profit relationship to reach our final equilibrium condition:

Marginal-revenue-product of labor $=$ price of labor

Marginal-revenue-product of capital $=$ price of capital

and so on for any number of factors.

Thus, our graphical analysis has arrived at the same final result as our common-sense reasoning of this chapter—which tells us that we will stop hiring more of a factor only at the point where the marginal-revenue-product it brings just matches its market price. This is what lies behind the firm's demand curve for a productive factor.

QUESTIONS FOR DISCUSSION

1. Explain what is meant by a production function. Use it to describe the law of diminishing returns. What would the production function be like if there were three factors of production? How would you write it down?

2. If the price of capital increases from $2 to $3, what will happen to the parallel lines of Fig. 4? Why will they be flatter? Why still parallel? What will happen to the new Least-Cost equilibrium point in Fig. 5? Does this agree with common sense?

3. What is the relation between the slope of the equal-product curve and marginal-physical-productivities? Show that the tangency condition of Fig. 5 is essentially the same thing as our previous marginal conditions for Least Cost. What trouble would tangency create for us if the equal-product contour were convex from above instead of being concave from above? (Hint: Would costs be at a minimum or maximum? What would you do about it?)

PRICING OF FACTORS OF PRODUCTION: RENTS
OF LAND AND OTHER RESOURCES

The price of pig,
Is something big;
Because its corn, you'll understand,
Is high-priced, too;
Because it grew
Upon the high-priced farming land.

If you'd know why
That land is high,
Consider this: its price is big
Because it pays
Thereon to raise
The costly corn, the high-priced pig.

H. J. DAVENPORT

The preceding chapter showed how the derived demands for productive inputs are determined for each firm facing given market factor-prices. This
chapter will show how the demands of all firms and industries are added together to form the aggregate market demand for the factor of production in
question. Such a demand curve, together with the supply curve for the factor,
will be found to determine its market price; in this way a market economy
determines the distribution of income to owners of the different factors of
production. The interesting special case of the rents to lands and to other
resources serves to illustrate these general principles. The following chapters
will provide still other important applications.

▶ AGGREGATE MARKET DEMAND CURVES FOR OUTPUT AND FOR EACH INPUT

Figure 1 shows how the demand for a given input, such as fertile corn land,
can be derived from the consumers' demand curve for corn. This assumes,
of course, that we hold constant the prices of such cooperating inputs as fertilizer, labor, and farm machinery. At each land-rent price prevailing in the
market place, any small farmer must decide on the Least-Cost combination of
the various inputs, and he must also decide on the Best-Profit scale of final output to throw onto the market. Therefore, each farmer will want to hire more

and more of corn land up to the point where its marginal-revenue-product is equal to its market rental.

We are dealing with a competitive industry in which the single farmer is too small to affect the market price of corn. In such a perfectly competitive industry, no one need worry about spoiling the market for the previous units of corn being sold; consequently, marginal revenue and price are the same thing. It follows that marginal-revenue-product will be exactly the same thing as marginal-physical-product times corn price. For such a special case of a perfectly competitive commodity market, economists often use the special name of "value of the marginal product" instead of marginal-revenue-product.

▶ FIVE PRINCIPLES OF DERIVED DEMAND

We shall now develop five principles to show what the degree of elasticity of derived demand depends on. In Chapter 28 we'll see that trade-union officials are very interested in these principles. For if it should turn out that the derived demand for labor were very inelastic, the union could hike wages and not fear much of a drop in employment.

The same principles apply to rent of corn land or any other factor demand, and we'll phrase this chapter's discussion in terms of an imposed increase in rent—brought about by fiat, or by contriving a drop in land supply. How inelastic is the derived demand curve for this factor input? We'll give the reasoning behind each of the five principles and then state that principle before going on to the next.

First, note that the higher becomes the rent of corn land, the less of it will be rented, and the less will be the total corn produced. This reduction in the supply of corn will force consumers to move up their market demand curve in Fig. 1a, and this will raise the price of corn. But the higher the price of

Demand for factors is derived from demand for the goods they produce:

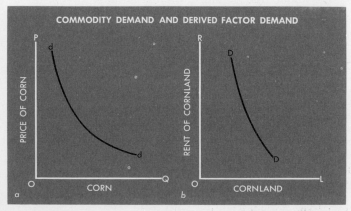

Fig. 1. The derived demand for cornland DD comes from the commodity demand for corn dd. Move dd up and up goes DD.

corn, the less will farmers find it necessary to cut down on their purchases of corn land and other factors. Therefore, a comparison of Figs. 1a and 1b shows us something interesting.

▶ 1. If the demand for the product in Fig. 1a is rather inelastic so that consumers will pay a much higher price before they cut down much on the amount they buy, then the derived demand for the factor of production in Fig. 1b will also tend to be rather inelastic.

　　Raising rent then won't much reduce land demand.

Second, if farmers are spending only a small fraction of their total costs on the renting of corn land, then a large increase in land's rental rates would still increase the total costs of producing corn very little, and the increase in rent would thus have very little effect in raising corn price or in cutting down on corn production. Hence,

▶ 2. The smaller is the proportion spent on a productive factor, the more inelastic the derived demand for it will tend to be.

Sometimes this principle is described as "the importance of being unimportant." When we come to study how a trade-union for one small craft, such as the electricians, can often raise their wages and not suffer much unemployment, this same principle will be seen to be in operation.

Third, even if corn land is a rather unimportant element of total costs so that corn production is not appreciably changed, there will still be some decrease in total land demanded by the farmers; for, as the last chapter showed, the farmers' new Least-Cost combinations of productive inputs will require them to *substitute* whatever other factors they can for corn land. Hence,

▶ 3. Other things being equal, the derived demand for any input will tend to be inelastic when the technical substitutability of other factors for it is very low.

So if fertilizer or machinery or manpower can quite easily make up for any reduction in land area, then a small increase in land rent will result in a very great reduction of the amount demanded of it and its demand will be elastic. If substitutability is low, then our third principle tells us that lack of substitutes will make its demand inelastic.[1]

Our fourth principle can be stated and then explained.

---

[1] Of course, we must not forget cross elasticity of demand. An increase in the price of corn land will tend to increase the demand for all of its substitutes. On the other hand, those inputs which "complement"—rather than "compete" with—corn land will have their demand reduced when the purchase of corn land is reduced. (Fencing might be an example.) And all factors, whether substitutes or complements, will tend to suffer a reduction in demand as a result of any output-effect on corn production necessitated by higher costs of production. All these effects can be expected to influence the prices of the other inputs.

▶ 4. The greater the changes induced in the prices of other factors, the more inelastic will tend to be the demand for the original factor whose price has initially
changed.

Thus, if an increase in land rent results in a great increase in the price
of fertilizer, then there will not be so great a substitution of fertilizer for land;
or if a rise in the rent of land causes the prices of fencing to be greatly
depressed, then the combined cost of land and fences will not have risen so
much, and there will not be so great a reduction in the use of land.[1]

The above four principles governing the inelasticity or elasticity of derived
demand were developed by Alfred Marshall, the distinguished economist we
met in an earlier chapter. They are important, and the reader should review
them carefully. They apply principally to the cases in his time considered to
be the most usual and important, namely, perfectly competitive industries.

Today, economists are aware of the factual importance of imperfect or monopolistic competition. And for such situations a fifth principle may be added:

▶ 5. The derived demand for any factor will tend to be inelastic when the imperfect
competitors hiring it wish to pursue, and are able to pursue, price policies that
cause their total production to change very little as a result of any increase in
factor-costs.

Thus, if oligopolists freeze their good's price, the rise in rent won't cause a
drop in goods demanded and hence there will be less drop in land needed.
Contrariwise, if a factor cost rise is used by oligopolists as the excuse for a
large rise in goods price, this will greatly cut down on sales and production
and lead to a very elastic derived demand for the factor.

On the other hand, if the monopolistic firm should greatly cut down on its
output—either because its sales drop off rapidly when it increases its price
or because it tries to pass on to the consumers a large part of the increase
in its unit costs—then its demand for all factors is likely to decrease strongly
in response to an increase in factor-price.

▶ FACTOR-PRICE DETERMINATION BY SUPPLY AND DEMAND

Up until now we have worked only with the demand curve for a factor, taking its market price as given to the demanders. But obviously it is *all the firms
together* who determine the factor's market price that each small firm faces.
Now we must see how the total demand curve of all for the factor, together
with the total supply curve for the factor, will interact to determine the equilibrium price tending to rule in the market place.

---

[1] Here is an alternative way of phrasing principle 4: Derived demand for one factor will
tend to be *inelastic* if all other factors are in *inelastic supply* to the industry.

Figure 2 shows the total demand curve for corn land, *DD;* it was arrived at by adding together each and every individual firm's demand curve.

Now it is one of the peculiarities of land that, unlike most things, its total supply is relatively fixed by nature and cannot be augmented in response to a higher price for it, and its total cannot be diminished in response to lower land rentals. (Of course, this is not strictly true. Land can sometimes be created by drainage, and the fertility of the existing land can be depleted by overcropping.)

Nonetheless, we can take the complete fixity of its supply as the characteristic feature of land. By tradition, we may confine our discussion to the "original and inexhaustible gift of nature" whose total supply is by definition *completely inelastic*. It was the price or return to such a factor that the classical economists of the last century called "rent." This differs from ordinary usage in which rent or rental is the money paid for the use over a period of time of anything—of a house, truck, etc.

In Figure 2, the supply curve for land *SS* is taken to be completely inelastic because of the fixity of its supply. The demand and supply curves intersect in the equilibrium point *E*. It is toward that factor-price that the rent of land must tend. Why? Because if rent rose above the equilibrium price, the amount of land demanded by all firms would be less than the existing amount that would be supplied; some property owners would be unable to rent their land at all; therefore, they would offer their land for less and thus bid down its rent.

Fixed land must work for what demanders will bid:

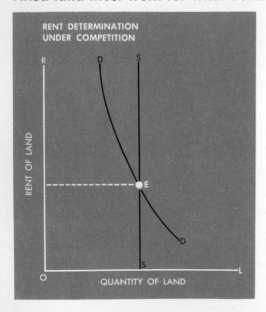

Fig. 2. Perfect inelasticity of supply characterizes the case of so-called "pure economic rent." We run up *SS* curve to demand curve to determine rent.

By similar reasoning, the rent could not long remain below the equilibrium intersection. If it did, you should be able to show how the bidding of unsatisfied firms would force the factor-price back up toward the equilibrium level. Only at a competitive price where total amount demanded of land exactly equals the total supply will there be equilibrium. It is in this sense that supply and demand determine any factor-price.

Note that the man who owns land does not have to be a particularly deserving citizen in order to receive this rental. A virtuous and poor landowner will be given exactly the same rental by competition as will a wealthy wastrel. It is the productivity of the land that is being paid for and not the personal merits of the landowner.

Even this productivity of the land is not something absolute. For example, what would happen if the price of corn were to fall greatly because people began to desire other goods? Then the derived demand for corn land would shift drastically downward and to the left. What will happen to the rentals received by landowners? After a time, rents must sink down to a new equilibrium intersection. The land is not less productive in a technical sense than it was before, and the landlords are neither more nor less virtuous than they were before. But factor demand and supply intersection has changed.

A factor of production like corn land is said to earn a "pure economic rent" because: (1) its total supply is regarded as perfectly inelastic; and for the moment we shall assume that (2) the land *has no other uses,* such as the production of sugar or rye. Adam Smith's great follower in England of the early 1800's, David Ricardo, noted that the case of such an inelastically supplied factor could be described as follows:

It is not really true that the price of corn is high because the price of corn land is high. Actually the reverse is more nearly the truth; the price of corn land is high because the price of corn is high! Its total supply being inelastic, the land will always work for whatever is given to it under competition. Hence the value of the land is completely derived from the value of the product, and not vice versa.[1]

▶ RENT AND COSTS: IMPLICIT VERSUS EXPLICIT RETURNS

Some economists even went so far as to say that "rent does not enter into the cost of production." The last paragraph shows that there is a grain of truth in this. But still this is very dangerous terminology. If you were a farmer trying to

[1] Land is not the only factor whose return may be considered as economic rent. For an example where most of a wage payment is a "pure rent," see Chapter 28. And in the short run, the supply of a machine or plant may be entirely fixed; thus a hydroelectric plant takes a long time to build, still longer to wear out. The return to any factor in temporarily fixed supply is sometimes called a *quasi-rent*—"quasi-" because in the long run, its supply need not be fixed. Those New England farmers who petitioned OPA for higher milk price because of higher cow prices were, without knowing it, illustrating rent and quasi-rent doctrines.

go into the corn-raising business, you would certainly find that the landlord has to be paid like anybody else. You would certainly figure in rent in your cost of production; and if you could not pay it, you would go out of business.

Even if you were a farmer who owned your own land, it would be a mistake to think that rent does not enter into your costs of production. After you had paid all your other bills, including wages to yourself at least as great as what you could earn elsewhere in the market, there would have to be left an amount at least equal to the market rental value of your land. For what if there were not such an amount? Then you would soon find that it would be better for you to rent out your farm on the open market and hire out your own labor to somebody else.

Sometimes economists call rent paid by a man to himself "implicit" rather than "explicit" rent. Very clearly, implicit rent is as much a part of long-run competitive costs as are any other costs, and the same can be said of the implicit wages or implicit interest earned on any other factors that you could sell rather than use personally.

▶ **RENT AND COSTS: RELATIVITY OF VIEWPOINT**

When some economists claim rent doesn't enter into society's cost of production, what are they driving at? They are saying: Since rent is the return to an inelastically supplied factor that would be supplied to the community even at much lower prices, the direction of causation goes as follows, "Goods prices really determine land price—rather than having land price determine goods prices."

We must avoid our old enemy the "fallacy of composition." What appears as a cost of production to each and every firm may *to the industry as a whole* be really a derived price-determin*ed* expense rather than a price-determin*ing* one. More than that, suppose we now assume that the corn-producing industry is just one of very many industries which can use the same land. Then to each *small* industry—such as the buckwheat or rye industry—the supply curve of land may appear to be almost completely horizontal or elastic. This is because that one industry may be too small a part of the total market picture to have any appreciable influence on land rents.

Now put yourself in the shoes of someone who takes the viewpoint of that industry as a whole. Will land then appear to be an element determining the price of rye? Or will it seem like a cost that is determin*ed* by the final price for rye? The answer must definitely in such a case be the former: To a small industry using relatively little of a factor, the factor-price is an important determin*er* of the industry's commodity price, and not vice versa. At the same time to the economy as a whole, the rent of a factor whose total quantity is inelastic can still be said to be more the *result* than the *cause* of the values of the various final products. (The Davenport poem hints at all this.)

To conclude: Whether rent is or is not a price-determining cost depends upon the viewpoint from which we look.

► HENRY GEORGE'S SINGLE-TAX MOVEMENT: TAXATION OF LAND "SURPLUS"

In the last part of the nineteenth century, a western frontier still existed in this country. As more and more people came here from Europe, each acre of land had more and more people to work it. In a sense, therefore, the land became more productive. In any case its competitive rental value certainly tended to rise. This created handsome profits for some of those who were lucky enough to get in on the ground floor and buy land early.

Nor was this true only in agriculture. Men still alive in the Middle West can remember when towns first began. They will tell you how they might have been rich if only they had recognized 70 years ago that the corner of State and Madison would eventually become the center of town and would grow tremenduously in value as a result of the great increase in urban populations.

Sites with good locations earn rents in the same sense that fertile areas do. Many people began to wonder why lucky landowners should be permitted to receive these so-called "unearned land increments." Henry George, a printer who thought much about economics, crystallized these sentiments in the single-tax movement. This had a considerable following a half century ago or more, and there are still some adherents to it; but it is not likely that anyone running on the single-tax ticket will again come so close to being elected mayor of New York City as did George in 1886. Nor is it likely that anyone will soon come along and write so persuasive a bible for the movement as did Henry George in his *Progress and Poverty,* a book which sold millions of copies.

This is not the place to attempt any assessment of the merits and demerits of such a political movement. But its central tenet—that land rent is in the nature of a surplus which can be taxed heavily *without distorting production incentives*—can be examined to illustrate one principle of distribution and taxation.

Suppose that supply and demand create an equilibrium land rent, as in Fig. 3 at E. Now what would happen if we were to introduce a 50 per cent tax on all land rents? Mind you, we are not taxing buildings or improvements; for that certainly would affect the volume of construction activity. All we are taxing is the yield of the naturally fixed supply of agricultural and urban land sites, assuming that this can somehow be identified.

There has been no shift in the total demand curve for land; firms are still willing to pay the same amount as before for the same amount of land. Hence, with land fixed in supply, the market price that they pay must therefore still be at the old intersection E. Why? Because supply has not changed and neither has demand. Because at any higher price than before, some land would have to go without any demanders. And hence in the absence of any monopoly on the part of landlords, rents could not permanently be raised to land users.

Tax on fixed land is shifted back on landlords, skimming off pure rent:

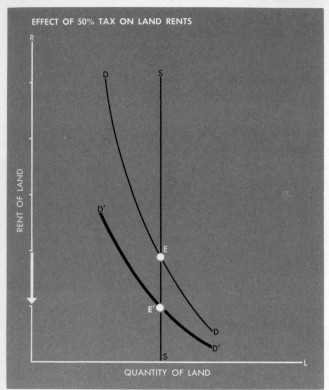

EFFECT OF 50% TAX ON LAND RENTS

Fig. 3. A tax on fixed land leaves rentals paid by users unchanged at *E* but reduces rent retained by landowners to *E'*. (What can the landowners do but accept less return?)

Of course, what the farmer pays and what the landlord receives are now two quite different things. As far as the landlords are concerned, once the government steps in to take its cut of 50 per cent, the effect is just the same as if the net demand to the owners had shifted down from *DD to D'D'*. Landowners' equilibrium return *after taxes* is now only as high as *E'*, or only half as high as *E*. The whole of the tax has been shifted backward onto the owners of the factor in inelastic supply! The landowners will not like this. But under competition there is nothing they can do about it, since they cannot alter the total supply and the land must work for whatever it can get.

Whether or not it is a fair thing to take away part of the return of those who own land is quite another question. Perhaps many voters will feel that such owners are not less deserving than are investors who have put their money into other things, but such a political question has no place in the present discussion. What is relevant is to point out that a similar 50 per cent tax, put upon a factor of production whose total supply is *not* completely inelastic, will certainly produce definite effects on the factor-prices charged in a competitive market. To some extent this tax would distort the pattern of production, and it would shift part of the burden *forward* onto the users of the factor and onto consumers. Thus, if the same acre of land were to be taxed differently when used for wheat rather than corn production, this would certainly have distorting effects on the price of wheat relative to that of corn.

▶ SUPPLY AND DEMAND FOR ANY FACTOR

The competitive determination of land rent by supply and demand is only one instance of the general analysis applicable to any factor of production. How is the rental value per week of a tractor to be determined in a competitive market? We first sum up the derived demands of all business firms for tractors. (Of course, these derived demands have behind them marginal-revenue-product considerations as shown in the last chapter, but this behind-the-scenes relation need not now concern us as we observe the aggregate market demand for this factor.)

In addition to the *DD* curve shown in Fig. 4, we must also have a supply curve such as *SS*. But there is now no reason why the supply curve should be perfectly vertical. It may now be positively elastic, rising upward toward the northeast—being dependent in the case of the tractors on their marginal costs of production. Or if the factor of production were labor, it might be that people would feel they could afford to work *fewer* hours as wages rise, so that the *SS* curve might eventually bend backward and northwestward from the vertical, rather than rising forward.

Factor supply and derived demand together determine income distribution:

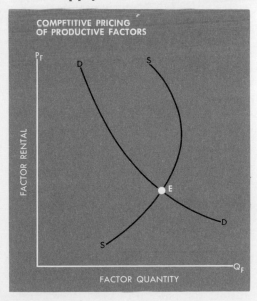

COMPETITIVE PRICING
OF PRODUCTIVE FACTORS

P_F

FACTOR RENTAL

FACTOR QUANTITY

Q_F

Fig. 4. Land's share in national income rises when its rent is bid up. Skilled and unskilled labor shares are, in competitive markets, determined by interplay of factor supply and demand. Same would hold for any factor.

In any case, whether the supply curve is vertically inelastic, positively elastic, or negatively elastic, there will be an *SS* curve as in Fig. 4. Where the demand and supply curves intersect, the final equilibrium factor-price will be set. And if the demand curve for the factor shifts upward, its market price will tend to rise; on the other hand, if the supply offered of any factor increases, so that the supply curve shifts rightward, then the factor-price will tend to fall.

In a competitive market economy, therefore, factor-prices and the distribution of income are not determined at random. There are definite forces of supply and demand operating to create high returns to scarce factors that are very useful in producing the things wanted by people with purchasing power. But the price will drop if more of any factor should become available or if other close substitutes for it are found or if people stop wanting the goods that a factor is best suited to make. Competition gives and competition takes.

▶ **FACTOR PRICING AND EFFICIENCY**

Competitive supply and demand helps determine the For Whom problem of society. Whether or not we like its answer to this distribution question—and in the case of rent Henry George certainly did not—we have to admit that it does contribute to an *efficient* solution of the How problem for society.

Thus, as a result of supply and demand in markets for goods and for factors, in America where land is plentiful and labor scarce we find extensive agriculture. In Europe or Asia, where people are plentiful relative to land, we find intensive agriculture.

Why? Because of government planning? No, not necessarily.

Rather it is the signaling of market pricing that results in efficient How. Land has to be auctioned off at a low price here; labor auctioned off at a high price here. So every farmer, seeking his Least-Cost combination lest he go bankrupt, substitutes land for labor. And abroad, cheap labor gets substituted for land. (More than that: with labor scarce here, we find that fussy vegetables which require much care get priced relatively higher than those which lend themselves to extensive methods. So the resulting high commodity prices tend to make us substitute the cheaper goods in our diet for the more expensive ones. Abroad the opposite commodity substitutions take place. Hence, the pricing system signals best commodity substitutions as well as best factor substitutions.)

Do you now believe that charging rent has a function—even if you later tax part of it away? Then you are ready to appreciate that some of the troubles in the real world come from the fact that there is no way to charge the appropriate rents. Here are some examples.

Item: The sea is free to all. So every one fishes in it until the fish are all killed off. If society could somehow charge rents for commercial fishing licenses, we might in the long run all be better off—including fishermen!

Item: Our roads get very crowded on weekends and during the rush hour. We usually can't charge tolls or rents. If we could, we might coax shoppers and people who are getting very little pleasure from driving to do their driving at some less crowded time.

Item: In a Boston suburb, the cost of collecting money from parking meters turned out to be just equal to the revenues raised by the 5-cent charges. Many said, "Let's cut out the meters." Three economic professors who lived in town argued that the point in making charges was to make the limited parking space go around and be divided among those (nickel voters!) who desired it most. The point of the meters was not, so said the economists, to raise money. Which was right? The group who said "Down with meters," or the learned professors?

Other examples of how charging rent leads to efficient How—even though it may lead to For Whom considered ethically dubious—could be given. But the point has been made.

► **CONCLUSIONS**

The same general principles determining land rent also determine the prices of all inputs; the rental of threshing machines or of trucks is determined in essentially the same way. We might even go so far as to say that wages are the rentals paid for the use of a man's personal services for a day or a week or a year. This may seem a strange use of terms; but if you think about it, you will recognize that every agreement to hire labor is really for some limited period of time. By outright purchase, you might avoid ever renting any kind of land. But in our society, labor is one of the few productive factors that cannot legally be bought outright. Labor can only be rented, and the wage rate is really a rental.

The next chapter will deal with the peculiar problems of wages and the labor market. Chapter 29 will analyze the problems of capital and interest, which will be shown to be important in determining the supply of durable goods available for rental and use.

SUMMARY

1. Factor demand curves are derived from commodity demand curves. An upward shift in the latter causes a similar upward shift in the former.

2. Five principles determine how inelastic the derived demand for any factor of production is likely to be. A factor's demand will tend to be very inelastic *(a)* to the extent that the demand curves for its final products are *in-*

elastic; (*b*) to the extent that it represents only a small, *unimportant fraction* of total costs of production of the finished products; (*c*) to the extent that it has no readily *substitutable* rival factors of production; and finally (*d*) to the extent that the *induced changes in other factors' prices* are large. A fifth principle may be added in the case of imperfect or monopolistic competition: Demand for a factor will tend to be most inelastic when the firms hiring it tend to pursue price policies that keep their total *output from changing* very much.

3. We add all the derived demands for a factor to get the aggregate demand curve. This, together with the specified supply curve of the factor, can be expected to determine an equilibrium intersection. At the equilibrium market price for the factor of production, the amounts demanded and supplied will be exactly equal—only there will factor-price have no tendency to change. Anywhere above the equilibrium price, suppliers will tend to undercut the market and to cause price to fall; anywhere below the equilibrium price, demanders will bid the price upward, restoring the equilibrium.

4. The unchangeable quantity of natural land is an interesting special case where the supply curve happens to be perfectly vertical and inelastic. In such a so-called *pure* rent case, competition will still determine an equilibrium market rental. But in this case, we are faced with a cost element that is more price-determin*ed* than price-determin*ing*; the land rent is more the result of the market prices for the finished commodities than their cause. Yet we must not forget that to any small firm, or to any industry too small to affect appreciably the total demand for land, rent will still seem to enter explicitly or implicitly into the cost of production just like any other expense. To such a small industry, rent appears to be as much price-determining as any other cost element.

From the standpoint of the community as a whole, the rent of an inelastically supplied factor will be reckoned in the national income at its full dollar value, like anything else. But below the veil of money, it still remains true that this factor would be willing to work for less if it had to, and in that sense its return is in the nature of a "surplus" rather than in the nature of a reward necessary to coax out the factor supply. This provides the basis for Henry George's "single-tax" proposals, aimed to tax the unearned increment of land value— and without any shifting forward of the tax to the consumer or distorting effects on production.

5. Whatever some may feel about the ethical nicety of its answer to the For Whom problem, proper factor pricing does under perfect competition lead to efficient solution of society's How problem. Indeed, *not charging rents* may cause inefficient overcrowding in many situations.

6. The general principles of supply and demand can also be used to explain the competitive price determination of all services other than those of land. In common everyday usage, we speak of rent or rental as the price paid for the use

of any input, whether the factor's supply curve is inelastic or not. The rental of all inputs—including the wages that have to be paid for the use of the services of human beings—are determined in a competitive system by supply and demand. But there are special peculiarities to the labor market, and also there are special problems connected with interest rates and capital valuations.

The Appendix to this chapter uses the simple case of an island community to illustrate how the marginal-products of different factors interact to determine the general pattern of factor supply and demand. Those who wish to move on directly to the next chapters may omit this bird's-eye view of distribution reduced to its lowest terms.

QUESTIONS FOR DISCUSSION

1. The demand for permanent waves is rather elastic. What can you say about the derived demand for beauty operators? Which of the four principles of derived demand does this illustrate? Give an example of an industry of very inelastic demand and inelastic derived demand for factors.

2. Only a few drops of Angostura Bitters are used in a cocktail. Would you expect the demand for them to be inelastic or elastic? Why? Most of a laundry's expense consists of wages. Would this be a factor favorable or unfavorable to a union request for higher wages? Why?

3. Few lubricants with the quality of oil exist. How is demand elasticity for oil affected by this fact? Why would a change in the price of oil from one state alone be expected to elicit an elastic demand?

4. Electricians in a textile plant realize that they are an unimportant part of total costs. This tempts them to ask for a wage increase. But they know that all the other unions in the plant will then insist on an equal pay increase. So?

5. You work for a public utility whose price is fixed by law. Why will demand for your services be more inelastic than if you worked for a competitive company that could raise its price? Suppose the regulatory authority will permit the utility to raise its price as costs rise; how will your conclusion about inelasticity be affected?

6. "Value of the marginal-product" is defined as MPP × price of the product; "marginal-revenue-product," as MPP × marginal revenue. Which of these two values is lower for a firm in an imperfectly competitive industry? In a perfectly competitive industry? (MPP = marginal-physical-product.)

7. Define the "pure rent" case. Explain the sense in which the price of such a factor is "price-determined" rather than "price-determining." Show that, nonetheless, an increase in the availability of the rent-earning factor will depress its return and lower commodity prices that use much of it.

8. What was the Henry George single-tax movement all about? Use a diagram to show what the effect would be of taxing pure rent.

9. Review your understanding of the following concepts:

derived demand

elastic and inelastic derived demand

inelastic product demand, "un-importance," lack of technical substitutability, inelastic supply of cooperating factors, monopoly price rigidity

price-determined expense versus price-determining expense

inelastic supply of God-given land, pure rent

single tax, backward shifting of land tax

factor price equilibrium

price signaling of efficient factor and commodity substitutions

How, For Whom, and rents

APPENDIX: BIRD'S-EYE VIEW OF MARGINAL-PRODUCTS AND DISTRIBUTION IN THE SIMPLEST CASE

The supplies and demands for all factors interact with each other and with the supplies and demands for all commodities. The result of this competitive process is a set of equilibrium factor and commodity prices and a set of equilibrium quantities for all inputs and outputs. No more than this need be said in an introduction to economics. However, many people feel happier about a new subject if they can work out carefully a simplified case. That is the purpose of this Appendix: to show how marginal-products can distribute society's product.

Basic Assumptions

Imagine an island newly discovered off the coast of Europe. Suppose it consists of 1,000 square miles of land of uniform quality, well-suited to the production of food. Think of food as being a single, composite commodity, and imagine that it is the only commodity anyone ever wants to produce and consume. Only two productive factors are needed to produce this food: land and labor. A known quantity of food will always result whenever any given quantity of land is worked by any given quantity of labor. We can assume that the ownership of the newly found land has already been determined. It will not matter if the owners live

on the island or are absentee landlords; the laborers who work on any parcel of land will operate efficiently in a routine manner without the need of any management.

If the island is conveniently near Europe so that workers can move back and forth across the water easily—travel cost is negligible, and it is as pleasant to live on the island as elsewhere—then the wage rate set in Europe will also be the wage rate that will ultimately have to prevail on our island. This may take a little time, since people will have to move to the island whenever wages there are higher than in Europe and back to Europe when wages are higher there than on the island. The island is not nearly big enough to change the general level of wages in Europe (just as a small bay in the ocean is so small that the level of water in it is determined by the level of water in the wide ocean rather than vice versa).

The common level of wages can be thought of as being paid in units of food. Or if we use a one-dollar market basket of food for our unit of food, we can think of real wages as being paid in ordinary dollars. For example, a man can be thought of as earning $1,000 per year or as earning 1,000 units of food per year.

Determination of Equilibrium

Now our stage is set. Initially, there are no workers at all on the island. But confronted with a $1,000 annual wage rate at which people can be drawn from Europe, the owners of land will now be able to arrive at their individual demands for labor. The total amount of labor demanded will be 1,000 times the amount demanded on each square-mile farm. This is because we are making the important special assumption that it is only the *proportion* of land to labor that counts, and not the absolute *scale*. Two hundred men, working on 2 square miles of land, would produce exactly twice the quantity of food obtained when one hundred men work on 1 square mile.

But what determines the demand for labor on each unit of land? Our theory of production earlier told us that every prudent employer will add labor to his land up to the point where labor's marginal-revenue-product is just equal to its wage rate. Because food is our only product, and because its price is perfectly fixed at the defined level of $1, it is clear that marginal-revenue-product and marginal-physical-prod-

uct are exactly the same thing: the former is one times the latter, and for brevity we can speak simply of marginal-product. So to find the demand for labor, we must first investigate marginal-product.

Laws of Marginal-Product

Figure 5 shows the extra production of food that results when we add successively more units of labor to the same square mile of land. The first few men have a very great marginal-product, about 3,000 food units or dollars per year, as shown by the very tall vertical slab marked (*a*). Because of the law of diminishing returns, we know that adding more men to the same unit of land will cause their marginal-product to fall. This is shown by the shorter vertical slab (*b*). As we add still more units of labor, the marginal-product falls still lower and lower. Finally, when we have 100 units of labor working, the very last unit of labor has a marginal-product of only 1,000 food units; and at 200 units of labor, marginal-product has fallen to less than 800 food units.

This marginal-product curve in Fig. 5 tells us all there is to know about our sim-

Each new man adds less marginal-product:

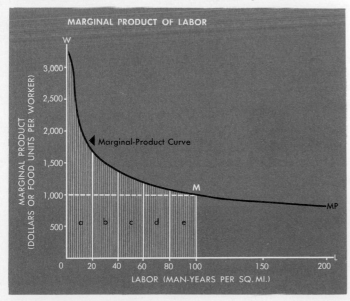

Fig. 5. Each extra man adds less and less to total product, as shown by the shorter and shorter vertical slabs. Summing all of these vertical slabs gives us the total product as an area.

ple production function—about the technical law which determines the quantity of food to be had from different quantities of land and of labor. We can read off from Fig. 5 not only *marginal*-product but *total* product, thus:

When there is zero labor, the food product is zero. When one man is put to work, we get a product of about 3,000 units as represented by a very thin slice on the left-hand side of slab (*a*). When 20 men are at work on our square mile, what is the total product? It is the sum of all the vertical slices making up the area of slab (*a*). Similarly, the sum of areas of the slabs, (*a*) + (*b*) + (*c*) + (*d*) + (*e*), must equal the total product being produced on each square mile by the joint cooperation of land and the stated quantity of labor, 100 units. This total works out to 150,000 units of food produced on 1 square mile of land by 100 workers.

The law of diminishing returns has told us that this total product is increasing as we add labor, but increasing at a decreasing rate. If we had wanted to avoid any diminishing returns, we should have had to increase land at the same time that we increased labor, so that the whole scale would have grown together with no change in any proportions.

Identity of Marginal-Product Curve and Demand for Labor

Now we can determine the demand for labor on each farm. Recall the rule that the prudent landlord must follow in our simple case: Hire labor up to the point where labor's marginal-product is just equal to the wage. Confronted with any wage rate that he must pay for the hire of labor, our landlord will simply go to the marginal-product curve of Fig. 5. At a high real wage, he will hire little labor; and when the wage level in Europe and elsewhere should fall it will pay him to put more labor to work.

Since the rule is to equate marginal-product with the wage, the marginal-product curve and the demand curve are one and the same. (Thus, if the Europe-set wage were 1,000 dollars or food units annually, then 100 laborers would be hired on each square-mile farm, as shown at the point *M* in Fig. 5.)

Total Demand and Supply

Now we can derive the island's total demand for labor. It is *DD* in Fig. 6. Since there are 1,000 square miles on the island, this curve is nothing but a 1,000-fold scale enlargement of the Fig. 5 curve of labor's marginal-product on a single unit of land. Because of the law of diminishing produc-

Behind society's demand is marginal-product:

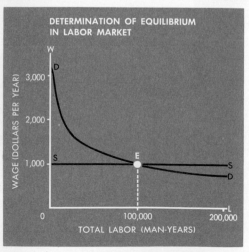

Fig. 6. Summing the marginal-product curves for all of the 1,000 square-mile farms gives us the total demand curve for labor. The supply curve is given by the wage-rate abroad. Equilibrium is at *E* intersection.

tivity, this demand curve is a declining one.

The long-run supply curve of labor can be indicated by SS and must be drawn horizontally at the wage level set to our island by Europe and the rest of the world. Where the curves of supply and demand intersect is our equilibrium E. It tells us in this case what we already know—that wages will be at the world-set level of $1,000 per year. But it tells us more than that: It also tells us exactly how many people will be employed on our island and how much will be the total production.

The equilibrium quantity of labor for the island will be 1,000 times the equilibrium amount demanded at the going wage for each 1-square-mile unit of land (or a total of 1,000 times 100 laborers = 100,000 laborers, as shown below E in Fig. 6). The equilibrium total product, or national income, will be 1,000 times the sum of all the vertical slabs of Fig. 5, or 1,000 times $150,000 = 150 million dollars.

Figure 7, which is a redrawing of Fig. 6, shows the total of national product as the shaded area ODEL. Of the 150-million-dollar total, it turns out that exactly two-thirds, or 100 million, goes as wages to labor; this is because each of the 100,000 laborers had to be paid 1,000 dollars or food units a year. Wages are shown by the area of the rectangle OWEL, its altitude being the wage and its base the number of workers.

Who gets the rest? Obviously, on each square mile of land, whatever product is left after the workers get paid off must go as a residual to the owner of the land. Who else could claim it under a system of private property? Each farm yields 50,000 food units to the landowner after 100 laborers each receive 1,000 food units.

How much then is total rent? Multiplying 1,000 times the rents received on each unit of land gives us the total rents received by all landowners. This is the remaining one-third of the total of national product, or 50 million dollars' worth of food. Total rents are shown by the triangular area WDE, which is a 1,000-fold enlargement of the similar triangular area of Fig. 5.

(To test his understanding of this, the reader should draw in the corresponding rectangle for wages and triangle for rent when the wage has fallen down to $800. With labor cheaper, every unit of land can then have more labor to work on it and hence its rent will go up. What area will represent the increase in rent? Will the total of wages have to go down just because the wage per worker has gone down? Explain why not in common-sense terms, and

Marginal-product principles determine factor shares of income:

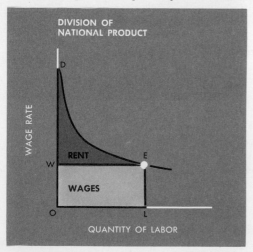

DIVISION OF
NATIONAL PRODUCT

WAGE RATE

RENT

WAGES

QUANTITY OF LABOR

Fig. 7. Total wages is rectangle's area: the wage-rate altitude times labor-quantity base. Rent gets what's left over, as shown by the residual triangle WED. Total product, the sum of wage-rectangle plus rent-triangle areas, is area under DE demand curve of society's marginal-product.

then see if you can show that the answer to this question depends on a comparison of certain areas. Which ones?) [1]

Competitive Equilibrium a Good Thing?

We've now completed a sketch of how the marginal-product theory "distributes" total product between two factors—land and labor—in a simplified one-good world.[2]

We've simply been observing how hard-boiled competition would work itself out under simple conditions. Just as the jungle has its laws without regard to right and wrong, so does the competitive market have its brute facts.

But did you notice one efficient thing that happened? Without a planning board, *society got its food produced in the most efficient way.* How did that happen? Well, efficiency certainly requires that the homogeneous land and labor everywhere be combined in exactly the same proportions. (Proof: Suppose Congress made half the country use much labor per acre, the other half little. The law of diminishing returns tells us that the shift of workers to the dense half causes a fall in the extra product they produce—a fall compared to what they could have produced higher up on their marginal-product curve when each had more land to work with. So equating marginal-products and factor proportions everywhere is the rule for efficient production. QED.)

---

[1] It happens in this example that the share of rent in the national product remains at about one-third after the increase in population and lowering of wage. This is a special case: A reduction in wages would always increase the absolute total of land rent, but total product might change by a greater or lesser percentage than did rent.

[2] Earlier editions showed what happens when lands differ in quality and earn "differential rents." And showed what happens when there are many factors other than land and labor, with supply curves of any shape. But all that proved long for a first book. An eager reader might try his hand at the hard last three discussion questions at the end of this Appendix.

Ruthless competition with only the commercially fittest surviving did bring about the desirable equality everywhere of factor proportions and marginal-products. How did it do this? By landlords' seeking maximum rents; by workers' seeking maximum wages; by market prices' being forced to lowest costs of production—these were the vital processes. (Warning: A tendency toward "increasing returns to scale" would have killed off perfect competition, and have brought in monopoly to spoil the whole story.)

We'll see again in Chapter 30's Appendix that competitive pricing may help efficiently solve the How problem of any society. We'll see that charging a rent for God-given land is necessary if such scarce land is to be rightly allocated.

All right. But does this mean that market pricing creates Utopia? Does it mean that a few landlords who may do nothing and who may have inherited their land from ancestors who first stole it—that such men should, as in our example, get one-third the nation's product? So asks the radical critic.

On this ethical question, economists' analysis of pricing does not pronounce. Our proof of competition's efficiency said nothing about For Whom output is to be produced. If workers owned land and collected the rent, things might have worked just as well. And remember Henry George. If the state owned the land, charging actual prices for it (or, as we'll see in Chapter 30's Appendix, possibly setting up fictitious accounting prices for land use) that too could be a way of getting efficiency.

The moral? Perhaps this: At this point, suspend judgment on the ethical problems of distribution—on the For Whom. And when you do begin to tackle such ethical questions, don't forget efficiency.

Conclusion: Intercommodity Substitution and Qualifications

It is not hard to show what happens when we drop the simplified case of a single product. As any factor, such as machine tools, becomes more plentiful, its marginal-revenue-product and rental will tend to fall. Not only will more of it tend to be substituted for other factors in each line of production—in addition, those special goods which happen to use much of this factor in their production will fall in price more than will prices generally. This relative price drop will tend to cause consumers to buy more of such cheapened goods, and in this way the derived demand for the factor will become even more elastic.

Thus, *in addition to intracommodity technical substitutability between factors, there is also intercommodity substitutability resulting from differential price effects.* (This suggests how distribution will be determined even when the continuous substitutability assumptions of the marginal-product theory of production break down. If factors must be used in fixed-proportions, their derived demands are still perfectly well determined. These demands, together with supply relations, help determine all prices. Intercommodity substitutions now become extremely

important, as do the supply conditions for the factors.) [1]

Finally, note this. To understand the different aspects of the problem of distribution in our island community is to begin to understand much of the history of the classical and modern theories of distribution and of competitive pricing. But it does not tell us much about the cases of monopolistic competition: (1) where there may be economies of scale that lead to a few firms gaining semimonopoly power and (2) where consumers may develop a special preference for products that can be produced only by factors owned by a single firm. As Chapter 30 shows, in these cases the firms may earn "monopoly profits" or "monopoly rents" which the attempted competition of other firms cannot take away from them. To "natural scarcity" is then being added artificial or "contrived scarcity"—brought about by someone's holding in his supply for fear of "spoiling the market."

---

[1] An example illustrates how intercommodity substitutions can determine factor-prices even in the worst case of fixed-proportions, *e.g.*, where 1 unit of machinery *and* 1 unit of labor are needed to produce a unit of wine and where 1 unit of machines *and* 2 units of labor are needed to produce a unit of bread. Assume that wine sells for $10 per unit and bread for $12. Bread differs from wine by $2 in price and cost; and in terms of inputs, it differs by what? By 1 extra unit of labor. Hence wages must be exactly $2 per unit (= $12 − $10), and machines must be priced at $8 per unit (= $10 − $2, or $12 − 2 × $2). So from commodity prices we can obtain factor-prices—even in this fixed-proportions case.

You will realize that the prices of wine and bread had also to be determined by supply and demand and will depend in part upon how much income goes to hungry laborers and thirsty machine owners and upon the initial supplies of the factors. For example, imagine that we started

with a supply of 200 machines and 300 laborers, and let us summarize the resulting general equilibrium.

If we had started with factors in a 1:1 ratio—say 200 of each—and *if* we require them to be fully employed, they would *all* have to go into wine production. We could not possibly produce any bread and still keep all our factors employed. Similarly, if our factor totals were in a 1:2 proportion—say 200 machines, 400 laborers—we should have to produce nothing but bread.

But we start with a halfway ratio—200:300. Common sense and simple algebra tell us that we must then split our machines half and half between the two industries, thereby using up the total of both factors in producing 100 wine units and 100 bread units. The prices of these supplies of goods would be then determined by the interplay of competitive supply and demand for the two goods and for the two factors, and thus we end up at the above equilibrium prices for goods and services. (NOTE: A factor-price can be made zero by some demand patterns, but this "free factor" possibility is neglected for simplicity.)

SUMMARY TO APPENDIX

1. In a simple world where food is produced by land and labor, the curve of labor demanded by the owner of one unit of land will be the curve of falling marginal-product of labor. The total demand curve for labor will be a 1,000-fold enlargement of the demand on each of the 1,000 square miles. Where the supply curve of labor intersects with the demand curve will be the equilibrium wage and quantity of labor. The total product left over from the harvest after the laborers have all been paid their wage is the *residual* left over for rent. Rent is represented by a triangular shape on labor's marginal-product diagram, while wages are represented by the rectangular area.

2. But intermediate texts show that the factors can all be treated perfectly symmetrically. We can hold labor constant and add land to it. Workers' demand for land at any given rental will be limited by the marginal-product curve of land. The aggregate demand for land is the magnification of the demand of each group of workers, the extent of the magnification depending upon the total number of workers.

The resulting equilibrium between the supply and demand for land will necessarily yield exactly the same marginal-product rental for land as was arrived at by the residual method. Otherwise, it would no longer be a matter of indifference as to

whether (*a*) landowners hire labor or (*b*) laborers hire land.

3. When many products are brought into the picture, we can go beyond the possibility of *intracommodity technical substitution* of other factors for a factor which has become relatively dear. In addition, there will now be *intercommodity substitutions* by the consumer, who will begin to buy less of the now dearer goods using relatively much of the expensive factor and who will buy more of the now cheaper goods using relatively little of it. Even in the worst case where the factor proportions are fixed within each industry, these differential commodity price changes can, together with the supply conditions for the factors, determine the pattern of distribution. Hence, the general theory of competitive supply and demand transcends the theory of marginal-products but in no way contradicts it.

4. So long as there is no technological tendency toward "increasing returns to scale," free competition will be self-policing. An invisible hand, so to speak, will lead competitive pricing to an efficient solution of society's How problem. But until we are supplied with ethical judgments about the ownership of productive factors—about the distribution of wealth—we must reserve judgment concerning how well competitive pricing solves the For Whom problem.

QUESTIONS FOR DISCUSSION

1. Explain how we can read off total product from the marginal-product curve. Show this would not be true if total output did not begin at zero when labor is zero.

2. "Constant returns to scale" means increasing all inputs in exactly the same proportion will increase output in exactly the same proportion. What would you suppose "increasing returns to scale" means? "Decreasing returns to scale"? Show that constant

returns to scale is not inconsistent with the good old law of diminishing returns.

3. Suppose the wage rate abroad rose from $1,000 to $1,500. Describe the new equilibrium level of employment, rent, total product, etc. Show that almost the same result could be created on the island even if the world wage level did not change but instead immigration was restricted. By about how much would it have to be restricted?

4. Suppose land and labor both have inelastic supplies. Which factor return is a pure rent? Is the resulting equilibrium determinate? Why and at what level?

5. What is meant by "technical substitution between the factors"? Give examples. What is meant by intercommodity substitutions? When different commodities use the factors in different relative degrees, show that an increase in any one factor will cause more of it to be used even if there is no technical substitutability.

6. Suppose there are three factors of production. What then?

7. Show that either of the two factors can be thought of as earning a residual. Explain why it is plausible to believe that this residual is the same thing as the factor's marginal-product. (Hint: Observe behavior of a fixed number of workers confronted with a given market rental for land. Show that with workers the fixed hiring factor and land the variable hired factor, the same final production and factor-price equilibrium must emerge. Illustrate with rectangles, triangles, etc.)

8. If a sheep always gives 100 pounds of mutton to 5 pounds of wool, and always costs $10 to raise, show that the prices of these joint products can be anything between $2 for wool with $0 for meat to $0 for wool with $0.10 for meat, depending on the strengths of their demands. Can you show that existence of a second breed of sheep, which gives 100 meat and 6 wool and costs $11 to raise, can make the pricing determinate? (Hint: If both breeds are used, wool must sell for exactly $1 per pound. Why? What is meat's price?)

28 COMPETITIVE WAGES AND COLLECTIVE BARGAINING

The labourer is worthy of his hire.
NEW TESTAMENT

A man is much more than a commodity. Yet it is true that men do rent out their services for a price. This price is the wage rate, and of all prices it is by far the most important. For the vast majority of the population, the wage is the sole determinant of family income; and when we remember that much of the income of farmers and of nonincorporated enterprises is in actuality a form of labor income, we realize that wages must constitute almost 80 per cent of the national income.

When the price of coffee or of typewriter ribbons changes, it is easy to remain calm and dispassionate; the effects on our welfare are relatively minor. But let my wage be cut by 5 per cent and I change from an affable philosopher into a raging malcontent. Because wages are prices that arouse vital human emotions, they are the proper study of the psychologist as well as the economist. The sociological importance of wages has economic implications which a student of the labor market must always keep in mind.

▶ WAGE LEVELS AND DIFFERENTIALS

Wage rates differ enormously. The average wage is as hard to define as the average man. An auto executive may earn one-half million dollars a year at the same time as a clerk earns $4,000 and a farm hand $2,000. In the same factory, a skilled machinist may earn $150 a week while an unskilled man gets $75. Part of any theory of wages must explain these differentials.

But important as these wage differences are, we must not overlook the vital question of the general wage level. Wages of virtually every category of labor are higher than they used to be half a century ago. Why? Wages are higher in the United States than they are for similar categories of labor in Europe, and they are higher in Europe than they are in Asia. Why?

What is supposed to determine wages under competitive conditions? This is the first problem we shall tackle. Then, in Section B of this chapter we shall investigate the effect of deviations from competitive conditions and analyze the economics of collective bargaining between trade-unions and employers.

A WAGE DETERMINATION UNDER PERFECT COMPETITION

▶ **EQUALITY OF WAGE—FOR IDENTICAL LABOR**

Let us begin by examining the simplified case of wages paid to a particular category of laborers all exactly alike in skill, effort, and every other respect. Then competition will cause their wage rates per hour all to be exactly equal. No employer would pay more for the work of one identical man than he would pay for his twin, and no worker would be able to ask more for his services.

How is this single market wage determined? If we know the supply and demand curves for these laborers—as in Fig. 1a—then the competitive equilibrium wage must be at E, the intersection point. You can by now supply the details of the process whereby wages are bid up or down to this equilibrium

Favorable resources and technology explain high American wages:

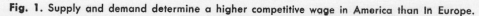

Fig. 1. Supply and demand determine a higher competitive wage in America than in Europe.

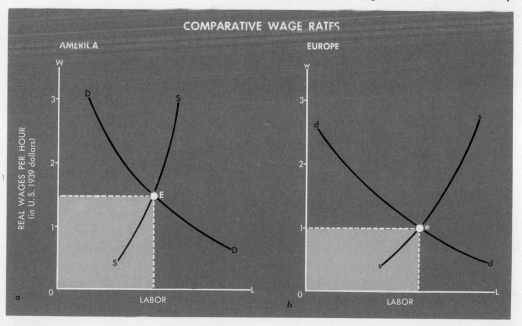

level. (It is important to note that we are interested in *real wages*—in what the wage will buy and not just in its money amount. Therefore in Figs. 1a and 1b we express wages in money units whose purchasing power over goods is held constant at the level of some particular year and place, *e.g.*, in terms of American dollars of 1939 or 1958 purchasing power.)

Imagine that Fig 1a represents the state of affairs in America and Fig. 1b that in Europe. Why are wages so much higher in America than in Europe? Is it because we have unions and they do not? Or because we have passed higher minimum-wage laws than the Europeans? Obviously, such factors have nothing to do with our simplified competitive world. A true, but superficial, answer would be: Supply and demand are such in America as compared with Europe as to lead to a higher wage here.

But *why* are supply and demand such as to lead to high American wages? What lies behind these schedules?

▶ NATIONAL RESOURCES AND HIGH PRODUCTIVITY

In the first place we note that the derived demand schedules for labor slope downward and to the right, going from northwest to southeast. One reason for this will occur to you at once: The law of diminishing returns suggests that adding more and more labor to the same American natural resources and land area will tend to diminish labor productivity and wages. Suppose you let American population increase so as to shift the supply curve SS far to the right in Fig. 1a. Then the wage might fall to the European level or even lower.

One important explanation of high American wages, therefore, lies in the sphere of economic geography: *Compared with the size of our working population, we are generously supplied with land, with coal, with iron, with oil, and with water power.* The per capita supplies of these vital sinews of modern industrial production are less in Europe and still less in many other regions.

▶ TECHNOLOGY, CAPITAL, AND HIGH PRODUCTIVITY

But economic geography does not tell the whole story. Two regions may be exactly alike in endowment of natural resources; but if one of them uses superior technological methods, its productivity and real wages may be much higher than the other's. In part, using superior technological methods involves better know-how, better applied science, better economic laws and customs, better management, and better work methods; in part, it is made possible by the relative abundance of capital goods—of man-made machinery, materials, and plants.

Just why the United States developed a superiority in know-how and capital availability is not well understood by economic historians. But the facts of this superiority are not subject to much dispute.

► **IMMIGRATION AND RESTRICTIONS OF LABOR SUPPLY**

This raises an obvious question: Why do not Europeans move from their low-wage area to our higher-wage area? We all know the answer from our history books. People *did* migrate to this country in great numbers during the three centuries prior to World War I. A few came to seek religious freedom, many came because they liked our system of government, but by far the greatest number came to the United States because they expected to better their economic condition here.

After World War I, laws were passed severely limiting immigration. Since then only a trickle of immigrants has been admitted. The reasons for the restriction of entry were primarily sociological rather than economic. The ethnic groups from Southern and Eastern Europe began to dominate the stream of immigration in the decades before World War I. Because of ensuing political resentments, quotas were set up, sharply limiting *all* immigration but greatly favoring Western Europe where most immigrants had come from in the earlier centuries.

This is our first example of interference with the free play of competition in the wage market. By keeping labor supply down, immigration policy tends to keep wages high. Let us underline this basic principle:

►   Limitation of the supply of any grade of labor can be expected to raise its wage rate; any increase in supply will, other things being equal, tend to depress wage rates.

Note that this principle holds for wage *rates,* paid per hour or year to any class of workers; it most certainly need not hold for the *total* of wages, paid to the class of workers as a whole. If we admit millions of migrants into this country, hourly wage rates might fall; but with so many more hours of labor being worked, it is quite possible—indeed, likely—that total dollars of wages earned would rise. As long as the demand curve for the workers in Fig. 1a has an elasticity greater than one, lowering their wage rates per hour can be expected to increase rather than decrease their total payroll earnings. (What if the elasticity were equal to one? Less than one?)

► **THE COUNTERLAW OF INCREASING RETURNS**

At this point we must be careful not to overstate the law of diminishing returns. Working against it, for a range at least, is a counterlaw: *the law of increasing returns* or of *economies of mass production.* One of the reasons the United States is so prosperous is that ours is so *large* a free-trade area. Modern technology increasingly requires larger and larger plants: unless you can produce a thousand electric refrigerators per *day,* you will not realize the full economies of mass production. So, with trade barriers in Europe, a small country like Belgium, which cannot be sure of selling even a thousand refrigerators per *month,* finds it difficult to have an efficient domestic industry.

Look to the automobile industry for a still more striking example of the importance of large-scale operations. General Motors, Chrysler, and Ford all produce in tremendous quantities. Even the smaller independents can be efficient only because they are able to buy tires, headlights, and countless parts from factories that sell to all the automobile companies; moreover, to seek large-scale economies there have had to be in the mid-1950's mergers between Studebaker and Packard and between Hudson and Nash. Europe's car makers hope the new Common Market there will give them some of the advantages of a larger market.

All this raises a question: Would the United States be better off in the 1960's if our population were cut by one-third, so that we had scarcely 100 million people? If you apply the law of diminishing returns uncritically, you will answer, Yes. But in view of the counterlaw of increasing returns, the answer is very much in doubt. Are we already regretting the bulge in births immediately following World War I? Will the revival in the birth rate after World War II tend to lower real wages in the future? Probably not, I should guess—provided we are able to import raw materials from abroad on a relatively free-trade basis.

Is postwar Europe overpopulated? Certainly some agricultural areas of extreme population density are. And if urban areas like the United Kingdom must for reasons of defense and security depend upon their own agriculture for much of their food, then a balanced reduction in population might increase their per capita welfare. But if a peaceful pattern of world trade can be re-established, will much be gained by moving people from European towns to Australian and Canadian towns? Nobody knows the answer—but that in itself suggests we must not expect too much from such a policy.

▶ THEORY OF THE OPTIMUM POPULATION

All this suggests a rather interesting theory of population. Why not have the best of both situations? Why not take advantage of increasing returns per capita as well as of diminishing returns? Specifically, why not aim at letting population grow up to the exact point where increasing returns end and decreasing returns begin? This point will give the highest level of real wages or real incomes and is called the "optimum population." Figure 2 illustrates how the optimum population is defined at the very top of the productivity curve.

Unfortunately, no economist knows in terms of actual numbers what the curve of increasing and diminishing returns looks like. Perhaps we in America should for purely selfish reasons welcome millions of new immigrants and

Incomes reach a peak where population is not too large or small:

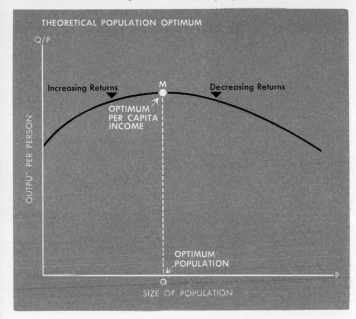

Fig. 2. At the point where decreasing per capita returns begin, output per person is at its very highest.

births. Or are we already beyond the point of optimum population? What if Congress were to appropriate billions in order to make a controlled experiment? Could it find out the answers to these important questions? Why not?

▶ THE IRON LAW OF WAGES: MALTHUS AND MARX

At the beginning of this book, in Chapter 2, we encountered the Malthusian theory of population. According to this theory, you should draw in on Fig. 1a a *horizontal* long-run supply curve of labor. This should be drawn in at the wage level corresponding to the lowest standard of living at which people will just reproduce their numbers. A century and a half ago, economics was called "the dismal science" because many classical economists believed that wages tended toward the bare minimum of subsistence. In our survey of the growth of populations by births and deaths, we have seen how unrealistic for the modern Western world is this notion of a bare-minimum long-run supply curve of labor.

A quite different version of the iron law of wages was provided by Karl Marx. He put great emphasis upon the "reserve army of the unemployed." In effect, employers were supposed to lead their workers to the factory windows and point to the unemployed workers out at the factory gates, eager to work for less. This unhappy spectacle, according to Marx, would be enough to depress wages to the level of a subsistence minimum.

Let us try to show this on our diagrams. Figure 1a is redrawn as Fig. 3. Suppose that the wage is at $2 per hour and employment is at the level indicated by the point A. Sure enough, there will be unemployment just as was alleged. The amount of unemployment would be represented by the distance between the labor supplied and demanded AB. In our simple, idealized model of competition, such unemployment could certainly be expected to put downward pressure on wages.

But does the basic Marxian conclusion follow? Is there any tendency for real wage rates to fall to a *minimum subsistence level* such as MM in Fig. 3? None at all. There is absolutely no reason why in our simple model real wage rates should ever fall below the equilibrium level at E. In a country well endowed with capital and natural resources, this competitively determined equilibrium wage might be a very comfortable one indeed as compared with wages in history and in most parts of the present-day world. In a less fortunate country, we should expect it to be lower.

Thus we reach an important principle: If competition in the labor market were really perfect, there would be no necessary tendency for wages to fall to any minimum subsistence level.

Employers might prefer to pay low wages. But that would not matter. In a competitive market they are unable to set wage rates as they would *like*. As

Karl Marx exaggerated power of reserve army of the unemployed:

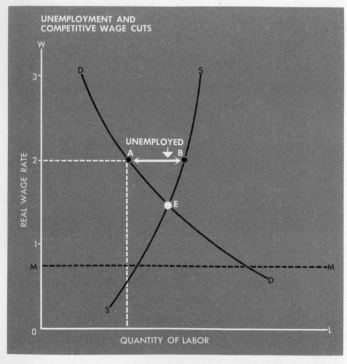

Fig. 3. Contrary to Marx, the "reserve army of the unemployed"—as shown by AB—need not depress real wages to the MM "minimum-subsistence" level. It can only depress competitive wages from A to E.

long as employers are numerous and do not act in collusion, their demands for any grade of labor will bid its wage up to the equilibrium level at which the total forthcoming labor supply is absorbed. The workers may aspire to still higher wages, but under competition they do not get what they would *like* either—as long as they do not act collusively to limit the labor supply, their wishes will not serve to keep wages from falling to the competitive level.

▶ **SHORTER HOURS AND SMALLER LABOR FORCE**

The law of diminishing returns makes it easy to understand why the trade-unions have favored restrictions on immigration. The same analysis helps to explain why they have pressed for (1) a shorter and shorter working week and more days of vacation per year; (2) restrictions on child labor, encouragement of early old-age retirement, and exclusion of women from some areas of labor; and (3) restrictions on degree of effort and speed-ups.

    The old labor jingle

> Whether you work by the week or the day,
> The shorter the work the better the pay

expresses the hope that workers can travel upward on the demand curve for labor.[1]

▶ **THE LUMP-OF-LABOR FALLACY**

It would be wrong to think that this economic analysis alone explains why unions pursue policies to restrict labor and effort. There is a related and still more powerful reason why workers fight for shorter hours. They fear unemployment; they tend to think the *total amount of work to be done is constant* in the short run. So what happens if a foreigner is put to work? Or a woman comes into the labor market? Or an old man refuses to retire? Or a fellow worker begins to work too efficiently? Or a machine replaces a man? The worker is apt to think that each and any of these events represents a threat to his own job and livelihood.

    This attitude is sometimes called by economists the "lump-of-labor fallacy." We must give this notion its due. To a particular group of workers, with special skills and status, the introduction of technological change may represent a real threat. Viewed from their personal standpoint, the lump-of-labor notion may not seem so fallacious.

    True enough, in a great depression, when there is widespread unemploy-

---

[1] Union policy today is by no means uniform in pressing for these restrictions upon supply. Of recent years, many unions have revised their views on retirement age, now opposing compulsory retirement at sixty-five. The AFL-CIO has recently gone on record in favor of a more liberal immigration policy for the United States. Some unions still featherbed, but others encourage increased productivity.

ment for years at a time, one can understand how workers may yield to lump-of-labor philosophy. But the lump-of-labor argument implies that there is only so much useful remunerative work to be done in any economic system, *and that is indeed a fallacy.* If proper and sound monetary, fiscal, and pricing policies are being vigorously promulgated, we need not resign ourselves to mass unemployment. And although technological unemployment is not to be shrugged off lightly, its optimal solution lies in offsetting policies that create adequate job opportunities, and not in restrictions upon production.[1]

► A THIRTY-HOUR WEEK?

There are, of course, still other arguments for or against cutting working hours from, say, 40 per week to 30. As our standards of living and productivity rise, it is only natural that we should feel we can afford more leisure. Historically, working hours have been progressively shortened, as we have already seen. But at this stage of history would American workers really wish to purchase 10 extra hours of leisure per week if this meant foregoing a sizable fraction of real and money income—say 20 per cent of what potentially might be earned? I wonder. The last decade of full employment has seen a great reduction in the agitation for the 30-hour week; this suggests that the *unemployment* rather than the *leisure* argument really carries most weight.

Moreover, when a union leader such as Walter Reuther of the United Auto Workers favors a shorter week, he at the same time asks that there be no cut in take-home pay. What worker could be against a free present of more leisure? We shall investigate a few pages later the degree to which unions can squeeze higher wages out of employers; so we need not discuss here these same arguments which are also used to favor the 30-hour week. But there is one argument that does bear directly on the question of hours.

During World War I and after, it was found that, when the working day was cut by 1 hour in 10, output did not fall by 1 in 10. Why not? Because output *per hour* increased. This suggests that a 25 per cent cut, from 40 to 30 hours a week, might not require an equivalent 25 per cent cut in take-home pay. But this is a far cry from the claim that workers can take an extra day per week off and not reduce total production. The Bureau of Labor Statistics has made careful studies of the available evidence, and these lend little credence to the extreme claims of proponents of the 30-hour week.

Saturday work will no doubt become rarer and rarer in American industry. Probably there will be a trend toward increased vacations with pay—not so much because the vacation will improve workers' productivity during the rest of the year but rather because people get a great deal of enjoyment out of summer and winter vacations. Taking more time off will be probably one

[1] See Chapter 35's detailed discussion of "automation."

of the ways in which we shall choose to enjoy the fruits of technological progress. No doubt, too, our grandchildren will choose to work a still shorter week.

▶ GENERAL SUPPLY CURVE OF LABOR

Let us return to our case of perfect competition. What is the supply curve of labor like? How does the wage rate affect population? How does it affect people's desire for a longer or shorter average working day? How does the wage level influence the number of people *not* in the labor force (via age of retirement, years of schooling, women workers, etc.)? Will higher wages enable and motivate people to work more effectively, or will they feel they can afford to take things easier?

These questions show that the supply of labor involves at least four dimensions: (1) population, (2) proportion of the population actually in the labor force, (3) average number of hours worked per week and year by workers, and (4) the quality and quantity of effort and skill that workers will provide.

Of these four labor-supply dimensions, the third is most subject to purely economic causation. We have already seen that, in the Western world, population has become dependent on sociological as well as economic forces. Deepseated customs and laws seem, also, to determine which population groups are in the labor force of the gainfully occupied.[1] While economic factors have some influence on the morale and incentives of workers, increasingly we are recognizing the vital contribution that the psychologist and social anthropologist can make to the study of team productivity in a factory.

▶ "SUBSTITUTION-EFFECT" VERSUS "INCOME-EFFECT"

This leads us to the interesting economic question: What effect will wage rates have on the number of hours worked per year? We have already touched on this in earlier discussions. A diagram may help to make the issues clear. Fig. 4 shows the supply curve of total hours that a group of people will want to work at each different wage. Note how the supply curve rises at first in a northeasterly direction; then at the critical point *C*, it begins to bend back in a northwesterly direction. How can we explain why higher wages may either *increase* or *decrease* the quantity of labor supplied?

Put yourself in the shoes of a worker who has just been offered higher

---

[1] The labor force tends to grow in depression: when a husband is thrown out of work, his wife and children may seek jobs. Tending to cancel this is the fact that women and other workers are, under prosperous conditions, attracted into jobs by plentiful employment opportunities. Actually during recent decades of prosperity there has been an increase in number of women who enter—and reenter!—the labor force.

At a high-enough wage we can afford to work less:

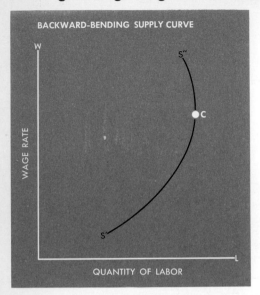

BACKWARD-BENDING SUPPLY CURVE

W

WAGE RATE

QUANTITY OF LABOR

Fig. 4. Above the critical point C, raising the wage rate reduces amount of labor supplied. (Income effect overcomes substitution effect.)

hourly rates and is free to choose the number of hours worked. You are torn two different ways: On the one hand, you are tempted to work some extra hours because now *each hour of work is better paid.* Each hour of leisure has become more expensive—hence you are tempted to substitute extra work for leisure. But working against this so-called "substitution-effect," there is an opposing "income-effect."[1] With the wage rate higher, you are, in effect, a richer man. Being richer you will want to buy more clothes, more insurance, better food, and more of other consumer goods. But most important for the present problem, *you will tend also to buy more leisure!* Now you can afford to take Saturday off if you want to; now you can have a week's vacation in the winter or an extra week in the summer.

Which will be more powerful, the substitution-effect or the income-effect? Or will they just balance each other and cancel each other out—so that the supply curve neither rises forward nor bends backward, but rises perfectly vertically and inelastically? There is no one answer. It depends upon the individual. In Fig. 4, from S' to C the substitution-effect outweighed the income-effect. But from C to S", the income-effect was the more important.

---

[1] See Chapter 23 for a discussion of "substitution-effects" and "income-effects" in connection with consumption. The income-effect of a wage increase is defined as its tendency to make you feel richer and able to afford more pleasurable leisure. Its substitution-effect is its tendency to make you want to react to the higher price of leisure—higher because of the higher hourly wage you now forego to get each hour of leisure—by substituting for leisure the new goods your pay will buy you. The two effects work against each other; when the income effect wins out, labor's supply curve bends back.

▶ **RENT ELEMENTS IN WAGES OF UNIQUE INDIVIDUALS**

Generally, one could expect that, after people receive a comfortable margin over what they consider to be conventionally necessary, further increases in wage will not bring forth further hours of work. This was tested by a tax lawyer who studied his professional and business friends in New York City to learn the effect on them of the heavy wartime taxes. Somewhat to his surprise, he discovered that taxes seemed to make them work harder so as to maintain their previous standards of living. Apparently, the short-run income-effect was more powerful than the substitution-effect. But probably most powerful were their nonmoney drives—their desire for achievement and their liking for their work. A Harvard Business School study has gathered similar evidence and so has a recent study of English accountants and solicitors.

As we shall see in Chapter 30 on profits, the most harmful effects on incentives of our increasingly high tax rates seem to involve risk taking and venture capital rather than in connection with the supply of effort by gifted people.[1] And as we saw in Chapter 27, all things considered, most of the high earnings of outstanding individuals can probably be classified as "pure economic rent." Babe Ruth earned $100,000 a year playing baseball, something he liked to do anyway. Outside the field of sports it is doubtful if he could have counted on earning more than, say, $5,000 a year at most. Between these two limits his supply curve was almost completely *inelastic,* and so we can term the excess of his income above the alternative wage he could have earned elsewhere *a pure rent,* logically like the rent to nature's fixed supply of land.

▶ **EQUALIZING DIFFERENCES IN WAGES**

Let us now turn from the problem of supply of labor in general and investigate the vital problem of *differentials in competitive wages* among different categories of people and jobs. Supply conditions now become all-important in explaining the tremendous wage differentials observed in everyday life.

When you look more closely at the differences among jobs, some of the observed pay differentials are easily explained. Jobs may differ in their unpleasantness; hence wages may have to be raised to coax people into the less attractive jobs. Such wage differentials that simply serve to *compensate for the nonmoney differences among jobs* are called "equalizing differences."

[1] According to some medical authorities, successful businessmen and professional people probably work too hard for their own good—as indicated in such groups by the high incidence of ulcers, coronary thrombosis, and similar diseases. After we have had high taxes for generations, will the harmful "substitution-effects" of high taxes outweigh their "income-effect" leading to more work?

Steeple jacks must be paid more than janitors because people do not like the risks of climbing flagpoles. Workers often receive 5 per cent extra pay on the 4 P.M. to 12 P.M. "swing shift" and 10 per cent extra pay for the 12 midnight to 8 A.M. "graveyard shift." For hours beyond 40 per week or for holiday and week-end work, one and a half times the base hourly pay is customary. And when you observe a doctor who earns $15,000 a year, you must remember that at least a part of this is an equalizing difference needed to induce people to incur tuition costs and endure the lack of pay for years.

Jobs that involve dirt, nerve strain, tiresome responsibility, tedium, low social prestige, irregular employment, much seasonal layoff, short working life, and much dull training tend to be less attractive to people. To recruit workers for such occupations you must raise the pay. On the other hand, jobs that are especially pleasant or attractive find many applicants, and remuneration is bid down. People like white-collar jobs, and so clerical wages are low.

To test whether a given difference in pay is an equalizing one, ask people who are well qualified for both jobs: Would you take the higher-paying job in preference to the lower-paid one? If it turns out that they are not eager to make such a choice, then it is fair to conclude that the higher-paid job is not really more attractive when due weight is given to all considerations, nonmonetary and monetary.

► NONEQUALIZING DIFFERENTIALS: DIFFERENCES IN LABOR QUALITY

If all labor were homogeneous, every observed competitive wage differential could be explained as an equalizing difference. But turn to the real world. True, some of the observed differentials can be regarded as equalizing. Yet you know that the vast majority of higher paid jobs are also *more pleasant,* rather than less pleasant. Most wage differentials cannot therefore be of the equalizing type. What then are they due to?

Are they perhaps due to the fact that competition is imperfect? Undoubtedly some observed differentials are of this type. Trade-unions or minimum-wage laws or a monopoly by the workers in a particular occupation can explain part of the existing nonequalizing differentials. If you removed these obstructions due to monopolistic or imperfect competition, people would flow into some of the higher-paid jobs and bring pay in these jobs into equality with that prevailing elsewhere. We shall analyze these interferences with competition in a moment.

But never forget that many of the observed differentials in wages have little to do with the imperfections of competition; they would still persist if there were no monopoly elements. Even in a hypothetically perfect auction market, where all the different categories of labor were priced by supply and demand, equilibrium would necessitate tremendous differentials in wages.

This is because of the tremendous *qualitative* differentials among people. You would not expect the competitive wage of a man to be the same as that of a horse or that of a horse to be the same as that of another mammal such as a cow. Then why should you expect one man to receive the same competitive wage as another man or woman? A zoologist may call us all members of the same *Homo sapiens* species, but any personnel officer who is trying to equalize the marginal-physical-product per dollar expended in every direction knows that people vary tremendously in their abilities and their contributions to a firm's dollar revenue.

There are about 70 million people in our labor force. There is no single factor of production called labor; there are thousands of quite different kinds of labor. If you are hiring men to shovel railroad trains out of a blizzard, it will probably pay you to lump together as one indistinguishable factor of production all adult males of certain ages who appear to be reasonably healthy, muscular, and sober. Similarly, the labor market will always group people into certain general classifications for purposes of wage determination. Even after groupings have taken place, there still remain many categories of labor, and their wage rates will have a wide spread.

▶ "NONCOMPETING GROUPS IN THE LABOR MARKET"

About 80 years ago, economists began to call these different categories of labor "noncompeting groups in the labor market." Instead of one single factor of production, labor was recognized to be many different factors. Economists expected as many different wage rates would result as there were noncompeting groups. Their instinct was sound, but there is some danger of misunderstanding their terminology.

In the first place, we must not think that in a perfectly competitive labor market the so-called noncompeting groups would disappear. We should still have different categories of labor—just as in the wheat market we have winter wheat, spring wheat, grade 2 red wheat, etc. Second, no one can doubt that these different groups are in some sense competing with each other. Just as I decide between hiring a horse or a tractor, so must I decide between hiring a very skilled, fast-working, high-paid worker and a lower paid, less skilled one.

The essential point then is this: The different categories compete with each other; yet they are not 100 per cent identical. They are *partial rather than perfect substitutes* for each other.

Workers can to some degree cross over from one category into another. If welders' wages were to become $100,000 a year, I might study the art and quit being a teacher. Or if I did not, others would. Therefore, even when the wages of the different categories of labor are different, quantitative wage differences are still subject to the laws of supply and demand. "Cross elasticity" of supply becomes very important: The wage amount that you have to pay to recruit foundrymen depends on what the near-by automobile industry is paying to men on the assembly line.

Or take the case of skilled surgeons. They receive high pay in all countries compared with butchers. Why? Because their work is important? Only in part on this account. For suppose (1) that every year as many babies were born with the capacity necessary for a surgeon as are born with the capacity necessary for a butcher, (2) that someone learned how to train surgeons in no time at all, and (3) that a surgeon's activities and responsibilities were not regarded as less pleasant or more taxing than those of a butcher. Then do you really think that surgeons would continue to receive higher earnings than butchers? And if you think the sanctity of human life is the important explanation, how do you account for the fact that the best plastic surgeons are higher paid than the best abdominal surgeons?

▶ GENERAL EQUILIBRIUM OF LABOR MARKET

In real life as we know it, things are not black or white. There is some mobility between different jobs; differences in wages will gradually over a long period of time tend to encourage greater and greater mobility; and it is never necessary for all workers to be mobile—a few movers are enough. But there will still remain certain permanent barriers to mobility that depend upon the irreducible differences in biological and social inheritance. Hence, wage differentials will still persist even in the long run.

How big will these differentials be? Suppose we made it easy for people to get the education they are fitted for and to travel from one region to another where their skills can be better used. And suppose we provided people with the best possible information about job opportunities and about their personal potentialities. Then differentials would be much reduced.

But such differentials as remain, how exactly are they determined? The answer is provided by supply and demand. *The market will tend toward that equilibrium pattern of wage differentials at which the total demand for each category of labor exactly matches its competitive supply.* Then and only then will there be general equilibrium with no tendency for further widening or narrowing of wage differentials. Table 1 sums up our conclusions.

Table 1. Competitive wage determination

Situation	Result
1. People all alike—jobs all alike	No differentials
2. People all alike—some jobs differ in disutility	Equalizing wage differentials
3. People differ, but each type of labor is in unchangeable supply ("noncompeting groups")	Wage differentials that are "pure economic rents" or "surpluses"
4. People differ, but there is some mobility between groups ("partially competing groups"; "cross elasticity" important)	General equilibrium pattern of wage differentials as determined by general demand and supply. (Includes 1–3 as special cases.)

B IMPERFECTIONS OF THE LABOR MARKET AND COLLECTIVE BARGAINING

Real-world labor markets are far removed from the ideal model of perfect competition. You can grade wheat into neat market categories, but you cannot do that with human beings. No auctioneer allocates workers to the highest bidders. Studies of areas such as New Haven, Connecticut, show that workers often have only the most imperfect knowledge of near-by wage rates. Nation-wide studies show that there are considerable short-run and long-run immobilities: Through ignorance, inertia, or attachment for a particular locality or job, workers may fail to move to higher-paying jobs; hence, wage differentials persist.

Wage stickiness. Two tests indicate that the labor market is imperfect. When there is a considerable increase in unemployment—as in the recession of 1954—do wage rates drop as they would in a competitive market? History answers, No. You may be every bit as capable as someone who has a job, and yet there is no way that you can take his job away by underbidding him. Just imagine going to Ford or any large corporation when the next depression comes, brandishing your degrees and certificates of I.Q. and excellence, and offering to work for less than they are paying. Could you get a job that way?

Wage policy of firms. The fact that a firm of any size *must* have a wage policy is additional evidence of labor market imperfections. In a perfectly competitive market, a firm need not make decisions on its pay schedules; instead it would turn to the morning newspaper to learn what its wage policy would *have* to be. Any firm, by raising wages ever so little, could get all the extra help it wanted. If, on the other hand, it cut the wage ever so little, it would find no labor to hire at all in a perfectly competitive labor market.

But just because competition is not 100 per cent perfect does not mean that it must be zero. The world is gray, not black or white—it is a blend of (1) competition, and (2) some degree of monopoly power over the wage to be paid. If you try to set your wage too low, you will soon learn this. At first nothing much need happen; but eventually you will find your workers quitting a little more rapidly than would otherwise be the case. Recruitment of new people of the same quality will get harder and harder, and you will notice slackening off in the performance and productivity of those who remain on the job.

Availability of labor supply does, therefore, affect the wage you set under realistic conditions of imperfect competition. If you are a very small firm, you may even bargain and higgle with prospective workers so as not to pay more than you have to. But if you are any size at all, you will name a wage for each type of job, then decide how many of the applicants will be taken on; and in terms of the number of applicants who respond, you may alter your wage rate over time. Even in the absence of unions, you will find that it is a perplexing task to decide on an optimal wage policy.

Is it best for you to try to pay the so-called "going wage"? (And if so, what exactly is meant by a "going wage"?) Or, like many large and prosperous companies, should you aim for the cream of the local labor market by paying higher than average wages? Or are you in a highly competitive industry so that you must try to squeeze what work you can out of low-paid people, knowing they will leave you once they can get another job?

▶ THREE WAYS THAT UNIONS TRY TO RAISE WAGES

Dropping the oversimplified picture of perfect competition, we can use economic theory to analyze how trade-unions operate. How might unions hope to raise wages in a particular industry? There are three main methods, all of them closely interrelated. (1) Unions can reduce the supply of labor. (2) They can use their collective bargaining power to raise standard wage rates directly. (3) They can cause the derived demand curve for labor to shift upward. These three devices are much alike and often reinforce each other, but there are also significant differences among them.

1. *Restriction of labor supply.* We have already seen that a union may restrict the supply of labor in order to travel upward on the derived demand curve for labor. Immigration barriers, maximum-hour legislation, high initiation fees, long apprecticeships, refusal to admit new members into the union or to let nonunion members hold jobs—all these are obvious restrictive devices that have been used in the past. In addition, there are other, more subtle restrictions on labor supply: explicit union limits on work loads (artificial limits put on number of bricks per day, width of paint brush, stand-by orchestras, number of looms attended, and similar "featherbedding" labor practices) and implicit understandings forcing a slowdown of the working pace.

2. *Raising standard wage rates.* Direct limitations on the labor supply are today no longer so necessary to unions, except to reinforce the ability of the union to secure a high standard wage rate and to enforce it. Union leaders have learned this important economic fact: If you can persuade or force employers to always pay a high standard wage, then the supply of labor will take care of itself. At the standard rate, employers will hire the number of men they want, and any surplus job applicants will be *automatically excluded* from the labor market.

Figures 5a and 5b contrast *direct* restriction of labor supply and *indirect* restriction via a high standard wage. In Fig. 5a the union cuts down supply from SS to S'S' by insisting on long apprenticeships and high training fees. The wage consequently rises from E to E'. (Test your understanding of this: Explain the effects on doctors' earnings of a policy that reduced the number

To raise pay, unions restrict supply and enforce standard wage rate:

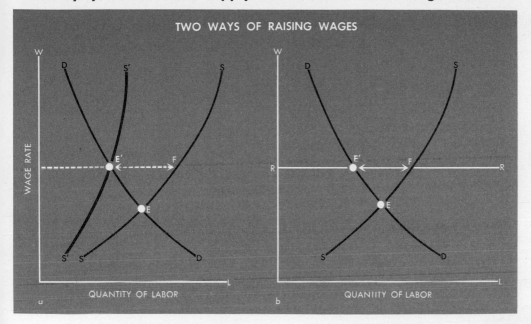

Fig. 5. Raising the standard wage to *RR* in (*b*) has exactly the same effect on wages as reducing the effective supply from *SS* to *S'S'* in (*a*); the workers from *E'* to *F* are excluded from employment in either case.

of students going through medical schools relative to the total population.)

Alternatively, in Fig. 5*b*, the union gets all employers to agree to pay wages no lower than the minimum standard rate, as shown by the horizontal line *RR*. Note that here, too, the equilibrium is at *E'*, where *RR* intersects the employer's demand curve. The workers from *E'* to *F* are as effectively excluded from jobs as if the union had directly limited entry. What now limits supply? It is the lack of job opportunities at the high standard wage rate.

This helps explain what used to puzzle many observers of modern unionism. At the same time that unions were liberalizing restrictions on union membership, wage rates were being pushed up by collective bargaining.

3. *Shifting the derived demand curve upward.* A union may hope to increase wages by any policy that improves the demand for labor. Thus, like the International Ladies' Garment Workers Union, it may study ways of reducing garment prices by improving productivity of labor and management or it may help the industry advertise its products. *Or* the union may agitate for a tariff to protect its industry, hoping thereby to raise the demand curve for domestic workers. *Or* it may persuade the government to pay higher rates on public contracts and to write make-work featherbedding restrictions into building codes. *Or* it may help the employers in an industry to maintain a

Some union policies try to shift the labor demand curve upward:

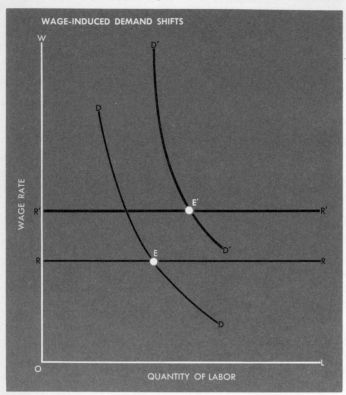

WAGE-INDUCED DEMAND SHIFTS

Fig. 6. Raising wages (from *RR* to *R'R'*), by making ill-fed workers stronger or resentful ones more energetic, in this case shifts the curve of demand productivity upward (from *DD* to *D'D'*), with employment actually increasing (from *E* to *E'*).

high monopoly price, with some of the extra profits going into higher wages.

Moreover, if collective bargaining raises wages, and if increased wages increase the productivity of labor, then labor will have shifted its own demand curve upward. Figure 6 depicts the case in which an increase in the wage from *RR* to *R'R'* itself results in an upward shift in the demand curve for labor—from *DD* to *D'D'*. Note that at the new equilibrium *E'*, both wage and employment have increased.

In the old days, the standard example of this was the case where workers were being paid so little that they were malnourished and therefore inefficient; higher wages might then have made them more effective and thus might have resulted in lower rather than higher production costs. Today in this country, few workers can be thought of as physiologically undernourished. But psychological elements are often as important as physiological. Many an employer has found that too-low wages are bad business even from a hard-boiled dollars-and-cents standpoint.

Moreover, it is often argued that high wages have a favorable "shock effect" on the employer's efficiency in the use of labor. One of the reasons advanced for the high productivity of American industry, even back in the nineteenth century when unions were unimportant, was the fact that high farm earnings made it necessary for industry here to develop good machine methods in order to be able to pay high wages and still stay in business. Adversity, in the form of a kick in the pants from unions or from fate in general, can at times galvanize a businessman into finding new improved ways of doing things. There is something to this shock-effect argument, but just how much nobody knows. It should, at any rate, be used with caution.

▶ WAGE INCREASES AND REDUCTIONS IN EMPLOYMENT

If raising wages means simply that you climb up the existing demand curve for labor, then employment will decrease in consequence.[1] This is because demand curves almost always slope upward and to the left.[2] The amount of unemployment created in a particular occupation by wage increases would depend upon the elasticity of the demand curve for that particular category of labor. We saw in earlier chapters that a factor demand is a "derived demand," and Chapter 27 discussed the five conditions that determine how elastic or inelastic the demand for labor might be. The following two cases will help to review and apply those principles.

Case of inelastic derived demand. Suppose that a particular building-trades union, such as the electricians', raises wages. Review the five principles to see which of them tells us that the drop in employment of electricians will as a result tend to be small in the short run. (1) Note that, in the short run, employers cannot substitute other factors—such as machines or plasterers—

---

[1] Intermediate economics texts and texts on labor problems show that, where an employer was previously possessed of monopoly-buying-power over labor, collective bargaining can—if not pushed to excess—right the balance, leading to both increased wages *and* increased employment. An employer with monopoly-buying-power is called a "monopsonist" after the Greek words for "single" and "buyer." Before unionization, the monopsonist who is on his toes will set his equilibrium wage at *MM* in Fig. 7. This will always be lower than the so-called competitive wage at *E*. Why will the monopsonist's equilibrium always be at a point like *m*? The monopsonist will not want to travel upward from *m* to *E* because he realizes that any wage increase beyond *m* will raise the wages paid to *already hired workers* by more than the extra revenue resulting from hiring the new men.

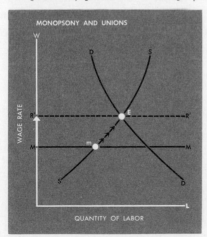

MONOPSONY AND UNIONS

Fig. 7.

When the union raises the wage toward *E* by collective bargaining, the monopsonist employer reluctantly travels up the *SS* curve. Note we do not travel up the demand curve *DD*. Wages and employment both rise together. (Query: What if collective bargaining raises the standard wage to a level *R"R"* that lies *above E*? What then will happen to employment? Draw in the arrows on the demand curve.)

[2] Cases have been noted where short-run demand is virtually completely inelastic.

for electricians. (2) Do not forget *the importance of being unimportant:* The total cost of a house will be little affected by a change in the wage rate of electricians alone. Will this fact tend to cause a strong or mild reduction of employment as a result of an increase in their wages? (3) Suppose there is a great housing shortage so that people feel they need homes desperately. How will inelasticity of demand for the final product, housing, affect the derived elasticity for electricians? (4) Suppose that all practicing electricians must be in the union so that an increase in wages is not followed by a great increase in the nonunion labor supplied. Will this inelasticity of supply of rival factors tend to make the demand for union electricians a steep one— or a relatively horizontal, elastic one which registers a great drop in employment as you climb up the demand curve? (5) Suppose finally that imperfect competition or public regulation will not permit the prices of houses to change much. Will this make for an inelastic or elastic demand for the factors that build houses? (Hint: all five conditions make for "inelasticity.")

Case of elastic demand. On the other hand, suppose you were a union leader in the glass-blowing industry. Suppose that labor costs are an important part of the total expense but that new mechanized processes exist which substitute machinery for men. Suppose, too, that a large part of the industry is not unionized, particularly those nonskilled workers who run the new machines. And finally, suppose that there are many commodity substitutes for glass—such as tin and paper. Can you apply our principles to show qualitatively (1) how elastic the demand for labor would then be, and (2) how disastrous it would be in terms of employment to raise wages in such a situation? Can you show why unions try to bargain collectively on an all-inclusive national scale, a whole industry at a time? (Hint: The demand for the products of *all* firms in the industry will be more inelastic than the demand facing any one firm alone, and also the threat of nonunion competition will then be less.)

▶ **UNION WAGE POLICY**

Actually the glass-blowers' union did belatedly see the need for wage cuts. Similarly, in 1931 the hosiery workers' union accepted a wage cut in order to stem the tide of nonunion competition. The shoe industry in Massachusetts has been losing firms to other less unionized rural areas; in the postwar period the union has taken account of the implied elasticity of demand for its laborers and has accepted lower earnings than would otherwise have been the case. So did the Studebaker auto workers in 1954. On the other hand, John L. Lewis' United Mine Workers' Union provides a clear-cut example of a union's raising hourly wages—even though this means a reduction in hours of work and a large increase in the sale of oil as a substitute for coal.

Some unions do take account of the effect of their wage demands on employment. But such self-imposed limits by unions on their own demands for wage increases operate feebly to the extent that (1) workers regard an increase in wage rates as always a good thing; (2) the union has regard exclusively for the interests of the workers who will continue to be employed after the wage increase, disregarding the interests of those who will become underemployed or the interests of those workers who potentially might be in the industry but are hardly aware of the possibility; and (3) the demand curve for union labor is actually inelastic *or is thought to be* inelastic.

▶ MANAGEMENT AT THE COLLECTIVE BARGAINING TABLE

Just as unions sometimes realize it would not be to their interest to get higher wages, managements sometimes take the view that an increase in wages would improve their long-run corporate earnings. But both of these views are exceptional. Usually at any collective bargaining conference, the workers are pressing for higher wages than management wishes to pay.

Thus, workers in a certain tool company may be receiving about $3 an hour base pay. The old collective bargaining contract with the union may be running out; a meeting has been called between the vice-president of the company in charge of industrial relations and the union bargaining representatives. The union asks for a 10 per cent wage increase, or 30 cents per hour. The employer offers a 5 per cent increase, or about 15 cents an hour. Perhaps the union does not expect to get the full 30 cents, and the company may know that it will have to increase wages by more than 15 cents.[1]

▶ THEORETICAL INDETERMINACY OF COLLECTIVE BARGAINING

What will be the terms of the final agreement? Unfortunately, this is one important subject that economic theory can tell us little about. The result depends on psychology, politics, and a thousand other intangible factors. As far as the economist is concerned, the final outcome is in principle indeterminate—almost as indeterminate as the haggling between two millionaires over the price to be paid for a rare oil painting.

In this case the final wage agreement might be anywhere between $3.15 and $3.30. Six main arguments will be appealed to during the bargaining: (1) If the cost of living is rising, the union economist will talk a great deal about the workers' *standard of living;* but if prices are falling, it is the employer who will bring up this fact. (2) If the company and industry have been prosperous, the union will stress *ability to pay;* but if the industry has been unprofitable, the employer will emphasize this fact. (3) If *productivity* has risen or fallen in the industry, this will be brought into the negotia-

---

[1] In 1958, part of the 30-cent wage demand might take the form of a demand for pensions and a welfare-insurance fund or a guaranteed annual wage, but the same principles apply.

tions by one of the interested parties. (4) If other firms in the same area are paying *going wages* higher or lower than this firm, this fact will be brought out. (5) Labor will extol the philosophy of high wages as a means of bolstering *purchasing power* and national prosperity; management will emphasize the higher cost aspects of wage increases. (6) If a *national pattern* of "fourth- or *n*th-round" wage increases of so much per hour has already been set by a few "key bargains" in large industries such as coal, steel, or automobiles, that will have great weight in the deliberations. (7) American workers and employers have grown accustomed to steady money wage increases. Almost as certainly as spring brings robins, it brings wage increases. So General Motors and many other firms build into their wage agreements a steady upward trend—the so-called "improvement factor." This may mean a 2- or 3-cent-an-hour wage boost each year in addition to any cost-of-living escalator wage clauses.

Most often labor and management will arrive at a new yearly contract after some days of negotiation; perhaps $3.24 will be the final wage reached by collective bargainers in our example. But sometimes they will get stalled—between, say, $3.23 and $3.25. A government mediator may try to narrow down the 2-cent disagreement. Or there may be an understanding that a disinterested "arbitrator" will render a decision, which both parties will accept. Unfortunately, economic theory cannot tell us how such an arbitrator will arrive at his final decision. All the previously mentioned factors will be weighed in his mind, plus the all-important question: What decision is likely to be acceptable to both sides?

▶ **STRIKES AND COLLECTIVE BARGAINING**

Usually, there will not be a strike or lockout. But at all times, everybody will be realizing that failure to reach agreement will mean a costly strike. Still, it may ultimately come to pass that management refuses to go above $3.23 while labor refuses to take less than $3.25. A "work stoppage" will result. Should we call this an "employees' strike" or an "employer's lockout"? In popular speech, it will certainly be referred to as a strike. But since either party knows it can end the work stoppage by agreeing to the other party's terms, we would call it either.

A strike hurts both parties badly: the workers may lose several weeks' pay; the employer's plant is almost sure to be completely shut down for the same period of time. Worse than that: the public generally suffers if the two parties cannot get together peacefully.

Radio news commentators ask why workers go out on strike just because of a 2-cent disagreement; they point out that it might take two or three years for the workers to recover—at 2 cents an hour—their loss of earnings during the strike. But the workers look at it differently. To them the employer caused the strike by his stubbornness. They point out that the employer will lose more by the strike than the extra 2 cents would cost him in many years' time.

Why then do both parties let the strike occur? The explanation lies in this vital truth: A strike is *not* really over just the last 2 cents of wage disagreement! The workers believe that the employer would not have been forced from $3.15 up even to $3.23 except for the threat of a strike, which hangs over the negotiation like a time bomb. It takes agreement by both parties to keep the bomb from going off. (Of course, this is brutal language. We all sincerely hope that the day will arrive when language far removed from conflict and strife will adequately describe the facts of industrial relations. But as would-be scientific observers we must not let our wishes sway our judgment.)

Threats become hollow unless occasionally carried out; a gun known to be loaded with blanks frightens no one. Both parties must show that they are truly prepared to incur at some point the costs of a strike. Thus, suppose the employer was deprived, voluntarily or by law, of the right to refuse any wage demand if it would bring on a strike. Would this cost him only 2 cents an hour? Obviously not. There would then be no reason why the union might not hold out for a 50- rather than a 25-cent wage increase. Similarly, if the union could never exercise the right to strike, why should not the employer offer $2 rather than $3 per hour if he can get labor at that rate?

▶ COLLECTIVE BARGAINING AND THE PUBLIC INTEREST

Within the framework of present legislation, the government does not interfere. Collective bargaining is usually carried on by voluntary cooperation of labor and management. The result is far from ideal, but it is not at all clear in the judgment of experts that more active government regulation and control would improve things. Nonetheless we do all know that collective bargaining in important and vital industries, such as transportation and steel, is "heavily affected with the public interest." To every labor dispute there are *three* parties, not *two*. When labor and management fight in key industries, the *public* is vitally harmed. Therefore, in every emergency situation, the voluntary conduct of collective bargaining will always be superseded whenever it leads to a tie-up of the nation's economy and a threat to the nation's security. The government will take over the railroads to keep them running; the courts will issue injunctions; the President may even draft men into the army.

But once the government has superseded voluntary collective bargaining, what principles are to be used in setting wages? Fact-finding boards are appointed, but that only reframes the question. Moreover, is the problem of defining a "fair wage" simply a factual question of economics? Or is it simply a political question of what public opinion will accept as a fair settlement? There are no easy answers that an economics textbook can set down in italic type. But we must stress that a stable and progressive economic system requires all parties to use self-control in exercising their political powers.

▶ QUALIFICATIONS

1. *Has unionization raised wages?* The advocates of organized labor claim unions have raised real wages; the critics criticize unions for having done so and having thereby distorted the efficient use-pattern of resources. Despite this agreement that unions raise real wages, the facts are not at all clear.

Since 1933, for example, low-paid, nonunionized occupations (such as domestic service and farm work) have shown greater percentage wage increases than have most unionized trades. Moreover, in this same period of tremendous organization of labor, there has been a general tendency toward higher wages—but with the differentials remaining about the same in *absolute* terms. This means that the percentage differentials are diminishing. (For example, suppose you are a unionist earning $2 an hour, and I earn $1 in a nonunion trade. Now let us both get a $1 increase; this leaves the absolute differential unchanged; but no longer do you get twice my wage—instead you receive $3 to my $2.)

Most countries do show a lessening of percentage wage differentials in recent decades, a trend probably in part quite independent of union trends.

It is true that the average wage in unionized industries is higher than the average wage in nonunionized industries. But that in itself does not prove that unions are responsible for the difference. The industries that are unionized tend also to be those dominated by large rather than small enterprise and by firms which use workers of higher than average skills. Even before they were unionized, these same industries paid higher than average wages.

Professor Arthur Ross of the University of California has studied the change in wage rates since 1933 in union and nonunion industries.[1] He finds that the industries most recently unionized do seem to show a slightly greater wage increase since 1933 than do similar industries either that have never been unionized or that had already been unionized prior to 1933. (That is, if we examine industries *A, B,* and *C,* all of which were paying about the same wages in 1933, then *A,* the recently unionized industry, seems to show a slightly greater wage increase than does *B,* the never-unionized industry, or than does *C,* the industry unionized before 1933.)

One warning: Such statistics on the differential movements of union and nonunion wages cannot give the whole answer to the question whether unions have raised wages. Labor spokesmen claim that unions help raise wages for the unorganized workers. Thus, a nonunion industry's policy may be to fol-

[1] A. M. Ross, *Trade Union Wage Policy* (University of California Press, Berkeley, 1948). See L. G. REYNOLDS and C. H. TAFT, *The Evolution of Wage Structure* (Yale University Press, New Haven, Conn., 1956) for references to confirming later studies by R. A. Lester, A. E. Rees, J. T. Dunlop, and others.

low any changes in the wage scale hammered out in unionized plants near by. If an industry raises wages in order to keep the union out, the union will get no credit for its influence in the figures. On the other hand, suppose the targets for union organizers are profitable, expanding, high-productivity, concentrated industries; then the union may be riding aboard a moving demand curve and be given credit for wage increases that would have occurred even in its absence. Which is cause and which is effect?

If we had a laboratory like the chemist, we might hope to set up experiments to determine which hypothesis is more nearly correct; but the social sciences being what they are, we can only wait for more data to accumulate and hope that they will throw light on this important question. The statistics on national income do not seem to reveal any great shift in the fraction of national income going to labor as compared with the preunion era.

2. *Pitfalls in the concept of a general demand for labor.* A second important warning must be given. It is legitimate to draw up a demand curve of the usual general shape for one small labor market; as long as all other prices and wages are more or less unaffected, it is indeed true that a higher money wage is the same as a higher real wage; it is true also that employment can be expected to fall off somewhat.

But we must never forget the fallacy of composition. What is true for any small sector of the economy need not be true for the whole aggregate. If all wage rates rise, it is preposterous to suppose that commodity prices will remain constant. Thus, doubling all money wages *might* well result in a doubling of all prices. Were that the case, the real wage would not be changed at all. And hence, in a diagram like Fig. 1, we should be moving neither upward nor downward on the demand curve. (Turn to Fig. 1 and note that the vertical axis represents real wages in dollars of *constant purchasing power.*)

We must never forget that wages are not simply costs: they also represent *incomes* of most of the population. Therefore, the sales revenue of business enterprises is vastly affected by a substantial change in wage levels. Since the demand for labor is a demand derived from the demand for business products, it is clear that every change in wages generally must shift the general demand curve for labor. Hence, it is exceedingly dangerous to argue in terms of an unchanged demand curve for labor.

To illustrate this pitfall, let us ask ourselves the following question: In 1932 when there was widespread unemployment, would an all-round cut in money wages have *increased* employment? Or, as claimed by the trade-unionists, would a decrease in general money wages have decreased "purchasing power" and *decreased* employment? To the extent that a halving of wages would result in a halving of all prices, of all money incomes, and of all money spending, the answer must be obvious. Such a completely balanced deflation would neither help nor hurt the unemployment situation. This serves as a warning against accepting the superficial claims of those critics of labor who argue in terms of simple *DD* curves and of those friends of labor who argue in terms of "purchasing power."

This whole subject is one of the most complex in all of economics, and it obviously cannot be settled in an elementary textbook—or for that matter in a newspaper editorial or after-dinner speech.[1] The CIO in the Robert Nathan report of 1946 claimed that higher money wages provided an important key to full employment; the AFL long made similar pronouncements. On the other hand, for a century wage cuts have been extolled as a panacea for depression. Both views may be wrong; the truth is that economic *theory* provides no conclusive answer.

We may cautiously conclude by quoting in turn from two leading students of labor economics, Chicago's Albert E. Rees and Yale's Lloyd G. Reynolds:[2]

We tend to overemphasize the role of the unions, both in . . . their own industries and . . . the economy as a whole. . . . The other two thirds may have their wages and salaries influenced by what the unions do, but I feel there are very strong independent forces on the demand side that govern their rates of pay. . . . Even in the . . . unionized [one third] there are some very weak or almost impotent unions that have had very little to do with the wages of their members. . . .

In a series of rough guesses, I would say perhaps a third of the trade unions have raised the wages of their members by 15 per cent to 20 per cent above what they might be in a nonunion situation; another third by perhaps 5 per cent to 10 per cent, and the remaining third not at all. . . . The high figures tend to be found, not in periods of inflation, but in periods of prosperity combined with stable prices. . . . In [an inflationary] period like 1946–1948, for example, the union people may even lag behind simply because of the rigidities involved in the collective bargaining process.

And Reynolds states the following conclusions of his researches:

Summing up these diverse consequences of collective bargaining, one can make a strong case that unionism has at any rate not worsened the wage structure. We are inclined to be more venturesome than this, and to say that its net effect has been beneficial. This conclusion will doubtless strike many economists as surprising. . . .

[1] Today most economic theorists believe that the favorable effects during recession of any over-all general wage cut will depend upon how it affects the balance of saving and investment, or total real demand. If (1) lower wages cause prices to drop and (2) people's cash and holdings of government bonds do not drop in proportion, then the increase in people's *real wealth* may have expansionary effects on the real propensity to consume and on employment. But falling prices may aggravate debts and bankruptcy and, by making people pessimistic, may harm investment; consequently, most advanced textbooks in economics seem to advocate expanding people's real wealth and real consumption schedule by means of expansionary bank and financial policy rather than by deflation. This is one of the rare cases where economists are more in agreement on policy than they are on analysis.

[2] The Rees quotation is from *Wage Inflation* (National Industrial Conference Board, New York, 1957), pp. 27–28; the Reynolds quotation, from REYNOLDS and TAFT, *op. cit.*, pp. 194–195.

Fears that complete unionization will bring seismic disruption of the wage structure do not seem to be well founded. . . . The countries with the strongest union movements appear to have a wage structure which is more orderly and defensible than the wage structure of countries where unionism has been weak.

SUMMARY

▶ A. COMPETITIVE WAGE DETERMINATION

1. In perfectly competitive equilibrium, if all men and all jobs were alike, there would be no wage differentials. The equilibrium wage rate would be determined by supply and demand. To the extent that country A has (1) more natural resources per worker than country B and (2) better productive methods (because of capital availability and technical knowledge), to that extent the competitive wage in A is likely to be higher than in B.

2. The law of *diminishing returns* suggests that a reduction of labor relative to natural resources might be expected to raise real wages. While this principle lies back of labor's immigration policy and similar restrictions, historical examples of economies of mass production point to the operation of a countertendency of *increasing returns*. In theory the *"optimum* population" size is at the point where the two countertendencies have reached a balance of maximum per capita income.

3. Under modern technological and institutional conditions, there is no tendency for population growth to push real wages down to a minimum subsistence level.

Pressure exerted on real wages by the so-called "reserve army of the unemployed" tends to depress real wages only to the *equilibrium* level. In the Western world at least this equilibrium wage is much above the physiological *subsistence* level and is increasing with every decade.

4. Fear of unemployment sometimes leads to acceptance of the "lump-of-labor" fallacy. This belief that there is only a fixed amount of useful work to be done may result from the experience of technological unemployment or depression. It lies behind much of the agitation for a 30-hour week, protective tariffs, and featherbedding work rules. But the problem of unemployment calls for public and private policies to furnish adequate job opportunities, and not for defeatist restrictionism. (See Chapter 35 on automation.)

5. The supply of labor has four dimensions: population size, percentage of people gainfully employed, average number of hours worked per week and per year, and quality of effort of workers. Of these, the wage rate affects primarily the number of hours. The others depend more on sociological factors.

6. As wages rise, there are two opposite effects on the supply of labor: The "substitution-effect" tempts each worker to work longer because of the higher pay for each hour of work; the "income-effect" exerts influence in the opposite direction—since higher wages mean that workers can now afford more leisure along with more commodities and other good things of life. Each individual person's tastes will determine which effect will dominate. But it is likely that for most people there does exist *some* critical wage above which further increases are likely to make the supply curve bend backward. The labor supply of very gifted, unique people is probably quite inelastic; their wages are likely to contain a large element of so-called "pure economic rent."

7. Once we drop our wholly unrealistic assumptions concerning the uniformity of people and jobs, we find that substantial wage differentials will characterize even a perfectly competitive labor market. "Equalizing wage differences," which compensate for nonmonetary differences in disutility between jobs, explain some of the differentials.

8. But differences in quality of various grades of labor are probably the the most important cause of wage differences. Although it cannot be claimed that labor consists of wholly "noncompeting groups," it is nonetheless true that there are innumerable categories of partially competing groups. When the relative wage of one category rises, there are substantial cross-elasticity effects on labor supply as some people switch to the improved-pay occupation. The final pattern of wages would, in a perfectly competitive labor market, be determined by the general equilibrium of the interrelated schedules of supply and demand. (Reread Table 1 to see how the different special cases fit into this pattern of general equilibrium.)

▶ B. IMPERFECT COMPETITION AND COLLECTIVE BARGAINING

1. In real life, labor markets are not perfectly competitive. Employers usually have some control over wages, but their wage policy must always be conditioned by the available supply of labor.

2. Unions try to affect wages by (*a*) restricting labor supply, (*b*) establishing standard rates via collective bargaining, and (*c*) following policies designed to shift upward the derived demand schedule for labor. Of these methods (*b*) is by far the most important today.

3. Relative increases in wages will in most industries usually result in less employment in those industries. This is based on the assumption of a movement *along* a given demand schedule (*i.e.,* there are no shifts in demand due to higher productivity, etc.). If the relevant demand curve is elastic, a given percentage increase of the wage rate will cause a *greater* percentage reduction in employment, and hence the total of wages earned will decline. If, however, demand in the operative range is inelastic, higher wages, though still resulting in *less* employment, will nevertheless mean an *enlarged* payroll. The five principles of Chapter 27 indicate what factors help to determine the degree of elasticity in any particular instance.

4. At the collective bargaining table the following are some of the determining factors around which argument is likely to center: (*a*) cost and standards of living, (*b*) ability to pay and profits, (*c*) productivity trends and improvement factors, (*d*) "going wages" paid elsewhere in the locality and in the industry, (*e*) the influence of higher wages on purchasing power and on the level of costs, (*f*) the "national pattern" as determined by "key bargains" in important industries. Economic theory cannot tell just what the final wage bargain will be; the terms of wage settlement are theoretically indeterminate.

5. Usually a compromise settlement will be possible, without government intervention, formal arbitration, or a strike. But the *threat* of strike is ever-present and conditions the whole bargaining procedure. Strikes hurt labor, management, and the public; but if either labor or management unilaterally gave up the right to strike or to veto wage increases, it would seriously weaken its own bargaining power.

In vital industries, however, the interest of the public transcends the individual interests and rights of the disputing parties; consequently, voluntary collective bargaining is on trial in such strategic areas and is subject to government controls whenever damaging work stoppages occur.

6. Historically, the extent to which unions have succeeded in raising wages is in doubt. Since 1933 union membership has greatly increased, but in this same period wage differentials seem to have remained about the same in absolute terms. There seems to have been here and abroad a narrowing of percentage wage differentials. While it is true that *recently unionized* industries seem to show slightly greater wage increases from 1933 to 1955, the quantitative difference is not great. Moreover, it is not clear as to which is cause and which effect. Heavily concentrated and expanding industries may have been targets for unionization, and the high wages may have been the result of factors associated with or causing unionization rather than the result of unionization as such.

7. A final warning is in order: We must beware of the fallacy of composition; we must be careful in ascribing to the *demand curve for labor in general* the shape characteristic of the *demand curve for one small category of labor*. Wages are more than costs; they also constitute much of the income of consumers, and they heavily react back upon the demand for the products of business. A general change in money wage rates can be expected to have important effects on prices. It is even possible that real wages will not change at all. To the extent that a general wage change is balanced by an equivalent percentage change in *all* prices, little substantive effect upon unemployment or jobs may result. In actual fact, a general wage change may have nonneutral effects on saving and investment and may harm or help employment. But this is one of the most thorny parts of advanced theory. Only a warning of the complexity of the problem need be given in an introductory work.

QUESTIONS FOR DISCUSSION

1. Explain how wage differentials would disappear in a perfectly competitive market where all people and jobs were exactly alike.

2. What factors of technology, economic geography, and legislation help to determine the level of real wages? Show how diminishing returns and countertendencies are linked up with the theory of optimum population. Be critical in making applications.

3. Is the Marxian iron law of wages the same as the Malthusian? Discuss.

4. Define and contrast "equalizing and nonequalizing differences in wages." Which of these two concepts would be exemplified by high wages that contained much "pure economic rent"? What about noncompeting groups?

5. Give a list of imperfections in the labor market. Show that not all are related to monopoly power or to trade-union organization.

6. State arguments purporting to show that there is not "equality of bargaining power" between boss and worker. What did the theory of competitive wages assume?

7. Give three ways that unions try to influence wages. Contrast the first two, and gauge their importance. How important is this chapter's method No. 3?

8. "Unions can raise real and money wages in a particular industry, but the result will be less employment." Evaluate the degree of truth in this statement, according to the elasticity of demand for labor. (Review Chapter 27's five principles of derived demand.)

9. Give a journalistic account of how collective bargaining might work in a given industry. How is the public interested in voluntary collective bargaining?

10. Do unions raise wages? Debate Rees versus Reynolds.

11. Explain the dangers involved in treating the general demand for labor just like a particular group's demand. Show wages are both costs and sources of demand.

12. Review your understanding of the following concepts:

optimum population	*standard rate*
subsistence wage level	*shock effect*
backward-bending supply curve	*derived demand*
income-effect versus substitution-effect	*collective bargaining*
	productivity, ability to pay, improvement factor, and wage round
rent element in wages	
equalizing and nonequalizing wage differences	*strike, lockout, work stoppage*
	percentage and absolute differentials
noncompeting groups	*purchasing power*
general equilibrium	

INTEREST AND CAPITAL

How to have your cake and eat it too: lend it out at interest.

ANONYMOUS

The last chapters have sketched the determination of the rents of resources and the wages of labor. Now in this chapter we turn to the third great category of productive factors, capital—and to the determination of its special price, which is called "interest."

Capital theory is one of the most difficult parts of economic theory. For this reason, an introductory treatment cannot hope to grapple with all the important issues. What strategy shall we follow then in treating capital theory? Experimentation in the earlier editions of this book suggests it is best to proceed as follows:

The main part of this chapter summarizes in an uncritical way the basic notions about capital and interest found in every standard treatment of the subject. Then at the end are briefly given some of the key qualifications that ought to be made concerning the oversimplified traditional treatment. For the Appendix is reserved a short synthesis between classical capital theory and modern doctrines of income determination.

▶ LAND, LABOR, AND CAPITAL

Our traditional account of capital theory begins with a rather arbitrary division of all productive factors into three categories. This trinity of factors consists of the following: (1) Natural resources provided by Mother Nature in fixed supply, which cannot be augmented or used up—the return of this inelastic factor we have called *rent* or "pure economic rent." (2) Human *labor* resources, not produced in response to economic conditions, but rather taken by the economist as determined outside his field by sociological and biological circumstances—the return of this human factor is called *wages* (inclusive of salaries for brain and managerial workers as well as for manual workers).

In the oversimplified traditional account, the above two factors are called "primary factors of production"—primary in the sense that they are determined largely outside the economic system itself. To them we must now add an "intermediate" factor of production: (3) capital goods, *produced by the economic system itself* to be used as productive inputs for further production of consumption and other goods and services. These capital goods can be long- or short-lived. They can be rented out in the competitive market just the way acres of land or hours of labor can be rented out. Their rents—or perhaps we might use the term "rentals," to avoid confusion with pure economic rent to natural resources in fixed supply—these rentals of capital goods are determined by the same demand conditions of marginal productivity that we have discussed in previous chapters.

However, in the traditional capital theory, the return or yield of capital is not taken to be the *rentals* of capital goods. What then is it? The yield of capital is the *interest rate per annum,* which is a pure percentage per unit time—independent of dollar or other value units. Of what is the interest rate 5 per cent per annum the yield or price? Obviously, it is the yield or price applied to the *dollar* value of capital goods. True, you cannot add together hammers and thread and locomotives and looms to arrive at any meaningful dimensional magnitude. But in competitive markets, each physical capital good has its dollar market value definitely determined by supply and demand.

Is there any reason why you can't add together the *dollar values* of diverse physical capital goods? No, dollars can always be added to dollars. And the resulting total is the money value of all capital assets.

▶ NET PRODUCTIVITY OF CAPITAL

Now we ask ourselves this question: Why do people ever bother to transform the primary factors of labor and land into intermediate capital goods or into capital? The answer: It is a technological fact of life that you *can get more future consumption product by using indirect or roundabout methods.*

To see this, imagine two islands exactly alike. Each has exactly the same primary factors of labor and land. Island *A* uses these primary factors directly to produce consumption product; she uses no produced capital goods at all. Island *B*, on the other hand, for a preliminary period sacrifices current consumption; instead she uses some of her land and labor to produce intermediate capital goods such as plows, shovels, synthesized chemicals, etc. After this preliminary period of net capital formation, she ends up with a varied stock of capital goods—*i.e.,* with a sizable amount of capital. Now let's measure the amount of consumption product she can go on permanently producing with her land, labor, and constantly replaced capital goods.

Careful measurement of Island *B*'s roundabout product shows it to be greater than Island A's. Why is it greater? Why does B get *more* than 100 units of future consumption goods for her initial sacrifice of 100 units of present consumption? That is a technological engineering question. The economist traditionally takes the following answer as a basic technical fact:

▶ There exist roundabout processes, which take time to get started, that are more productive than direct processes.

From this basic technological fact we can now draw an important economic conclusion: Capital has a *net productivity* that we can express in the form of a percentage per annum; and the only reason you don't take further advantage of this opportunity to get more product is because you must cut down on present consumption if you are to speed up capital's rate of growth.[1]

▶ **DEFINITION OF NET PRODUCTIVITY OF A CAPITAL GOOD OR INVESTMENT PROJECT**

We need an exact definition of the net productivity[2] of any capital project. How do we get a percentage rate per annum that we can use to make comparisons between such diverse physical items as locomotives and looms, gadgets and gasoline, brooms and bonds, ships and stock-share prices, mills and mortgages, punchcards and patents? Money has generally been the measuring rod that we've used to make diverse physical goods commensurable. And capital theory is no exception. It is no accident that the capital market is often called the "money market." It is there that bonds and shares are bought and sold. There that money is borrowed and lent. There that assets which bring in future dollar receipts are given a current capitalized value.

And it is money that we use to decide whether the productivity of roundabout methods in one area is more deserving of investment than that of roundabout methods in another area. How do we use money?

We calculate first the original dollar cost of the factors you buy to begin each roundabout process. Then we calculate the total receipts that the round-

---

[1] Some early economists made a "naïve" mistake: they pointed to the fact that capital goods add to production and therefore have *positive rental values* in the market place. From this fact of "gross productivity" of capital, they tried to prove there must be a positive interest rate. Böhm-Bawerk, a distinguished Austrian authority on capital, pointed out more than half a century ago that this "naïve productivity theory" is logically faulty. Why? Because a capital good's positive rentals might conceivably add up over its lifetime to just enough to buy primary factors to replace itself; *i.e.*, depreciation on a tool might just equal its rental with nothing left over for interest. Böhm-Bawerk correctly insisted: For there to be a positive rate of interest, capital goods must have (and they do have!) rental productivities which add up over their lifetime to *more* than their replacement (or depreciation) costs; it is this *net* productivity of capital that contributes to the explanation of a positive interest rate.

[2] Since 1936 many economists follow Keynes and use the term "marginal efficiency of capital" for what is here called "net productivity." Actually, Yale's Irving Fisher had 30 years earlier given the name "rate of return over cost" to this same concept; and more carefully than Keynes, Fisher concentrated on "the marginal rate of return over cost," which is the same concept applied to the *new* "marginal" investment projects (or "marginal extensions" of old investment projects) that just pay and that are carried on until they are just equal to the market rate of interest.

about methods give. We know very well that the receipts total must add up to more than the original cost total, else there is no net productivity—gross productivity, yes, but not net productivity. Having satisfied ourselves that there is indeed a positive net productivity, we need a way of measuring it quantitatively so as to make diverse projects comparable—projects involving apples and oranges, projects involving 50-year bridges and 5-month beer. Our final solution is to look for a measure that is a *percentage per annum*.

We end up defining the net productivity of a capital project thus:

▶   A capital or investment project's net productivity is that annual percentage yield which you could earn by tying your money up in it. What is the same thing, the project's net productivity is that market rate of interest at which it would just pay to undertake it. (Example: this 50-year bridge with a net productivity of say 8 per cent won't be worth building if the market rate of interest is 9 per cent. But when the market interest drops to 8 per cent or below, you'll build the bridge.)

Here are some examples. A machine that lasts one year costs me $100. I can rent it out for one year (to others or to myself) for $110. So subtract $100 of my original principal from the gross receipts of $110. Then convert the remaining $10 to a percentage net productivity by dividing it by the money capital tied up in the machine: $10/$100. This gives the answer: Net productivity equals 10 per cent per annum. (What if the gross receipts had been $120? Or only $100? Calculate the implied net productivities.)

Example: A 1-million-dollar loom that never wears out will fetch annual market rentals equal to one-twentieth of its cost to build or buy. If you could count on all this lasting forever, show that its net productivity is exactly 5 per cent per annum. Proof: Since it never wears out, all its gross receipts of one-twentieth of $1 million = $50,000, can be treated as if they are net. So $50,000/$1,000,000 = 5 per cent per annum, net productivity. (If you could buy it for 25 times its perpetual annual yield, what would the net productivity be? For 30 times, or for so-called "30 years' purchase"?) [1]

---

[1] Here is a harder example. A machine (or patent or annuity) that costs $1,000 today will pay you gross annual receipts of $110 each year starting next year and continuing for exactly 10 years. What is the net productivity of such a project? Answer: Since $100 is needed each year to pay back the original principal, it is only the excess of receipts above this "depreciation" that gives rise to positive net productivity. By what should we divide $110 − $100 = $10 per year, in order to get a percentage figure? Not by $1,000, since most of the time we have gotten some of our original principal back by virtue of the early installment receipts. With the installments of receipts being always equal, we on the average have about half our money back and half still invested. So we try dividing by $500 = half of $1,000. Thus, an approximate calculation of net productivity gives $10/$500 = 2 per cent per annum. To get an exact answer we would need bond tables of compound interest. These give an exact answer of 1.77 per cent, a little less than the 2 per cent approximate answer. (Exercise: Calculate approximate net productivities if receipts were $105, or $115, or $100.)

More advanced economics and accounting books show that the exact "net productivity" or "marginal efficiency" or "yield" of an asset is always that rate of compound interest which will discount all its future receipts into exact equality with its initial cost. See the Appendix for some further discussion of discounting and capitalization.

▶ BIRD'S-EYE VIEW OF INTEREST DETERMINATION

We now see what determines interest rates over time. If Robinson Crusoe (or a communist dictator or the average citizen in a free economy) cuts down on current consumption, capital formation can be high and capital goods will grow in number. The more capital goods there are, the lower will tend to be their net productivities. Why? Because of our old friend the law of diminishing returns: with population and natural resources unchanged, when you add more and more physical capital goods—or, what is closely related, when you make production more and more roundabout and time-consuming—you will add to total product, but at a decreasing rate.

When you have built the bridges, dams, factories, and production lines that yield a net productivity of 20 per cent, you have then to go on to investment projects with lower net productivities. The market rate of interest that can be earned on investments will thus fall, and this will be the signal for investors to undertake projects which were previously unprofitable at the earlier higher rates of interest.

Two kinds of thrift are involved. First, people must be resisting the temptation to eat up the capital that was amassed in the past; they must be "abstaining" from consuming more than their current incomes, abstaining from making net saving become negative. Second, if there is to be positive capital formation, the community must be willing to undergo "waiting"— waiting in the sense of giving up consumption goods now in return for more consumption goods in the future.

All in all, saving-consumption decisions plus the technical net productivity of capital goods are needed to explain behavior of interest rates over time.

As we shall see, the government—through its monetary and fiscal policies— is also an important determinant of investment and interest rates. Robinson Crusoe could never have his saving desires thwarted by a paradox of thrift, because for him an act of saving and an act of investing are one and the same thing. But in a free market that uses money, an attempt to save more than would be invested at full employment could in a world of sticky wages and prices result in a lowering of actual saving. To the extent that government fiscal and monetary policies succeed in maintaining full employment without inflation, we are closer to the Crusoe case—but only to that extent.

And in any case, every time the government prints money or causes the Central Bank to print new Federal Reserve notes or to undertake expansionary open-market operations and legal-reserves changes—every time that these things we've already studied happen, there is an immediate effect on the interest rate and on the availability of funds for real capital formation. Then too, every time the government raises its taxes relative to expenditures, it cuts down on people's disposable incomes and on the amounts they try to save out of the economy's full-employment income.[1]

So two economies in which private individuals and corporations show the same thrift propensities may develop very differently over a decade or century depending upon the government policies being followed.

▶ GRAPHICAL DETERMINATION OF INTEREST

Supply and demand diagrams can amplify this survey of interest determination. But in the field of capital theory, they become rather complicated. At this point we can greatly simplify the exposition of the traditional theory if we agree to concentrate on the case where all physical capital goods are exactly alike. Of course, in the real world, they're not all alike; therefore, more advanced textbooks have to go through a rather lengthy discussion to show how the diversity of capital goods is to be handled.[2]

By concentrating on the special case of identically homogeneous capital goods, we gain real insight into the traditional theory at a low cost in terms of reading effort. Throughout the rest of this chapter, let's agree to use a big C and write Capital (instead of capital) whenever we want to call attention to the fact that we are talking about the physical stock of homogeneously identical capital goods.

Figure 1 illustrates how the interest rate is determined in traditional capital theory. Curve *DD* shows the demand curve for the stock of Capital. Remember how the demand for labor was formed from the marginal productivity curve for labor. Similarly, the demand for Capital is a "derived demand"—derived ultimately from the value of the extra consumption goods that extra Capital makes possible. The demand for Capital is made up from its net productivity curve (which can be reckoned as a percentage per annum).

Diminishing returns. We see the law of diminishing returns applies to

---

[1] If a government is overeager in its fiscal and monetary policies, it may create inflationary price rises. With people slow to spend their money incomes just received, the rise in prices may cheat them out of consumption. This process of artificially induced high capital formation economists often call "forced saving." It illustrates the great importance for investment of social fiscal and monetary policies. Of course, social security and similar programs can directly affect thriftiness.

Don't think the government has unlimited powers. It can print money or create bank credit and bring interest rates down to any level. But it can't do these and leave prices unchanged! Too-easy money will, at full employment, create inflationary gaps and rising prices. A balanced doubling or millionfold increase of prices would—all transitional effects of price changes neglected—greatly increase interest receipts; but it would at the same time greatly increase all capital values. Hence the interest rate, which is a pure number because it is the ratio of two dollar values, may be unaffected by mere price-level change of a balanced type. (Sweden's great economist of fifty years ago, Knut Wicksell, developed an interesting theory of *Interest and Prices,* based on the fact that when the Central Bank sets too low a market rate of interest it will generate cumulative price inflation that ends only when the market rate is again in alignment with the "real" interest rate compatible with full-employment price stability.)

[2] See the Appendix for some further discussion of this problem.

Capital as well as to other factors; that explains why the *DD* curve slopes downward—*e.g.*, at levels where Capital is very scarce, there are some very profitable roundabout projects that yield 12 or more per cent per annum. Gradually, through thrift, capital formation takes place and the community finds it has exploited all the 12 per cent projects; with total labor and land fixed, diminishing returns to the varying Capital have set in. The community must then invest in 11 and 10 per cent projects.

In Fig. 1, capital formation has taken place in the past until the existing supply of the stock of Capital is given by the vertical supply curve *SS*. The equilibrium rate of interest must in the short run take place at the intersection of the *DD* demand curve and the *SS* short-run supply curve. Here's why. Below the equilibrium interest rate, there would exist too many investment projects; the community's stock of Capital is just big enough to take care of the projects yielding the shown equilibrium interest rate of 8 per cent.

Short-run equilibrium. Why is the equilibrium at *E* only a short-run equilibrium? Because 8 per cent is a rather high rate; and even though Capital is currently scarce enough to keep us at *E*, people would probably there want to go on saving part of their income. This means the community will have capital formation continuously going on; so as time passes, the community will be moving southeast on the *DD* curve as shown by the arrows.

Capital demand intersecting supply determines interest rate:

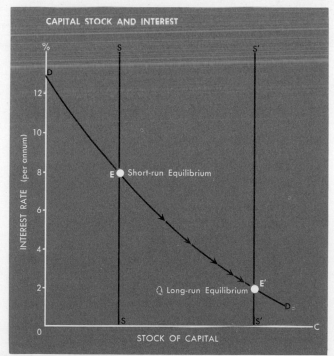

Fig. 1. Existing supply of Capital intersects net productivity schedule to determine short-run equilibrium interest rate. Long-run equilibrium interest rate is at *E'* where net saving ceases.

Specifically, (1) we move east because the accumulating amount of positive investment and capital formation means that the capital stock and the short-run supply curve is being pushed more and more rightward. (In each new short run, the curve will again be vertical but farther to the right.) Now why does the interest rate move downward? (2) We move downward because the law of diminishing returns tells us—other things such as labor, land, and technology remaining unchanged!—that the net productivity of the increased stock of capital goods falls to ever lower percentages.

▶ LONG-TERM STEADY-STATE EQUILIBRIUM

The equilibrium at E is in the nature of a short-run equilibrium, short-run in the sense that people are still saving at the interest rate shown there. Capital is still growing; we are still moving down the DD curve. The interest rate at E is just big enough to keep us growing at the rate we are growing. But the interest rate at E is not yet low enough to choke off all desire to save, not yet low enough to make the community's average propensity to consume equal to 100 per cent of income.

It is at E' that long-run equilibrium is finally achieved. Again, the existing stock of Capital is being auctioned off in the market for the highest short-run interest rate it can fetch. (You run vertically up the $S'S'$ supply curve and read off the E' interest rate.) But now interest is so low that the net saving is zero; now Capital stops growing and the supply curve no longer shifts rightward. The arrows converge on E': at higher interest Capital would grow through positive saving and investment; at lower interest Capital would decline through positive disinvestment and dissaving. So E' represents stable long-run equilibrium.[1]

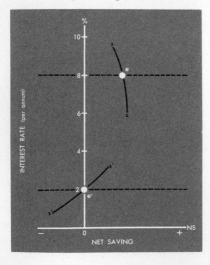

Fig. 2.

[1] In the third edition, saving-investment supply-demand diagrams were pictured along with Fig. 1's stock of Capital diagram. To save space, the story they tell about E' as contrasted to E can be shown in Fig. 2. The 2 per cent long-run equilibrium corresponding to E' of Fig. 1 is marked e' here. Note that at so low a rate, net saving-investment is exactly zero. So Capital neither grows nor declines. But at e, the short-run equilibrium that corresponds to the 8 per cent of Fig. 1's E, the schedule of what people want to save and invest registers positive Capital formation—which is why we keep moving down DD from E to E'.

As was discussed in Part Two and in Chapter 8, the level of income and employment is an important determinant of how much people will want to save when faced with each interest rate. Hence, the ss and $s's'$ curves must be thought of as shifting with different income levels, and more complicated diagrams are needed to tell the whole story. Also, statistical and theoretical studies suggest that interest is not a terribly important factor in influencing the propensity to save: some people save more as the interest rate rises, much

This completes the traditional account of capital and interest theory and the core of our chapter. Before proceeding to criticize and qualify its oversimplifications, we can use the traditional theory to clear up some ancient debates about interest.

▶ INTEREST FAIR OR UNFAIR?

Pointing out that money is "barren," Aristotle said it was unfair to charge positive interest for loans. Many sophisticated medieval Schoolmen followed him in this view that interest represents unjustified usury. Indeed, throughout the Middle Ages, interest was forbidden by canon law; and many were the dodges and devices to get around these restrictions.

How do we answer this view? First, we could point out what has been shown in earlier chapters—that holding a cash balance often does serve a useful function for which people will gladly pay up to a point. But let's meet the issue head on. Let's make the realistic assumption that when I borrow money from you, my purpose is not to hold onto the cash: instead I use the borrowed cash to buy capital goods; and, as we have seen, these intermediate capital goods are so scarce as to create a net product over and above their replacement cost. Therefore, if I didn't pay you interest, I'd really be cheating you out of the return that you could get by putting your money into such productive investment projects!

Consumption loans. Still there will arise in your mind the question of loans made for consumption rather than investment purposes. Suppose I, a poor man, borrow from you, a rich man, so that I can eat more today or pay a hospital bill. (1) Is it fair that I should have to pay you interest? (2) How do such consumption loans affect the short-run and long-run equilibrium interest rates? The answer to the second question will help answer the first.

Consumption lending is today less important than productive-investment lending; therefore, productive investment primarily determines the statistics of interest rates. None the less, to the extent that there is a desire to borrow now for present consumption purposes, we can take this into account in Figure 1. If some people want to dissave, their consumption borrowing will make the community less thrifty as a whole than it would otherwise be. So we find the SS curve of the stock of capital shifting more slowly rightward; and we thereby progress more slowly downward on the DD curve from E toward E', with interest not falling so fast or far as it would otherwise do.

Now we can treat the fairness question. Are we assuming that there is effective competition in the money market for consumption loans so that no

---

like what is shown in $s's'$; but when interest rises, there are some who feel they don't have to save as much to achieve their retirement and other future goals—as shown by the backward bending part of ss; then too, many save automatically from habit and depending upon institutional arrangements, and for them our curve should be quite vertical or inelastic. All these conflicting tendencies make for a rather vertical aggregate curve.

one—rich or poor—can take unfair *monopoly* advantage of anyone else by preventing him from borrowing at the cheapest available terms? If we explicitly assume effective competition, then it is hard to see why there is anything more unfair about loan transactions between rich and poor than there would be in other competitive transactions between rich and poor—*e.g.,* when a rich butcher sells a poor consumer a pound of meat. Of course, the poor man would rather pay nothing for the meat than have to pay a positive price. But being a scarce good, the meat commands a positive price and one that changes with supply and demand. If the existing distribution of income seems unfair to the populace, the field of taxation would seem to offer the best remedies— not interference with competitive loan or other market transactions.

▶ PRODUCTIVITY OR IMPATIENCE?

Some people like to find a single cause for everything, and such people ask: "Is interest caused by the productivity of capital? Or by the fact that savers must be paid for the unpleasant task of 'abstinence' or 'waiting'? Which is more important: opportunity to invest or impatience to spend?"

Our previous paragraphs and our supply-and-demand diagrams show this is a false antithesis. *Both* factors operate to determine the time path of interest: the productivity factor works through the *DD* curve; the impatience to spend, or the tendency to prefer the present to the future, limits the growth of Capital by slowing down the rightward shift of the *SS* curve. Just as both blades of a scissors are needed to cut—so that you can't say one blade rather than the other is doing the actual work—similarly both factors, impatience *and* productivity, interact to determine the behavior of interest rates.[1]

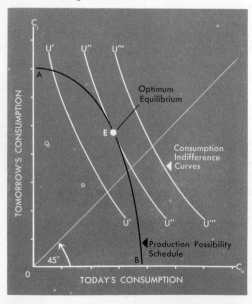

Fig. 3.

[1] Those who have mastered the indifference-curve graphs of Chapter 23's Appendix can use the accompanying Fig. 3 graph to see that positive interest is caused by two factors: (1) a vertical bias of the *AB* production-possibility schedule between present and future consumption goods, and (2) a general vertical bias of the typical consumer's indifference contours between present and future consumption goods. Hence, the tangency-equilibrium at *E* has a slope steeper than 1.0, corresponding to positive interest. The experienced reader will recognize that these can be related to Böhm-Bawerk's three famous causes for interest. His third cause, technological superiority of roundabout processes, and his first cause, the expectation by the typical consumer that his future dollars will have lower marginal utility because his income will be higher in the future (as a result of technological progress or of the productivity of roundaboutness), relate to factor (1). Böhm's second cause—systematic time preference by consumers for present rather than future goods, for rational reasons of life's uncertainties or for irrational reasons—relates to (2).

► A ZERO INTEREST RATE POSSIBLE?

In a world of perfect certainty, it is hard to see how people could ever save enough to bring the net productivity of capital all the way down to a zero interest rate. As long as there is a single hilly railroad track left, it would pay at a zero rate of interest to make it level. Why? Because in enough years, the savings in fuel would pay for the cost. As long as any increase in time-consuming processes could be counted on to produce any extra product and dollars of revenue, the yield of capital could not be zero. Also, as long as any land or other asset exists with a *sure perpetual net income*—and as long as people are willing to give only a *finite* amount of money today in exchange for an infinitely large amount of income spread over the whole future—then we can hardly conceive of the rate of interest as falling all the way to zero.[1]

A zero rate of interest is a little like an "absolute zero of temperature" in physics. We can imagine getting close to it, but we can hardly imagine actually reaching the limiting state of a zero rate of interest. Thus, interest is a basic phenomenon that would not disappear even in the most ideal economic world.

► INTEREST UNDER SOCIALISM?

Our economic analysis suggests that a person is superficial if he thinks that interest is solely a monetary phenomenon of predatory capitalism. Students of planning in a centralized socialistic society have discovered that even such a society must introduce a concept like the interest rate into its plans. Every known society has, since Eden, had some limits on its supply of capital. Every society, therefore, has the important task of screening out investment projects, giving first priority to those that are most immediately productive of the things that society wants. Even in Utopia, you simply can't do everything at once.

How, then, does the screening out among possible projects take place, so that definite priorities can be given? Clearly, there is no alternative but to consider (1) how much of present resources are to be used, and (2) how much of future useful products will be created. To reduce all the alternative patterns into a final single figure is not easy; but something like our earlier calculation of net productivities must be made. Unless you are satisfied to toss a coin or proceed by guess and by gosh in your collectivist's society, you have to introduce first those investment projects with the higher net productivity.

(To test your grasp of this Irving Fisher diagram, rule out factor (1) by making AB "symmetrical around the 45° line," and rule out factor (2) by making the indifference curves "symmetrical around the 45° line." Having ruled out net productivity and time preference, prove that the equilibrium interest rate must then be zero.)

[1] Under realistic conditions of uncertainty, we must qualify the above. Before you have recovered the costs of leveling the roadbed of the railway, airplanes might make them obsolete —or earthquakes might undo your work. In 1932 people expected and experienced zero or negative returns from most capital projects.

When much investment has gone into these in the past and diminishing returns has brought down the yield, you can go on to lower-net-productivity projects.

At some point, therefore, something like the interest rate necessarily comes in. A recent study by Dr. Norman Kaplan (*Journal of Political Economy*, 1952) showed that the social engineers of the Soviet Union are anxious not to be denounced as capitalistic apologists, yet they need some form of interest rate for making efficient investment calculations; as a result, about a dozen different accounting methods are in vogue there for introducing a thinly disguised interest-rate concept into Soviet planning procedures.

▶ SOME MAJOR QUALIFICATIONS

Now the main task of this chapter has been completed. This traditional account of capital theory is in need of some important qualifications; and this chapter concludes with only brief mention of the more important qualifications. The Appendix provides further discussion.

Disturbing factors. In real life you cannot hold other things constant. The long-run equilibrium would no doubt soon be disturbed. For example, someone will undoubtedly turn up with a new invention: this technological change will often shift the old *DD* schedule upward.[1] You can then verify that interest will rise from the old stationary-state level; and you can draw in a new *DD* curve and use it to show how positive net investment will again bring the law of diminishing returns into play and give us new southeast arrows. Again, you can find a new long-run equilibrium.

But again new inventions will come along and disturb the equilibrium. This explains why economic historians do *not* observe steadily declining interest rates as diminishing returns lead toward a zero-saving long-run equilibrium. Instead new inventions are constantly coming along to raise interest rates. Some economists have likened the process to a plucked violin string: other things being equal, the string will gradually come to rest; but before this can happen, some outside event or invention comes along to pluck it once more and to set it again into motion.

Uncertainty and expectations. Our exposition of the traditional capital theory has assumed perfect foresight. This is a serious oversimplification. In real life no one has a crystal ball to read the future: all evaluations of capital and all investment decisions, resting as they do on estimates of future earnings, must necessarily be guesses—accurate guesses based on much thought and information in some cases, wild guesses in other cases, but in every case uncertain guesses. Each day we wake up to learn our expectations were not

---

[1] Some inventions may be "capital saving" and shift *DD* downward, often tending to lower interest. (Note that inventions may also destroy some capital by making it obsolete; and changes in consumer tastes can have similar disturbing effects.)

quite accurate and have to be revalued; each night we go to bed realizing that the next morning will have some surprises for us.

The next chapter will show how significant uncertainty is for profit theory. Here, in connection with interest and capital theory, we must note an important effect of uncertainty: investors' optimism about future yields and risks can change markedly in a very short time; and hence Fig. 1's *DD* curve will be very *shiftable*. It will shift with changes in opinion and rumor; with changes in population trends; with changes in technology and innovation; and with changes in many other factors.[1]

Shifts in schedules with income. Even without disturbing outside factors, there is a serious drawback to traditional schedules. *Changes in the level of real income profoundly shift the saving and investment schedules at each rate of interest.* (Only recall our long statistical and theoretical discussions of Part Two dealing with the propensity to consume and save out of different levels of income. Also recall our discussions of investment induced by increases in the level of income relative to fixed capacities of capital—or what is closely related, the "acceleration principle" of our business-cycle chapter.)

Shifts of the basic schedules represent serious weaknesses in the traditional theory. Many classical economists of a century ago were unaware of this problem because they had the comfortable view that chronic unemployment was impossible. They didn't always know why they believed full employment was inevitable. But they did believe that "supply always creates its own demand and general overproduction is an impossibility."[2]

A neoclassical synthesis. At this point the impatient student will burst out: "Why waste our time with classical notions based on the absurd assumption that full employment always spontaneously maintains itself? We know that there are enough stickinesses of wages and prices in the real world to make unemployment possible: the newspapers confirm this and so do the history books; and you devoted Part Two of your text to detailed analysis of the principles of income determination. So why now bring up ancient (and irrelevant) history?"

How to reply? Readers are not interested in general analysis for its own sake. They want to know whether the traditional capital theory has any

---

[1] To illustrate the subjective volatility of the *DD* schedule, recall a remark once made by Keynes. He characterized the 1929 crash as "a sudden collapse in the marginal efficiency [*i.e.*, net productivity] of capital"—a true albeit surface explanation.

[2] *E.g.*, some believed in a miraculous law of conservation of market purchasing power: what wasn't spent in one direction they said *had* to be spent in another. A more defensible version of the theory claims that if only wages and prices were never sticky, then flexible decreases in all prices and wages would ultimately so increase the real purchasing power of the coin and currency in each man's pocket as to reduce his thriftiness enough to restore full employment. The modern version of this hyperdeflation theory is associated with Cambridge's A. C. Pigou, who does not recommend it for policy purposes. Advanced readers will note that this "Pigou effect" does *shift* the *ss* schedule in Fig. 2 and therefore in no way forestalls the need to qualify the oversimplified traditional capital theory.

relevance to modern actual life. Fifteen years ago, the author wouldn't have known quite what to say. But today one can give a confident reply along the following lines:

By proper use of monetary and fiscal policies, nations today can successfully fight off the plague of mass unemployment and the plague of inflation. With reasonably stable full employment a feasible goal, the modern economist can use a "neoclassical synthesis" based on a combination of the modern principles of income determination and the classical truths.[1] Paradoxically, successful application of the principles of income determination does result in a piercing of the monetary veil masking real conditions, does dissipate the topsy-turvy clashes between the whole and the part that gave rise to countless fallacies of composition, and does finally validate the important classical truths and vanquish the paradox of abortive thrift.

▶ PUBLIC AND PRIVATE POLICY IN DETERMINING CAPITAL FORMATION

Concretely, how does the neoclassical synthesis enable us to use the valid elements of the traditional theory? Here is its basic contribution:

Fiscal and monetary policies interact with private thrift to determine how fast society builds up its capital. For consider a successful pattern of full employment equilibrium without inflation. Recall that this requires the saving and investment curves of Chapter 12's theory of income determination to be intersecting at full employment, with no inflationary gap and no deflationary gap.

But the community's propensity-to-save-out-of-income curve will crucially depend upon budgetary fiscal policy. To see this, suppose tax rates are very high, so that revenues collected at full employment are very high relative to expenditure, with the budget being overbalanced. Suppose too that the taxes fall most heavily on the relatively thriftless lower income groups. Then the community's propensity-to-consume schedule will be a low one at every level of national income, including the full-employment level. The amount not consumed (equal to net personal saving plus the government surplus) will then be very great at every level and—what here interests us—will be great at the full-employment level of income.

Will such a depressed consumption level cause unemployment? Not if the neoclassical synthesis is working. Aggressive easing of monetary policy (open market purchases, lowered reserve requirements, lowered discount rate, possibly aggressive selective credit programs, etc.) will push the community's investment schedule upward. Result: tight fiscal policy plus very expansionary monetary policy have given us a full-employment income characterized by very high capital formation and relatively low consumption.

Work out the opposite mix of monetary and fiscal policies appropriate for

[1] This use of the word "neoclassical" represents an extension of its earlier conventional meaning. Instead of confining the term to those economists who perfected, but remained within, the classical traditions, we now apply it to a wider synthesis of classical verities and the modern theories of income determination.

Mix of monetary and fiscal policy determines rate of capital growth:

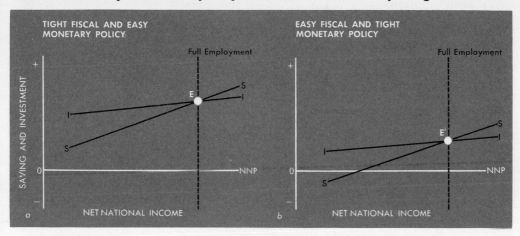

Fig. 4. By tight fiscal and easy monetary policies, the first economy is causing full-employment saving and investment to reach equilibrium at *E*, with rapid rate of capital formation. The second economy uses easy fiscal policy (low taxes and deficits) matched by tight monetary policy to create a low saving and investment (high consumption) full-employment equilibrium.

a community that seeks a high-consumption low-investment full-employment income. Figure 4 shows the alternative rates of capital formation in two alternative societies, each characterized by the same degree of private thrift (as measured by family budget studies at each level of disposable income). Note the resulting differences in capital formation. Do you see that diminishing returns would be operating to bring down interest more rapidly in the high-investment society?

A sobering public responsibility. We conclude, then, with two reminders. The neoclassical synthesis can banish the paradoxical possibility of thrift becoming abortive and can in this sense validate the classical notions concerning capital formation and productivity. On the other hand, modern societies necessarily are pursuing monetary and fiscal policies—and it is these public policies that to an important degree do shape the resulting pattern of high-employment consumption and investment.

This power over the community's rate of capital formation should constitute a sobering responsibility for the voters in any modern democracy.

SUMMARY

1. We can apply *primary* factors of production, land and labor, in indirect ways by introducing *intermediate* productive factors called *capital goods*. It is taken as a technological fact that this "roundaboutness" yields a *net productivity* over and above all replacement costs, expressible as an annual interest percentage, and subject to the usual law of diminishing returns. (Be sure to read again the exact definition of net productivity, a vital concept.)

2. The interest rate is the device society uses to screen out investment projects that are most urgent and economical. When interest is high, only projects with highest net productivities can qualify. Gradually after much past capital formation has invoked the law of diminishing returns, the interest rates will be falling. This provides the signal for introducing capital projects with lower net productivities.

3. Thrift, in the sense of *abstaining* from consuming past capital accumulations and *waiting* for future consumption goods rather than current ones, interacts with the technical net productivity of capital goods to determine the developing pattern of interest rates and capital formation. Outside a Robinson Crusoe or collectivist world, government monetary and fiscal policies play an important role in this process.

4. The long-run equilibrium rate of interest is classically that at which investment is zero and capital ceases to grow. In the absence of technological or other change, long-run equilibrium is reached when capital has grown so much that its lowered interest yield is just low enough to coax out no net saving. Here productivity and impatience are just balancing each other. At all times—in both the short and long run— (*a*) saving decisions involving impatience and time preference are interacting with (*b*) technological productivity conditions to determine the behavior of interest rates. Both blades of the scissors are involved.

5. This traditional theory, oversimplified as it is, enables us to see how consumption loans affect interest, how interest figures even in a socialist state, and how the fairness of positive interest is to be appraised.

6. Important qualifications to the oversimplified traditional capital theory are further discussed in the Appendix and include the following: Lack of perfect foresight means that the net productivity schedule is very shiftable as expectations, technology, and income levels change. Also, a classical theory that ignores shifts in national income does need correction.

7. Fortunately, we can adopt a *neoclassical synthesis* of the valid elements of the traditional classical capital theory and the modern theories of income determination and effective demand. According to this rather optimistic—and somewhat oversimplified!—view, a great variety of compensating monetary and fiscal policies can succeed in maintaining inflationless, reasonably full employment. With stable employment being assumed, Figure 4 gives the needed qualification to the traditional theory: and it reveals that public policy has great responsibility for determining whether the composition of the full-employment national income will be heavily weighted toward investment or toward consumption; this means that the Central Bank and the legislature between them shape the environment within which thriftiness works itself out, as the Appendix further discusses.

QUESTIONS FOR DISCUSSION

1. List a number of capital goods or assets. Which are "circulating capital" (*i.e.,* consumable within 1 year)? Which "fixed capital"?

2. Contrast three "prices" of capital: (*a*) rental of a capital good; (*b*) market price of the good; (*c*) interest yield on the value of a good.

3. Give some examples of efficient roundabout processes.

4. Describe short-run equilibrium interest rate with Capital stock fixed. What determines the rate of Capital growth? The long-run equilibrium?

5. Is interest fair? Can it be zero under (*a*) capitalism, or (*b*) communism?

6. How do innovations and expectations affect traditional interest theory?

7. Is there one saving schedule independently of income? Of fiscal policy?

8. Interpret the "neoclassical synthesis." Contrast full employment involving "tight money" and "easy fiscal policy" with an opposite full employment.

9. Irving Fisher wrote a book with the title *The Theory of Interest.* He gave as its subtitle *As Determined by Impatience to Spend and Opportunities to Invest.* Explain what these mean. Defend the following: "Fisher should have added 'and as affected by government monetary and fiscal policies.'"

10. Review your understanding of the following concepts:

various meanings of capital	*time preference, abstinence, and*
net productivity (or marginal	*waiting*
efficiency) of capital	*uncertainty and technological*
indirect, roundabout methods	*change*
and diminishing returns	*neoclassical synthesis and pub-*
interest rate per annum	*lic responsibility for rate of*
short- and long-run equilibrium	*capital formation*

APPENDIX: THEORETICAL ASPECTS OF INTEREST, MONEY, AND POLICY

Here, very briefly, can be mentioned some elaborations and qualifications to this chapter's discussion.

Measuring Capital Value

How do we handle the realistic fact that capital goods are diverse and not homogeneous? To answer this, ask the following:

"How does the competitive market place handle the problem of diverse looms, machines, raw-material inventories, etc.?"

Common-sense observation tells us that brokers and bankers never bother to add together a pound of vacuum tubes and a dozen of electric motors. Bids and offers in competitive markets set dollar price tags on all assets, whatever their tangible or intangible forms; and these dollar totals, as we have seen, can be added together.

How is the present dollar value of any capital good or income stream to be measured? We shall find that the market rate of interest enables us to "capitalize" any future money payments into a "present discounted value."

A careful reader may be troubled, saying: "To explain interest in Fig. 1, you use the concept of a homogeneous magnitude called Capital. Now you tell me that the total of actual capital can be evaluated only after we know the interest rate. Isn't there a vicious circle here?"

There is a circle, but it turns out to be a virtuous circle rather than a vicious one. What does logic tell us about the circularly dependent statements: "I am twice your age. You are 20 years younger than I"? Clearly, these circularly dependent conditions can be *simultaneously* solved for the determinate unique solution: "I am 40, you are 20."

Similarly, in a perfectly competitive capital market which involves no frictions, there would always be going on bids and offers for all capital goods and all tangible or intangible income streams. There would then *simultaneously* be determined (1) the capitalized prices of all assets and (2) the unique current market rate of interest (expressed as the same percentage yield per annum on all the riskless assets).[1]

The problem, then, of defining a homogeneous measure of capital is not one that the people in the market place would ever find insoluble. I should also add that the market place never finds it necessary to separate out "intermediate" and "primary" factors: actually, nature's land and other resources will also be part of the capitalized assets bought and sold in the market place —whether or not new resources can be found or produced. These, and many other problems that economists argue about, turn out not to be problems of the real world; they are only problems that arise from too brief expositions of economics textbooks.

Capitalization of Perpetual Annuities or Income Streams

To see how assets are capitalized, let's first look at the simplest case of a piece of land or an annuity contract that is certain to pay you the same number of dollars each year from now until eternity. It turns out we can quite easily write down the formula for the present capitalized value, V, of any permanent income stream of $1 per year or $N per year. We ask, "How many dollars put out every year at the market rate of interest i per annum will give us exactly the same return of $1 per year or $N per year?" The obvious answer is summarized in the rule:

$$V = \frac{\$N}{i}$$

where V = present capitalized value (often called "present discounted value")

N = permanent annual return

i = interest rate expressed as a decimal (such as 0.05 or 5/100 or 5 per cent, etc.)

Thus, if the interest rate will always be 5 per cent, any permanent income will sell for exactly 20 (= 1 ÷ 5/100) times its annual income. (In the Middle Ages, they called this "20 years' purchase" and thus got around the taboo against interest. Show that 2 per cent interest means 50 years' purchase; 4 per cent, 25 years' purchase; etc.)

Market Capitalization of Assets Equals Their Present Discounted Value

Now we can go beyond the simple case of perpetual annuities to the general case. Un-

---

[1] In real life there are always some frictions and imperfections of competition. Perfect foresight being absent, different assets will turn out to have different yields. At any one time there will be a whole spread of interest rates on different assets depending upon people's views of their riskiness. However, the yields at any one time would all become unique if foresight were perfect.

der conditions of absolute certainty, anyone can borrow or lend as much as he wishes at the single competitive market rate of interest. Every asset must be yielding that same market rate of interest. This equality of yield results from the way competitors bid up or bid down the market price of any asset—whether it be a bond, a stock, a patent, a going business, a corner lot, or any earning stream of net rentals whatsoever.

What exactly is the formula for the capitalized market value of *any* asset? Our answer here can be brief:

Under absolute certainty, every asset will be capitalized *by the price bids of buyers and sellers* in the market place at the *present discounted value* of all its future net receipts.[1] These dollar receipts cannot simply be added up regardless of the date when they are received. The farther off in the future is a given dollar receipt, the less it is worth today. Why?

Because the positive market rate of interest means that all future payments must be *discounted*. A building far off looks tiny because of space perspective. The interest rate produces a similar shrinking of time perspective. Even if I knew you would pay my heirs $1 in 999 years from now, I should be foolish to advance you more than a cent today. To see why, let's review the arithmetic of this discounting process.

At 4 per cent interest I can set aside about 96 cents today and it will grow to $1 within the year. Hence, the *present discounted value* of $1 payable a year from now is today only 96 cents (or to be exact $100/1.04 = 96\frac{16}{104}$ cents). The present discounted value of $1 payable in 2 years' time is only about 92 cents or $1/(1.04)^2$. Similarly, any table of compound interest will show that money, invested and reinvested at 4 per cent compound interest, more than

[1] By *net* receipts we mean all the cash dollar rentals received from the asset *minus* all cash outlays for materials, repairs, etc. To count in interest and depreciation expense (along with using discount and reckoning in each initial cost of assets) is shown in more advanced discussions to involve double counting.

doubles itself in 20 years' time. Then what must be the market value today of $1 payable in 20 years? The present discounted value is less than 50 cents.[2]

You may raise the following objection: "It is all very well to know how to evaluate a single dollar payable at some specified date in the future. But most assets involve a bundle of dollars payable in some installment pattern over future years. How does the market place evaluate such assets?"

This is a perfectly valid question. An asset such as a bond does pay equal installment coupons for a long time and then pays you back your principal. A truck probably gives you a bundle of receipts that decrease as it gets older and begins to need repairs. A piece of land may be paying you a certain rental, not once, but in every year. Except for single-payment loans, we must always evaluate a bundle of receipts.

But the way to arrive at any asset's present discounted value is straightforward. We let each dollar stand on its own feet; we evaluate the present worth of each part of the stream of future receipts—giving due allowance for the discounting required by its payment date. Then we simply *add together* all these separate present discounted values. And thus we have arrived at the asset's capitalized market value—or what is often called its "present discounted value."

Figure 5 shows this graphically for a machine that earns steady net annual rentals of $100 over a 20-year period and has no scrap value at the end. Its present value is not $2,000 but only $1,359. Note how much

[2] The general rule for present discounted values is the following: To figure out the value today of $1 payable t years from now, ask yourself how much must be invested today at compound interest to grow into $1 at the end of t years. Now we know that at 4 per cent compound interest any principal grows in t years proportionally to $(1 + 0.04)^t$. Hence, we need only invert this expression to arrive at the final answer. Therefore, the *present discounted value* of $1 payable t years from now is only $1/(1 + 0.04)^t$. What if the interest rate were 6 per cent? Or i per cent?

Future dollar receipts are today discounted:

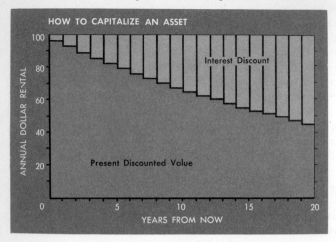

Fig. 5. The present value of a machine giving net annual rentals of $100 for 20 years (with interest rate given as 4 per cent) is shown by the lower area. The upper area has been discounted away.

the later dollar earnings are scaled down or discounted because of the time perspective we have been talking about. The total area remaining after discounting (the lightly shaded area) represents the total of the machine's *present discounted value*—its capitalized market value.[1]

Acting to maximize present discounted

---

[1] Can you now verify our $V = \$N/i$ perpetuity formula? In high school algebra we learn to sum a convergent geometric progression

$$1 + K + K^2 + \cdots = \frac{1}{1 - K},$$

for K any fraction. If you set $K = \dfrac{1}{1 + i}$, you can with a little work verify our capitalization formula for a permanent income stream: write out *all* the discounted terms

$$\frac{\$N}{1 + i} + \frac{\$N}{(1 + i)^2} + \cdots$$

$$= -\$N + \$N \left\{ 1 + \frac{1}{1 + i} + \left(\frac{1}{1 + i} \right)^2 + \cdots \right\}$$

$$= -\$N + \$N \frac{1}{1 - \dfrac{1}{1 + i}} = \frac{\$N}{i}. \text{ QED.}$$

But note that common-sense economics give us an equally convincing proof: At interest i, $\$N/i$ is the only sum *whose earnings will exactly match* the $\$N$ per year of permanent income.

value. Our formula tells us how to write down in our balance sheets the value of any asset once we know how that asset will be used. But note that an asset's future receipts usually depend on our business decisions: Shall we use a truck 8 or 9 years? Shall we overhaul it once a month or once a year? Shall we replace it with a cheap nondurable truck or an expensive durable one?

There is one golden rule for giving correct answers to these and all other investment decisions.

▶ Calculate the present discounted value resulting from each possible decision. Then always act so as to achieve the largest present discounted value. That way you'll have more wealth, to spend however and whenever you like.[2]

Net productivity once again. Note that the lower the interest rate the more durable will be the products and the more roundabout will be the methods on which people

---

[2] This rule shows that business decisions in an ideal capital market would be independent of the decider's personal consumption-saving time preference. Why? Because it's always better to be able to sell out now for a larger money sum than for a small sum—no matter how you decide to spend on consumption.

will finally decide. Why? Because a lower interest rate will discount less heavily the far-future receipts of roundabout processes; and thus such investment projects will for the first time become worth while.

For any investment project—a particular bridge or oil refinery—we can calculate how low interest must fall for the project in question to become just worth while. (Thus, at 10 per cent interest a 50-year bridge over the Hudson River might not pay. But at, say, 6 per cent it might just pay.) And don't forget that all investment decisions depend on guesses about the future.

Rents Regarded as Interest: A Digression

We have spoken of national income as being composed of wages, rents, and interest. Or briefly we can speak of it as labor incomes and property incomes. However, the total of property income can, under ideal conditions, be regarded as interest.

The reason is as follows: After any rent-producing factor of production—land, machinery, or any other—has been capitalized, its rental earnings will appear in the form of interest. The $40 of annual net rentals that I received from a parcel of land will appear as a 4 per cent interest return on the $1,000 capitalized market value of the land. The net rental earned by a truck (over and above replacement and other expenses) will likewise appear in the guise of interest on its capital value. To the investor, these interest returns are indistinguishable from any other interest earnings.

This shows that *all* property incomes could be expressed as interest. From this viewpoint, we could think of the national income simply as *wages plus interest*.[1] (The important thing is not to count any net rents twice: Do not count in land rents and

------

[1] As a matter of fact, if we could legally buy and sell human beings and the rights to their future earnings, then wages too might be capitalized. That done and with all nonwindfall profits "capitalized," *all* the national income might be called interest!

also the interest on the land's money value.)

Money, Interest, and Public Policy

Our final brief task is to suggest how the classical theory of interest fits with the modern theory of effective demand.

Do changes in the amount of money affect the interest rate?

If you believed that employment was always full and that changes in money always resulted via a strict "quantity theory" in proportional changes in *all* prices, then interest rates would indeed be independent of monetary policy. This extreme classical version of neutral money is today believed applicable to short-run events by nobody. (Some economists would grant it a measure of long-run validity, even today.)

In Part Two we saw that an alternative to holding earning assets is holding money as an asset. Suppose people make no change in their current propensities to save and consume out of a given income when faced by a given interest-rate structure. But suppose they do decrease their desire to hold cash. Then they bid for existing stocks, bonds, and titles to earning assets. This raises capital values and immediately *lowers interest rates;* it also may set capital to growing at a more rapid rate; but only after a time period of higher investment can the volume of real capital goods have appreciably increased. Unless offset by contractionary fiscal policy, all this will raise employment and/or expand wages and prices.

Note that the Central Bank can create exactly the same chain of events by engaging in expansionary monetary policies. (Recall Chapter 16's open-market operations, reserve-rate and discount-rate changes, etc.)

How do we reconcile this increase in investment that results from no change in personal thriftiness with classical notions? We do so by recognizing that moving interest downward and relaxing credit generally may raise employment and real income, and thereby shift the saving propensities of Fig. 2 and of earlier chapters—thus sending us faster down Fig. 1's *DD* curve, et cetera.

Synthesis of Classical Theory of Interest with Theory of Income Determination: Review

The neoclassical synthesis referred to earlier shows how private and public thrift patterns interact. It shows that private thrift need no longer be feared lest it cause a depression and paradoxically abort itself. It deals with a well-running system that is kept near inflationless full employment by matching Central Bank and fiscal policies.

Thus, if we desire a high-investment full-employment condition, the Central Bank uses its bag of tricks to increase investment. Of course, given the community's private thrift patterns and technological-expectational investment patterns of the moment, we can stay at the full-employment level aimed at by the Central Bank only if Congress adopts a compensating fiscal policy.

What are the requirements of this compensating fiscal policy? Taxes and expenditure must be just contractionary enough to affect disposable incomes enough to cut the consumption propensity down to equality with full-employment product minus investment. (Describe what Central Bank and fiscal authorities must do to create full employment with high consumption.) [1]

---

[1] Intermediate texts will show you what happens when independent fiscal and monetary policies are followed. Then income and employment (and possibly the price level) will become important variables. For the benefit of advanced readers Figs. 6a and 6b have been added, to throw light on this more general case. Both plot levels of interest rates vertically against the level of real income. Both contain the curve BB which shows for each interest rate and for a given fiscal policy what will be the level of income generated (through our old friend the "multiplier") by the marginal efficiency of investment level appropriate to the designated interest rate. This BB curve slopes southeast because low interest begets high investment which begets high income.

Figure 6a summarizes each monetary policy by showing the *level of interest* that the Central Bank authorities insist on ending up with. Note that of all the horizontal lines (AA, A'A', etc.) only one will end us up at the full-employment point E once the fiscal policy presupposed by BB is given.

Figure 6b shows the same thing, but on the assumption that each different monetary policy is expressed in terms of setting a specified fixed *level of money*. Thus M'M' corresponds to less total money created by the Central Bank than does MM. Each of these "equal-total-money" curves slopes upward. Why? Because higher incomes require more money for transactions and this leaves less money to bid down securities' yields. Note that MM is the only money level that will exactly realize the full-employment goal E.

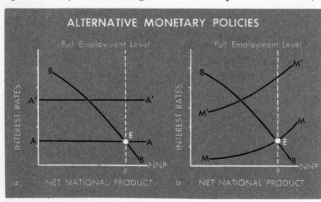

More advanced texts show that (1) fiscal policy operates primarily on BB, as do changes in personal thriftiness and in investment's marginal efficiency; on the other hand, (2) monetary and debt-management policy primarily act to shift AA or MM, as do changes in people's liquidity preferences concerning desirability of holding cash or earning assets. See A. H. HANSEN, *Monetary Theory and Fiscal Policy*

Fig. 6.

(McGraw-Hill, New York, 1949), Chap. 4. Oxford's J. R. Hicks first gave the Fig. 6b interpretation of Keynes' *General Theory*.

SUMMARY TO APPENDIX

1. No impossible task of measuring Capital ever faces a competitive interest market. Under perfect competition all foreseen future income streams are capitalized, and there is never any need to distinguish between "primary" and "intermediate" factors. All current earnings that appear in national income can be alternatively expressed as interest (rather than as net rentals) to the extent that these earnings can be legally capitalized into property values by purchase and sale and by pledged loans.

2. The simple formula for present capitalized or discounted value of a permanent N-per-year income stream is $PV = \$N/i$, where $1/i$ is the "number of years' purchase."

3. The general way of capitalizing any future income stream involves separately discounting each of its future dollar receipts payable t years in the future by applying the discount factor $1/(1 + i)^t$.

4. Every productive decision is made so as to *maximize present discounted value.* This means that no one will invest in a project whose net productivity is lower than the market rate of interest. The net productivity of a project is that critical rate of interest at which the project just pays, because the positive receipts when discounted just add up to equality with the (discounted) costs. The marginal efficiency schedule giving the total demand for investment slopes down as low interest coaxes out more investment.

5. Few today think the interest rate will be unaffected by changes in total money. Especially in the short run is the level of income a variable, and it is untrue to think that money changes all prices in the strict proportionality demanded by the simplest quantity theory. Increases in money (or decreases in people's desire to hold idle money) will bid up security prices, lower interest, raise investment, and expand money and/or real incomes.

6. But the classical analysis can be usefully applied if we make the neoclassical assumption that Central Bank and fiscal policies will be so meshed as to preserve stable high-employment levels without undue inflation. (The Central Bank, so to speak, sets interest to the desired investment level, and the fiscal authorities regulate taxes and expenditures to validate the needed thrift. Of course, both policies are to be *simultaneously* applied.)

QUESTIONS FOR DISCUSSION

1. How do you reckon capitalized or present discounted market value?

2. Give reasons why higher interest rates might reduce investment demand.

3. What does higher M do to interest? Why? What does higher income do? Explain why *independent* monetary and fiscal policies need not lead to full employment. Show there is more than one investment rate compatible with full employment because of changing fiscal policies.

4. Review your understanding of the following concepts:

> *capitalized value or present discounted value of an asset*
> *discounting*
> *30 years' purchase*
> *perpetuity or perpetual annuity*
> *maximization of present discounted value*
> *neoclassical synthesis*

30 PROFITS AND INCENTIVES

> *The world will always be governed by self-interest. We should not try to stop this, we should try to make the self-interest of cads a little more coincident with that of decent people.*
>
> SAMUEL BUTLER

In addition to wages, interest, and rent, economists often talk about a fourth category of income: profit. Wages are the return to labor; interest the return to capital; rent the return to land. What is profit the return to? Economists do not always agree on the answer. A graduate student recently checked over a number of modern textbooks and came up with 14 different answers!

What shall we do? Examine all 14 answers? Add a fifteenth? The obvious thing is to give a common-sense description of what people generally mean when they speak of profits. Let us call a spade a spade. If profit is a miscellaneous catchall category, let us recognize it as such. And let us be satisfied to notice what are some of the important elements contained in the usual definitions of profit.

We shall first discuss the main definitions of profit. The usual profit figures bandied about will not check with any of these, as we shall see. Then, after analyzing the main notions about profit, we'll conclude the chapter with a summary of the role profit and loss play in the market pricing solution to society's problems: What, How, and For Whom.

▶ REPORTED PROFIT STATISTICS

When a U.S. Department of Commerce or United Nations statistician gives newspaper reporters a figure involving profits, what does he usually mean? First, he means *corporation earnings*—whether they are paid out as dividends or retained as undistributed profits. (In some reports he includes and in some he excludes corporate profit taxes, and sometimes he "adjusts" corporate profits for changes in evaluation of inventories due to price-level changes. So you must be careful in using published statistics.) He may also give the reporters a second figure that has the flavor of profits about it, namely, *income of unincorporated enterprises* (farmers, self-employed, doctors, partnerships, etc.).

We know how he arrived at such a statistical figure of profits for a corporation or unincorporated enterprise. From the sales revenue of the firm, he subtracted the firm's costs: its cost of materials, wage payments to employees, bond interest, land rents, etc. What is left goes into the figures as profit.

▶ FIRST VIEW: PROFIT AS "IMPLICIT" FACTOR RETURNS

To the economist, such statistical profits are a hodgepodge of different elements. Obviously, part at least of reported profits are merely the return to the owners of the firm for the capital supplied by them. Thus, part may be the return to the personal work provided by the owners of the firm—by the farmer and his family, by the doctor, by the partners, or by corporate executives who also happen to be principal stockholders. Part may be the rent return on self-owned natural resources; part the equivalent of interest on the owner's capital.

This shows us the first principle about profit: Much of what is ordinarily called profit is really nothing but interest, rents, and wages under a different name. *Implicit* interest, *implicit* rent, and *implicit* wages are the names economists give to this part of profit—*i.e.,* to the earnings of *self-used* factors.

▶ SECOND VIEW: PROFIT AS THE REWARD TO ENTERPRISE AND INNOVATION

Suppose we lived in a dreamworld of perfect competition, where we could read the future perfectly from the palms of our hands and where no innovations were permitted to disturb the settled routine of things. Then the economist says there would really be no profits at all! Here's what he means.

The statistician might still be reporting some profit figures to the press; but we know that, under these ideal equilibrium conditions, the *implicit returns* to the labor and property supplied by owners *would exactly swallow up all the profits reported*. Why? Because owners would hire out their factors on the market if they did not get equal rewards from using them in their own businesses. And because people who previously were hiring out their labor and property services would soon go into business for themselves if they knew they could earn more in that way.

Perfectly free entry of numerous competitors would, in a static world of perfect knowledge, bring price down to cost and squeeze out all profits above and beyond competitive wages, interest, and rent.[1]

We do not live in such a dreamworld. We never shall. In real life somebody must act as boss and decide how a business shall be run. Competition is never

---

[1] If people like running their own business, they may gladly take lower implicit wages. If, by contrast, people dislike having to boss other people and take responsibility for management decisions, then management wages may have to be higher.

perfectly perfect. Somebody must try to peer into the future to decide whether there will be a demand for shoelaces or what will be the price of wheat. And in the world as we know it, there is a chance for a man with a brand-new idea to invent a revolutionary machine or a softer soft drink—to promote a new product or find a way to lower costs on an old one.

Let us call the man who does any of these things an *entrepreneur* or *innovator*. Although it is hard to draw the line, let us distinguish him from the bureaucratic executive or manager who simply keeps an established business running. Many economists—such as the late Joseph Schumpeter, Harvard's Austrian-born economist—do not think of profit as simply the wages of management: they think of the wages of management as wages—implicit or explicit, and high as they may be in the competitive market for gifted managers. They think of *profit as the return to innovators or to entrepreneurs.*

Today it is easier for us to understand this distinction than it used to be half a century ago. We are all acquainted with huge corporations that are run by managers who own less than 1 per cent of the common stock. Even though these executives run the business, they are paid wages much like anybody else. Management of this type is a skill not different in kind from other skills—such as being able to keep books or supervise a production process. People who possess this skill are bid for in the market place, and like any other factor, they move into those jobs where they will receive the highest wages.

The innovator is different. Though he may not always succeed, he is trying to carry out new activities. He is the man with vision, originality, and daring. He may not be the scientist who invents the new process, but he is the one who successfully introduces it. Maxwell developed the scientific theory of radio waves, Hertz discovered them experimentally, but Marconi and Sarnoff made them commercially profitable. On the other hand, De Forest, who discovered the triode tube, also sought to put his inventions into commercial use. But he went broke a number of times and on each occasion disappointed the hopes of investors who had put money into his enterprises.

Many try; a few succeed. The dollars earned by the successful innovators are defined by some economists—like Schumpeter—as profit. Usually these profit earnings are temporary and finally are competed out of existence by rivals and imitators. But while one source of innovational profits is disappearing, some new clever innovation is being born. So altogether these profits will continue to exist.

▶ THIRD VIEW: RISK, UNCERTAINTY, AND PROFIT

If the future were perfectly certain, there would be no opportunity for a bright young man to come along with a revolutionary innovation; everything would be already known. This shows that innovators' profits are closely tied up with risk and uncertainty. Frank Knight, a famous University of Chicago economist of the last 40 years, has an important theory that *all true profit is linked up with uncertainty*.[1] Innovators' profits, discussed in the preceding section, represent one important category of uncertainty-induced profit.

Go to Knight with the story of a broker who guessed that wheat would rise in price and who thereby made a million dollars over the week end. Knight probably would nod and say, "That's what I mean. If the future were perfectly certain, the market would have discounted in advance the coming shortage of wheat and these profits would not have arisen." Or go to Knight with the story of a broker who lost his shirt betting wheat would rise in price. Knight would probably reply, "Profits can be negative as well as positive. Uncertainty causes a spread between what people *expect* will happen and what *does actually* happen. The amount of this discrepancy is profit (or loss)."

In examining any profit figures, we must always keep uncertainty and risk in mind. We saw in earlier chapters that some low-grade risky bonds may appear to be yielding 8 per cent at the same time that high-grade safe bonds yield only 3 per cent. But if the chances are that 1 out of 20 low-grade issues will default on their principal in the coming year, then you are kidding yourself if you think that these bonds are a better buy. Actually, the extra 5 per cent is no more than enough to cover the risk of default.

While people who buy lottery tickets face uncertainty, the promoter of the lottery faces no risk. He knows he will come out ahead. Similarly a large insurance company may rely on mathematical laws of probability to reduce its relative riskiness. Why? Because the different risks tend to be canceled off against each other if the numbers are large enough. To the extent that we can eliminate uncertainty by pooling risks, the problem of profits fails to arise. It arises only for the irreducible minimum of riskiness that remains.

In some years, the total of losses may be greater than the total of profits. Risk bearers then as a whole have paid out to labor, to capitalists, and to landowners more than those factors would have earned if the future had been certain. In another year, the algebraic total of Knight-defined profits may turn out to be positive—so that the factors of production have then received less than they would have if the future were certain. A big question is this: Are risk bearers on the whole overly optimistic? As a class do they lose money and subsidize the other factors of production? Or are risk bearers as a class overly pessimistic—as claimed in most economics textbooks—so that profits represent a net positive payment for the service of risk bearing?

Knight does not claim to know the answers, and neither does anyone else. But this much is clear: If we regard profit as the return caused by uncertainty, then profit is not simply a fourth factor return like wages, interest, or rents. Profit is *part* of these factor returns. A worker who is unlucky enough to have

---

[1] FRANK H. KNIGHT, *Risk, Uncertainty and Profit* (London School of Economics and Political Science, Series of Reprints of Scarce Tracts, No. 16, 1933).

picked a trade that becomes obsolete can also suffer losses. Glass blowers displaced by the machine are a standard example of the difference between what actually happened and what people expected to happen. Or a man who by chance studied nuclear physics may find himself unwittingly playing the role of a lucky entrepreneur. Because of uncertainty, a landowner may also experience windfall gains or losses; and in that sense, part of his rents may be positive or negative profits. Same is true of the capitalist betting on different industries.

These "capital gains or losses" are bred by uncertainty, and they cannot be predictably expected to recur again and again. Many experts would not admit that they are income; in England, capital gains as such are not taxed at all. In this country they receive very special treatment: Capital gains on assets owned more than 6 months are taxed at half the rate of ordinary income or even lower; they can never be taxed at more than a 25 per cent rate, and you'll recall that additional ordinary income can be taxed 90 per cent or more.

▶ FOURTH VIEW: PROFIT AS A "MONOPOLY RETURN"

The author once discussed in a classroom these three aspects of profit: (1) profit as *implicit* rents, wages, and interests; (2) profit as the temporary return to daring, but unforeseen *innovations;* and (3) profit as the divergence —thrown up by the fact of *uncertainty*—between what people had *expected* to happen and what actually happened. A student came up to him after class and complained: "Your discussion has confused me. Now I don't know what it is that I'm against."

Probably he, like many men in the street, had in mind a fourth notion about profit. He thought of *profit as the earnings of monopoly*. Like most people, he probably had a grossly exaggerated notion of how much of each dollar that we spend on an automobile or a pork chop goes to profit receivers—according to any of our definitions. Most likely, he thought that about 50 per cent of each dollar goes to wealthy monopolists; the truth is that, even in terms of the catchall statistical definition, corporate profits after taxes are less than *one-fifth* of corporations' wage payrolls.

▶ PERFECT COMPETITION REDEFINED

Still if we are to be objective, we must not close our eyes to this fact: In the world as we know it competition is not "perfect." Let us recall again what perfect competition means as rigorously defined by the economist. It does not simply mean that there should be at least two sellers of a product. It is not enough that two companies should compete over the radio in proclaiming the superlative merits of their respective goods; it is not enough that there be partial substitutes for the products sold by any particular business firm. Even if the firm is trying desperately to expand its production and sales at its publicly quoted price, this does not ensure perfect competition in the economist's strict sense. Perfect competition is a much stricter condition than any of these—or than all of them put together.

▶ *Perfect competition means that each seller has absolutely no control over price;* it means that his demand curve is perfectly horizontal and *infinitely* elastic; it means that no person is able to control any significant fraction of the total of any category of productive resource.

We have seen in Chapter 24 and elsewhere that this is a far cry from the real world. Almost all firms, except farmers, can raise or lower their prices without losing or gaining *all* the customers in the market. Instead their demand curves are somewhat tipped, and there is a discrepancy between price and marginal revenue. Most market situations are imperfectly competitive—a blend between competition and monopoly. (So nearly universal a condition is by no means necessarily illegal or immoral: but, as we have already seen, imperfections of competition do have effects on What, How, and For Whom that we must recognize.)

When we go on to examine the ownership of productive factors, we see that no two factors are quite alike. Your abilities as a worker and those of your neighbor are somewhat different. If we define your precise pattern of abilities as a separate factor of production, then we must admit that you do own and control an appreciable fraction of the total of that unique factor of production —100 per cent, in fact. Or you may be the sole owner of the patent to a particular process. Or you may own the only site where the river narrows down to its most suitable place for a bridge. Or there may be no acre of Iowa farm land quite like yours.

Let us see how this ties in with imperfect competition. Your neighbors are a little different from you, certainly. But in all probability they are enough like you so that the wage rate for your services would not be appreciably different even if you *withheld* some from the market. You really do not possess any appreciable monopoly power because the demand for the factor you own is for practical purposes infinitely elastic.

The same is true of your acre of good Iowa corn land. If you let half of it stand idle, the price of corn would not be affected; and the derived price for your land would be unchanged even though you and your family know that there is really no other farmstead quite like it.

And note this: If the land is sufficiently fertile, you will, of course, be making quite a living off your farm. Perhaps you may even be in the top 2 per cent of the income distribution. Even though competition is perfect, this rent return to the land you own can *not* be competed away by rival farmers. As long as the Good Lord made only a limited amount of fertile Iowa farm land, it will earn a rent for its owner—regardless of how he originally acquired title to the land. *Competitively determined rents are the results of a natural scarcity.*

► **"CONTRIVED SCARCITIES" VERSUS "NATURAL SCARCITIES"**

It is quite a different matter if the demand for one of your factors of production is negatively inclined rather than infinitely elastic. (Let us review what this means: It means that, when you raise your price, you still can sell *some* of your factor; this is the sense in which you have some monopoly control over price.) If you are the sole owner of an important patent, it will pay you to charge a price so as to limit its use. If audiences swoon to your singing as to nobody else's, then you will have to remember that, the more you sing, the lower will be the price the market will pay for your singing. If you own the best site for a bridge, then you must be careful not to sell anyone else the lot next to it; otherwise, he will be able to offer the bridgebuilders a site nearly as good as yours, and this will limit the dollars you can derive from yours. Part of the rent you earn on Nature's bridge site has a monopoly element in it by virtue of your withholding its use for fear of spoiling your dollar market.

What does all this add up to? It means that, *as soon as there is an appreciable deviation from perfect competition, it will pay you to take account of the fact that you will spoil the market the more you offer of your factor.*

Any prudent firm takes account of the loss on all previous units resulting when it sells an extra unit of product, and it is its marginal revenue—lower than price because of the loss on previous units—which a prudent firm concentrates on. So with you as the owner of a factor. You are interested in the *marginal* or *extra revenue* that the factor brings you. You will not withhold *all* the factor from the market—that would bring you in *no* revenue at all. Nor will you provide so much of the factor that it becomes a free good and brings in no revenue. As a quasi-monopolist or imperfect competitor, what should you do? You will withhold just so much of that service as will bring its marginal revenue down to zero.[1]

Our principle is this: *Under imperfect competition, it pays people to limit the supply of their factors.* By definition, natural scarcities are such that nothing can be done about them. But under imperfect competition, we encounter in addition so-called *contrived scarcities.*

► **MONOPOLY EARNINGS AS THE RETURN TO "CONTRIVED SCARCITIES"**

Hence, the fourth view of profits as a monopoly return is often reformulated in the economic textbooks to read as follows:

Part of what is called profit is the return to a "contrived scarcity."

This return takes the form of rent, wages, or interest, depending on the na-

---

[1] Of course, there may be some discomfort to you in rendering the service, or you may have the opportunity of selling the service in some other market—as in the case where you could use your bridge site to grow corn. In these cases, you will obviously equate marginal revenue to some defined marginal *cost* rather than to zero.

ture of the factor in question and on the contractual relations set up to handle the particular situation. (For example, an investor may buy the bridge-site land at the full capitalized value of its monopoly earning power. To him, the return will seem to be interest.) So monopoly profits are inextricably tied up with wages, interest, and rent.

▶ **ETHICAL ATTITUDES TOWARD PROFITS**

Any sampling of public opinion shows some hostility toward profit. A scientist recently asked a random sample of businessmen if they "tried to maximize their profit." To a man they all denied this firmly, perhaps because they pictured a profit maximizer as some kind of chiseling extortionist or miser. But then the scientist asked the same businessmen whether they thought any change in their present price policies could be counted on to make them better off in the long run. To a man, they all replied that they were already doing as well as they could hope to do.

It is misleading to talk about "a profit system." Ours is a *profit-and-loss* system. Profits are the carrots held out as an incentive to efficiency, and losses are the kicks that penalize using inefficient methods or devoting resources to uses not desired by spending consumers.

Within the framework of law and custom—where it is both illegal and uncustomary to put sand in sugar—what does the pursuit of profit mean? It means that the businessman, like anybody else, is trying to get as much as he can for the resources at his disposal. This is not different from what a worker is doing when he changes occupations or joins a union. If competition is perfect, the businessman will end up with no *excess profits*. If competition worked perfectly, the attempt by all to reap excess profits would result in none succeeding. Competitors would have to run hard in order to stay in the same place! This is a paradox, but it is true nonetheless.

Would the competitive disappearance of profits mean that the businessman's land, acumen, sweat, and financial investment go without reward? No, certainly not. Even under perfect competition, his factors would earn wages, interest, and rent. Much of the hostility toward profit is really hostility toward the extremes of inequality in the distribution of money income that comes from unequal factor ownership; this should be kept distinct from hostility toward profit created by imperfections of the competitive process.

▶ **THE IMMEASURABILITY OF PROFIT**

How large are these four different categories of profit? We have no way of knowing. It would be nice if we could say that so many billion dollars of the reported total of profit is implicit wages, so many billions implicit interest, and so many billions implicit rents and, of the remainder, so much is innovator's profit and so much is the algebraic total due to uncertainty generally. It would be nice, too, if we could divide the total of all factor incomes into two separate parts: (1) the return to so-called contrived scarcities and (2) the competitive rent return to so-called natural scarcities.

But probably we shall never be able to do this with precision. And what good would it do us if we could? Well, for one thing, some reformers believe that, if only Congress could easily identify every situation of an illegally contrived scarcity, it might hope to bring about a more efficient use of resources.[1] Or some citizens may think that, if Congress could identify the temporary profits due to innovation, it might try to tax them more heavily. And some may agitate for reversal of the present light treatment of capital gains and propose that Congress tax the profits arising from uncertainty more heavily than it taxes ordinary income.

► EFFECTS OF TAXATION ON PROFITS

But even if you are opposed to high profits, you know that taxing profits will raise grave problems. Such legislation will have many effects on the economic system, and we had better examine these effects hardheadedly before making up our minds on how far to go in this direction. Let us examine some of the effects of taxing each of the four different kinds of profit.

1. Suppose you pass a law taxing a corporation's implicit interest more heavily than the explicit interest it pays out to bondholders. What are the consequences likely to be? To answer this, we do not have to put ourselves into a trance, for the American corporation income tax is just such a law.

Standard Oil has to pay the government about half of each dollar earned on the capital supplied by its stockholders; on the capital it raises through bond flotations, it does not have to pay corporate taxes. (That is, Standard Oil can deduct from its taxable income each dollar of bond interest, but it *cannot* deduct any dollars paid out in dividends or plowed back as undistributed profits). What is the result? If Standard Oil is just indifferent between bond or stock financing, it will tend to rely on bonds in order to make its capital earnings show up as explicit rather than implicit interest. (The reader may work out the following similar problem: When I quit my job for a week in order to paint my house, I switch from explicit to implicit wages and the latter is not

---

[1] Wherever contrived scarcities exist, they distort the optimum pattern of resource use. They may also create high earnings for the people involved. But high earnings do not always follow. Thus, under imperfect or monopolistic competition, there may be many taxicabs or grocery stores. Each owner may have a sloping demand curve and may be setting a price in excess of marginal cost. Yet there may be so many imperfect competitors that none of them is earning more than he could get in a perfectly competitive industry. Wiping out the imperfections and illegally contrived scarcities might improve the pattern of production, but it still might or might not have much effect on the relative distribution of income. See Fig. 3, p. 487.

taxed as personal income. What tendencies would you attribute to this feature of our tax system?)

If hostility to profit makes you tax implicit returns, you should realize this will change (and often distort) people's decisions.

2. The case of taxing innovators' profit is even clearer. Taxing a retired innovator's income may seem to have no distorting effects. But we must not forget the young innovator who can then no longer look forward to reaping a tidy sum from his new ideas. He may decide to take that civil service job or remain thirteenth vice-president of a bank. You cannot tax the results of an old innovation without affecting the prospects of an as-yet-unborn innovation.[1]

3. If Congress taxes risky activities more heavily than routine activities, what can any reasonable person expect to happen? People will naturally tend to avoid venturous fields and to gravitate toward routine, steady ones. Yet all of us—rich and poor alike—have a great stake in promoting vigorous exploration of new ways of doing things. Not only has scientific and technological innovation been the secret of our material progress, but in addition the investment associated with venturesome projects is just what the doctor orders to avoid depression and mass unemployment.

As we have seen, our present income tax already discriminates against venture capital. It is true that income taxation is being improved by introducing systems of "averaging income" over more than one year; but until further reforms are made, it remains partially a case of "heads I lose, tails the government wins." The losses brought to me by uncertainty cannot be fully offset against my gains, and taxing profits still more heavily would increase the harmful effects on venture capital.

This conclusion that our ordinary income tax on personal and corporate income discriminates against risk taking has to be substantially qualified when we take into account present light taxation of capital gains. Tax experts know that many investors, particularly high-income investors, deliberately seek out risky investments: oil drilling, common-stock buying, new growth companies, patents, etc. Why? Because they expect that the lucky gains from such ventures will be taxed at less than half rate, while many of their costs can be charged off against high-taxable income.[2]

---

[1] Incidentally, this provides a partial defense of patents. Society deliberately gives a man a monopoly; this contrivance permits him artificially to keep something *partially* scarce. But society hopes the offered bribe of temporary monopoly will encourage the invention of things that would otherwise be 100 per cent scarce.

[2] Thus, a movie star will borrow from a bank to drill for oil; he knows his interest will be paid 91 cents on the dollar by the government through his tax saving; he knows he can deduct his intangible drilling expenses on the same 9-cent-to-91-cent basis; he knows too that when he finds oil, he can sell it and pay only 25 per cent long-term capital-gain tax—or, holding on to the successful oil well, he can collect tax-free $27\frac{1}{2}$ per cent oil-depletion allowance.

The above capital-gain loopholes are today widely used.[1] Hence, some say that our present tax system, far from penalizing risk taking, improperly encourages people to do too much of this sort of thing. And others say, "We can't have too much risk taking if we want to make progress. Capitalism breathes through the tax loopholes." No simple answers can be given in this controversial field.

4. In advocating taxation of monopoly profits you may think you are on more solid ground. But how can you decide what fraction of any company's profits are attributable to these so-called contrived rather than natural scarcities? In 1920 the American Viscose Company dominated the rayon field with its patents, and it earned 156 per cent on its capital. Perhaps the courts might identify cases like this as monopoly profit; perhaps not. But such simple cases are the exception, since we have seen that returns to alleged contrived scarcities are intermingled with all factor returns. Monopoly profits may already have been capitalized and may appear in the guise of interest, or they may take the form of high wages.

Moreover, the best cure for monopoly is not to transfer its earnings to the state, as Louis XV and other despots used to do with their salt and match taxes. If a factor is not naturally scarce, why keep it artificially scarce? Where the government can recognize illegal monopoly, it should deal with it by court action or by public-utility regulation. It would seem sounder policy to wipe out excessive monopoly profits by price cuts than to transfer them by taxation.

▶ INCENTIVES, SURPLUSES, AND EQUITY

Voters often favor measures that tax the rich relatively more than the poor and that tend to reduce inequality of income.

Within the framework of constitutional government, it is the privilege of the electorate to press for what they regard to be ethically the good life. But in weighing what they consider to be the ethical advantages of a more equal distribution of income, the public should rationally face what may be some of the concomitant effects on venturesomeness, efforts, and thriftiness.

▶ PROFIT NOT NECESSARILY A SURPLUS

The prevailing hostility toward so-called profits shows that there is a fifth—and fallacious—definition of profit running around in the back of most peo-

---

[1] A 1953 Harvard Business School study suggests the rich men it studied were able to keep their tax rates down to 50 per cent on the average, and taxes pushed some toward venturesome investment. "Appreciation-minded investors . . . may have been so stimulated by the tax structure to seek out investments offering unusually large capital gains potentialities, such as promising new ventures, as actually to increase the flow of capital to such situations." J. K. BUTTERS, L. E. THOMPSON, L. L. BOLLINGER, *Effects of Taxation: Investment by Individuals.*

ple's minds. They think of profits as being *the unnecessary surplus* that factors earn. Our earlier discussion of the rent earned by inelastically supplied land shows that "taxable surpluses" may indeed occasionally exist. And if we examine the case of *any* factor of production, it must be clear that, every time you raise prices in order to coax out the last or marginal unit, you are in part creating a kind of extra surplus for all the factors already employed.[1] (Thus in World War I the government raised the price of copper so as to bring inefficient mines into operation; in doing this, it created high earnings for the more efficient mines.)

Every factor income, therefore, has in it both elements of (1) *surplus* and (2) *incentive payment*. But that does not mean that you can take the 400 billion dollars of national income and divide it up into two parts—say 100 billion dollars of taxable surplus and 300 billion dollars of incentive payments. *The two are hopelessly intertwined;* and unless you were to make a study of each and every factor or commodity unit and were to name a different price for each unit—as was done by OPA for the copper industry in World War II—you would have no way of hitting at the surplus without at the same time doing damage to incentives.

The fifth notion of profit as a surplus must therefore be handled with care.

▶ A SERMON ON PROFIT AND WHAT, HOW, AND FOR WHOM

Back in Chapter 3 we surveyed how a price system helps solve society's basic problem of What, How, and For Whom. In Part Three we studied the tools of supply and demand that determine competitive market price. And we examined some of the important effects of monopolistic imperfections of competition.

This final chapter on profit culminates Part Four's discussion of how pricing determines distribution of income—how factor pricing determines both society's How and its For Whom (and at the same time the cost to consumer of What goods they can consume). It is fitting here to summarize the role of profit and loss in the over-all pricing process. The Appendix gives a complete review, but the essentials can here be briefly stated.

1. Each person seeks his own advantage. Workers seek highest wages. Landlords, highest rents. Capitalists, highest interest returns. Some of these factor returns will be implicit returns and be called profits. Still other returns may arise from innovation and/or uncertainty, and for those reasons be called profit.

2. In the most general sense, profit-seeking is simply self-advantage seeking. Does this all lead to a jungle—"red in tooth and claw," and chaotic? Not if

---

[1] In more advanced texts, Alfred Marshall and others term this "producers' surplus," which is closely analogous to the "consumers' surplus" of Chapter 23.

there are complete checks and balances. These checks and balances are most complete if competition is perfect; incomplete if competition is imperfect.

3. Where competition is perfect, or nearly so, there results a pattern of order. A pattern of efficiency. But not, mind you, any proven condition of Utopia— with the poor become prosperous and the rich brought down to a mean level.

Of course, shirkers get low incomes. And earnest people, born stupid and with weak muscles, also get low incomes for all their earnestness. Smart go-getters get high incomes. Highly intelligent altruists, who seek the well-being of other people, themselves get low incomes. Smart girls, born of smart and lucky fathers, get high incomes. Stupid girls, born of smart and lucky fathers, get high incomes. Those who get a good education from five to twenty, or five to twelve, stand to gain at the expense of those who don't. So it goes.

4. Where a democracy doesn't like the For Whom pattern that results from *laissez faire,* it puts in tax changes, school and other expenditures, fiats and subsidies, to change the pattern. This helps some incomes, hurts others.

These redistributions are acquired at a cost. What cost? The cost of distortions of incentives, distortions which may somewhat lessen the efficiency of the most efficient market system. Also, there are the costs involved in tax collection and transfer.

5. Profits and losses signal the advantages to other people. When a man is doing what someone in society wants, he finds his wage or profit return rising. So he keeps on doing this. If he overdoes it, he gets penalized. Or, through no fault of his own, he gets penalized when some one better comes along. He may then get kicked into the next best thing for him to do.

Where knowledge is imperfect, a man may make money by correctly guessing the future. If he thinks wheat will be scarce in Kansas, he ships wheat there; or grows more wheat there; or makes a bet about wheat's scarcity on the board of trade, and by making this bet activates someone else to grow more wheat, eat less, or ship more.

In a free pricing system, each man may use his initiative to create a new product or process. If his guess about the future is wrong, he stands to lose. And so do all the people who guessed that he was right—his workers who gave up other jobs, his capitalist backers, etc. If he turns out right, he strikes it rich; and his rival may go to the poorhouse. Any entrenched way of doing things can, under freest competition, be bested and changed.

Profits and high factor returns are the bait, the carrots dangled before us enterprising donkeys. Losses are our penalty kicks. Profits go to those who have been efficient in the past—efficient in making things, in selling things, in foreseeing things. Through profits, society is giving to those who have piled up a record of success the command over new ventures.

To understand this last point imagine a bureaucrat board that awards money to people who apply to it for new projects. If a man was very successful in his last five projects, the board is likely to be favorable toward his new application.

Well, profits that a man with high innovating abilities has piled up from the past do automatically give him the go-ahead signal for the future. (But in life, and in the case of the bureaucratic board, how do you get your first start?)

Profits are the report card of the past, the incentive gold star for the future, and also the grubstake for your new venture.

6. Under perfect competition a man could get ahead only by doing things of value to himself or to someone else. With knowledge perfect, he couldn't spread lies about fake uranium mines and make money that way. He couldn't make false advertising claims. He couldn't be a monopolist, cutting down on his output by equating Marginal Revenue to Marginal Cost $(MR = MC)$. Instead he'd have no control over market price and he'd be doing what the utopian invisible hand says everyone has to do if the pricing system is to be 100 per cent efficient: namely, he'd be equating Price to Marginal Cost $(P = MC)$. And he couldn't be making monopoly profits from contrived scarcity, because under perfect competition there are no monopoly positions.

And if a pricing system were really utopianly perfect in its working, no one would be pouring smoke into the air without being made to pay the cost that such smoke imposes on the rest of the community. No one would refuse to do basic research for fear that he could never tap its full advantage to society and thereby recover his own private research costs. All "external" benefits or costs connected with every activity would be correctly counted in. So when each maximized his own advantage, the checks and balances of perfect pricing would ensure that the benefit of all with money votes was being efficiently achieved.

7. The above remarks show that you'd be wrong to say: The trouble with perfect competition is that it has never been tried. For could it ever be tried? Can we institute perfection? Monopoly aside, can we banish "external effects?"

Obviously, no one can institute perfection. And obviously no one can identify the existing world with perfect competition, or identify a government-do-nothing world of *laissez faire* with perfect competition.

To the degree that public action can (*a*) lessen monopolistic imperfections, (*b*) increase imperfect knowledge, and (*c*) bring total social benefits and costs into closer alignment with private benefits and costs—to this degree will there be a creative role for the state. Of course, all such action has its costs. And these must be carefully weighed in connection with each extension of government and retention of past function.

Our sermon on pricing is at an end. Taking into account the real world as we know it, students of the modern economy realize why it has to be—from its very nature—a mixed economy. Competitive pricing must carry most of the burden of solving society's What, How, and For Whom. But constructive public policies are needed to keep the system competitive and to provide the favorable environment within which private initiative can achieve the common good.

SUMMARY

1. Profit is a highly miscellaneous category. In national income statistics, it is the total of lumped-together corporate earnings and the income of unincorporated enterprises. But really we must distinguish four profit concepts.

2. Much of what is called profit is really *implicit* interest, rent, and wages payable for the productive factors provided by the owners of the business.

3. The special category of *high temporary earnings resulting from innovation* is often termed profit by many economists. Routine management earns wages, they say, but profit may accrue to genuine entrepreneurship.

4. Uncertainty is the all-pervading fact of life. It makes innovation possible and also creates positive and negative divergences between what factors expect to earn and what they actually end up earning. Knight and other economists define profit and loss as the *unforeseeable discrepancies created by uncertainty*. Whether the algebraic total is positive or negative will depend upon luck and upon the unanswerable question: Are people on the whole overoptimistic so they accept too many risks? Or are they overpessimistic so a positive price is paid for the limited supply of risk bearing, as many texts claim?

5. Still another definition of profit is: the return accruing as the result of a monopoly position. This concept is sometimes varied to describe profit as part of the return resulting from a "contrived scarcity."

6. The taxation of any of these categories of profit can be expected to have definite repercussions, some undesirable from any viewpoint. A fifth notion of profit as *an identifiable and taxable surplus rather than incentive payment* is oversimple. If the public wishes to pursue what it calls equity or an ethically more desirable distribution of income, let it face and weigh what some of the distorting effects on incentives may cost.

7. Profit or advantage seeking does, under perfect pricing conditions, lead to efficient How. If the distribution of initial wealth, abilities, and opportunities were made ethically optimal and if these were no externalities, then the checks and balances of perfect competition could lead to a best solution of society's What, How, and For Whom.

In a mixed economy, public policies try to provide needed correctives and checks and balances and try to help align social and private benefits—in short, to promote the best environment within which private initiative can function.

QUESTIONS FOR DISCUSSION

1. Define "implicit" factor earnings. Contrast them with other profits concepts.

2. Give cases of innovation. Of risk taking. How will taxes affect them?

3. What is meant by perfect competition? By imperfect competition? Can you specify a monopoly profit that all will think bad? Can you ever separate natural and contrived scarcities? Why try?

4. Give ethical and incentive aspects of taxing so-called profits or higher incomes generally. (*E.g.,* corporate income tax favors bond finance. So?)

5. "Profit seeking is ugly. Even if it were efficient—and I deny that it works out that way—I'd be against it. Give me medieval charity or Zuñi brotherhood, but deliver me from the market." Do you disagree?

6. "If the Lord gives a man strength, brains, and energy, then he's been given much. So he deserves lower material income—not higher." Contrast with "To each according to his ability—according to his marginal-product."

7. Review your understanding of the following concepts:

reported statistics of profits

implicit versus explicit factor returns

wages of management, reward for risk taking

innovation, uncertainty

capital gain, ordinary income

imperfections of competition, monopoly, contrived versus natural scarcity

rent and surplus, incentives

initial distribution of wealth

ethical questions

external effects and divergence of private and social benefit and cost

APPENDIX: REVIEW OF COMMODITY AND FACTOR PRICING: GENERAL EQUILIBRIUM AND THE PARABLE OF IDEAL WELFARE PRICING

Part Three and Part Four are done. Now we can review by putting the pieces together and by studying the parable of pricing in an idealized welfare Utopia.

Review of Pricing

We have seen (1) how competitive supply and demand operate in a *single* market; (2) how the relative utility or indifference preferences of the individual lie behind his demand curves; (3) how total, marginal, and unit costs lie behind the competitive supply curves; (4) how the technical production function relating output to factor inputs lies behind the cost curves, which have been minimized by the firm's demanding inputs until their marginal-physical-products are proportional to factor prices; (5) how these marginal-physical-products and marginal-revenue-products summed for all firms provide the "derived demands for the factors"; (6) how these derived demands for land,

labor, or capital goods interact with their market supplies to determine factor prices such as rent, wages, rentals,[1] etc.; and finally (7) how the pursuit of profit and avoidance of loss furnish the motive force behind the whole competitive process—but how paradoxically under statical conditions free of uncertainty and innovational change, competitive profits (other than implicit factor returns and wages of management) would tend to zero.

Simultaneous mutual determination. Look at these seven steps. Each follows the other in the list—(1) and then (2) and then (3), until finally we come to (7). And in the textbook chapters they follow in about the same order.

But in real life, which does come first?

---

[1] This list and Fig. 1 skip the additional fact that capital goods rentals are capitalized so that they can be expressed in terms of interest.

Is there any order and sequence, with prices being determined in single markets on Monday, consumers evaluating preferences on Tuesday, businessmen reckoning costs on Wednesday, and marginal-products on Thursday? Obviously not. All these processes are going on at one and the same time.

That's not all. These different processes don't go on independently side by side, each in its own little cell careful not to get in the way of the other. All the processes of supply and demand, of cost and preference, of factor productivity and demand—all these are really different aspects of one vast simultaneous *interdependent* process.

Thus, the supply curve for wheat met in the first chapter of Part Three is itself the resultant of the cost calculations given at the end of Part Three, and of the production considerations given at the beginning of Part Four, and of the process of wage and rent and interest determinations given at the end of Part Four. Actually, you can take any one of the seven steps in the outline and draw arrows connecting it causally *with each and every other step.* (Try it; give interpretations of the interdependent links.)

Figure 1 tries to give a summary picture of the interdependent system which economists call "general equilibrium."

You will remember from the very first chapter on national income a circular flow diagram showing plumbing pipes carrying dollars clockwise from business to families and from families to business. That gave what economists call the "aggregative" or "macroeconomic" picture of the nation's grand totals.

Now look at Fig. 1. It too gives the circular flow of dollars. But this time we take a more microscopic approach—what economists call the "microeconomic" picture. Now we don't talk about the grand total of factor incomes; instead we show derived demand by business for skilled labor, for unskilled labor, for good vineyard land, etc. Likewise, we don't speak of total consumption; we specify; we show the consumer's demand for coffee, for tea, for shoes, etc.

Note that in the lower loop we have for each factor *both* a supply and a demand.

(Query: Which does business provide? Which do consumers provide?) In the upper loop, you see *both* a supply and demand for each good.

Thus, we can give an optimistic answer to the logical purist who asks the embarrassing question: "Your economic system isn't determinate until you have found conditions to determine a price *and* a quantity for *each* output and for each input. Do you have enough simultaneous conditions (or equations) to make your interdependent equilibrium system determinate?"

Fortunately, we can answer: "We do have for each output or input *both a supply and a demand condition.* So we can hope that the system will by trial and error in the market place finally settle down—if left undisturbed!—to a determinate competitive equilibrium."[1]

And we can say: "The final competitive equilibrium is an 'efficient' one. Output is being maximized; inputs are being minimized; people who like apples are not being given oranges, or vice versa. From so efficient a final point, you can no longer make everyone better off. You can help Joe only by hurting Moe."

Figure 1 here is the final development of the figure given back on p. 41 of Chapter 3, when we first asked how a price system goes about solving What, How, and For Whom. Only after mastering the tools of Parts Three and Four, could we give this culmination of our original inquiry.

Qualifications. Mind you, all the above proceeds on the basis of some heroically abstract assumptions: no monopolies, no imperfections, no dynamic innovations or unforeseen disturbances, no governmental distortions, and so forth. Figure 1 therefore is like the no-friction model of the physicist;

---

[1] Leon Walras, a French economist of three-quarters of a century ago, is usually credited with the discovery of general equilibrium. But W. S. Jevons of England, C. Menger of Austria, Alfred Marshall of England, J. B. Clark of America, Vilfredo Pareto of Italy, K. Wicksell of Sweden all made significant contributions, and even in Adam Smith you can find the germ of the idea if you look hard enough.

What, How, and For Whom is determined by general equilibrium pricing:

Fig. 1. The clockwise money flow is broken up to show consumer demand meeting industry supply at A to determine equilibrium price and quantity of each good. Similarly, derived factor demands of business meet public's supply of factors at E to determine equilibrium factor-prices and amounts. (Interpret what is going on behind B, D, F, and H—and inside C and G—and compare this with the What, How, and For Whom of Fig. 1 on p. 41.)

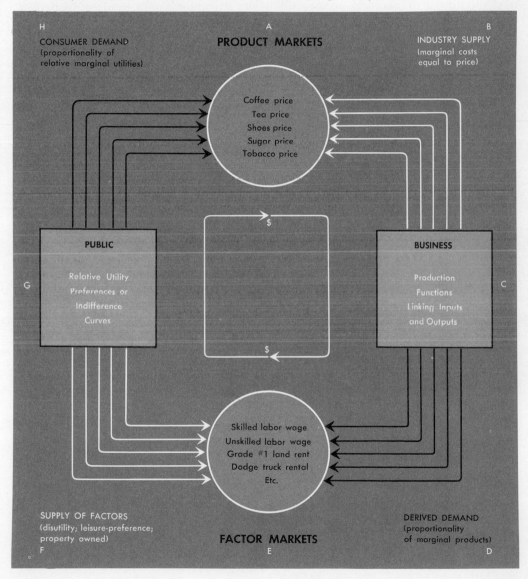

it is not a picture of the real world as we know it when we step outside the library and rub elbows with real live breathing people on the street.

Yet, even though every engineer knows he must meet friction, he does find the frictionless model a valuable tool in throwing light on complicated reality. So with our ideal competitive model. In the longer run, many imperfections turn out to be transient. *The competitive model, therefore, may suggest in its over-simple way some interesting hypotheses that turn out to have a measure of long-run validity!* (Example: An invention cuts cost of aluminum; the competitive model says price will fall and pressure will be put on use and price of steel; the sophisticated student of imperfect competition says the real world is not perfectly competitive, so no hard-and-fast conclusion can be drawn. Nonetheless, bet with him the above result will happen *in the long run*—and probably you will win his money. A sure thing? No, but still a good bet.)

Parable of Utopian Pricing

We economists are twitted that our books always harp on Robinson Crusoe. True enough: we do find that the economic decisions of a single man furnish a dramatic way of simplifying our basic principles. But these days, we have an even more dramatic device for illustrating the fundamental facts of economic life: we use the example of a fully collectivized society. This retains the same simplicity of ultimate decision making, but at the same time it gives us social interactions between people that the Crusoe model lacks. The contrast between such a model and our realistic everyday world is, of course, enormous. And therein lies its value. By examining the logic of such a model, we get new insight into the nature of our own pricing system.

Let's turn, therefore, to see how our economic analysis of pricing can be applied to a noncapitalistic system. In analyzing the problem of pricing in a planned socialist state, we kill two birds with one stone:

1. We get one of the best possible reviews of the over-all working of an ideal *capitalistic* price system.

2. We gain an introduction to problems of "welfare economics," *i.e.*, the study of what is considered right and wrong about any economic system. This depends, of course, upon ethical points of view, which are themselves a-scientific. But the economist, as a disinterested observer, may help to throw light upon how successfully an economic system realizes any suggested ethical *goals*.[1]

A Dilemma for Centralized Planning

The earlier chapters of this book have shown how a system of market prices operates so as to solve the basic economic problems of What, How, and For Whom. To drive home a better understanding of what all this really means, make a mental experiment. Suppose you were given the job of writing down the blueprints of a completely planned economic system. How would you set about this problem?

First, let's suppose you are interested in giving people what they want, not in telling them what they ought to want. Obviously, you cannot give them everything they want: land, labor, capital goods, and technological knowledge are limited in amount. So you will have to make compromises and choices.

You may say to yourself: This is obviously a complicated mathematical problem, calling for the use of lots of high-powered electronic high-speed calculating machines. But remember that you will have to deal with the millions of items that are to be found in department stores, with thousands of grades of productive factors, and with numerous individuals and families. The number of unknowns of the mathematical problem will be in the millions, and the number of steps in its solution in the billions of billions. No known set of calculating machines can begin to tackle such a problem.

You are stumped. And discouraged. Perhaps you will lower your sights and stop being a perfectionist. Instead of giving people exactly what they think they want, you may decide that there will be only a few types of, say, shoe styles and sizes, and so forth, so that the calculation problem will be simplified. Or you may start to give people goods that you find it convenient to give them.

One thing is clear: If centralized plan-

---

[1] For example, he may be personally opposed to an equal distribution of income, but that doesn't prevent him from measuring the degree of success in reaching this common ethical goal.

ning means that one centralized person must have in his mind all the myriad intricacies of detail, then it is an impossible job to do with any efficiency. So you will naturally begin to experiment with various devices to decentralize the job. And quite probably you will finally end up by introducing a pricing system in many ways like that of capitalism. How might such a pricing system work?

Pricing in a Socialist State: Consumption Goods Prices

Many socialists have insisted that, in their new society, the consumer should still have *freedom of choice* and would not have dictated to him the relative amounts of different commodities which he is to "enjoy." As in the capitalist system each person will receive a sum of money or abstract purchasing power which he can spend among different commodities as he wishes. Thus, vegetarians will not have to eat meat, and those who most prefer meat will be able to exert their preference.

How will relative prices between salmon and Spam or any other consumers' goods be set by the socialist state? Generally speaking, prices will be set with the same double purpose as in a capitalist society: (1) just high enough to ration out the existing supplies of consumers' goods, so none are left over and none are short; and also (2) just high enough to cover the socially necessary extra costs of producing the goods in question—or, in technical terms, prices are to be set equal to relative "marginal utilities" and "marginal costs."

The Distribution of Income

So far the process has worked much like the capitalistic system. However, socialism, almost by definition, means a society in which most land and capital goods or nonhuman resources of all kinds are owned collectively by society and not individually by people. In our society an Astor who owns 500 parcels of New York City land which each produce $4,000 of net rents per year will receive an income of 2 million dollars per year—which may be 1,000 times what a

night watchman is able to earn, and 200 times what the average skilled engineer can earn. In a society where most property is owned collectively and not distributed with great inequality among different individuals, an important source of inequality of the distribution of income would be removed.

Many people profess to hold the ethical and philosophical belief that different individuals' wants and needs are very much alike, and that the present market mechanism works inadequately because the rich are given so many more votes in the control of production than the poor—which makes the market demand for goods a poor indication of their true social worth. Such people with a relatively equalitarian philosophy will welcome the great reduction in the spread of incomes between the lowest 90 per cent of all families and the highest 10 per cent. They will argue that taking away $1,000 from a man with an income of $100,000 and giving it to a man with an income of $2,000 will add to social well-being. After the distribution of income between families has been determined correctly, according to society's fundamental (a-scientific) value judgments, then and only then will it be true that the dollars coming on the market will be valid indicators of the value of goods and services; and only then will they be serving to direct production into the proper channels and goods into the right hands. So goes the argument.

How is what is considered the proper, ethical distribution of income to be achieved aside from the negative act of wiping out unduly high property incomes? Perfectionists have two answers: (1) in part by letting people get some of their income in the form of wages; but (2) in large part by having these wages supplemented by receipt of a lump-sum *social dividend payment*. This cash payment would presumably be pretty nearly the same for most average families; but even in an equalitarian society, there might be differences to compensate for different numbers of children, age and health, and so forth.

It is an ethical rather than a scientific question as to just how large each person's final income ought to be. As a science, economics can concern itself only with the best means of attaining given ends; it cannot prescribe the ends themselves. Indeed, if someone decided that he preferred a feudal-fascistic kind of society, in which all people with little black moustaches were to be given especially high incomes, the economist could set up the pricing rules for him to follow to best achieve his strange design. He would be told to determine his social dividend payments so as to achieve the required optimal distribution of income, after which each dollar coming on the market could be regarded as correctly representing (that eccentric person's) true social values.

The social dividend differs from a wage because it is to be given to each individual *regardless of his own efforts*. That is why it is called a "lump-sum" dividend. Any bonus based upon productivity or effort is to be treated as a wage. We have not yet seen how wages are to be determined. But before doing so let us first turn to another important problem.

Pricing of Nonhuman Productive Resources and Intermediate Goods

What should be the role of land and other nonhuman productive resources as an element of cost in an ideal socialist state? Some people would say that such nonhuman resources should not enter into cost at all; that only human sweat and skill is the true source of all value; and that any extra charges based upon the cost of land or machinery represent a capitalistic surplus which the owners of property are able to squeeze out of the exploited laboring masses by virtue of the private monopoly of ownership of the means of production. This view is sometimes loosely spoken of as the "labor theory of value," and it is usually attributed to Karl Marx, the intellectual father of communistic socialism. Learned scholars dispute over just what Marx meant by the "labor theory of value," and whether he meant it for a socialistic economy in the short or long run.

We need not enter into this dispute. However, it is important to note that, in

its simple form, *the labor theory of value will lead to incorrect and inefficient use of both labor and nonlabor resources in even the most perfect socialist society.*

So long as any economic resource is limited in quantity—*i.e.*, scarce rather than free—the socialist planners must give it a price and charge a rent for its use. This price need not, as in the case of the Astor millionaire under the capitalistic system, determine any individual's income. It can be a purely bookkeeping or accounting price set up by the planners, rather than being a market price. But there must be a price put upon the use of every such resource.

Why? First, we must price nonhuman resources to ensure that society is deciding How goods shall be produced in the best way, so that we really end up out on the true production-possibility curve of society and not somewhere inside it. It would be absurd to get rid of the capitalistic system with its alleged wastes due to unemployment, and then by stupid planning end up far inside of society's true production potentialities.

Related to the above point is the second need for all resources to be given a value if correct prices are to be charged to consumers for those final goods that use up a great deal of scarce resources. In other words, for society to find itself in the best of all possible positions along the production-possibility curve, we must price such consumption goods as food and clothing so as to reflect their true relative (extra or marginal) costs of using up scarce resources. Otherwise, the free choice exerted by consumers on their dollar spending will not truly reflect their own or society's best preferences.

The Example of Land Rent

These two reasons are difficult to grasp. However, let us try to make the necessity for land pricing clear by considering a single example. Suppose there are two identical twins in a farming Utopia. What if one were to produce wheat on an acre of good land, and the other to produce less wheat by the same year's work on an acre of bad land. If they are identical twins, working equally hard, we would certainly have to agree that their wage rates ought to be the same.

Now, if wages were to be treated as the only cost, in accord with the labor theory of value, then the same price could not be charged for the two different outputs of wheat, even though the kernels of wheat were identical. The good-land wheat would have involved low labor costs and will have to sell for less than the poor-land wheat.

This, of course, is absurd. A well-wishing social planner might try to get around the dilemma by charging the same price for both, perhaps losing money on the poor-land wheat and gaining on the other. Or what is almost the same thing, he might say "Let us pay the twin on bad land lower wages than his brother, so as to keep the costs of the two wheats the same; but then let us make the richer brother share his wages with the poorer."

Such a solution is not absurd, but it falls short of achieving the desired best results; maximum production and equal pay for equal human effort. In particular, it fails to shift more labor on to the more productive land.

The only correct procedure is to put an accounting price tag on each land, with the good land having the higher tag. The prices of both kinds of wheat will be equal, because the land cost of the good-land wheat will be just enough higher than that of the poor-land wheat to make up the difference.

Most important of all, the socialist production manager must try to minimize the combined labor and land cost of producing each kind of wheat. If he does so according to the marginal-product principles discussed in Part Four, he will accomplish something new and important and undreamed of by the simple believer in the labor theory of value.

He will find it pays to work the good land more intensively, perhaps with the time of $1\frac{1}{2}$ men until the extra product there has been lowered by the law of diminishing returns so as to be just equal to the extra product of the $\frac{1}{2}$ man's time on

the poor land. Only by putting a price upon inert sweatless land are we using it, and sweating breathing labor, most productively! The price or rent of land rises so as to ration its limited supply among the *best* uses.

Note too that the most finicky humanitarian will have nothing to complain of concerning our solution. By transferring labor from one plot of land to the other until its marginal productivity has been made equal, we get the largest possible total production of wheat.[1]

The two brothers are paid the same wages because they have worked equally hard. But their wages are not high enough to buy all the wheat since part of the cost of the wheat has come from (bookkeeping) land charges. However, the people through their government own the land equally. The land's return does not go to any property owner, but is available to be distributed as a lump-sum dividend to both brothers according to their ethical deserts.

By putting a proper accounting price or rent on land, society has more consumption than was otherwise possible.

If we turn now to the production of more than one consumers' good, it will be obvious that their cost prices must be made to reflect the amount of socially limited land and machinery which they each use up. A field crop like potatoes requires little labor and much land as compared to an intensive garden crop like tomatoes. If we price each good on the basis of labor costs alone, potatoes will sell for too little and too much land will be forced out of tomato production. Everyone will end up worse off!

One last point concerning the final determination of a product's cost and price. After the costs of all necessary factors of

---

[1] As earlier discussions of marginal productivity have shown, *total product will be at a maximum only when labor has been transferred from the land where its marginal-product is low to the good land where its marginal product is high.* Every such transfer must necessarily yield us extra product, until finally no further increases in output can result when the marginal-products have been equalized in the two uses.

production have been added together to arrive at total cost, the planning authorities must set their prices at the extra or marginal cost of new units of production. Or more accurately, the socialist managers of a plant must behave like a perfect competitor: they must disregard any influence that their own production might have on market price, and must continue to produce extra units up to the point where the last little unit costs just as much as its selling price. For many industries, such as railroads where unit costs are constantly falling, setting marginal costs equal to price will imply that *full* average costs are not covered. In a noncapitalistic society the difference would be made up by an (accounting) grant from the state. For if a railroad system is worth building, it is worth being utilized to the full.[1]

Summary of resource pricing. Correct social planning requires that all scarce resources, whether human labor or not, be given accounting prices at least. The final costs of consumers' goods should include the sum total of *all* extra costs necessary to produce each good; or, in short, should equal *marginal cost*. The demand for consumers' goods is really an indirect demand for all productive resources, a demand which can be kept in proper check only by putting appropriate valuations on productive resources.

Otherwise, society's valuable nonhuman —and human!—resources will be incorrectly allocated, and the market pricing of finished goods will not lead to maximum consumers' satisfaction. It is to be emphasized that the accounting prices of land and other

---

[1] The long-run question as to whether to build a railroad in the first place may involve an "all-or-none decision," which cannot be made step by step. In such a case, there must still be a balancing of the extra (or marginal) advantage and extra cost to society of the enterprise. But for such a big step, price is no longer a good indicator of total welfare, since—as we saw in Chapter 23—there is always an element of consumer's surplus in the total amount of goods a person consumes, over what he's paid for them. Welfare may go up as price and total value go down.

nonhuman resources need not, in a socialist state, be part of the incomes of anyone. In the language of the visionary critic of private enterprise: no one is "exploited" by having a property owner skim off part of the final product. Instead, the contribution of capital and land to production is given to people in the form of the *social dividend*.

The Role of the Interest Rate in a Socialist State

We have seen that the interest rate has an important function in a capitalistic, socialistic, or any other kind of economic system. Capital goods have a "net productivity." So long as resources can be invested for the present or the future, it will be necessary to make important decisions with respect to capital. Shall we apply present land and labor to the production of a corn crop this year or to apples 15 years from now? Shall we have grape juice today or wine 10 years hence? Shall we replace a worn-out printing press by a new expensive one which yields its services over a period of 20 years, or buy a cheap one that will only last 14 years? Every one of these questions can be answered only by using an interest rate to relate future and present economic values. Without such an interest rate, the existing stock of fixed and circulating capital cannot be devoted to its best uses; and whatever amount of national income society has decided to invest in capital formation cannot be embodied in the best form without such an interest rate.

The interest rate acts as a sieve or rationing device: all projects that can yield 6 per cent over time are undertaken before any that yield only 5 per cent.

It should be added that most economic writers on socialism do not think that the rate of interest should also determine—as it does in our economy, to some degree— the rate at which capital growth is to take place at the expense of current consumption. The decision as to how much should be saved would be determined by the state "in the light of national and social needs" and not by the "haphazard" notions of individuals with respect to the future. But the level of social saving and capital growth once having been determined, the interest rate must be used to allocate scarce "capital supplies" optimally and to determine the order of priority of alternative projects.[1]

Wage Rates and Incentive Pricing

We must now return to the problem of how the socialist planners would set wage rates, and then we are done. If the amounts of labor of all kinds and of all skills were perfectly fixed, there would be no reason why labor should not be given accounting prices just like any other productive factor. Workers would receive no wages at all. They would then receive all the national income in the form of an enlarged *social dividend*.

However, if people are to be free to choose their own occupation and given a choice between working a little harder and longer in return for extra consumption goods, then it will be necessary to set up a system of *actual market wages* at which people can sell their services. These rates may differ depending upon the irksomeness and unpleasantness of the job; and unlike our system, the pleasanter jobs may be the lower paid, and the ditchdiggers or garbage collectors may have to be higher paid to attract people into their jobs. Occupations that require much training and skill will receive high pay, but much of that pay may be spent by the state in providing the education necessary to acquire those skills. Piece rates may often be used under socialism, and a worker with a 10 per cent higher productivity may receive higher wages. Workers will in every case be offered wages equal to their marginal or extra productivity.

Therefore, it is not necessarily true that all incomes will be at a dead level in the socialist state. They will differ somewhat as a result of two distinct factors: (1) society's appraisal of the "needs and worth" of different individuals—as reflected primarily in the size of the individuals' lump-sum *social dividends,* and (2) the need for wages to differ to provide incentives and to compensate people for extra disutility and effort. Incomes would not differ, however, because of inequality in the ownership and inheritance of property. Wage rents (like Babe Ruth's) could be heavily lump-sum-taxed, exactly like Henry George's surplus land rents.

Summary of Socialist Pricing

1. A socialist system could make use of four different kinds of pricing: (a) consumer-goods prices, (b) wage and incentive rates, (c) accounting prices of intermediate goods, and (d) final lump-sum dividends (when positive, subsidies; when negative, taxes). The first three groups of prices would be determined by supply and demand.

2. To give people free choice among consumers' goods, market prices would be set for such goods. Similarly, to provide freedom of choice of occupation, to give people incentives, and to provide compensation for differences between occupations, wage rates would have to be set to correspond to (marginal) productivities and disutilities.

3. Accounting prices would have to be set on all nonhuman productive resources to ration them in their best uses where their (relative) marginal productivities are equal and highest. Similarly, there would have to be a rate of interest to ration the existing and growing stock of capital among its best uses. Any consumption good would be produced up to the point where the full marginal cost of production (necessary to attract all resources from other uses and from leisure) is just equal to the price.[2]

---

[1] There is no logical reason why individuals who are willing to forego present for future consumption should not be permitted to do such voluntary extra saving and receive an interest return equal to the net productivity of capital.

[2] The decentralized managers of industries would achieve this result by seeking to maximize their net algebraic profits, measured in accounting points or actual dollars, but with *all* prices taken as given parameters. (NOTE: Under cost conditions suitable for viable *laissez faire,* this type of behavior is actually policed by competition; but where bureaucrats "play the game of competition," there may be a hard administrative problem to make sure they do behave in the prescribed parametric manner.)

4. Lastly, the final distribution of income would be made to correspond to what society regards as the ideal distribution pattern by means of payment of a lump-sum social dividend to people, depending upon "need and wants" but not—like a wage—on effort or performance. Presumably in a socialist society, it would be felt that a much more nearly equal distribution of income will be necessary before the dollar votes of consumers can be expected to reflect true social preferences. However, this is a nonscientific, ethical question. And we could use the same economic principles to make blueprints for an *ine*galitarian Utopia.

5. None of these processes except the last requires detailed comprehensive planning by a central agency. Mathematicians would not have to be called in to solve thousands and thousands of simultaneous equations. Instead, the decentralized planners would proceed by successive approximation, by trial and error—setting provisional market and accounting prices and cutting them or raising them depending upon whether available supplies are piling up or running short.

It would be naïve to think that any actual socialist society would succeed in reaching the ideal equilibrium positions described above. Errors of foresight would inevitably be made. Existing vested interests, anxious to preserve their security in a dynamic world of change, would resist and sabotage such change in the same qualitative fashion as they have done in historical societies. There is great reason to doubt that politicians and the electorate would pay much attention to the incentive mechanisms outlined in the preceding pages. The importance of this discussion is that it teaches us how to appraise the mechanical efficiency of pricing in a *non*socialist society![1]

---

[1] A brief history of welfare pricing doctrines may be of interest. From Smith's time at least, men saw beauty in the laissez-faire mechanism and inferred that it must have teleological significance in giving efficiency. But they were often uncritical; and often they overlooked the assumption that dollar votes were to be distributed in the ethically desired way; and they could not prove what they believed. Around 1900 Pareto

Welfare Economics in a Free Enterprise Economy

On the basis of the above general principles of pricing, we are in a position to see what friendly and unfriendly critics think is wrong in our present system, or not necessarily right from various ethical viewpoints. Critics list the following possible deviations from the social optimum:

1. The existing distribution of property, income, education, and economic opportunity is the result of past history and does not necessarily represent a perfect optimum according to the ethical philosophies of Christianity, Buddhism, paganism, the American creed, or other ideologies. Defenders of the capitalist system point out that such deviations from the optimum distribution of income can be corrected by appropriate tax policies, if that is desired. There are always, however, some costs to be incurred in our capitalistic system from such policies because of effects upon incentives, risk taking, effort, and productivity.

2. The widespread presence of monopoly elements in our system and the limited appearance of perfect competition mean that production is rarely being pushed to the optimum point of equality of marginal cost to price; because the elasticity of demand is not infinite under imperfect competition, production is pushed only to the point of equality of marginal cost to marginal reve-

---

showed that an ideal socialism would have to solve the same equations as competitive capitalism. Around 1920, Ludwig von Mises, perhaps unaware of Pareto's proof, set forth the challenging view that rational economic organization was *logically* impossible in the absence of free markets. Fred Taylor of Michigan, A. P. Lerner of England and Chicago, and Oscar Lange of Poland answered Mises with the view that socialism could conceptually solve the problems of economic organization by a decentralized process of bureaucratic trial and error—"playing the game of competition" and "deliberately planning not to plan." F. A. Hayek has argued that this answer overlooks the problem of giving *each man the initiative* to better the existing order, and that only with actual free enterprise do you efficiently utilize the dispersed information that each of us may possess.

nue. Because of the fear of "spoiling the market," monopoly price is too high and monopoly output is too low.

This is related to a further evil under imperfect competition when entry of new firms into an industry is very easy. There may then tend to be an inefficient division of production among too many firms; the price charged is too high, but because of wasteful use of resources, no one need be making any profits.[1]

3. Finally, of course, as shown in Part Two, under a laissez-faire system, there may be great wastes due to unemployment and the business cycle. Consumers, labor, farmers, and business together with public fiscal and monetary policy must be mobilized in a never-ending war against this greatest of modern scourges—this poverty that has no real cause but stems only from an intricately misbehaving monetary society.

---

[1] Another evil, discussed in more advanced economic writings, is the fact that individual firms, in making their decisions, don't take into account some possible effects of their production decisions on other firms or industries. In digging his oil well, Pat doesn't mind that he may be robbing Mike's oil pool; and the same with Mike—with the result that less oil is obtained in the end, and with more cost. Because of such so-called "external diseconomies" (or occasionally, "external economies") apparent "private mar-

ginal costs" do not reflect true "social marginal costs"; and certain lines of activity deserve to be contracted and others to be expanded. Compare A. C. PIGOU, *Economics of Welfare* (Macmillan, New York, 1932). The paradox that really perfect competition would discourage people from inventing (since they would know their profits would disappear) can be understood in terms of external economies. My pecuniary reward from an invention may be much less than its social value after it has been widely imitated.

SUMMARY TO APPENDIX

1. In a pure unmixed competitive society, the economic problems of What shall be produced, How, and For Whom are solved in an intricate, interdependent manner by the impersonal workings of the profit-and-loss market system. Every economic variable depends upon every other, but all tend to be simultaneously determined at their general equilibrium values by a process of successive approximations involving adjustment and readjustment.

2. Unless a socialist economy were uninterested in efficiency and economizing, or in freedom of choice of goods and jobs, it would have to institute a system of pricing. However, some prices would be purely accounting or bookkeeping figures; in addition, the

final determination of the distribution of income would involve an outright social dividend, given to everyone by the explicit a-scientific decision of government and society.

3. From the standpoint of welfare economics, it is seen that our own capitalistic system may depart from what is considered a social optimum in three main ways: through improper distribution of income, through monopoly, and through fluctuations in unemployment.

It is the present writer's belief as exemplified throughout the book, that all these evils can be ameliorated by appropriate policies, within the framework of the capitalistic system.

QUESTIONS FOR DISCUSSION

1. Summarize how a pricing system works to solve the three fundamental economic problems. Illustrate the interdependence of these three problems.

2. Discuss the four kinds of prices in a

planned, socialist state.

3. What do you deem to be imperfections in the present economic order? Virtues? What defects would plague a collectivist society?

4. Review your understanding of the following concepts:

interdependence, general equilibrium, determinate final economic equilibrium, efficient final equilibrium

labor theory of value versus proper pricing of nonhuman resources

interest rate in capitalism and socialism

lump-sum, social dividend

wage rents

accounting prices versus actual prices

monopoly restrictions, wastes of excess capacity

"external" divergences between social and private benefits and costs

welfare economics, ethical distribution questions

part

5

INTERNATIONAL

TRADE AND

FINANCE

THE 31 BALANCE OF INTERNATIONAL PAYMENTS

What the Periodic Table of Elements is to the chemist, the Balance of Payments is to the international economist.

W. S. JEVONS

In the earlier chapters of this book we took international trade more or less for granted. Here in Part Five we wish to analyze explicitly the interesting economic problems arising as soon as an economy engages in foreign trade.

The present chapter and its Appendix deal with the monetary mechanisms involved in international trade. Then the next two chapters concentrate on the basic real factors that underlie international trade and are often obscured by the monetary veil which covers all international transactions. These basic real factors are involved in any rational appraisal of the problems raised by tariffs and other barriers to the international division of labor. In the final chapter we put all these principles to work to help us understand the contemporary international economic scene.

We'll find that international trade is important for the following basic reason: Foreign trade gives us a "consumption-possibility schedule" that is further northeastward than our own domestic production-possibility schedule! (Example: Brown men in Malaya give us rubber; we give monocled Englishmen wheat; Englishmen give Malayans cotton shirts. *Each of us ends up consuming more than he could alone produce!* That's the essence of foreign trade. So simple. Yet so hard for congressmen and voters to remember.)

Our task in Part Five is to study the mechanics of all this. Foreign exchange rates. Balance of international payments. Foreign lending and giving. Tariff duties on imports, import quotas telling how much oil you can bring into the United States. The so-called "principle of comparative advantage," which tells what kinds of trade will take place and why. And finally the international economic problems of 1960: Dollar shortage? The Common European Market

Foreign aid. The International Bank and the International Monetary Fund.

Abstract economic problems? No, the news that's breaking on tomorrow's front page.

▶ FOREIGN EXCHANGE RATES

First, how does trade take place? If I buy maple sugar from Vermont or pig iron from Pittsburgh, I naturally want to pay in dollars. Also, the farmers and steel producers I buy from expect to be paid in dollars, because their expenses and their living costs are all in dollars. Within a country, economic transactions are simple.

But if I wish to buy an English bicycle, matters are more complicated. I must pay in British money, or what is called "pounds sterling," rather than in dollars. Similarly, an Englishman must somehow get dollars to an American producer if he wants our merchandise. Most Americans have never seen a British pound note. Certainly they would accept pounds only if they could be sure of converting them into American dollars—dollars to spend or save.

Clearly, therefore, exports and imports of goods between nations with different units of money introduce a new economic factor: the foreign exchange rate, giving the price of the foreigner's unit of money in terms of our own.

Thus, the price of a British pound is in 1958 about $2.80. There is, of course, a foreign exchange rate between American money and the currencies of each and every country: 50 cents for a Philippine peso, less than one-fourth of a cent for a French franc, etc.[1]

Given the foreign exchange rates, it is now simple for me to buy my English bicycle. Suppose its quoted price is £20 (*i.e.*, 20 British pounds). All I have to do is look up in the newspaper the foreign exchange rate for pounds. If this is $2.80 per pound, I simply go to a bank or post office with $56 and ask that the money be used to pay the English bicycle exporter. Pay him what? Pounds, of course, the only kind of money he needs.

Whether I use the post office or a bank or a broker is of no particular importance. In fact it is all the same if the English exporter sends me a bill requesting payments in dollars. In any case, he ultimately wants pounds, not dollars, and will soon trade the $56 for £20. (Needless to say, we are neglecting commission charges and the cost of money orders.)

You should be able to show what a British importer of American grains has to do if he wants to buy, say, a $2,800 shipment from an American exporter. Here pounds must be converted into dollars. Why? How?

---

[1] There are also foreign exchange rates between the pound and the French franc, etc. But these rates between other countries need not interest us much, particularly since in a free competitive market the pound-franc rate can be simply calculated from the pound-dollar and franc-dollar rate, because sharp-eyed international arbitragers see to it that relative "cross rates" do not get out of line.

▶ HOW THE FOREIGN EXCHANGE RATE IS DETERMINED

So much at present for foreign exchange rates. Unless you are an expert, you need not worry further about mechanical details. Still your knowledge will be incomplete unless you understand the basic economic forces working behind the scenes. How are banks, post offices, and brokers always able, here and abroad, to exchange pounds for dollars and dollars for pounds?

The answer lies in the fact that international trade is largely a two-way street. Goods are being traded for goods, just as in a horse swap. When we import, we offer dollars for pounds. When we export, the English offer pounds for dollars. All this is true enough. But what are the mechanisms of foreign exchange?

There are two interesting cases of exchange rate determination: (1) the case of a *freely fluctuating* foreign exchange rate, and (2) the case of a *stable* exchange rate, determined by government adherence to the gold standard or by some other explicit government program.

For a century of peace, the gold-standard stable-exchange case was most important. But the free-exchange case is simpler to describe; and in recent years it has been gaining somewhat in importance.

Free exchange rates. Have you ever bought tourist currency in a black market abroad? Then you have an idea how supply and demand determine the exchange rate. When many foreigners want to get hold of dollars, they offer American tourists a lot of foreign money for our currency and the price of foreign exchange goes down. In the opposite case, where many Americans have an avid desire to buy French pocketbooks and perfumes, the strong dollar demand for foreign currency sends the foreign exchange rate up.

But let's not talk about black markets. Let's talk about white markets. Take the years from 1919 to 1925. England had gone off the gold standard after World War I. So what determined the foreign exchange rate of dollars and pounds? *I.e.*, what determined the dollar price of a pound? When Uncle Ben, wanting to buy wool socks, read the rate $4.10 per pound in the *New York Times,* where did that 1920 exchange rate come from?

Figure 1 gives a simplified supply-and-demand picture of determination of a free exchange rate. Each day's foreign exchange rate is set by that day's supply and demand. Next month, if *DD* shifts upward and *SS* doesn't change much, then Uncle Ben will find a new exchange rate of $4.20 or more. So it goes in a free market: price clears the market.

Gold-standard stable exchange rate. The Appendix discusses this in more detail. But let's go on to the gold-standard case. Actually, back in 1925 Winston Churchill (remember him?) put England back on the gold standard at the prewar "mint-parity" rate of $4.87 per pound. How did he do that?

Did Churchill, like King Canute who foolishly ordered the ocean tide to

Demand bids up, supply bids down, a free foreign exchange rate:

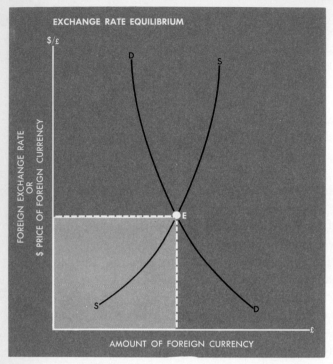

EXCHANGE RATE EQUILIBRIUM

$/£

FOREIGN EXCHANGE RATE
OR
$ PRICE OF FOREIGN CURRENCY

AMOUNT OF FOREIGN CURRENCY

Fig. 1. Behind our *DD* is our desire to import British goods, buy British securities, visit the Bard's grave, etc. What is behind their *SS* supply of £ to be traded for $?

recede, simply declare: "Pound sterling, I command thee to sell at $4.87"? He did not. What a laugh that command would have got in the London City or gotten in Wall Street. What does Uncle Ben care for an English chancellor of the exchequer anyway?

Here's what Churchill did. His Government offered to buy gold at a fixed pound price, and to sell gold at about that same price. So the pound price of gold was definitely stabilized at that mint price—not because Winnie said so, but because he bought and sold at that price.

Now it so happens that America was, all through those years, also on the gold standard. What was Cal Coolidge's Treasury Secretary Mellon doing in 1925? He was offering to buy gold at about $21 an ounce and offering to sell gold at about the same price. So the price of the dollar was also fixed in terms of gold.

Now let's put the two countries together. Things equal to the same thing are equal to each other, we learn in school. The same applies in the economic world. *If* the dollar is fixed in price relative to gold; and *if* the pound is fixed in price relative to gold; and *if* you allow free shipment of gold between nations in either direction—a big if—then it follows as the night the day that the pound and dollar must be in a fixed exchange rate to each other. The

1925 stable exchange rate or "mint parity" worked out to about $4.87 per pound and lasted until the Great Depression. (Check your understanding by this example: The United States pays $35 an ounce for gold in 1958. The United Kingdom pays £12½. So the exchange rate is $2.80 per pound.)

Again you'll have to read the Appendix for details of how this all works out. You'll see that the gold standard imposes certain "rules of the game" upon countries. Still it did tie the world together, making foreign trade just as easy between nations as domestic trade between New York and California.[1]

► EXCHANGE "DEVALUATION" AND "DEPRECIATION" DEFINED

You read in the papers that the dollar was devalued by Franklin Roosevelt in 1933; that the pound was devalued in 1949 from $4.02 to $2.80; etc. What does "devaluation" mean? And how does it compare with the term exchange "depreciation"? What do I mean when I say that the franc is depreciating relative to the dollar? We now have the background to define these terms.

We say the pound is depreciating relative to the dollar when the dollar cost of a pound is going down in the foreign exchange market. *E.g.*, we can now buy one pound for $2.80 rather than $4.00.) We say the pound appreciates when its foreign exchange rate goes up. (*E.g.*, a pound rises in cost from $2.80 to $2.90.) Plainly then, in a free exchange market where the exchange rate fluctuates from day to day, the foreign exchange rate is constantly appreciating or depreciating. Of course, for countries that are undergoing astronomical inflations, this tends to be a one-way street: since you can buy less and less of their goods with their currency, their foreign exchange rate tends chronically to depreciate.

Devaluation of a currency is a term usually reserved to mean a change in its value relative to gold. Example: Suppose every country were on the gold standard; and one bright fall morning, suppose every country were to double its buying-and-selling price for gold. Then we could speak of a world-wide devaluation. But note this: the pound, franc, dollar, and every other currency would have moved *together;* there would be no change in the foreign exchange rate of one against the other. Devaluation would have taken place, but absolutely no depreciation. In short,

► Depreciation of a currency usually refers to any drop in its foreign exchange rate relative to other currencies. Devaluation usually refers to a change in a currency's value relative to gold, and usually to a rare once-and-for-all event of some magnitude rather than to a day-to-day fluctuation.

What are important economic effects of a devaluation? When one country

[1] Note that Uncle Ben never bothers to look in the paper for the price of California dollars; they always sell for $1 of New York money now. But back in the days before the telegraph, when it was costly to carry goods or news to a distant spot within the country, there used to be varying exchange rates for dollar funds in different parts of the country. Ask great-grandpa.

goes off the gold standard and others stay on the gold standard, its currency usually depreciates relative to the others. If it goes back onto the gold standard with each of its units of money worth less in gold, it has gone through a devaluation.

Such a combined depreciation and devaluation has important effects on its physical exports and imports. What are these effects? If England cheapens her pound from $4.20 to $2.80, I find that her books, whisky, sweaters have become cheaper to me. So? So I buy more of them, traveling down my ordinary demand curve for English goods.

That's not all. John Hicks, professor of economics at Oxford, has his demand for American goods affected by the devaluation of the pound. He finds American jazz records have gone up: the albums he used to buy for £1 now cost him 50 per cent more, or £1 10s. So? So he buys less American jazz records: he substitutes Purcell disks; he takes up cricket or the English horn; etc. Devaluation makes him travel up his demand curve for American goods. The moral is clear:

► Devaluing a country's currency tends to increase its physical exports and to decrease its physical imports.

When does a country devalue and why? It will try to devalue, or will have devaluation thrust upon it, when it is having serious "balance of payments" difficulties—when the value of the goods and services it exports tends chronically to fall behind the value of the goods and services it imports. For a while it may export gold to make up the gap; or nice friends abroad may make it loans. But eventually it may find itself running short of foreign currencies at the existing exchange rate.

It may then devalue. Why might that improve the situation? Recall that devaluation cuts down on its physical imports. This will save it foreign currency and work in the corrective direction. Recall too that devaluation will expand its physical exports. This too will work in the right direction, tending to give it more foreign currencies.[1]

► **THE INTERNATIONAL BALANCE OF PAYMENTS**

Exactly what do we mean when we speak of a country's balance of payments? We mean the balance between export of goods and import of goods. Between gold coming in and out. Between capital loans (or "I.O.U.'s") going in and out. Between gifts and foreign aid. And between all these taken together.

The balance of international payments summarizes these important relations. Understand it and you have a pretty good idea of a country's foreign trade.

[1] International-trade texts show that the demand for its exports must have an elasticity of greater than one if the change in exports is to help the trade balance.

The U.S. Department of Commerce keeps official records of all international transactions during a year: of merchandise exported and imported, of money lent abroad or borrowed, of gold movements, of tourist expenditures, of interest and dividends received or paid abroad, of shipping services, etc. They all go to make up the balance of international payments—which is simply a double-entry listing of all items, drawn up in such a way that it must always show a balance.[1]

The balance of international payments is conveniently presented in three sections:

I. Current account
    Private
        Merchandise (or "trade balance")
        Invisibles
            Transportation (shipping services, etc.)
            Travel expenditure (tourists, etc.)
            Income on investments (interest, dividends, etc.)
            Private gifts (immigrants' remittances, etc.)
            Miscellaneous services
    Governmental
        Government export of military goods to allies
        Unilateral grants of United States government (aid programs, military aid, etc.)
II. Gold movements (out and in)
III. Capital movements
    Private
        Long-term
        Short-term
    United States government

Balance on current account. The totality of items under (I) is usually referred to as the "balance on current account." This important magnitude summarizes the difference between our total export of goods and services and our total import of goods and services. In fact it is nothing but an old friend of ours from the national income chapter under a different name: the balance on current account is exactly the same thing as what we called "net foreign investment" in the various national product and income accounts; if the current balance is positive, America is performing net positive foreign investment; if the current balance is negative, we are disinvesting abroad on balance.

In a moment, we shall see how any positive surplus balance on current ac-

---

[1] Smuggling and some innocent items elude the record keepers, so it is almost always necessary to introduce a miscellaneous category of omitted items just large enough to preserve a formal balance.

count is "financed"—or, more precisely, is offset—by gold and capital movements shown under (II) and (III). But before doing this, let's describe briefly the major current items, which are seen to fall under the headings of Private and Governmental.

Centuries ago, when *merchandise* items predominated, writers used to concentrate on this narrow category alone. If merchandise exports were greater than merchandise imports, they spoke of a "favorable balance of trade"; if imports exceeded exports, they spoke of an "unfavorable balance of trade." This is not a very good choice of terms, since we shall see that a so-called "unfavorable" balance of trade may be a very good thing for a country.

In addition to the so-called "visible" merchandise items, we must not forget the important role played these days by the "invisibles." These consist of such things as shipping services which we provide for foreigners or which they provide for us, American tourist expenditures abroad, our earnings from abroad, and the gifts that immigrants send back home. If you think about it, you will realize that an invisible item like the expenditure of an American for a drink in Paris has the same effect on the final balance of payments as does his import of French wine to be drunk here at home in America. And if we provide shipping insurance service to foreigners, that too acts just like one of our merchandise exports.

A good way to decide how *any* item should be treated is to ask the following question: Is the item, like one of our merchandise exports, providing us with more foreign currencies? Or is it, like one of our merchandise imports, causing us to use up our stock of foreign currencies and making it necessary to get more foreign currency? The first, or export-type, item is called a "credit item"; the import-type is called a "debit item."

To show how this rule works, ask the following question: How shall we treat income on investments received by Americans from abroad? Clearly they are credit items like exports in that they provide us with foreign currencies. The reader can reverse the argument to show that the interest and dividends which foreigners receive from us must be treated like debit items—like imports, they use up foreign currencies.

At this point a look at Table 1 will be helpful. It presents official data on the balance of international payments of the United States for 1956. Note its three main divisions into current, gold, and capital items; in addition, it has a last item to account for statistical errors and omissions. Each row is numbered to make reference easy.

Then after each item has been listed by name in Column (*a*), we list in Column (*b*) the credits—*i.e.*, the amounts of those items that are like exports in earning us foreign currencies. Next in Column (*c*) are listed the debits—*i.e.*, the amounts of the items that use up foreign currencies because of our need to pay for imports, etc.

We keep records of all exports and imports, of gold movements and capital movements:

Table 1. Balance of international payments of the United States, 1956 (in millions of dollars).

No.	Items	Credits	Debits	Net Credits (+) or debits (−)
	(a)	(b)	(c)	(d)
I	Current:			
	Private:			
1	Merchandise (adj.)	$17,321	$12,791	+$4,530
	Invisibles			
2	Transportation	1,619	1,432	+ 187
3	Travel expenditures	705	1,275	− 570
4	Income on investments (interest, dividends, etc.)	2,658	618	+ 2,040
5	Private remittances			− 503
6	Miscellaneous services	1,215	784	+ 431
7	Current private balance			+$6,115
	United States governmental:			
8	Exports of military goods and services to allies	2,605		+ 2,605
9	United States government military aid payments to allies		2,605	− 2,605
10	Other grants and payments		1,829	− 1,829
11	Expenditures abroad by United States military		2,910	− 2,910
12	Current government balance			− 4,739
13	Net balance on current account			+$1,376
II	Net gold exports (+) or imports (−):			− 306
III	Capital account, net exports of our I.O.U's (+) or net imports (−):			
	Private:			
14	Long-term			− 2,039
15	Short-term			+ 903
16	Total private capital movements			− 1,136
17	United States government			− 626
18	Net balance on capital account			−$1,762
19	Errors and omissions			+ 692

Thus, in 1956 our merchandise exports gave us credits of 17,321 million dollars; but our merchandise imports gave us debits of only 12,791 million dollars. The net difference between credits and debits is in this case 4,530 million dollars. It is shown listed in the last column, Column (d), of the first row. (Be sure you know why the algebraic sign is shown $+$ rather than $-$.) Even today one hears this export merchandise surplus called by the misleading title, "favorable balance of trade."

The reader can interpret each line of the invisible items. He will know why the American tendency to travel abroad results in a negative—or net debit—entry under travel expenditures. He will also know why gifts by private Americans to relatives or charities abroad serve to use up foreign currencies and are listed as debits in line 5. (Of course, in their balance of payments, foreign countries would think of our debit as their credit; and they would think of these last two items as "making more dollars available" to them.)

Table 1 shows that as far as the private current items are concerned, the effect of the invisible items was to reinforce our surplus of credits over debits —primarily because of our interest and dividends from abroad.

How were foreigners able to pay for our 6,115 million dollars surplus on private current account? They would be tempted to call this a "dollar shortage"; and Table 1 shows that in 1956, as in the years since the Marshall Plan began, it was our government aid programs that filled the "dollar gap."

Indeed as we look at the United States government unilateral payments, we see that they register a total debit amount of 4,739 million dollars! These come primarily from our expenditure abroad on our armed services: thus, when our quartermaster buys meat in England to feed American airmen based in the United Kingdom, this appears as a debit item in row 11. Aside from our military expenditures abroad, our other government grants—for economic development abroad, etc.—also helped substantially to fill the dollar gap. It's worth noting that our shipment of guns and military supplies to our allies have no effect on the international balance: this is because the listing of these as a credit in line 8 is just matched by the offsetting debit entry in line 9 that goes under the name of our military aid to allies.

Combining private and governmental items, what is the final Net Balance on Current Account? Uncle Sam's unilateral payment programs fell short in 1956 of matching our tremendous surplus on private current account. How far short? By the 1,376 million dollars shown in line 13's net balance on current account. Thus, in 1956 we were running a surplus on current account of more than a billion dollars—despite vast government aid programs. This current surplus, we'll see, means we were lending abroad more than a billion dollars in 1956. This current surplus is the important figure for net foreign investment which the national income statistician reckons as one of the four basic components of GNP, as we saw back in Chapter 10.

Gold movements. It is to be stressed that neither the balance of trade nor the balance of current items has to be necessarily in perfect balance. Only the *total* balance of international payments must be always in balance. This is because any lack of balance of current items must be exactly matched by an opposite balance of the capital and gold items. Why? Because whichever of our sales abroad are not matched by swaps against goods and gifts must be paid for by gold or must be owed to us.[1]

Turning to the gold movements, see that we imported 300 million dollars of gold from abroad in 1956—to be exact, 306 million dollars. This debit item went a small part of the way to offsetting our surplus on current account. (You will never have any trouble deciding whether a gold movement is a credit or debit if you firmly remember that you can treat export or import of gold exactly like export and import of any other commodity: shipping gold abroad gives us foreign currencies just as does any merchandise export, etc.)

For many years after Franklin Roosevelt raised the price of gold from \$21 to \$35 an ounce back in the early 1930's, America was a vast importer of gold. It has been only in the hot and cold war years that we have been an exporter of gold, and as we saw in earlier chapters, our current gold stock remains very high—above 20 billion dollars, which is a significant fraction of all the gold that exists in the world.

Capital movements. Since gold does not fully make up our surplus on current account, we must turn to capital movements. After all, what you don't pay for, you must owe for; and when we run a surplus, what we don't get paid for, we must be owed.

It is easy to decide which are credit and which debit items in the capital accounts if you use the following rule: Always think of America as exporting and importing *capital securities,* or for short exporting and importing I.O.U.'s. Then you can treat these exports and imports like any other exports and imports. When we lend abroad, is it a credit or debit? Obviously, we are importing I.O.U.'s—and imports always give rise to debits. So the answer is, Debit. Similarly when we are borrowing from abroad on balance, this creates a net credit. If you don't follow this rule, you'll find yourself getting confused: when we lend abroad you'll be tempted to think of us as exporting capital abroad and thereby earning a credit. This is wrong: we're then importing I.O.U.'s and these imports are debit *offsets* that enable us to be paid for our surplus of credit exports in the noncapital accounts.

Table 1 shows that in 1956 America was a net foreign lender: we were

---

[1] Even if our *trade* were in balance with *all* the rest of the world, there probably would not be balanced merchandise trade with any one country, such as Britain. On the contrary, it is usual and desirable for us to sell more to Britain than we buy from her; for Britain to sell more to the East Indies than she buys from them; and for the East Indies to sell more to us than we sell to them. This example of triangular trade is just one instance of the profitability of multilateral trade. As discussed in a later chapter, standards of living all over the world would deteriorate if international trade were pressed into the mold of bilateralism, with insistence upon a perfect balance between the countries in every pair.

lending or investing abroad more than foreigners were lending or investing here. Table 1 shows that our net short-term borrowing was more than offset by long-term private and government lending, leaving us with 1,762 million dollars of net lending in line 18. As a matter of definition this net lending plus our gold imports must exactly match our surplus on current account (plus errors and omissions).

Of what importance is it that we had in 1956 positive net foreign investment of about 1½ billion dollars? To the Federal Reserve money manager worried about 1956's inflationary pressures, positive net foreign investment was one more contribution to his inflationary gap computations, giving him multiplier headaches. To the marginal worker, who can find work only when the economy is humming, the positive net foreign investment perhaps meant his first steady job since the 1953–1954 recession.

The items in the balance of payments are the stuff economic life is made of.

▶ STAGES OF A COUNTRY'S BALANCE OF PAYMENTS

Historically, the United States has gone through three of the four stages typical of the growth of a young agricultural nation into a well-developed industrialized one. Review of this history will consolidate understanding.

1. *Young and growing debtor nation.* From the Revolutionary War era until just after the Civil War, we imported more than we exported. England and Europe lent us the difference in order to build up our capital structure. We were a typical young and growing debtor nation.

2. *Mature debtor nation.* From about 1873 to 1914, our balance of trade appears to have become favorable. But growth of the dividends and interest that we had to pay abroad on our past borrowing kept our balance on current account more or less in balance. Capital movements were also about in balance, our new lending just about canceling off our borrowing.

3. *New creditor nation.* In World War I, we expanded our exports tremendously. At first, private American citizens made loans to the warring Allied powers. After we got in the war, our government lent money to England and France for war equipment and postwar relief needs. We emerged from the war a creditor nation. But our psychological frame of mind had not adjusted itself to our new creditor position. We passed high tariff laws in the early 1920's and again in 1930. Because we refused to import, foreigners found it difficult to get the dollars to pay us interest and dividends, much less repay principal.

So long as we remained in this third stage of being a new creditor country; so long, that is, as we kept making *new* private foreign loans all through the 1920's, everything momentarily appeared all right on the surface. We could continue to sell more than we were buying, by putting most of it "on the cuff." The rest of the world met our export surplus by sending us gold and by sending us I.O.U.'s. As long as Wall Street bankers could interest Main Street in foreign bonds, everything seemed rosy. But by 1929 and later, when Americans would no longer lend abroad, the crash finally came. International trade broke down. Debts were defaulted. America, as much as the rest of the world, was to blame.

4. *Mature creditor nation.* America has not yet succeeded in adjusting herself to moving into the fourth stage of being a mature creditor nation. England reached this stage some years ago. And as in all such cases, her imports exceeded her exports. Before we feel sorry for her because of her so-called "unfavorable" balance of trade, let us note what this really means.

Her citizens were living better because they were able to import much cheap food, and in return did not have to part with much in the way of valuable export goods. The English were paying for their import surplus by the interest and dividend receipts they were receiving from past foreign lending.

Fine for the English. But what about the rest of the world? Weren't they worse off having to send exports to England in excess of imports? Not necessarily. Normally, the capital goods that England had previously lent them permitted them to add to their domestic production—to add *more* than had to be paid out to England in interest and dividends. Both parties were better off. Nineteenth-century foreign lending was twice blessed: it blessed him who gave and him who received.

Of course, things were not always quite so smooth. Some investments proved unwise. Political problems of colonies and nationalism complicated the situation. And as we shall see, after World War I the whole process broke down.

▶ **BASIC SIGNIFICANCE OF INTERNATIONAL CAPITAL MOVEMENTS**

Let us return now to the problem of capital movements. If political problems of nationality and domestic problems of unemployment did not enter the picture, then the fundamentals of international lending would be easy to understand. We could easily cut through the fog of money and finance and concentrate upon the real aspects in terms of goods and resources.

How does capital grow within a country? By our diverting labor, land, machinery, and other resources away from the production of current consumption goods. Instead, we plant trees, drain rivers, build new machinery and buildings. All these add to our future income and consumption.

We are postponing present consumption for future consumption; in fact, for an even *greater* amount of future consumption. Where does the increase in future consumption come from? From the fact that *capital goods have a "net" productivity.* This productivity is the real side of the interest rate.[1]

Different parts of the world have different amounts of resources: labor, minerals, climate, know-how, etc. Were it not for ignorance or political bound-

[1] See Chapter 29.

aries, no one would push investment in North America down to the point of 3 per cent returns *if elsewhere there still existed 6 per cent opportunities.* Some capital would certainly be invested abroad. This would give foreign labor higher wages, because now the foreign worker has more and better tools to work with. It would increase foreign production. By how much? Not only by enough to pay for the constant replacement of used-up capital goods, but in addition by enough to pay us an interest or dividend return on our investment. This interest return would take the form of goods and services which we receive from abroad and which add to our standard of living. An all-wise scientist would probably approve of the process. It would make sense to him because capital is going into the regions where its productivity is highest.

When would we be repaid our principal? So long as we are earning a good return, there is no reason why we should ever wish to have it repaid. However, the once backward country may finally become rather prosperous. It may wish to pull in its belt as far as consumption is concerned, and to use its savings to buy out our ownership in its factories, farms, and mines. But suppose that we are rich, with plenty of savings and with so much capital at home that our rate of interest is low. We will not particularly wish to sell out or be repaid. We will raise the selling price of our farm and factory holdings abroad. In other words, we will be content with a smaller percentage interest return. Thus, there is no necessary reason why a country should ever be paid off for its past lending, unless it has become relatively older and poorer.

When nationalism rears its ugly (or beautiful) head, matters change. Within the United States, interest and dividends may stream from South to North and West to East until doomsday. A few people may grumble about absentee ownership; but the courts and police are there to see that property rights are respected. Not so between nations. When a country is poor, it may be anxious to borrow. After it has become richer, it becomes unhappy to have to pay dividends and interest abroad. It chooses not to remember that its prosperity stemmed in part from its past borrowing. More than an economic burden is involved; politically, countries don't like the principle of absentee ownership by "furriners." Therefore, they are prone to insist upon getting rid of their international liabilities—paying them off at a fair price, at an unfair price, or often by outright default.

Economics and politics mix in ways too complicated to discuss in this book. Some say "trade follows the flag." Others say the flag follows trade. Some say the pursuit of economic gain is the primary motive behind the imperialistic search for colonies. Others claim that national power (offensive and defensive) is an end in itself; that economic well-being is sacrificed to this end; and that economic resources are sought for their contribution to military strength (offensive and defensive) rather than for their contribution to economic well-being. According to this view, without wars and nationalism, anyone could invest and trade anywhere; all sensible people would prefer to live in small countries unhindered by costly military establishments and colonial administration. At the opposite extreme is the view that victory in battle, rather than comfortable living, is the only worthy end in life; the foreigner is of no importance compared with the fatherland; he can be stripped of his goods and land, and he can be made to work for the "super-race," so that the latter can have its cake and cannons too. The world of the last few centuries lies somewhere in between these extreme cases.

► FINANCIAL VERSUS REAL ASPECTS OF FOREIGN LENDING

Let us turn from politics back to economics, to see how these processes take place in financial terms. Money throws a veil over the real aspects of capital movements. Usually a foreigner borrows *money* from us rather than capital goods directly. He gives us an I.O.U. in the form of a bond, note, or stock certificate. We give him dollars. If he simply holds the dollars or puts them in an American bank or invests them in an American security, then there has been no net·capital movement at all. We have some form of his I.O.U.; he has some form of ours. In the capital movements section of the balance of payments, the difference just cancels out. Only when he uses the receipts of the loan to import goods and services (or gold) in excess of his exports to us has a real and a financial capital movement taken place.

When the time comes for interest payment, the foreigners must sell us more goods than they buy in order to get the extra dollars to remit to us. Our balance of international payments then will show an import surplus, balanced by the invisible credit item, interest and dividends.

Should we feel glad or sorry when we are exporting more than we are importing? If we never had to worry about unemployment, we would certainly regret having to give away goods that might better serve our own well-being. Only the consolation of later receiving goods in return could serve to compensate us for this present loss. Altruism aside, if we could look into a crystal ball and see that the investment were sure to go sour later and never be repaid either in principal or interest, then we should certainly conclude that the capital movement was a bad and not a good thing.

A century ago, John Stuart Mill properly stressed that it is imports and not exports that add to a nation's well-being. Before World War II, countries were so badly handling the problem of maintaining full employment that they began to turn the cart before the horse and to treat exports as if they were an end for their own sake. Fortunately, nations are learning how proper monetary and fiscal policies can bring back to validity the fundamental principles of classical economics. And to this degree Mill's sensible stress on imports will come back into its own.

SUMMARY

1. Buying or selling abroad presupposes a foreign exchange rate between home and foreign currencies. Supply and demand sets each day's free exchange rate; but two countries on a gold standard have a stable foreign exchange rate set by the stable prices at which they each buy and sell gold. (Appendix gives details.)

2. The balance of international payments refers to all the transactions that use up foreign exchange or make foreign exchange available to us. It relates the total of our exports of goods and services to our imports. Our export of goods, services, gold, or I.O.U.'s are credit items, making foreign currencies available to us. Our imports of those items are debits, using up foreign currencies.

3. Our net balance on current account comes from adjusting our merchandise trade balance for "invisible" service items and from taking into account our unilateral government aid programs. The final net balance on current account is the important national-income concept of net foreign investment. It has to be offset by gold shipments and short- and long-term capital movements.

4. As a nation passes from the "young debtor" to the "mature creditor" stage, its balance of trade and balance of current account items undergo a series of changes which you should understand.

5. No problem in international finance is more important than that of understanding the real and the monetary aspects of capital movements in their effect upon the industrial development of nations.

QUESTIONS FOR DISCUSSION

1. Contrast free and stable foreign exchange rates. Explain each.

2. Draw up a list of items that belong on the credit side of the balance of international payments, and another list of items that belong on the debit side. What is meant by a favorable balance of trade? How does the trade balance differ from the balance on current account? Why the term "invisible items"? What is the difference between short-term and long-term capital movements?

3. Construct hypothetical balance sheets for a young debtor country, a mature debtor country, a new creditor country, a mature creditor country.

4. A Canadian railroad company floats bonds in England and uses the proceeds to buy tracks and locomotives. How would the English balance of payments be affected by this capital movement? Later the loan is repaid with interest; what effect then?

5. "Foreign lending causes war. Foreign giving postpones war. Free foreign trading prevents war." Comment.

6. Comment on Stuart Chase's "common-sense formula": "The stuff we produce, as a nation, plus the stuff we import, less the stuff we export, is a measure of our standard of living."

7. Review your understanding of the following concepts:

gold standard versus free exchange rate

currency depreciation and devaluation

balance of international payments, trade balance, current account, government aid items

"favorable balance"

invisibles

gold movements

I.O.U.'s, capital movements

net foreign investment

historical capital movements, financial and real, in politics and in economics

APPENDIX: A FEW MECHANICS OF INTERNATIONAL FINANCE

Without going into details, we may briefly survey how exchange rates, prices, and trade are determined (1) under *freely flexible* exchange rates, and (2) under the *gold standard* or some other regime of stable exchange rates.

Freely Flexible Exchange Rates

From 1919 to 1925, the price of the pound fluctuated from day to day, going from almost $5 down to $3. Such a rate is determined by the interplay of competitive supply and demand for foreign exchange. When Americans wish to import or travel, their demand for pounds tends to push up the rate—say from $3 to $3.10. Any other American debit item, such as our desire to lend abroad (*i.e.*, import I.O.U.'s!) has the same effect.

Any credit item, on the other hand, such as our exporting to Britain, adds to the supply of pounds, because foreigners then need dollars. This tends to depress the price of foreign exchange or pounds. Brokers and bankers keep their ears glued to the telephone in order to follow the tug of war of supply and demand acting on flexible exchange rates.

We need not go into details of the exact mechanism, except to note one important tendency: When the price of foreign exchange rises, there are usually strong forces making for self-correction and helping to keep it from rising indefinitely. Similarly, there are self-correcting forces tending to limit a decline in the exchange rate.

Thus, if our imports become too large, we bid up the price of pounds. But at $4 per pound rather than $3, Americans find that British dishes and cloth have greatly increased in cost to us. Our imports are discouraged, which tends to correct the situation or at least to keep the exchange rate from rising further. More than that. Now an Englishman can get more dollars for his pounds. Consequently, even if American industries do not change their dollar price tags, the British will be encouraged to take more of our exports once the dollar has depreciated. This is an additional factor operating toward restoring the equilibrium of exports and imports and limiting the magnitude of the exchange-rate variation.

Show that, just as a depreciation of the dollar tended to create an American export surplus and to correct an import surplus, so will an appreciation of the dollar tend to encourage American imports and discourage

American exports and to be self-correcting and self-limiting. (Hint: Let the pound fall to $2.50. Why will it not fall farther?)

Determinants of Supply and Demand

It is all very well to say, as we have just been saying, that supply and demand determine a flexible exchange rate. But if we want to probe deeper behind the scenes to ascertain what makes supply and demand act as they do, we shall find that the level of the exchange rate depends upon at least the following four fundamental factors.

1. The *strength of our desires* for foreign goods and services relative to their desires for our goods and services. The greater our desire for their goods, the higher will be the price of foreign exchange be bid. The dollar will tend to depreciate in value and the pound to appreciate.

2. *The more our national income rises,* the greater will be our demand for imports. This will tend to make the dollar depreciate. On the other hand, high foreign national income makes the dollar appreciate, or what is the same thing, makes the price of foreign exchange cheaper for Americans. All this comes about because a country's "propensity to import" increases with national income in much the same way that its willingness to consume does.

3. The higher our *prices* and *costs* are, relative to the foreigners', the greater will be our imports, relative to exports. Therefore, high American prices and low foreign prices usually mean a high price for foreign exchange. After World War I this third factor, then considered most important of all, was called the "purchasing power parity" theory of exchange rates. According to this theory, the relative change in exchange rate between two countries will—other things being equal! —be proportional to the relative change in our prices compared to those abroad. Or,

$$\text{Foreign exchange rate} = \frac{\text{American prices}}{\text{foreign prices}}$$

This theory is most useful when one of the two countries has suffered a tremendous inflation that has tended to raise most of its

prices by almost the same percentage. If everything else is exactly the same, except that it now takes 100 times as much foreign money to buy things, then what should we expect about the exchange rate (the price of a unit of foreign currency)? We should expect it to probably find its level at about one one-hundredth of the previous rate.[1] (Do you see why?)

4. Finally, the foreign exchange rate will be higher, the more Americans wish to lend abroad, the greater the payments we have to make on past debts or on war-punishment reparation payments, and the less willing foreigners are to hold dollars. When our investors develop a desire to hold foreign I.O.U.'s, bonds, stocks, bank deposits, or currency—then they will bid up the foreign exchange rate. The reader can work out the reverse case, where payments into the United States tend to lower the foreign exchange rate.

This last factor of capital movements is intimately tied up with *speculation* in foreign exchange. If only merchandise exports or current items were involved, the foreign exchange rate might be sluggish and change very little. Unfortunately, when the price of the pound drops from $3 to $2.96, many people begin to be afraid that it may fall still farther. Therefore, they try to get out of pounds and into dollars. But the increased sale of pounds and reduced demand for pounds, resulting from jittery short-term speculative capital movements, tends to push the pound down farther. Thus, small movements of the exchange rate are often amplified in a self-aggravating way by "hot money," which rushes from country to country with every rumor of war, politics, and exchange rate fluctuation. When such "capital flight" gets started in one direction on a large scale, exchange rates may move chaotically.

Debate over Flexible Exchange Rates

There is much to be said for flexible ex-

---

[1] The fall during inflation of the German mark, the Greek drachma, the Italian lira, the French franc, and the Chinese dollar, and other foreign exchange rates are all good examples.

changes. Each country is free to pursue its own internal economic policies, leaving the exchange rate to take care of itself. However, there are also important disadvantages. With the exchange rate varying wildly from month to month, the volume of international trade and lending is greatly discouraged. A producer would naturally prefer to sell and buy at home rather than to be betting continually upon the foreign exchange rate.[1]

A further disadvantage of fluctuating exchange rates results from the fact that each change in rates disturbs the existing situation in export and import markets. When suddenly the dollar depreciates, our exporters are helped and our importers are hurt. When the dollar appreciates, the reverse happens. This contributes toward unemployment, windfall profits and losses, and instability.

Advocates of free exchange rates have replies to these criticisms: "When trade doesn't balance, someone has to make adjustments. Better that the adjustments should come from exchange rate drops having direct effects to encourage exports and discourage imports than that government should introduce quotas and nasty direct controls over imports. And better that the exchange rate should be allowed to fall today than that its rate should be temporarily pegged, with every speculator knowing it can go in but one direction and therefore doing all he can to take advantage of the inevitable day when the exchange rate is devalued."

Stable Exchange Rates

The alternative to free exchange rates is a government policy of making the economy adjust to a fixed stable rate. The simplest way to do this is not to pass a law or edict but rather to come into the market with a big enough supply or demand for foreign exchange to keep the rate stable. Usually governments do this through so-called "exchange stabilization funds." There is no rea-

son why a wealthy eccentric private citizen might not attempt to stabilize, say, the dollar price of Belgian francs. He, or any governmental fund, would have to start out with a huge pile of both dollars and Belgian francs (or with commodities like gold or wheat that could be converted by sale into either currency). Then to stabilize the price of the franc, he would simply instruct his brokers to bid dollars for francs whenever the price tended to fall, and to sell francs for dollars whenever the price tended to rise. So long as he did not run out of either francs or dollars, and so long as he stood ready both to buy and to sell francs at a given dollar price, then the franc-dollar exchange rate would be perfectly stable at that level.

Of course, even a multimillionaire might not be rich enough to do this for very long. A government, or the International Monetary Fund, is in a more powerful position. However, even the most powerful government will not be able to stand up against the ocean's tide and maintain any given exchange rate—unless it is able to influence prices, costs, and other conditions *so as to make private supply and demand for foreign exchange just about balance at the "pegged" rate.* Otherwise it will eventually be drained of all its holdings of one of the currencies— and then bingo! the rate can no longer be held steady.

Historically, the so-called "quasi-automatic gold standard" was a still more important method of stabilizing exchange rates and of thereby facilitating international trade. Let us turn to it.

Workings of the Gold Standard

To go on the gold standard a country need consult no one. Its Treasury must do two simple things: (1) agree to buy all gold brought to it at a given price—say $35 an ounce, in the case of the American Treasury —and (2) be willing to sell gold freely to all comers at the same price of $35 per ounce. The result: the dollar price of gold becomes perfectly fixed, at a level called "mint parity."

As far as a single country is concerned, that is all there is to it. But where does the

---

[1] See Chapter 22 on speculation for the possibility of reducing risks by "hedging" in a "futures market." Unfortunately, prior to 1958 foreign exchange markets had not been well enough organized to make this very helpful.

foreign exchange rate enter the picture? As soon as a second country (say Britain in addition to the United States) goes on the gold standard, then the *price of gold in terms of pounds* is also stabilized. To keep the arithmetic simple, let us work this out using a $3 rather than $2.80 pound.[1]

Of course, things equal to the same thing must be equal to each other. If a dollar is $\frac{1}{35}$ ounce of gold and a pound is $\frac{3}{35}$ ounce of gold, then the price of a pound in terms of dollars must be 3. This is not simply a question of arithmetic, but of hard practical business sense. If I want to buy pounds in order to import from Britain, I will never pay more than $3 for them. Why? Because I can take three crisp American bills and get from the United States Treasury $\frac{3}{35}$ ounce of gold. I ship this gold to London, where the English Treasury gives me a crisp pound note. You should be able to work out the reason why an Englishman will never supply pounds for less than $3.

Thus, with each currency tied to gold, they become tied to each other at a fixed exchange rate. But with one minor qualification. There is approximately a 2-cent shipping, insurance, and interest charge involved in transporting this much gold between New York and London. Therefore, supply and demand can bid the pound price up to $3.02 before it becomes profitable for Americans to export gold. This is called the American gold-export point (or the British gold-import point). As an exercise, you may show that the British gold-export point is at about $2.98, and that the exchange rate is free to wobble around the hypothetical $3 mint parity point within the range set by the two gold points.

The Equilibrating Specie-Flow-Price Mechanism

To this point the process has been completely mechanical. But the alert reader will worry, as the "mercantilist" writers of the

seventeenth and eighteenth centuries did, over this: What prevents the exchange rate's always being forced to the gold-export point of one of the countries until the one-way drain finally uses up all its gold reserves and forces it off the gold standard?

The answer was first discovered two centuries ago by the Scottish philosopher David Hume. He claimed there was an automatic self-correcting "specie-flow-price" mechanism at work. According to him, Americans need not worry if they are importing more than they are exporting and are losing gold or specie. Here's why. (1) The gold pouring into England will proportionately increase the amount of English money. (2) The increase in English money will (via the quantity theory of money and prices) cause a proportionate inflationary increase in British prices. Also, (3) the gold flowing out of America will cause a proportionate contraction of our money supply. (4) Again, via the quantity theory, this will cause a proportionate deflationary fall in American prices.

As a result of these four steps, there will be a double-edged tendency toward correcting the outflow of gold. (5) With British prices high relative to our own, Britons will begin to buy more of our exports. (6) Similarly, with our low prices, it will now pay us to buy less of their imports. Thus, the situation will finally correct itself. The changes in relative price levels caused by the flow of gold will remedy the adverse trade balance and choke off the one-way flow of gold before it has gone very far. Therefore, said Hume, there is nothing to worry about.

Today we are not so sure. England may not want to have an inflation, and America may not like the idea of having a deflation just because the impersonal gods of the gold standard dictate it.

Besides, since Hume's time, banking and finance have become more elaborate. Now that gold coins are no longer the important part of our money supply, the process is not automatic. Instead the Treasury and the Central Bank are supposed to "follow the rules of the gold-standard game." When gold flows out, this is to be a signal for us to put

---

[1] Thus instead of using the 1955 price of £12½ per ounce, imagine that the United Kingdom buys and sells gold freely at 35 ÷ 3 pounds or £11⅔ per ounce.

on the deflationary brakes. For example, we should increase tax collections relative to expenditure; discourage private investment by raising the "discount" and other interest rates; tighten up on bank reserves by Federal Reserve open-market sales of securities or by raising legal reserve ratios put downward pressure on wages and prices. In short, deliberately create a depression and deflation.

You should be able to list the inflationary steps that the rules of the game would impose on the country receiving gold. You will then be in a position to understand how, and why, countries refused to play the rules of the gold-standard game in the years after World War I. They did this to avoid inflation or deflation. But, with this further result: the one-way drains of gold were not corrected, and finally the gold standard broke down.

However, the breakdown was not due simply to the willful disregard by nations of the rules of the game. In part the breakdown came because the gold standard is a "fair-weather system" that works best when only small strains are placed upon it. In the jittery, troubled period since 1914, with erratic capital movements and political upsets, the strains were anything but small.

Finally, from a technical economic viewpoint, we are no longer so optimistic as Hume was about the efficacy of the specie-flow-price mechanism. The weaknesses of the quantity theory have already been pointed out in earlier chapters. Also we have seen that prices and costs are often sticky in capitalistic countries.[1]

Income Effects and the "Foreign Trade Multiplier"

For all the reasons earlier discussed, the gold standard probably would have broken down

and been abandoned long ago, were it not for an important equilibrating process not dreamed of in Hume's specie-flow-price philosophy. In recent years economists have emphasized that *income changes in the two countries help to restore equilibrium*. If our exports go up, then even without any price changes, we now have a higher national income. Part of this higher income we shall want to use to buy more imported goods. Thus, (1) to some degree, an increase in exports will directly induce an increase in imports via income, no matter what happens to prices. But, (2) when we analyze in detail the full multiplier effects of our increased income, we shall see that the induced increase in imports is only *partial* rather than being equal to the original increase in exports. There is still some need for prices or exchange rate changes to restore equilibrium. The details of the argument follow; but they can be skipped at a first reading.

Let us turn then to the multiplier analysis of foreign trade. We have seen that new domestic investment creates primary jobs and income and that the spending and respending of this new income give rise to a chain of secondary multiplier effects. New exports have exactly the same multiplier effects. They raise incomes directly, but in addition they set up a chain of further spending and respending.

Thus, a billion dollars' worth of new export orders to New England machine-tool factories will create 1 billion dollars of primary jobs and income. Then workers and owners may respend perhaps two-thirds of their new income on the consumption products of Indiana and California; two-

---

[1] Still worse, there is a possibility that the Hume price changes could make the situation worse rather than better if international demands turn out to be inelastic rather than elastic. In such cases, lowering the prices of American export goods will not expand our sales much; therefore, Englishmen will actually offer fewer pounds for dollars rather than more pounds. Similarly, if the American demand for

British goods should be very urgent and inelastic, raising British prices may force us to demand more pounds rather than less. Thus, the price reaction to a depreciation of the dollar may be a perverse rather than an equilibrating one: The dollar would have to depreciate still further; or paradoxically, currency appreciation might in this perverse case wipe out a country's import deficit.

thirds of this extra income is in turn respent, etc. The process comes to a halt only when the total adds up to

$$3 = 1 + \tfrac{2}{3} + (\tfrac{2}{3})^2 + \cdots = 1/(1 - \tfrac{2}{3})$$

times 1 billion dollars, or to 2 billion dollars of secondary consumption expenditure in addition to the 1 billion dollars of primary expenditure.

Besides introducing a multiplier effect of exports into the picture, international trade has a second important effect. Higher American national income will increase our imports, let us say by one-twelfth out of every extra dollar. This means that our chain of induced domestic purchasing power will peter out quicker than in the above example. At each step, these imports act as "leakages," just like the marginal propensity to save.[1]

Therefore, out of the original 1 billion dollars of income in the export industries, perhaps only $\tfrac{7}{12} (= \tfrac{2}{3} - \tfrac{1}{12})$ rather than $\tfrac{8}{12}$ will be respent on *American* consumption goods (in Indiana, California, and so forth). And so it will go at each stage. The whole

multiplier will now add up only to

$$1 + \tfrac{7}{12} + (\tfrac{7}{12})^2 + \cdots$$

or only $2\tfrac{2}{5} = 1 \div (1 - \tfrac{7}{12}) = 1 \div \tfrac{5}{12}$ instead of to 3. This is because $\tfrac{1}{12}$ of our extra $2\tfrac{2}{5}$ billion dollars of generated income—or $\tfrac{1}{5}$ of a billion dollars in this case—tends to go abroad for extra imports.

If we look at our multiplier formulas we find that this is a general rule:

▶ So long as some fraction of income at every stage is leaking into domestic savings, a new dollar of exports will never be able to lift income by enough to call forth a full dollar of new imports.[2]

---

[1] If you apply the foreign trade multiplier analysis to a small city or country, you will find that the secondary multiplier effects upon the workers of that region are almost negligible, since almost all extra income leaks out to other regions.

[2] Suppose that each extra dollar of income is always split up into the three fractions: c for American consumption goods, b for America's propensity to import goods from abroad, a for the remaining amount going into saving. Then let exports go up by one unit. The multiplier tells us that our income will go up by $1/(1 - c) = 1/(b + a)$. Multiplying this extra income by the fraction b, we get induced imports of $b/(b + a)$, which is certainly less than our original one of new exports—to the extent that the marginal propensity to save, a, is positive.

If there is any induced domestic investment, it can be thrown in with c and our result will still hold for any "stable" system with positive "leakage," a.

INTERNATIONAL TRADE AND THE THEORY
OF COMPARATIVE ADVANTAGE

*The benefit of international trade—a more efficient employment of
the productive forces of the world.*

J. S. MILL

Again and again we have seen how specialization increases productivity and
standards of living. Now we must show exactly how this works out in the field
of international or interregional trade, going behind the façade of international finance.

Why did the United States specialize a century ago in the production of
agricultural goods and exchange these for the manufacturing output of
Europe? Why is she today able to export highly complex mass-produced goods
to the far corners of the globe? Why is the agriculture of Australia so different
from that of Austria or Belgium? How great would be the costs of complete
self-sufficiency to a modern country? How do all countries benefit from trade?

The key to the correct answers to such questions, and many more, is provided by the theory of comparative advantage or comparative cost. Developed
more than a century ago by David Ricardo, John Stuart Mill, and other English followers of Adam Smith, the theory of comparative advantage is a closely
reasoned doctrine which, when properly stated, is unassailable. With it we are
able to separate out gross fallacies in the political propaganda for protective
tariffs aimed at limiting imports. At the same time, it helps us to identify the
germs of truth that sometimes pop up in the heated claims for protection.

▶ DIVERSITY OF CONDITIONS BETWEEN REGIONS OR COUNTRIES

For simplicity, therefore, let us imagine two countries or continents, each endowed with certain quantities of natural resources, capital goods, kinds of labor, and technical knowledge or know-how. The first link in the comparative-
cost chain of reasoning is the *diversity in conditions of production between*

different countries. Specifically, this means that the production possibilities of the different countries are very different. Although people could try to produce something of every commodity in any region, it is obvious that they would not succeed; or, if they did succeed, it would be only at a terrific cost. With hothouse procedures and forcing methods, wine grapes could perhaps be grown in Scotland; but the cost in terms of economic resources would be exorbitant, and the resulting product would hardly be fit to drink anyway.

Even if by chance two countries can both produce the same commodities, they will usually find that it pays for each to concentrate its production especially on some goods and trade them for other goods. If we consider trade between, say, the northern temperate zones and the southern tropics, this proposition will seem true and trite. Of course, resources near the equator are more productive in the growing of bananas, and of course northern resources are better designed for wheat growing. Everyone can readily see that in this case specialization and trade will increase the amount of world production of both goods and also each country's ability to consume both goods.

It is not so immediately obvious, but it is no less true, that international trade is mutually profitable even when one of the two countries can produce *every commodity* more cheaply (in terms of all resources) than the other country. One country has an *absolute advantage* in the production of every good; the other country has an absolute disadvantage in the production of every good. But so long as there are differences in the *relative* efficiencies of producing the different goods in the two countries, you can always be sure that even the poor country has a *comparative advantage* in the production of those commodities in which it is relatively most efficient; this same poor country will have a *comparative disadvantage* in those commodities in which it is more than averagely inefficient. Similarly, the rich, efficient country will find that it should specialize in those fields of production where its absolute advantage is comparatively greatest, planning to import those commodities in which the highly inefficient country has the least absolute disadvantage.

Thus, trade between America and Europe in food and clothing is mutually advantageous even if America should be able to produce both these items more efficiently (in terms of all economic resources). Moreover, barter between America and Asia is especially advantageous to us even though the Indian laborer receives only a fraction of the real wages going to productive American labor. We shall see in a moment how this paradox is possible.

A traditional example used to illustrate this paradox of comparative advantage is the case of the best lawyer in town who is also the best typist in town. Will he not specialize in law and leave typing to a secretary? How can he afford to give up precious time from the legal field, where his comparative advantage is very great, to perform typing activities in which he has an absolute advantage but in which his relative advantage is least? Or look at it from the secretary's point of view. She is at a disadvantage relative to him in both activities; but her relative disadvantage is least in typing. Relatively speaking, she has a comparative advantage in typing.

▶ A SIMPLE CASE: EUROPE AND AMERICA

Let us illustrate these fundamental principles of international trade by a simplified example. Consider America and Europe of a century ago, and concentrate on only two commodities, food and clothing. In America land and natural resources were then very plentiful relative to labor and capital; but in Europe, people and capital were plentiful relative to land.

This contrast is best seen if we look at the *intensive* agriculture of a country like Belgium. There, in order to get the greatest possible output, small plots of land have to be cultivated assiduously by many people and much fertilizer. Compare this with the extensive agriculture of early America: here one family cultivated many acres and national product was maximized by each man's "spreading himself thin" over the virtually free land. A Belgian farmer would have thought this wasteful. But in view of the relatively high cost of our labor or capital and the low cost of land, it was not. It was prudent.[1]

Of course, if surplus population could have all migrated from Belgium to the United States, real wages here would have tended to fall toward equality with rising wages there; and high land rents there would have fallen toward equality with rising rents here. Actually, this would have tended at the same time to increase *total world production*. Why? Because the transfer of workers from their poor Belgian farms to rich American farms would increase their productivity. This follows from the fundamental law of diminishing returns.

But let's be selfish and hard-boiled. Let's suppose that immigrants from abroad are to be kept out of the United States in order to keep labor scarce here and wages high. From this same selfish point of view, should the United States also impose a protective tariff designed to keep out imports from abroad? Or should it not? To answer this important social question we must measure carefully the amounts of food and clothing that will be produced and consumed in each country (1) if there is no international trade, and (2) if trade is permitted to follow its own course.

▶ THE LAW OF COMPARATIVE ADVANTAGE

David Ricardo, stockbroker and self-made millionaire, expert on the theory of land rent and of currency, came up in 1817 with the first simple proof that international specialization pays for a nation. This is the famous theory of comparative advantage or, as it is sometimes called, the theory of comparative

---

[1] This disregards the practice of burning out the natural fertility of the soil by overuse, and also the destruction of forests, giving rise to floods and soil erosion. From a social point of view, such exhaustion of natural resources undoubtedly was a great waste. Even now conservation programs in lumber, oil, and farming leave much to be desired.

cost. The remainder of this chapter will describe this very important theory.

For simplicity Ricardo worked with only two countries. We'll call them America and Europe. For simplicity he worked with only two goods. We'll call them food and clothing. For simplicity Ricardo chose to measure all costs in terms of hours of labor. We'll do the same, recognizing that more advanced texts and our Appendix can give some of the needed qualifications when our simple assumptions are relaxed. The germ of truth in the principle of comparative advantage will still remain.

Table 1 shows that an hour of American labor can produce 20 units of food. Or it can produce 6 clothing units. What about Europe? An hour of European labor can produce 10 units of food, or it can produce 8 units of clothing. Now the whole theory of comparative advantage is based upon a careful study of these four labor productivities: on the ratio of 20 to 6; on the ratio of 10 to 8. (Ratios like these we'll write in the usual manner as 20/6 and 10/8.)

Before-trade equilibrium. First suppose there is no trade. What price ratios will rule in America? Evidently clothing will be dearer than food because less clothing can be produced by a labor hour. How much dearer? The ratio of clothing price to food price must be exactly 20/6 in isolated America. (Verify this by setting American wages at \$2 per hour or at any other rate; show that food's production costs will always be six-twentieths of clothing's dollar cost.)

What about Europe before trade? There the ratio of clothing price to food price must be exactly 10/8. (Why not 8/10?) In the absence of trade, each continent happily produces both food and clothing for its own consumption; and the indicated price ratios prevail.

To make or buy? Now open up trade. (Forget all transport costs, tariffs, foreign exchange, and think of pure barter.) America now must ask herself, Should we make our own clothing? Or should we buy it from abroad, trading food for it? (Every businessman who seeks maximum profit is always asking: Shall I make my own power, or is it cheaper to buy it from someone else?) America's problem is this: Shall we use our labor directly in the domestic production of clothing? Or can we better use the same labor in indirectly producing clothing—by first producing food and then exporting that food in exchange for more clothing imports than we could ourselves produce with the labor involved?

Comparative advantage depends on four crucial labor productivities:

	In America	In Europe
Food	20	10
Clothing	6	8

Table 1. American and European labor productivities (in good units per hour). Because 20/6 is greater than 10/8, America will have to export food for clothing. (What does 8/10 > 6/20 mean for Europe?)

Now suppose America is a new and small continent. Even when we open up trade between her and Europe, she can't possibly be a big enough trader[1] to supply all the European market for either good. So Europe even after trade will have to go on producing both goods and will have to go on exchanging the goods at her clothing-to-food cost ratio 10/8. Europeans are exchanging the goods at that price ratio: and hence in a free-trade market Americans can fetch home 8 units of clothing at a cost of 10 units of food exports.

Alternatively, how much food does it cost America if she shifts her labor to produce 8 clothing at home? Does 8 clothing cost her less than 10 food at home—in which case America would certainly refuse to export food for clothing? Or does 8 clothing cost America at home more than 10 food—in which case she'll find it beneficial to get her clothing indirectly by trade? Since each clothing unit costs America 20/6 of food units, and since you can easily calculate that 20/6 (= 10/3) is greater than 10/8, America will find it cheaper to get clothing by trade.[2]

After-trade equilibrium. So after trade America will end up producing no clothing at all. She will specialize, devoting all her resources to the production of food. And she'll export some of her food production in exchange for imports of clothing. Thereby, she'll end up able to consume *more of clothing and more of food!* America's real national income will have gone up. American real wages will be higher as a result of the efficient international division of labor. What about her prices? Now America will end up in an equilibrium clothing-to-food price ratio different from her domestic 20/6 cost ratio. The relative prices charged within American cities will be the international price ratio of 10/8 at which trade takes place.

What about Europe's equilibrium after trade? She's so big that trade hasn't been able to change her price ratio. She still produces both food and clothing. To be sure, she doesn't produce quite as much food as before, instead importing some in exchange for clothing. In our example Europe hasn't gained anything from her partial specialization and trade; but she hasn't lost anything either. Her prices and real wages end up exactly the same as before trade.

▶ ABSOLUTE ADVANTAGE, OR COMPARATIVE ADVANTAGE?

If an engineer looked at this example, he might say: "It stands to reason America will produce food and import clothing. Look at the four productivity numbers. American labor is absolutely more productive than European labor in the production of food (20 is greater than 10). And European labor is more productive than American labor in the production of clothing (8 is

---

[1] Ricardo did not begin with the special assumption that one country is "small." But it turns out that such a case is a little easier for beginners to understand. Later we drop this special assumption and let both countries be about the same in size.

[2] In short, our clothing firms will find it cheaper to get 8 clothing by sending 10 food abroad than to have to sacrifice *more than 20 food* to produce 8 clothing at home!

greater than 6). So just as the tropics trade bananas to the temperate zone in exchange for wheat, so does each country produce that good in which it has an *absolute productive advantage,* swapping for goods in which it has an *absolute* disadvantage."[1]

The engineer is right. But superficial. For if we go back to our arithmetic, we see that the benefit to America has nothing to do with *absolute* advantage: we never had to compare the numbers 20 and 10, or the numbers 6 and 8. We only had to compare the domestic *ratios* 20/6 and 10/8. This is what Ricardo's readers found really surprising and at first could not believe. (Some congressmen still can't grasp this principle!)

Comparative advantage vindicated. To show that only comparative advantage and not absolute advantage is important, let's imagine that Europe's labor productivities go up a hundredfold. Let poor backward America keep the same productivities. A barefoot congressman might then say: "European labor is so productive, it can undersell us in every line. Foreign producers will have lower labor costs than we can hope to compete with. Not only will we lose our export markets, but in addition we'll be inundated with both food and clothing. Let's erect an iron tariff wall to protect the American real wage, the American real national income."

I don't know quite what the engineer would say. Perhaps he'd say: "European labor is absolutely more productive in both goods than America. So I find it hard to envisage a profitable swap."[2]

Well, both the congressman and the engineer are wrong. As Ricardo showed, it still pays for America to calculate whether she should produce clothing at home or trade food for it. Only now she compares Europe's ratio 1,000/800 with her own food-costs-per-unit-of-clothing 20/6, and America still finds it cheaper to get her clothing by barter with Europe. (Note that the absolute productivity levels of Europe—as dramatized by the two new zeros in the hundredfold improvement in her productivities—cancel out of her ratio; 1,000/800 is no different from 10/8; or, for that matter, if we killed off Europe's productivity, no different from 0.10/0.08.)

So no matter how absolute advantage may have changed, as long as *comparative* advantage is unchanged, America will in the long run specialize and trade exactly as she did before. Her equilibrium price ratios, real wages, and real income will have benefited exactly as before from trade. So long as exports are bartered for imports, our American labor can't be undersold in every line by the absolutely more productive foreign labor—nor could it be undersold *in every line* by miserably paid, absolutely unproductive Asian labor.

[1] The engineer could add that real wages in America end up in our example higher than in Europe if you measure them primarily in food; but lower if you measure them in clothing.
[2] If he were more sensible, he might say: "If it can, American labor ought to migrate to Europe, where it can produce and earn more." But we follow Ricardo in ruling out movements of factors between countries or regions; it is free international trade in goods we study.

Without doubt, labor employed in the American clothing industry can be undersold by imports. This was true before Europe got its hundredfold productivity improvement, and it is still true; that clothing can't in the long run compete is a fact of comparative, not of absolute, advantage. This means that clothing employers cannot pay American workers the high money and real wages that food employers can pay them. That's why clothing manufacturers go bankrupt and workers drift to the food industry.

▶ A DIGRESSION ON MONEY WAGES AND MONEY PRICES

Some people can see all this when it is worked out in terms of barter. But they are obsessed by the notion that in actual money terms America will always be undersold by Europe in every line. They fear our exports will disappear, our imports will soar, and our balance of payments will never be able to come into a stable equilibrium. So let's briefly work the same thing out in money, as did the classical economists. Suppose America uses dollars for her money; these could be gold coins weighing $\frac{1}{35}$ ounce of gold. Suppose Europe measures all her prices and wages in terms of pounds rather than dollars. Suppose we stick to $£1 = {}^{2.8}\!/_{35}$ ounce of gold, so that the foreign exchange rate will always give $£1$ equal to $2.80 in price. And suppose we first go back to the four productivities of Table 1.

Before trade, let America have lots of gold. Let our wages then be $2 an hour. (Show that our food and clothing prices then have to be $0.10 and $0.33⅓ respectively. Use Table 1.) Before trade, let Europe's wages be much less than a pound, say $£^2\!/_7$; or, in American terms, let Europe's hourly wage be $0.80. (Verify that her initial labor productivities of 10 and 8 must then give her food and clothing prices equivalent to $0.08 and $0.10 respectively.)

Now open up trade. Initially Europe's food price is less in dollars than America's ($0.08 is less than $0.10). And her clothing price is less than ours ($0.10 is less than $0.33⅓). So *at first* she does undersell us.

Here is what happens at first. We export no merchandise; we import much merchandise; we pay for the difference by exporting gold. And transitionally, we might have a depression. Transitionally too, Europe has a great boom, with overfull employment and an inflationary gap.

But what happens after a while? Much gold flows to Europe. Europe's money supply rises. The income multiplier is hard at work in Europe. Her wages get bid up because of the strong domestic and foreign demand for her goods. And these demands are backed up by plenty of gold. So her wages, and of course her prices, begin to rise in terms of gold (or pounds or, for that matter, dollars).

You should be able to trace out the opposite transitional happenings in America. Gold is leaving the country. Nothing is being produced in America. Men find no work at the old $2-an-hour wage: no work in the food industry; no work in clothing. So what happens to American money wages, if they are not kept sticky by fiat, custom, or unions? American hourly money wages fall. How much must they fall? With American food initially costing $0.10 as against Europe's costing $0.08, America's wages certainly need not fall more than 20 per cent. For when they fall more than that, American food can undersell European.

So once America's wage drops 20 per cent relative to Europe's rising wage, we can find a lasting equilibrium.

To be specific, suppose America's wage drops a little less than 20 per cent of $2, ending up at, say, $1.70 per hour. Suppose Europe's wage rises a little, going from $0.80 an hour to $0.85. Now American food costs $0.08½ (= ⅟₂₀ of $1.70) and Europe food costs exactly the same 0.08½ (= ⅟₁₀ of $0.85). Then we've found an equilibrium at which both share the food market. What about clothing? Europe's cost is $0.10⅝ (= ⅛ of $.85), and this is clearly less than what would be America's cost of $0.28⅓ (= ⅙ of $1.70). So America produces no clothing, the textile industry having gone past its so-called "peril point" and into oblivion.

Then this must be the final equilibrium. America specializes in food, exporting some in exchange for European exports of clothing. Gold no longer flows either way. American and European money wage and price levels have been linked by trade. Each has full employment and lives happily ever afterward enjoying the benefits of trade. Finally note: the congressman was right that free trade might lower American *money* wages; but he forgot that American prices will then fall on the average even more than wages—so that *real* wages were raised by the international competition. And he failed to notice that it was precisely this fall in our money wages and prices that made it impossible for us to be undersold in every line.

To complete this digression which shows the equivalence between the barter and the simple money models, the reader should work out the same transitional analysis that would be necessary if we opened up trade with a Europe whose absolute productivities have now increased a hundredfold relative to America's. (*I.e.,* replace 10 and 8 of Table 1's Europe column with 1,000 and 800.) Undoubtedly, the deflationary strains on our economy would this time have to be very much greater during the transition. And we would rightly hear much talk of "pound shortage," reminiscent of European postwar complaints about "dollar shortage." But note that, regardless of absolute advantage, there still could be found a final ratio of European and American money wage rates at which the barter and money equilibrium of *comparative* advantage could always be permanently maintained.[1]

[1] Thus, with Europe's productivities 1,000 and 800 in food and clothing, America's hourly wage might have to fall to, say, $0.17 (or less), with Europe's wage rising to $8.50 (or more). Once each area's money wages and prices have adjusted to reflect absolute productivities, the comparative productivities or advantages will determine the pattern of profitable specialization and trade. (With effort you can work out all final prices.)

▶ BENEFIT OF TRADE TO ALL

Return now to the simpler barter discussion, knowing that it has been vindicated. The time has come at last to treat Europe a little more generously. By
making America so small, we gave Europe none of the advantage of trade.
Let's work out a happier example for Europe. One possibility at this point
would be to make America very big and Europe very small; but such an example would teach us no new principles.

So let's make both places about the same in size. Specifically, let's suppose America is large enough relative to Europe so that after America decides
to export food to Europe, she is able by specialization in food to capture *all*
the European food market. Mind you, this will make Europe very happy. Why?
Because she will go through the same kind of reasoning as America did:
Europe will learn that it always pays her to get her food by indirect trade
trade whenever she can import food for less cost in clothing (and in labor or
money) than she can produce it at home.

Each area ends up producing the good in which it has a comparative
advantage, exporting that good in exchange for imports of the good in which
it has a comparative disadvantage. And you'll find the final food-to-clothing
price ratio has to end up somewhere in between America's 20/6 cost ratio and
Europe's 10/8 cost ratio.[1] Both countries end up better off, each able to consume more of food and more of clothing.

How is this miracle accomplished? You can't get something for nothing.
Where does the extra consumption come from? The bright engineer will fi-

---

This discussion of monetary effects has been framed in terms of a gold standard. We could
just as easily have assumed a freely fluctuating exchange rate between the pound and dollar,
rather than the fixed $2.80 rate. Then money wages in each country could be held absolutely
constant throughout, with all the adjustments taking place via a depreciation of the dollar
relative to the pound. Thus, if we hold America's hourly wage at exactly $2 and Europe's at
exactly £¼ (or 5 shillings), Table 1 implies that the exchange rate must find its ultimate
equilibrium at £1 = $4, rising to this level so that food can cost exactly $0.10 in both places.
After the hundredfold increase in Europe's productivities, fixed money wages would require the exchange rate to rise to no less than £1 = $400—no doubt with considerable transi-
tional effects! In a dynamic world, where one country's productivities have a tendency *always*
to outstrip the other's, there might be a chronic tendency for the laggard's exchange rate to
depreciate. (Some economists attribute Europe's "dollar shortage" to faster technological improvements in American productivity. See Chapter 34's discussion of "dollar shortage.")

[1] What is the same thing, the price ratio always ends up between 10/3 and 10/8. Just where
in between? At 10/4, 10/5, 10/6, or 10/7? At exactly 10/8, or exactly 10/3? Each would like to
have it end up near the other's cost ratio, thereby gaining for herself the maximum benefit
from cheap imports. Ricardo never worked out just where in the crucial interval the final
price ratio would fall. Apparently he was content to explain the qualitative character of trade
and specialization and not to worry about its quantitative amount. His friend James Mill
had a precocious son, John Stuart Mill, who later showed that the final price ratio is determined by the relative strengths of reciprocal supply and demand in the two areas. If
American and European demand for food is brisk relative to world supply, that will tend to
raise food's price relative to clothing's—as the Appendix shows.

nally see the point. "If each country specializes in that good in which it has a comparative advantage," he'll point out, "then total American and European labor end up producing a *larger world total of both goods.* So the gains from more efficient world production can be shared in the form of more consumption opportunities to both places."

▶ QUALIFICATIONS AND CONCLUSIONS

Of course, comparative advantage holds for any two countries, not just for America and Europe. (Ricardo used England and Portugal in his examples.) And for any two goods. (Ricardo used cloth and wine rather than food and clothing.) The Appendix shows how the principle of comparative advantage can be generalized to handle any number of goods; and more advanced books show how it can handle any number of countries or regions.

Transport costs too can be treated, as can movements of productive factors between regions. Instead of using simple labor cost examples, we could easily measure costs in terms of "doses" of labor, land, and capital goods of fixed proportions. It is possible also to allow for changing factor proportions and diminishing returns. For all this and more, see the Appendix.

Perhaps a more serious defect of comparative advantage is its statical assumptions. The theory assumes away all stickiness of prices and wages, all transitional inflationary and deflationary gaps, all balance-of-payments problems. It pretends that when workers go out of one industry they always go into another more efficient industry—never into chronic unemployment. No wonder that this abstract theory sold at a discount during the Great Depression. Recently its prestige has been coming back. To the extent that we can in the future count on the successful neoclassical synthesis, which mobilizes modern theories of money and fiscal policy to banish chronic slumps and inflations— to that extent will the old classical theory of comparative advantage come back into social relevance.

If theories, like girls, could win beauty contests, comparative advantage would certainly rate high in that it is an elegantly logical structure. Indeed one must admit that it is a highly simplified theory. An oversimplified one, as far as our rushing out to make immediate applications to real life is concerned. Yet for all its oversimplification, the theory of comparative advantage has in it a most important glimpse of truth. Political economy has found few more pregnant principles. A nation that neglects comparative advantage may have to pay a heavy price in terms of living standards and potential rates of growth.

SUMMARY

1. If two countries have different production conditions so that their comparative costs are different, it is clearly to their separate selfish advantages to trade regardless of whether their real wage levels are different. Each country specializes in the commodity in which it is relatively most efficient. The commodity producible at a comparative disadvantage in a country will of course be wanted in some amount by its consumers; but the country in question will find it more efficient to take resources out of *direct* domestic production of that commodity and put them instead into the lines of greatest advantage. Think of such diverted resources as creating the wanted goods *indirectly,* in the sense that exports turned out by the resources can be more advantageously bartered for the wanted goods in question. A country following comparative advantage is simply acting like any prudent business which buys things from outsiders if it cannot produce them as cheaply itself.

2. Profitable trade can take place between countries, where *each* has an absolute advantage in one good. But equally profitable trade can take place between a country and another country that has an *absolute* advantage over it in the production of every good. What counts in determining the pattern of efficient specialization is *ratios* of advantage—i.e., *comparative* not absolute advantage. To be sure, changes in absolute advantage may have important transitional monetary effects on wages, prices, and the balance of payments.

3. In international exchange one country need not gain at the expense of another. The benefits from trade are mutual. All countries can gain. This is possible because the total of world production is increased by international specialization along the lines of comparative cost.

4. Precisely how these total gains will be split up between the participating nations depends upon the reciprocal supply-demand situation. We can state with confidence that the final terms of trade, or price ratio, will fall somewhere between the divergent domestic cost ratios of the two countries. Whether it will fall near to one's original cost ratio and thereby give most of the benefits to the other, cannot be told in advance.

5. Comparative cost or advantage is a highly simplified theory, but a highly important one with numerous applications.

QUESTIONS FOR DISCUSSION

1. "If we can buy a good cheaper abroad than we can produce it at home, it is to our advantage to do so." Is this consistent with comparative advantage?

2. State in a page the meaning of the theory of comparative advantage.

3. Can you apply that theory to trade between people within a country?

4. Replace Table 1's (20/6; 10/8) by (20/20; 10/8). Show that this productivity increase in American clothing production will change America's comparative advantage over into clothing, and that we will begin to import food. Describe the possible final equilibrium and the transitional "dollar shortage."

5. Can a country once have a comparative advantage—say in electric generating equipment—and then lose it? What then *will* happen? Should it?

6. Explain the difference between comparative and absolute advantage. Verify that barter and money lead to the same final equilibrium.

7. Why might a new continent have a comparative advantage in food?

8. What happens if two countries are exactly alike? Explain.

9. Review your understanding of the following concepts:

absolute versus comparative advantage

personal and regional diversity and specialization

money and labor costs

labor productivities

price and cost ratios

gold flows and exchange rates

equilibrium price ratio

enlarged world production

APPENDIX: COMPARATIVE ADVANTAGE AMPLIFIED AND QUALIFIED

Our discussion of comparative advantage has, up until now, followed Ricardo and measured all costs in terms of labor. Modern economists know that the theory is still valid even if you don't want to assume a labor theory of value. The production-possibility or transformation curve that we used in Chapter 2 to discuss guns and butter is the tool that enables us to dispense with labor units: users of the production-possibility curve choose to measure the cost of clothing in terms of the food we must sacrifice to get more clothing. (This is often called "opportunity cost" in more advanced texts.)

The first part of this Appendix works through in detail the America-Europe food-clothing case, showing that absolute labor costs are quite irrelevant to the problem. Then some important extensions of the assumptions are carried through in the remainder of the Appendix.

America Without Trade

In Chapter 2, we saw that every economy has a production-possibility (or transformation) schedule indicating how much of one commodity, food, can be produced if all resources are diverted to it; also how much of the other commodity, clothing, can be produced if all resources are diverted to its pro-

duction; and how either good can be transformed into the other—not physically, but by transferring resources from the production of one to the other.

For simplicity, let's suppose food can always be transformed into units of clothing in America at the *constant ratio* of 10/3. For each 10 units of food sacrificed, we can always get 3 units of clothing. Let's further assume that, when all resources are diverted to food production, America will have altogether 100 (million) units of food.[1]

Then, clearly America can, if she chooses, have 90 units of food and 3 units of clothing, 80 and 6 . . . or finally 0 of food and 30 of clothing. We may put this in the form of a schedule, as shown in Table 2.

This may be plotted in Fig. 1, just as was done in Chapter 2, Fig. 3. The solid line *AK* is the production-possibility curve. This new production-possibility curve is a straight line, whereas the earlier one was rounded, being of convex curvature when looked at from

---

[1] You should realize that labor is never mentioned in the following discussion. But if you wanted to relate this discussion to Ricardo's labor treatment, you'd merely have to assume America has exactly 5 million labor hours in all. (Hint: Use Table 1.) And later you'd assume Europe has 10 million labor hours.

Domestically, America can sacrifice food for clothing:

Table 2. Production-possibility schedule of America (10/3, constant-cost ratio)

	AMERICA	
Possi-bilities	Food, millions	Clothing, millions
A	100	0
B	90	3
C	80	6
D	70	9
E	60	12
F	50	15
G	40	18
H	30	21
I	20	24
J	10	27
K	0	30

Without trade, consumption is tied to domestic production:

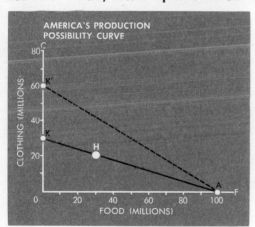

AMERICA'S PRODUCTION POSSIBILITY CURVE

CLOTHING (MILLIONS)

FOOD (MILLIONS)

Fig. 1. The constant-cost line AK shows America's domestic production possibilities. The new line AK' indicates an increased ability to produce clothing, and means that America can move northeast from AK, enjoying more of both goods.

above. The straight-line production-possibility schedule has been introduced in order to keep the argument simple; any tendency toward what is called "increasing (relative marginal) costs" has been deliberately assumed away. The returns of food for clothing sacrificed are instead always to be given by the constant-cost ratio 10/3, instead of having relative costs rise in a more realistic fashion. Constant costs have been assumed only to simplify the argument—to relieve the

student from having to remember many different cost ratios. As will be seen later, this will not seriously affect the validity of the argument. Where a few qualifications are needed, they are later made.

So far we have been talking only about production. However, if the United States is isolated from all trade, what she produces is also what she consumes. Let us suppose, therefore, that the emphasized quantities, H, of Table 2 and Fig. 1 represent the amounts produced and consumed by America in the absence of trade; or in numerical terms America then produces and consumes 30 units of food and 21 units of clothing.

Why was this particular combination decided upon rather than one of the other possibilities? We know from earlier chapters that in a competitive system nobody "decides" upon this, but that the price mechanism, operating through supply and demand for goods and services, determines What shall be produced, How, and For Whom. Well, the starred quantities are the What. Very little need be said here about the How, except for the obvious remark that agricultural food production will require more land relative to labor than will more highly fabricated clothing output. As to the For Whom, we need only remark parenthetically that scarcity of labor in the United States will mean rather high wages for workers, while superabundance of land here will mean low rents (per acre) for landlords.

Let us proceed to introduce Europe into the picture. Before doing so, it will pave the way for the later argument to interject a question. What would happen if some American (perhaps Eli Whitney, inventor of the cotton gin, will do as an example) should make a clever invention so that each 10 units of food could be transformed into 6 rather than 3 units of clothing. Would America be potentially better off? The answer is obviously, Yes. The production-possibility curve has shifted outward and upward and is now shown by the broken line, AK', in Fig. 1. (Show that America could now go from H to a new point H' and have *more of both* food and clothing.)

Europe Without Trade

We can now do for Europe exactly what was done above for America; but with an important difference. Europe's plentiful endowment of labor relative to land would give her a different cost or transformation ratio between food and clothing. She would have less of a comparative advantage in food and more in clothing. For her, each 10 units of food may be transformable into, say, 8 units of clothing. She gets 5 more than was true of the United States because of her comparative advantage in clothing. However, in terms of food, America gets $10/3$ or 3.33 units for each unit of clothing sacrificed; while Europe's comparative disadvantage in food production gives her only $10/8$ or 1.25 units of food for each sacrificed unit of clothing. *The important thing to concentrate upon is the difference in the two cost ratios: 10/3 for America and 10/8 for Europe.*

Let's still keep the two continents isolated from each other. What is Europe's exact production-possibility schedule? Let us suppose that Europe's population is so large and her land area is such that before trade she was producing and consuming 50 units of food and 80 units of clothing. This fact, plus the constant-cost ratio, 10/8, tells us all we have to know in order to draw up Europe's complete production-possibility schedule as in Table 3. Check this against the production-possibility line of Fig. 2.

Domestically, Europe too can produce food or clothing:

EUROPE		
Possi-bilities	Food, millions	Clothing, millions
A	150	0
B	100	40
C	50	80
D	0	120

Table 3. Production-possibility schedule of Europe (10/8 constant-cost ratio)

Europe's production possibilities favor clothing:

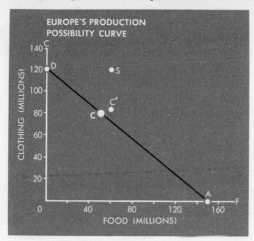

Fig. 2. Before international trade, Europe is on her domestic production-possibility curve at C, consuming just what she produces. (Disregard the points C' and S until later in the chapter.)

The Opening Up of Trade

Now, for the first time, let's admit the possibility of trade between the two continents. Food can be bartered for clothing at some *terms-of-trade*, i.e., at some *price ratio*.[1] To dramatize the process let's suppose there stands in mid-ocean an impersonal auctioneer, whose business it is to balance supply and demand—offers of clothing, and offers of food. He does this by calling out to both countries an exchange rate or price ratio between food and clothing. Until supplies and demands are balanced, he keeps the bidding going. When he finally hits on the equilibrium price level *at which supply and demand balance,* he raps his gavel three times and says, "Going, going, *gone!*" But only then.

Probably, he will suspect in advance that Europe is going to specialize on clothing production, in which she has a comparative advantage, and that she will wish to export part of her clothing production in exchange for food imports. But he has no idea what the final exchange ratio or "terms-of-trade" between food and clothing will be—whether it will be 10/3, 10/8, 10/5, 10/6, or anything else. For that matter, if the auctioneer is very

[1] Terms-of-trade (or an exchange ratio) of say 10 food for 6 clothing means that clothing is more expensive than food, with the price ratio (clothing price) / (food price) $= 1\frac{2}{3} = 1\frac{6}{10}$.

new at the game, or very stupid, he may think that the final equilibrium exchange level or terms-of-trade will be 10/1 or 10/12.

Actually, neither of these last two can be the final exchange ratio. He would soon learn this from bitter experience. For let him tell America and Europe that they can get all the clothing they want in exchange for food at the rate of only 1 unit of clothing for every 10 units of food. What will America do? By producing at home, she can get 3 units of clothing for each 10 of food. Clearly she will not be sucked into trading food for clothing on those terms; she would rather remain self-sufficient.

That is only half the story. Why shouldn't America go to the other extreme and export clothing in exchange for food imports? Each 1 unit of clothing gets her 10 units of food from the auctioneer. What will 1 unit of clothing get here at home in domestic food production? Obviously, from Table 2 and Fig. 1, only $1\frac{0}{3}$ or 3.33 units of food. At 10/1, therefore, America should certainly shift all her resources to clothing production; she should export some of her surplus clothing in return for food imports.

Now, what about Europe? At home she gets only $1\frac{0}{8}$ or 1.25 units of food for each unit of clothing. At 10/1, she too will want to trade clothing for food. We see, therefore, what a green hand the auctioneer was. By calling out 10/1, he brings a flood supply of clothing on his head and only demands for food. Since he has no supplies of either good up his sleeve, he must now change his tactics. He must raise the price of food relative to the price of clothing. He had better try the ratio 10/2, or perhaps even 10/9. You are now in a position to reason out why neither of them will do: why 10/2 will still bring out a tidal wave of clothing; and, on the other hand, why 10/9 represents the opposite error, in which there is a tornado of food.

Clearly, *the final exchange ratio cannot be outside the original two-country limits of 10/3 and 10/8!* Anywhere in between is a possibility—with America following her comparative advantage and specializing in food, and Europe following her comparative advantage and specializing in clothing.

Recapitulation

We are now at a breathing space. Let's review exactly what we've proved:

1. If nature endows two regions or countries unequally with factors of production, the *relative* costs of transforming one commodity into another domestically will probably be different for the two areas. (*E.g.*, a land-rich area will have a comparative advantage in food and other land-intensive goods. A labor-rich area's comparative advantage will be in labor-intensive goods.)

2. Under free trade, goods will exchange for each other at a price ratio somewhere *intermediate* between the domestic cost ratios of the two countries.

3. Each country will specialize in the commodity in which it has a comparative advantage, exporting its surplus of that product for imports from abroad.

4. Each country is made better off by trade and specialization: if America can get, say, 6 units of clothing for each 10 units of food traded, she is certainly better off than when she domestically transforms 10 units of food into only 3 units of clothing; Europe does better when she trades 6 units of clothing for 10 units of food than when she domestically transforms 8 of clothing into 10 of food. The

same would be true if we had picked any other trading ratio than 10/6—so long as it is between the limits 10/3 and 10/8.

5. Trade is *indirect* production. Trade is efficient production. Efficient production is always better than inefficient production. (Note that the advantage of trade has nothing to do with *relative wage rates*. Under free trade, each country's wage tends to be pulled up to the higher levels of productivity of its export industry and not down to the low-efficiency level of its import industry.)

Exact Determination of the Final Price Ratio

Just where in between the domestic cost ratios will the terms-of-trade settle down? Some of Ricardo's immediate followers were foolish enough to say, "We split the difference between the two countries' cost ratios, or in this case pick 10/5½ as the equilibrium ratio."[1]

Actually, as John Stuart Mill, the third great classical economist (after Smith and Ricardo) showed a little later, *the exact final level of the terms-of-trade in between the two cost ratios will depend upon the strength of world supply and demand for each of the two commodities.* If people have an intense desire for food relative to available supplies of food and clothing, the price ratio will settle near the upper limit of 10/8; if clothing is much demanded by both countries, the final price ratio will settle nearer to 10/3.[2]

Mill did what our auctioneer would have to do. He drew up a schedule showing supply and demand at *each possible price ra-*

---

[1] Or would they have said halfway between $10/3$ and $10/8$, giving us $110/48$—which corresponds to $10/4\frac{4}{11}$? Both answers are equally foolish.

[2] Also, if America were very small relative to Europe, so that its supplies made hardly a "dent" on the market, then the price ratio might even stay at 10/8. America would then be specializing in food and importing clothing, but all America's food exports would amount to so little that Europe would still have to produce some food for herself. This is possible only at a price of 10/8. America would in this case get all the gains from international trade. It pays to have a large (different!) neighbor.

America specializes in food, imports clothing:

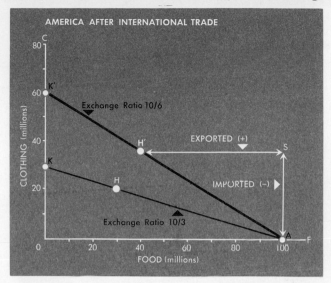

Fig. 3. The line *AK* represents America's domestic production-possibility curve; the line *AK′*, her new consumption-possibility curve when she is able to trade freely at the price ratio 10/6 and in consequence has decided to specialize completely in the production of food (at *A*). The white arrows from *S* to *H′* and *A* to *S* show the amounts exported (+) and imported (−) by America. As a result of free trade, she finally ends up at *H′* with more of both goods than before at *H*.

tio:[1] how much food America would wish to export and how much food Europe would want to import; and at the same time, how much clothing Europe would be willing to export at each price ratio in comparison with the amount of clothing America expected to import. At one, and (usually) only one, intermediate price ratio, exports and imports will balance. At this equilibrium price, exports and imports will "mesh" (or match), quantitatively as well as qualitatively; the auctioneer and Mill will heave a sigh of relief, and trade will continue indefinitely until tastes or technology have changed.

For our numerical problem it has been assumed that the equilibrium terms-of-trade ratio is 10/6, a little nearer to Europe's pretrade ratio than to America's.

America concentrates her production com-

---

[1] This schedule would differ from the ordinary supply and demand schedules for wheat, tea, or automobiles observed in Chapter 19 only in the fact that the price of, say, clothing is not expressed in money terms, but in barter terms, *i.e.*, in terms of food. Similarly, it is not money that is offered for clothing but food. We can either say that America supplies food and Europe demands food, or we can just as well say that America demands clothing and Europe supplies clothing.

pletely on food. In Fig. 3, America is production-wise at *A*. But since she can now trade freely at 10/6, America is no longer limited to her old production-possibility curve. By trading, she can now move on the solid line *AK′ just exactly as if a fruitful invention had been made.* Is America made potentially better off by trade? Indeed she is. Just where she will stop on this solid line, which we may call her new *consumption-possibility* curve, depends upon the workings of her internal price system. It has been assumed that this causes her to stop at the point *H′*, where 40 units of food and 36 units of clothing are consumed. The white arrows show America's exports (+) and imports (−).

All this is summarized in America's rows of Table 4. This important table should be studied very carefully. To understand it thoroughly is to understand the doctrine of comparative costs.

As a result of specialization and trade, America has become better off; she has more food and more clothing to consume. The same is true of Europe. What is the black magic by which something seems to have been got for nothing? The rows marked World, which represent the sum of the

International trade makes larger world production possible:

Table 4. Summary showing specialization and gains from trade according to comparative advantage

Area compared	Exchange ratio of food for clothing P_c/P_f	Food production	Food consumption	Food exports (+) or imports (−)	Clothing production	Clothing consumption	Clothing exports (+) or imports (−)
Situation before trade							
America	10/3	30	30	0	21	21	0
Europe	10/8	50	50	0	80	80	0
World	none	80	80	0	101	101	0
Situation after trade							
America	10/6	100	40	+60	0	36	−36
Europe	10/6	0	60	−60	120	84	+36
World	10/6	100	100	0	120	120	0
Gains from trade							
America	—	—	+10	—	—	+15	—
Europe	—	—	+10	—	—	+ 4	—
World	—	+20	+20	—	+19	+19	—

American and European rows, give the answer. *World production of both goods has been stepped up by specialization and trade.*

Actually, the sixth row gives the data the auctioneer would be most interested in. He is assured that equilibrium has been reached by two facts shown there: (1) World consumption of each product is identically equal to world production—no more, no less; and (2) the amounts that each country exports are just balanced by the amounts that the other country wishes to import. Thus the price ratio 10/6 is the right one.[1]

This completes our explanation of com-

[1] The auctioneer could have made up a whole book full of such tables, each page corresponding to a different price ratio. But only one page is the right one, because at all other prices the algebraic total of exports and imports would not cancel out. Thus, at 10/7, America's desire for clothing imports would surpass Europe's willingness to export clothing. The world as a

parative advantage. You might test your full understanding by filling in on Fig. 2 for Europe everything that has already been filled in for America on Fig. 3. Why does Europe's new consumption-possibility line, made possible by trade, pivot around the point D on the vertical axis? Draw in the arrows to S representing the amounts exported (+) and imported (−) as was done in Fig. 3. Note that Europe's arrows match America's but are opposite in sign. Why is this quantitative meshing of exports and imports necessary at equilibrium? The eager reader could add to the example all labor measurements. Finally note: comparative advantage, not absolute labor advantage, is the all-important thing.

whole would be trying to consume more clothing than had been produced. Since the auctioneer has no inventories to draw upon, he would have to turn the pages toward a higher price for clothing and a lower price for food. On the right page the price ratio would be an equilibrium one, and exports would balance imports.

Many Commodities

Very briefly we must now show what happens when we remove some of the oversimplifications made in the above discussion. The conclusions are not essentially changed, and even the changes in details are usually not too difficult.

First note that up until now we have simplified the discussion by considering only two commodities: food and clothing. Obviously, food stands for many different items (beef, milk, etc.), and the same is true of clothing. Moreover, the advantages of exchange are equally great when we consider the thousand and one commodities that can and do enter into all phases of international trade.

As is shown in advanced textbooks,[1] when there are many commodities producible in two countries at constant costs, they can be arranged in order according to their relative advantage or comparative cost. For example, the commodities automobiles, flax, perfumes, watches, wheat, and woolens might be arranged in the following comparative-advantage sequence:

From the beginning we can be almost sure of one thing. The introduction of trade will cause America to produce wheat and Europe perfume. But where will the dividing line fall? Between automobiles and flax? Or will America produce flax and Europe confine herself to watches, woolens, and perfumes? Or will the dividing line fall on one of the commodities rather than between them, so that, say, flax might be produced in both places at the same time?

You will not be surprised to find that the answer depends upon the comparative strength of international demand for the different goods. If we think of the commodities as beads arranged on a string according to their comparative advantage, the total demand and supply situation will determine where the dividing line between American and European production will fall. Then, an increased demand for automobiles and wheat, for example, may tend to turn the terms-of-trade in direction of America and make us so prosperous that it will no longer pay us to continue to produce our own flax. Also, there is the possibility that a new scientific

AMERICA ←——┼————┼————┼————┼————o————┼——→ EUROPE
     Wheat   Automobiles   Flax   Watches   Woolens   Perfumes

This means that wheat costs are lowest relative to all other commodities in America; Europe has its greatest comparative advantage in perfumes; its advantage in watches is not quite so great, etc.

discovery permitting America to grow flax on the desert might rearrange the order[2] of the comparative advantages of the different commodities and alter the pattern of specialization and trade.

---

[1] For example, G. HABERLER, *Theory of International Trade* (Macmillan, New York, 1937).

[2] This ordered array of goods might have arisen from the following numerical data, which are presented only for the curiosity of the more advanced reader and which have nothing to do with the above discussion. As before, it is not necessary to measure costs in terms of money or labor but only in terms of the relative commodities into which any good can be "transformed." Suppose that we choose to measure the costs of every good in both countries in terms of woolens, which is

Goods (1)	American cost ratio, in terms of woolens (2)	European cost ratio, in terms of woolens (3)	Comparative European costs, in terms of American costs (3) ÷ (2)
Automobiles	1,000	3,000	3.0
Flax	0.8	1.6	2.0
Perfumes	5.0	3.0	0.6
Watches	50	75	1.5
Wheat	0.2	0.8	4.0
Woolens	1.0	1.0	1.0

selected arbitrarily because it comes last alphabetically. Then our data might be arranged alphabetically as in the accompanying table. This means that in America one must give up the production of 1,000 units of woolens to get 1 automobile, while in Europe the cost of 1 automobile is the sacrifice of 3,000 units of wool production;

Many Countries

So much for the complications introduced by many commodities. What about many countries? Europe and America are not the whole world. And even they include many separate so-called sovereign nations.

Introducing many countries need not change our analysis. As far as any one country is concerned, all the other nations with whom she trades can be lumped together into one group as "the rest of the world." The advantages of trade have nothing specially to do with state boundaries. The principles already developed apply between groups of countries and, indeed, between regions within the same country. In fact, but for historical accident, they would be more applicable to trade between our Northern and Southern states than to trade between the United States and Canada.

From the standpoint of pure economic welfare, the slogan "Buy American" is as foolish as would be "Buy Wisconsin," or "Buy Oshkosh, Wisconsin," or "Buy South Oshkosh, Wisconsin." Part of our great prosperity has come from the fortunate fact that there have been no restrictive customs duties within our vast 48 states, and we have formed a great free-trade area.

There is, however, one new aspect introduced by the existence of many countries. America may find it very profitable to trade indirectly with Europe. America sells Europe much, including finished commodities like machinery. It buys little from Europe. But it does buy rubber and raw materials from the East Indies. They in turn do not usually buy goods from America. However, they do buy clothing and other goods from Europe. Thus, we have a very advantageous triangular trade, as shown in the accompanying diagram.

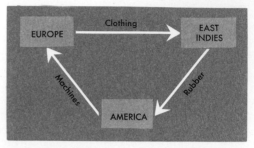

The arrows indicate the predominant direction of exports.

What would happen if all countries tried to sign bilateral trade agreements with each other, so that America could not and would not buy from the Indies unless they bought an equal amount from us? And so forth with every two nations? Clearly, trade would be cut down severely. Imports would balance exports, but at the level of whichever is the lower. Each trading land would end up worse off.

Increasing Costs

Returning again to two countries and two commodities, we must now drop the assump-

---

Therefore, the comparative cost of automobiles in Europe is three times that in America, and so forth for the other goods.

Obviously, Europe's relative cost advantage is greatest in perfumes and least in wheat; in between, the commodities are arranged as shown above in the text. The fact that the figures in the last column are predominantly greater than 1 in no way reflects on the efficiency of Europe, but results from the accidental fact that we chose woolens as our common denominator in which to express costs. Had we selected wheat or watches, the opposite would have been the case and yet none of our results would be any different—except for a "scale factor" (such as converts inches to feet or yards).

Technical note: Anyone who feels he must bring in labor productivities can write the respective products of America's hour of labor as $A, B, C, \ldots$, and of Europe's hour of labor as $a, b, c, \ldots$. The whole analysis can then be worked out in terms of comparative ratios of the form $A/B, C/B, \ldots$, and $a/b, c/b, \ldots$; to explain trade patterns it is never necessary to compare absolute advantages between countries $A/a, B/b, \ldots$, etc. Of course, if he wants to compare money and real wages, these absolute advantages are necessary: it can be shown that the ratio of European to American money or real wage must fall between the least and greatest of $A/a, B/b, \ldots$—just *where* between depends on the working out of reciprocal demands.

tion that costs are constant. The production-possibility curves of Figs. 1, 2, and 3 should better have been convexly bent, as they were in Chapter 2. It is no longer possible to specify a single cost figure for each country.

America is better endowed on the whole for food production than Europe; still, after a great amount of American food is produced, the cost of *extra* food will begin to exceed that of Europe. Even after American competition has drastically lowered the price of food relative to clothing, a little of the best land in Europe will be able to hold its own in food production. In the same way, that first little bit of American clothing production which can be produced at low costs will continue even after international trade has reached an equilibrium level. However, any attempt to expand American clothing production further would entail higher extra costs and competitive losses.

We may summarize the modifications in international trade made necessary by increasing costs as follows:

---

[1] For the geometrically minded, Fig. 4 may be helpful, although most of us will probably do better to skip over it. It shows America's condition before and after trade when increasing costs prevail. The production-possibility curve is now convex. Before international trade, America is consuming and producing at the point H. The domestic price ratio is 10/3, just equal to the ratio of extra costs of getting (at H) a little more clothing for a little sacrificed food. This is shown by the slope of the AK curve at H.

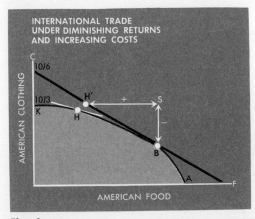

INTERNATIONAL TRADE UNDER DIMINISHING RETURNS AND INCREASING COSTS

Fig. 4.

▶ As a result of international trade, each country will tend to specialize, as before, in the commodity in which it has the greatest comparative advantage; and it will export some of that commodity in exchange for the other country's surplus exports. But because of increasing costs, specialization need not be complete: something of both commodities may still be produced in either country, because even the less favored commodity may have low enough costs to compete when its production is small.[1]

International Goods Movements as a Substitute for Labor and Factor Movements

Having acknowledged the law of increasing costs described in Chapter 2, we must also examine the implications of the related law of diminishing returns within the two countries.

After international trade takes place, re-

After trade, when the common price ratio is 10/6, American production shifts to B, toward less clothing but not away from clothing altogether. The new production point, B, will be reached as a result of competition, because the slope of the curve there—*i.e.*, the ratio of costs of extra clothing for extra food—is 10/6, or just equal to the common international price ratio. At B, and only there, will the value of America's national product (evaluated at the 10/6 price ratio) be at a maximum.

The straight line represents the new consumption-possibility curve to which America can get as a result of trade. It is straight and not bent because the auctioneer offers to trade freely, giving America at the 10/6 ratio as much or little clothing for food as she wishes. The final levels of consumption, determined by supply and demand, are given by the point H'. As before, the arrows indicate exports and imports.

There are still gains from trade. But because of diminishing returns and increasing costs, there is not so much specialization as before and not quite such large gains. Note that at the equilibrium point, where no further trade is possible, relative (extra or "marginal") production costs in the two countries are equal, each to the common price ratio 10/6.

sources in Europe flow from food to clothing production. Because clothing requires relatively much labor and little land, the pressure of population on the limited land of Europe is relieved. Land is no longer so relatively dear; rents fall compared to wages. In America the reverse happens after trade: concentration upon food production in which labor is economized and land heavily utilized tends to raise rents relative to wages.

In each case the free international movement of goods has effects which are partly like those following from the free international movement of factors of production. Just as the movement of labor from Europe to America would relieve the scarcity of labor in America and of land in Europe, so the movement of clothing from Europe to America and of food from America to Europe tends to make the superabundant factor in each country less abundant, and the scarce factor less rare.

The person who has most clearly emphasized how commodity trade partially relieves the scarcity in all countries of the less abundant factors of production is the Swedish economist and public financier Ohlin (pronounced O'Lean).[1] He has made the following important addition to the classical doctrine of comparative cost:

Free movements of labor and capital between countries will tend to equalize wages and factor prices. *However, even without any movements of productive factors across national boundaries, there will often result a partial (but not necessarily complete) equalization of factor prices from the free movement of goods in international trade.*

It is clear, therefore, that, although international trade increases national product in England, it may at the same time so reduce the share of particular groups that they are made worse off. Thus, the large British landowners who a century ago constituted the backbone of the Conservative or Tory party may have been selfish in opposing the famous repeal of the English corn law tariffs

in 1846, but they were not necessarily unintelligent in making their unsuccessful last-ditch fight to retain protective tariffs on imported grains.

Decreasing Costs and International Trade

If economies of mass production are overwhelmingly important, costs may decrease as output expands. This would strengthen the case for international exchange of goods. In fact, decreasing costs are a second great factor—in addition to differences in comparative costs—explaining why specialization and trade are profitable. For, as was discussed in Chapter 3, large-scale specialization is most fruitful when there is a widely expanded market. In fact, even if there were no differences in comparative cost between two countries, it would pay for them to toss a coin to decide who was to produce each of two goods subject to increasing returns or decreasing costs. Complete specialization would increase world production of both goods. This may be illustrated by our example in Chapter 3 of the two identical Indian twins who, despite their similarity, still find it advantageous to specialize to reap the efficiencies of mass production.

Moreover, there is one very practical aspect of international trade under decreasing cost. Peculiarly under such conditions is competition likely to break down and be succeeded by monopoly or imperfect competition. By excluding foreign competition, protective tariffs only serve to consolidate the position of the monopolist. This is recognized in the old slogan: "The tariff is the mother of trusts." Freer international trade is often an effective, and an efficient, way of breaking up such monopoly positions.[2]

Differences in Tastes or Demand as a Reason for trade

Two reasons have been given thus far for international trade: (1) differences in com-

---

[1] BERTIL OHLIN, *Interregional and International Trade* (Harvard University Press, Cambridge, Mass., 1933).

[2] Still, one must admit that decreasing cost situations might under free trade lead to bigger monopolies; and that decreasing cost situations may have in them some of the valid elements of the "infant-industry" argument.

parative costs between regions and (2) decreasing costs.

For completeness, a third obvious possible cause for trade may be mentioned. Even if costs were identical in the two countries and increasing, trade might take place as the result of differences in *taste*.

Thus, it might pay both Norway and Sweden to produce fish and meat in about the same amounts. But if the Swedes have a relatively great fondness for meat and the Norse for fish, then a mutually profitable export of meat from Norway and fish from Sweden would take place.

Both parties gain from this trade. The sum total of human happiness is increased, just as it is when Jack Spratt trades fat meat for his wife's lean. Both get some "consumer's surplus" from the swap.[1]

---

[1] Even two individuals with identical amounts of two goods and the same tastes may in rare instances trade. Two sailors, each with a fifth of

Transportation Costs

Up to this point, we have neglected the whole problem of transportation costs. The economic costs of moving bulky and perishable goods lessen the extent of profitable regional specialization.

The effects are like those produced by the passage of artificially restrictive tariff legislation. As is discussed in the next chapter, many of these effects are harmful to national economic welfare. In the case of transportation costs, the evil is unavoidable, whereas protective tariffs or artificial barriers to interregional trade within a nation are squarely the responsibility of man.

---

rye and a fifth of gin, might toss a coin to decide which is to have 2 fifths of gin and which 2 fifths of rye. You should reason out why the same might be true of herring and chocolate, but not of corned beef and cabbage. This fourth cause of trade is primarily only a curio.

33 THE ECONOMICS OF TARIFF PROTECTION AND FREE TRADE

> *To the Chamber of Deputies: We are subjected to the intolerable competition of a foreign rival, who enjoys such superior facilities for the production of light that he can* inundate *our* national market *at reduced price. This rival is no other than the sun. Our petition is to pass a law shutting up all windows, openings and fissures through which the light of the sun is used to penetrate our dwellings, to the prejudice of the profitable manufacture we have been enabled to bestow on the country. Signed: Candle Stick Makers.*
>
> F. BASTIAT

It would be absurd to try to decide whether God exists or not by counting on one hand all the arguments in the affirmative, and on the other hand all the arguments in the negative—and then to award the decision to the side with the greater number of points. It would be no less absurd to evaluate the case for tariff protection by a simple count of unequally important pros and cons.

Indeed, there is essentially only one argument for free or freer trade, but it is an exceedingly powerful one: namely, *unhampered trade promotes a mutually profitable international division of labor, greatly enhances the potential real national product of all countries, and makes possible higher standards of living all over the globe.* This was elaborated upon in the previous chapter.

How do tariffs or trade impediments affect all this? Putting on a tariff duty discourages imports and raises prices to the domestic consumer. By killing off the fruitful international division of labor, it "protects" the relatively inefficient domestic producer.[1]

---

[1] See the brief Appendix to this chapter for a graphical demonstration of how a tariff affects prices and quantities.

672

The arguments for high protection against the competition of foreign imports take many different forms. They may be divided into three categories: (1) Those that are definitely economically false, some so obviously and palpably as hardly to merit serious discussion, but some whose falsity can be detected only by subtle economic reasoning. (2) A few arguments for protection that are without validity in a perfectly competitive "classical" static full-employment world but that contain some kernels of truth in a world of sizable nations subject to underemployment and undergoing economic development. (3) Finally, certain noneconomic arguments that may make it desirable national policy to sacrifice economic welfare in order to subsidize certain activities admittedly not economically efficient.

▶ NONECONOMIC GOALS

Let's begin with the last, for they are most simply disposed of. If you ever are on a debating team and are given the assignment to defend free trade, you will strengthen your case at the beginning by conceding that economic welfare is not the only goal of life. Political considerations are also important. Thus, it may be necessary to become partially self-sufficient in certain lines of activity at great cost because of fear of future wars.

An example is the production of snythetic rubber. If synthetic rubber capacity is considered necessary for national defense and if the needed amount of capacity is not able to survive under free trade, the economist cannot assert that national policy should be against protection to this industry. But he can suggest that a *subsidy* to domestic production might be preferable to a tariff: This would bring the domestic price down to the international price instead of raising the price to the consumer up to the domestic cost; also the subsidy would show clearly what the total costs of national defense are and would better enable the public to decide whether the game is worth the candle.

The question of a national policy to foster the American mercantile marine is a similar one. Doubtless the United States does *not* possess a comparative advantage in building or operating a merchant fleet. As soon as American seamen, through trade-unions or on their own, insist upon living conditions and wages remotely resembling those in Detroit factories, then we cannot compete with English, Dutch, Japanese, and Norwegian ships. If we give no weight to America's "glorious seafaring tradition"—a long way back!—and consider purely economic welfare, the correct policy is obvious. If America has a comparative advantage in factory production, let men go to Detroit factories where their real productivity is high. American international trade will not suffer by being carried in other countries' bottoms.

However, if national defense makes a large merchant marine necessary, that is another matter. Mail subsidies and subsidies for building ships with the extra speed to escape submarines may then be justified.

The problem of deciding how much to spend in peacetime on national defense is always a perplexing question, especially since armament races are both *cause* and effect of international disunity. The economist can claim no special competence to advise on this problem. He can point out that selfish economic interests often wrap themselves in the flag and try to justify uneconomic projects in terms of national defense. He can ask suspiciously: Was the recent increase in tariffs on Swiss watches really justified by our defense needs for precision workers? Or was this a case of political pressure? With even less confidence, the economist can point out that mutually profitable international trade may help to promote international understanding and unity and that political interferences with trade have in the past provided some of the frictions that made war inevitable.

In conclusion, it is well to point out other noneconomic goals that may deserve consideration. Society may feel that there is some special sanctity about farm life, or something worth preserving in the way of life of the "stout agricultural yeoman or happy peasant." (It is to be doubted that all people who rhapsodize in this fashion have ever lived on a farm.) Or some groups may agree with the Soviet Union and the church that rural living is worth fostering because the country has a higher birth rate than the cities. Or the day may arise when decentralization of population will be necessary because of the threat to our concentrated eastern seaboard cities of self-guided hydrogen bombs. In all such cases subsidies rather than tariffs seem called for. A tariff is simply one rather indirect clumsy form of subsidy that draws attention away from the evil in need of a remedy.

Don't be left with the impression that the political noneconomic arguments are all in favor of tariffs. They're not. Every congressman and editor knows that America has a tremendous diplomatic interest these days in winning friends and allies. And nothing is so disruptive to our popularity abroad as our reputation for being a high-tariff country. We don't deserve that reputation as much as we used to. So it's all the more to our political interest to resist many of the pressures that make for restrictions to international trade.

▶ GROSSLY FALLACIOUS ARGUMENTS FOR TARIFF

Keeping money in the country. To Abraham Lincoln is sometimes attributed the remark, "I don't know much about the tariff. But I do know that when I buy a coat from England, I have the coat and England has the money. But when I buy a coat in this country, I have the coat and America has the money."

There is no evidence that he actually ever said this. But it does represent an age-old fallacy typical of the so-called "mercantilistic" writers of the seventeenth and eighteenth centuries who preceded Adam Smith. They considered a country lucky which gave away more goods than it received, because such a "favorable" (!) balance of trade meant that gold would flow into the country in question to pay for its surplus of exports over imports.

In this day and age it should be unnecessary to labor the point that, while an increased amount of money in the hands of one person will make *him* better off, doubling the money in the hands of everybody in a full-employment economy will only serve to raise prices. Unless the single individual is a demented miser like King Midas, the money makes him better off, not for its own sake but for what it will buy or bid away from other individuals. However, for society as a whole, once full employment is reached, new money cannot hope to buy any new goods.[1]

A tariff for higher money wages. Today it is agreed that extreme protection can raise prices and attract gold into one country, if all other countries do not retaliate with tariffs. The tariff may even increase *money* wages. But it will tend to increase the cost of living by more than the increase in money wages, so that *real* wages will fall as labor becomes less productive.

One could go on endlessly giving examples of protectionist fallacies that every thoughtful person can explode in a minute by subjecting them to analysis. This does not mean that such crude fallacies can be dismissed as unimportant. Actually, they are most important of all in shaping legislation, the other fancier arguments simply being used as window dressing.

Tariffs for special-interest groups. The single most important motivation for protective tariff is obvious to anyone who has watched the "logrolling" in Congress when such legislation is on the floor. It is the well-known "give-me." Powerful pressure groups and vested interests know very well that a tariff on their products will help *them,* whatever its effect on total production and consumption. Outright bribery was used in the old days to get the necessary votes; today powerful lobbies are maintained in Washington to drum up enthusiasm for the good old crockery, watch, or buttonhook industry.

Economically the case for freer trade may be strong. But politically the case for protection tends to exert undue pressure. Why? Because freer trade helps everybody a little, while protection helps a few people a lot. Does it matter politically that the bad of protection outweighs the good? Not if those few who benefit from protection (or who are kept by protection from suffering harm) are politically active day and night in pressing for their cause. It is much harder to organize the masses of consumers and producers to agitate for the even larger gains that they get from an efficient pattern of national spe-

---

[1] Of course, the gold might be spent abroad. But this perfectly sensible way of improving welfare by importing was precisely what the mercantilist "bullionists" were arguing against.

cialization and trade.[1] If political votes were in exact proportion to *total* economic benefit, every country would selfishly legislate most of its tariffs out of existence.

▶ SOME LESS OBVIOUS FALLACIES

A tariff for revenue. First, there is the claim that the tariff should be used to raise government tax revenue. Actually, a customs duty on imports is only one form of regressive sales tax, and a peculiarly obnoxious one. A customs duty or tariff is especially bad because it distorts economic resources away from their best uses. If the people who advance the revenue argument were really sincere, they would advocate a sales tax which would also fall on domestic production. But this would provide no protection at all.

To clinch the point, only remember that a really prohibitively high tariff, which perfectly "protected" us from imports, would collect no revenue at all! Back in 1890, the so-called "billion-dollar Congress" found itself with a surplus of tax revenue over expenditure. Since there was no debt to retire, Congress found the situation embarrassing. It finally solved the problem of excessive tariff revenues not by lowering tariff rates but by *raising them so high* as to reduce the total of revenue collected.

Tariffs and the home market. A second argument, which by itself is on the whole false but whose fallacy is rather difficult to spot, goes as follows: "Farmers should support a tariff for industry because that will gain them a large home market for their products." Henry Clay, the perennial candidate who turned out to be neither "right" nor "President," often advanced this argument a century or more ago.

Its falsity can be seen from different points of view. First, by cutting down industrial imports we are really at the same time indirectly tending to cut down our farm exports. Thus the farmer is hurt directly. "But," Clay might remonstrate, "what about the extra home market for farm produce?"

Well, what about it? Our detailed example of comparative cost showed that isolation from foreign trade decreases the total of national product or real income. The total domestic demand for farm products will certainly be less at a low level of real income than at a high level. So unless it can be buttressed by one of the quite different arguments for protection coming later, the slogan about "creating a home market" is seen once again to be fallacious.

Competition from cheap foreign labor. A third argument for protection has been the most popular of all in American history because it appealed to

[1] There is perhaps one exception to this perverse political fact. Recently the powerful export industries have come to realize that *their* interest is served by freer trade. (Remember, more imports mean more exports!) So they have begun to agitate within the traditionally protectionist NAM and Republican party against protectionism.

the large number of labor votes. According to its usual version, "If we let in goods produced by cheap pauper foreign labor—by Chinese coolies who live on a few cents' worth of rice per day or by low-paid Japanese textile workers —then the higher standard of living of American workers cannot be maintained." So stated, the argument cannot stand up under analysis.

We have seen that trade is mutually profitable even if one country can produce every good more cheaply in terms of resources than the other. The important thing is comparative advantage, not absolute advantage. In the last analysis, trade boils down to two-sided barter. One country cannot indefinitely undersell the other in every line of merchandise.

Earlier we have shown that full employment at home need not depend in the long run on foreign trade. If, then, everyone in this country remains fully employed at his most suitable occupation, is it not to *our selfish advantage* for the workers of other countries to be willing to work for very little? Or to put the matter another way: the comparative-cost doctrine shows that we benefit most by trading with countries like China or the tropics which are *very different* from ourselves, rather than with countries like England or Germany which are like our own industrial economy![1] As a further criticism of the pauper-labor argument, there is the remarkable fact that the analysis of comparative advantage, summarized in the last chapter, shows that absolute wage levels had nothing to do with the long-run increase in national income that resulted from trade.

So much from a theoretical point of view. If we turn to the real world, we find the arguments to be even more incorrect. In Europe and in Asia the workers beg for tariffs saying, "Protect us from the 'unfair competition' of high-paid, efficient American workers who have skill and machinery far better than our own." The rest of the world lives in mortal fear of competition from American mass-production industries. The English protectionist claims that the American worker in Bridgeport, Connecticut, who is paid $3 per hour is more than three times as efficient as the English worker who gets paid 95 cents an hour. This is perhaps an overstatement but it is near to the important truth: high American real wages come from high efficiency and do not handicap us in competing with foreign workers.

Thus far we have had nothing but adverse criticism for the "cheap pauper foreign labor" tariff argument. To be perfectly honest, and without honesty there can be no science, we must admit that it may have an iota of possible truth. The Ohlin proposition of the last Appendix suggested that free trade

[1] This argument must be qualified and amplified. Backward countries, so poor that they have little real purchasing power with which to import, at best can export little to us. Most trade today is between industrialized countries. As a backward country advances industrially, it buys more from industrial countries, and not less; but perhaps not proportionally more, and perhaps there is *less surplus per dollar of trade* accruing to both parties.

in goods may serve as a partial substitute for immigration of labor into the United States. This implies that labor scarcity in the United States could be alleviated by our international specialization on labor-economizing products and that real wages might actually fall under free trade. Real national product would go up, but the relative and absolute share of labor might go down.[1]

Although admitting this as a slight theoretical possibility, most economists are still inclined to think that its grain of truth is outweighed by other more realistic considerations. Of course, particular laborers such as Waltham watchmakers might be hurt by removing a tariff. Nobody denies that. But since labor is such an important and flexible factor of production with many alternative uses, it seems likely that other laborers would gain more than they lose and that labor as a whole would share in the increased national product resulting from trade.

A tariff for retaliation. Some people admit that a world of free trade would be preferable to a world of tariffs. But they say that so long as other countries are so foolish or so wicked as to pass restrictive tariff legislation, there is nothing that we can do but follow suit in self-defense. Actually, however, a tariff is much like an increase in transportation costs. If other countries were foolish enough to let their roads go to ruin, would it pay us to chop holes in ours? The answer is, No. Analogously, if other countries hurt us and themselves by passing tariffs, we should not add to our own hurt by passing a tariff.

To make sure that you grasp the point that our tariff harms us as well as the foreigner, you should realize that there are four gains when the Hull trade-agreements program succeeds in getting another country and ourselves to lower tariffs reciprocally. The other country's tariff reduction bestows gains (1) on us, and (2) on them. Our tariff reduction adds two more gains: (3) for ourselves, and (4) for them.

The only possible sense in the argument, therefore, that we should retaliate when a foreign country raises tariffs, is that our threat of retaliation may deter them from raising tariffs; and our promise to reduce tariffs may persuade them to reduce theirs. This would justify our passing an occasional tariff as a bluff; but whenever our bluffs do not seem to cause foreigners to reduce their tariffs, we should give them up.

Most realistic students of political science believe from their studies of history that retaliatory tariffs usually cause other countries to raise theirs still higher, and rarely provide an effective bargaining weapon for multilateral tariff reduction.

---

[1] The advanced student may be referred to the paper by W. F. Stolper and P. A. Samuelson, "Protection and Real Wages," in *Readings in the Theory of International Trade* (Blakiston–McGraw-Hill, 1949), p. 333 (reproduced from *Review of Economic Studies*, Vol. 9, November, 1941, pp. 58–74). A study of Harvard's W. Leontief finds that in America capital rather than labor seems to be the relatively scarce factor! If correct, this is an argument for raising American real wages by lowering tariffs.

The "scientific" tariff. This is one of the most vicious arguments for a tariff; vicious because it often sounds plausible and moderate, but if taken literally, it would mean the end to all trade! According to the usual form of this argument, tariffs should be passed to "equalize the cost of production at home and abroad." We saw in the preceding chapter that all of the advantage from trade rests upon *differences* in cost or advantage. If tariffs were passed raising the costs of imports to that of the highest American producer, no goods would come in at all.[1]

There is nothing scientific about such a tariff. It is a grave reflection on the economic literacy of the American people that this least defensible of all protectionist arguments has had tremendous political importance in our history, and has even been written into law upon occasion.

Peril-point tariff argument. The scientific tariff might, if consistently applied, wipe out all trade. In our recent congressional debates a related argument has become increasingly important. This is the peril-point provision in our trade agreements. Here's how it works. America is to keep tariff duties low on an industry. However, if this results in so many imports that the very existence of that domestic industry is threatened, we have reached the so-called "peril point." When that point has been reached, America is to increase duties or tighten quotas so as to keep our domestic industry from disappearing altogether or from becoming perilously small.

What about this argument? While it may sound moderate, note that its basic philosophy runs completely counter to the economic theory of comparative advantage. Our nation gains from trade by *specializing*—i.e., by giving up certain activities and moving their resources into other industries in which we have a greater comparative advantage. The industries in which we have a great comparative disadvantage should never have come into existence. And suppose an industry formerly had a comparative advantage but has lost it —because other industries have had greater technological improvements, because the domestic factors it uses have become more expensive through becoming more valuable elsewhere, because factors for that industry have become relatively cheaper abroad, or for any other reason. Then this industry *ought* to be imperiled! It ought to be killed off by the competition of our more productive industries. It ought to reach the peril point, and pass the peril point.[2]

This sounds ruthless indeed. No industry willingly dies; no region gladly undergoes conversion to new factor uses. And in truth any line that is imperiled is probably already a sick industry with a past history of suffering. So

[1] With nonconstant cost the scientific tariff formula is indeterminate. A zero tariff may equalize foreign costs with those of our few most efficient producers. Where draw the line?

[2] Of course, national defense and other valid arguments for tariffs might apply; but if they do, it is *those* arguments and not the peril-point argument that have to be respected.

the already weak industry and region feels it is being singled out to carry the burden of getting the country into a more productive configuration.

Perhaps a best policy then is to introduce tariff reductions gradually, so that factors will have time to move. In addition, some have suggested financial aid from the public purse and subsidies to retrain and relocate factors of production: it is argued that this would speed the transition, share the burden among strong and weak, and perhaps lessen effective opposition to the needed reorganization of national production. Bicycles, watch manufacture (as distinct from domestic assembly of Swiss movements), oil, briar pipes, wool growing, china, textiles, and large generating equipment are some of the weak sisters who feel imperiled. Political pressures have forced protective concessions to many of these.

Fortunately, in a growing economy the ineffective industries gradually dwindle in importance relative to the dynamic effective ones. Fortunately too, the strength of our export industries and the effective use of fiscal and monetary policies have kept over-all employment opportunities high, so that with good conscience the nation can strive for the increase in real income made possible by specialization according to the principles of comparative advantage.

▶ **THE FOREIGNER WILL PAY OR TERMS-OF-TRADE ARGUMENT**

After dealing so long with fallacious tariff arguments, we find it refreshing to come now to a possibly valid one—which hopes to shift the terms-of-trade against the foreigner. Indeed it is about the only argument that would be valid even under statical conditions, and it goes back 125 years to John Stuart Mill. Paradoxically, valid arguments for protection seem mostly to have come from free traders, not from protectionists!

If we put a tariff on rubber, Mill would argue, that will raise the price here over its price abroad. But with our demand now curtailed and with us an important demander of rubber, the price abroad will be bid down.[1] So part of the tariff really falls on the foreigner. (To test yourself, show why a very small country couldn't use this argument.)

All in all then, a judicious tariff might improve an important country's so-called *terms-of-trade* (which are defined as the ratio of a country's export prices to her import prices).

Warning: A prohibitive tariff, which suits the protectionist who really is against all trade, could never be justified by this terms-of-trade argument. Why? Because killing off all trade would kill off all the advantage you get from shifting the terms-of-trade in your favor. Mill and modern economists, therefore, insist that the "optimal tariff" is one just large enough to improve your terms-of-trade, and just small enough to keep your physical exchange of

[1] See the Appendix for a graphical demonstration that our tariff can lower world price.

imports and exports at the level most favorable to your own country.[1] Most economists think that all this would imply rather small tariff rates for most countries. And they hasten to point out that when all nations pursue such terms-of-trade tariff policies, the world pattern of production and exchange becomes less efficient. So most (if not all) nations tend to end up worse off under such beggar-my-neighbor policies.

▶ ARGUMENTS FOR PROTECTION UNDER DYNAMIC CONDITIONS

At last we are arriving at a point in the protection versus free trade debate where those in favor of tariffs can begin to score some weighty points. Three important arguments fall in this category: (1) that a tariff may help to reduce unemployment, (2) that tariffs may create diversified industries more immune to risk, and (3) that temporary tariff protection for an "infant industry" with growth potentialities may be desirable.

Tariffs and unemployment. Historically, one of the strongest arguments for protection has been the desire to make or preserve jobs. We earlier discussed the favorable multiplier effects of exports and foreign investment on jobs and domestic spending, and also the unfavorable "leakage" effects of imports. So there is no denying that beggar-my-neighbor high-tariff policy might increase employment in the short run before other nations retaliated.

But can we accept such measures as a valid part of our national full-employment program? Isn't freer trade much like a scientific discovery of new machinery and methods? Both represent increases in our *potentially producible* level of real national output; but either *might* in the short run tend to lower our actual *attained* level of output and employment. And yet, there is no need, either in the short or the long run, to tolerate a gap between actual and potentially producible product: for that represents an unnecessary frittering away of the gains from progress.

How then do we meet the arguments concerning unemployment because of too low tariffs? We refute these arguments just as we refute arguments concerning "technological unemployment." We point out the existence of domestic monetary and fiscal policies that can successfully *and efficiently* solve the problem of economic slump. (Recall our hundreds of earlier pages on all this.) If workers displaced by imports can find other jobs in a buoyant labor market, this protection plea loses its force.

Once again, we realize how vitally important it is to insist on a "neoclassical synthesis" that employs the tools of modern income analysis to create the favorable environment for stability and growth which is vitally necessary if the classical principles of economics are to be relevant and valid.

[2] The argument is exactly like that of a domestic monopolist who raises his price above marginal cost, but doesn't raise it sky-high, instead stopping where $MR = MC$.

Diversification to reduce terms-of-trade risk. Comparative advantage might tell a country to specialize completely on one good or a few goods. So she is to put all her eggs in one basket. But then what would happen if the prices of those goods drop? Or if her export prices oscillate? The country would find any such variations in her terms-of-trade very destabilizing to her real income. And she might be left stuck with an industry that has become permanently unprofitable.

To avoid the perils of "monoculture," Latin-American economists advise the introduction of tariffs. Just as an investor in securities diversifies to reduce risk, rather than keeping all his eggs in one basket, so they believe a country should use tariffs to induce diversification.

This argument certainly deserves careful examination. Note that it assumes that private citizens are neglecting to take account of the riskiness in future prices of the industries they put their money in. This argument has to assume that the government is better informed than private investors, or at least that the government is more farseeing than private investors in taking account of the future perils of price drops and price gyrations. For, if the future risks are genuine and are foreseen by private investors, those investors will not be misled by temporarily high profits into investing in these few industries; in truth, such industries will not then have a genuine long-run comparative advantage, and there will be no effective tendency to specialize in them.[1]

At this point a related Latin-American argument for tariffs should be mentioned. Dr. Raul Prebisch, chief economic adviser to post-Perón Argentina and to the United Nations' Economic Commission for Latin America, argues that the long-run terms-of-trade are always shifting against agricultural products. So nations who specialize in them are betting on the wrong horse. He argues their governments should instead put on tariffs aimed at building up manufacturing industries whose future terms-of-trade will be more favorable.

Is it true that farm products have declined relatively in price historically and will decline in the future? We can't be sure. First, the quality of manufactured goods has been increasing more than that of staples; so there might be an optical illusion in any fancied terms-of-trade trend. Second, the fact that food has become cheaper in Europe doesn't mean it has necessarily dropped in price in the New World: the steady cheapening in transport costs of the last century could mean that food prices have risen in both places, only the differential having dropped. Third, there is the counterargument, used by Europeans to justify their tariffs against foods, that agriculture is

---

[1] Suppose private employers do foresee the risk, but think they can fire workers when export prices drop, thereby throwing the burden of the unemployed workers on the state. Then we face a genuine so-called "external diseconomy" which might justify government intervention in the form of tariffs, quotas, or other programs. Also recall the limited conditions under which the foreigner-will-pay argument has terms-of-trade validity.

more strongly affected by the law of diminishing returns than is industry. So with population burgeoning all over the world, such Europeans argue that the future terms-of-trade of food will *improve*. Both sets of economists can't be right; if one tariff argument is valid, it undermines the other. Fourth, if past and future drops in food prices are caused by even greater drops in real food costs, because agriculture undergoes great technological improvements, then long-run comparative advantage might still validly tell nations to specialize in food to improve its real income. Finally, even with food prices falling, it might be that you'd minimize your losses by specializing on food.

All in all, no easy answer can be given. Why not? Because the valid kernel of this argument is really an argument about what will be the *future* comparative advantage of the countries in question. To the degree that governments are smarter than private investors in discerning threatening trends to the terms-of-trade, a valid case can be made for their interfering with free market forces. But if government is wrong in its comparative-advantage forecasts,[1] the loss in real income to the nation can become very considerable. And the nation may find its rate of development slowed down rather than speeded up.

Tariffs for "infant industries." Alexander Hamilton in his famous "Report on Manufactures" stated this argument very clearly; it is also associated with the name of a nineteenth-century German economist, Friedrich List; and it has received the cautious blessing of John Stuart Mill, Alfred Marshall, the late Professor Frank W. Taussig, and other orthodox economists.

According to this doctrine, there are many lines of activity in which a country would really have a comparative advantage, *if only it could get them started.* If confronted with foreign competition, such infantile industries are not able to weather the initial period of experimentation and financial stress. But given a breathing space, they can be expected to develop economies of mass production and the technological efficiency typical of many modern processes. Although protection will at first raise prices to the consumer, once the industry grows up, it will be so efficient that costs and prices will actually have fallen.

There is certainly something to this, at least as a theoretical possibility. Taussig in a careful historical study[2] came to the tentative conclusion that the American silk-manufacturing industry represented a successful case of the infant-industry argument. That is, silk manufacturing finally developed a comparative advantage; it finally grew up so that it could stand on its own feet

[1] Colin Clark has argued that Australia was all wrong in the postwar period in not pushing staple production more. Depending upon the fluctuating quotations for wool and meat, Clark or those he criticizes appear to be ahead in the debate.

[2] F. W. TAUSSIG, *Some Aspects of the Tariff Question* (Harvard University Press, Cambridge, Mass., 1931, rev. ed.).

even were the tariff to be removed. But the same could not be said about the woolen worsted industry. This industry came into being because of tariff protection; but seemingly it never did reach the point where it could utilize our so-called "Yankee mechanical ingenuity" as effectively as other industries. It represented, therefore, a baby that never grew up.

Unfortunately for the practical importance of this argument, even promising baby industries cannot swing many votes. It is not they who tend to receive protection from Congress but rather the old and powerful vested interests who have never shed their diapers for, lo, these many years.[1]

The "young-economy" argument. Probably, the infant-industry argument had more validity for America a century ago than it does today, and has more validity for present-day backward nations than for those which have already experienced the transition from an agricultural to an industrial way of life. In a sense such nations are still asleep; they cannot be said to be truly in equilibrium. All over the world, farmers seem to earn less than industrial workers. Consequently, there is everywhere a relative growth of industry and a decline of agriculture. Populations migrate cityward, but this movement is not rapid enough to achieve an equilibrium of earnings and productivity. A strong case can be made for using moderate protection to accelerate these economically desirable long-run trends. Such a defense of protection might better be called a "young-economy" rather than an infant-industry argument.

One final word. Please note that the infant-industry or young-economy arguments are not contradictory to the principle of comparative advantage. On the contrary, their validity rests upon the presumption of an induced, dynamical shift of the production-possibility curve outward and in direction of a new comparative advantage in the lines needing temporary protection.

► QUOTAS AND THE INVISIBLE TARIFF

Up until now, this chapter has usually spoken of tariffs. But almost everything said would apply equally well to any other impediments to trade. Thus, quotas have all the bad effects that tariffs do; and often quotas are much more restrictive than tariffs. Note too that any increase in transport costs will have many of the same effects upon advantageous exchange as will artificial government impediments.

Finally, we should mention the so-called "invisible tariff." In many countries, and the United States is no exception, the complicated administration of the customs can be as bad as the monetary duty that has to be paid, or worse. If an importer's shipments are unduly delayed, if a foreigner's exports to us are refused admittance for complicated reasons of health or of failure to comply with arbitrary regulations, then such red tape can be as harmful to

---

[1] Perhaps an exception is provided by certain war industries such as chemicals and optics, which got a start when World War I cut off German competition.

trade as outright tariffs or quotas. The United States has been working to-ward simplification of customs administration, but it still has a long way to go.

This completes our discussion of the tariff controversy. No fair-minded reader who takes the trouble to think the matter through can fail to see how shallow are most of the economic arguments for tariff protection. The only serious exception is the infant-industry or young-economy argument. It is not surprising therefore that economists—who are supposed to agree on almost nothing—were unanimously opposed to the extreme tariff rates in the Smoot-Hawley Tariff of the early thirties and have been overwhelmingly in favor of the Hull Reciprocal Trade Agreements and the proposed ITO (International Trade Organization) aimed at lowering trade barriers.

SUMMARY

1. The case for freer trade rests upon the increased productivity which international specialization according to the law of comparative advantage makes possible. Higher world production is made possible, and all countries can have higher standards of living. Trade between countries with different standards of living is likely to be especially mutually profitable.

2. Most arguments for tariff protection are simply rationalizations for special benefits to particular pressure groups and do not stand up under analysis.

3. An important exception is provided by the need to favor certain uneconomical lines of activity for reasons of national defense. Perhaps an outright government subsidy would be preferable in such cases.

4. The only other exception of any practical importance,[1] aside from the argument for a tariff to relieve unemployment, is provided by the case of infant industries or young economies that need some temporary protection in order to realize their true long-run comparative advantages. And generally, to the degree that public planning for development can discern long-term trends better than the free market can, tariff and other interventions might turn out to be beneficial.

QUESTIONS FOR DISCUSSION

1. What do you think is the single most favorable argument for a tariff?

2. Make a list of fallacious tariff arguments. How would you outline the various arguments for and against tariffs?

3. "Import quotas and exchange controls are much like tariffs." Discuss.

4. Comment critically on the infant-industry and young-economy arguments. What is their relation to comparative advantage?

[1] The foreigner-will-pay argument, for all its theoretical prettiness, is probably of limited actual importance for most single countries.

5. Mention some noneconomic considerations relevant to tariffs.

6. Relate the peril-point argument to last chapter's theory of comparative advantage.

7. Review your understanding of the following concepts:

*tariff protection, custom duty and
   quota*

scientific tariff and peril point

national defense arguments

terms-of-trade

invisible tariff

*infant industry and young
   economy*

APPENDIX: GRAPHICAL ANALYSIS OF A TARIFF'S EFFECTS

Figures 1 and 2 apply the tools of supply and demand to show what will be the effects of a tariff duty of $1 on each unit of corn imported. Our conclusions are these.

If we have previously been importing some corn, the tariff will (1) almost certainly raise price here, but not by more than $1—say by $0.75. The tariff will (2) tend to

Free trade importing lowers home price:

Fig. 1. Without trade, equilibrium is at the two autarky points *a* and *A*. To find free-trade equilibrium, move *FF* horizontal line up or down until you find price level at which export and import just match.

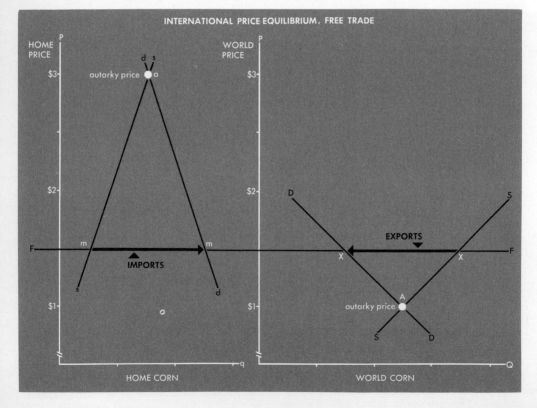

lower the corn price abroad, probably by a good deal less than $1—say by $0.25 (= $1 − $.75). So long as the tariff doesn't become prohibitive, shutting out all imports, it must (3) cause the discrepancy between home price and price abroad to be exactly equal to itself, namely, $1.

What are effects on quantity as distinct from price? Reduced imports mean production will rise a little at home, and corn land will get higher rents. Consumption will fall at home because of the higher price, and more advanced texts show that the harm to the consumer will not be matched by the government's revenue and benefit to producers. Abroad consumption will rise a little and quantity supplied will drop a little.

Now to read off these conclusions from the diagrams. Note that *a* and *A* show the autarky equilibrium points that would prevail here and abroad were all trade prohibited.

To find the free-trade equilibrium price configuration, construct a horizontal line *FF* depicting equal prices at home and abroad. Now move the *FF* level up or down until—what? Until our import bracket *mm* (representing the excess of domestic demand over domestic supply) just matches their export bracket *XX* (representing the excess of their supply over demand). This happens only at $1.50 free-trade equilibrium. (Check this.)

Now, in Fig. 2, we replace the horizontal *FF* line F————————F by the line-with-a-joint-in-it *TRFT* T————————$|^{R}_{F}$————T. Note the trick of the diagram is to make the joint *RF* just equal in size to the amount of

Tariff reduces imports and raises home price:

Fig. 2. To find equilibrium with $1 duty, construct the *TRFT* curve with bent-joint equal to duty. Then move *TRFT* up or down until you find *exact level at which exports and imports match* while at the same time prices differ by the duty.

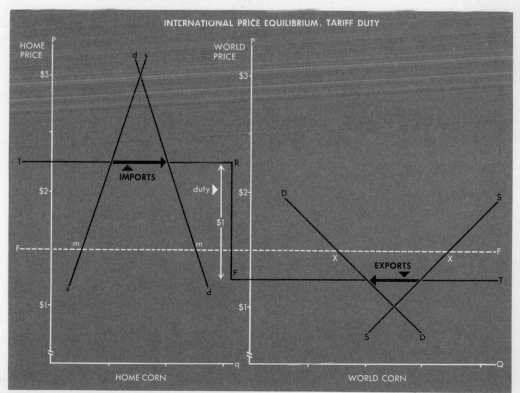

the tariff duty—in this case, $1. Why do we do this? Because the after-tariff equilibrium must give home price higher than price abroad by the exact amount of the duty being paid on our imports.

What use is $TRFT$? We move it up or down until we find equality between our import bracket and their export bracket. Check that this lowers imports and means $2.25 home price and $1.25 foreign price, with most of the duty (but not all) going to raise our price. To test yourself, show that a tariff of more than $2 will be prohibitive, killing all trade and leading to autarky equilibrium.[1]

---

[1] Intermediate texts can use this same diagram to show effects of an exchange rate devaluation —provided you logarithmically interpret the vertical scales. Then RF represents the devaluation of the dollar relative to foreign currencies, raising our prices and lowering theirs, and decreasing our imports and their exports.

34 CURRENT INTERNATIONAL ECONOMIC PROBLEMS

MISS PRISM: *Cecily, you will read your Political Economy in my absence. The chapter on the fall of the rupee you may omit. It is somewhat too sensational. Even these metallic problems have their melodramatic side.*

OSCAR WILDE, *The Importance of Being Earnest*

We must now turn to the main international economic problems facing the United States and the rest of the world in the years ahead. How can we understand the important facts? Which economic policies must we avoid? Which policies must we follow?

► EXPORTS AND JOBS

Talk to a businessman whose memory goes back 45 years. He will point out that exports have always been a stimulating factor along with domestic private or public investment. He will recall the years 1915 and 1916, before we entered World War I, when France, Russia, and England suddenly became avid customers for our exports. We sent them goods in return for barren gold and fancy gilt-edged certificates. The result: a shift from American depression to great prosperity. Or in the period after we entered World War I, when our shipments of useless shot and shell increased, again there resulted all the apparent trappings of prosperity booms—high prices and many jobs.

During the 1920's, when we were making many foolish private loans to the rest of the world and whooping it up for tariffs allegedly to "protect the American workers' standard of living," one of the contributing factors to our favorable balance of saving and investment seemed to be heavy foreign lending. Like domestic private investment or government deficit expenditure, the foreign trade balance was adding more to total money spending than it was subtracting. The hard-boiled businessman sums it up: "Of course, many of our foreign loans later turned sour and investors lost their money. But while we are shipping goods abroad, jobs are created. It doesn't matter as far as *current* jobs and prices in the twenties are concerned whether the loans 10 years later will turn out good or bad, or whether they represent public or private gifts." Or, as Leon Fraser, who used to be president of J. P. Morgan's First National Bank of New York, put it: "It is better to have lent and lost than never to have lent at all."

▶ **FOREIGN INVESTMENT AND INFLATIONARY PRESSURES**

Our Part Two's income analysis will help us evaluate such expansionary effects of foreign investment. Remember how, back in Chapter 12, the "multiplier" worked out? It began with, say, a 1-billion-dollar increase in domestic investment, in government spending, *or in net foreign investment.* That created 1 billion dollars of jobs on the first round. Then those workers and employers spent ⅔ billion dollars of this on the second round. The workers and employers who produced those goods proceeded in turn to spend two-thirds of their ⅔-billion-dollar income. And so it went in a multiplier chain. But we found the total spending did add up to a definite total, given by $[1 + ⅔ + (⅔)^2 + \cdots] = 3$ billion dollars in all.

That multiplier is what we are now seeing in operation here: when foreigners buy from us more than we from them, the balance of saving and investment is shifted toward an intersection that gives a higher American national income.

Is that a good thing? It all depends. If previously you have been having a deflationary gap, new foreign investment will be a good thing in that it will give jobs to the unemployed and expand your production. Example: In 1914 there was a mild slump here; so Europe's war demand for our goods started a multiplier process that worked itself out in terms of more jobs and goods.

But what if new foreign demand impinges at a time when you already have *too much* demand, when you already find yourself with an inflationary gap?

Then the multiplier process will still work itself out in an expansionary way. But now what can expand? Employment can't much expand—there's already a labor shortage. Output can't expand—machines are already working overtime and foremen despair of finding new men to hire. Something has to give in to the multiplier. What? It is prices that will have to be bid up.

In short, when domestic demand is already excessive, expansion of our exports relative to our imports will add to inflationary pressure. At such times new foreign investment is, from our stability viewpoint, a bad rather than a good thing.

Do you think this an academic, unrealistic case? It's not. From 1945 to 1948 we had too much domestic demand at home. Yet Europe needed our help to get back on her feet after the war. We gave it: we made gifts; we made loans; we sold goods in return for gold. Result: some increase in our inflationary pressures; some further rise in our already zooming price levels. The same thing happened back in 1915–1917. The 1914 European demands were good because they got us out of our little recession. But by 1916 we were getting too much of a good thing, and our foreign investment began to be multiplied into paper price increases rather than into real expansions of output. Thus, even before we got into the war, we had a real inflation.

▶ THROW ONE LOAF ON THE WATERS TO GET TWO LOAVES?

The betting odds seem against the world's soon going back to the slump conditions of the Great Depression. But we'd better not be too smug, better not be too quick to forget the important lessons of the 1930's. Reviewing that experience might even help us to avoid it in the future.

When jobs are scarce everywhere, each country tries to export its unemployment. How? By buying rail or ship tickets for the unemployed? No, only a few countries which let in foreign workers on temporary permits can hope literally to export their unemployed. (Switzerland does send back Italian workers when jobs get scarce—but this is an exceptional case.) The way countries try to export their unemployment is by adopting "beggar-my-neighbor" policies designed to *discourage imports* and *encourage exports*.

Of course, one country's exports are another's imports. So all can't succeed in developing a trade surplus. But all can try. And all trying, all can end up worse off.

We'll see how beggar-my-neighbor policies work in a moment. But first let's ask why a rational nation will try to export goods rather than import them. Why, outside a lunatic asylum, would you want deliberately to give away goods rather than get them? And if you should run into someone foolish enough to try to give you goods, why aren't you sane enough to gladly help him achieve his object of charitable exporting?

The answer lies, of course, in a failure of the neoclassical synthesis. It stems from being in that paradoxical topsy-turvy land of mass unemployment. Recall Chapter 12's discussing the paradox of thrift that could characterize so crazy a world: the attempt of individuals to increase their saving will, in a world of unemployment, often result in *less actual* saving and investment because of harmful effects on income and employment.

Here we meet with what might be called the "paradox of international charity." As compared to doing nothing at all to cure depression unemployment, you may find it better to increase exports and refuse imports. Better from the standpoint of creating new jobs? This is an obvious enough possibility. What may not be so obvious is the fact that such giveaway programs may actually give you more domestic consumption! Just how? Through the multiplier: you throw away the first 1 billion dollars of goods; but remember that the remaining $[\frac{2}{3} + (\frac{2}{3})^2 + \cdots]$ dollars $= 2$ billion dollars of new output consists purely of domestic coinsumption![1] So this paradox, however second-best as policy, does have to be recognized as a possibility.

▶ BEGGAR-MY-NEIGHBOR POLICIES

A little knowledge is a dangerous thing. Suppose that you are a congressman who has grasped this possibility of creating jobs and domestic consumption by increasing exports and refusing imports. You might immediately set about to create a favorable balance of trade for the United States. You might begin to follow one or all of the following beggar-my-neighbor policies:

1. Up protective *tariffs* on imports; promote "Buy American" campaigns.

2. Better still, pass a law setting low *import quotas,* so that not more than a specified amount of each good can be shipped to us.

3. Or, taking a leaf from Hitler's Nazi book, introduce comprehensive *exchange control:* so that every import must receive a special license; exports are to be subsidized; bilateral trade agreements are made with each country, limiting the direction and degree of trade and serving as a political weapon of intimidation or bribery. An elaborate system of regulations is set up, making foreigners pay different prices for the dollars they need for each different kind of good—depending upon what the "traffic will bear," etc.

4. *Depreciate the dollar* as much as possible, so that foreigners can buy our exports very cheaply, while pounds and francs are made so expensive as to discourage our importing. In other words, the more we succeed in depreciating the dollar compared to all foreign currencies, the greater the exports we are able to give away and the fewer are the imports we are willing to take. If other countries do not retaliate, this depreciation of the dollar will cheapen the dollar relative to foreign currencies and will enable us to give away exports in exchange for no imports.[2]

---

[1] An example may help. Legislate a giveaway program that expands General Electric turbine exports. Boston workers get first-round jobs—just as leafrakers get first-round jobs when you introduce boondoggle antidepression programs. The Boston workers, by respending, create new jobs in Ohio and elsewhere. Final real score: first-round United States production thrown away abroad just like the wasted first-round boondoggle output; but in both cases considerable expansion of United States production and consumption from all the later rounds.

[2] Raising the United States price of gold above $35 an ounce would "devalue the dollar" but wouldn't depreciate it relative to other currencies if they also raised their mint prices for gold. Because the British Empire (and the Soviets) mine gold, such a devaluation might help foreigners get more dollars.

(A fifth way a country can expand its exports relative to its imports is to offer foreigners sound or unsound *international loans* at low interest rates; or even more, to make them huge gifts—financed by the Treasury or by gullible private investors. But the foreign country is not necessarily beggared as a result.)

A good congressman should be able to think up a few more devices, but these are the most important policies to be followed by a country that hopes to solve its unemployment problem at the expense of its neighbors: *i.e.,* by a country whose motto is "A short life and a merry one. Export and be happy, even though an international financial crash is brewing."

Any intelligent person who agrees that the United States must play an important role in the international world will strongly oppose the above policies, because they all attempt to snatch prosperity for ourselves at the expense of the rest of the world.

But suppose we are hard-boiled or, to put it crudely, selfish. We still must regard these beggar-my-neighbor policies as rather foolish. Why?

One does not need much intelligence to see that foreign nations will not stand idly by while we attempt these policies. They too have economics textbooks and legislators. They too, during a great depression, will be following beggar-my-neighbor tactics; they too will be raising tariffs and introducing import quotas and exchange control; they will be trying to depreciate the pound (or the franc as the case may be) so that the dollar will appreciate in value. In short, they'll be trying to up their exports and cut imports.

What is the result when all countries try to beggar their neighbors in this way—when all try to climb on each other's shoulders to see the parade? Obviously, we cannot succeed in exporting to England more than she is exporting to us, while *at the same time* England is succeeding in exporting to us more than she is importing. Our mutual attempts to develop favorable balances of trade are worse than canceling. International trade drops to the lowest level of exports and imports. Both nations are worse off.

Again, how can we succeed in getting the pound-dollar foreign exchange rate up to $4 per pound (a "depreciation" of the dollar) at the same time that the English are succeeding in depreciating their pound down to far below $4 per pound? We both can't succeed. To elaborate the obvious further, how can we lend to Britain (net) in the next depression at the same time that she is lending (net) to us? Indeed, with legislators of both countries on their toes, we cannot even succeed in giving away goods to each other. For, if free supplies began to come in from abroad, more American workers would be thrown out of jobs—a condition no red-blooded American could permit.

What is the final moral? Evidently, that a strong, important country like the United States cannot sensibly regard international trade as a way of solving any future unemployment problem. We cannot. And we should not if we could.

But we cannot. Other countries will retaliate to our beggar-my-neighbor tactics, with the result that we shall all be much worse off.[1] Between 1960 and 1975, our choice should never be between (1) doing nothing about unemployment, or (2) trying to export our unemployment abroad by restrictive trade policies in the hope of getting favorable secondary multiplier effects.

Instead we must aim at a superior third choice whereby (3) we conquer the problem of unemployment by domestic policies and use international trade only to increase our present and future standards of consumption, or to serve our political aspirations and responsibilities.

International "boondoggling" would be no better or worse than scattering leaves and raking them; but if it were the only alternative, some might find it better than nothing. Still, doesn't the whole process remind you of the first savages who had to burn down a house to roast a pig?

Surely we should always be able to get something useful for our 1 billion dollars of work on the first round. Instead of throwing useful goods into the ocean, so to speak, why not use them for domestic consumption or domestic capital formation? Or if we feel that it is to our national interest and preference to help out the consumption and development of foreign nations, let us make sure that it does really help them out. This is just common sense, just as it is clearly better for the government to build useful dams and hospitals rather than to rake leaves or construct pyramids. Both policies may lead to extra jobs and extra induced private consumption, but one leads to a greater total of useful production than the other.[2]

▶ AMERICAN GOALS AND INTERNATIONAL COOPERATION

Economic isolation will not work. On this, if on no other proposition, $99\frac{44}{100}$ per cent of all economists are agreed. Nevertheless, isolationism may again rear its head, because nations who ignore history are condemned to repeat it. Let us turn to the problems the United States must face in the years ahead.

Let us assume that we all want to aim at the twin goals: full and efficient employment at home, with a rising standard of living and productivity; and peaceful, profitable trade relations with our neighbors on a durable basis. To achieve these goals we must face and solve the following main problems.

---

[1] If our neighbor abroad has overfull employment and inflation while at the same time we have unemployment, the above beggar-my-neighbor policies may then paradoxically be pleasing to both of us.

[2] Recall the "neoclassical synthesis" whereby successful income stabilization validates the classical principles of economics.

▶ FULL EMPLOYMENT AT HOME

The United States can make its greatest single contribution to sound economic relations by adopting such domestic public and private policies as will keep its real national income high and growing. In the past, America was long the important plague center of unemployment. By letting our national income slump off, we let our imports fall to low levels, while still striving to export. "America sneezes and Europe gets pneumonia!" economists used to say. As a result of trying to solve our unemployment through a favorable balance of trade, we used to deflate and impoverish the rest of the world. This invited retaliatory foreign restrictions; and all nations lost in the mad game of beggar-my-neighbor.

The least we can aim at is to do a pretty fair job of keeping American employment and income high—by means of *domestically created* purchasing power. With reasonably full employment at home, we shall be in a position to welcome goods sent to us as dividends and interest on our past investments and as repayment of principal. With full employment, we can welcome anything that enables us to raise our living standards by importing more *cheaply* and fully. With full employment, we can gradually reduce our artificial protective barriers and subsidies to relatively inefficient American industries.

If all other nations were doing a perfect job of keeping their employment full, their prices stable, and their international payments in healthy balance, they would say to us: "If you want to be a good neighbor, don't generate an inflation which—like the flu—will seep abroad and infect us."

But other countries aren't in so perfect a position. As we'll see, most of them are undergoing inflations of their own. So, paradoxically, in their franker moments they say about us: "If only the United States would have a domestic inflation at least as great as our own. Then her costs would rise and she'd buy from us about as much as we're always tempted to buy from her."

Just before he died, Lord Keynes thought that America would solve the so-called "dollar shortage" by having a greater internal inflation than the rest of the world. That turned out to be a poor guess. We'd like to be a good neighbor—but there is a limit to what you can expect even of the best-intentioned neighbor, and having a domestic American inflation just to be neighborly seems beyond our limit!

▶ FOREIGN LENDING AND THE INTERNATIONAL BANK

The United States is more developed industrially than the rest of the world. South America, the Orient, and other regions of the world could profitably use our capital for their industrial development. Such capital could be expected to increase their production by more than enough to pay generous interest and repay the principal.

But private American citizens are loath to lend. Though American corporations will build branch plants abroad and will invest in oil or mineral resources, substantial private lending through Americans' buying foreign bonds or stocks died some time in 1929, perhaps forever. Yet American citizens have savings which they would be glad to lend if such capital transactions could be made safe; and the American nation would benefit by a higher future standard of living from such sound foreign lending.

Therefore, the leading nations of the world (except Soviet Russia) have come together to form the International Bank for Reconstruction and Development and its sister institution, the International Monetary Fund. As its name implies, the International Bank is formed to provide sound long-term loans for reconstruction and development. (The International Fund is concerned, as we shall see shortly, with short-term credit and the cooperative stabilization of foreign exchange rates.)

The International Bank is easy to understand. The leading nations subscribe to its initial 9 billion dollars of capital stock in proportion to their economic importance. The United States quota is about one-third, or 3 billion dollars. The bank can use its capital to make sound international loans—to people or countries whose projects seem economically sound but who cannot get private loans at reasonably low interest rates.

So far, each country has been called upon to put up only 20 per cent of its full quota, and it is not planned that the members will have to put up the remaining 80 per cent. Obviously, this is not much money on international standards. The International Bank's true importance arises from something greater than the loans that it can make out of its own capital. More important is the fact that it can float bonds and use the proceeds to make loans. (It has successfully floated bonds in the United States, in Switzerland, and elsewhere.) The bonds are safe because they are backed by the credit of all the nations (up to their 100 per cent of quotas). Also, the International Bank can *insure* loans in return for a ½ or 1 per cent premium; private parties can then put up the money knowing that the Bank's credit is behind the loan.

As a result of these three ways of extending long-term credits, we can expect to see goods in the years ahead flowing out of the United States aimed at international development. If sound, these loans will be repaid in full. If some go sour, the loss will be paid out of the Bank's interest or premium earnings. If still more go sour, the loss will be spread over all the member nations—not on Uncle Sam alone. While the loans are being made, Uncle Sam will be getting jobs (and, if spending is already too great, some increase in inflation problems). When the loans are being "serviced" or repaid, America should have an import surplus of useful goods.

Has the Bank been a financial success? Decidedly. If anything, the Bank may be too conservative in its practice of lending to self-liquidating projects.

In addition to the International Bank to which many nations belong, the federal government has set up its own Export-Import Bank. This also makes foreign loans: *e.g.,* an American exporter who wants to sell machine tools to Brazil may be helped to do so by the Export-Import Bank. Many of these loans are "tied loans"; *i.e.,* our Congress has insisted that the proceeds all be spent *directly* in this country. We criticize this sort of restrictive practice in others but practice it ourselves.[1]

The Eisenhower administration has also set up an International Finance Corporation. As a subsidiary to the World Bank, it helps provide venture capital for economic development.

Later Table 1 will show the postwar government loans of the United States.

▶ STABLE EXCHANGE RATES, FREER TRADE, AND THE MONETARY FUND

When exchange rates vary from day to day, the risks of international trading become so great that its volume is reduced. World specialization and productivity is reduced. Also, when every nation tries to engage in competitive exchange depreciation, all end up worse and world trade ends up on its back.

The gold standard, while it operated, kept exchange rates constant. But (as is shown in Chapter 31's Appendix) it made each country a slave rather than a master of its own economic destiny. As long as we stuck to its rules, we had to inflate ourselves whenever the rest of the world said inflate; and deflate ourselves when the rest of the world had a depression. Of course it had some advantages, but alas, poor gold standard! It was a casualty of World War I, and since then all the king's horses and all the king's men couldn't put it together again, and many wouldn't want to if they could.

The International Monetary Fund along with the International Bank grew out of 1944 international conferences held in Bretton Woods, New Hampshire. It hopes to secure the advantages of the gold standard without its disadvantages; *i.e.,* exchange rates are to be relatively stable, but international cooperation is to replace the previous automatic mechanism; also, countries are to be spared the need for making adjustments that involve deflating themselves into drastic unemployment. It hopes to lessen need for direct import controls.

In 1947 the Fund set postwar exchange rates for most of its members. (The dollar was set equal to 0.889 gram of gold, the British pound to 3.581 grams— with a resulting exchange rate of $4.03 per pound.) But King Gold is tolerated only as a constitutional, rather than an absolute, monarch. And in 1949 most of the British Empire and Western Europe depreciated their currencies 30 per cent, so that the pound was stabilized at $2.80.

---

[1] Not only do tied loans distort the direction of international trade, but in many cases they are quite unnecessary. If part of our loan is used abroad, say in England, rather than here in the United States, then the extra dollars put in the hands of the British will probably cause them to take some of our exports. International trade is multilateral rather than bilateral.

It is too much to expect there will be a perfect balance of international transactions in these troubled days. Quite clearly some countries will for a while sell more abroad than they buy—even after taking into account long-term foreign lending and aid. Others will be running into adverse trade balances and debt. How then can stable exchange rates be maintained?

Here is where the International Fund comes in. It provides short-term credits for the debtor countries. The Fund tries to set up rules and procedures to keep a country from going on year after year, getting deeper into debt. After a country has been piling up debts for a considerable period, certain financial penalties are applied. More important, the Fund's directors consult with the country and make recommendations for remedying the disequilibrium. But, they do not tell a country it must create a depression for itself in order to cut its national income down to such a low level that its imports will finally fall to within its means. Instead, the country is permitted on its own hook first to depreciate its currency by 10 per cent. This will tend to restore equilibrium in its trade by expanding its exports and contracting imports.

If this is still not enough to correct the so-called "overvaluation" of the debtor country's currency, the Fund authorities may, after proper consultation, permit still further depreciation of the debtor country's exchange rate. But note this: all changes in rates take place in an orderly way. Most of the time, we have international stability. And there is also provision for flexibility when needed—which is better by far than waiting for a big international blowup or breakdown.[1]

Let's discuss briefly and without going into the mechanical details how the International Fund is able to extend short-term credits. First, all the member nations must pay in certain initial quotas which are set in proportion to national income and the volume of international trade. The United States quota is about one-third of the total and equals $2\frac{3}{4}$ billion dollars. At least 75 per cent of each country's quota is payable in its own currency; the rest is payable in gold, but not beyond 10 per cent of a country's official holding of gold and American dollars.

Ordinarily a country will go along paying for its imports by means of its exports or long-term borrowing. But suppose these are not large enough, and the country—say, England—is in need of short-term credit from the Fund. How does the Fund enable such a debtor country to get hold of, say, dollars? It does this by extending "purchasing rights." It simply permits the British to buy with British currency some of the Fund's own holdings of dollars. To keep the

---

[1] A growing number of economists think that freely fluctuating exchanges will work out better in the end than will stable exchange rates. Better to make adjustments every day than put them off, they argue, and devaluations will be foreseen and are unlikely to be "orderly."

Fund from getting loaded up with pounds and stripped of its dollars, in any 12-month period, the British are not permitted to buy an amount greater than one-fourth of their original quota. And the Fund will never hold more than twice the original quota number of British pounds.

After the British balance of payments has improved, they are expected to buy back with gold (or with dollars) the pounds they have sold to the Fund. Thus, the Fund need never run out of dollars or any other currency; especially if it stimulates corrective action to prevent continuing disequilibrium.

Everyone admits the Fund has been rather a disappointment. The postwar strains turned out much larger than people realized in 1944; and the Fund's resources have been inadequate to cope with the disequilibriums. Fortunately, its function has been met in part by the European Payments Union, which was set up after the Marshall Plan aid program to provide short-term credits and clearings for the European nations; and by the Organization for European Economic Cooperation (OEEC), which has provided for consultation. Within the British Commonwealth the sterling area has coordinated the trade relations of this "key currency" area.

▶ **MARSHALL PLAN, MILITARY AID, AND OTHER PROGRAMS**

Table 1 shows how enormous have been the American aid programs. After the United Nations Relief and Rehabilitation Administration (UNRRA) had helped meet the immediate postwar emergency needs, we introduced our dramatic Marshall Plan program for European recovery. Subsequently, our aid shifted toward grants to the North Atlantic Treaty Organization (NATO) and other military alliances. (Thus, the "Truman Doctrine" brought financial aid to Greece when threatened by communism. Even Red Yugoslavia has received aid, as did the Nationalists in China, the South Koreans, and the French in Indochina.)

Undoubtedly, the motives for many of these programs were our fear of communism. Full stomachs may not save a democracy; but empty ones can seal its doom. And putting modern guns into the hands of our friends will both help their defense and save American soldiers' lives.

However, a close study of the events leading up to the Marshall Plan will show that America in the postwar has also had strong "do-good" motivations. Call this altruism if you wish. Or call it long-run expediency. We recognize that the globe holds 15 non-Americans to every American, making our very future depend upon a stable international order. Close study of the facts will in any case discredit the hypothesis that we embraced aid programs because that was the only way to prevent a great depression crisis at home. On the contrary, we gave most at times when domestic inflation problems were most

For relief, recovery, development, and military security, we gave:

Table 1. U.S. Government postwar foreign aid (billions of dollars). Notice how our initial loans have been replaced by military grants. And notice the Marshall Plan aid in the middle years. Are you surprised that Europe has received almost two-thirds of the total? (Source: U.S. Department of Commerce.)

	1945–47	1948–50	1951–53	1954–56	Total Postwar Period
Net nonmilitary grants	4.8	12.3	5.9	5.2	28.2
Western Europe	1.7	9.2	3.5	1.9	16.3
Asia, Africa & Near East	1.8	2.8	2.2	2.9	9.7
Rest of world	1.3	0.3	0.2	0.4	2.2
Net government loans	7.7	1.7	1.7	−0.2	10.9
Western Europe	6.6	1.5	0.8	−0.6	8.3
Asia, Africa & Near East	0.6	0.1	0.4	0.4	1.5
Rest of world	0.5	0.1	0.5	0	1.1
Net military grants	0.7	1.1	8.5	8.3	18.6
Western Europe	0	0.3	6.0	5.1	11.4
Asia, Africa & Near East	0.7	0.7	2.2	3.0	6.6
Rest of world	0	0.1	0.3	0.2	0.6
Net total, grants and loans	13.2	15.1	16.1	13.3	57.9

pressing; and one of the gravest costs of our aid was this aggravation of our contemporaneous internal scarcities.

▶ POINT FOUR: THE BOLD NEW PROGRAM

Aside from providing substantial material aid to foreign countries, there is one thing we can do that may help them a great deal and yet cost us very little, namely, help other countries acquire the technical know-how that will enable them to increase their levels of productivity and living standards. This is known as the "Point Four Program" because it was first enunciated as the fourth point in the Truman 1949 inaugural address. There is no better way to describe it than to quote:

Fourth, we must embark on a bold new program for making the benefits of our scientific advances and industrial progress available for the improvement and growth of undeveloped areas. . . . I believe that we should make available to peace-loving peoples the benefits of our store of technical knowledge in order to help them realize their aspirations for a better life. . . . We invite other countries to pool their technological resources in this . . . world-wide effort for the achievement of peace, plenty, and freedom.

In addition to these government plans, we have been privately exporting our "know-how" abroad. Many of our largest companies are establishing branch factories abroad; often the capital is largely raised abroad, with Americans supplying the technical knowledge. Some shortsighted people raise their hands in horror at the thought of our helping foreign nations to become our industrial competitors. They seem to forget the statistical fact that international trade is largest between developed industrial nations, not between us and backward countries.

▶ **FREER MULTILATERAL TRADE**

In review, note that we've discussed (1) maintenance of high employment at home, (2) long-term international lending by the International Bank, (3) short-term credits by the Fund and other stabilization organizations, (4) American aid and military programs, and (5) the Point Four Program of technical aid.

Only after these problems have been faced is there much point is discussing the problem of (6) getting freer trade and convertible currencies, whether through the proposed International Trade Organization (ITO) or through the General Agreement on Tariffs and Trade (GATT).

The Cordell Hull reciprocal trade program for reducing American and other tariffs has now been with us for more than 20 years. And contrary to the widespread view, our high 1930 tariffs have been substantially cut (in some cases they have been halved and then halved again). As a result, careful measurement of the degree to which all the nations of the world restrict trade will show that in 1958 the United States is up near the top of the list of "relatively free traders." To be sure, we ought (in our interest and that of others) to go even farther; and admittedly, the rest of the world can never know when Congress will increase tariffs. Still, many who talk about American trade policy should study the true situation as it now is and not be victims of cultural lag.

Earlier chapters have discussed how much more productive multilateral specialization is in comparison with bilateralism. Indeed Oxford's Sir Donald MacDougall finds that in actual prewar practice the classical theory of comparative advantage shows up in the statistics in the following way: England and America seem not to trade much with each other; primarily, it is in the third markets of the world that England outsells us in the lines where she has comparative advantage; and we outsell her in those markets in lines where we have comparative advantage.

All stand to gain if fruitful multilateral trade can be restored.

► THE COMMON EUROPEAN MARKET AND FREE-TRADE AREA

One way of getting trade impediments down is for several countries to form a customs union. Within such a union, tariffs and quotas might be reduced or banished; but they might still persist with respect to external trade. History provides us with many examples. The 48 states of the United States can be thought of as a large customs union. A century ago the many independent German states formed a *Zollverein* or customs union. More recently, Belgium, Luxembourg, and the Netherlands formed the Benelux union.

Most interesting for the future is the Common Market of Europe: in 1957 Belgium, France, Italy, Luxembourg, the Netherlands, and Western Germany signed treaties to create a Common Market (and at the same time the six countries signed a second treaty to create a common nuclear energy pool, Euratom). Subject to some exceptions, each nation over a 12- to 15-year transition period is to gradually eliminate tariffs and import quotas on nonfarm goods produced within the area; to set up a common tariff against goods from countries outside the Common Market; to allow free movement of capital and labor; and to set up a European Investment Bank with quota contributions from each country, whose purpose is lending for economic development. Farm goods are not yet included, and the difficult·problem of overseas territories of the European nations is not yet clarified. Moreover, there are still numerous qualifying clauses.

This Common Market could become the second-largest free-trade area in the world. If Great Britain were to join it, there would be a powerful impetus to large-scale production and exchange in Europe. Britain herself is hesitant because she already belongs to the Commonwealth sterling bloc, which itself tried in the 1930's to promote internal trade between its members by favorable tariff rates in the form of "Imperial preference." When a way is found for Britain to join the Common Market and yet keep her close ties with Australia, Canada, India, and other Commonwealth countries, this could become the largest free-trade area in the world.

Some economists have worried whether the lowering of tariffs between countries of a bloc is truly a movement toward a more efficient world pattern: "Won't there be a danger that the lower-than-average tariffs between the countries in the union will distort the 'normal' pattern of trade even more than it is already being distorted by separate nations' tariffs? Won't the difference between the ins and the outs be magnified and represent as serious a distortion as the previous situation?"

Other economists have replied: "Two wrongs don't make a right. If you can't get rid of trade impediments everywhere, at least get rid of them where you can. Then maybe a few great customs unions can ultimately merge into a world-wide free-trade area."

No definitive answer will cover every case. As an economist and betting man, I'd have to venture the guess that lowering of tariffs in Europe could have such good effects there on the division of labor as to make the whole experiment a very worth-while one.

▶ DOLLAR SHORTAGE?

This chapter can end with the big open question of our time. Is there a "dollar shortage" of a lasting sort, which will for a long time keep other nations from freeing their trade and making their currencies freely convertible?

What does dollar shortage mean? We can all use more dollars: that's as true of professors and grocers in Cambridge, Massachusetts, as of professors and grocers in Cambridge, England. Dollar shortage must mean something more than that.

Sir Dennis Robertson, Cambridge University's distinguished economist, gives this definition of dollar shortage:[1]

> What it seems to mean is a persistent tendency on the part of the populations of the world outside North America to spend more in that region than the sum of what they are earning in that region and what the inhabitants of that region are disposed to lend to them or invest in their borders under the play of ordinary economic motive.

Robertson thinks the symptoms of the dollar-shortage disease are continuous pressure on the international reserves of other countries, persistent direct import controls that they impose on their citizens, and a series of special gifts and loans by the United States and Canada. He first lists as a cause of the disease the wartime disorganization of European and Asian production. Along with those who attribute the dollar shortage primarily to the tendency for foreigners to live too high and to their propensity to overinflate their currencies, Robertson makes the further point: ". . . what are politely called 'balance of payment difficulties' do not necessarily drop from heaven . . . any nation which gives its mind to it can create them for itself in half an hour with the aid of the printing press and a strong trade union movement."[2]

However, he and many economists here and abroad suspect that dollar shortage may be the symptom of a more fundamental condition that had already asserted itself over the last quarter century and holds regardless of war: namely, the allegedly higher rate of technological progress in the dollar countries than in the rest of the world. As invention brings down our costs faster than foreign costs, we tend to outsell them and to create balance-of-payments problems for them—in brief, dollar shortage. As fast as adjustments are

[1] D. H. ROBERTSON, *Britain in the World Economy* (G. Allen, London, 1954), p. 53.
[2] *Ibid.*, p. 56.

made to this process by having our money wages rise relative to theirs—as envisaged by the theory of comparative advantage of Chapter 32—new inventions come along and recreate the dollar shortage. So goes the argument.[1]

The orthodox economist tries to answer each one of these arguments. He counters fact with fact, theory with theory. It would be tedious to go over all this ground. And unnecessary. For the orthodox economist rests his case on one general principle. He argues:

"If foreigners' demand for dollars is outrunning the supply available to them—no matter what the reason for this, no matter what the amount of this—there is always a simple cure. Depreciate all currencies relative to the dollar enough—and you are sure to cut down on imports from America enough and to expand exports to America enough to restore balance. At the new depreciated exchange rates, dollars will be neither short nor in superabundance."

Sir Geoffrey Crowther, long-time editor of the influential *London Economist* and the first (back in 1937!) to coin the term "dollar shortage," gave in 1957 the following reply to this argument:[2]

In currency matters, we shall continue to have Two Worlds, as we do now. Neither more nor less. On the one hand, it will not prove possible to dismantle the controls and defences that separate the Dollar Area from the Eastern Hemisphere. And on the other hand the very substantial degree of freedom of payments that now exists in the Eastern Hemisphere can be expected to continue.

. . . The maladjustments are far too large for the normal mechanisms [of exchange depreciation and internal changes in prices and credit conditions] to cope with. . . . The world has an urgent and swelling demand for American products. . . . On the other side of the fence, the demand of the United States for the products of the Eastern Hemisphere is neither very elastic nor very urgent. . . . The increased imports of raw materials on which the United States will depend will come either from Canada or the Caribbean area . . . relatively little from the Eastern Hemisphere.

Like many economists, Crowther goes on to argue that closing the dollar gap by depreciating the pound and other currencies relative to the dollar would have to result in a tremendous depreciation—greater than nations will tolerate. Why is so great a depreciation implied? Because Americans are thought to have an inelastic demand for imports from abroad, and Europe and the rest of the world to have an urgently inelastic demand for our exports. Result: to get rid of dollar shortage, exchange rates and terms-of-trade would have to move tremendously against Europe. Rather than risk that happening, the world will stay in two camps—the dollar area and the pound area.

---

[1] Robertson gives the analogy of a servant to an ingenious scientist. He loses his job as cook when the boss invents an automatic cooker. So he turns to shoe shining—only to lose that job from a new invention. Instead of turning to trash-bin emptying, mightn't the servant be better off to turn his back on the scientist, cultivating his own garden? *Ibid.*, pp. 58–59.

[2] G. CROWTHER, *Balances and Imbalances of Payments* (Harvard Graduate School of Business Administration, Boston, 1957), pp. 34, 44–48.

No one can give a firm evaluation of these competing views. So let's turn to the recent facts. Figure 1 shows how enormous the "dollar gap" appeared to be in the early postwar years. The right line shows our current surplus balance on private account. How was this met? Largely by our making vast loans and vast gifts. But even that did not meet the problem, and Fig. 1 does not tell the whole story. Behind the scenes there were stringent exchange controls in most countries. A citizen there had to get a permit to import; and permits were kept low in number. You couldn't take your money out of the country without a permit; and these were granted only in special cases. Undoubtedly, were it not for quotas, tariffs, and exchange controls, Fig. 1 would record a worse United States surplus on current account.

Note that by 1948, our Marshall Plan aid met more and more of the private

Will the dollar gap end, making government aid and loans unnecessary?

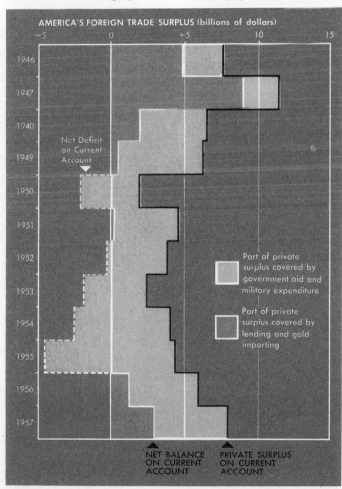

AMERICA'S FOREIGN TRADE SURPLUS (billions of dollars)

Part of private surplus covered by government aid and military expenditure

Part of private surplus covered by lending and gold importing

Net Deficit on Current Account

NET BALANCE ON CURRENT ACCOUNT

PRIVATE SURPLUS ON CURRENT ACCOUNT

Fig. 1. The medium shading shows that the early postwar surplus of our exports over imports was financed by large foreign investment. In 1956–1957 Americans again had positive net foreign investment or positive net balance on current account. But in Korea years, you'll note that government-aid programs filled the current gap; and the dotted lines show the years when net foreign investment was actually negative, government aid then more than making up the gap.

Dollar and gold reserves are no longer so desperately low:

Table 2. Foreign gold reserves and dollar holdings (billions of dollars). There has been substantial growth everywhere, but the Sterling Area has gained less than would be required by the expansion of world prices and trade. (Source: *Federal Reserve Bulletin*.)

Area	1928	1938	1948	1956
Sterling area	1.4	3.9	2.9	3.9
Western Europe	4.8	7.3	5.8	14.1
Latin America and Canada	1.5	1.3	3.9	6.7
All other	1.0	1.3	5.8	6.7
Total outside United States	8.7	13.8	18.4	31.4

surplus; less strain, therefore, was placed on our foreign lending and on foreigners' sending gold to us. By 1950, the Korean war and boom finally reversed the postwar dollar shortage: we still ran a private surplus, but our military expenditure and government-aid programs more than made up for it. Now foreigners had to lend to us, and we had to send them gold. But in 1956 and 1957, there was again a resurgence of the private gap.

Table 2 shows the great improvement from 1948 to 1956 in foreign gold reserves and dollar holdings. So we end with a vital question: Has the world turned the corner of the dollar shortage? And will our imports continue to rise relative to our exports so that our private accounts can approach current balance in those days ahead when the world becomes more peaceful and we can reduce our military programs?

This is our problem as much as Europe's. For as Sir Dennis Robertson points out, just as it takes two to make a quarrel or to make a baby, so it takes two to make a dollar shortage—we in the United States as well as the rest of the world.

The least we can do is act so as to bring nearer the reality implied by the attractive slogan: Trade, not aid.

SUMMARY

1. Expanded exports relative to imports will have multiplier expansionary effects on a country. If previously it had unemployment and excess capacity, the result will be more jobs and output. If previously it had inflationary pressures, the result will be an intensification of those pressures.

2. The beggar-my-neighbor policies of the depressed thirties, by which each nation vainly tries to export its unemployment abroad, are self-defeating. There should be no need for the United States in the next decade to rely on such bad-neighbor policies. Domestic fiscal and monetary weapons are strong enough to meet any instability problems we might face.

3. The International Bank, the International Monetary Fund, important Marshall Plan and military-aid programs, Point Four, the reciprocal trade program for tariff reduction, the Common European Market—all these are important factors in the postwar bid for more rational world trade.

4. The "dollar shortage" is the big open question of our time. Among its causes are wartime disorganizations; the tendency for others to have more rapid inflation than America; their attempt to emulate our higher living standards and to develop themselves ever faster; the fact that their currencies are "overvalued," with their having to have recourse to direct import restrictions; etc.

But the most long-lasting factor is the alleged tendency for America to be the pace setter in technological change. This continuing process of new inventions is continually upsetting the adjustments that comparative advantage is making to past inventions, so that the dollar shortage chronically remains.

Orthodox economists argue that a sufficiently great exchange rate depreciation would end the dollar shortage. But it is argued against them that the resulting depreciation and deterioration of Europe's terms-of-trade might have to be so great as to be intolerable. In any case, most experts agree that the dollar shortage is as much an American as a world problem and that we should do all we can to expand our imports.

QUESTIONS FOR DISCUSSION

1. "In 1935 it was better to export goods in exchange for useless gold than to do nothing." Discuss critically. Would your answer be different in 1942 or 1958?

2. How does the multiplier analysis apply to international trade?

3. Define, describe, and criticize beggar-my-neighbor policies.

4. Contrast and compare the International Bank and Fund.

5. Draw up a list of what you consider our most important postwar economic problems. If you were in Congress, what would you do about them?

6. What effects do you expect from the Common Europe Market?

7. "Not one single American industry should be sacrificed in the name of the ITO's program for realizing freer multilateral trade." Do you agree?

8. Describe the extent of our postwar aid to the rest of the world. Was this merely "generosity"? Did generosity play an important role?

9. What is your Point Five Program for the future?

10. Stage a debate on "the dollar shortage."

11. Review your understanding of the following concepts:

net foreign investment and the multiplier

various beggar-my-neighbor policies

domestic and international boondoggling versus the neoclassical synthesis

International Bank and Fund

Marshall Plan and other aids

Point Four

customs unions

lower tariff moves

dollar shortage

part

6

CURRENT

ECONOMIC

PROBLEMS

35 ECONOMICS OF TECHNOLOGY

Energy = mass × (speed of light) ^{2}
ALBERT EINSTEIN

The automatic machine is the economic equivalent of slave labor.
NORBERT WEINER

One of the striking features of the modern world is the rapid pace of science and technology. Are we in a new Industrial Revolution? In a Second Industrial Revolution? Or in a continuing Industrial Revolution? If you read the newspapers or listen to the speeches that scientists make when they take off their white laboratory coats, you might think we are indeed in a new era. You might wonder whether all the old rules of the game don't have to be scrapped and all the ancient principles of economics rewritten.

The more dramatic philosophers of the new order divide off into two quite opposite camps. On the one hand there are the prophets of doom who see in the development of "automation" a displacement of man: robots are soon to take over, throwing the worker out of his job; like Frankenstein who created a monster he couldn't control, modern science has unleashed social forces more destructive than the hydrogen bomb itself.

Against this alarmist view, there are the sweet optimists. They can prove by arithmetic—or, if this doesn't convince, they can cite the facts of history—that technological improvements can't help benefiting every last man, woman, and child. They point out that auto factories hire more men than the buggy shops ever did; and they deduce from this that technological unemployment is quite impossible and can never happen again. QED! The more poetical members of this optimistic camp look forward to a new age of plenty, when we shall all wear glass neckties, have pushbutton homes, spend most of the week in week-ending, and discuss (through high-fidelity microphones) the great books of

711

fifth-century Athens, or perchance spend our leisure peering at pancake-thin TV sets to see who wins the 64-million-dollar question.

In this chapter we subject the two fateful topics of nuclear energy and automation to sober economic analysis. The economic tools of income determination and of efficient relative pricing, far from being obsolete, turn out to be precisely what is needed for a careful study of these important developments.

▶ ENERGY TRENDS

We begin with the question of nuclear or atomic power. Every child realizes that modern civilization rests on the use of power: Stone Age man used his muscles; early historic man used horses and oxen; classic and medieval man used water mills, windmills, and ship sails. Then came the so-called Industrial Revolution. Man learned to convert heat into steam; steam into motion; motion into electricity; and electricity into light, motion, or heat.

It is a commonplace that each one of us in a modern economy has hundreds of horsepower at his disposal. (See Fig. 1.)

Until now coal has been the most important energy source. While coal and capitalism have been inseparable, more recently oil and natural gas have in America outstripped coal. Besides these so-called "fossil fuels"—called "fossil" because oil, coal, and gas were formed aeons ago from decayed animal and vegetable life—hydroelectric power provides the cheapest source of electricity to those places that happen to have sharp water drops. (*E.g.*, TVA in the

High incomes and high per capita power consumptions go together:

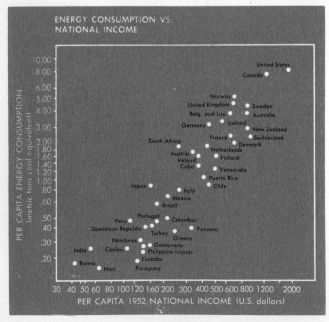

Fig. 1. While energy is but one of the needed elements for prosperity, the tendency for real incomes and average energy consumptions to grow together is striking. (Source: United Nations.)

South, Bonneville and other Western dams, Canadian and Central African waterfalls.)

Today America's power consumption grows at a rate of more than 5 per cent per year. So voracious is the appetite of modern living for power that fossil fuels are becoming scarcer and dearer. And the best hydroelectric sites tend first to be used; which means that further power sources are to be had only at higher and higher costs. At our present pace the world by A.D. 2000 will be consuming power at ten times today's rate, and it will then be in sight of having used up much of its cheapest conventional power sources.

W. Stanley Jevons, a leading economist of the nineteenth century, predicted just a century ago that England would lose her dominant position because her coal mines would become exhausted.[1] And in every decade some geologists have prematurely mourned the end of our petroleum reserves, only to find their predictions refuted by new finds. So we must not be too alarmist. Yet we must face the fact that English mines are now very deep and picked over, that American wells have to be drilled deeper and deeper, and that more and more of them are dry holes. Some Middle East wells produce in a month what a good Texas well would take 10 years to produce.

▶ NUCLEAR ENERGY BY ATOMIC FISSION

Plainly the world is ripe for a new energy source. Luckily, physicists around 1939 discovered that neutrons could split heavy elements (such as uranium or thorium) by fission into lighter elements, with the parts resulting from the fission turning out to have less mass or weight than the whole had had. By the Einstein equation quoted at this chapter's head, any destruction of mass must be accompanied by a tremendous liberation of energy. Secret war research was thus able to develop the atomic bomb used in Japan.[2]

In physics, energy is energy. In economics, the packaging of energy much affects its value. Thus, to get a big explosion at one place, armies will pay billions of dollars for the same kilowatthours that any steam plant could over a time produce for thousands of dollars. Nuclear energy becomes economically important for peace to the extent that it is possible to have controlled chain reactions which release energy continuously in usable form. Fortunately, even before the bomb was made, Fermi and other physicists showed at Chicago

[1] He recommended that she pay off her internal public debt at once so as to compensate for the impending exhaustion of the coal mines—which shows that even a great scholar can partially confuse internal transfers and genuine resource burdens!

[2] Physicists also believe that the sun's energy comes from *fusion* of the light element hydrogen into the heavier element helium, but with a loss of mass and great release of energy. Again the Einstein equation. This suspicion has been confirmed with the development by the United States and the Soviet Union of the hydrogen bomb. Peaceful use of such a thermonuclear fusion reaction to generate power was discussed at the Atoms for Peace conference at Geneva in 1955, and British and American scientists a few years later reported achieving by magnetic means the terribly high temperatures needed to create controlled fusion.

that slow chain reactions could be made self-sustaining with a release of energy in the form of heat; and they have since learned how to control and utilize fast reactions.

So just when fossil fuels are threatening to become scarce, the world has found a new potential source of energy from fissile fuels—uranium and thorium. A generation ago the Oklahoma Indians got rich from oil; now some New Mexico Indians have been lucky enough to find uranium promoters eager to buy their land for prospecting.

Uranium and thorium are quite common in nature, geologists estimating that the first 3 miles of the earth's crust contains some million million tons. Since Einstein's equation suggests that complete fission of a pound of uranium is equal in energy release to the burning of 14,000 tons of coal, some sensationalists have begun to talk of a new age of abundance based on practically free, inexhaustible energy from fission. They talk of new autos, which are to come from the factory with built-in fissile fuel no bigger than a pea, and which will never have to be refueled throughout their lives.

▶ **THE SOBER ECONOMIC AND SCIENTIFIC FACTS**

Every scientist knows better. Much of the uranium in nature appears in so dispersed a form as never to be profitably recoverable. On the optimistic assumption that new methods will reduce the cost of recovery from moderately low-grade ores to not more than $100 per pound of metal, we can roughly estimate recoverable fissile fuels to be only one forty-thousandth of the total—or 25 million tons of uranium and 1 million tons of thorium in all. And probably only one-third of this would in practice end up split. Yet even this could ultimately yield more than 100 times the energy of all recoverable fossil fuels.

Every scientist also knows that material the size of a pea is below the "critical size" needed to sustain a nuclear chain reaction. Fermi's first Chicago nuclear reactor or "pile" filled an indoor tennis court. And we all know how dangerously radioactive are fission processes, so that an atomic auto might have to carry 6 feet of solid concrete as a *shield* against dangerous radiation.

The sober economic and scientific facts are then these.

1. Natural uranium and thorium have to be found at great expense. (Canada, the Congoland, and the western United States are a few of the important localities.) It has to be mined and separated at great expense.

2. Of all natural uranium, only $\frac{2}{3}$ of 1 per cent is in the form of so-called U^{235} from which bombs and reactors can best be made. It was an expensive job at Oak Ridge, Tennessee, to separate out physically this U^{235} from the bulk of so-called U^{238}. At Hanford, Washington, the Atomic Energy Commission used nuclear reactors to convert U^{238} into another more fertile fissionable material called "plutonium." Most commercial nuclear reaction will in America come

from use of so-called "enriched" fissionable fuels—not from natural U^{238} but from U^{238} plentifully mixed with U^{235} or with plutonium. Because these enriched materials are the raw material for military bombs, the government will have to be the source of them. At what cost will civilian producers be able to buy them? At full cost to the government? Or below cost? And what safeguards will be needed to make sure that no civilians or foreign governments use the enriched materials to make illicit bombs?

3. Most of the world has no enriched fissile fuels. That is why England is launching a great program, which will in the beginning use nuclear reactors to convert natural U^{238} into plutonium. This process will also give off heat that can generate electric power. (At Hanford, Washington, this heat was wasted, being dumped into the Columbia River.) The best English reactors will thus be double-purpose reactors, producing enriched fissile fuels as well as useful energy.[1] Whether an English reactor will be commercially profitable evidently will depend on how much the government pays for the plutonium that it buys for military purposes and for later use as enriched fissile fuels.

4. The capital costs of nuclear reactors are very high. Reactors generate heat above 1000° F., requiring new heat-resistant metals and delicate handling. They require much shielding, much remote-control handling. To control the dangerously radioactive liquids and gases of their coolants, you have to develop absolutely airtight pumps, blowers, valves, etc. Even small leaks would be deadly. Built-in safety features, needed to protect lives and to make the operation commercially insurable, require advanced techniques and are colossally expensive. Moreover, as running time goes on, the reactor gradually poisons itself; so you have to perform an expensive cycle of pumping out and reprocessing its contents.

5. Talk of free energy and abundance overlooks an important fact. Today 65 to 75 per cent of a public utility's costs are for *distribution* of energy. Even if the utility could get its energy for nothing, the reduction in ultimate cost to the homeowner and factory owner would be modest. And power itself is but 4 to 7 per cent of modern production costs. These facts alone rule out talk of a "new era."

▶ THE OUTLOOK FOR NUCLEAR POWER

Figure 2 compares the cost curves of a nuclear and conventional power plant after fossil fuels have become dearer and nuclear technology has advanced.

---

[1] The useful energy from nuclear reactors will for the foreseeable future consist mostly of heat, which can then be converted into electricity via steam engines and generators—or can be used, as in England's Calder Hall, directly to warm offices and homes. Direct conversion into electric power seems not yet to be scientifically feasible. When fissile as well as fossil fuels are exhausted some centuries hence, direct conversion of sunlight—by focusing mirrors, storage tanks, chlorophyll-like plant and inorganic reactions, solar batteries, etc.—might be used.

Not for decades will nuclear energy outcompete coal and oil:

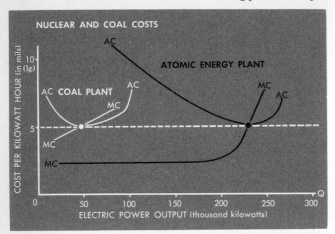

Fig. 2. The black cost curves show hypothetical average and marginal costs for future large-scale nuclear power stations. Even with coal's average costs comparable, the lowness of pre-capacity marginal cost for the nuclear plant suggests it will tend to be kept continuously operating, with stand-by coal plants being used to meet peak loads. (Can you figure out why this is likely?)

Gradually, under these conditions, more and more of our energy will come from fissile fuels. But fossil fuels will still, in all probability, continue to dominate. Most experts expect nuclear energy will be introduced so gradually as to minimize shock effects and transitional disturbances. As we make our breakfast toast, we won't know or care that some of our electricity came from the atom.

Note that the giant nuclear-power stations probably won't much cheapen power. Rather is nuclear energy likely to save us from the age of greater poverty that fossil-fuel exhaustion would otherwise have entailed. In short, successful nuclear energy will eventually hold down the price of coal. Finally, note that energy from coal and from atoms is shown with about the same unit costs in Fig. 2. This is not by coincidence. It is because the price or "economic rent" of coal, although it will rise, will remain just low enough to keep coal's dwindling supply competitive.

▶ GOVERNMENT PROGRAMS HERE AND ABROAD

What about nuclear energy for the underdeveloped countries of the world? Will Alaska, Argentina, and other places far from cheap fossil fuels be the first

World power needs are outstripping visible conventional energy sources:

Energy Source	Reserve (billion tons of coal equivalent)
Coal and lignite	3,000
Oil and gas	300
Oil shales and tar sands	150
Hydroelectricity	2.5 (per year)

Table 1. Recoverable world energy reserves. Despite the fact that we have been getting more efficient in using fuels, conventional fuel costs can be expected to rise. (Source: 1955 Geneva Atom Conference.)

to benefit from atomic energy? When you recall nuclear energy's high capital costs and its delicate technology, your answer becomes, Probably no. Nor will developed countries like the United States and U.S.S.R., which have plentiful coal and oil, have the most to gain from nuclear energy.

Who then will gain? Perhaps England, a developed country now running out of coal, will be the one to push atomic energy ahead at the fastest pace. Certainly in the late 1950's she has been the most vigorous in starting development programs, having tripled her program targets and now aiming for a 5- to 6-million-kilowatt nuclear capacity by 1965.

Nuclear energy will be commercially so uncompetitive for a long time that governments will undoubtedly have to subsidize most development programs. American atomic-energy programs, financed by the federal government but often run on contract by such large companies as General Electric and du-Pont, represent a new social hybrid: hardly capitalism, hardly socialism. Even the large private utilities,[1] which have banded together on more than 20 American projects, realize that it is the knowledge they gain rather than the commercial power which will be profitable to them in the near future. But that knowledge will be available to all; whereas the risks they take of freezing on one of the many kinds of reactors would fall on themselves.[2]

Without government aid atomic energy is not yet a commercially profitable venture. Energy from fusion will come, but don't expect it tomorrow.

▶ SPECIAL USES OF NUCLEAR PRODUCTS AND ENERGY

The immediate future of nuclear energy we have seen will not be in mass production of electric power. There it won't yet compete for a couple of decades more. But the atom does have an important role to play when it comes to special, expensive packagings of power.

Here are a few examples: (1) bombs, where expense counts little; (2) submarines, where the ability to stay under water indefinitely, without having to recharge batteries and replenish oxygen or refuel, is all-important; (3) merchant and naval ships, which can make long trips without refueling; (4) locomotives and other massive engines; (5) mobile emergency power plants, to be used in earthquake, flood, and military crisis; (6) giant airplanes, which can fly long ranges without refueling. Because of the need for massive shielding, our cars will not soon be run by the atom; and some experts are still skeptical that an atom-powered airplane or locomotive makes much sense.

[1] Pennsylvania already uses some atomic energy; and New England, Michigan, Idaho, and other regions have modest programs under way. There are so many different kinds of reactors to have to choose from, and the scientists learn new facts so fast, as to make each project a serious gamble. No wonder private enthusiasm has been waning.

[2] There may be involved here a so-called "external economy," where private and social advantages diverge and which economists have long recognized as calling for modification of *laissez faire*.

Indeed, if you stick to the cold facts, the atom nucleus has by 1958 been truly an economic success in but three applications: (1) for bombs, where it has been a veritable tour de force; (2) for submarines, where the *Nautilus* and *Seawolf* have been highly successful; (3) for production of radioactive isotopes, which fight cancer, trace down bodily ailments and processes, date trees and fossils, test metals, and control numerous industrial processes.

The American atom program has been the largest government spending program of all times. The billions of dollars spent have produced tremendous results, tremendous for potential good and tremendous for potential evil. At this awesome point, the economist must—and not unwillingly!—turn the matter over to the political scientist and statesman.

▶ AUTOMATION: WHAT'S IN A NAME?

The word "automation" has just penetrated into the dictionaries. It was coined in 1947 by Del Harder, vice-president of Ford Motor Company, to mean "automatic handling of parts between progressive production processes." Example: Use of special handling or transfer machines that link together in a sequence long lines of boring and reaming tools for machining auto engines.

At about the same time, John Diebold, a Harvard Business School graduate and management engineer, shortened the word "automatization" into automation. Diebold stressed the use of control devices that operate by means of "feedback." Examples: When I see my arrow strike the target to the left, I feed back this observed error signal to make a rightward correction in my bow. Similarly, my thermostat starts the house furnace when room temperature errs below the desired level, and shuts itself off when temperature errs upward. Oil refineries and chemical plants have long been automatically regulated and programmed from beginning to end by similar control devices. Your gasoline and arsenic were produced "untouched by human hands."

Automation has still other meanings. Giant electronic calculators, which are a millionfold faster than hand machines, have simplified data processing and record keeping. A pretty machine does the work of a hundred even prettier girls. Some modern digital computers can beat a good player at checkers; none can yet beat a champion; none can yet play a really good game of chess; at simple games like ticktacktoe the machine plays a perfect game. The day is near when every time a teen-ager buys a pair of overalls in a Seattle J. C. Penney store, the cash register will send an electronic message to New York to keep the chain's inventory records up to date; and this message may trip off reorders to an Oshkosh factory. Numbers recorded on magnetic tape can make a milling machine or lathe turn out intricate copies of a master pattern.[1]

[1] Besides these examples of digital (or numerical) computers there are numerous examples of "analogue computers": thus a wind tunnel duplicates the conditions an unbuilt plane will

Still, if you want to throw an apostle of automation into a rage, tell him that it's nothing but old-fashioned mechanization and mass production on a bigger scale. Tell him that ages ago James Watt used feedback in his steam-engine governor, which has rotating fly balls that rise with centrifugal force of too rapid motion and thereby open a valve to release steam and control engine speed. Tell him that looms have since 1801 been "programmed" by Jacquard punched cards to weave intricate patterns. Point out that so-called "servomechanisms," which permit amplification and control of power, have been used to steer ships since 1872. And remind him that Dr. H. Hollerith, realizing in the nineteenth century that it was beginning to take more than 10 years to analyze each decennial census, invented the modern IBM punch-card system.

We don't have to take sides on this issue. Whether you think automation is something new, or think it represents a great postwar quickening of developments already known in principle, you must admit it is a force to reckon with. Maybe Henry Ford II, when he has to bargain collectively with UAW's Walter Reuther over the alleged effects on workers of automation, sometimes regrets that his vice-president ever conjured up the word.

▶ DISPLACEMENT OF LABOR?

Automation will presumably increase productivity. Otherwise it wouldn't be installed. Does this mean it will reduce the total need for labor, creating mass unemployment? Back in the depression of the 1930's, long before we knew the name of automation, there was much fear of "technological unemployment." Should we again start worrying that modern man will become obsolete?

Norbert Wiener, MIT mathematician and one-time prodigy, who coined the name "cybernetics" (from the Greek word for "helmsman"), has pronounced in the following dramatic way:

The industrial revolution up to the present has displaced man and the beast as a source of power. . . . The automobile factory of the future . . . will be controlled by something like a modern high-speed computing machine . . . [which] plays no favorites as between overall and white collar labor. . . .

Thus a new war will almost inevitably see the automatic age in full swing within less than five years. . . . We can expect an abrupt and final cessation of the demand for the type of factory labor performing repetitive tasks . . . an intermediate transitional period of disastrous confusion. . . . Industry will be flooded with the new tools to the extent that they appear to yield immediate profits, irrespective of what longtime damage they can do.

. . . Let us remember that the automatic machine, whatever we think of any feelings it may have or may not have, is the precise economic equivalent of slave labor.

---

face; a laboratory network apes the conditions of transmission lines a thousand miles long. Related to feedback and automation, there are also the new fields of "information" theory, systems analysis, and operations research.

Any labor which competes with slave labor must accept the economic conditions of slave labor. It is perfectly clear that this will produce an unemployment situation, in comparison with which the present recession and even the depression of the thirties will seem a pleasant joke.[1]

This quotation involves both the principles of income determination at the aggregative level and the principles of relative pricing at the detailed level of commodity and factor markets. Its first two paragraphs raise questions about automation's short- and long-run impacts on employment and purchasing power. The quotation's last paragraph raises question about the ultimate market pricing of labor even after the transition is over. First we must use Part Two's tools of income analysis. Then we can apply the price analysis tools of Parts Three and Four.

▶ **THE FORWARD LOOK**

Ever since workers tried to "sabotage" technical advance by throwing their wooden shoes or sabots into the new machines, there has been a fear that the same total work, if performed more efficiently, would require less man-hours to do. A doubling of productivity means a halving of employment—*if* total product remains the same.

In the Great Depression men readily believed total product would remain the same, that desired output would fail to grow with the growth of productivity. This view makes you look at unemployment in the following way: "Why did those unemployed workers over there lose their jobs? Which machines displaced them?" And so forth.

Modern students of income determination follow a more fruitful attack. They say: "Regardless of why those men lost their jobs, why aren't there enough *new* jobs for them? What fiscal and monetary policies are needed to create the new dollar purchasing power necessary for them to be hired anew?"

"Satchel" Paige, a great baseball player, once said: "Never look backward; someone may be gaining on you." This is good advice in economics too. Don't look back to find what caused past layoffs. Look forward to see what you have to do to restore high employment. This is much more efficient.

Better still, this approach means you don't have to decide whether the pessimists are right who argue that inventions will kill off more jobs than they create; or whether the optimists are right in expecting inventions to stimulate so much new consumption and investment spending as to more than make up for the reduction in labor requirements per unit of output. Need we care which is right? *In every case we know that high employment without infla-*

[1] NORBERT WIENER, *The Human Use of Human Beings* (Cambridge, New York, 1950), pp. 180, 181, 186, 188, 189.

tion will require monetary and fiscal policies of the correct magnitudes. If the pessimists happen to be right in one year, *expansionary* monetary and fiscal policies will be then needed to restore the stable equilibrium. And modern governments do know how to implement such needed policies. If the optimists are right in any period—so that technological change is whipping up too much consumer and investor spending—then a government with the will to act does know how to carry out *contractionary* monetary and fiscal policies.

► **THE INCOME-DETERMINATION ANALYSIS OF TECHNOLOGICAL UNEMPLOYMENT**

To apply this fruitful approach, we can use the saving and investment diagrams of Chapter 12. Or what is the same thing, and a little more convenient here, we can use the consumption + investment + government spending approach, looking for income equilibrium where the $C + I + G$ schedule just intersects the 45° helping line. The next page's diagrams illustrate this.

Suppose that automation makes labor 30 per cent more productive. This means the same full-employment labor force could produce 30 per cent more real national product; hence, the FF full-employment line of Fig. 3a is now shifted rightward 30 per cent to $F'F'$. Let's make the worst possible assumptions: (1) that government leaves its expenditure G as it was; and that the new machines are so cheap and short-lived that they can be introduced just by using up the depreciation allowances of the wearing-out machines, so that (2) net investment I is no greater than before; finally, that automation gives people the same things for less but doesn't whet their appetites for new gadgets, which means that (3) the propensity to consume schedule (and to save!) will be exactly the same as before in terms of disposable income.

In short we assume the $C + I + G$ schedule has none of its components shifted as a result of automation. Then the schedule must continue to intersect at the same E point as before. But whereas this E point was previously a full-employment equilibrium, now it represents a point of 30 per cent unemployment! A large fraction of the populace is now out of work completely, and many are working only part time. Were this to become the case, who can doubt that unions and the government would agitate to cut the length of the working week and to sabotage new methods and machines?

But even this worst case can be cured by proper therapy. Here's how. Let the Federal Reserve fight this slump by making credit much cheaper and much more freely available. (Recall open-market purchases, lowering of reserve requirements, lowering of discount rates, etc.) What will this do to the I schedule? Push it up. At the same time, let the government cut down on the heavy taxing it was doing in the previous full-employment situation. This will increase people's disposable incomes, will increase their consumption spend-

The income determination diagrams before and after automation:

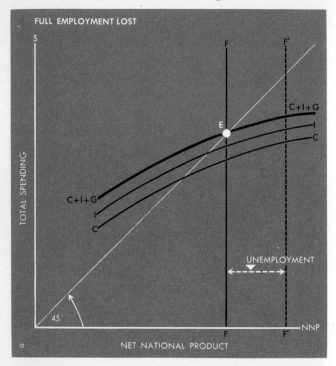

Fig. 3a. If inventions raise productivity 30 per cent, FF shifts 30 per cent rightward to F'F'. Were C, I, and G not to change, the intersection would still be at E, but now with 30 per cent unemployment.

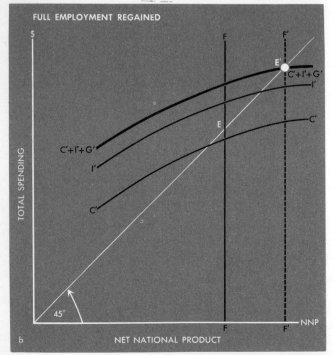

Fig. 3b. Expansionary monetary policy will raise I. Expansionary fiscal policy will lower taxes, raise disposable incomes, and shift up the consumption schedule. Full-employment equilibrium will be restored at E', where C' + I' + G' has been shifted upward the right amount.

ing, and thus shift upward the C part of the $C + I + G$ schedule. (Maybe I will be further shifted too.) Without increasing government expenditure directly, we can thus shift the $C + I + G$ schedule far enough upward until the new $C' + G' + I'$ schedule intersects the 45° line at the new full-employment level E'. Alternatively, a public-works program or other expansion of G could be used to help shift $C + I + G$ up to the target level, if the people feel they need public services more than extra C and I.

Figure 3*b* shows how these upward shifts have restored the full-employment equilibrium. By proper policy we have converted the machine from a curse to a blessing. People now enjoy 30 per cent more output. They aren't forced into bread lines. They aren't made to work short hours. They don't have to take Mondays off because the limited work has to be shared. They don't have to throw their cigarette cases into the works of the new machinery to protect their jobs and take-home pay.

You should be sure you know how to use the same diagram to handle the case where automation or new inventions spontaneously increase investment a great deal and spontaneously tempt people onto an upward-shifted consumption schedule. You can then show how the desired E' equilibrium could come about spontaneously. Indeed, to test.your powers, you should analyze the extreme case where automation causes too great a burst of investment and consumption spending. You should then show how contractionary monetary and fiscal policy would be needed to wipe out the inflationary gap and to bring the new $C + I + G$ schedule back to the proper intersection.

▶ HOW TO EASE TRANSITIONAL SHOCKS

Personnel experts counsel a company to introduce automation gradually so as to minimize the number thrown out of work. With a gradual enough introduction of automation you can simply stop hiring new workers. There are always some quitting anyway, and you can let these bring the labor force down gradually to the new desired level. Or it is even better if you can introduce automation at the time of an upswing in total production. Careful advance explaining to the workers and planned retraining programs can allay many real and fancied threats to workers' security.

Yet when all this has been done, there will still be some workers hurt by any new technique. They have invested in skills that are now obsolete; their built-up job seniority has been wiped out. Too, if the needed over-all fiscal and monetary policies are not followed, all the careful planning at the company level will merely serve to transfer the burden to the rest of the community. If many firms were simultaneously to stop hiring new workers, letting their labor force shrink as people quit, the needed new job opportunities for school graduates and for those who quit other jobs would be seriously impaired. Hence the problem of coping with the employment effects of automation is primarily one of national policy, not one of company tactics.

▶ TECHNOLOGICAL CHANGE AND THE DISTRIBUTION OF INCOME

The supposition that modern government will use its fiscal and monetary weapons to avoid mass unemployment and galloping inflation frees us to examine the more interesting long-run question: What will automation and other technical advances do to the distribution of our growing national income? Will it lower wage rates relative to rents? Will it raise interest rates? Will it raise skilled wages relative to unskilled? Will it cause profits to go sky-high? The tools we used in Parts Three and Four to analyze commodity and factor pricing must now apply.

Profits? First, is it likely that the share of profits—meaning by this simply corporate income—will be sent up by technological change?

No simple answer is possible. Recall that Western society has been in a gigantic Industrial Revolution for a century and a half, and that the inventions of recent years do not show any great quickening in the trends of productivity. (Engineers, who respect facts in their own laboratory, unaccountably prate of "Second Industrial Revolutions" without looking at the masses of facts on productivity gathered by the Bureau of Labor Statistics to see whether the facts have heard about the news.) Remember too that the share of labor in the national income has been remarkably constant over the last century, showing if anything a slight tendency in recent years to increase rather than decrease.

Study of the facts of history and of the present do not, therefore, suggest that profits will be the main beneficiary of technical change.

Does reason confirm the testimony of fact? Sitting in your armchair, can you think of any reason why one manufacturer could grab the benefit from automation to the exclusion of all others? Doesn't it seem more likely that improved techniques come from many rival sources; that the government is subsidizing much research and development, with their fruits free for all to imitate; that patents are less important today than they used to be? If these things are so, we should expect technological change to create temporary profits for some innovators; to create losses for many competitors whose goods, equipment, and methods become obsolete. But our less-than-perfectly competitive system seems unlikely to become appreciably more monopolistic as a result of automation.[1]

Reason then makes us expect the costs of goods to be bid down over the longer run, and the prices of productive factors needed for modern technol-

---

[1] To the degree that automation favors large-scale production, this might need qualification. But some think automation may finally make for more flexible small-scale production.

ogy to be bid up. Profits as such would hardly seem the primary beneficiary of automation.

Natural-resource returns? This raises the question of the likely demand for the various productive factors. Will natural resources be more eagerly demanded in the future?

I suspect that we may be in for such a trend. Just look at the growth of Canada, a great producer of raw materials like oil, iron ore, uranium, copper, timber, and nickel. Latin America, the Middle East, and Africa too are learning how hungry the high-employment modern economy is for raw materials. Certainly many of our richest men have been getting their fortunes from discovery and ownership of important natural resources.[1]

Capitalist returns? It takes intricate machines to make intricate machines. So one of the effects of invention could be to impute a higher economic value to existing stocks of physical capital goods. This could show itself in higher interest rates; or, even with lower interest rates, it could show itself in the form of higher imputed market rentals from capital goods and higher capitalized market values for them.

Still one would feel that in the longer run a plentiful supply of capital formation would permit the duplication of scarce physical capital goods and would tend (at least once the pace of invention stopped accelerating) to cheapen the services of such capital goods.

Higher wages? We are left then with the inescapable fact that if profiteers, interest receivers, and resource owners all seem unlikely to get the lion's share of the fruits of technological advance, there is only labor of brain and muscle left to reap its share of the harvest. Somebody's real wages will then have to go up. If man can produce a robot slave, the net product of that slave must be man's.

The economics of slavery is perhaps more complicated than would at first seem to be the case. Modern research shows that ante-bellum owners of slaves did reap substantial real incomes from the productivity of slave labor. Far from decaying of its own weight, slavery appears from the records of auction-market quotations and from accounting statements of slave users and slave breeders to have been a highly profitable industry.[2] And ask yourself this tricky, but suggestive, question: If all whites could be owned by Negroes, how could any Negro worker who could find the land to breed white slaves on have his earning power wiped out by the competition of slave labor?

Thus, the parable of the machine as a slave by no means implies that automation is likely to lower average real wages.

[1] To the degree that science learns to chemically synthesize nitrate, rubber, rayon, nylon, and other fabrics out of ubiquitous local materials, there could be a reverse trend away from higher resource earnings.

[2] See ALFRED H. CONRAD and JOHN MEYER, "The Economics of Slavery in the Ante-bellum South" in National Bureau of Economic Research's 1957 Conference on Income and Wealth.

▶ UNCERTAIN RELATIVE WAGE TRENDS

To be sure, not all wages have to go up equally. Some types of labor could actually be competed down; but that would have to be because some other factor returns had gone up.

We should perhaps expect engineers and technicians, who are needed to design and maintain automatic equipment, to be very much in demand and to have their wages relatively bid up. Certainly in the late 1950's there has been much talk of the engineer shortage, brisk recruitment each June at engineering colleges, and considerable labor pirating of young engineers. The defense effort figures importantly behind this demand; knowledge that the Soviet Union is beginning to train more technicians and scientists than we do and is forging ahead in the missile and satellite fields has produced a sense of urgency which threatens to reach down even to the level of training more and better high school science teachers.[1]

Automation may tend to lessen the differences between white-collar clerks and blue-collar factory workers: already their differences are becoming blurred; often both wear sport shirts in a literal as well as figurative sense.

Unskilled labor, despite the alleged obsolescence of muscle power, today earns more than it ever did before: a longshoreman or ditchdigger makes more today in Western society than skilled workers can earn by muscle or brain in backward countries, and today he probably has at his command more of most consumption goods than any prince of the royal blood had centuries ago. Automation could even make machinery so foolproof in operation as to economize on I.Q. rather than requiring more of it. No one really knows.

The science journalists and engineers who pontificate about the wage and skill trends implied by automation are mostly spinning the tale out of their own heads. They may well be right later. But up to this date the Bureau of Labor Statistics has not been able to detect a worsening of the position of semiskilled labor relative to the highly skilled. And wages for clerks have been rising rather faster than the average—giant computers notwithstanding. Highly skilled labor seems, if anything, barely to be holding its own. And most professional incomes are not growing quite so fast as wages generally.

All we do know is this: average real wages do continue—in union and nonunion industries—to grow rather steadily each year. We should be rash to say

---

[1] Columbia's George J. Stigler, studying the engineer shortage in 1957 for the National Bureau of Economic Research and the National Science Foundation, has announced the paradoxical fact that, despite all the frenzied recruitment and talk of engineer shortage, engineers' incomes have actually been falling behind those of doctors and growing recently less rapidly percentagewise than those of teachers. Could the engineering shortage be a myth? See D. M. BLANK and G. J. STIGLER, *The Demand and Supply of Scientific Personnel* (National Bureau of Economic Research, New York, 1957).

that this fact is exactly what economic theory would suggest, but we can honestly say that it is not out of line with the supply-and-demand analysis derived by our production and distribution analysis of Part Four.

SUMMARY

1. High-level modern economies are based on plentiful use of power. Traditional fossil sources of power (coal, oil, and gas) and hydroelectric sources threaten to become more expensive in the decades to come. So energy from nuclear fission or fusion looms just over the horizon.

2. Despite much enthusiastic talk, nuclear energy will come in very gradually, supplementing rather than supplanting conventional fuels. Capital costs will be high; costs of natural and enriched fissile fuels will be dependent on government programs; value of fissile by-products, such as plutonium and enriched U^{235}, will much depend on military considerations and government decisions; safety problems and technological difficulties with high temperatures and new materials will undoubtedly be overcome gradually.

3. As fossil fuels become more expensive and as the nuclear techniques improve, reactors will begin to take over a fraction of the total power load. Countries with developed technology and high fuel costs, such as Britain, may lead the way. Coal and nuclear power will coexist for a long time, with the latter gradually setting the price for the former. Then thermonuclear fusion will probably take over. Much more rapid will be the use of the atom's nucleus to give special packagings of power—as in the submarine and ship—and to produce useful radioactive substances. No new age of plenty looms ahead, but rather the hope of continued evolution toward higher living standards.

4. The name "automation" is more dramatic than the diverse facts it describes. Before and after the war there has been a great increase in use of integrated automatic and control processes, which often use "feedback" and electronic calculating components. Yet men (and women) are still needed to design, make, program, maintain, and correct machines. And no significant acceleration in the pace of productivity change is yet to be found in the overall statistics on labor productivity.

5. The modern tools of income analysis make us look forward to policies needed to assure new jobs rather than look backward to reasons why old jobs disappeared. This analysis enables us to be neutral on the question whether automation will spontaneously create more new investment and consumption spending than it destroys. In either case national income analysis specifies the contractions or expansions in monetary and fiscal policy needed to prevent chronic unemployment or inflation.

6. Fear of chronic unemployment aside, we can study the likely long-run impact of automation and technical change on relative wages, profits, interest, and natural-resource prices. Neither facts nor theories suggest that monopoly profits are likely to grow in percentage importance. Nor would rises in interest rates or in returns to existing capital goods seem likely to be exhaustive beneficiaries. This suggests that wages and natural-resource returns are likely to grow at least in proportion to productivity increase. Laborsaving devices primarily producible by labor cannot outcompete labor and lower real wages: the slave is slave, not master.

7. Changes in the structure of occupations and in relative wages may come from automation. Possibly engineers, technicians, and supervisors will grow in relative economic importance. But we can't be sure even of this, since modern gadgets may become more foolproof and more economical of intelligence and specialized trainings. The statistical facts have not yet borne out the trends popularized by the science-fiction writers.

QUESTIONS FOR DISCUSSION

1. How much does electricity cost in your region? How is it generated?

2. List ways that cheaper power might dramatically raise living standards.

3. Write a prediction of world power growth. In what ways are fossil and fissile fuels alike? In what ways different? What about fusion and use of sunshine? Show how military and civilian atom use will be related by the problem of natural versus enriched fissile fuels.

4. Contrast the marginal-cost pattern of fissile and fossil fuels. What do low precapacity marginal cost and high overhead nuclear costs suggest?

5. "The word automation is like 'six players in search of an author.' The name covers a multitude of old and new phenomena." Do you agree? Argue.

6. List reasons why automation might create unemployment. List reasons why it might create jobs. Try to draw up a balance sheet, but show in any case what programs might promote high employment without inflation.

7. What are automation's transitional impacts at the plant and individual level?

8. Evaluate the Wiener quote critically. Where *might* he be right? Where do you think he is *likely* to be right? Where wrong?

9. Review your understanding of the following concepts:

nuclear or atomic energy

fission and fusion

fissile and fossil fuels

enriched fissile fuel (U^{235} and plutonium) versus natural U^{238} and thorium

automation and technological change

transitional versus long-run effects

fiscal and monetary programs

wage and nonwage benefits

36 ECONOMICS OF WAR AND DEFENSE

> *This is the way the world ends*
> *This is the way the world ends*
> *This is the way the world ends*
> *Not with a bang but a whimper.*
>
> T. S. ELIOT

Why study so unpleasant a subject as economics of war? At least three important reasons suggest themselves.

1. We live in unsettled times: experts who insure life and property tell us the risk of war is real and substantial. A sad fact, but not one we can ostrichlike ignore. And even if war does not come, national defense programs will be with us for the rest of our lives.

2. As economists we want to analyze war and defense problems for a selfish reason: our tools and principles really do work. Economics really does help win a war. You don't believe it? You think economic principles all become old-hat the day war is declared? Well, Adolf Hitler seems to have made precisely this mistake. After the war when our intelligence teams took over the German files and records, they uncovered a shocking ignorance of the basic principles of national income and economic mobilization. Dr. Hjalmar Schacht, the so-called wizard of German finance, let his obsessive fear of inflation sway the advice he gave on how much of an economic effort the Fatherland could "afford"—with the fatal result that Germany never did devote to war as large a fraction of her total resources as we did in England and America.

3. Finally, we must study the economics of war in order to understand the economics of peace. Here is one more example of the rule: *To learn about normal functioning, you must study pathological cases.* Certainly, nothing could be more pathological than the sight of two great powers waging total

war on a global scale; and yet the very size of the operation creates for us almost the controlled conditions of a laboratory experiment.

Do you want to study inflation? Great wars, alas, provide our most clear-cut examples. Do you wish to measure the potency of public finance? Then examine the fiscal record of wartime here and abroad. Do you doubt that the pricing system is constantly regulating the What, How, and For Whom of economic life? Then take a look at the intricate problems the War Production Board and Office of Price Stabilization must face when hot- or cold-war emergencies cause temporary suspension of the relatively free pricing system.

▶ FALLACIES ABOUT FINANCE

Today every schoolboy knows more about war economics than did the great statesmen and financiers of pre–World War I. Sir Norman Angell's best seller of that day, *The Great Illusion,* correctly pointed out that neither side could end up economically better off after an expensive modern war. The public interpreted this to mean that the war touched off by the summer assassination of Archduke Ferdinand would have to be over by Christmas, 1914. Four long and dreadful years proved the falsity of this economic guess.

But people learn slowly. Again in the summer of 1939 many pundits predicted that Hitler wouldn't go to war. Why not? Because he couldn't afford to. Why couldn't he afford to? Because Germany, according to usually reliable sources, had already spent the little gold she held. And of course with only one week's supply of gold, she couldn't hope to wage a war; etc. . . .

Today we know that war is a *total* national effort. Gone are the days when princes chivalrously jousted with each other; when a few mercenary soldiers engaged in limited battles, while the general populace went about its ordinary business of producing and consuming the national income. We moderns are astonished to read in the history books that an Englishman did not dream of interrupting his wintering on the French Riviera just because one of the minor wars between England and France was going on.

Of course, you don't fight a total war with gold.[1] You can't hurl paper bills at the enemy's trenches. You need guns and bullets, airplanes and bombs, submarines and torpedoes, missiles and warheads. You must block the enemy from his food supply and try by bribes or force to keep the few remaining neutrals from sending him strategic raw materials.

In short, we fight wars today with the *real national income*—with all of it.

---

[1] Do the leaders of the Soviet Union understand modern economics? According to the Bank for International Settlements at Basle, Russia produces one-seventh of the world's gold. Except for a little that sneaks into Switzerland or has been publicly sold to the Bank of England and other central banks, this gold seems to be hoarded by the Russian government. Could it be that the Kremlin gives too high grades to the outmoded Marxian theory concerning the importance of commodity-money? Could it be that hatred of the capitalistic system is insufficient for an understanding of it?

► **THE SINEWS OF WAR**

World War II confirmed what the economic theorist had learned during World War I: The sinews of war are the sinews of peace. That block of nations wins which has the greatest Gross National Product: *i.e.*, which has the most manpower in uniform and in military production; the most plentiful capacities and supplies of oil, steel, power, transport, coal, and light metals; and finally, the most advanced technology and industrial know-how.

Figure 1 gives rough estimates of the comparative strength of the Iron Curtain countries relative to the United States and Britain. The estimates are for 1958, and are moderately reassuring to us. But most of us have a long time still to live. And what we should like to see are similar figures for 1965 and 1975. Of course no one—not even the experts who spend all their time studying the facts about the Soviet Union—can more than guess as to the distant future. Still we do know that the planners in the Soviet Union are putting full steam ahead on their program of industrial expansion: some experts attribute to them a 6 per cent rate of expansion, which is double ours and which could give them by 1975 production equal to ours. But can they maintain this pace? Some doubt it. But no one doubts their progress in science.

► **REAL SOURCES OF THE WAR EFFORT**

There are but four sources from which an expanded war effort can come: (1) expansion of total output; (2) sacrifice of civilian consumption to release land, labor, and capital goods to the defense programs; (3) cutting down

The sinews of war are the sinews of peace:

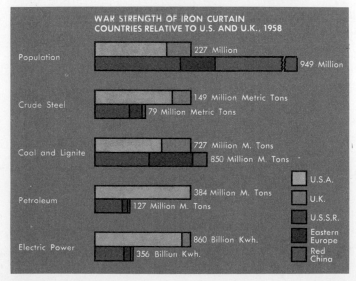

WAR STRENGTH OF IRON CURTAIN
COUNTRIES RELATIVE TO U.S. AND U.K., 1958

Population — 227 Million / 949 Million

Crude Steel — 149 Million Metric Tons / 79 Million Metric Tons

Coal and Lignite — 727 Million M. Tons / 850 Million M. Tons

Petroleum — 384 Million M. Tons / 127 Million M. Tons

Electric Power — 860 Billion Kwh. / 356 Billion Kwh.

U.S.A.
U.K.
U.S.S.R.
Eastern Europe
Red China

Fig. 1. The Iron Curtain nations are still behind in economic strength. But will the gap narrow? And how do you give a rating to international ballistic missiles and manmade satellites?

on gross capital formation, thereby releasing for defense resources that would otherwise go either to maintaining and replacing old capital or to producing net new capital goods; (4) getting goods by new borrowing from neutral nations abroad, or what amounts to the same thing, by selling them our holdings of their securities and letting them pay back what they owed us at the war's beginning. Let's look at each of these sources in turn.

1. *Expanding output.* If the economy has been depressed, unemployed men and machines can provide the slack for an increase in war or defense output. From 1939 to 1941, this was an important factor in the American defense program. However, in the 1960's no well-running nation will tolerate chronic deflationary policies and large-scale unemployment. So not much can be expected from this source in the future.

Nevertheless, even during normal full-employment times only part of our total population is gainfully employed in the labor force. We can vastly increase our total wartime manpower (includes womanpower, of course) in the following ways: Boys and girls can leave school and college early, working directly for the war effort or releasing someone else. Older people can put off retirement, or even come back from retirement. Housewives and women who work at home can take jobs while their husbands, fiancés, and friends are in the army and war plants. World War II showed that expansion of the labor force is especially important for a rich country like the United States, where a large fraction of the population does not normally work for pay.

An equally important expansion of manpower comes from our all working longer hours. Thus at one Cleveland plant during the war, people worked 84 hours a week—no less than 12 hours a day, every day of the week! And throughout industry the 40-hour normal week was augmented by overtime work. Round-the-clock shifts were the rule, with many a schoolteacher and factory worker holding down two jobs. Again, a rich country whose people normally enjoy much leisure can put on a fast wartime sprint by working longer hours to a degree not open to a poor country.

Not only can a war economy expand total man-hours; it can also try to increase output by raising the *productivity* of each man-hour. Economies of large-scale production may increase productivity—especially if you can concentrate on producing standardized shoes or equipment for the army and the populace. Capital, which ordinarily rusts away during the night, can do double or triple duty on extra shifts. By cutting down on various conveniences and services, retail stores can vastly increase the customers served by one clerk, thereby releasing manpower to military production or the armed services. Patriotism and the feeling of peril may cause workers to step up their pace, and managers and engineers to intensify their search for new methods. All this can greatly increase the total output available for the war.

2. *Converting civilian goods to war goods.* As a second source of output,

some civilian goods and resources can be *directly* converted to war programs: *e.g.,* the machine tool that builds tanks rather than trucks, the chauffeur who becomes a navigator. But most often, civilian goods are *indirectly* transformed into war goods. How? By the process of shifting productive factors from civilian to war output: *e.g.,* a whole radio factory with all its men and tools may turn to producing radar and walkie-talkies. Of course, it may take time to convert butter to guns—just when time is scarce.

What the war effort gains out of a fixed total, the public as consumers must lose. Just when those of us left on the home front are working hardest, we must consume least: we eat less and worse; we accept inferior goods; we pass up pleasure trips and make the old clothes do; we try to make our scarce gasoline drive our smooth-tired and aging cars as many miles as possible.

With everyone in the family working, and many working overtime, our *money* incomes are at a maximum. But our *real* consumable incomes have to be at a minimum, and in the national interest there must not be things for us to spend our money on! At such a time, when the total available for consumption is at a bare minimum, the voters often insist that it be distributed more evenly among the populace than in days of "normalcy."

3. *Capital formation for war use.* As much as one-eighth of the resources of society may be devoted during normal times to net capital formation—to producing new tools, new buildings, and new inventory. During the war such net investment can be cut down to the minimum: the resources released can go to the war effort. But that is not all. In normal times resources are being used to maintain and replace old capital equipment. And if we are willing to run down our capital, these resources too can be diverted to the war effort. Thus, all components of gross investment—including capital depreciation as well as net capital formation—can be tapped for a temporary war program.

During the last war, no one could build homes and stores, or paint and maintain his property. The only investment and construction permitted by the government was that related directly to the war effort—or related indirectly to it, as in the case of temporary housing for congested defense areas. The nation milked its capital, passing up normal additions to the civilian capital stock. Naturally we ended up with older and dingier homes, with roads in bad shape, with threadbare clothing and equipment—all sacrifices made in order to increase the current national product devoted to the war.

And don't forget irreplaceable raw materials. The rich Mesabi iron range of Minnesota went to war in 1917 and 1941 but won't go to war again. It's gone! Just another illustration that using up society's resources faster than they would be used up in peace is a third real source of the war effort.

4. *Foreign sources.* Today's trend is toward global wars: most neutral countries of World War I found themselves one by one involved in World War II; perhaps the next great conflict will involve two great blocks, with still fewer

neutrals. Taking the viewpoint of all the allied nations in a block, there may be no foreign areas from which substantial outside economic help can come. Certainly the enemy will not provide you with economic resources. And how you divide the burdens among allies—admittedly a major and vexing problem —is a problem within the family and quite a different one from outside aid.

Nevertheless, foreign borrowing was important in both world wars. England lost in World War I much of her foreign holdings. In World War II she lost much of the remainder; and—equally serious—after she had liquidated her holdings of property in India and elsewhere, she ran up huge sterling debts that she has had to honor gradually in the postwar.

Were another war to come, it is hard to envisage any European neutrals from whom the free nations could borrow. But some nations in Asia or Latin America might conceivably stay out of the conflict, and we might hope both to borrow from them and to permit repayments from them of such securities of theirs as we own. True, this would leave us poorer after the war than would otherwise have been the case. Why then rely on international borrowing? Because such international borrowing does provide a source for stepping up the military pace.

Remember, too, that this is a chapter on *defense* as well as one on *total* war. There is no need to rule out borrowing from third parties when you are engaged in limited battles in one region, as was the United States in Korea.

▶ **QUANTITATIVE ESTIMATES OF WAR POTENTIAL**

To summarize the major real sources of the war effort, let's hazard some rough quantitative guesses. Suppose our peacetime GNP is 500 billion dollars when war breaks out. How much of a war effort could we carry on? Neglecting unemployment, we still might expect an expansion of total output of one-fifth or of 100 billion dollars through increases in man-hours and productivity. Normal consumption activity of families and the government could be curtailed—releasing perhaps another 150 billion dollars to the war effort. If gross private investment usually averages about one-seventh of the GNP, we could hope to divert most of this to the war effort—picking up from this source, let's say, one-tenth of GNP or 50 billion dollars. Assuming but few neutrals in a world conflict, we can neglect foreign borrowing.

Where then do we come out? Table 1 gives a residual of 300 billion dollars to the war effort, equal to fully half the expanded 600 billion dollars wartime GNP. These of course are only rough and hypothetical guesses; but they are consistent with the World War II experience of Germany, the United Kingdom, and the United States, and they may err on the side of conservatism.

Note that Table 1 does not tell us how the total sacrifices are to be allocated among different families and businesses. That we shall discuss in the final

How the war GNP compares with the peace GNP:

Major components	Prewar situation	Wartime situation
Private consumption and government (includes normal defense)	$430	$280
Gross capital formation (purely civilian and domestic)	70	20
Net foreign investment	*	*
War effort	0	300
Gross National Product	$500	$600

Table 1. Hypothetical sources for economic war effort. (In billions of dollars; asterisk indicates less than 10 billion dollars.)

third of this chapter, when we grapple with our taxation and monetary policy; and the discussion of rationing and direct controls in the next third of this chapter will also bear on the interpersonal allocation of the war burden.

▶ **DETAILED ALLOCATION OF WAR RESOURCES: THE PROBLEM**

So far we have been talking about aggregates of national product. They are important, but here in the middle third of this chapter we must dig deeper. For, just as you can't hurl coin or paper money at the enemy, you can't defeat him in battle by throwing totals of real national product at him. Thousands and millions of detailed decisions must be made concerning just what shall be the best division between sea and air power; just how many tanks and guns of each kind are to be produced; just how many spare razor blades each infantryman shall carry; and so forth.

Does this exaggerate the minuteness of the items and the multiplicity of decisions? When you stop to think that the builder of one bomber has to keep track of 15,000 separate parts and components, and when you generalize this to the myriad of goods and services that must be produced in the war years, you realize how tremendous the task of organizing a war effort really is. No few planners in Washington can hope to cope with its working details; all that those at the top can do is lay down the broad outlines.

▶ **BASIC RELIANCE ON THE PRICING MECHANISM**

How, then, does the vast job get done? Recall how the half million items in the Sears Roebuck catalogue get produced. Not by a central plan. Not by antlike instinct. How then? Primarily by the almost miraculous coordination of a pricing system, of a market system.[1] Along with every other resource in the nation, the pricing mechanism too must go to war. So basic is its function, so omnipresent is the influence of the pricing system, that we are in danger of

[1] Recall the earlier discussion of pricing in Chapter 3 and in Parts Three and Four.

overlooking it entirely. Remember then that all the tools of supply and demand, of cost curves and production, apply directly to war economics.

If the war is a limited one, the government may introduce few emergency interferences with the price mechanism. This doesn't mean the government can neglect taking economic action: as we shall see in the final third of this chapter, it is particularly when the government is relying on free use of the pricing mechanism that it must successfully solve the problems of wartime taxation and monetary policy. For let us never forget that market prices respond to dollar votes. To whose dollar votes? To any dollar votes. And what does this imply? It means the government must take dollar votes away from consumers, and must divert the effective dollar votes in the direction of essential war goods. So, aside from direct fiats, the government must solve the fiscal and monetary problems—as will be discussed shortly.

▶ NO FIATS, ALL FIATS, OR WHAT?

Judging from the experience of every single one of the belligerent countries in both world wars, we must consider it likely that every country will go beyond a free pricing system in any serious struggle for its national survival. Every businessman, every labor leader, every politician, every man in the street takes this for granted. But the economist can take nothing for granted in his own field. If the pricing system works quite efficiently in peacetime, why not rely solely on it in war?

Indeed, a few reputable economists have followed their logic to its ultimate conclusion. "Tolerate no wartime fiats interfering with supply and demand," they say. To the practical man of affairs who regards the betting odds in favor of some wartime government controls as virtually certain, this view may seem of only academic interest. Still a textbook is the one place to explore, at least briefly, academic matters.

An absurd case will test the extreme view and elucidate the issue. Why draft soldiers? Instead of using coercive fiats, why not bribe men into the army by raising your offering price until you get the millions of men you need? Do you think this preposterous? Do you think that even when the government raised the wages of battle-duty soldiers to 1 million dollars per year it might not get the needed number? Then, the answer to the dilemma is clear: increase your bid to 2 million dollars, until at a high enough equilibrium price you coax out a sufficient supply. So the argument goes.

Perhaps you will object, "There isn't enough money in the community to pay 10 million soldiers each 2 million dollars; that adds up to 20 million million dollars, which is 40 times as great as our total GNP of 500 billion dollars and we still haven't paid for their guns and uniforms or for the necessary food of defense-plant workers."

As an economic theorist, I still have the following answer for you: "Let's put a tax of 2 million dollars on each young male whose blood pressure and general health meet certain specifications. Knowing he must pay this, and knowing that only the army pays wages of such amount, what will such a young male do? He will—for he *must*—accept the army employment."

Now, what have we accomplished? By free use of the pricing system, plus heavy reliance on the traditional powers of the government to tax, we have indeed succeeded in recruiting our army. But now we must ask ourselves whether the result is really much different from the strongest use of government fiat—namely, coercing a man to risk his life to save his country.

Just because we draft men into the army, don't think logic compels us to use direct controls everywhere else, or anywhere else. Still the analytic lessons to be gleaned from this extreme case would seem to be the following:

The changed conditions of war must create great changes in the *relative* prices arrived at in free markets. Some people would gain; some would lose. If the government had ideally efficient taxing powers, it could take from the winners and compensate the losers so as to end up with the nation's desired final outcome. But all taxing involves frictions and inefficiencies; so, in principle, it is quite possible for you to introduce more inefficiencies into the economic system by avoiding fiats than come from fiats alone. So goes the argument.

Does this mean we should go to the other extreme and rely completely on fiats, dispensing with the price mechanism? Rather, most statesmen and economists would probably draw the middle-of-the-road conclusion:

It is mostly a matter of degree. Depending upon the duration and extent of the emergency, nations rely on different degrees of temporary controls. In and of themselves controls are evils to be invoked only when their alternatives involve greater delay or ineffectiveness.

At this point a textbook writer must flash the signal: Stop, look, and listen —controversial area! So examine the issues with care and carefully scrutinize the arguments on both sides.

▶ **WARTIME GOVERNMENT CONTROLS**

We may list the principal government controls in order of their likelihood of being established; *i.e.,* the last listed controls are least likely to be introduced, while the first listed are likely to be introduced in even a moderate emergency.

1. *Allocation of strategic materials and granting of priorities.* A production board issues permits for aluminum, steel, magnesium, and other scarce materials essential for the military and for defense production. Before firms can supply buyers who have no priorities, they must set aside supplies to honor the needs of essential users who have priorities. Often different orders or classes of priorities are given out. This is because of the tendency for each class of pri-

ority to be overissued—so that unless you have an AAA-Essential priority you may not get your needed amount at the time you need it.

2. *Selective credit controls.* The Federal Reserve Board may use its powers to put limits on home mortgage borrowing, increasing the percentage of down payments and making borrowing terms generally less favorable. It may discourage installment buying by increasing down payments and shortening amortization periods for furniture, consumer durable goods, and charge-account loans generally. It may try to discourage stock-market speculation by increasing margin requirements, from 70 to 85 per cent or even to 100 per cent. Necessarily these measures bear down hardest on the man without much cash. In the post-Korean period they proved very potent, and for this very reason finally aroused considerable opposition.

3. *Particular price controls.* Goods that are especially in demand or short in supply may have their prices frozen; *e.g.,* auto prices may be held down to some maximum by order of a price stabilization authority. It may issue orders covering not only goods but also services (such as housing rentals).

4. *General price freeze.* Particular maximum prices have a way of spreading: if you control bread prices you soon feel you must control dough prices. When you find yourself issuing so many special price regulations that the unregulated good begins to be the exception, you may have recourse to a *general* price stop. This puts the burden of the proof on any price increase, and was resorted to in World War I, in World War II, and in 1951 following the Korean emergency. Various formulas for permitting limited price increases may be applied, with all price increases requiring approval by the authorities.

5. *Wage controls.* At the same time that goods are becoming scarce, labor probably becomes scarce. A war labor board is likely to freeze wage rates, requiring approval for any further increases in wage rates or "fringe benefits" (vacations with pay, pensions, health benefits, etc.). The authorities may make their approvals of increases depend upon the permitted rise in controlled prices of the goods consumed by labor. When soldiers are dying, wages are deemed subject to control; when wages are controlled, prices and profits are deemed subject to control. Thus direct controls tend to ramify.

6. *Consumer rationing.* Keeping prices from rising is a little like controlling the temperature in your home by not letting the thermometer rise. You are tackling symptoms, rather than removing the fundamental scarcity brought on by war. What can the government do to keep the unsatisfied demanders, who cannot get goods at the official prices, from putting upward pressure on prices or from spilling over into illegal "black markets"? It may finally introduce ration tickets or coupons. Then to buy sugar or gasoline you will need tickets as well as money: by this rationing device, the demand can be cut down to the level of supply available at the frozen prices.

In the first stages of rationing, there may be separate tickets for each of the principal scarce goods. But at a later stage when everything is scarce, it may be more efficient to introduce point rationing. This is almost like introducing a new kind of money: in return for so many brown stamps, you can have so much pork; for a different number of brown stamps, you can have so much beef. This point system gives people a measure of free choice in spending their total brown stamps; it does this in the hope that the supplies will go to those who want and need them most. Where clothing rather than meat is concerned, blue ration stamps may provide the points of currency. And still other colors may be used for other constellations of scarce goods.

Of course, the logical conclusion of this use of artificial points would be—what? Perhaps to wipe out all money for the war's duration, replacing the prewar currency by an entirely new temporary money in amounts geared to the emergency situation? In its extreme form this has nowhere been introduced. And it need not be. For reflection and our later analysis show that properly handling the tax and fiscal policy of the government may let us do without many of these direct controls; proper fiscal and banking policies may permit our ordinary money to function reasonably well during the war emergency.

7. *Direct manpower controls.* If the emergency is very grave, the manpower authorities may go beyond drafting young men into the army; they may introduce direct restrictions on the freedom of civilians—women, old folks, everyone—to pick their own jobs. By threatening to draft those not in essential lines, the government coerces people into desired channels. By requiring all hiring to be done through official placement agencies and by steering job applicants into essential industries, production can be guided into the crucial wartime areas.

Some nations have gone farther and laid down by fiat just where unattached workers of given age and sex must work. But thus far in the United States no emergency has seemed grave enough to require such stringent action.

▶ ECONOMIC ANALYSIS OF CONTROLS

With the possible exception of controls that simply freeze prices, all our direct controls can be given a simple interpretation in terms of supply and demand. They all tend to shift demand curves for less essential civilian goods downward and to the left, and to shift the supply curves for essential war goods rightward. With what result? With a resulting tendency to keep prices of both kinds of goods from rising as much as would otherwise be the case. (To be sure you understand this, go back to Chapter 20's Fig. 2 to see how consumer rationing affects supply and demand. Show that priority allocations have the same effect on the market for strategic materials.)

Symptom treating. Fixing maximum prices by itself does nothing to increase supplies of scarce goods. Were the government weak and the citizenry not law-abiding, such price fixing would probably fail to limit the demand. The upward pressure on the legal price, created by the fringe of unsatisfied demanders, might send the market price (now a "black-market price") upward—thus rendering the price freeze nonoperative. Still in the United States, the United Kingdom, Scandinavia, Germany, and many other countries, experience shows that price controls can be made to work. Of course, there will always be some lawbreaking; and the longer the controls are in effect and the less the national emergency, the greater will be the strain on the regulations.

However, assuming that direct controls are perfectly enforceable, we must still raise the question: Do they tackle only the symptoms of scarcity? Does suppressing an inflation accomplish anything?

These are hard questions to answer briefly. Probably the man in the street regards direct controls as being more important than they are, and perhaps professional economists think them less important than they are.

Price controls do affect symptoms. But an inflationary situation is a psychological situation, and every psychiatrist will tell you that, where human psychology is concerned, affecting symptoms may have genuine effects on the patient's condition. Believing prices frozen, people sometimes relax their frantic buying. Thus after general price controls were introduced in 1951, the wave of post-Korean consumer spending did subside—so much so that the controls seemed scarcely needed. It must be frankly admitted that no one knows how much credit to give for this to these price controls as against the monetary, fiscal, and extraneous events taking place at the same time.

The wartime "disequilibrium system." There is an additional important effect of price controls. Professor J. Kenneth Galbraith of Harvard University developed an interesting hypothesis out of his World War II experience as Deputy Price Administrator of the Office of Price Administration.[1] He sets up the notion of a "disequilibrium system" that remained in almost miraculous equilibrium: (1) Firms, particularly large ones, have to "administer" their prices even in normal times; so under regulation they largely followed the law, with only the little ones doing much cheating. (2) Consumers were primarily law-abiding, and when they couldn't spend their money on durable consumers' goods and other scarce items, they didn't let their money spill over into other goods but rather *let it spill over automatically into induced saving. I.e.,* price controls did go beyond symptom treating and did really help to close the gap of inflation by automatically creating a larger volume of wartime saving.

General-price-rise fallacy. Before leaving the difficult subject of direct controls, we must point out a common instance of the fallacy of composition. Letting the price of oranges rise so as to clear their single market can indeed be expected to solve a scarcity of oranges. And that's the end of it. But suppose *everything* is scarce in time of war; and suppose you have not introduced the needed fiscal and monetary policies. Then you must beware of the seductive

---

[1] J. K. GALBRAITH, *A Theory of Price Control* (Harvard University Press, Cambridge, Mass., 1952).

analogy which says that you can apply to all market prices the reasoning valid for one small part.

Why is this analogy fallacious? Because in the case of all markets, a price rise does not end the story. Why not? Because the rise in general prices will automatically and immediately result in an increase in the total incomes of all of us in the country. Then in the next period we have more income to spend. So prices must rise again. And away we go in a vicious circle of "open inflation" which keeps from period to period recreating an inflationary gap.

If neither suppressed nor open inflation provides the answer to war finance, what then is the answer? We shall have to find it in the realm of over-all fiscal and monetary policy, to which we now turn.

► WAR FINANCE: FISCAL POLICY AND MONETARY POLICY

In the first part of this chapter we analyzed the true sinews of war and the genuine economic sources for the real national product needed to wage a war. In the second part we discussed how market prices and controls determine the correct allocation at the microscopic level of these real aggregates. In this final part, problems of over-all monetary finance now come into focus.

We shall see that the government must adopt a tax program that will (1) prevent inflation and inflationary pressure during the war, (2) lessen inflationary pressure after the war or toward the end of a long war, (3) allocate the wartime sacrifices among the populace in the manner deemed most equitable by the country and its legislators, and (4) provide as much incentive as is needed for people to expand effort and ingenuity. Compromises among these different goals will of course have to be made.

Early in this chapter we learned that the real burden of a war can be shifted to future generations in but two ways: by depleting capital and not adding to it during the war; and by real borrowing from abroad and having to repay in real goods after the war. Neither of these operations is directly connected with the simple question: Shall we handle the monetary finance of war by taxing or by borrowing? Once you avoid the mistaken identification of the shifting-real-burden-through-time problem and the taxing-or-borrowing problem, don't conclude: Wartime taxation doesn't matter. It does matter —as we shall now see.

► TAXATION TO PREVENT CURRENT WARTIME INFLATION

Since World War I economists have given this advice to politicians and the public:

Raise more revenue for war expenditure from taxes; raise less than you have been doing from issuing bonds.

Do this for the fundamental reason of reducing the rate of price inflation or of inflationary pressure. That is, tax in order to cut down on civilian spending; tax so that resources will be voluntarily released to the war effort; in short, tax to prevent too many money votes from coming on the market and bidding up prices or putting pressure on price ceilings.

This follows from common sense. In Table 1 the government wants 50 per cent of the peak wartime Gross National Product. But it is the people as a whole—land, labor, and capital—who are producing the gross product. And —so long as taxes aren't brought into the picture—100 per cent of it is going to them as spendable income. With 100 per cent of the national income to spend and only 50 per cent of it available in the form of civilian goods to be bought, what will people do? You know the answer. They will bid up prices; and unless administrators are omnipotent and omniscient, resources will be sucked out of the war effort and back into civilian goods. Only the enemy would like that.

There is really but one way out. *Tax and tax heavily so that the war goods expenditure can be financed with dollars that would otherwise go for civilian goods.* Could this mean the war should be financed without any deficit, completely from taxes and not at all from borrowing? Taken by itself, our argument can certainly call for a balanced war budget.[1]

▶ NATIONS' FAILURE TO TAX IN BOTH WARS

Table 2 shows that nations have not followed to the letter the economist's advice to pay for war largely by current taxes. France was a victor in the first war, and yet her taxes were only 4 per cent of the total. Imperial Germany lost the first war; but she did hold off the powerful alliance against her for four long years; and when final defeat came, it was in battle and not due to her failure to raise more than 12 per cent of her war costs from taxes. In the first war, the United States raised only 30 per cent of total cost from taxes; the rest came from a rise in national debt, which rose from practically nothing to what was then regarded as the colossal figure of 26 billion dollars.

By World War II governments were more closely following the advice to tax. Yet, the country that depended relatively most on taxes, Canada, still had to rely 43 per cent on borrowing. Our own record in the United States was

[1] It could even require the government to raise taxes by more than its expenditure, thereby running a wartime surplus. This is because starting out from full employment, we cannot be satisfied to give the public back *in expenditure* an amount *equal* to what we collect from them *in taxes;* for, after all, that would leave them with unchanged incomes and unchanged private expenditure on real resources. To get the public actually to *cut down* on their real spending, we might have to tax them *more* than we pay out in war expenditure. However, since it is politically too difficult even to approach a balanced budget, we needn't spend much time on the goal of *over*balancing the war budget. To review the deflationary effects of taxes reread Chapter 12, Section C, and also fiscal policy discussions of Chapters 17 and 18.

In the last war nations taxed more:

War	United States	United King-dom	Can-ada	Ger-many	France	Rus-sia
World War I	30	29	16	12	4	4
World War II	45	52	57	35	not avail-able	not avail-able

Table 2. Percentage of war expenditures raised by taxation. Economists think the after-war inflation would have been less had we relied less on war-time deficits.

better than in the first war, but we still paid for less than half the war effort in current taxes. By the end of the war our national debt had grown fivefold, reaching a quarter of a trillion dollars by 1945, which went beyond 12 months' national income.

According to our analysis, (1) diverting extra product to the war while (2) failing to tax away people's extra income generated by that extra product should (3) raise United States prices and produce inflationary pressure. Why didn't it in 1940–1945? Well, in part it did: prices did rise a little; and there were certainly many signs of at least mild inflationary pressure. But the economist must confess that there was a puzzling absence of the disaster predicted by a crude version of his theory.

The answer must apparently be found in the potency of direct controls mentioned earlier, and the increase in civilian voluntary or involuntary saving. (Recall Galbraith's almost-too-good-to-be-true "disequilibrium system.")

▶ WARTIME TAXATION TO PREVENT POSTWAR INFLATION

Though we partially suppressed inflation during the war, after the war the nation tired of direct controls and their potency diminished. When most controls were finally repealed, there was a belated upward surge of prices; and today most of us think of each prewar dollar as the equivalent of about two of our postwar dollars. So we had our war inflation *after,* not during, the war.

This suggests a second important argument for wartime taxation:

Tax during the war lest by deficit-financing you create an ever-increasing amount of currency or bonds that people may try to spend in the postwar, or later in the war if it drags on. Even if you can suppress the wartime inflation, the financial claims that pile up because of failure to tax may plague you in the postwar—particularly since after a war people will have many important needs and wants that had to be postponed during the war. (If you fear deflation after the war, this argument goes into reverse.)

▶ DISADVANTAGES OF HEAVY WAR TAXES

If common sense tells us taxing is desirable to prevent inflation during and after the war, why do nations stubbornly refuse to pay for war largely by taxes? There must be some good arguments against using taxes. A few follow:

1. *Pain of taxation.* Taxes hurt. They take away spendable income and make us do without. This is a strong political argument against heavy wartime taxation. Of course, you will note that it misses the crucial point of our earlier discussion and Table 1: civilians do without because the nation's war effort needs resources; it is the war activity and not the tax bill that puts the burden on the civilian community as a whole—and if there were no taxes but goods were doled out by fiat, the same war effort would impose the same total burden on the civilian community.

2. *Interpersonal impact of taxation.* Table 1 deals only in totals and tells nothing about how much different families sacrifice. Some families find their incomes before taxes little changed by the war and may already be near the minimum of subsistence. If the government wants to take half the GNP for war and pay completely by taxation, it will have to legislate very steep tax rates and such a family will find itself very hard hit. Such a man and wife will write to their congressman and say: "We prefer rationing and suppressed inflation. We think you should raise taxes most on those who have had an increase in earnings attributable to the war."

Their congressman may be sympathetic toward some kind of "excess-profits" or "increment-of-income-over-prewar" taxation. However, if he is a man of experience, he knows how hard it is to identify profiteering due to the war; and he knows that taxing heavily those with rising incomes may most favor those already wealthy and may tend to lower social mobility and initiative.

3. *Adverse incentive effects.* This raises a final objection to exclusive reliance on heavy taxation. The country wants each person to give his best of effort and ingenuity. Heavy war taxation may mean that each bit of extra effort will have most of its fruits taxed away from the individual; consequently we may lose output if we rely completely on taxes.[1]

To answer this argument you may be tempted to say: "The war economy can't afford to give up real goods to reward people for making extra effort." But what about the alternative of rewarding the ingenious eager beaver by giving him a claim on postwar output rather than leaving him with a worthless receipted bill for taxes paid? In effect that is what bond financing can do.

▶ GENERAL CONCLUSIONS ON TAXING

We may summarize the tax issue. On the one hand we should tax heavily to prevent current and subsequent inflation; and we should tax in a pattern aimed at the desired sharing of the war sacrifices and burdens. But on the

---

[1] Excess-profits taxes and high income taxes point up the conflict between "equity" and "incentives." During war the clash may be less because heavy taxes, at the same time that they discourage effort at the margin, do make people feel poorer and therefore often willing to work harder. In advanced economic theory this is known as a clash between "income-effect" and "substitution-effect."

other hand, heavy taxing away of the fruits of effort may harm wartime incentives and output; so a case can be made for some reliance on borrowing —to give people extra rewards in the postwar for their extra wartime exertions.

Note that, by relying on borrowing, we change the postwar pattern of income distribution in favor of those who are permitted to accumulate bonds rather than having their surpluses taxed away from them. The postwar redistribution comes about through interest and principal payments on the war debt. The taxation needed to make such transfer payments will necessarily have some distorting effects on the postwar economy. And, as we saw in Chapter 18, these distortions are the true burden of an internally held debt.

As is usual in economics, war finance is a case where things are not all black or white: there are some valid arguments against too heavy reliance on wartime current taxing. If you could imagine a controlled experiment in which one nation taxed 100 per cent while an exactly similar nation paid for an exactly similar war partially by borrowing, suppressing inflation by more stringent direct controls, what could you confidently predict from economic theory? That the virtuous taxing nation would necessarily fare better? Unfortunately economic theory is not that exact.

What economists would mostly agree on is a more moderate statement—that warring nations often for political reasons tax less than the optimal amount.

▶ WARTIME MONETARY AND DEBT-MANAGEMENT POLICY

In a total war, governments are virtually certain to rely on borrowing and fiats. The pressure on resources is then likely to be very great. But paradoxically, monetary policy is not likely to be then so crucial; it is in a more limited war, when the pressure on resources is not so great, that monetary policy may be most important. Why this paradox? Because during limited war we probably would put on the brakes by conventional Central Banking techniques in order to discourage private investment. But in an all-out engagement, private civilian investment would, no doubt, already be under severe direct controls; so in a sense there would be less need then for Central Banking tight-money interest policies.

The mechanics of contractionary Central Banking policy were reviewed in Chapters 16 and 17 of Part Two. The Federal Reserve Banks can follow a policy of open-market operations that will keep Member Bank reserves tight —so tight as to cause the interest yield on old and new government bonds to be very high. With interest rates high and with bank credit so tight that bankers are doling it out very sparingly to would-be borrowers, there will be downward pressure on civilian investment. In fact there may be some downward pressure on necessary defense investment; and this is an argument for supplementing over-all credit restraint with selective controls that favor essential and penalize unessential activities.

Will a tight credit policy cut down on consumption as well as on invest-ment? Except in the areas of borrowing that can best be reached by the selec-tive credit controls mentioned earlier, little reduction in the propensity to consume (and increase in the propensity to save) seems to result from manip-ulation of interest rates. Why? Because it seems to be a fact of statistical experi-ence, and it is also a conclusion of the economic theory of consumption, that the elasticity of consumption with respect to interest rates alone is of unknown sign and presumably of small degree. It is primarily in the investment realm that monetary policy's favorable results are to be found.

During World War I countries generally let interest rates rise as the war continued; and yet prices rose. In World War II, countries generally relied much less on tight-interest policies, relying more on fiscal policy and more on direct controls; *e.g.*, in the United States interest rates were pegged at fixed levels from 1942 until after the war. So unimportant was the role of monetary policy regarded that in the middle of the war a threat was made to take away the air-conditioning system from the Washington Federal Reserve Building and to transfer it to an "essential war agency" like the War Production Board.

However it is a safe prediction, based on postwar experience, to expect more reliance on tight-money policies in any future limited war. Here is but one example. After the Korean incident the United States Treasury and Federal Reserve Board came to an "accord": as we saw, this gave the "Fed" freedom to tighten up on the cost and availability of credit as a device to help curb inflation.

▶ **DEBT MANAGEMENT DURING THE WAR**

So far we have said nothing about the way in which the wartime budgetary deficit is to be financed. By printing new money? By printing new bonds and selling them to the public? By printing new bonds and selling them to the Member Banks? By printing new bonds and selling them directly or indirectly to the Federal Reserve Banks?

Obviously during a serious war emergency, the government must do every-thing it can to get people to cut down on their consuming and investment. If patriotic bond campaigns can get them to cut spending, such campaigns are to be recommended. But to the extent that such campaigns succeed only in getting people to hold their old and new savings in the form of bonds rather than currency or bank deposits—to this extent, bond campaigns do not lessen the need for current contractionary fiscal policy. (During the war there is probably no particular advantage in having people hold bonds rather than deposits. But after the war, won't people who have committed their savings more largely to bonds be a little slower to rush out to spend than those who have simply added to their cash and deposits?)

We may suppose that the appeals to patriotism and the promotion of bond sales is carried as far as possible. And we may suppose a tight monetary policy, which we have seen raises the interest return on bonds, may further encourage people to hold their savings in the form of bonds rather than nonyielding cash and bank deposits. But even when all this is done, in all probability the government will still have bonds that must be sold elsewhere.

What the government cannot sell to nonbanks it must sell to the banks. But banks can buy only as many bonds as they have reserves to justify. Typically, therefore, the Treasury will sell part of the war debt to the Federal Reserve Banks and part to the Member Banks.[1]

The important thing is not the numerical ratios in which bonds go to commercial banks and the Central Bank. Primarily remember this: The money managers can carry on war borrowing in a regime of high interest rates or of pegged lower interest rates. And the Treasury and Federal Reserve can between them decide to put the emphasis on short-term borrowings or longer-term borrowings.

During the war emergency, the decision as to how tight to make money may not be so important as it will become in the postwar. Then, regardless of the wartime composition of the debt, the monetary authorities will have to decide on how much tightness to produce in the credit markets. For more of this, see our earlier discussions of the mechanisms of monetary policy.

▶ SUMMARY OF MONETARY AND DEBT POLICY

We may summarize debt and money policy by the following brief statements:

Taxing, direct and selective controls, plus patriotic campaigns, all aim to cut down on spending. Monetary credit tightness aims to cut down on inessential investment. The resulting accumulating savings of the nation can then be matched by large government deficits. The new bonds will be taken in part directly by the public or indirectly by their insurance companies. But only in part. The remaining amounts will have to be sold to the banking system—with the Federal Reserve Banks taking part in order to provide the needed reserves for the Member Banks to be able to take on the other part. The really fundamental question is always: How tight is credit to would-be spenders, and how much are they able and willing to spend out of their current incomes after taxes? All else is secondary detail.

---

[1] Suppose required legal reserve rates average about 20 per cent; and suppose the banks already have barely enough reserves to take care of their essential borrowers. Then as the government runs a war deficit year after year, it will probably have to sell about one-fifth of the bonds it can't sell to the public to the Federal Reserve Banks. When the government spends the deposit created for it at the Federal Reserve Banks, this will cause somebody's deposit in the Member Banks to go up; and this will give the Member Banks enough new legal reserves to buy the other four-fifths of the new bonds that the Treasury has to sell inside the banking system. (Review Chapters 15, 16, and 17 if this seems strange. And note: If legal reserve requirements were reduced to one-seventh, only one-seventh of the bonds need be sold to the Federal Reserve Banks.)

▶ **EPILOGUE: A BLITZKRIEG?**

Generals, we are told, have the fatal weakness of preparing for the last war. Economists face the same danger. World War II was not like World War I. Why should World War III be like World War II? What about the hydrogen bomb and the intercontinental ballistic missile?

America and Europe are urban economies. Wipe out 300 cities in the first hour of the war and you immobilize most of their populations—moreover, that part of the population most important for war production and defense.

Pinpoint your attack against key steel mills, oil refineries, aluminum plants, power stations, rail yards, and ship docks—and what is left of the sinews of war? Of what avail then our high peacetime Gross National Product?

There is no blinking these stern facts. What follows from them? It goes without saying that every attempt has to be made to keep there from being another total war. How? Disarmament? Build-up of retaliatory strength so no enemy will ever dare attack? Recourse to "limited" warfare? Dispersion of our cities and strategic industries? Construction of expensive early-warning radar systems? Stockpiling of essential matériel in underground caches and construction of subterranean armament factories?

You know these important questions cannot be decided in terms of economics alone. What the economist can do is to give two important insights.

Postblitz pricing. First, since the possibility of a blitzkrieg cannot be ruled out, *defense planners should be evaluating military resources not in terms of present market values but rather in terms of their true values to the economy on the day after a bad continental bombing.*

What does this mean? It means that steel in a place unlikely to be bombed has what the insurance underwriters in Lloyd's of London would call a much higher "actuarial value" than does steel in a vulnerable spot. The same holds for refinery capacity, jet-fuel inventories, etc.

Why can't businessmen, responsible to their stockholders, be expected to take this postbombing view in making their decisions? Because they know, if they've learned anything from history, that after a great emergency no society lets those people lucky enough to be left with crucial resources auction them off for whatever they're then worth. Just imagine the cries of "Profiteer!" that would follow. Result: Prudent businessmen won't use postbombing valuations in making their strategic decisions, and the pricing system may have to be supplemented by hardheaded government defense planning.

Affording what you must. The second general insight the economist can give is this: Defense is an expensive business. It uses up resources. It adds to inflationary pressures. It causes administrators and congressmen economic headaches. But that doesn't mean we should cut it back. We should cut it back only when it's not needed. It's the duty of public leaders to suffer headaches —in a necessary cause.

An elder statesman once said, "Inflation is worse than Stalin." The neo-classical synthesis, which insists upon the potency of monetary and fiscal programs, suggests that any inflationary pressures resulting from our needed defense *can* be offset—if there is a will to do so.

Experience suggests that there are no basic reasons why we cannot afford more economic defense if the situation truly calls for it. And most experts believe economic principles bear out these facts of experience.

SUMMARY

1. Wars are fought with real national product, not with monetary symbols. The sinews of war are real resources: steel, oil, . . . , etc. The four real sources of an expanded war effort are: expanded total output, sacrifice of civilian consumption, sacrifice of gross capital formation, and foreign loans involving real borrowing from abroad. Don't confuse the real-burden-shifting-through-time problem with the tax-or-borrow problem. They are distinct.

2. The thousands and millions of microscopic real decisions concerning real totals are largely made—even during wars—by the market and pricing mechanism. But the more serious the war, the greater the likelihood of the government's introducing such direct controls as allocations and priorities, selective credit controls, individual price controls, general price freezes, wage controls, rationing, and manpower regulations. Many of these direct controls operate directly to limit demand; but some primarily seem to tackle symptoms. Yet during the war, effective control of symptoms may, as in the so-called "disequilibrium system," affect genuine causes; and direct controls may have redistributive effects not easily attainable from conventional taxation.

3. Increased taxes are needed during war to curb dollar votes by civilians, in order to release resources to the war effort. Aside from their current deflationary impact, wartime taxes prevent the accumulation of liquid wealth (currency, deposits, insurance assets, bonds, etc.) that may create inflationary pressures later—after the war or toward the end of a lengthy war.

4. Nations in fact have not relied fully on current wartime taxes. Heavy taxes do have harmful incentive effects on current wartime efforts, and an economic case can be made for using loan finance to provide for rewards in the postwar to those who create extra income during the war.

5. Conventional contractionary monetary policy can, by making credit dear and unavailable, contribute toward curtailing private investment spending. Depending upon patriotic campaigns and the interest policy introduced, the banking system will nevertheless still be confronted with a larger or smaller total of bonds that have to be bought. If Member Banks are to have needed reserves to buy bonds, the Federal Reserve Banks will have to buy a fraction of the created debt. How much must be sold to the banks will depend of course on general tax and monetary policies adopted. These are fundamental.

6. A third world war raises the problem of an all-out blitzkrieg. This makes postbombing evaluations and pricing a must for defense planners. And it raises the question of how much defense an economy can really "afford."

QUESTIONS FOR DISCUSSION

1. After reading this chapter, what fallacies about war economics can you list? What is superficially attractive about each, and what is fallacious?

2. Without detracting from the personal glories of Ulysses S. Grant and Robert E. Lee, show how an amateur economic historian would compare the real national incomes of the North and South in 1860 and what he would conclude about the betting odds on which side would win the Civil War. Give a historical case where the economic underdog won. (Hint: Fall of Rome?)

3. Using Table 1, draw up a list of the four sources from which the 300-billion-dollar war effort comes, showing the quantitative importance of each.

4. If a defense effort is solely guided by *pricing,* describe the changes.

5. Make a list of the different direct controls used in time of war. In terms of supply and demand and other economic principles, show how each is supposed to work.

6. Describe how Galbraith's "disequilibrium system" closed the inflationary gap by automatically creating a high enough propensity-to-save schedule. What if people had tried to spend on other goods the money they couldn't spend on the unavailable goods? If wars come close together, people are likely to remember the inflation of the last war. Will they then behave in the convenient manner described by Galbraith?

7. The Nazi occupiers of Belgium and Norway confiscated the plates to print money and flooded those economies with newly printed currency. What problems did this create for their postwar governments? How might you call in or freeze the old currency, issuing new to people according to some graduated confiscation formula?

8. Give arguments for and against heavy wartime taxing. In what ways are "incentives" and "equity" in agreement or disagreement?

9. Why is there a postwar inflation threat? How is this likely to be affected by (*a*) heavy current taxing; (*b*) patriotic wartime voluntary saving; (*c*) sale of bonds to people rather than to banks or the Central Bank; (*d*) a forced wartime loan?

10. Review your understanding of the following concepts:

the sinews of war and peace
real sources of a war effort
pricing versus fiats
allocations, price and wage
    controls, rationing

shifting war burdens to future generations
wartime tax, debt, and money policies
postbomb pricing or evaluations
what an economy can "afford"

37 PROBLEMS OF ECONOMIC GROWTH AND DEVELOPMENT

I believe in materialism. I believe in all the proceeds of a healthy materialism,—good cooking, dry houses, dry feet, sewers, drain pipes, hot water, baths, electric lights, automobiles, good roads, bright streets, long vacations away from the village pump, new ideas, fast horses, swift conversation, theatres, operas, orchestras, bands,—I believe in them all for everybody. The man who dies without knowing these things may be as exquisite as a saint, and as rich as a poet; but it is in spite of, not because of, his deprivation.

FRANCIS HACKETT, *Ireland*

All the economic principles we have learned can now be brought to bear on perhaps one of the most challenging problems of the next quarter century—the problem of underdeveloped economies. There are about 3 billion people in the world. And at this moment two-thirds of them are hungry—literally hungry, even though it be right after meal time: only someone who has been pursuing beauty or health on a temporary diet of 1500 calories per day will know how food can fill one's dreams and every waking thought.

For our conscience' sake we are impelled to help. In addition, history teaches us that men do not always starve quietly.

▶ DEFINING UNDERDEVELOPMENT

Writers used to speak of "backward" nations, which naturally irritated the people of those lands. The United Nations to avoid offense sometimes used the roundabout expression "less-developed" nation. Today most people adopt the expression "underdeveloped" nation. What do they usually mean by the term? Many alternative definitions have been given but most seem to involve the following:

751

An underdeveloped nation is simply one with real per capita income that is low relative to the present-day per capita incomes of such nations as Canada, the United States, Great Britain, France, and Western Europe generally. Usually an underdeveloped nation is one regarded as being capable of substantial improvement in its income level.

Of course, every country is underdeveloped in the sense that it is not yet perfect and hence is capable of being improved still further. And even the so-called advanced countries were once underdeveloped by our definition and had to go through the process of development. Table 1 gives a picture of the relative stages of development of the different countries in the late 1950's.[1] Less than one-sixth of the world's population live in the Highly Developed Group (A); just over one-sixth live in the Intermediate Group (B); fully two-thirds live in the Underdeveloped Group (C).

Note that the Soviet Union now falls in the Intermediate Group. About one-third of the world's population live beyond the Iron Curtain. How are those people divided among the groups? Recalling the vast population of China, we find two-thirds of the Iron Curtain peoples falling in the lowest Group C, and none in Group A. Little wonder, then, that economic development is a lively subject on both sides of the Iron Curtain.

▶ CHARACTERISTICS OF UNDERDEVELOPED ECONOMIES

To bring out the contrasts between advanced and underdeveloped economies, imagine that you are a typical twenty-one-year-old in one of the underdeveloped countries, be it the little Central American country of El Salvador or the huge subcontinent of India. You are poor: even after making generous allowance for the goods you both produce and consume, your annual income averages less than $100 per head, as against $2,000 per head of your fellow man in America; perhaps you can find cold comfort in the thought that only one in ten of the human race averages more than $600 per year. To each of your people who can read, there are four like you who are illiterate. Your life expectancy is only half that of the average man in the advanced country: already two or three of your brothers and sisters have died before reaching adulthood; and though your mother has had fewer children than did your grandmother, thanks to imported medical techniques more of your brothers and sisters have lived to maturity, and with them you must compete for subsistence.

You work with but one-twentieth the mechanical horsepower of your prosperous fellow human. As a citizen of Asia, Africa, or Latin America, you and your fellows constitute 65 per cent of the world population; but you must divide up among you only 17 per cent of world income. You brood over the fact

[1] The author has relied heavily on the valuable study of the Council on Foreign Relations: EUGENE STALEY, *The Future of Underdeveloped Countries* (Harper, New York, 1954).

Most countries fall in the underdeveloped category:

Table 1. Countries grouped by level of economic development. (Source: Eugene Staley, *The Future of Underdeveloped Countries*, Harper, New York, 1954.)

A. Highly developed	Africa *(continued)* :	Americas *(continued)* :
Australia	Angola	Mexico
Belgium	Belgian Congo	Nicaragua
Canada	Cameroons	Paraguay
Denmark	Egypt	Peru
France	Ethiopia	
Germany	French Equatorial Africa	Asia:
Netherlands	French West Africa	Afghanistan
New Zealand	Ghana	Borneo
Norway	Kenya	Burma
Sweden	Liberia	Ceylon
Switzerland	Libya	China
United Kingdom	Madagascar	Formosa
United States	Morocco	India
	Mozambique	Indochina
B. Intermediate	Nigeria	Indonesia
Argentina	Nyasaland	Iran
Austria	Northern Rhodesia	Iraq
Chile	Ruanda-Urundi	Jordan
Cuba	Sierra Leone	Korea
Czechoslovakia	Southern Rhodesia	Lebanon
Finland	Sudan	Malaya
Hungary	Tanganyika	Nepal
Ireland	Tunisia	New Guinea
Israel	Uganda	Pakistan
Italy		Philippines
Japan	Americas:	Saudi Arabia
Poland	Bolivia	Syria
Portugal	Brazil	Thailand
Puerto Rico	British West Indies	Turkey
Spain	Colombia	Yemen
Union of South Africa	Costa Rica	
U.S.S.R.	Dominican Republic	Europe:
Uruguay	Ecuador	Albania
Venezuela	El Salvador	Bulgaria
	Guatemala	Greece
C. Underdeveloped	Haiti	Rumania
Africa:	Honduras	Yugoslavia
Algeria		

that the United States, with 6 per cent of the people, enjoys 40 per cent of the world income; and that Europe, with 25 per cent of the people, enjoys another 40 per cent.

▶ **URGENCY OF THE PROBLEM**

There have always been differences between rich and poor. Why worry especially about the problem of underdeveloped countries? We can list a number of reasons, all vital.

1. *Widening differentials.* In contrast to the narrowing of income differentials within the advanced nations, the divergence between advanced and underdeveloped countries is probably now widening rather than narrowing. Canada, the United States, and Western Europe have increased their production per head since 1938 by 40 per cent. Many authorities believe that living standards in India, Indonesia, and certain other underdeveloped countries have actually deteriorated during the same period.

2. *Ideological struggle.* In the modern ideological war between the free and the communist worlds, the communists regard the underdeveloped regions as our Achilles' heel of weakness. They ceaselessly agitate in such lands, never failing to point out the poverty there, never failing to contrast it with our wealth, never failing to remind the people there of real and fancied evils of "colonialism."

Alas! experience does not bear out the easy generalization, "Fill the stomachs of people and they will refrain from going communistic." Not necessarily: men in utter misery often seem incapable of revolting; and the big revolutions of the past (such as the French and Russian) have largely taken place at a time when some economic progress had already been achieved.

Nonetheless, to turn our backs on the problem of development is to court future disaster. Harvard's distinguished economic historian, Alexander Gerschenkron, has drawn the following important lesson from history:[1]

The Soviet government can be properly described as a product of the country's economic backwardness. Had serfdom been abolished by Catherine the Great or . . . in 1825, the peasant discontent, the driving force and the earnest of success of the Russian Revolution, would never have assumed disastrous proportions, while the economic development of the country would have proceeded in a much more gradual fashion. . . . The delayed industrial revolution was responsible for a political revolution in the course of which the power fell in the hands of a dictatorial government to which in the long run the vast majority of the population was opposed. . . . The paramount lesson of the twentieth century is that the problems of backward nations are not exclusively their own. They are just as much problems of the advanced countries. It is not only Russia but the whole world that pays the price for the failure to emancipate the Russian peasants and to embark upon industrialization policies at an early time. Advanced countries cannot afford to ignore economic backwardness.

To reinforce this point, tick off the advanced countries in *A* of Table 1.

[1] Alexander Gerschenkron, "Economic Backwardness in Historical Perspective," in Bert F. Hoselitz, editor, *The Progress of Underdeveloped Areas* (University of Chicago Press, Chicago, 1952), pp. 27–29.

Can you find a single one in which a successful violent proletarian revolution has taken place?

3. *Great expectations.* Within the underdeveloped countries, people are today acutely aware of their poverty. And they don't like it. What's more, they insist on doing something about it.

This was not always so: a century ago the Emperor of China sent a message to the King of England saying that his country neither needed nor desired economic improvement. Look at today's frantic efforts in China and mark the contrast. In the ancient formula

$$\text{Happiness} = \frac{\text{material consumption}}{\text{desire}}$$

Thoreau's counsel to hold down the denominator now gives way to insistence on increasing the numerator of material real income.

So perfect are modern instruments of communication that people everywhere know about—and often envy—the comforts of modern Western life. No longer do they shrug their shoulders and accept as the divine will of Allah their relative poverty. Most important, this increased awareness comes at a time when the role of government is highly developed. Today, when people want something done, they are likely to turn to government and to insist that programs be adopted toward the desired goal.

Reporting in his book *Strange Lands and Friendly People,* Justice William O. Douglas emphasized what he heard everywhere from the Mediterranean to the Pacific: We want better health; we want land reform, the breaking up of landowners' holdings; we want better methods of land cultivation; we want industrialization; we want our political rights as individuals. It is easy to see that men want these things for natural individualistic reasons. But economic welfare is not the only reason why men desire development. Justice Douglas and others observe that modern peoples desire development also for reasons of *nationalism:* people want their country to be powerful, to be respected, and—let us face it—to be feared. Thus, the English and Dutch may have brought sanitation to their former colonies; they may have thereby increased people's life spans and material well-being. But they did at the same time set up exclusive clubs whose front doors were barred to the native citizenry. "Freedom from contempt" is one Pakistani's way of describing the goal of his nation.

4. *Desired markets.* Altruism and political motivation aside, advanced economies have a selfish interest in growth of underdeveloped nations to provide markets for international trade. Writers who thought it foolish for us to help our competitors to develop were answered by the following argument: The statistical facts of history reinforce one's common-sense expectation that other countries will *import more from us as their national incomes grow*—a fact which has been inferred again and again by those who have studied the evi-

dence. Therefore, so the argument goes, we should favor economic development in order to expand our exports.

This argument is factually valid and does successfully refute false theories
of those who oppose development. But the issue is more complicated than any
simple statement can do justice to. Why after all do we want more trade?
Surely not for the sole purpose of increasing our mere dollar sales: we cannot
long continue to export without importing or lending; and our only valid selfish reason for wanting development abroad rests on *our desire to have foreign
economies grow up which display those differences in comparative advantage
that our earlier chapters have shown to be the sole basis for fruitful international exchange.*

Reverse the usual formulation and you will be more nearly correct: Rational self-interest makes us want other nations to develop so we can *import*
from them goods that we can less economically produce at home; *i.e.,* whenever our resources can produce exportable goods that will exchange for more
imported goods than can be directly produced at home with these same resources, then and only then is international trade truly advantageous. Here is
a single instance. The United States (and other advanced economies) have
great need for raw materials. The Paley Raw Materials Study found that with
each passing decade the needs will greatly grow, from our present 10 per cent
dependence to 30 or more per cent by 1975. To summarize:

Only to the degree that economic development abroad improves our "terms-of-
trade"—defined in the widest sense of import prices to export prices and calculated
over what they would otherwise be in the absence of development—is there validity to
the argument that we should further development in order to "expand markets."

In leaving this point, we must admit that the developing countries may not
wish to concentrate on the industries that will be of greatest interest to the
advanced countries. Hence we face a real possible clash of interests.

5. *Need to avert slump by economic imperialism?* The above analysis found
the selfish interests of the capitalistic nations to lie in the area of imports. To
modern Marxian economists this seems to set things upside down. Though
Karl Marx himself never worked out a theory of imperialism, his follower
Lenin set forth a view at the beginning of this century. The Lenin theory of
economic imperialism can be crudely summarized:

Wealthy capitalistic nations always face at home a worsening oversaving crisis. To
keep their profits from falling and to stave off ever-increasing depression crises, they
must dump goods abroad. Solely for this selfish reason do they seem to favor development of backward countries. In actual fact, they will end up enslaving the native peoples in bonds of "colonialism," probably even starting wars among themselves in their
rivalry for colonies.

What do we make of this view? Can it be refuted by the numerous studies
which show that in actual historical fact colonial activity was more motivated

by power politics than by selfish economic gain? Actually, instead of the flag's universally following trade and the profiteers, careful historians have discovered that governments usually took the initiative, later prodding businessmen into developing economic interests in areas of vital political interest to the government in question. Surely, it would be fruitless here to study the interplay of political and economic motives and tedious to try to draw up the detailed balance sheet of historical help and harm by advanced nations to underdeveloped ones.

Fortunately, we can meet the issue squarely without settling these ancient questions. Twenty-five years ago the world was in a great slump that economists only imperfectly understood. Then we might have been frankly troubled for an answer to the neo-Marxian theory of imperialism. Now we do know better.

In Part Two we studied the dynamics of national income determination. We learned that modern nations have an arsenal of fiscal and monetary programs which are effective in avoiding great depressions. We learned that there is never any need to create domestic purchasing power by foreign trade: modern governments possessed of full constitutional powers to regulate money, taxation, and budgetary expenditure can always fight unemployment by programs that are directly useful and make sense for their own sakes. Just as we never have to dig holes and fill them up to fight unemployment, so we never have to buy prosperity by throwing goods abroad.

6. *Exploitation of colonial peoples?* Followers of Karl Marx today realize that his prediction of falling real wages or "the law of immiseration of the masses" turned out dead wrong. English, American, French, German, and Scandinavian real wages have all been rising steadily under capitalism.

How can a Marxian explain this? By attributing the higher wages to trade-union and ameliorist reform movements? That would indeed be a bitter pill for revolutionary socialists to swallow and would in any case not explain the rise of wages in the most capitalistic country of all—America.

So for lack of better explanation, many Marxians try to explain the high wages of the advanced nations in terms of exploitation of the colonial peoples. Men drive new cars in Dayton, Ohio, because Burmese peasants starve. So goes the argument. Is there anything in it?

Because economics is not an exact science, we certainly can't dismiss this view without careful study of history's complicated facts. And we should lean over backward in appraising any charge aimed at ourselves. Having said this, I must record the view that the bulk of the evidence tells against this notion that the high Western standard of living depends in an important way on its trade with underdeveloped countries. Indeed, if nylon and synthetic rubber are followed by similar inventions, we may see the West even less dependent on such trade in the future.

7. *Plain altruism.* Finally, it is only the simple truth to mention disinterested altruism as an important motive for helping underdeveloped countries. What is the evidence for this? Examine public-opinion polls in the advanced countries. Recall that long before the ideological tension with Russia, America introduced its "good neighbor" program toward Latin America; recall Franklin Roosevelt's 1941 statement of the third of his Four Freedoms—"freedom from want . . . everywhere in the world."

The same ethical urges toward providing minimum standards for all, which have been politically important *inside* all the advanced countries, spill over in logic and in political fact to the problem of providing economic opportunity for peoples abroad. Altruism is not something we can with grace dwell on at any length, but ignore it and predictions on political events will lose some accuracy.

▶ **DIAGNOSIS AND THERAPY**

We have described the general problem of underdevelopment and cleared the ground of important fallacies. Now we can turn to the constructive task of discovering why countries are poor and what can be done to hasten their growth and development.

The most fruitful approach is through analysis of the four economic fundamentals: population, natural resources, capital formation, and technology.

▶ **POPULATION PROBLEMS**

Mere growth in numbers does not necessarily mean development. Indeed, as writers since Malthus have warned, unbridled increase in numbers is likely to invoke the law of diminishing returns and to work against increases in per capita living standards. Admittedly, we do find many underdeveloped countries repeating the pattern of the eighteenth- and nineteenth-century developing economies: improved medical technology (*e.g.,* sanitation and in our day cheap DDT) first reduces the death rate; and with birth rates remaining high, population rapidly grows.

Puerto Rico, Bali, and numerous other modern instances underline the twin lessons: first that much of the increase in output made possible by technological advance may be spent on duplication of numbers; and second that modern science, operating on disease faster than it operates on food, might in the future keep people from dying from germs—only to threaten them with death from famine as they vie with each other for insufficient food.

An economic textbook can no more than mention the big question being asked by demographers. Will birth rates fall in developing countries as they did in older countries? And before living standards actually deteriorate?

Improving human resources. Since labor is an important factor of production, there is much constructive programming to be done in this area. When planners draw up blueprints for hastening economic development, they write down the following specific programs:

1. Control disease and increase health and nutrition programs both to make people happier and to make them more productive workers. So don't look on hospitals and sewage projects as frills or luxuries.

2. Educated people make more productive workers. So budget for schools and other programs to reduce illiteracy. Beyond reading and writing, train people in new techniques of agriculture and industry. Send your best minds abroad to bring back knowledge of engineering, medicine, and business.

Disguised unemployment. One important source for permitting development is the better utilization of manpower. In poor countries, particularly rural ones, there often exists a large part of the manpower pool who do almost nothing because there is nothing for them to do. They may not be counted in the census of unemployment, but they can scarcely be called employed; they live with their kinfolk, and when a boom or a development plan comes along sweeping them into productive city jobs, there is almost no reduction in the product back on the farm. The same phenomenon of disguised unemployment is met in advanced countries, both in the subsistence farming regions and in the city streets where men eke out a bare existence doing door-to-door selling whenever productive jobs are unavailable.

To best solve this unemployment and underemployment problem, governments often find it desirable to pursue expansionary fiscal and monetary policies—even though these raise problems of inflation and of deficit in the balance of international payments.[1]

▶ **NATURAL RESOURCES**

Poor countries typically have been poorly endowed by nature, and such land and minerals as they do possess must be divided among densely teeming populations. The romantic notion of overlooked geographical areas rich in resources has pretty much been exploded by geographers. Generally speaking, people have already settled in the most productive regions.

True, geologists are still seeking and finding new hidden resources; and there are authenticated cases where control of malaria by DDT has reclaimed from the jungle hundreds of square miles of fertile Indian land. Against these cheerful considerations is the fact that many underdeveloped countries are rapidly depleting their mines, their topsoil, and their irreplaceable natural resources. Moreover, as we've seen, many of the present-day resources of tropical countries are becoming obsolete in competition with science's creation of syn-

---

[1] Harvard's G. Haberler and Chicago's T. W. Schultz dispute the view that most underdeveloped countries have much disguised unemployment. Schultz thinks Latin America has little —in comparison even with the United States.

thetic substitutes from cheap substances found in abundance within the advanced countries: thus nylon killed the silk industry, impoverishing millions; if synthetic rubber replaces natural rubber, eastern Asia will find itself unable to maintain even its present standard of living, low as that is.

Economic geographers are agreed that further development largely comes from better use of existing resources. Gone are the opportunities of a Columbus; and gone is the open door beckoning the poor of the older regions, begging them to migrate to the fertile prairies of North and South America or to the empty regions of Australia and New Zealand.

Of course, the quip still holds: "There's nothing wrong with any poor country that discovery of oil can't cure." Venezuela, Iraq, Saudi Arabia, Iran, and Kuwait are obvious examples.

Land reform. Even without creating or finding new land, nations can make better use of the land they do have. The medieval village was divided into little postage-stamp strips of land that you could hardly turn around on, and each man might have to live off the produce of one or two such strips, distantly located from each other. The same is still true in many parts of the world. It took from the thirteenth to the eighteenth centuries for the painful, and bitterly resented, *enclosure* movement in England to break up the common lands and to gather together into efficient larger-scale plots the land of the country. In the process, many peasants were dispossessed and had to go to the city slums. The ruthless, and not altogether successful, "collectivization" of Russian agriculture in the 1920's provides an analogous case. China's collectivization seems to have gone more quickly. The displacement of dust-bowl farmers during the 1930's by the tractor has, of course, been dramatically portrayed in John Steinbeck's best seller, *The Grapes of Wrath*. In many parts of the world, this same painful process of consolidating too small holdings is still to be consummated.

And at the other extreme, we see in many underdeveloped countries landholding in huge estates that are too large for efficiency. The tenant farmer has no incentive to improve the property, knowing that he can be dispossessed at any time and learning from bitter experience that little of the fruit of his initiative will ever accrue to him. The landlord in turn has no incentive to improve the property, never knowing whether an irresponsible tenant will waste and dissipate the costly resources placed at his disposal.

As the communists well know, the situation is explosive, and agitation for land reform signifies a rising ground swell of public sentiment not long to be denied. Theodore W. Schultz, eminent agricultural economist, has well said: Successful reform that puts land in the hands of owners who can count on the fruits of their own enterprise has again and again in country after country almost literally "turned sand into gold."

The problems of natural-resource development merge with the problem of improved technology and with the problem of improved capital-goods capacity for utilizing and discovering natural resources.

▶ CAPITAL FORMATION

The fingers and brains of men in the underdeveloped countries are much like the fingers and brains of their more prosperous brethren. But the latter in the advanced nations work with a plentiful supply of capital goods built up over the years. To pile up net capital formation requires, as we have earlier seen, a sacrifice of current consumption. But there's the rub: underdeveloped countries are already so poor as to be near the minimum of subsistence; they feel that they cannot—and in fact, they do not—save a very large share of their current national incomes.

Thus, in the advanced nations, from 10 to 20 per cent of income may go into capital formation; but in the underdeveloped nations, the rate of saving and investment may be less than 5 per cent. According to some estimates, the current rate of net capital formation in Indonesia may be less than 5 per cent of total real income (inclusive of nonmonetary items). Merely to provide for the rapidly growing population the primitive tools and housing now enjoyed can eat up most of this saving. And what is left then for economic development?

Until we learned how to prevent mass unemployment, many economists worried about oversaving in advanced countries. But for underdeveloped countries the problem is often the classical one of *under*saving: more precisely, the problem is underinvestment in productive instruments capable of increasing their rate of economic progress.

Why don't these countries save more? The answers are only too easy.

Low saving rates: poverty. Poor people on the bare edge of subsistence will not save much. This is the No. 1 reason.[1]

Inequality and saving. But there are other complicating factors. Within underdeveloped countries not all people are poor. Indeed, to an outside observer the contrasts between rich and poor, aristocrat and peasant, seem even sharper than in the advanced countries. You may be tempted to conclude from this: Much as inequality of wealth is an evil, it is a necessary evil if we are to get the needed saving. You may even argue that capitalism itself was able to develop so fast because of a certain ruthlessness in the economy which permitted a few energetic ones to prosper mightily and to plow back their gains into more and more investment.

Admittedly, there is much truth in this. But remember too—as has been pointed out by such great scholars as Max Weber, Tawney, and Sombart—a special *middle-class philosophy* grew up in the days of our Industrial Revolu-

---

[1] Cambridge's P. T. Bauer claims that no matter how poor some groups are they do save: the Chinese in Malaya, the Lebanese in South America, the East Side immigrant bound to rise.

tion. In oversimplified terms, the Reformation developed the "Protestant ethic," placing allegedly Spartan emphasis on thrift and money-making—with this important result, that the rich really did serve as effective instruments of progress. Subsequent research has found many holes in this sweeping Weber-Sombart-Tawney thesis: the Italian cities, the Rhineland, many parts of the Lowlands were Catholic, and yet they show similar rates of progress and development. Unless many other groups are blanketed in as "honorary Protestants," no ironclad rule can be stated. And within the Reformation countries, such as England or Scotland, some have argued that it was the nonconformist sects, unfashionable and outside the Established Church, who were most prominent in developing engineering, technology, and commerce.

Without settling this historical question, we have to admit that there lives on in many of the underdeveloped countries the older feudal tradition with its contempt for commerce, industry, and thrift. The rich live well.[1] Their great estates provide jobs for many personal servants. Much of the time they live abroad: a statistician has seriously argued that the expenditures in Paris during the last century of Hungarian or Brazilian noblemen on champagne and other items would have financed many a railroad and factory. Or consider the case of a Middle Eastern country where rich oil has been struck—for a country the nearest thing to being born with a silver spoon in its mouth. A computation estimated that, of 500 million dollars received by the chieftain of one such region, less than 100 million was funneled into long-term improvement, the rest going for air-conditioned Cadillacs, palaces, and gold hoards.

Whether or not they agree with the argument that society should deliberately foster inequality in the interests of more rapid progress,[2] fiscal experts point out that underdeveloped countries generally do already have "regressive" tax systems primarily dependent on excises.

Qualitative distortion of investment. There is a further problem. Not only is saving and investment *quantitatively* low in these countries; equally serious is the fact that the *qualitative composition of investment* is often bad from the standpoint of national development. Thus, too much of the limited saving of India goes into hoarding of gold and of jewelry, imported legally or illegally into the country and using up its scarce foreign exchange. Many underdeveloped countries, such as Brazil or Chile, suffer from chronic inflation—hence, there is a natural tendency for people to invest in real estate and in hoarding of inventory. When you can make 20 per cent on your money by hoarding goods, why seek an additional and problematical few per cent from manufac-

---

[1] Thorstein Veblen's *The Theory of the Leisure Class* stresses "conspicuous consumption" and other socioeconomic patterns.

[2] Sociologists tell us the family system in many cultures puts a more discouraging tax on thrift and initiative than any governmental tax: If saving and working means simply that more of your cousins' cousins will feel free to live off you, why bother?

turing? Thus, no less than 55 per cent of Brazil's 1947 investment was in the form of construction. And observers are struck with the fact that, in many of the poorest regions of the world, luxury apartment dwellings seem to mushroom up, at the same time that industry is languishing for lack of new equipment. Still another qualitative dissipation of the limited saving in an underdeveloped country comes from the frequent tendency of the wealthy to pile up their savings abroad, legally and illegally, thereby making them unavailable to the nation for its internal development.

Emulating the prosperous foreigner. There is another reason why saving comes hard in present-day poor countries. Even if you discover that they are now little poorer than was England in the heyday of its Industrial Revolution, you cannot expect them to match England's saving rate. For Englishmen then, poor as they were, still were the most prosperous people in the world. We all know that there is a great human urge "to keep up with the Joneses," to imitate the standard of life we see in our prosperous neighbors. The underdeveloped peoples today constantly have thrown before them the comforts of life in the advanced countries: they see our movies and magazines; they meet our tourists; their students bring back the glad tidings. Little wonder, then, that they find themselves spending a high percentage of their incomes in an attempt to enjoy some few of the things we enjoy in abundance.

Nor is this true simply on the private front. Within the realm of government, nations that are scarcely emerging from the stage of feudalism are quite unwilling to go through the stage of laissez-faire capitalism. They see and emulate social security programs in the advanced nations; minimum-wage legislation; factory safety and maximum-working-day legislation; trade-union movements; etc. As one delegate to the United Nations crudely put the matter: "We have boys' incomes, but we have men's appetites. Whether we can afford the humanitarian legislation of the advanced nations, we are going to insist on getting much of it." Of course, all this too makes for high levels of government activity—not high in relation to advanced countries, for we've seen on page 113 that the latter spend about 25 per cent of their national product on government while the underdeveloped countries often spend about 10 per cent, but high in relation to the historical experience of the advanced countries when they were undergoing development. And aside from its expenditure, the government regulations in many of these countries do put obstacles in the way of entrepreneurs: *e.g.,* high minimum wages and pension costs in Italy may simply freeze into complete idleness many workers who could contribute at least something to the national product.

Capital from abroad. If there are so many obstacles to domestic-financed capital formation, why not rely more heavily on foreign sources? After all, did not England in the nineteenth century invest heavily in the United States, Canada, Australia, and Latin America? Did not France before 1914 invest heavily in Czarist Russia? And did not Germany invest heavily in Eastern Europe? Doesn't economic theory tell us that a rich country which has used up all its high-interest investment projects can benefit itself and at the same time benefit a poor country abroad—if only it will shift investment to the high-interest projects not yet exploited abroad?

Actually, prior to 1914 economic development did proceed in this natural fashion. Britain in her heyday did save about 15 per cent of her national income, investing fully half this amount abroad. If the United States were to match these percentages today, we should *every year* have to lend and invest privately almost 30 billion dollars, or several times the combined Marshall Plan and foreign aid programs of the federal government, Export-Import Bank, International Bank, and all the rest!

For many reasons we moderns cannot expect great things from foreign investment. After all, was the pre–World War I pattern so natural, or was it perhaps the special result of fortuitous historical coincidences? Thus, loans from Europe to the New World typically went together with migration of European peoples to those same new lands: Englishmen went along with their money, so to speak, to the American colonies, Canada, Australia, and other dominions. Notice that the same pattern of laws and customs prevailed in the capital-importing countries as in the capital-investing country.

Remember, too, the ante-bellum world was an unbelievably cosmopolitan one. You could travel everywhere with no passport. You could migrate freely from country to country. You could expect there to be low tariffs and no trade quotas. You knew the international gold standard would let you transfer capital from place to place at your slightest whim. You knew your property was safe abroad from government confiscation: back in those days few dreamed of questioning the sanctity of private property, and those nationalistic countries which did raise such questions could be easily intimidated by dispatching cruisers for off-coast maneuvers. Finally, you could buy up—literally buy up—dictatorial governments in many backward countries, and bribe them into giving you extremely favorable long-term mining and other concessions.

Sounds like an investor's paradise, doesn't it? Of course, if you examine the historical facts more closely, you find things were not really quite so rosy: foreign investments often did go bankrupt, there being insufficient commercial demand for the railroads built across the plains of North America and elsewhere. Also, the people in the countries importing capital do not from their historical utterances seem to have been too happy over this investor's paradise. But the system did work. And as we look back today, it appears often to have conferred *mutual benefits* on both the advanced and backward areas.

Now all this is ancient history. The ante-bellum world is gone for good. Never was nationalism stronger than today. Never have borrower and lender been so agreed: the underdeveloped countries are agreed not to sell to foreigners long-term rights in the development of their countries, no matter how advantageous the price; the developed countries are agreed it would be rash to buy bonds and stocks from backward countries in the old carefree pattern.[1]

Does this mean we must rule out substantial foreign capital investment programs? Not completely. But to be realistic, we must search out new instrumentalities for carrying them on. Often these will involve agreements between governments, or various government guarantees of private ventures. Always foreign investment will have to take into account the rising tide of nationalism.

▶ **TECHNOLOGICAL CHANGE AND INNOVATIONS**

In addition to the fundamental factors of population, natural resources, and capital formation, there is the vitally important fourth factor of technology. Here we can strike a cautiously optimistic note. Here the underdeveloped countries have one possible advantage. To be sure, they live "lonely and afraid, in a world they never made." But for precisely this reason, they can hope to benefit by copying the more advanced technology of the developed nations.

Imitating technology. The new lands do not have to develop still unborn Newtons to discover the law of gravity: they can read about it in any book. They do not have to go through the slow meandering climb of the Industrial Revolution: they find in every machinery catalogue wonders undreamed of by the great inventors of the past.

Japan, Germany, and Russia well illustrate all this in their historical developments. Japan joined the industrial race late: at the end of the nineteenth century she sent her students abroad, aping Western technology. Her government took an active and creative role in stimulating the pace of development, building railroads and utilities, and taxing heavily the newly created increments of land value resulting from the improvements in agriculture. A few energetic, wealthy families were permitted to develop vast industrial empires, while at the same time the general population was made to work, and work hard, in order to earn its living. Without relying on net foreign capital imports, Japan in a few decades had moved into the front rank both as a military power and as an industrial nation.

Only after the Revolution of 1848 did Germany really accelerate her industrialization. As Thorstein Veblen claimed, Britain was in a certain sense handicapped because she had her Industrial Revolution so early: this froze her in many lines to older and obsolete modes of production. Arriving late at the feast, Germany was under no such handicap. Through government aid to her universities, German science soon became preeminent in mathematics, physics, chemistry, and engineering. Fifty years ago, most American professors of these

---

[1] Even in friendly Canada, citizens have been resenting the vast postwar investment by large United States corporations!

fields—and of history, economics, and philology too—went to Germany for their postgraduate degrees. German prowess in organic chemistry, optics, glass, and electrical equipment was unsurpassed until the two wars set her back.

Russia too illustrates the possibility of fast development through technological imitation. The very fact that the Russians claim to have invented everything is taken by the rest of the world as a sign of her basic insecurity and realization she had entered the race late. As we saw earlier, Czarist Russia was undergoing rapid economic development some 60 years ago: French bankers, encouraged by their government, were selling to individual Frenchmen large quantities of Czarist government bonds; their proceeds were going in part to building up railroads and other industries.

All this was too late to put off the Bolshevik Revolution that followed her World War I defeat by Germany. And after that, the Soviet Union could of course no longer tap foreign sources for capital. To force the pace of industrial development, she ruthlessly cut down on current consumption in her repeated Five-year Plans following 1928. At first she relied heavily on foreign engineers; and at all times since, her scientists have shown a close interest in the technological literature appearing abroad. She does not have to send out spies to get such data, for most of it appears all the time in our open periodicals.

Finally, the case of the United States itself provides an optimistic example to the rest of the world. Until Hitler made us a present in the 1930's of many of the best Continental scientists of all faiths, we could not honestly boast of having quite reached the very front rank in the field of pure science. Yet for a century, our applied technology was admittedly outstanding. Examine one by one the key inventions in the automobile. Where did they originate? Mostly abroad. And yet Henry Ford and General Motors have always greatly outproduced the rest of the world. "Yankee ingenuity" is a phrase that explains nothing; but it does refer to a real phenomenon.

Interplay of technology and capital. It is all very well to speak of underdeveloped countries' copying advanced technology. But haven't we overlooked something important? Isn't advanced technology embodied in the form of complex capital goods? And haven't we already seen that those countries are short of capital? So how can we expect them to copy better technology?

Certainly there is much truth in these suggestions. Technological change and capital investment do go hand in hand. Often they are inseparable. All the same, we are right to treat them as analytically distinct—albeit related—processes. Here is one of many examples to show why.

Farming is inefficient in many backward countries. You see peasants breaking up the soil by the same primitive methods their ancestors were using back in the time of David and Solomon. Perhaps an ingenious light plow—something simple that would cost no more than a dollar and would pay for itself in the first month—can be found that will both lessen the total amount of capital needed and greatly increase output. This shows how technological innovation can often be capital-*saving* rather than capital-*using*.

Moreover, even in the poorest countries, some gross capital formation is always going on as things are wearing out and are being replaced. Why replace them with the same thing? Why let much of the economy's capital go into mere *duplicative projects?* Surely, it is much better to embody the newly available investment funds in the form of more efficient technological implements. Thus we see how the interrelated factors of capital formation and technology can be mutually reinforcing.

Entrepreneurship and innovation. We've made it sound easy for an underdeveloped economy, haven't we? All they have to do to telescope into a few years the scores of years it took us to develop is this: Go abroad and copy our efficient methods. Bring them back and put them into effect at home. Then sit back and wait for the extra product to roll in.

Of course it doesn't work out this way. People in the underdeveloped countries know this from bitter experience. Yet the same illusion keeps cropping up among the people in the so-called advanced countries. Too often we think we can send a few technical experts on a short junket to a poor country: after surveying the field for a month or so, they can write up their recommendations for improvement, and then the neatly typed report they leave behind can be "implemented." And so the problem of development is solved.

Sometimes in connection with particular technological processes, experts have indeed been able to work wonders in this sweet and easy way: thus, an American expert on tanning was sent out to Libya to advise them on some of their difficulties, and in short time he did diagnose their chemical troubles and come up with an effective cure. But technologists soon discover that this sort of quick miracle is exactly what cannot be accomplished in connection with the *development of a whole economy.* Indeed the typical pattern is one of complete disillusionment: after spending several months surveying an underdeveloped country, the expert is thoroughly impressed with the thousands of cultural and economic barriers to progress; so much so that he comes back with a hopeless feeling of defeat. This pessimistic conclusion is probably just as wrong in its way as was the opposite optimistic illusion.

Experience shows development is truly a hard and slow process. But not an impossible one. To hasten its evolution there must develop spontaneous entrepreneurship and innovation on the part of the peoples directly involved. Remember many of these peoples begin with a contempt for dirty, hard work— a contempt they often inherit from the colonial elite who used to rule over them. Often too they have a contempt for business—for money-grubbing and production. Gradually, they must develop for themselves—within their own mixed cultural pattern—a creative group of producers alert to try out new ways of doing things.

Why place the emphasis on creative innovation? Because it is by no means a cut and dried task to adapt advanced foreign technology to an underdeveloped country's own use. Remember the advanced technology was itself developed to meet the special conditions of the advanced countries. What are these conditions? High money wage rates; laborers scarce in number but plentiful in industrial skills; plentiful capital inherited from the past; mass production; etc. These are not the conditions prevalent in the underdeveloped country.

Time and time again experience has shown us how easy it is to get a foreign loan to put up a model factory in Turkey or Burma. Often it is imported piece by piece from abroad and embodies the latest wrinkles of Western technology. Yet with what result? With high production and sales exceeding costs, so as to yield a comfortable profit which can be plowed back into further industrialization? Only too rarely. Often such imported grandiose projects turn out to be extremely unprofitable. The factory that is optimal for New York may in Ankara or Rangoon be a fiasco.

This task of creative innovation is not one for rugged individualism alone. The government can do much to set up extension services in every agricultural province for consulting with farmers on the best seeds, methods of cultivation, tools and implements. By setting up vocational schools and training courses in machine methods—yes, and in bookkeeping too—the government can itself creatively innovate.

▶ CASE STUDY OF DEVELOPMENT: ALERTIA ON THE MARCH

To end our discussion, let us consider a concrete case of an underdeveloped country. How does it go about stimulating economic growth?

Impatient planners anxious to force the pace of development must always remember that people are people, not inanimate objects. Ignore their customs and their ancient prejudices only at your peril; rather you must add to pure economics generous doses of sociology and anthropology, proceeding in an evolutionary rather than discontinuous manner. And remember, each nation is different. No master plan will fit all underdeveloped countries.

Alertia (rhymes with inertia) is poor and populous. Long dominated by a European power, it finally won freedom from colonial status. But political freedom did not itself raise the economic standard of life. Now the government has set up a Planning Committee in the Cabinet to draw up a Plan for Development.

With the help of experts from the United Nations, estimates of national product have been prepared. The Technical Assistance Program of the U.S. Department of State has sent missions to help improve technology; in agriculture, the Food and Agriculture Organization (FAO) has helped develop better methods of cultivation.

Tax policies. The government has revamped the tax system, increasing revenues substantially. Yet it knows it cannot make a really modern tax system like that of Canada or the United States work. Here are some of the reasons: widespread illiteracy; primitive accounting methods; a tradition of trying to cheat the government by underdeclaration of personal and corporate income; corruption and inefficiency in its own civil service; great importance of nonmonetary transactions on self-sufficient farms; etc.

Expenditure policies. Despite these obstacles the government does collect a good deal of revenue, much coming from the exporters of a few staples enjoying a brisk postwar market. Part of this money it uses for important "social overhead capital" projects: roads, schools, hospitals, power dams and river development, railroads, soil improvement, and conservation. While many of these projects are extremely valuable, they create intangible benefits that cannot be expected to yield pecuniary profits to private investors; some of these projects are too large for the limited private capital markets; and still others will yield their ultimate return too far in the future for private investors to take much of an interest in them. In addition, the government spends on current projects to train workers, advise farmers, and help businessmen.

Foreign experts have told Alertia how vital "social overhead capital" had been in the development of today's advanced economies. Paul Rosenstein-Rodan, who originated the term, uses it to refer not only to roads, dams, and railroads but also to sewers and "indivisible" public utilities—to all the environmental conditions needed if private industry is to be able to "take off the ground." He compares successful development to airplane flight: to develop you need a break-through into a minimal pace of growth, just as an airplane has to go beyond a certain speed if it is ever to get off the ground at all.

Public loans. Some of the government revenue is given to a Finance Development Corporation: this makes loans to private applicants, choosing those most likely to be socially profitable. Finally, some of the revenues are used to retire public debt, thereby permitting the Central Bank and commercial banks to expand their loans to new private ventures.

Inflation and development. Earlier the government faced considerable inflation. Partly this was because of international price rises; but partly it was because inflation came from the government's forcing the pace of economic development faster than it could increase its tax revenues. The Cabinet reminded itself how the older capitalistic nations had floated their industrial revolutions on a rising price level, tending thereby to subsidize the active entrepreneurial classes at the expense of the creditor *rentier* class and the wage earners. Reminding itself of this, the Cabinet was willing to countenance a little inflation, hoping thereby to speed up development—and, incidentally, to lessen "disguised unemployment."

However, it soon met limitations in the inflating process: at the same time inflation increased investment, inflation distorted its qualitative composition into real estate and inventory speculation. And after people got used to inflation, they saved less. Why? Because they anticipated that further price rises would melt the real value of their savings. All in all, therefore, the government is now trying to lessen its reliance on inflation as a stimulant to development. The Prime Minister sometimes gets a little impatient with students who have studied depression economics abroad and don't seem alert to the different realities at home.

Diversification and protection. Bitter experience has warned Alertia to beware of putting all her export hopes on a few staple crops. New substitutes abroad, and cyclical changes in foreign demand and supply there, have resulted in great ups and downs for Alertia; so she has come to regard "monoculture" as a condition to be avoided. Instead, she is trying to diversify her industries and agriculture and to lessen her dependence on imported foods.

To this end she has introduced tariffs and protective quotas, claiming in justification the "infant-industry" and "young-economy" arguments of standard international trade theory.[1] Many within the country doubt whether every one of the protected activities has as yet outgrown its swaddling clothes—in particular, the modern imported steel mill seems always to require government subsidy. However, friendly critics are reserving judgment until the future shall have revealed what the new comparative-advantage situation is.

Breaking vicious circles. Sometimes the Cabinet Minister for Economic Development gets discouraged. He feels caught in a vicious circle: poverty creates want, want destroys thrift, absence of capital formation prevents improvement, limitation of mass demand makes new mass-production projects unappealing, absence of mass production makes poverty—and so the vicious circle goes.

However, by the same token and because of the very interconnectedness of the various economic processes, once Alertia can make a break-through on any front—*e.g.,* once a new dam makes power and irrigation possible—there tend to be favorable repercussions throughout the length and breadth of the economy. These "external economies"—to use the phrase of the economic theorist—can break the vicious circle and lead to accelerating spirals of development. After each small success, the Cabinet Minister reflects: "The advanced nations once faced our same problems, and gradually, step by step, they did somehow succeed in achieving development."

[1] Alertia has had to choose between what Jacob Viner, Princeton's distinguished economist, calls the "sentimental" and "aristocratic" approaches. She knows she cannot at one and the same time hope to improve the productivity and well-being of *every* sector of the economy. So Alertia has chosen to stint many of them, instead investing heavily in a few aristocratic "nuclei" of what she hopes will one day be efficient, viable industries.

Beyond economics. It is too soon to know how the desperate race between Alertia's rising population numbers and her development program will turn out. Great issues are still debated politically: How much shall government do? How much, private industry? How much reliance should she place on domestic rather than foreign sources? To what degree shall she give first priority to industry rather than agriculture? How can she most quickly and optimally adapt foreign technology to her own resource situation, which involves much unskilled labor, little land, and great capital shortage?

However, the biggest problems go beyond economics. They involve the sociological tensions between the old culture and the new. The elders in Alertia take a dim view of materialistic trends. Many of the young people—especially those who have recently poured into city slums—have lost their old roots and have not yet developed new roots: thus, insecurity, crime, and disorganization raise difficult problems.

All in all, to the visiting anthropologist and economist, Alertia presents a fascinating spectacle. No one knows quite where she is going. But to everyone this much is clear: she is on her way.

SUMMARY

1. Most of the world consists of underdeveloped countries: countries with low per capita incomes relative to the most advanced economies; countries capable of improvement but at the present time diverging from the growth rates of the advanced nations. The increasing political self-consciousness of such countries, plus the eagerness of the communist ideology to help them "skip the capitalistic stage of development," reinforces our own self-interest in finding new sources of mutually advantageous trade—not, mind you, new objects for imperialistic make-work programs. All this, and altruism too, make the development problem of major interest to us.

2. The key to development rests in the four fundamental factors: population, natural resources, capital formation, and technology. Population raises sociological problems of explosive growth in numbers as death rates fall before birth rates fall; the Malthusian devil of diminishing returns stalks the underdeveloped realms. On the constructive economic agenda, improving the population's health, education, and technical training has high priority. The pool of "disguised unemployment" in country and city provides an important manpower source for extra product.

3. Even in densely populated areas, discovery and better utilization of natural resources can help offset the law of diminishing returns. Land reform raises tremendous problems of transition. The process of capital formation—

of investing in soil conservation, irrigation, drainage, and improvement—interacts with the natural-resource category, just as it does with population—through investing in people.

4. Rates of productive capital formation in underdeveloped countries are low because of (*a*) poverty, (*b*) lack of a bourgeois ethic stressing frugality and acquisitiveness, (*c*) qualitative distortion of saving outlets toward unproductive hoarding of precious objects and idle inventory, and toward luxurious real estate or money markets abroad, (*d*) emulation of consumption standards of advanced nations, (*e*) nationalistic barriers to importing capital on terms acceptable to investors in the advanced countries.

5. Technological change interacts with, and is embodied in, new capital goods. Nevertheless, it is a distinct process—and one which offers much hope to underdeveloped nations inasmuch as they can copy from advanced nations. The historical experience of Japan, Russia, Germany, and the United States shows that the process of adapting to one's own fruitful uses the methods developed elsewhere is not easy. It takes a degree of entrepreneurship and creative innovation. And one of development's most pressing tasks is to hasten internal growth of the entrepreneurial and commercial spirit, so scarce in many cultures.

6. The case study of a developing economy (Alertia) sets out the detailed acts of governments in the usual programs: surveying national income and resources; setting up goals in an over-all plan; reforming tax systems to check inflation and finance social overhead capital projects; setting up finance corporations to make loans to important private projects; creating a fiscal surplus so the banking system can finance more capital formation without producing hyperinflation; arranging foreign loans and technical assistance programs from governments, international agencies, and private foreign corporations; fostering infant industries by protective devices in the hopes of developing new comparative advantages and lessening dependence on monoculture; and many other programs too numerous to list.

QUESTIONS FOR DISCUSSION

1. Would you expect everyone to agree with the praise of material well-being expressed in the quotation at this chapter's beginning? What would Buddha think of modern plumbing as one of the goals of life? What would one of his modern followers think of plumbing *after* becoming accustomed to it? Can scientists decide the true view in such matters? Why not?

2. Bishop Berkeley, writing in the eighteenth century, wrote a pamphlet that described the miseries of Ireland and showed Ireland then met every

modern test as to what constitutes an underdeveloped country. Though of more fertile soil than Denmark, Eire did not until recently show material progress. What do you think were the reasons? What might have been done to improve the situation?

3. Bertrand Russell is one of the greatest philosophers, logicians, and writers. Yet the following words of his are agreed by all competent historians to be absolutely wrong in asserting that the Industrial Revolution worsened living standards: "The industrial revolution caused unspeakable misery both in England and in America. I do not think any student of economic history can doubt that the average happiness in England in the early nineteenth century was lower than it had been a hundred years earlier; and this was due almost entirely to scientific technique." Actually real per capita incomes increased. Why the widespread contrary notion?

4. Briefly list the principal contrasts between life in America and in a typical underdeveloped country. Give your own diagnosis of the historical reasons for the difference.

5. Write down important factors bearing on development; then show where each falls into the outline involving the four main factors of population, . . . , and technology.

6. Suggest some constructive policies to improve net capital formation and entrepreneurship in backward lands. Evaluate each.

7. Write down two parallel case studies: one of a country that tries and fails to develop, and the other of a successful development pattern. Explain why one fails and the other succeeds. Are you sure that wiser policies would have changed the story?

8. Assume that present-day efforts toward development succeed widely. What will the world look like when you are at the retirement age?

9. "The study of underdeveloped lands is the best approach to the study of what advanced lands have done—and need to do!—to grow." Evaluate.

10. Review your understanding of the following concepts:

characteristics of underdevelopment

interest of advanced countries in development of others

population, resource, capital, and technology factors

inequality, poverty, emulation, foreign lending and capital formation

entrepreneurship

inflation and development

social overhead capital and vicious circles

38 ALTERNATIVE ECONOMIC SYSTEMS

Your old men shall dream dreams, your young men shall see visions.

OLD TESTAMENT

▶ **THE CRISIS OF CAPITALISM**

After World War I, new governments were set up all over Europe. By 1927 any impartial observer would have said that the future of the capitalistic way of life appeared serene and assured. Yet within a half-dozen years, country after country succumbed to dictatorship; totalitarian fascist governments covered the map of Europe. The depression decade of the 1930's finally ended in a great world war.

Fifteen years after World War II, what is the outlook? The world is divided into two great blocks: Soviet Russia with her satellites of Eastern Europe and Asia stand within the Iron Curtain; and outside is the rest of the world. But the nations outside the Iron Curtain are far from homogeneous. Labor-Socialist governments are now ruling, or have recently been ruling, in Britain, in Australia and New Zealand, and in all of Scandinavia. Various forms of dictatorship still linger on in Spain, Portugal, and Latin America. France, Germany, and Italy have within them noisy and articulate left-wing political parties. The awakening nations of Asia and Africa do not view the world with laissez-faire-tinted glasses.

Only the United States and Switzerland and a few other countries remain as islands of capitalism in an increasingly collectivized world. And even here, the scene is drastically changed: ours is a mixed system of private and public initiative and control; and in these disturbed days, a mixed system of a peace and a war economy.

Every new dispatch reminds us that the capitalistic way of life is on trial. Not only must it perform adequately—more than that, it is required to perform superlatively. Mass unemployment here at home would have disastrous repercussions upon our prestige abroad, to say nothing of the internal political unrest that a slump would involve. And a faltering rate of our growth and development would count against us.

▶ A BOUQUET OF ISMS

Men have always had visions of a more perfect society: Plato's Republic, Sir Thomas More's Utopia, Marx's Dictatorship of the Proletariat, and so on without number. It is only too easy to look at concrete present-day imperfections and then to contrast them with the ideal features of a vaguely defined Utopia. Beyond agreeing on the faults of the present order, different schools of reform have little in common.

At the one extreme, we have the anarchists who believe in no government at all; at the other, the apologists for an all-powerful collectivized, totalitarian, communistic social order, where the first person singular is all but replaced by the first person plural. Within the field of socialism itself, we find many subdivisions: Christian socialism, state and Marxian socialism, guild socialism, Fabian (or evolutionary) socialism, and many others.

In the popular mind, socialists are characters who meet in a cellar lit by a candle thrust in an empty wine bottle to plot a bloody revolution, or at least to brew bombs sent in laundry parcels to government officials and capitalists. Or the term "socialist" is frequently used as a disparaging stereotype to discredit anyone who believes in social security, progressive taxation, bank deposit insurance, some other social improvement, or free love.

Whatever the strength of radical parties abroad, in America no third party has ever been able to develop in any strength.[1] The American Socialist party runs a candidate for the presidency every election—along with the Prohibition party—but gains only a negligible fraction of the vote. The Communist party never could gain any sizable vote, either under its own name or in disguise.

If we look at the picture in Europe, we find the names of almost all the parties have the word "socialism" in them. But this does not mean much: a party like France's Radical Socialists turns out to be anything but radical, being one of the conservative parties. Even Hitler's fascistic party took the name of "National Socialism."

Often, however, the leading European "liberal" parties can be characterized as "social democrats." For example, the Labor party in Britain, the German Social Democratic party, the ruling parties in Sweden and Norway— all of these claim to be in favor of gradual, nonrevolutionary extension of socialism by peaceful and democratic methods.

It is clear, therefore, that we do not have to master all of the thousand and

[1] Theodore Roosevelt's 1912 Bull Moose party was primarily an offshoot of the Republican party. Old Bob La Follette's 1924 Progressive party was by far the most successful third-party effort, and yet he was able to carry only his home state, Wisconsin. Henry Wallace's 1948 Progressive party was a complete failure.

one different "isms" in order to understand the world today. It is enough to understand something of (1) relative *laissez faire* or private enterprise, (2) socialism, (3) communism, and (4) fascism. There is no hard and fast boundary between these; it is a matter of degree. Moreover, we cannot even range these along a line, with fascism at the extreme right wing and communism at the extreme left wing. In some ways—although neither would admit it—communism and fascism have much in common.

Most of this book has been concerned with describing the capitalistic system, so we may turn briefly to the others.

▶ FASCISM

This is easier to characterize politically than economically. Whether in Hitler's Germany, Mussolini's Italy, Franco's Spain, Salazar's Portugal, or Perón's Argentina, fascism is usually characterized by a one-man dictatorship, by one political party with all others abolished, by the disappearance of civil liberties of the type granted in our Bill of Rights. Fascistic movements are always highly nationalistic, often with the emphasis placed upon a vaguely defined "master race" which exploits and persecutes minority groups. In the words of Mussolini, fascists are urged to "live dangerously"—to value war and national power as ends in themselves. The individual is to be secondary to the state.

On the economic side, Mussolini's fascism happened to toy with the notion of a "syndicalist" or "corporate" state; each industry and group of workers was organized in a syndicate, and these were to meet and bargain and plan how the economy should be run. However, this syndicalism has never come to much and has not been especially characteristic of other fascist regimes.

Almost all of them are against free and militant trade-unionism; almost all give the central government great regulatory power over every sphere of economic life. Some work hand in glove with religious authorities; others are anti-church. Often capitalists and the lower middle classes contribute to the initial strength of fascist movements; but later when the fascist movement begins to take on—as they sometimes do—revolutionary aspects, the capitalists may regret the Frankenstein's monster that they have helped to create.

Their only consolation lies in the fact that one of the earmarks of a fascist regime is opposition to communism; often it sails into power by exaggerating the immediate likelihood of a bolshevik revolution, and after coming into power the threat of communism is used as an excuse for the suppression of all democratic processes.

▶ MARXIAN COMMUNISM AND SOVIET RUSSIA

Travel eastward from New York, and if you continue long enough you will return to it from the west. Move far enough to the right, and you will round the circle and encounter the extreme left-wing communist movement. For three-quarters of a century after Karl Marx and Friedrich Engels issued their 1848 Communist Manifesto, numerous international socialist conferences were held; but outside the British Museum, not much was accomplished.

In 1917, the big moment arrived. Czarist Russia was knocked out of the war by the Germans. Lenin, a follower of Marx, was transported in a sealed railroad car across Germany and into Russia. Aided by Trotsky, a one-time New York inhabitant, Lenin's Bolsheviks snatched power from the more moderate regime that had overthrown the monarchy. Preaching peace, promising land for the peasants and a dictatorship of the proletariat, the followers of the red hammer and sickle gained adherents in the navy and army and forcibly took power.

There followed what John Reed (later buried in the Kremlin) called "ten days that shook the world." The meeting of the democratic Constituent Assembly, only few of whose elected representatives were procommunist, was forbidden. An army was organized and trained by Trotsky, and successive towns were won over to the revolutionary forces—often by strategic capture of the water and power supply alone. Then there followed a great civil war between the Red and White armies, the latter aided by Poland and Western powers. In the end, the officers of the White army ended up chiefly in Paris, driving taxicabs and drinking vodka to the memory of Czar Nicholas.

The world expected a Russian collapse. But the communist regime persisted—not without experiencing horrible famines, in which literally millions perished. Aristocrats and bourgeoisie were ruthlessly "purged" and "liquidated"—new words for age-old processes.

The Communist party was the only permitted political party; only a few per cent of the population could belong to this elite group; it elected the members of local "soviets" of factories and farms. These elected representatives to still higher soviets, until at the very top, over all the federated Union Republics, stood the Council of People's Commissars of the Supreme Soviet of the U.S.S.R. (Union of Soviet Socialist Republics).

The Soviet leaders had no blueprint to guide them. Marx had confined himself largely to the faults of capitalism, revealing very little of what the promised land was going to be like. It was not even on the timetable that backward Russia, which had hardly emerged from feudalism into capitalism, should experience its revolution before the downfall of the top-heavy industrialized nations. During the 1920's, Lenin compromised with capitalistic enterprise in the NEP (New Economic Policy). But in 1928–1929, the first Five-year Plan for industrialization of manufacturing and collectivization of agriculture was introduced. This was followed by a second Five-year Plan.

Because of the rapid pace of capital formation, war preparedness, and the state of Russian technology, consumption was severely rationed throughout these years. Workers had ration cards that were honored at specific stores, but money continued to be used. Excess money income could be spent only upon special goods at higher prices than the basic ration. Real and money wages differed between occupations, with piece rates and incentive pay for higher productivity becoming more and more dominant.

Joseph Stalin, one of Lenin's many lieutenants, finally won out in the struggle for power after Lenin's death in the early 1920's. Trotsky and other old-line revolutionaries were accused of plotting with foreign powers against the Soviet Union, and in the middle 1930's a tremendous purge of generals and officials culminated in the sensational Moscow trials—sensational because all the defendants vied with each other in beating their breasts and avowing their own guilt. After the Chamberlain-Hitler appeasement pact, Nazi Germany and Soviet Russia in 1939 signed a nonaggression pact, which lasted until Hitler—flushed with his victory over Poland, and France—attacked Russia.

With the aid of fanatical patriotism and United States lend-lease, the Russians traded their blood for the Germans' until few Germans were left. After the defeat of the Axis, the short-lived comradeship with the Western powers flickered out, and the world now stands in the shadow of the hydrogen bomb, with Russia trying to spread her influence over Europe and Asia, and with the British, the Atlantic nations, and ourselves bent on stopping her.

In the postwar Stalin's one-man rule became more and more paranoid, and his 1953 death brought in the inevitable revulsion of feeling. What seemed to be a thaw set in under the committee rule of Khrushchev, and sprigs of criticism began to push up their sprouts. But the Poles, Hungarians, and Leningrad students learned the hard way that winter was not quite over.

So much for this thumbnail sketch of Soviet political development. Economically, the Communist regime is far removed from any profit system of individualism. A State Planning Commission—the Gosplan—deals with two of the three basic economic problems: What goods to produce, and How to produce them. It is concerned with the location of industry, with the relation of industry to agriculture, and the relation of consumer goods to producer goods. Factories, land, and capital equipment are owned by state enterprise. Private property is limited to dwelling houses, furniture and personal effects, and what the workers may save from their earnings. The problem of For Whom rests with an Economic Council, which sets wage rates. Piecework rates are widely used, with an elaborate system of incentive bonuses, as a stimulus to increased output. Inequality of incomes, wealth, and inheritance is presumably less than in a capitalist society, although other inequalities may arise through special privileges granted to party members. Prices of consumer goods are set by the government and maintained by state stores and cooperatives.

The Russians claim that they have "industrial democracy." This is clearly a different commodity from political democracy as we know it. Even defenders of the Soviet Union will admit that expressions of opinion against the government or the Communist party will not be tolerated. Free press—in our sense—is forbidden. Even if a majority of the Russian people were to prefer their form of government, no one should blind himself to its great differences from our own concepts of democracy and freedom.

▶ **SOCIALISM**

In defining fascism or communism, we were able to point to Nazi Germany or Soviet Russia. Socialism cannot be so easily described. Of course, we can describe the Swedish socialist government or the British Labor party's program, but these do not have such dramatic contrasts with our system. They represent a middle way.

Nevertheless, there are at least a few elements that seem to characterize socialist philosophy:

1. *Government ownership of productive resources.* The role of private property is gradually to be lessened as key industries such as railroads, coal, and even steel are gradually nationalized. Unearned profits from increases in land value are also limited.

2. *Planning.* Instead of permitting the free play of profit motives in a laissez-faire market economy, coordinated planning is to be introduced. Sometimes the program of "production for use rather than profit" is advocated; advertising expenditure on gadgets is to be wiped out; workers and professional people are to develop instincts of craftsmanship and social service so that they will be guided by other motives than those of our "acquisitive society."

3. *Redistribution of income.* Through government taxing powers, inherited wealth and swollen incomes are to be reduced. Social security benefits and cradle-to-grave welfare services provided by the collective purse are to increase the well-being of the less privileged classes.

4. *Peaceful and democratic revolution.* As distinct from communism, socialism often advocates the peaceful and gradual extension of government ownership—revolution by ballot rather than by bullet. This is often more than a tactical move; rather a deep philosophical tenet of faith.

British socialism. A brief look at British socialism will point up the modern issues. Just when Adam Smith's classical economics had won the day from its mercantilistic and feudal predecessors, English intellectual opinion began to move beyond *laissez faire* and toward socialism. A key example is John Stuart Mill, who was brought up by an eighteenth-century exponent of utilitarian individualism, but who had by the last half of the nineteenth century turned to socialism. And in the twentieth century, university and night-school intellectuals were won to the Fabian doctrines of the inevitability of gradual socialism. Equally important, the socialist views of Bernard Shaw and Beatrice and Sidney Webb had also become the views of the trade-union movement.

All this was hidden until World War I. After that war, the Liberal party was ground away between the millstones of the Conservative and Labor parties. And after World War II, Labor finally came into power with a strong majority. Its early goals included: (1) vast extension of welfare services by the state—to which Conservative governments in large degree have acquiesced; (2) heavy redistributive income and estates taxation—in which to a degree the Conservatives also acquiesce; (3) extensive centralized planning, including stringent regulation of land use and zoning; and finally, (4) a fairly sweeping program of nationalization—beginning with coal, power, and railroads, and reaching in the doctrines of the left wing of the party beyond steel to many branches of wholesaling and distribution, engineering, ordnance, and so forth.

With the return of the Conservatives to power, the electorate stands in the late 1950's somewhat undecided as to how far to carry socialism. The Labor party itself stands divided: this shows itself in debates over the extent to which nationalization should go and the degree to which reliance shall be placed on market mechanisms. At the intellectual level, now that so many of the goals set up years ago in *Fabian Essays* have been realized, there is much soul-searching going on; and challenging, new Fabian essays are hard to write. Is mere "new-dealism designed to make capitalism work well" enough? And can it command the idealistic enthusiasms more sweeping reforms are able to fire?

Nor is this quandary unique to Britain. In Sweden, Norway, Denmark, Australia, and New Zealand, the so-called "middle way" of moderate labor socialism has now been in power, or near to it, for a quarter of a century.[1] Yet every one of these economies begins to look more and more like what the United States itself has become after three decades of administration by Franklin Roosevelt, Harry Truman, and Dwight Eisenhower.

► A TWENTIETH-CENTURY PATTERN?

What do all these economic societies have in common? First, they all see that collectivism in Europe and Asia has not been a sufficient condition for economic prosperity or for political well-being. Second, all try to ameliorate the

---

[1] Degree of public economic direction is a trait that ranges from a laissez-faire society through a collectivist communist regime. But a survey of history shows that this classification must not be confused with the degree of political freedom and democratic civil liberties. Fascist regimes have often passed socialistic measures, and communist bureaus have suppressed personal freedom. On the other hand, Britain, Scandinavia, and other socialist countries have retained all the familiar civil liberties and individual political freedoms that are guaranteed by our own Constitution.

It is one thing to tell a corporation what it may charge for electric power, and quite another thing to tell a man what he can say, what he can believe, or how he must worship. But some will ask: Can political freedoms be held when the state limits economic freedoms? History and anthropology have not yet given a conclusive answer to this question.

extreme inequalities of consumption that would characterize thoroughgoing *laissez faire*. Third, all resolve to use the fiscal and monetary powers of the nation to modify the ups and downs of employment and prices.

Very great differences of degree and of kind still remain, of course. But perhaps it is most important to note that the vital likenesses listed above are part of the *conservative* political parties' programs in all these countries. Thus, when Labor loses in Australia and New Zealand, the winning party has no thought of dismantling the above basic programs. When Denmark or Sweden are ruled by a coalition government, the same truth holds. In the United Kingdom the Conservative government too adheres to these same basic precepts. And in the United States, not only the Republican platform, but the actual day-to-day operations of a Republican-dominated Congress act to preserve and strengthen social security systems and to offset inflationary or deflationary forces that keep our economy from the path of economic progress.

Writing a textbook some 30 years ago, one could not have said all this: looking around at the shrinking international trade network, at the collapsing banking structure, at the grim specter of poverty midst plenty, some might then have despaired over the future of free societies. Careful, dispassionate study of the economic statistics and annals of the years since then enables one to take quite a different and more optimistic view.

Even more important for a textbook writer: modern economic analysis does provide us with a "neoclassical synthesis" that combines the essentials of the theory of aggregative income determination with the older classical theories of relative prices and of microeconomics. In a well-running system, with monetary and fiscal policies operating to validate the high-employment assumption postulated by the classical theory, that classical theory comes back into its own, and the economist feels he can state with renewed conviction the classic truths and principles of social economy!

The reader who has stuck this far now has a general knowledge of the economic analysis that is used all over the world—in the United States, Britain, Western Europe, Latin America, Africa, Asia—everywhere except beyond the Iron Curtain, where Marxian economics is the official monopoly. In a brief Appendix the family history of present-day economics is shown: where modern economics came from, and the names of a few pivotal economists.

▶ **AN OPTIMISTIC LAST WORD**

In earlier chapters we have seen how our modern economy operates. Throughout, we have subjected the economy to a searching examination, pulling no punches when it came to taking note of friendly and unfriendly criticisms of the working of the economic system. In this chapter we have glanced briefly at a variety of alternative systems such as communism, fascism, and socialism.

Our own mixed enterprise system is not perfect. No system is. But its imperfections can certainly be ameliorated within our existing framework of ideas and institutions.

It is too easy to compare the obvious imperfections of our known system with the ideal perfections of an unknown planned order. And it is only too easy to gloss over the tremendous dynamic vitality of our mixed free enterprise system, which, with all its faults, has given the world a century of progress such as an actual socialized order might find it impossible to equal.

We may conclude on a note of profound optimism. The American economy is now in better shape than it ever was in the past. At the present time, possessing only 6 per cent of the world's population, it produces some 40 per cent of the world's income. And with all its defects, it has behind it a long-term record of the most rapid advance of productivity and living standards ever achieved anywhere.

Our mixed economy—wars aside—has a great future before it.

QUESTIONS FOR DISCUSSION

1. Make a list of a number of isms, describing each and outlining its history.

2. Describe your own vision of Utopia. Does it differ from the present?

3. Compare and contrast fascism and communism. What is the relation of socialism and capitalism to each?

4. Discuss the development of the Labor party in England, and its postwar activities.

5. "I'd rather starve in free America than live off the fat of the land under totalitarian communism." Are these your sentiments? Amplify.

6. "For all its talk of planning and production for use, Russia uses its resources less efficiently than the United States and has a slower rate of progress." Evaluate objectively.

7. Review your understanding of the following concepts:

anarchism, fascism, socialism,   *centralized planning*
    communism   *mixed system, freedoms, democracy*

APPENDIX: THUMBNAIL SKETCH OF HISTORY OF ECONOMIC DOCTRINES

Economic analysis has come from two main sources: from philosophers, and from practitioners interested in the policy problems of their day.

The family tree of economics on the back endleaf gives a few key economists with dates of their work. It shows that earliest doctrines are to be found in the writings of Aristotle, the Bible, and indeed in the unwritten folk culture of every people; and in the writings of such medieval Schoolmen as St. Thomas Aquinas, theology and practice were combined in a comprehensive codification of the "just price."

Braintrusters to the Prince: The Mercantilists
But the very name of economics stems from the Greek word that more nearly signifies what is today "home economics" and shows that management decisions—how to buy and sell, to produce and exchange—were always part of economics. And once men came together and the state began to regulate them, pamphleteers interested in current reforms were the principal developers of economic analysis.

Thus, as the modern age dawned and the national state emerged, advisers to the prince wrote pamphlets about gold, about discouraging imports and encouraging exports, and about thousands of minute fiats to control the economy. These so-called "mercantilists," however we may laugh at their ideas and the crudeness of their pamphlets, were advancing the tools of economics and paving the way for Adam Smith's reaction against them and for the classical advance.

A Digression on The Physiocrats and Leontief Input-Output
No sketch should fail to mention the French physiocrats, who just before the 1789 revolution put great stress on land as the source of all net product (*produit net*) and whose great leader François Quesnay first pictured

the circular flow of economic life and of what we should today call the national income.[1]

Indeed Quesnay's *Tableau économique* has today been perfected in the form of the so-called "input-output money flow" system of Harvard's Wassily Leontief. Most nations now try to gather such statistics showing what fraction of each industry's value-of-product is spent on the input labor and on inputs bought from other industries.

Table 1 of page 785 gives an oversimplified example of the several-hundred-industry table that the government and Leontief have prepared for the American economy. Here is its general idea. Each industry is listed twice: in a row as an output; in a column as a needed input. Agriculture and manufacturing are sample industries. In addition we treat the final consumption of households as an extra column, and the labor or other primary factors of production supplied by households as an extra row. These are the numbers that enter into national income or net national product and are italicized. (In practice Leontief also includes government, foreign trade, investment, and many other complications.)

The gross value of agriculture output is shown by the boldface $240 (billions) twice: at its row's right as the sum of all the places where farm output went—$140 as input to manufacturing plus $100 directly consumed by households as food; and at its column's bottom as the sum of the $160 cost it paid for labor input (and other household factors) and the $80 cost it paid for manufacturing inputs (chemical fertilizers, etc.).

Give a similar interpretation of the $280 gross total for manufacturing.

The table also shows our old friend national income. With no government or in-

---

[1] The rest of this section can be skipped at a first reading.

vestment in the picture, NNP of $300 equals the sum of the third column's italicized final products; or alternatively NNP equals the sum of all factor-cost or values added shown in the third row's italics. (NNP definitely doesn't include the intermediate purchases of one sector from another; the gross bold-face total of $520 definitely involves double-counting.)

This input-output table is more than a record of past history. How does Leontief or a planner hope to use it? *He hopes to use it to forecast the effects of changing consumptions.* Thus, suppose a war were to send final manufacturing consumption up from $200 to $300, leaving food consumption unchanged at $100. How much labor would each industry need? How much intermediate input? Leontief would use a giant electronic computer to show that the answer is the one given in the new table of the footnote.[1]

---

[1] All details aside, his key assumption is that $80/240 = \frac{1}{3}$ of agriculture receipts will always be spent on manufacturing input, with the remaining $160/240 = \frac{2}{3}$ always spent on labor input. Similarly $140/280 = \frac{1}{2}$ is the fraction that manufacturing will always spend on its needed agricultural input, the remainder being spent on needed household primary factors. Taking this into account, Leontief uses algebra to compute the gross amounts of each good needed as intermediate inputs and for final consumption. And he, with the Labor Department's help, can translate all this into manpower requirements. The table abbreviated from p. 785 will change from

0	140		100	240
80	0		200	280
160	140		300	
240	280			520

to wartime

0	200		100	300
100	0		300	400
200	200		400	
300	400			700

Remark: To avoid simultaneous equations, Leontief can use a "multiplier" method. Each

From Quesnay to Leontief is a long way. What's the connection? Just this: Quesnay thought of *land* as the primary factor input to be put in the table's third row italics. He, like Malthus and later classical economists, thought of people as being reproduced to order. *I.e.,* he puts labor and household's consumptions *within* northwest block of the Leontief table, like any other *intermediate* industry. Since the physiocrats supposed laborers were produced by food in the way that horses are produced by fodder and machines by steel, no wonder then that they ended up tracing all "surplus consumption" (*produit net*) in the end to land, all labor and worker consumption being treated as an intermediate good.

Adam Smith and the Classical School

Adam Smith's 1776 *Wealth of Nations* represents the beginning of modern economics. From start to finish it is an attack upon the governmental regulations and other interferences with free competition inherited from the mercantilists. Like the physiocrats and the contemporaneous admirers of Newton's physical system, Smith perceived harmonious order in the real world: if only free competition could operate, an "invisible hand" would lead to perfection. There's really a lot more to Smith than this—*e.g.,* he was for the underdog, not for big business —but so brief a sketch has to be superficial.

David Ricardo and John Stuart Mill are principal exponents of the classical school. They developed and perfected the Smithian insights. Thus, Ricardo elaborated on the notion that most costs could be decomposed into labor costs; and he explained how capital accumulation matched by population

---

manufacture requires $\frac{1}{2}$ of agriculture as input, and each of these in turn requires $\frac{1}{3}$ of manufacture as its input; so indirectly each manufacture requires $\frac{1}{2} \times \frac{1}{3} = \frac{1}{6}$ of extra manufactures to produce itself. So $(1 + \frac{1}{6} + (\frac{1}{6})^2 + \cdots)$ adds up to 1.2, which is the needed expansion of bold face manufacture for each 1.0 expansion of italics manufacture. This way he can fill in the new war table.

Leontief's input-output brings Quesnay's tableau up to date:

	Agriculture	Manufacturing	Household final consumptions	Gross totals
Agriculture		140	*100*	240
Manufacturing	80		*200*	280
Household labor and other factors	*160*	*140*	——	
Gross totals	**240**	**280**		520

Table 1. Input-output money flows (in billions of dollars). Sum of italicized final items will give national income or product. Each industry's output is listed twice—by row and by column. Each row shows what happens to its boldface output. Each column shows its needed inputs. (Fill in the proper NNP.)

increase would raise land rent, until finally the law of diminishing returns would bring down profit (or interest rate) so low as to kill off all saving and lead to a steady-state subsistence-wage economy with no further growth.

The classical economists were saying what the rising business class liked to hear. And they were listened to. True, they tended to be dogmatic; to think you could deduce the laws of economics the way you deduce the laws of arithmetic and logic—without ever looking at the real world of markets; to think that there wasn't much governments could do to repeal the "iron law of wages" and the other inevitable consequences portrayed by their "dismal science." Ironic then that a sensitive man like John Stuart Mill, once his stern father was dead and just as the 1848 first edition of his *Principles of Political Economy* had codified the classical system, should have turned toward socialism and reform.[1]

---

[1] The classical doctrines were rejected on the Continent by many: by romantics who despised capitalism, and later by the so-called "historical school" who despised a priori theories and tried to replace them by detailed (and often dull) factual studies. Friedrich List, a German writer of around 1840, is typical of some aspects of romanticism; his arguments for tariffs have carried weight, and some of his nationalistic followers became apologists for fascist economics.

Marx's "Scientific" Socialism versus Utopian Socialism

Each age produces men with a vision of a more perfect world—one in which goods ceased to be scarce, where altruism replaced selfishness, where inequality was replaced by equality or by property owned in common. A few representative nineteenth-century names are Robert Owen, wealthy English manufacturer who backed utopian colonies here and abroad; Simonde de Sismondi, who believed that capitalism would periodically suffer from too little consumption and purchasing power; Charles Fourier; H. de Saint-Simon; P. J. Proudhon; and many others.

Karl Marx felt contempt for such utopians, just as he did for vulgar apologists of capitalism. Writing in exile, he studied the works of Ricardo and particularly stressed the labor theory of value—that labor produces all value and if not exploited would get it all. He thought he could turn upside down Hegel's philosophy of matter's being mind. Instead he gave an "economic interpretation of history" in which the conditions of pro-

---

In America, the historical school took the form around World War I of the institutionalist group, headed by Wisconsin's John R. Commons and by the defrocked professor Thorstein Veblen. Today all economists pay lip service to the need both for facts and for logical reasonings about factual hypotheses.

duction shape all ideology and in which the class struggle operates through the successive stages of feudalism, capitalism, inevitably toward a dictatorship of the proletariat —to be followed by a "withering away of the state" and a final classless equilibrium.

For capitalism Marx forecast falling real wages, falling profit rates, and underconsumption leading to greater and greater business-cycle crises. He looked for increasing monopoly control, imperialism, and finally inevitable revolution, and he naturally spurned mere reform of the capitalistic system.[1]

Twentieth-century Economics

There were many crudities in the classical analysis. After 1870, the type of material given in Parts Three and Four of this book were developed—with the single name of Cambridge's Alfred Marshall quite typical of the period. (In Sweden K. Wicksell, in France L. Walras, in Italy V. Pareto, in America J. B. Clark, in Austria K. Menger and E. Böhm-Bawerk are typical of this movement.) Marshall's 1890 *Principles of Economics* followed Mill's as the textbook of several generations.

By the 1930's two important advances were

made. Harvard's E. Chamberlin and Cambridge's Joan Robinson analyzed monopolistic or imperfect competition. And Lord Keynes (formerly John Maynard Keynes) laid the basis in his 1936 *General Theory of Employment, Interest and Money* for income-determination theory.[2] Simon Kuznets at the nonprofit National Bureau of Economic Research pioneered the statistical measurement of national income, and this has been carried on by the Department of Commerce and the United Nations. Harvard's Alvin Hansen, and others, perfected the fiscal policy implications of the income-analysis tools.

Today most economists in the Free World attempt what is in this book called a "neoclassical synthesis": *i.e.,* by effective monetary and fiscal policies they try to make a marriage between the classical microeconomics of Smith and Marshall and the macroeconomics of modern income determination, combining what is sound in each approach. Economists who use these same tools range in their political beliefs from conservatives like London's Lionel Robbins to New Dealers like Alvin Hansen. But they all call a spade a spade.[3]

---

[1] Marx's economic tools split up a goods revenue PQ into labor cost, V; into profit, S; and into a catchall of such earlier stages' costs as depreciation and intermediate materials, which he labeled C. Marx thought that a developing rise in C/V would cause the profit rate S/PQ to fall (provided S/V doesn't rise enough to offset!). Careful critics of all political complexions think this is a sterile analysis both of capitalism and socialism. But try to persuade 1 billion people of that.

[2] The Scandinavians Ohlin, Myrdal, and Frisch pioneered here too—as did Poland's Kalecki and America's J. M. Clark.

[3] J. A. SCHUMPETER, *History of Economic Analysis* (Oxford, New York, 1954) is the standard reference work on all this. Those who dare not tackle its 1,200 pages may find ERIC ROLL, *A History of Economic Thought* (Prentice-Hall, Englewood Cliffs, N.J., 1956, 3d ed.), a useful substitute.

INDEX